To Jim,
With best wishes,
A. V. Huff Jr.

Christmas 1995

ι

Greenville

Greenville

The History of the City and County in the South Carolina Piedmont

Archie Vernon Huff, Jr.

UNIVERSITY OF SOUTH CAROLINA PRESS

For Kate

© 1995 by the Greenville County Historical Society, Inc.

Published in Columbia, South Carolina by the
University of South Carolina Press

Manufactured in the United States of America

99 98 97 96 95   5 4 3 2 1

Library of Congress Cataloging-in-Publication Data
Huff, Archie Vernon, 1937–
   Greenville : the history of the city and county in the South
Carolina Piedmont / Archie Vernon Huff, Jr.
      p.   cm.
   Includes bibliographical references and index.
   ISBN 1-57003-045-6
   1. Greenville (S.C.)—History. 2. Greenville County (S.C.)—
History. I. Title.
F279.G79H84 1995   95–4363
975.7'27–dc20

Contents

Illustrations

Preface

Methodist Bishop Francis Asbury visited Greenville County, in the upstate area of South Carolina, a number of times in the early nineteenth century. In October 1801 he recorded his impression of the area: "I fear there is more gold than grace."[1] Eighty years later Ellison Capers, the rector of Christ Church, noted: "Business is first and last, and everything must bend to business."[2] Business—or the economy—has without doubt been the major element in forming the history of the city and county of Greenville. Prior to the American Revolution the Cherokee Nation utilized the area primarily for hunting. Then, in the late eighteenth century, the early settlers eagerly carved farms and plantations from the former Cherokee domain. During the antebellum period, Greenville was atypical of much of the South—a staple agriculture was not developed, slavery was tangential to its economic life, and the area was strongly Unionist until just prior to the Civil War. Greenville's experience during Reconstruction was similar to the rest of the South, but it soon became a center of the Southern cotton textile industry and a leader in the New South. As textiles grew in importance, so did cotton production—both dominated the economy until after World War II. Since 1945 the growth and diversification of industry has been the major theme of the Greenville story.

Another aspect of the history of Greenville has been its lack of cohesion. During the Cherokee era, two major paths crossed the land—one across the north, the other across the south. Settlers clustered in those two areas as well as around the falls of the Reedy River—the site of the town of Greenville. After the Civil War the black community developed its own identity, and the urban population expanded. The textile industry at this time created a new class of mill workers which helped to shape the life of the region. By the end of the nineteenth century the city of Greenville dominated the area. All of these groups were overshadowed by the business elite, but each area and group maintained its own identity and made its contribution to the life of the region.

The political life of Greenville prior to 1860 was atypical of South Carolina in one important aspect. In the heat of the nullification crisis Greenville became a center of unionism and remained so until the pressure of the slavery controversy created a secessionist majority. But during the

Civil War sentiment in Greenville remained divided. After Reconstruction white Greenville became overwhelmingly Democratic, but with a split into factions (as did much of the solid South). Since 1945 the politics of Greenville has been a major factor in shaping South Carolina.

As far as religion is concerned, a strong evangelical Protestant tradition developed. Though Presbyterians formed the largest single denomination in the antebellum period, the separate Baptist and Methodist camp-meeting traditions dominated the region. The emergence of Holiness and Pentecostal churches in the late nineteenth century strengthened the conservative, revivalistic nature of religion in the area by challenging and at times threatening the emergence of liberal Protestantism in the city. In the last half of the twentieth century the resurgence of fundamentalism has become a major factor of religious life.

Culture in Greenville mirrored that of the region. The colleges and the city of Greenville combined by the end of the nineteenth century to create a small, but generally conservative, cultural community. In the twentieth century this community improved the quality and availability of its cultural life, but remained traditional—not innovative.

The presence of a small African-American population relegated race relations to secondary importance. As in the South generally, the institutions of slavery and segregation dominated life in Greenville until the civil rights movement in the 1960s. After Reconstruction, the existence of a very small middle class and the exclusion of black workers from the textile industry left African Americans defenseless against discrimination and periodic violence. In the wake of the civil rights movement, Greenville moved to end segregation in a peaceful, but grudging, manner. Nevertheless, black Greenvillians made substantial contributions to the community and the nation.

No historian works alone, and any historian of Greenville County is indebted to a host of fellow workers from the beginning. When Lauriston Blythe, who was then president of the Greenville County Historical Society, first approached me in 1987 about this project, I was immediately interested. Already my esteemed colleague at Furman, Albert Neely Sanders, had begun to collect a great amount of material for writing a history of Greenville County. When his health would not allow him to continue the project, Albert Sanders graciously gave me the material which he had meticulously organized.

A number of students of local history have published their work. I am indebted to the general studies of Colonel Stanley S. Crittenden, James M. Richardson, Frank M. Barnes, Laura Ebaugh, Alfred S. Reid, Choice

McCoin, and the collaborative work of Nancy Vance Ashmore Cooper and Judith T. Bainbridge. The *Proceedings and Papers of the Greenville County Historical Society* is an invaluable source on many important topics. Too late for inclusion in this book was the massive collection of sources for the upper part of the county by Mann Batson.

Many libraries and archives contain material on Greenville, and their staffs have been unfailingly helpful. The South Carolina Room of the Greenville County Library is an amazing repository of local history, and its former director, Penny Forrester, made its resources and her own collection readily available. The South Carolina Department of Archives and History is the custodian of many state and local records; thanks go to Alexia Helsley and the Search Room staff and Mary Watson Edmonds and the Historic Preservation staff. Allen Stokes and his co-workers at the South Caroliniana Library at the University of South Carolina were always ready to suggest material from their vast collection on the state's history. Farther afield, the Manuscript Division of the Library of Congress provided unexpected resources, and the R. G. Dun and Company ledgers in the Baker Library of the Harvard Graduate School of Business Administration are a gold mine of local business information from the nineteenth century.

The James B. Duke Library of Furman University was my "home away from home" for an entire year of research and writing. J. Glenwood Clayton, Steve Richardson, Lisa J. Pruitt, Carolyn Lancaster, Nancy R. Lewis, and Lilli Ann Dill were helpful day after day and brightened the spirits of this often weary scholar.

In addition, Furman University provided gracious assistance in this project. Dean John H. Crabtree granted a year of leave from teaching, and John M. Block, chair of the history department, supported me in every way. Carolyn Sims, faculty secretary in the department, is always helpful, but in this case she cheerfully transferred files from one computer format to another.

Year after year the Dana Fellows Committee, and later the Furman Advantage Program, granted funds for student research assistants whose work is buried in the footnotes. Stephanie Brewer investigated the names on the 1790 census. Thomas A. Wall, Jr., deciphered the Civil War correspondence of the Neves family, and Timothy Hicks read the Greenville newspapers for the Reconstruction era. Erin Snyder and Jennifer Brown mined the newspapers for the New Deal and World War II.

This work is the brainchild of the Greenville County Historical Society. At the end of his term as president, Lauriston Blythe became chair of the Publications Committee and has remained in that capacity. He has had the counsel of Yancey Gilkerson, William N. Cruikshank, and J. Glenwood Clayton.

Individual members of the society have given generously of their time, family collections, and financial resources. On one occasion William N. Cruikshank was host to a luncheon to which a number of Greenvillians came and brought with them their memories and documents. A large number of society members made specific contributions to the research and publication fund. In addition, local foundations and groups were most generous, including the Community Foundation of Greenville, the Dorothy H. Beattie Foundation, the Frances O. and William H. Beattie Foundation, the Stone Foundation, the Symmes Foundation, John I. Smith Charities, the Historic Greenville Foundation, the Open Book, and the Junior League of Greenville, Inc.

Brenda Hays, executive secretary of the society, took on the task of assembling the photographs. She had the assistance of Choice McCoin, the staff of the Greenville County Library, Oscar Landing, the volunteers at the Coxe Collection, Richard Sawyer, Joe Jordan, and numerous others. Frederick C. Holder gave invaluable help on the details of the Cherokee and colonial periods. He read the first two chapters, suggested corrections, and gave continuing moral support. From her voluminous notes and records, Anne McCuen freely shared her findings. William N. Cruikshank, Yancey Gilkerson, and Judith T. Bainbridge read preliminary drafts of the manuscript and made helpful suggestions. The final responsibility for this work, as always, rests with the author.

The staff of the University of South Carolina Press has been unfailingly helpful. The readers of the manuscript skillfully improved successive drafts, and the copy editors and staff personnel speeded the work toward publication.

My deepest debt is to my family. My wife, Kate, and my children, Vernon and Mary, have sacrificed a husband and a father to this project far too many times. I can only be grateful for their support.

Notes

1. Francis Asbury, *The Journal and Letters of Francis Asbury,* ed. Elmer T. Clark, 3 vols. (New York, 1958) 2: 311.

2. Greenville (S.C.) *News,* March 15, 1881, cited in David L. Carlton, *Mill and Town in South Carolina, 1880–1920* (Baton Rouge, La., 1982), 28.

Greenville

CHAPTER ONE

Cherokees and Settlers on the Frontier of Empire

Greenville County came into existence by an act of the South Carolina legislature in 1786. The county is about 795 square miles and lies in the northwestern area of the state, on the North Carolina border. But long before there was a Greenville County, the verdant mountains and rolling landscape had already nurtured prehistoric animals and successive groups of American Indians and shaped both the British colonial frontier culture and the society of the new American nation.

Formation of the Land

The formation of the land itself was a complex and sometimes violent process that stretched over millions of years. Some six hundred million years ago the land that is now Greenville County was part of an island off the coast of what eventually became North America. In a massive geological shift about 470 million years ago this island collided with the continent and created a fault line now called the Brevard Zone. Eventually the continent drifted eastward into northwest Africa and became part of a supercontinent (Pangea). At this stage, 350 million years ago, tremendous heat below the surface of the earth transformed the igneous and sedimentary rock of the region and thrust it upward to form the Blue Ridge Mountains. As North America separated from the larger land mass and settled into its present location, more heat and pressure forced molten material upward into cracks in the earth's surface. This new material eventually cooled into deposits of granite among the crystalline schists and gneisses that predominate in the region.[1]

Originally much higher, the southernmost chain of the Blue Ridge Mountains wore down to a height of just over 3,000 feet above sea level. South of this chain are a series of monadnocks (single mountains that tower over the surrounding hills and valleys). To the west in what became Pickens County is an example: Table Rock Mountain. This mountain is naked rock on three sides and was described by architect Robert Mills in 1826 as "a sublime and awful spectacle." Farther east is another example of a monadnock: Glassy Mountain, whose rocky slopes are wet with water which freezes in winter and "reflects the rays of the sun with a dazzling lustre." Hogback Mountain, a monadnock nearest Spartanburg County, is distinctive for its fertile plateaus. More nearly central to the area is Paris Mountain which is more than a mile in length and meanders east and south until it tapers into Piney Mountain on its southern end. South of the monadnocks, the sloping hills spread into gently rolling countryside.

The hills and valleys of Greenville are watered by a series of streams that arise in the mountains, and then fall swiftly through narrow banks. All the creeks and rivers eventually flow into the Broad River and become a part of the great Santee system that empties into the Atlantic Ocean 250 miles away. The largest river in Greenville is the Saluda, which forms its western boundary and falls some 500 feet within the county. The Reedy River arises near Paris Mountain and flows into the Saluda. The Enoree River, whose source is northeast of Paris Mountain, flows into the Broad River, as do the South and Middle Tyger Rivers and the South Pacolet River in the northeastern section of the county. These swift rivers would eventually lure textile mill builders into the region. But for millions of years clay and loam from the heights of the Blue Ridge flowed down these streams. This erosion, assisted by moderating temperatures and ample rainfall, eventually gave the mountains their rugged, but rounded, appearance. Left in the mountains were younger soils that lacked accumulations of clay beneath the surface. By contrast, in the Piedmont lies either sandy loam or a thick clay subsoil covered by a stiff crust that resists erosion.

During the ice ages, when the environment was cooled by glaciers farther north, vegetation grew along the upper reaches of Greenville that was similar to the hardwoods found as far north as New England—oak, chestnut, hemlock, white pine, beech, and yellow birch. South of the these mountains oak, hickory, and pine grew in more profusion; along the rivers and streams alder, cottonwood, and sycamore flourished.

Prehistoric Animals and American Indians

The earliest residents of the area were prehistoric animals, followed by American Indians. During the Pleistocene Epoch, which began two million years ago, herds of mammoths, mastodons, bison, and caribou appeared in North America and eventually roamed into the southeast. These herds dominated animal life in the region until the end of the last Ice Age some ten to twelve thousand years ago. By the time these animals disappeared, however, a new form of life arrived—humankind.[2]

The first wave of American Indians crossed the Bering land bridge from Asia into North America between 40,000 and 30,000 B.C. These Paleo-Indians moved south from Alaska down the Cascade-Sierra Mountains, into the Western Plains, and reached the southeast about 12,000 to 10,000 B.C. These earliest immigrants came in search of the great beasts of the last Ice Age. When they arrived, the Wisconsin Glacier still covered much of Canada, but it was receding and the climate was becoming warmer. Whether the mammoths and mastodons moved farther north in search of cooler weather or became extinct in the warmer environment is not clear. Nevertheless, by about 8000 B.C.—the beginning of the Archaic period—the large animals had disappeared. The Indians continued to gather vegetables, fruits, and nuts, and turned to hunting smaller game. Between 1000 and 100 B.C. these Indians imported innovations pioneered by those living along the Ohio and Mississippi Rivers—settlement into towns which were built around structures for burial and storage of food. In nearby fields the Indians began to cultivate and harvest crops. Pottery, which had appeared prior to 1000 B.C., became more common. Between 1000 B.C. and about A.D. 1650 the Indians became more and more sedentary.[3]

The Cherokee Nation

By the time of European incursion the land that became Greenville County was part of the domain of the Cherokees, who occupied an area stretching from the Seneca River in South Carolina north into Tennessee and west into Georgia. Their towns were autonomous, though European travelers divided them into two groups—the *ayrate* (low) people and the *ottare* (mountainous) people. British colonial authorities further divided them into the Lower Towns of northwestern South Carolina and northeastern Georgia, the Middle Towns of western North Carolina, and the Overhill Towns of east Tennessee.[4]

Though the number of towns and their locations varied from time to time, some sixty-four have been identified. In the late seventeenth century the towns were confederated under the supremacy of Chota, the capital of the Overhill Towns, and its leader, known as the First Beloved Man. In 1700 the towns contained six thousand Cherokee warriors compared to the combined white and black population of seven thousand. But a smallpox epidemic in 1738 reduced the Indian population by half. In 1764 John Stuart, the British Indian superintendent, estimated that there were only 2,750 fighting men and a total population of 13,500.[5]

The Cherokees were described in the *Travels* of naturalist William Bartram, published in 1791, as "by far the largest race of men I have seen, their complexions brighter and somewhat of the olive cast, especially the adults; and some of their young women are nearly as fair and blooming as European women." Their features were "regular and countenance open, dignified and placid." Their eyes "though rather small, yet active and full of fire; the pupil always black, and the nose commonly inclining to the aquiline."

> The Cherokees in their dispositions and manners are grave and steady; dignified and circumspect in their deportment; rather slow and reserved in conversation; yet frank, cheerful and humane; tenacious of the liberties and natural rights of men; secret, deliberate and determined in their councils; honest, just and liberal, and are always ready to sacrifice every pleasure and gratification, even their blood, and life itself, to defend their territory and maintain their rights.[6]

The Lower Towns were located in present-day South Carolina west of Greenville along the streams and rivers of what are now Oconee and Pickens Counties and in the northeastern tip of Georgia. The larger settlements included Keowee, two towns by the name of Estatoe, and Tugaloo. Towns and villages stretched from west of the Savannah River to near present-day Pickens. The number of towns and villages varied from as few as six or seven to as many as fourteen. New ones were built as older ones declined in importance or eventually disappeared. Central to each town was its domed town house set atop a low, earthen mound and containing the sacred fire. Nearby were the gaming yard and the ceremonial square ground where the entire town population gathered for seasonal festivals in honor of the Creator God. Scattered about were as few as twenty or as many as two hundred gabled houses built of white clay and cane. There were also winter houses, each covered with hides and earth and warmed by a smoldering fire. In the spring and summer, each family worked the fields allotted them by the council. The harvest was stored in corn cribs in town. In the fall and winter, hunting parties left the villages and moved into designated hunting areas where they secured their meat supply for the remainder of the year.[7]

Northeast of the settled areas lay the hunting lands of the lower Cherokees—stretching east of the Saluda River, including what is now Greenville County. About 1660, according to one tradition, the Catawbas settled near Rock Hill. The Cherokees considered them intruders, and the two nations met in a fierce all-day battle at Nation Ford to determine control of the land. After significant losses on both sides, the Cherokees and Catawbas agreed to live in peace. The Catawbas accepted the Catawba River as their western boundary, and the Cherokees accepted the Broad River as their eastern boundary. The land between the rivers was designated as common hunting land. This tradition is not entirely accurate because the Catawbas did settle west of the Catawba River. There is no evidence that the Cherokees ever settled east of the Saluda. But the area between the Saluda and the Broad Rivers was left free of permanent settlement.[8]

The Early Landscape

The land that became Greenville County was part of the Cherokees' and Catawbas' hunting preserve. The creeks and rivers were bordered with thick canebrakes, sometimes stretching for miles across the countryside. On ordinary soil the cane grew no higher than 6 feet, but in highly fertile areas it grew 20 feet to 30 feet tall. Only place names like Reedy River or the Great Cane Brake, site of the Revolutionary encounter in southern Greenville County, remain from this earlier landscape. The virgin forests consisted of massive trees with little undergrowth. According to early Piedmont settlers who lived south of Greenville, "the trees were generally larger [than at present], and stood so wide apart that a deer or buffalo would be easily seen at a long distance—there being nothing to obstruct the view but the rolling surface."[9]

But the landscape was not entirely dominated by forests and canebrakes. There were vast prairies "destitute of trees, and as luxuriant in grass and flowers as any prairie of modern times." Many of these open areas, later known to white settlers as "old fields," were created by the Cherokees who burned large areas of the forests for hunting herds of wildlife.[10]

Animals were plentiful and varied. Buffalo roamed in large herds through the open lands and forests. Logan puts the date of their disappearance at about 1775. The elk probably disappeared about the same time. Deer and turkeys were seldom out of the sight of hunting parties, while panthers, wolves, bears, catamounts, and wildcats prowled in the swamps and thickets. Bears were so numerous, according to Logan, that in one season a settler could kill enough to make some 3,000 pounds of bacon. There were beavers on every creek and stream. Greenville still boasts Beaverdam Creek, Wildcat Creek, and Panther's Fork, as well as the Middle Tyger River. The name Lickville is reminiscent of the salt licks frequented by the buffalo and deer.[11]

Indian Remains

As late as 1784, when Greenville land was officially opened for settlement by the state, sites of Indian activity were identifiable. On the Checharoa River, part of the North Fork of the Saluda, a "Town House" served as a landmark. Also on the Checharoa was Uscetie's Camp. Oyl Camp gave its name to Oyl or Oil Camp Creek.[12] Traces of these camps were visible in the nineteenth century. The best-known example was a site within the city of Greenville near the falls of the Reedy River. Stephen S. Crittenden, in *The Greenville Century Book*, recalled that "in his boyhood [in the 1830s] the great number of Indian arrow heads, mostly of white flint rock, were scattered in the fields around the village." He especially remembered them in "certain localities," such as "the fields between the old McBee homestead [at the top of McBee Avenue] and Reedy River, and those in what is now embraced in Washington and other streets." In the twentieth century large numbers of artifacts have been recovered at Camp Greenville, near the North Carolina line, and smaller sites throughout the county.[13]

Indian Paths

A network of paths crisscrossed the region around Greenville. In a study of major southeastern Indians paths, American ethnologist, William E. Myer, wrote that these pathways were created by the buffalo, the elk, and the deer. These paths traced the journeys of the animals to springs, salt licks, and fords across the rivers. Native Americans first used the trails to stalk the animals to their sources of food and water. Eventually the paths were connected to travel between towns and nations. Using these paths, the Indians could travel hundreds, even thousands, of miles across the continent very quickly. The paths, according to Myer, "followed the lines of least resistance; they avoided rough, stony ground, briars, and close underbrush." The high ground was used where possible, with natural drainage to either side. Sections of these same paths later became the routes of pioneer wagon roads, railroads, and eventually interstate highways.[14]

Local Indian paths no doubt preceded the development of wagon roads such as the White Horse Road west of the city of Greenville and the Buncombe Road to the north. Two, perhaps three, major paths crossed Greenville County. The upper path ran northeast across northern Greenville County originating at Keowee Indian Town in present-day Oconee County and leading to a juncture with Indian paths in southwestern Virginia. This path followed the approximate route of S.C. Route 11 east of Pleasant

Ridge State Park, north of Tigerville, then passed into North Carolina. In northwestern Greenville County, just east of the Saluda River, this path forked into an upper and lower branch. The upper branch passed westward across the Saluda River and continued on to Estatoe Indian Town in northern Pickens County and southwest to Sugar Town and Keowee Town. The lower branch ran southwest to near Socconee Town, west of present-day Pickens, before curving westward to Keowee.[15]

More important for the subsequent development of Greenville County was the lower path which connected the Cherokee Path to the west (often incorrectly called the Keowee Trail) with paths near the Catawba Nation. The lower path through Greenville County crossed the Enoree River from the east and ran roughly parallel to U.S. Interstate 85, though farther south. After it crossed the Saluda River, the lower path joined the Cherokee Path near the headwaters of Twenty-Eight Mile Creek in present-day Anderson County.[16]

Myer lists a third major Indian path which entered Greenville County from the north through Saluda Gap and passed into Spartanburg County near Greer. In the nineteenth century this path became the route of the state road which connected upstate South Carolina with Columbia and Charleston. This path does not appear on the early maps.[17]

The Coming of the Spanish and the British

In the sixteenth century the lands of the Cherokee Nation became part of the struggle for international supremacy among the nations of Europe. This struggle began with the Spanish. In 1540 the conquistador Hernando de Soto marched across the Midlands of South Carolina from the Savannah River to the Wateree River and northward into the Catawba Nation. Only in North Carolina did de Soto turn westward and encounter the Cherokees. Twenty-six years later a detachment of troops under the command of Juan Pardo marched northward from Santa Elena, the Spanish capital of La Florida on the South Carolina coast. The detachment followed the trail of de Soto and likewise encountered the Cherokees in western North Carolina. Based on current research, it is unlikely that these expeditions crossed present-day Greenville County.[18]

The British were the ones destined to challenge the Indian occupation of South Carolina and to make Greenville the frontier of empire. The British settled Charles Town in 1670 and may have traded with the Cherokees of the Lower Towns within fifteen years. By 1714, at any rate, there were at least four traders living among them. Anthony Park, one of the early settlers in Newberry, stated in 1758 that white men had been living among the Cherokees for more than half a century. But these early traders probably centered their activities in the towns rather than the seasonally occupied hunting lands.[19]

When South Carolina became a royal province after the revolution against the Lords Proprietors in 1719, the colonial government on the coast actively cultivated the friendship of the Native Americans in the interior. This interest was spurred by the devastating war with the Yemassees in the low country and the appearance on the Gulf Coast of the French who immediately began to court favor with the Creeks and the Cherokees. In response, the government in Charles Town abolished private trade with the Indians and created a public monopoly under the control of the Commons House of Assembly—an arrangement which lasted until the crown intervened in 1756. Then in 1730 Sir Alexander Cuming, an eccentric aristocrat, visited the Cherokees and on an impulse invited a group of warriors to visit London. There the Indians signed a treaty pledging their allegiance to the British crown and agreeing to peaceable trade with the king's subjects. Though the warriors had no official standing, the treaty did cement Cherokee relations with the British government.[20]

The British on Cherokee Land

The earliest effort of the British to obtain Cherokee land in what is now Greenville County occurred in January 1747 when John and Thomas Turk and Michael Taylor of Augusta County, Virginia, petitioned South Carolina Governor James Glen to allow them to purchase land from the Indians for resale to potential settlers from Pennsylvania and Virginia. On February 12, 1747, Indian agent George Pawley and the leaders of the Lower Towns signed a deed opening Cherokee hunting lands to settlement. The boundary established in the deed stretched from the Savannah River to Long Canes Creek as far north as the Indian path from Ninety Six to Keowee, before turning east to join the Saluda River. At the Saluda River the line extended north to a point along the lower path connecting the Cherokee Path to the Catawba Nation. The price for the land was £189 sterling which was paid in ammunition. The immediate effect of this cession was to open land along the Indian path just north of Ninety Six, but it marked the first time that Greenville land was mentioned in negotiations between a British province and the Cherokees.[21]

Meanwhile Virginia, to the north, was showing considerable interest in trade with the Indians. In 1751 both the Cherokees and the Catawbas sent deputations to Williamsburg to discuss opening trade. In response, Governor Glen in Charles Town immediately initiated a series of meetings with the Cherokees, culminating in a conference at Saluda Old Town in June 1755 on the eve of the French and Indian War. Glen hoped to achieve several goals at Saluda—cement relations in light of the increasing French threat, tie the Cherokees more closely to Charles Town than Williamsburg, and open more Indian land in upper South Carolina to settlement. On his part Glen promised to strengthen Fort Prince George which the province had constructed on the Seneca River in 1753 and build a new post, Fort Loudoun, on the Little Tennessee River. In return the Cherokee leaders formally recognized the sovereignty of George II over their lands. But it is highly unlikely that the Cherokees thereby intended to open more land to settlement. By 1758, in fact, they were complaining that settlers were living so near their hunting lands that there were no longer enough deer to feed and clothe them. Such encroachment was one of the factors leading to the Cherokee War of 1760–1761. The fighting decimated the Indian population and devastated many of the Middle and Lower Towns. The Treaty of Fort Prince George, which concluded the conflict on September 23, 1761, defined the upper limits of settlement as 40 miles southeast of Keowee. The boundary was never formally established, but it would have run from the Savannah River to the Saluda River just north of DeWitt's Corner. A definitive boundary had yet to be drawn.[22]

The Indian Boundary

Such a boundary between the settlers and the Cherokees did emerge, but it arose in London out of concern for the empire as a whole, not in America where the primary focus was on the welfare of individual provinces. During the Seven Years War (1756–1763), known in America as the French and Indian War, the British had faced an alliance of the French with a number of Indian nations. Members of the Privy Council became convinced of the need for closer ties with the Indians. Such ties were easier to cultivate after 1756 when Indian affairs were taken out of the hands of the provincial governors and placed directly under Indian superintendents appointed by the crown. An important step in conciliating the Indians would be to end further British incursion on Indian lands. Early in 1763 Lord Egremont, secretary of state for the Southern Department (which included the American colonies), proposed a boundary that would define the farthest western limit of British settlement. After a month of discussion by the Privy Council, George III issued the Proclamation of 1763 in October, fixing a temporary line along the crest of the Appalachian Mountains. Meanwhile, Egremont instructed the new superintendent of Indian affairs in the South, John Stuart, to convene a conference of British governors with representatives of the Indian nations. At the meeting in Augusta in November 1763 the issue of the boundary was raised. Only the line between Georgia and the Creek Nation was settled at that time, but in the following months the Cherokees of the Lower Towns sent complaint after complaint to Charles Town about hunters and settlers violating their land. Governor Thomas Boone ordered the trespassers driven out and their houses burned. The commander of Fort Prince George proposed that the Indians themselves seize the traps and pelts of the hunters and drive them away.[23]

On January 8, 1765, Governor Boone recommended to the Commons House of Assembly in Charles Town that the South Carolina section of the boundary be determined in cooperation with the Cherokee leaders. On October 19 the chiefs formally ceded to the British all land south of DeWitt's Corner, near present-day Due West. In the spring, on April 24, 1766, Edward Wilkinson, former factor in the Indian trade at Fort Prince George; John Pickens, a surveyor representing the province; Alexander Cameron, the deputy Indian superintendent; six Cherokee leaders; and thirty Cherokee warriors met at DeWitt's Corner. These men ran the line southwest to the Savannah River, then returned, and laid off the boundary northeast to the Reedy River. In 1766 the Reedy River was assumed to mark the boundary between North and South Carolina. The section of the line from the Saluda River to the Reedy River survives today as the southern boundary of Greenville County.[24]

Governor Boone officially proclaimed the boundary on June 2, 1766, "strictly enjoin[ing] and requir[ing] all persons whatever, who have either willfully or inadvertently seated themselves upon any lands in this province northwestward of the boundary line . . . reserved to the Indians, to remove themselves from such settlement." These earliest known settlers on Greenville land were described in a report to London by Alexander Cameron, the deputy Indian superintendent. He found that "about Saludy, there are several Houses within four miles of the line, and one house within one mile of it. On the North Carolina side of the Reedy River [within the confines of present-day Greenville County], there are three or four families settled." Only one he mentioned by name, William Turner, who owned a plantation of 750 acres "on Saludy below Ninety Six" and had a number of slaves. Turner, according to Cameron, had "settled a Cowpens and Plantation on the above Indian lands, altho' he very well knew, that Mr. Wilkinson by [Lieutenant] Governor [William] Bull's orders, removed a settlement off the same tract last year." Turner was likely grazing cattle in the canebrakes and old fields along the Reedy River and had erected a cowpens nearby. It was common practice for British slaveholders who grazed cattle on the Carolina frontier to use their slaves as cowboys. If such activity were practiced by William Turner on Greenville land in 1766, it was not tolerated for long. Cameron reported to London that he "sent a warning to remove [them] without loss of Time, otherwise, I should take upon me to drive them off, and distribute part of their cattle among the Indians, as a tax belonging to them, etc."[25]

Two years later, in 1768, Indian Superintendent John Stuart found it "remarkable that in going hence to the Frontiers I rode at times 30 and 40 miles without seeing any house or hut." Yet the area near the line was full of inhabitants who were mostly emigrants from the Northern colonies. These immigrants traded with the Indians, according to Stuart, "by bartering rum for Horses, the Chiefs complained of this as the source of many disorders." Young warriors were "encouraged to steal horses from the Neighboring Provinces besides the danger of committing outrages when intoxicated which may involve their Nation in trouble. These back settlers pay little or no regard to Law or Government."[26]

Stuart informed Governor William Tryon of North Carolina that the Indian boundary in South Carolina was complete and suggested that the line north of the Reedy River be marked under his auspices. At first, Tryon hesitated. He was fearful that too much land claimed by his province would be surrendered to the Indians. In June 1766 he proposed a solution that would serve his own interests—surveying the line in two parts. The first survey would run the line due north from the Reedy River to the top of Tryon Mountain; the second would run it northeast from Tryon Mountain to Chiswell's Mines in Virginia. The second segment would preserve North Carolina land already designated as Mecklenburg and Tryon Counties. The governor became so enthusiastic about his proposal that by the end of July 1766 he volunteered to inaugurate the survey personally. So, on June 1, 1767, Tryon and the three North Carolina commissioners (John Rutherford, Robert Palmer, and John Frohawk) met Alexander Cameron and the representatives of the Lower Towns (led by Ustenaka, or Jud's Friend) on the proposed boundary at the South Tyger River. In a formal address, Tryon proposed running a line "between the western frontiers of North Carolina and the Cherokee Indian hunting grounds." Ustenaka replied:

> The man above is he who made the land and His Majesty over the water desires that the white people and [ourselves] should mutu-

ally possess it. As I said before the man above is head of all, he made the land and none other, and he told me the land I stand on is mine and all that is on it. True it is the deer, the buffaloe and the Turkeys are almost gone . . . the white people eat hogs, cattle and other things, which they have here, but our food is farther off, the land here is very good land, it affords good water, good timber and other good things but I will not [covet] it . . . as we are going to make a division, I want to do what is fair and right.[27]

The commissioners began their work at the Reedy River on June 4 (the king's birthday), and surveyed the line north to Tryon Mountain. The governor issued a proclamation on July 16, requiring any persons living west of the boundary "to remove from thence by the first day of January next: that no persons on any pretense whatsoever may disturb the said Indians in the quiet and peaceable possession of the lands to the westward of the aforesaid Line, or presume to Hunt thereon, or any other way or means to give them uneasiness." He gave notice that no land would be granted within 1 mile of the line and forbade surveyors from putting the dividing line on their plats.[28]

Americans failed to accept the Indian boundary as permanent. In Virginia George Washington urged fellow speculators to mark western land so they might claim it once the Proclamation of 1763 was withdrawn. As late as 1774 Virginia Governor Lord Dunmore permitted the survey of land west of the line, much to the consternation of officials in London. In South Carolina, despite the repeated warnings of British officials concerned with Indian policy and the governor, a series of individuals attempted to secure tracts of Greenville land while it was still beyond the boundary. Cherokee leaders seemed willing to part with the land since white settlement had already pushed game animals far back into the mountains.[29]

Efforts to Secure Greenville Land

The first of these individuals attempting to secure land was none other than Alexander Cameron, the deputy Indian superintendent, who earlier had been responsible for removing interlopers from the very land he secured. A Scot, Cameron held a commission as an ensign in the British Army and had served for a year at Fort Prince George (1762–1763). He settled on a land grant on Long Canes Creek in 1763 and was employed by John Stuart as a commissary. In 1768 he became deputy superintendent. Cameron fathered a child by a Cherokee woman, and, according to his own account, a group of chiefs offered him a tract of Greenville land in February 1768 so that his child could be educated and raised as a white man. Though Cameron countered that such a grant was against British law, the Cherokees persisted. Both Stuart and Lord Hillsborough, secretary of state for the Southern Department in London, condemned Cameron's acceptance of the land. Indeed, Stuart assured Hillsborough that Cameron had not occupied the land and that it remained Indian territory. But when Patrick Calhoun, deputy surveyor of South Carolina, made a plat of the area in 1770, he labeled a rectangle approximately 10 miles square as "Land Reserved for an Indian Boy begotten by a White Man Alexander Cameron." Perhaps the legal fiction of the grant to the child made the transaction more acceptable. The land stretched from the Indian boundary on the east to the Saluda River and included all but the upper reaches of Golden Grove Creek. At some time before the American Revolution Cameron used the land to graze cattle. Cameron reported to Stuart on August 31, 1776, that the Americans had seized a "good stock of cattle and horses from the Golden Groves." When Judge Henry Pendleton purchased a tract on Golden Grove Creek in 1784, the land was designated "Cammeron's Cowpens." Though Alexander Cameron never attempted to register a deed for the land himself, it was included on the Calhoun plat of 1770 and used by Cameron until he was driven out during the war.[30]

Richard Pearis

The most significant effort to secure Greenville land—and the most successful—was made by Virginia Indian trader Richard Pearis. Born in Ireland in 1725, he was the son of George and Sarah Pearis who immigrated to the Shenandoah Valley of Virginia with three sons and a daughter. George Pearis was a devout Presbyterian and a man of considerable property. By 1750 Richard owned 1,200 acres of land near Winchester. He and his wife Rhoda had three children—Richard, Elizabeth, and Sarah. Three years later Pearis was trading with the Cherokee Nation and served as an Indian agent for Governor Robert Dinwiddie. He formed a partnership with Nathaniel Gist, and they opened a store for trade with the Overhill Towns at Fort Robinson on Long Island in the Holston River, the site of present-day Kingsport, Tennessee. The partnership soon dissolved, but Pearis continued his trading activities. As early as 1754 Pearis was traveling in South Carolina among the Cherokees of the Lower Towns. Like other traders, Pearis fathered a child by a Cherokee woman; Pearis named this child George. During the Seven Years War Pearis led a company of 130

Cherokee warriors under the command of Major Andrew Lewis. At the conclusion of the war in 1763, Pearis served as Indian agent for Maryland.[31]

In October 1768 at a congress with Indian leaders at Hard Labor Creek, near Ninety Six, John Stuart proposed extending the Indian boundary through Virginia along a line east of some white settlements. Virginia Governor Lord Botetourt and the House of Burgesses opposed the move, and Stuart proposed a second congress be held at Cameron's plantation, Lochaber, near Ninety Six, in October 1769. Since Stuart seemed adamant about the location of the boundary, the Virginia commissioners—Andrew Lewis, Richard Pearis's old commander, and Dr. Thomas Walker—employed Pearis and Jacob Hite to sabotage the meeting at Lochaber.[32]

A neighbor of Pearis in Virginia, Hite was the son of Joist Heydt (Heidt or Hite), a land speculator who had settled in the Shenandoah Valley in 1731 on a grant of 100,000 acres. The younger Hite began the traditional ascent to prominence in colonial Virginia politics by serving as a justice of the peace, a member of the county court, and eventually as sheriff. Two of his sons, John Jr. and Thomas, later served in the House of Burgesses.[33]

Hite, a member of the frontier gentry, and Pearis, with his long experience among the Cherokees, were ideal for the mission. Hite forged a series of letters from the Cherokee leaders, including one from Oconostota, to Lord Botetourt indicating their willingness to cede land to the province. The letters, dated June 14, 1770, were presented to the governor on August 17, by Saluy, young warrior of Estatoe, who was in collusion with Hite and Pearis. The effort came to naught, but Pearis and Hite used the mission to look after their own interests. Saluy reported to Botetourt that the Cherokees had known Richard Pearis for many years and wished to grant land to him, his son George, and Jacob Hite in gratitude for past services, as well as future trade.[34]

The deed conveying 12 square miles to Richard Pearis was signed on July 29, 1769, by Cherokee leaders from the Lower Towns and surveyed by William Gist on August 2, in the presence of "fourteen chiefs and Seventy other Indians." The land, resurveyed by Patrick Calhoun in 1770, lay north of the Cameron grant and extended from east of the Reedy River to west of the Saluda River. Though Pearis testified after the Revolution to the British Loyalist Claims Commission that he settled in South Carolina in 1768, the date of this initial deed and a letter by Indian interpreter John Watts, dated May 17, 1770, places Pearis in present-day Greenville two years later, though not yet as a permanent settler. According to Watts's letter to John Stuart, Pearis arrived with three wagons loaded with goods, including a number of guns, and traded the guns for another tract of land.

Watts warned Stuart: "I take him to be a very dangerous Fellow who will breed great disturbances if he is let alone for he will tell the Indians any lies to please them."

Trouble was already brewing over the land grant. In June 1770 Pearis and Hite traveled to the Lower Towns to secure a more substantial title, since the previous deed had not been approved by the chiefs of the Cherokee Nation. The two men secured the further cooperation of Saluy at Estatoe by promising him a trip to England and a lifetime pension. Then the two men crossed the mountains to secure the approval of the chief at Chota. Alexander Cameron tried to intercept Pearis and Hite, but he was hindered by torrential rains. He sent a message to Chota warning the chiefs against signing any document and waited at Fort Prince George to arrest Pearis on his return. Saluy's intervention secured the approval of the chiefs at Chota, and Pearis and Hite avoided Cameron by returning directly to Virginia. Stuart could only chastise the chiefs for their complicity and urge both Tryon and Botetourt to convince Pearis of his error. Both efforts were fruitless. Not until a permanent boundary between North and South Carolina was determined was there any serious attempt by royal officials to stop Pearis.

The Boundary Between North and South Carolina

Pearis was not the only problem. During the 1760s settlers had increasingly moved into the back country west of the Catawba lands. Some of these residents of present-day York, Cherokee, and Spartanburg Counties had grants from North Carolina and some from South Carolina. But, which province had jurisdiction? Tryon wanted the boundary run from the Catawba Nation west to the Reedy River, but South Carolina challenged his contention. Eventually, the question was referred to the Board of Trade in London. On April 24, 1771, the board recommended to the Privy Council that commissioners from the two provinces survey the line from the Catawba River west to the Indian boundary. As usual, imperial affairs moved slowly, so it was not until May 1772 that the commissioners began the survey. The surveyors worked until early June, when the South Carolina party returned to Charles Town. This group had drawn what is still the boundary between the two states—from southwest of Charlotte to the eastern boundary of Greenville County. The old Indian boundary line north of the Reedy River, laid off by Governor Tryon, now lay in South Carolina and the future of Greenville lay with South, not North, Carolina. Now the attention of the Indian officials turned to Pearis's land.[35]

Trouble with the Pearis Grant

Within three months of the completion of the provincial boundary, in September 1772, John Stuart brought up the matter of the Pearis grant to Governor Charles Montagu in Charles Town. The superintendent produced evidence to show that Pearis had secured his title by generously plying a number of the younger leaders with liquor. On the advice of the attorney general, Montagu and the council urged Stuart to prosecute Pearis and Hite under a South Carolina statute of 1739 which forbade private ownership of Indian land by British citizens.

Unaware of Stuart's action, Pearis began to sell parcels of the land he had received, as well as trade with the Indians. Cameron wrote Stuart on September 21, 1772, that Pearis was dividing his land into tracts and selling them to Virginians for large sums of money. Pearis gave Hite one-third of the land, some 30,720 acres, and Hite purchased a second tract of 19,280 acres. Colonel John Neville and his son, residents of Winchester, Virginia, purchased 11,000 acres (which Hite eventually bought) to bring his Greenville holdings to 61,000 acres. Baylis Earle, Hite's friend and business associate from Winchester, purchased 500 acres from Pearis in 1771 for £100 Virginia currency. Joshua Pettit purchased at least 500 acres of land about 2 miles south of the fork of the Saluda River that he subsequently sold to John Armstrong on what has been known ever since as Armstrong Creek. By August 1775 Jonathan Clark was living on the Saluda River, perhaps on land purchased from Pearis.[36] In trading with the Indians, Pearis was not only buying deerskins but purchasing horses which the Indians were stealing from nearby white settlements. Pearis sent the horses to Virginia, according to Stuart, in order to avoid having the former owners identify them.

Stuart reported to London that Pearis and Hite were tried in the recently established circuit court at Ninety Six in November 1773 and found guilty of holding Indian land in violation of state law. Pearis surrendered his deed, but on December 21, 1773, he secured another deed from three leaders—Oconostota, Willinawa, and Ewe—for the 12 square miles, plus an additional tract of 57,840 acres east of his land stretching to the Indian boundary. This time the land was granted to Pearis's Cherokee son, George. Four months later George, who had taken the oath of allegiance as a British citizen, sold the one hundred and fifty thousand-acre tract of Greenville land to his father for £500, reserving 50,000 acres for himself. According to Cameron's report to Stuart, the deed was drawn by the future patriot leader, Edward Rutledge. But by the spring of 1774 Rutledge and the rest of Charles Town were more concerned about the legality of taxation without representation than titles to Indian land. As for Pearis, he did not register these deeds until the American Revolution was well under way.

The earliest surviving map of Greenville dates from this period, when another British citizen attempted to secure land in the area. Edward Wilkinson managed the South Carolina agency in the Lower Towns from 1762 to 1765, and the following year he was appointed provincial commissioner to survey the Indian boundary from the Savannah River to the Reedy River. He continued to trade with the Indians, and they owed him a considerable amount of money. At the congress at Lochaber the Cherokee chiefs proposed giving Wilkinson land to satisfy the debt. Though Stuart—and Wilkinson himself—objected, the chiefs proceeded with their plan. On November 1, 1770, less than five months after Pearis had secured his second deed, Oconostota and Willinawa appointed Little Carpenter and Terrapin to supervise a survey of the land. These men secured the services of Patrick Calhoun, the deputy surveyor of the province, who laid off a tract of 177,907 acres. It was divided into two parcels. The smaller section of 19,671 acres was south of the Cameron grant and bounded by the Indian line on the east and the Saluda River on the west. The larger section, running from Cameron's grant north to the mountains, excluded Richard Pearis's land. The Saluda River, the Indians argued, made a more logical boundary with the white settlers than a line of blazed trees through the forest. Stuart was quite sympathetic with Wilkinson's desire for payment. He reported to Lord Dartmouth, the secretary of state for the Southern Department, that Wilkinson, unlike Pearis, took no clandestine or underhanded steps to secure the land. Nevertheless, the Indian superintendent did not favor any grant so close to the Lower Towns. He proposed that the king grant Wilkinson land in Georgia to satisfy the Indian debts. Wilkinson sailed to London and personally laid his petition before Dartmouth. Though Secretary Dartmouth heard it, he denied the request. Eventually the trader received a grant of land in Georgia. Meanwhile, Pearis and Hite moved to Greenville.[37]

Pearis and Hite in Greenville

Sometime after 1770 Richard Pearis settled permanently on his Greenville land. Along with his wife Rhoda, his son Richard, and two daughters, Elizabeth and Sarah, Pearis and twelve slaves began to clear some 100 acres of land at the falls of the Reedy River. On this plantation, which he called the Great Plains, they sowed fields with grain and planted orchards of apple, peach, and plum trees. Pearis built a substantial house and a large store with an assortment of Indian goods on the hill east of the falls. Close by were a kitchen, smoke house, stables, dairy, blacksmith shop, and a slave quarter. Water was readily available at a spring to the south at the foot of the hill. On the Reedy River, Pearis built a grist and sawmill. What came to be known as "Pearis's waggon road" crossed the river above the falls and led west to the Saluda River, bringing the Cherokees to his store. On his Enoree and Saluda estates, Pearis constructed smaller settlements. Likely spread among them were herds of cattle and hogs, in addition to horses, mares, and colts.[38]

Sometime after November 1775 Jacob Hite and his family left Virginia to settle on the tract he had purchased from Pearis. With Hite came his second wife, Frances Madison Beale; a son by Hite's first marriage, James; and three daughters, two of whom are known as Susan and Eleanor. The Hites came with slaves, pack animals, and wagons loaded with furniture, silver, farm tools, and books. They settled on the Enoree River near the Indian boundary and lived in relative comfort.[39]

Settlers on Greenville land in the years just before the Revolution were relatively few, though there are hints in the existing records of more. James Pritchard with his wife Eleanor and four children—Elizabeth, William, James, and Mary—purchased land from the Cherokees. Robert Pearis, the brother of Richard, owned a tract either by gift or purchase. Baylis Earle purchased land from Richard Pearis in 1771, joining his brother, John, his father, Samuel, and his father-in-law, John Prince, who settled east of the Indian boundary. Sometime between 1773 and 1775 Baylis and John Earle moved to the North Pacolet River just over the line in North Carolina. Tradition locates the Gowen, Howard, Fisher, and Dill families in the valleys near Hogback and Glassy Mountains.[40]

Settlement East of the Boundary

A decade before, in the 1760s, settlers had moved just east of the Indian boundary in what was then called the New Acquisition—lands previously claimed by North Carolina. Many of these settlers would migrate to Greenville after the Revolution. One group of Scotch-Irish from Pennsylvania and Virginia settled along the branches of the Tyger River in 1761, and a second group came by way of Charles Town, settling in the open highlands nearby. As early as 1765 these settlers erected a log meeting house for worship, though they did not formally organize Nazareth Presbyterian Church until 1772.[41]

On the South Tyger River, about 1 mile east of the Indian boundary, Anthony Hampton settled with his family between February and April,

1774. With them came Anthony's daughter, Elizabeth, and her new husband, Richard Harrison. The elder Hampton was a Virginia native who had lived since 1754 at Town Fork on the Dan River in North Carolina, near the Moravian settlement at present-day Winston-Salem. Besides the production of wheat and tobacco, Hampton engaged in land speculation. Between 1771 and 1773 three of his sons—Preston, Edward, and John—moved to the Carolina frontier where they traded with the Cherokees and nearby settlers and surveyed land. Anthony Hampton never filed for a land grant, perhaps because he settled too close to the Indian boundary.[42]

No matter whether these settlers lived within the Indian boundary or beyond it, they faced the threat of attack by the Cherokees. Those that came as early as 1761 knew first-hand the stories of the war parties that descended upon the back country during the Cherokee War of 1760–1761. For protection the settlers constructed stockades in which the families in the immediate vicinity could gather in time of danger. There were more than a score of these forts across the northwest area of the province. In the dozen or so forts between Augusta and the Tyger River, as many as fifteen hundred persons gathered in January 1761. On the Enoree River, four hundred refugees crowded into one fort alone in May. As settlers moved into the New Acquisition or onto Greenville land between 1761 and the outbreak of the Revolution, they made sure there was shelter in case of attack. Only a description of Fort Prince, built in present-day Spartanburg County by John Prince, has survived. This fort was circular and about 150 feet in diameter—with upright timbers 12 feet to 15 feet high. Around the perimeter was a ditch from which earth was packed against the stockade. Beyond the ditch was an abatis of heavy timbers. In the stockade itself were port holes for the use of the riflemen inside.[43]

Just over the line in North Carolina on the North Pacolet River, the Earle family built Earle's Fort, and at the intersection of the Indian boundary with the North Carolina line stood the Block House (first mentioned as the western terminus of the provincial boundary survey in 1772). Farther south, near present-day Gowensville, was Gowen's Fort, and not far from the site of Greer was Wood's Fort, sometimes called Thompson's Station. Only fragmentary references survive about a fort on the ridge between Reedy River and the little fork of the Reedy and Pearson's Station on the South Tyger River. When the alarm came, the settlers dashed to these forts and from them returned home when the danger was past. They lived on the frontier of the British empire, and while the governments in London or Charles Town might come to their aid in an all-out war, these frontier people were responsible for their own security on a daily basis.[44]

American Problems with Britain

While the people on the northwest frontier were faced with the problems of survival, the leaders of the province in the low country were locked in a struggle with the London government over the issue of home rule. An increasing number of Carolinians took the position that the charter to the Lords Proprietors guaranteed them all the rights of Englishmen and that their representative body, the Commons House of Assembly, served them in the same stead as the House of Commons for the empire as a whole. When the government in London began to tighten imperial mercantile regulations and adopted heavier customs duties at the end of the Seven Years War in 1763, low country merchants, planters, and artisans began to protest taxation without representation. A series of local disputes, such as the election law controversy and the support of John Wilkes's suit against the crown in London, intensified ill feelings between the South Carolina Commons House and successive royal governors.

The Regulator Movement

The back country had its own political quarrels, but it was more concerned with taxation without representation in Charles Town than in London. Land on the frontier was taxed at the same rate as the rich plantations in the low country, but the back country had neither representation in the Commons House nor local courts. When a group of back country landowners organized themselves as Regulators in the summer of 1767 to stop lawlessness on the frontier, they petitioned the Commons House for circuit courts, a written legal code, parishes with churches and schools, and county lines surveyed as far as the Indian boundary. The Circuit Court Act of 1769 redressed their grievances and created the Ninety Six District in the northwestern section of the province. That same year Patrick Calhoun, the deputy provincial surveyor, was elected to represent the new district in the Commons House. These old animosities flared up again during the American Revolution when many Loyalists, including Richard Pearis, were denounced as "Scopholites"—a term used in the 1760s to identify the Regulators.[45]

The Coming of the Revolution

The events that finally sparked open revolution against Great Britain in the South Carolina low country were the passage of the Tea Act by Parliament in May 1773 and the arrival of HMS *London* in Charles Town on

December 21 loaded with 257 chests of tea. The general meeting of the disaffected populace in Charles Town that followed on July 6, 1774, was the first of a series of revolutionary gatherings that led to formation of an independent state government. In 1775 the South Carolina Provincial Congress met, and eight years of war began. Both British Loyalists and American patriots were well aware that they needed allies in the back country—not only to support their causes, but also to keep peace with the Cherokees lest they have to fight two wars simultaneously. While no more than one-fifth of the free population of South Carolina became Loyalists in any sense during the Revolution, perhaps the strongest concentration of supporters of the crown lived in the Ninety Six District between the Saluda and the Broad Rivers, southeast of the Indian boundary. In July 1775 the patriots in Charles Town sent a mission to the back country, led by planter William Henry Drayton, to persuade their fellow citizens to subscribe to the revolutionary Association of the Provincial Congress.[46]

The Struggle for the Back Country

Recognizing the need to cultivate the friendship of the Cherokees, Drayton proposed that Richard Pearis, initially friendly with the revolutionary party, arrange a meeting for him with the chiefs. Always eager to turn any opportunity to his advantage, Pearis expressed his willingness to assist Drayton if the patriot would defray his expenses and intercede on his behalf with the sheriff at Ninety Six who was about to seize Pearis's property for a debt he owed to a Charles Town merchant firm. Drayton reported to the revolutionary leaders that Pearis had offered to secure such an arrangement with land at bargain prices. Drayton refused the land, but he intervened with the Ninety Six authorities to stay the confiscation of Pearis's property for several months. Pearis then escorted four Cherokee leaders to the Congarees, near the present site of Columbia, for a meeting with Drayton. There the patriot leader gave Pearis a message to deliver to a subsequent gathering of Cherokee leaders at Sugar Town in October. By fall the British Indian officials were likewise soliciting Cherokee support. Alexander Cameron challenged George Pearis at the meeting at Sugar Town, reminding the Indians how the elder Pearis had attempted to defraud them in the past.[47]

Both the British and the patriots attempted to pacify the Indians by supplying them with needed ammunition for hunting. In October 1775 the patriot Council of Safety in Charles Town ordered 1,000 pounds of powder and 2,000 pounds of lead sent to Keowee, where Richard Pearis agreed to distribute it to the Cherokees. Meanwhile, Pearis was vying with

Edward Wilkinson for appointment as one of the patriot commissioners to the Indians. When the leaders in Charles Town selected Wilkinson, Pearis soon switched his allegiance to the British. The ammunition from Charles Town never reached the Cherokees because a force of Loyalists under Patrick Cunningham, who lived on the Saluda River south of the Indian boundary, captured the wagon train before it reached Ninety Six. When patriot Major Andrew Williamson attempted to recapture the powder with five hundred militia members, he was defeated by fifteen hundred men under Cunningham's command—including Richard Pearis.[48]

At the outbreak of hostilities, the militia in the Upper Saluda District, east and south of the Indian boundary, was under the command of Colonel Thomas Fletchall of Union. When Fletchall adhered to the British cause, Captain John Thomas gathered the patriot officers of the regiment at his home on Fairforest Creek on September 11, 1775, to organize a separate militia unit. Thomas (born in Cardiff, Wales, in 1720) had migrated with his family to Chester County, Pennsylvania. He was at Fort Duquesne with General Braddock in July 1755. Shortly afterwards he moved to South Carolina—first to the Camden District and then to Fairforest Creek around 1762. As the patriots gathered at Thomas's house, a letter arrived from William Henry Drayton, then at Ninety Six, urging Thomas to rally the patriots. Thomas replied that he could not raise an entire regiment, since that large a force would strip the frontier of defense. But he promised to recruit as many as possible from every company.[49]

The Snow Campaign

The patriot leaders in Charles Town planned to break the strength of the Loyalists in the Ninety Six District once and for all. The leaders entrusted patriot Colonel Richard Richardson from south of Camden with this mission. On December 8, 1775, Richardson issued a declaration to the Loyalists under Cunningham's command demanding both their surrender and the ammunition originally destined for the Cherokees. Richardson raised three thousand men, including John Thomas's group (by then designated the Spartan Regiment), and marched in pursuit of Cunningham's force. By December 12 he captured Richard Pearis and eight other Tory leaders. On December 21 Richardson had five thousand troops, including a large detachment from North Carolina, at his camp at Hollingsworth Mill on Rabun's Creek just south of the Indian boundary. He ordered thirteen hundred men under Colonel William Thomson of St. Matthew's Parish to pursue the Loyalists into Indian territory. The winter weather was severe, and the men, according to Richardson, had few heavy clothes, badly worn shoes, and no tents.[50]

Thomson and his men marched 25 miles through the night to the Loyalist camp at "the Brake of Canes." This site is about 7 miles southwest of present-day Simpsonville. The patriot force surrounded the camp long before sunrise. At dawn on December 22 Thomson and his men attacked the surprised Loyalists—still in their tents. According to Richardson's report, the Loyalist commander Patrick Cunningham escaped on his horse bare-backed and without his breeches, shouting to every man to shift for himself. There were only a few casualties in the Battle of the Great Canebreak—one patriot wounded and five or six Loyalists killed. The patriots were out for blood, but Thompson restrained his men. They seized the ammunition, originally destined for the Cherokees, and took 130 prisoners. On December 23 the patriots returned to Richardson's camp where the patriot commander forced the Loyalists to sign a document, promising to forfeit their estates if they took up arms again. Snow fell for thirty hours—accumulating between 15 inches and 2 feet. Richardson broke camp on Christmas Day, dismissed the North Carolina troops, and marched toward the Congarees—ending what came to be known as the Snow Campaign. The prisoners were sent to Charles Town, and the patriot victory ended the Loyalist threat to the area for the time being. The next attack, when it came, would be primarily at the hands of the Indians.[51]

Indian Attack on the Frontier

Both the British and patriot officials continued to win the favor of the Cherokees without unleashing them against the frontier settlements, but both groups ultimately failed. In May 1776 rumors of Indian attack forced settlers in the northwest into their stockade forts. Preston and Edward Hampton, the brothers of Wade Hampton, who were probably in the pay of the patriots in Charles Town, countered the rumors by boasting openly in the Lower Towns where they traded that a patriot force was on its way to capture Alexander Cameron and other British sympathizers in the Cherokee Nation. On May 17 Cameron, with some twenty Loyalists and a band of Cherokee warriors, captured Preston and Edward Hampton, then released them after they took an oath of neutrality.[52]

In late May 1776 a delegation of Shawnees, Delawares, and Mohawks from the Ohio country arrived in the Overhill Towns. This delegation reported that patriots in the North were raising armies to attack them and urged their Southern brothers to join in resistance. The Cherokees decided that the time had come to fight. Cameron abandoned his strategy of re-straint and asked only that the chiefs remain within the Indian boundary and spare the Loyalists, as well as all women and children. Reports of Chero-kee attacks along the frontier began to circulate in South Carolina. In mid-June Preston Hampton, with orders to capture Cameron, led a party of twenty-three men into Indian territory, and in a subsequent fight Hamp-ton and four of his compatriots died. Also killed by midsummer was James Hite, the son of Greenville settler Jacob, while on a mission in the Lower Towns to kill or capture Cameron. He met a war party near Estatoe that scalped and killed him.[53]

On the morning of June 30 a war party of Cherokees and Tories rode into the Hampton settlement just east of the Indian boundary. This war party killed Anthony and Elizabeth Hampton and the infant son of their daughter, Elizabeth Harrison. According to one account, the baby had been left with them while his mother went to visit a neighbor, Mrs. Sadler. Elizabeth Harrison and Mrs. Sadler watched from the nearby canebrake, where they had hidden, and then quickly rode to Wood's Fort for help. By the time help came, the raiders had left, but not before they stopped at Preston Hampton's house and killed his two children. His wife was found several days later, wandering through the woods. Her mind never recov-ered from the trauma of the event.[54]

Jacob Hite and his family died in the onslaught on July 1. He had already declared his support for the patriot cause, but he believed that his long-standing friendship with the Indians would save him from attack. Tradition has it that one of the daughters of Richard Pearis, who had been engaged to the recently killed James Hite, went to warn the Hites when she heard of the impending raid. But Jacob Hite was killed, his two daugh-ters Susan and Eleanor disappeared, and his wife Frances was kidnapped. Frances Hite's body was discovered by the militia under the command of Colonel Andrew Williamson on August 9, in a deserted Indian town. A similar fate befell the Hannon family on the North Pacolet River just over the line in North Carolina.[55]

Many of the Cherokee war parties were joined by Loyalists. One, a Captain York, rode into the white settlements to recruit British adherents to join the Cherokee raids. Richard Pearis's plantation at the falls of the Reedy River became a staging area for these attacks. During the first week in July, according to a report sent by Alexander Cameron to the Board of Trade in London, one hundred patriots were killed and numerous women and children captured on the Greenville frontier. Of the raiding parties, only two died.[56]

Campaigns Against the Indians

Such depredations along the Southern frontier aroused the new state governments to action. President John Rutledge in Charles Town began corresponding with the presidents of the Virginia Convention and the North Carolina Council about a joint campaign against the Cherokees. He authorized Andrew Williamson to raise a force in the Ninety Six District to attack the Lower Towns and urged North Carolina to join Williamson against the Middle and Valley Towns. At the same time, Virginia prepared to move against the Overhill Towns.[57]

The frontiersmen along the Indian boundary did not wait for authorization from the patriot leaders in Charles Town or New Bern. Captain Thomas Howard, born in 1760, and eventually a resident on upper Greenville lands, gathered a force at the Block House, located on the Indian boundary at the North Carolina-South Carolina line. His objective was to attack a party of Indians and Loyalists under the command of Big Warrior, encamped at what has been known ever since as Big Warrior Gap. Howard enlisted the assistance of a friendly Cherokee, Skyuka, who led the patriots behind the Loyalist encampment through what is now known as Howard's Gap, east of Big Warrior. Howard's force surprised the Indians and killed and wounded a large number. After the Battle of Round Mountain, the Indians buried their dead and covered the common grave with a mound of rock.[58]

By July 17, only five hundred patriots had gathered at DeWitt's Corner to join Williamson's command. There was considerable hesitancy among the men to leave their families in the poorly defended forts on the frontier. Williamson's mission was to repeat the scorched-earth policy of the Cherokee War of 1760–1761. "Cut up every Indian cornfield," William Henry Drayton wrote him, "and burn every Indian town. . . . For my part, I shall never give my voice for a peace with the Cherokee Nation upon any other terms than their removal beyond the mountains."[59]

As Williamson marched toward the Lower Towns, he detached one hundred men under Captain Leroy Hammond to burn Richard Pearis's plantation, which he termed "a rendezvous for the Indians and Scopholites." Hammond was instructed to join Colonel Thomas's Spartans and Lieutenant-Colonel Ezekiel Polk's North Carolina troops in attacking Pearis's Great Plains. Afterwards, the forces would march to Keowee where Williamson would be waiting. Williamson and Thomas were both strong-willed and did not always work in harmony. "I have wrote [sic] and sent him express upon express," Williamson reported, "to no purpose. It is really disagreeable to have any connexion with such men." Nevertheless, Thomas joined forces with Hammond and Polk and burned the Pearis plantation. They seized the slaves and stock and transported them to Fort Prince, where they were sold at public auction on July 16, 17, and 18 (bringing £7,733 in South Carolina currency). Meanwhile Pearis, released from prison in Charles Town, appeared in Williamson's camp on July 18. He was treated politely, but with no special welcome. Shortly thereafter Pearis petitioned the legislature for compensation for his loses and received £700. Two years later the legislature granted Thomas and Polk immunity from any further claims filed by Pearis.[60]

Because of their extended action on the Reedy River, Thomas and Polk failed to meet Williamson at Keowee on August 2, but the burning of Pearis's plantation had frightened the Indians. Williamson continued his march and, by August 22 had burned all the Lower Towns. Simultaneously, General Griffith Rutherford of North Carolina marched through the Middle and Valley Towns, and the Virginians destroyed the Overhill Towns. The Cherokees were now ready to negotiate.[61]

The Treaty of DeWitt's Corner

The patriots concluded two treaties with the Indians—one at Long Island in the Holston River for North Carolina and Virginia, and one at DeWitt's Corner for South Carolina and Georgia. Negotiations began at DeWitt's Corner on May 7, 1777. Williamson, Hammond, Drayton, and Daniel Horry, representing South Carolina, met with three Georgia commissioners and eight Cherokee chiefs. By the terms of the treaty, signed on May 20, the Cherokees acknowledged "the conquest of all the Cherokee lands, eastward of the Unacay Mountain . . . and the Cherokee Nation in consequence thereof do cede the said lands to the said people, the people of South Carolina." All the land previously reserved to the Cherokees in South Carolina was transferred to the state except for a strip of territory in what is now Oconee and northwestern Pickens Counties. The treaty was contingent on the ultimate victory of the patriots in the War for Independence, but the Cherokees were no longer a major threat on the frontier.[62]

Civil War on the Frontier

For a year and a half the fighting shifted to the northern and middle states. Not until December 1778, when the war in the North reached a stalemate, did the British renew the fighting in the South. On December

29 Savannah fell, and on May 12, 1780, the American army surrendered Charles Town. Subsequently, the British established garrisons in Georgetown, Camden, Ninety Six, and Augusta to control the back country. State militia units under the command of Thomas Sumter, William Hill, Andrew Pickens, and Francis Marion resisted whenever and however they could. Near the former Indian boundary, the patriot settlers were normally out of British reach, but they were in constant danger from Loyalists and the savage onslaughts of those whom Benjamin F. Perry later referred to as "plundering renegades, called 'out-layers,' who belonged to no party, or any party." They possessed, he wrote, "all the meanness of civilization, without any of the heroism of a savage life." This infighting among the patriots, the Loyalists, and the "outlayers" reduced life on the frontier to continual terrorism.[63]

The terrorism intensified during the summer and fall of 1781 after the British abandoned the garrison at Ninety Six. Patriot victories at Kings Mountain in October 1780 and at Cowpens in January 1781, led Lord Cornwallis to reduce the British presence in South Carolina and march toward Yorktown in Virginia. American troops lay siege to Ninety Six, from which the British withdrew in July. Without strategic support, the Loyalists on the northwest frontier launched their own offensive.

Two of the most infamous local leaders shared the same epithet, "Bloody Bill." The more widely known was William Cunningham, a cousin of the respected brothers—Robert, Patrick, and David—who were planters on the Saluda River north of Ninety Six and supporters of the crown. Like Richard Pearis, "Bloody Bill" Cunningham was at first a patriot and then a Loyalist. He served in the Loyalist militia until the British withdrew from Ninety Six in July 1781. Thereafter, in the summer and fall of 1781, with a band of sixty recruits known as "the Bloody Scout" from the region between the Saluda and the Enoree Rivers, Cunningham captured a number of frontier forts and attacked an armed party of patriots south of the Saluda. He then systematically pillaged and looted the area south of the former Indian boundary.[64]

At the same time, "Bloody Bill" Bates led a force of Loyalists and Indians that terrorized the frontier farther north. According to Perry, Bates attacked Gowen's Fort in November 1781. After a brief engagement, Bates offered the defenders protection, and the fort surrendered. Some were put to torture, though the majority were killed on the spot. A few, including Major Buck Gowen, were forced to march into the hills to be later killed, but they eventually escaped. One of those marked for torture was a young man named Motley or Matlow, whose family had already been killed. As he was being chained to a stake, young Motley appealed to Bates, once his neighbor, for mercy. "Damn you," Bates replied, "I have nothing to do with you." Motley broke away, was wounded in the thigh, and escaped through a canebrake. Years later, according to Perry, Bates was arrested for stealing horses and placed in jail in Greenville. Motley gathered a few neighbors and rode into Greenville forcing their way into the jail and dragging Bates outside. Before Motley shot Bates, he exclaimed: "Die, scoundrel, and receive the punishment your hellish life has merited." The former Loyalist, in Perry's words, "fell without uttering a syllable, and was buried where he fell, at the prison door." Motley was never prosecuted for the murder of "Bloody Bill" Bates. John B. O. Landrum, in a less romantic account, placed the attack in November 1781 at Wood's Fort, or Thompson's Station, as it was sometimes called. He connected the story of the Motley family with a raid on their farm, not the fighting at Wood's Fort.[65]

Jane Thomas and Dicey Langston Springfield

The closing days of the Revolution produced not only villains, but heroines as well, two of whom lived in the Greenville District after the war. Jane Thomas, a native of Pennsylvania, married Colonel John Thomas in 1740 and moved to Spartanburg about 1762. Though Colonel Thomas commanded the Spartan Regiment in the early years of the war, he took British protection as did many other patriot leaders after the capture of Charles Town in 1780. That fall, however, he raised another patriot militia group, was arrested by the British for breaking parole, and was jailed at Ninety Six. His son, John Thomas, Jr., then took command of the new Spartan Regiment. Meanwhile, Jane Thomas accompanied her husband to Ninety Six to look after him while he was in prison. One evening she overheard talk of a Loyalist attack on the Spartan Regiment. To warn her son, Jane Thomas rode all night from Ninety Six to Cedar Springs, where the regiment was encamped. When the Loyalists attacked during the night of July 13, 1781, it was they who were surprised and defeated.[66]

Laodicea (Dicey) Langston Springfield, born in 1766, lived on Duncan's Creek in what is now Laurens County with her parents, Solomon and Sarah Bennett Langston. According to her obituary in the Greenville *Mountaineer,* she "took an active part in the struggle and performed many daring deeds." Family tradition filled out the story. During the raids of 1781 she learned that the community in which her brother James lived was about to be attacked by Loyalists. To warn him, she walked miles through the night—wading swamps and creeks up to her neck. On another occasion she protected her elderly father from Tory raiders by throwing herself between him and the Loyalists. Once she refused to give information to Tories. "Shoot me, if you dare," she said, "I will not tell you." In 1783, after the war, she married Thomas Springfield, and they settled in upper Greenville District near present-day Travelers Rest.[67]

In 1782, after Cornwallis's surrender at Yorktown, there was only scattered fighting along the frontier. "Bloody Bill" Cunningham led a second raid on the Saluda River, but this time he was defeated by a party of patriots. The newspapers reported the defeat of a group of Loyalists from the "Indian Ground" under the command of a Colonel Black in the Ninety Six District. But rumors were rife that Britain was ready to end the hostilities. On December 14, 1782, the British troops formally evacuated Charles Town, and the Revolution in South Carolina was over. Greenville land was no longer the frontier of the British empire.[68]

Notes

1. Early nineteenth-century descriptions of Greenville County include John Drayton, *A View of South-Carolina, As Respects Her Natural and Civil Concerns* (Charleston, 1802, 1972) and Robert Mills, *Statistics of South Carolina* (Charleston, 1826, 1972), especially 17–103, 571–75. Geological studies funded by the state at mid-century are Michael Tuomey, *Report on the Geology of South Carolina* (Columbia, 1848) and Oscar H. Lieber, *Report on the Survey of South Carolina* (Columbia, 1859). A popular survey is found in Guy A. Gullick, *Greenville County: Economic and Social* (Columbia, 1921), 29–33. The most recent treatment of the state's geography is Charles F. Kovacik and John J. Winberry, *South Carolina: A Geography* (Boulder, Colo., 1987).

2. Leland Ferguson, "The First South Carolinians," *South Carolina Wildlife* 21: 5, 14–24; Leland Ferguson, "Indians of the Southern Appalachians Before DeSoto," in "The Conference on Cherokee Prehistory," David G. Moore, assembler, (Swannanoa, N.C., 1986), 1–6.

3. Ibid.

4. The standard treatment of the American Indians in this region is Charles Hudson, *The Southeastern Indians* (Knoxville, Tenn., 1976). An older book, but still useful, is Chapman J. Milling, *Red Carolinians* (Columbia, 1940). Most recent for this area is Ferguson, "Indians of the Southern Appalachians." The highly disputed question of whether the Cherokees are connected with the Paleo-Indians or migrated into the region later is discussed in Roy S. Dickens, Jr., "The Origins and Development of Cherokee Culture," in Duane H. King, *The Cherokee Nation: A Troubled History* (Knoxville, Tenn., 1979), esp. 26–28.

5. Eighteenth-century accounts of the Cherokees by Europeans include James Glen, "A Description of South Carolina" in *Colonial South Carolina: Two Contemporary Descriptions,* ed. Chapman J. Milling (Columbia, 1951), 3–104; James Adair,

History of the American Indians, ed. Samuel C. Williams, (Johnson City, Tenn., 1930, 1968); and Henry Timberlake, *Lieutenant Henry Timberlake's Memoirs, 1756–1765,* ed. Samuel C. Williams (Marietta, Ga., 1948). Population figures can be extracted from Glen, 68; Adair, 227; and Louis DeVorsey, Jr., *The Indian Boundary in the Southern Colonies, 1763–1775* (Chapel Hill, N.C., 1966), 19–20. A readable study is David H. Corkran, *The Cherokee Frontier: Conflict and Survival, 1740–62* (Norman, Okla., 1962).

The problem of identifying Cherokee towns is treated in Betty Anderson Smith, "Distribution of Eighteenth-Century Cherokee Settlements" in Duane H. King, *The Cherokee Nation* (Knoxville, Tenn., 1979). An invaluable account for this area is Forest Acres/McKissick Quest Program, *Cherokee Villages in South Carolina* (Easley, 1990).

6. William Bartram, *The Travels of William Bartram,* ed. Francis Harper (New Haven, Conn., 1958), 306–7.

7. A useful summary of Cherokee life and culture in the eighteenth century can be found in Corkran, *Cherokee Frontier,* 306–7.

8. One version of the tradition from a manuscript now lost was reported by Philip E. Pearson in 1842 and cited in Douglas S. Brown, *The Catawba Indians: The People of the River* (Columbia, 1966), 29–30. See also John H. Logan, *A History of the Upper Country of South Carolina from the Earliest Periods to the Close of the War of Independence* (Columbia, 1859), 16.

9. This somewhat romantic view of the early Piedmont landscape appears in Logan, *Upper Country,* 2–15.

10. Logan, *Upper Country.*

11. Ibid., 15–34, cites stories of early wildlife.

12. Commissioner of Locations, Ninety Six District North Side of Saluda River, Plat Book A, 71, 50, 57. Greenville County Mesne Conveyance Records, S.C. Department of Archives and History, Columbia, S.C. (microfilm).

13. Stanley S. Crittenden, *The Greenville Century Book* (Greenville, 1903), 6. Though little formal archeological work has been done on American Indian sites in Greenville County, the Institute of Archeology and Anthropology, University of South Carolina, maintains a file of sites. See for example *S.C. Institute of Archeology and Anthropology Notebook 13 (1981): 23; 15 (January–August, 1983): 1–2, 19; 18 (1986): 1–4. Tommy C. Charles, in S.C. Institute of Archeology and Anthropology Notebook 13 (1981): 2ff.,* surveyed collections of Indian artifacts. He describes what is known of the collections of A. S. Powell and Charles F. Schwing, now dispersed or destroyed.

14. William E. Myer, "Indian Trails of the Southeast," *42nd Annual Report of the Bureau of American Ethnology, 1924–1925* (Washington, D.C., 1928), 727–857.

15. The paths through present-day Greenville County can be traced on two early maps: Henry Mouzon, "An Accurate Map of North and South Carolina With Their Indian Frontiers" (1775), and B. Romans, "A General Map of the Southern British Colonies in America . . . With the Neighboring Indian Countries" (1776).

Copies can be found in the Seaborn Map Collection, Oconee County Library, Walhalla, S.C.

16. Mouzon and Romans Maps. The lower path appears as the Lower Cherokee Traders' Path in Gary C. Goodwin, *Cherokees in Transition: A Study of Changing Culture and Environment Prior to 1775*. Research Paper, Department of Geography, No. 181 (Chicago, 1977), 89.

17. Myer designates the paths as Trail 77, Lower Cherokee Trading Path prior to 1775; Trail 37, The Old Cherokee Path to Virginia; and Trail 78, South Carolina State Road to the North. Myer, "Indian Trails," 772–77.

18. Charles Hudson, Marvin T. Smith, and Chester DePratter, "The Hernando DeSoto Expedition: From Apalachee to Chiaha," *S.C. Institute of Archeology and Anthropology Notebook* 19 (1987): 18–28; Chester DePratter, Charles Hudson, and Marvin T. Smith, "The Route of Juan Pardo's Explorations in the Interior South East, 1566–1568," *Florida Historical Quarterly* 61 (1982–1983): 125–58.

19. Verner W. Crane, *The Southern Frontier, 1670–1732* (New York, 1928, 1981), 40–41. Milling, *Red Carolinians*, 266–67.

20. Milling, *Red Carolinians*, 277.

21. DeVorsey, *Boundary*, 113–15; Robert L. Meriwether, *The Expansion of South Carolina, 1729–1765* (Kingsport, Tenn., 1940), 123–25, 195.

22. Milling, *Red Carolinians*, 281–85; David Duncan Wallace, *South Carolina, A Short History, 1520–1948* (Chapel Hill, N.C., 1951), 172–73, 179–81. For the 1761 line, see DeVorsey, *Boundary*, 114, fig. 15.

23. DeVorsey, *Boundary*, 27–36.

24. David K. Eliades, "The Indian Policy of Colonial South Carolina, 1670–1763" (Ph.D. diss., University of South Carolina, 1981), 247–49; DeVorsey, *Boundary*, 124–30.

25. DeVorsey, *Boundary*, 131–32; Meriwether, *Expansion*, 133; Peter Wood, *Black Majority, Negroes in Colonial South Carolina from 1670 through the Stono Rebellion* (New York, 1974), 30–31.

26. DeVorsey, *Boundary*, 133.

27. Ibid., 97, 101–2.

28. Ronald E. Bridwell, "Acquisition and Conflict: A History of South Carolina's Western Lands, 1763–1784" (M.A. thesis, University of South Carolina, 1968), 47–48; DeVorsey, *Boundary*, 108–9.

29. John C. Miller, *Origins of the American Revolution* (Stanford, Calf., 1959), 76.

30. A detailed account of the Cameron grant, based on Colonial Office Papers, British Public Record Office, and the General Thomas Gage Papers, William L. Clements Library, University of Michigan, can be found in Bridwell, "Acquisition and Conflict," 63–69. See also John R. Alden, *John Stuart and the Southern Colonial Frontier, . . . 1754–1775* (Ann Arbor, Mich., 1944), 298.

31. The most thorough treatment of Richard Pearis's career can be found in Mrs. Beverly T. (Mildred E.) Whitmire, "Richard Pearis, Bold Pioneer," *The Proceedings and Papers of the Greenville County [S.C.] Historical Society* 1 (1962–1964):

75–85. Unfortunately Mrs. Whitmire's work was prepared as an address and does not contain her documentation. For Pearis in Virginia, see W. Neil Franklin, "Virginia and the Cherokee Trade, 1753–1775," *East Tennessee Historical Society Publications* 5 (1933): 22–28 and William W. Abbott et al., eds., *The Paper of George Washington* Colonial Series, 3–4 (Charlottesville, Va., 1984), passim. For Pearis's initial contacts with the Cherokees and Catawbas in South Carolina, see *Documents Relating to Indian Affairs, 1754–1765*, in *The Colonial Records of South Carolina*, ed. William L. McDowell, Jr. (Columbia, 1970), 15–16, 20.

32. Corkran, *Cherokee Frontier*, 55–56; Bridwell, "Acquisition and Conflict," covers the Pearis story in detail, 77–102.

33. A careful study of Hite, both in Virginia and South Carolina, is Mildred E. Whitmire, "A Man and His Land: The Story of Jacob and Frances Madison Hite and the Cherokees," *Magazine of the Jefferson County* [Va.] *Historical Society* 44 (December 1978): 37–58.

34. This account closely follows Bridwell, "Acquisition and Conflict," chapter 7.

35. The provincial boundary is treated in Alexander S. Salley, *The Boundary Line Between North Carolina and South Carolina*, Bulletin of the Historical Commission of South Carolina, 10 (Columbia, 1929), and Bridwell, "Acquisition and Conflict," 49–62.

36. Petition of George Hite, February 8, 1784; Petition of Anne Armstrong, February 28, 1784; and Grant to Baylis Earle, March 20, 1784 in *Journals of the House of Representatives, 1783–1784, State Records of South Carolina*, ed. Theodora J. Thompson and Rosa S. Lumpkin (Columbia, 1977), 411–12. 578; Affidavit of Jonathan Clark, August 21, 1775, in Robert W. Gibbes, *Documentary History of the American Revolution* (New York, 1855, 1972) 1: 147–48.

37. The story of the Wilkinson tract is found in Alden, *John Stuart*, 300, and Bridwell, "Acquisition and Conflict," 70–76. After Wilkinson's death, his family secured 3,200 acres from the state. *The Statutes at Large of South Carolina*, ed. Thomas Cooper and David J. McCord (Columbia, 1836–1840) 4: 645–46.

38. Testimony of Colonel Richard Pearis and Major Christopher Neely, August 25, 1786, and William Cunningham, March 21, 1786, Loyalist Claims Commission, Audit Office 12, 49: 203, 305, 307, 312–13, British Public Record Office (photostats in S.C. Room, Greenville County Library, Greenville, S.C.). The location of Pearis's house has been identified by Ann McCuen as being on Main Street to the rear of the present Carpenters' Brothers Drug Store. Benjamin F. Perry cited the location in the Greenville *Enterprise*, September 6, 1871. The designation of "Pearis's waggon road" appears in a number of sources including *The Statutes at Large of S.C.* 4: 661–68 and 7: 211.

39. Whitmire, "Hite," 40–42; *S.C. House Journals, 1783–1784*, 411–12.

40. Plat Book A, 21 (Samuel Earle); *S.C. House Journals, 1783–1784*, 411–12, 578; Joseph E. Birnie, *The Earles and the Birnies* (Richmond, Va., 1974), 35–50; James M. Richardson, *History of Greenville County, South Carolina* (Atlanta, Ga., 1930), 34; James A. Howard, *Dark Corner Heritage* (Greenville, 1980), 3–4. Family tradition also locates the Nathaniel Austin family in Greenville in 1761. For the

family claim, see James W. Austin and Josephine M. A. Knight, *The Austin and Allied Families,* 2nd ed. (Atlanta, Ga., 1972), 3–4, and Aurelia Austin, *Captain Nathaniel (Nathan) Austin of Gilder Plantation, South Carolina* (Atlanta, Ga., 1986), passim. The earliest records indicate that Austin owned land on Rabun's Creek in Laurens County before January 1, 1789, and on Gilder's Creek in Greenville County by August 8, 1789, Deed Book C, 208, 164, in Sarah M. Nash, *Abstracts of Early Records of Laurens County, South Carolina, 1785–1820* (Fountain Inn, S.C., 1982), 47, 44.

41. S.C. Writers Program, *A History of Spartanburg County* (Spartanburg, 1940), 15–16.

42. Bridwell, "The South's Wealthiest Planter: Wade Hampton I of South Carolina" (Ph.D. diss., 1980), 10–16, 31–36; family tradition is recounted in Virginia G. Meynard, *The Venturers: The Hampton, Harrison, and Earle Families of Virginia, South Carolina and Texas* (Easley, S.C., 1981), 58–69.

43. Meriwether, *Expansion,* 234–36; Richard M. Brown, *The South Carolina Regulators* (Cambridge, Mass., 1963), 8; Logan, *Upper Country,* 28–32.

44. John B. O. Landrum, *Colonial and Revolutionary History of Upper South Carolina* (Greenville, 1897), 30–34; Richardson, *Greenville County,* 34; Plat Book A, 75 (Jordan), 122 (Dutton), 56 (Thompson).

45. Brown, *Regulators,* 124; the report of patriot Colonel Richard Richardson after the Snow Campaign lists "R'd Pearis, Scopholite Captain, Ninety Six," Gibbes, *Documentary History* 1: 249.

46. The events of the American Revolution in South Carolina can be followed in any of the standard accounts: Wallace, *Short History,* or the more detailed Edward McCrady, *History of South Carolina,* vols. 3 and 4 (New York, 1901, 1969). A short, readable account is Lewis Jones, *The South Carolina Civil War of 1775* (Lexington, S.C., 1975). The role of the Loyalists is the subject of Robert S. Lambert, *South Carolina Loyalists in the American Revolution* (Columbia, 1987), esp. 306–8.

47. Drayton, "An Address to the Inhabitants of the Frontier Settlements," Journal of the Second Council of Safety, December 6, 1775, S.C. Historical Society *Collections* 3 (1859): 53–57; Bridwell, "Acquisition and Conflict," 105–7.

48. Bridwell, "Acquisition and Conflict," 113–18; Congress created five Indian commissioners, but appointed only two. South Carolina was empowered to appoint three. Pearis was passed over for Wilkinson, George Galphin, and Robert Rae. James H. O'Donnell III, "The Southern Indians in the War for Independence, 1775–1783" (Ph.D. diss., Duke University, 1963), 31, 33.

49. Landrum, *History of Spartanburg County* (Atlanta, Ga., 1900), 134–37; "John Thomas, Jr.," *Biographical Dictionary of the South Carolina House of Representatives,* ed. Walter B. Edgar and Louise Bailey (Columbia, 1974–1992) 3: 708–9.

50. McCrady, *History* 3: 94–97. The documents, including Richardson's, are in Gibbes, *Documentary History* 1: 224–25, 239–53.

51. McCrady, *History* 3: 94–97.

52. O'Donnell, "Southern Indians," 65–66, 69; Bridwell, "Acquisition and Conflict," 122–23; Bridwell, "Hampton," 48–49.

53. O'Donnell, "Southern Indians," 66–68; Joseph Johnson, *Traditions and Reminiscences Chiefly of the American Revolution in the South* (Charleston, 1851, 1972), 458–59; Whitmire, "Hite," 38–39; Bridwell, "Hampton," 55.

54. Landrum, *Upper South Carolina*, 86–89, 94–95; Bridwell has carefully collated the evidence and gives a reasonable account of the Hampton massacre in "Hampton," chapter 2.

55. Johnson, *Traditions*, 459; Whitmire, "Hite," 42–43; Bridwell, "Acquisition and Conflict," 125–26.

56. Bridwell, "Aquisition and Conflict," 125–26.

57. O'Donnell, "Southern Indians," 73–74; Bridwell, "Acquisition and Conflict," 126.

58. Landrum, *Upper South Carolina*, 96–97; Howard, *Dark Corner*, 5–11.

59. O'Donnell, "Southern Indians," 75–76.

60. Gibbes, *Documentary History* 2: 24–27; E. F. Rockwell, ed., "Parallel and Combined Expeditions Against the Cherokee Indians in South and in North Carolina [Ross Journal]," *The Historical Magazine* (October 1867) 213; Bridwell, "Acquisition and Conflict," 128–29; Whitmire, "Pearis," 82–83. After Pearis's plantation was burned, his family went to Augusta, and he went to Florida where he served in the loyalist militia. He joined the British during the siege of Charles Town, was later stationed at Ninety Six, and eventually was captured by the patriots at Augusta. After the Revolution, Pearis lived in East Florida and later in Nassau near Robert Cunningham, whose daughter married Richard Pearis, Jr. The elder Pearis died in 1794. Whitmire, "Pearis," 83–85. Pearis filed a substantial claim for losses in the Revolution and received "a handsome reward of £5,624 and an annual allowance of seventy pounds." Lambert, *Loyalists*, 268.

61. Gibbes, *Documentary History* 2:32; O'Donnell, "Southern Indians," 75–98, contains a detailed account of the entire campaign.

62. O'Donnell, "Southern Indians," 120–22. The text of the treaty is published in Archibald Henderson, "The Treaty of Long Island of Holston, July 1777," *N.C. Historical Review* 8 (1931): 76–78.

63. Benjamin F. Perry, *The Writings of Benjamin F. Perry*, ed. Stephen Meats and Edwin T. Arnold (Spartanburg, 1980) 1: 12–13; Perry's work on the Revolution in the up country in collected in ibid., 1: 3–123. The work was earlier collected in part in Johnson, *Traditions*, 419–72.

64. Lambert, *Loyalists*, 206–10; Landrum, *Upper South Carolina*, 341–59; Perry, *Writings* 1: 119–23; McCrady, *History* 4: 77–79.

65. Lambert, *Loyalists*, 224; Perry, *Writings* 1: 4–7; Landrum, *Upper South Carolina*, 359–63. J. D. Bailey, *Some Heroes of the American Revolution* (Spartanburg, 1924, 1976), 227, also identifies Wood's Fort as Thompson's Station.

66. Landrum, *Upper South Carolina*, 110–11; Elizabeth F. Ellett, *The Women of the American Revolution* (New York, 1849) 1: 250–62; Landrum, *Spartanburg County*, 134–43. The site of the John Thomas house and cemetery is on S.C. Route 11, near Lake Cunningham. Mrs. Beverly T. (Mildred) Whitmire, *The Presence of*

the Past: Epitaphs in Greenville County, South Carolina (Baltimore, 1976), Cemetery 80.

67. Obituary of Laodicea Springfield, Greenville (S.C.) *Mountaineer,* June 10, 1837, cited in Brent Holcomb, comp. *Marriage and Death Notices from the Up-Country of South Carolina* (Columbia, 1983), 44. Ellett, *Women* 1: 284–91 traces the accounts to Perry who heard them from a member of the family. Whitmire, *Presence,* Cemetery 158, locates the Springfield place on the Tigerville Road near Travelers Rest.

68. McCrady, *History* 4: 628–31; Lambert, *Loyalists,* 221.

CHAPTER TWO

The Creation and Settlement of Greenville County

In less than a decade after the American Revolution the state of South Carolina opened the former Cherokee land for settlement and established Greenville County. As settlers moved into the area, they created an agricultural society and laid the foundations for their economic, political, religious, and cultural life.

Incorporating Cherokee Land into the Ninety Six District

By the Treaty of DeWitt's Corner of May 20, 1777, the Cherokees formally ceded most of northwestern South Carolina to the self-proclaimed independent state. But the struggle with Britain prevented the state government from any immediate action to incorporate the new territory. Not until March 28, 1778, did the General Assembly in Charles Town ratify an act declaring that "the lands lately ceded by the Indians to this State . . . [were] within the district of Ninety Six, and that the magistrates of Ninety Six district have full power and authority to exercise as much jurisdiction within the same as they are empowered to do within any part of the said district of Ninety-Six." But the newly ceded territory was hardly in the forefront of the concerns of the war-weary government in the low country. In fact, the act incorporating the land into the Ninety Six District was entitled "An Act for Completing the Quota of Troops to be Raised in this State for the Continental Service; and for Other Purposes Therein Mentioned." A number of people had taken refuge in the former Indian land in order to escape service in the Continental Army, and the territory was annexed to the Ninety Six District for the sole purpose of placing these people within the reach of the law. Not until the War for Independence was over did the legislature further utilize the land.[1]

Sale of Greenville Land

South Carolina emerged from the Revolution free from British rule, but nearly bankrupt. The report on the war expenditures to Congress in

1789 indicated that South Carolina's indebtedness was by far the largest of the states—$5,386,232. Only Massachusetts and Virginia reported as much as half of the amount owed by South Carolina. Less than two months after the British evacuated Charles Town, the Ways and Means Committee reported to the state House of Representative that £10,000 could be raised through land sales. Not only would the income enrich the treasury, but the tax base of the state would be considerably broadened. Such optimism proved well founded, for Governor William Moultrie informed the legislature four years later: "Near four Million Acres have been granted since the opening of the Land Office, the purchase money of which when paid into the Treasury, will in addition to our Ancient Grants, by a very moderate Tax on Land, Negroes, and other property as usual, soon Sink the public Debt."[2]

The most vocal champion in the legislature for the development of the back country was Judge Henry Pendleton, a native of Virginia, who moved to South Carolina and was admitted to the bar in 1771. In April 1776 he was elected to the bench, and three years later he began to serve in the legislature, representing first St. David's, then Saxe Gotha in the back country. In 1784 Pendleton purchased 640 acres of Greenville land on which he maintained a residence and twenty-one slaves. After his death the legislature renamed Augusta County in the newly opened land "Pendleton" in his memory.[3]

During the 1783 session Judge Pendleton presented to the House a report from the Ways and Means Committee that recommended the sale of vacant lands belonging to the state. Again and again, he pushed the unwilling legislature toward the creation of a land office. But not until the following year did he gain an important ally. On February 2, 1784, Governor Benjamin Guerard outlined his proposals to the new session of the General Assembly, including opening a land office. On March 21 the legislature ratified an act outlining the method of surveying and granting vacant land. The act empowered the legislature to elect a commissioner of locations in each circuit court district "who shall take and receive the original entry of all vacant lands." In the Ninety Six District, however, two commissioners were appointed—one for the north side of the Saluda River and the other for the south side. The commissioners were required to keep their offices at or near the center of the district and keep them open six days a week. They were empowered to employ a deputy surveyor to locate and stake out the lands for sale. Within two months the surveyor must deliver a plat to the commissioner of locations, and in three months the original plat must be sent to the office of the surveyor general in Charleston. No land warrant could be issued until May 21, 1784, two months after the act became law. On that day individuals were eligible to purchase a maximum of 640 acres at the rate of £10 sterling for each 100 acres. Treasury indents which had been issued in payment for service in the militia during the Revolution could be used to purchase land. On every third Friday of January, April, July, and October the governor was authorized to sign the warrants. On March 25, 1784, a joint session of the General Assembly elected Colonel John Thomas of the Spartan Regiment, then sixty-three-years-old, the commissioner of locations for the north side of the Saluda River.[4]

In clear, precise language the statute provided that "all grants and surveys passed on or made for lands lying beyond the Indian boundary . . . before the passing of this Act, shall, and are hereby declared to be null and void." In regard to the land claimed by Richard Pearis, the action was consistent with the confiscation of Loyalist property. But there were others who held or claimed land either from Pearis, such as the Hites, or from the Cherokees, such as Edward Wilkinson who had served the patriot cause during the Revolution. On February 3 George Hite, on behalf of the heirs of Jacob Hite, submitted a claim for 61,000 acres of land between the Reedy and the Enoree Rivers. On February 23, 1784, Anne Armstrong, for herself and her children, petitioned for the recovery the 500 acres on the Saluda River purchased by her husband, John, in 1775. Elizabeth Wilkinson and her three sons submitted a claim for the estate of her husband Edward, one of the continental Indian superintendents, on March 18. The same day the heirs of John Pritchard—his widow Eleanor and four children—submitted a claim. On March 20 Baylis Earle filed a claim for 500 acres he purchased from Pearis in 1771. By legislative act on March 26 the claimants received grants of land. Six Hite heirs received 6,000 acres, the four Wilkinsons 2,560 acres, and the five Pritchards 3,200 acres. Anne Armstrong and Baylis Earle each received 500 acres. The Hite, Armstrong, and Earle grants were located in what became Greenville County.[5]

On May 21, 1784, the first day that land could be granted under the new law, Colonel Thomas began receiving applications, probably at his home on Fairforest Creek in present-day Spartanburg County. To assist him, he had selected a group of deputy-surveyors—including William Benson, Robert J. Hanna, George Salmon, Thomas Lewis, James Seaborn, Andrew Thomson, Jonathan Downs, David Hopkins, Philemon Waters, Bernard Glenn, John Bowie, W. A. Thomas, and Minor Winn.[6]

The initial survey was made for James Hamilton between nine and twelve o'clock of the first morning the Location Office opened. Hamilton secured the maximum amount of land under the law—a tract of 640 acres on Reedy River known as Pearis's Shoals. That same day Colonel Thomas Brandon of Union purchased the site of the city of Greenville—400 acres on Reedy River including Richard Pearis's plantation. A native of Pennsylvania, Brandon had come to South Carolina and served in the Revolution, first as a major, then colonel, in the Spartan Regiment. He also served in the legislature at various times from 1776 to 1799. Brandon became one of the major landowners in the up country; his Greenville land was only a small part of his 8,097 acreage.[7]

Brandon was one of a number of prominent citizens who speculated in the newly opened lands, but who seldom became residents there. Not as successful as Brandon in land speculation was Colonel Richard Winn of Fairfield who acquired the 640 acres on Reedy River known as the Great Cane Break (where he had fought during the Great Snow Campaign in 1775). Winn eventually owned 3,316 acres, but he sold the Great Cane Brake tract two years after purchasing it. Eventually he was forced to pay his creditors some fifty thousand dollars, and in 1812 he left the state. Not as wealthy as Brandon and Winn was Judge Aedanus Burke who acquired 640 acres on Golden Grove Creek on May 25, 1784. An Irish native, he was an officer in the Revolution until he was elected associate judge in 1778. After the war he became a champion of republican ideals and an antifederalist in the struggle to ratify the federal Constitution.[8]

Less prominent, but much more numerous, were the veterans of continental service who applied for the bounty grants of 200 acres offered by the state. On March 21, 1784, five days before the statute was enacted opening vacant lands, the legislature issued grants in any districts to the officers and soldiers of the South Carolina Continental Line, as well as the navy and the three independent companies. On October 15, 1784, the first two bounty grants of Greenville land were recorded. James Bradley received 200 acres on Golden Grove, and Robert Prince, heir of Robert Prince Pate, received 200 acres on branches of the Enoree River north of Pearis's Mountain. By 1799, when the last bounty grant was recorded, some 6,032 acres of Greenville land had been awarded to veterans.[9]

The land in Ninety Six District north of the Saluda—including Greenville—filled rapidly. Between May 21, 1784, when the land was opened, and January 19, 1785, when the first plat book was filled, Thomas issued warrants for 1,036 tracts of land. Two hundred forty-four warrants, totaling some 97,036 acres, were issued the first day. Not all of that land was actually settled; indeed, 15,028 acres of the initial claims were never surveyed. As many as a dozen of the warrants issued for Greenville land the first year indicated previous settlement. A few referred to claims prior to the Revolution—by Richard Pearis, his brother Robert, and the Hite family. Others indicated improvements that were likely made by squatters during or subsequent to the War for Independence. These squatters filed for land under the new law, but only after the land on which they had first settled was claimed by others. For example, Baylis Earle's tract on the Reedy River included Stephen Ford's improvements, while Ford secured another tract on the Reedy Fork of Reedy River. William Benson's land on the south fork of Reedy River included Sheril's improvements, but Philip Sheril purchased 200 acres on Mush Creek. John Langston claimed 639 acres on Langston Creek of Reedy River near Pearis's Mountain, while John Young purchased 640 acres on Reedy River known as Langston's Improvements. Archibald Dill did secure the 400 acres on which he had originally settled on a branch of South Tyger River.[10]

Land grants not only followed the waterways but also the sites of Indian settlements or camps. George Salmon, one of the deputy surveyors, claimed 640 acres "on both sides of Checharoa River of Saluda well known by the name of Usetie's Camp." Benjamin Clark purchased 200 acres on the same river "including the Town House." On the middle fork of Saluda River John Brandon's 640 acres included "the mouth of the Oyl Camp Creek."[11] At least two Indian paths figure in the earliest land warrants. John Davis claimed 250 acres on the Enoree River "about Two miles below the Lower Indian path." Joseph Dunn received 236 acres on the Checheroa River of the Saluda "on the lower Indian path." Dunn's land was probably located on the lower prong of the upper path to Virginia.[12]

With the rapid granting of land, the population in what became Greenville County rose dramatically. From May 1784, when the Location Office opened, to the first federal census in 1790, the number of people increased from perhaps a dozen families to 5,888 whites and 615 blacks— a total of 6,503. By that time, however, the most desirable land was gone, and in 1791 the legislature revised the land act in order to entice settlers to less attractive tracts. Land was made available to anyone who paid the fee for surveying and registration. But instead of benefiting small landowners, the revised policy encouraged speculation. Large surveys were made of lands already granted and settled, and Governor Moultrie informed the legislature that he had refused to sign several such grants. Finally, on May 10, 1791, the General Assembly closed the Land Office for a period of four years and ordered that no one person was eligible to receive a single grant for more than 500 acres. The land rush in South Carolina was, in effect, over.[13]

The Division of Greenville Land

The teeming, newly opened lands had no effective local government. The judicial districts, which were created in 1769 in the wake of the Regulator movement, provided only circuit courts and sheriffs. On March 24, 1785, the legislature divided the circuit court districts into counties. In each county, a court of seven justices of the peace convened quarterly to hear civil cases in which damages did not exceed £50 and all criminal cases, except those involving capital crimes or corporal punishment. The justices licensed taverns and supervised roads, rivers, bridges and causeways. Each court elected a sheriff and a clerk who would register deeds and draw jury lists. The county was authorized to erect a courthouse, jail, pillory, whipping post, and stocks. The law provided that these county buildings should stand on 2 acres of land acquired by either purchase or donation.[14]

By a legislative act of March 17, 1785, the Ninety Six District was divided into six counties, including Abbeville, Edgefield, Newberry, Laurens (at first named Hereford), Union, and Spartanburg. For administrative purposes, Greenville land was divided between Spartanburg and Laurens Counties. According to the act, the land "to the northwest of the road commonly called Pearis's waggon road up to Saluda River, and thence up to the south fork thereof, shall be annexed to and included in Spartanburgh county." The land southeast of "the said waggon road and Saluda river and the fork of Saluda, down to the old Indian boundary, shall be annexed and included in Laurens county." The Laurens County Court convened on the second Monday of March, June, September, and December, while the Spartanburg court met a week later on the third Monday.[15]

Though the minutes of the Laurens Court have not survived, the records of the Spartanburg County Court indicate the active participation of Greenville residents. Among the seven justices who constituted the court were John Ford, who later became a state senator from Greenville County, and Colonel John Thomas, Jr., the clerk of court who eventually became a Greenville planter. At the first session of the county court in March 1786, George Salmon, one of the deputy surveyors and a resident on the North Saluda River, served on the grand jury, and Isaac Morgan, who had purchased the site of Jacob Hite's place on the Enoree River, sat on the petit jury. The only case involving a Greenville resident to come before the court during the session of March 1785 was the successful effort of James McElhaney from the South Saluda to attach the goods that John James of Indian Creek had put up to secure the bond of Robert and Isham Foster.[16]

Life in Early Greenville

As the elected officials began to shape political and legal institutions for the newly opened land, the landowners were carving farms and plantations out of the old Indian territory. George Salmon, one of the deputy surveyors, is typical of the large landowners. Born in Amelia County, Virginia, in 1754, Salmon had moved to the Ninety Six District by 1773 in time to witness the deeds transferring land from the lower Cherokee chiefs to George Pearis, and eventually to Richard Pearis. During the Revolution Salmon served in the state militia, sometimes as commissary and quartermaster. He became deputy surveyor for the lands north of the Saluda in 1784 and applied for 640 acres in the valley of the North Saluda in full view of the Appalachian Mountains. On March 10, 1785, he married Elizabeth Young, a substantial landowner in her own right. They became the parents of seven children. Salmon built a log dwelling which still stands on the property. It is typical of two other surviving houses of the period that are preserved at the Roper Mountain Science Center. Originally one and a half stories, the Salmon house was constructed of chestnut and oak logs and chinked with clay with two doors and a single window. On one end was a chimney with a five-foot fireplace. A corner stair connected the first floor with the loft above. The floor of the loft consisted of pine boards some 12 inches wide, supported by $2\frac{1}{2}$ inches by $6\frac{1}{2}$ inches rafters inserted into pine logs built into the walls. In 1790 Salmon owned a single slave; four years later his plantation included 5,006 acres.[17]

The furnishing of such a plantation prior to 1800 is reflected in the estate inventory of Robert Maxwell, the sheriff of Greenville County and the Washington District, whose property included 2,116 acres and twelve slaves. In the dwelling house itself the fireplace contained a set of fire dogs, shovel and tongs, and a skillet. Over the fireplace hung a "rifle gun." There were two chairs of some quality and a desk, which held some fifty to sixty volumes. Maxwell's unusually large library reflected his concern with the law and religion. He owned Blackstone's *Commentaries* and the code of laws. There were three Psalm books, a copy of Dodridge's hymnbook, three volumes of *The American Preacher*, two books of sermons, and "Barkett on the New Testament." Of more general works there were two volumes of maps, a volume of the *Annual Register*, the *Universal Gazette*, and a book of poetry.[18]

For dining there was a mahogany table and six Windsor chairs, as well as twenty-six plates of Queens ware, twenty-five spoons, and a case of knives and forks. There were also three pewter dishes and six plates, a coffee pot, and a teapot. The drinking habits of the family was reflected by a "case of bottles." Bedrooms were furnished with bedsteads and mattresses. In addition, the master of the plantation had a case containing "rasors[,] Base & Brush."[19]

While the fireplace in the main house served for cooking at first, a separate kitchen later boasted a pot and hook, five dutch ovens, a spider, and a frying pan. There were also work tables, basins, two wash tubs, two churns, and two iron spice mortars. Two spinning wheels and three wheels for cotton were supplemented with wooden cards and a loom for weaving. The blacksmith shop contained wedges, awls, a branding iron, a hand saw, a drawing knife, three quarter augurs, and a grindstone. Tools for planting included two plows, twelve shovels, six axes, broad hoes, grubbing hoes, and two mattocks. Livestock included 136 hogs, 35 sheep, 50 head of cattle, and geese and ducks in abundance. Eight horses included "Jack the Bachelor" and "Gilding Derby." Transportation for the farm and family consisted of a stage wagon, two smaller wagons, and an ox cart. The major cash crop was wheat, of which there were 111 bushels listed in the inventory.[20]

By 1790 there were 615 blacks in Greenville County, accounting for 9.5 percent of the population. Of these, 606 were slaves and nine free blacks. The James McGlothlin family accounted for four free blacks, and there were five in the household of Martin Mahafee, a white male. Of the 606 slaves, 243 (46 percent) lived on farms with one to four slaves, fifty-nine (11 percent) lived on farms with five to ten slaves, and ninety-three (18 percent) lived on farms or plantations with eleven to twenty-one slaves. There were 155 slaveholders in the county (16 percent of the heads of households). According to the later definition of a planter as an individual who owned twenty or more slaves, there were only two planters in Greenville—John Blassingame (twenty slaves) and James Harrison (twenty-one slaves). By far the largest number of slaveholders, fifty-five (35 percent), owned only one slave.[21]

The Creation of Roads

Connecting these developing farms and plantations were animal trails and Indian paths. But the major corridors crossed Greenville land from east to west, and the new inhabitants petitioned the county government for roads running north and south. In its role as road commission, the Spartanburg County Court, at its December 1785 session, ordered that a road be laid out from the middle fork of the Saluda to the county line, between Reedy River and Brush Creek. This road connected the Middle Saluda settlement with Pearis's wagon road. Appointed overseers of the road were Wood, Salmon, John Foster, Sr., David Kelley, and James Richey; warners were Thomas Bramint, William Right, and James McElhaney. Presumably all these individuals lived on or near the road. A second road was opened from James Alexander's to James McElhaney's, connecting the settlements in the southern part of Greenville with Pearis's wagon road. The overseers were John Alexander, William Ursary, Jeremiah Dutton, and Randolf Casey. James Nicols was appointed to inspect the road.[22]

Richard Harrison and His Store

The mercantile center of the area that became Greenville County was the store operated by Richard Harrison near the Great Cane Brake on the Reedy River. His experience as a merchant had begun prior to 1774 when he served as a storekeeper for Lanier and Williams on Town Creek in piedmont North Carolina. He married the daughter of Anthony Hampton and moved to the South Tyger River with the Hamptons on the eve of the Revolution. After the destruction of his house during the Hampton Massacre in 1776, he settled in Fairforest in present-day Union County. At Cross Keys, where the roads to Charleston and Augusta intersected, Harrison opened a store with his brother-in-law, Wade Hampton I. The partnership lasted only a year, when Charleston fell to the British and the war returned to the up country. Harrison served in the militia until June 1782, when he reopened his store. His surviving account book records transactions from 1783 to 1798. Harrison served as a merchant and factor for the Union, Spartanburg, and Greenville areas, as well as banker, surveyor, planter, and land speculator. In June 1783, for example, he transported 154 pounds of deerskins to Charleston; that fall he made three shipments of tobacco, which totaled 5,932 pounds.[23]

Baylis Earle's account is typical of those doing business with Harrison. On October 5, 1783, Earle purchased 6 yards of linen cloth, 3 yards of ribbon, two spools of thread, and a snuff box. The following day he purchased 22 yards of linen, 21 yards of striped cloth, $3^{1}/_{2}$ yards of narrow broadcloth, as well as two papers of pins, two razors, seven skeins of thread, a silk handkerchief, and a second snuff box. The total cost was £9 7s. 3p. On January 18, 1784, Harrison entered in Earle's account credit for 16 pounds of butter and 294 pounds of tobacco, and the "remainder of your Tobacco sent last winter," which was very likely recorded in a previous account book. The banking functions of Harrison's store are illustrated in the account of William Young, who purchased 1½ gallons of rum in June 1783. Credited to his account was 9s. 4p. by Samuel Jackson on April 28, 1784, and 5s. by Archer Smith in 1785. In May 1785 Harrison paid Young £4 7s. for George Salmon.[24]

When the Location Office opened in May 1784, Harrison began to purchase Greenville land. First, he bought 791 acres on the Reedy River, and two years later he secured the Great Cane Break tract from Richard Winn for £320 sterling. Eventually he is reputed to have owned 15,000 acres in the Carolinas and Tennessee. In 1790 he was the largest slaveholder in Greenville County, with twenty-one slaves. A member of the first Union County Court in 1785, Harrison moved to the Great Cane Break and began construction on Cripple Creek of what was no doubt the most handsome house in Greenville County. The work lasted eighteen months. The house contained thirty thousand bricks, which took sixty days to mold and fire. One-third of them were glazed to make a bonded pattern. The house had ten windows, for which hinges were purchased in Ninety Six. The exterior doors and shutters were painted "egg yellow oker." There were six parallel doors. The downstairs rooms were paneled with walnut, and the other rooms whitewashed.[25]

Richard Harrison opened his store, and soon was shipping tobacco and hemp—not to Charleston, but to Augusta on the Savannah River. His own fields grew tobacco, oats, corn, and wheat, as well as foodstuffs, flax, and cotton for domestic use.[26]

Religion in Early Greenville

The early settlers of what became Greenville County quickly organized religious and educational institutions. The earliest church was a Methodist society organized in 1785 by a group of families who owned land along the Reedy River just north of the Indian boundary. Among them were the Sullivans, Arnolds, Camps, Chandlers, Gores, Hamiltons, Martins, and Ragsdales from Virginia, and the Dunklins from the South Carolina low country. They joined families already settled in nearby Laurens County—the Bowmans, Bollings, Choices, and others. On land belonging to Charles Sullivan near the Reedy River these settlers built a "pole chapel." Peter Ragsdale, on a trip back to Virginia, persuaded his brother-in-law, Mark Moore (a Methodist lay preacher), to return to South Carolina, lead the society, and teach the children in the community. Moore registered a deed for land in Laurens County, dated January 28–29, 1785. Precisely at that time Francis Asbury, the newly elected bishop of the Methodist Episcopal

Church in America, was on his way from Baltimore to organize Methodism in South Carolina, a major manifestation of the eighteenth century evangelical revival. That spring, the annual conference created the Broad River Circuit in South Carolina, which no doubt included the Grove, the chapel that stood on the Sullivan plantation of the same name. In 1786 Mark Moore was admitted to the itinerant ministry and later became the rector of Mount Bethel Academy in Newberry County—the first school established by the South Carolina Conference in 1795.[27]

A Presbyterian congregation was established by a group of Scotch-Irish settlers in Greenville in 1787—the Peden, Alexander, and Nesbit families. John and Peggy McDill Peden were natives of County Antrim, Ireland, from which they emigrated in 1773. They settled initially in Spartanburg near Nazareth Presbyterian Church with their seven sons and three daughters. After the Revolution, they moved to Chester. But their sons, John, Samuel, and David Peden, along with James Alexander and James Nesbit, purchased Greenville land. Alexander donated land near his home for a church, and according to tradition it was named Fairview for their church in County Antrim. The first ruling elders of the congregation were John and Samuel Peden and James and John Alexander. The first sermon under care of presbytery was preached by Samuel Edmondson on April 10, 1787. He had been licensed in 1773 by the Hanover Presbytery in Virginia (the center of the New Side revival which grew out of the Great Awakening). The first regular minister of Fairview Church was John McCosh, a native of Ireland, who was assisted by Robert McClintock.[28]

Baptist churches were organized shortly thereafter. They were part of the Separate Baptist movement, which had originated before the Revolution in Connecticut as an outgrowth of the Great Awakening. The Separate Baptist leadership eventually moved to piedmont North Carolina, and Philip Mulkey established a Separate congregation in South Carolina on Fairforest Creek in the 1750s. From Fairforest, the Separates established churches across the up country. Reedy Fork Church, near the Methodist and Presbyterian churches, was organized prior to 1789, when it was admitted to the Bethel Association. In 1790 the church reported a membership of thirteen, including John Ford, one of the delegates to the association and Greenville County state senator from 1791 to 1795. When Reedy Fork Church closed in 1792, part of its congregation joined Horse Creek Church, which had been constituted in 1789 with twenty-eight members. A decade later it became Fork Shoals Church. In northern Greenville County, the Head of Enoree Church was organized about 1789. In 1791 it had forty-seven members. The pastor, Thomas Mersick, said to have been born in

North Carolina in 1756, was converted to the Baptist way at the age of seventeen. He was excommunicated by the church for immorality in 1793 and replaced by Abraham Hargess. The Head of Enoree Church flourished and counted among its membership a large number of ordained and licensed ministers who served a number of branches—including the Main Saluda, Middle Saluda, Reedy River, and Second Reedy River Horse Neck Churches. The mother congregation was incorporated by the legislature as the Head of Enoree Baptist Society in 1799. Eventually it adopted as its name, Reedy River Church.[29]

The Formation of "Greeneville" County

The rapid settlement of Greenville land and the creation of local economic and cultural institutions foreshadowed the restlessness of the inhabitants between the Saluda River and the old Indian boundary at being annexed to Spartanburg and Laurens Counties. On March 8, 1786, less than a year after annexation, Daniel Huger, a low country planter who represented the up country district between the Broad and Catawba Rivers, arose in the state Senate to present a petition from residents of the newly opened land requesting the formation of new counties. The following day a committee composed of Huger, Colonel William Hill, and Major Zachariah Bullock reported favorably on the petition. The bill made its way through both houses and was ready for ratification on March 22:

> Whereas, the inhabitants of the new ceded lands on the north side of Saluda, below the Indian line have experienced many inconveniences, by being annexed to some of the counties heretofore established;
> I. Be it *ordained*. . . . That a county shall be established in the new ceded lands, by the name of Greeneville, and shall be bounded by Saluda River and the south fork thereof, the old Indian boundary, the North Carolina line, and shall be entitled to county courts to be held on the third Monday in February, May, August, and November; which courts shall hold, exercise and enjoy the several powers and jurisdictions which are by law vested in the said county courts heretofore established.[30]

The use of the terms "county" and "district" in South Carolina is confusing from the end of the Revolution to the adoption of the state Constitution of 1868. The County Court Act of 1785 created county courts and corresponding election districts. Until 1791 Greenville was a part of the Ninety Six judicial district; then it was transferred to the Washington District. After fifteen years of experimentation, the General Assembly passed the Circuit Court Act of 1800, which abolished the county court system. From 1800 to 1868 the counties became judicial and election districts. So Greenville County (1786–1800) became Greenville District (1800–1868). Counties did not reappear in South Carolina until 1868.

Origin of the Name of Greenville County

While there is no contemporary evidence for the origin of the name of Greenville County, it seems clear that the legislature was following current practice in selecting names from its recent Revolutionary experience. The spelling, "Greeneville" County, in the ordinance creating the county and as late as the House Journal of March 28, 1787, confirms the intention of the legislature to honor General Nathanael Greene. At the age of forty-four, Greene was in the last year of his life. A native of Rhode Island, he had served George Washington in the Northern Department as quarter-master-general, and after Horatio Gates's disastrous defeat at Camden in 1780 he became commander of the Southern Department. In the closing years of the war, Greene successfully opposed Lord Cornwallis's British troops in the Carolinas and coordinated the South Carolina militia forces under such independently minded commanders as Andrew Pickens and Thomas Sumter. Greene sacrificed his personal fortune to keep the army from starvation, and once the fighting was over, both South Carolina and Georgia granted him extensive tracts of land in gratitude for his services. South Carolina honored the general in 1785 by naming the town of Greenville at Long Bluff on the Great Pee Dee River in his honor.[31]

Uncertainty over the origin of the name of Greenville County began as early as 1826, with the publication of the *Statistics of South Carolina* by Robert Mills. "The name of the district, it is believed," Mills wrote, "was derived from the physical face of the country, presenting a remarkably verdant appearance." In October of that same year, however, John C. Calhoun, speaking in Greenville, offered a toast referring to General Greene: "The village of Greenville picturesque and lovely in its situation, may it so prosper as to be worthy of the memory of him whose illustrious name it wears." Benjamin F. Perry, who did considerable research on the early history of Greenville in the nineteenth century, accepted the Nathanael Greene theory.[32]

In the twentieth century another theory was proposed by Alexander S.

The Vardry Mill, 1873–1943. Courtesy of Richard Sawyer.

Sketch of Home of Dicey Langston Springfield, on Tigerville Road near Travelers Rest, ca. 1784. Courtesy of Joyce Howard Ellis.

Site of Pearis's Great Plains Plantation, Reedy River Falls, ca. 1770–1776.

George Salmon House, on Highway 414 west of U.S. 25, ca. 1784. Courtesy of John N. Walker.

Prospect Hill, home of Lemuel Alston and Vardry McBee, ca. 1788. Courtesy of Greenville County Library.

Portrait of Elias Earle, ca. 1820, oil on canvas, 35 x 28 inches. Collection of the South Carolina State Museum.

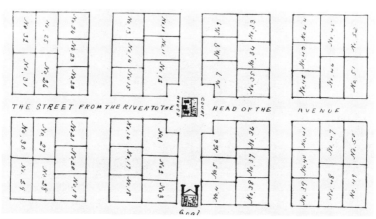

Plat of Pleasantburg, 1797. Courtesy of Greenville County Library.

Salley, Jr., longtime secretary of the state Historical Commission. In the 1946 edition of the *South Carolina Legislative Manual,* he wrote that Greenville was named for "Isaac Green who ran a mill in Reedy River about which the town grew." James M. Richardson, in his *History of Greenville County, South Carolina* in 1930, discredited the Isaac Green theory: "Against the Isaac Green origin the evidence seems even stronger than against Nathaniel [sic] Greene. The public records show that Isaac Green secured his first land grant . . . during the fall of 1785, and the legislative act naming the county passed March 22, 1786, less than six months after Isaac Green came into the county, and long before he built a mill on Reedy river." Richardson supported the "verdant appearance" theory of Robert Mills.[33]

The First County Court and Courthouse

On March 20, 1786, anticipating the creation of the county, the General Assembly elected nine members of the Greenville County Court: John Ford, Ambrose Blackburn, James Blassingame, Thomas Jenkins, Thomas Lewis, Lemuel J. Alston, Isaac Morgan, Obediah Hooper, and Henry M. Wood. Two days later, Wood was moved from last to second in the list, indicating the likelihood that the names were listed by seniority. Most were sizeable landowners whose holdings averaged 1,183 acres. Their holdings ranged from Blassingame's 3,966 acres in six tracts to 194 acres owned by Blackburn on Golden Grove Creek. Though there was no effort to have representation from all sections of the county, Morgan lived on the Enoree River in the east, Hooper on Armstrong Creek to the west, and John Ford in the south. Only the northern part of the county was not represented.[34]

Because the minutes of the Greenville County Court have not survived, it is impossible to know for sure where the justices assembled for their first session on the third Monday in May 1786. In all likelihood, the court convened at the plantation of John Ford, the senior justice of the peace, on Golden Grove Creek. Ford served in the Revolution and rose to the rank of major in 1781. At his death in 1795, he owned nine tracts of land in Greenville, Spartanburg, and Union Counties—totaling over 1,658 acres. He and his wife, Ann, were the parents of eight children who survived him. His local political preeminence was clear by his election to the state Senate in 1791. A Baptist, Ford served as a delegate from Fork Shoals Church to the Bethel Association that same year.[35]

It is probable that the county court continued to meet at Ford's plantation and built the first county courthouse and jail there. According to a petition to the legislature filed by George Foster in 1792, "the place . . . being one of Notoriety, the Justices of the Original Appointment, at the time appointed by Law, for the first court, thought proper to assemble there. The Gentleman there Resident being himself an Influential Member of the Court [John Ford], found but little difficulty, in procuring a Majority in favor of its continuance."[36]

Indian Unrest and the Militia

The creation of Greenville County was accompanied by warfare with the Indians on the Georgia and Tennessee frontier. Although the Cherokees had confirmed their wartime cession of land to South Carolina in the Treaty of Hopewell on November 28, 1785, the attacks left the people of Greenville fearful and unsettled. On December 17, 1786, a small band of Creeks killed three whites just west of the Tugaloo River. The next year, in August 1787, the Creek Nation declared war on the Georgia frontier. General Andrew Pickens requested assistance from Governor Thomas Pinckney, who authorized the raising of two regiments of militia—one from the south side of the Saluda River in what became Pendleton County and one from the north side in Greenville. On October 18, 1787, Pickens met with the leaders of Greenville County to organize the new regiment. One of these leaders was Henry Machen Wood who became lieutenant-colonel in the regiment. Wood was a native of Virginia and had acquired 1,913 acres and twelve slaves. A horseman in the militia during the Revolution, he served as justice of the peace in Spartanburg County in 1785 before becoming the second-ranking member of the Greenville County Court. In 1797 he became sheriff of the Washington District.[37]

Pickens ordered Colonel Wood to prepare a roster of all men eligible for militia service and divide them into three equal divisions. The 560 men who constituted the Greenville regiment of the Ninety Six Brigade received orders from Pickens to prepare to defend the frontier at a moment's notice.[38]

On November 11, Pickens received word from Governor Pinckney that he planned to inspect the up country militia in December. Pickens called the Greenville militia to assemble "in the most central and convenient place" in the district on December 14. After reviewing the troops, Pinckney officially notified Pickens that he had appointed the general to serve as South Carolina's representative on the commission appointed by Congress to negotiate a settlement with the Creeks. Pinckney thus became the first governor of the state to visit Greenville, and his letter to Pickens from "Greeneville County" is the oldest extant letter that bears a Greenville return address.[39]

Greenville Votes to Ratify the Constitution

In the midst of the Indian unrest, Greenville County voters gathered to cast their ballots for delegates to the state convention in Charleston on May 12, 1788—called to ratify the new federal Constitution. Elected to represent the "North side of Saluda" were Samuel Earle, Lemuel J. Alston, and John Thomas, Jr. In the first vote of the convention on May 21 Earle and Alston voted with the up country delegates to postpone a decision on the Constitution until October. The following day, Earle and Thomas, voted with the rest of the up country against a second consecutive term for president of the United States. But on May 23, on the final vote to ratify the Constitution, the three Greenville delegates voted "aye." Unlike most of the up country, the delegates from Greenville and Pendleton voted unanimously for the new national government. Precisely what the motives of the Greenville delegates were is not clear, but Andrew Pickens, who was not a delegate, made no secret of his disillusionment with the Confederation Congress. He clearly preferred a strong central government that could deal decisively with the ever-present Indian threat. Robert Anderson, a delegate from Pendleton, was unable to attend the ratifying convention because he was on alert as colonel of the county militia. As late as 1806, Lemuel J. Alston, one of the Greenville delegates, was denounced in the congressional campaign as a Federalist. At any rate, in 1788 the Greenville delegates perceived that their well-being was tied more closely to Charleston and the national interest than most of their up country neighbors, and they cast their votes for the new federal Constitution. This strain of nationalism would reappear in the antebellum period in the struggle over nullification and secession.[40]

While the loss of the minutes of the county court obscures much of the early political organization of Greenville, the records of the legislature indicate that Robert Maxwell was elected sheriff, tax collector, and assessor in 1788, and on January 16, 1789, Henry Machen Wood was recommissioned lieutenant colonel and commandant of the state militia. Maxwell, a native of Ireland, had migrated to South Carolina by the mid-1770s. He married Mary, the daughter of Colonel Robert Anderson (a large landowner and political leader in the Ninety Six District). Maxwell himself eventually owned over 2,000 acres and twelve slaves and lived in the Golden Grove on Grove Creek. He served as sheriff of the Washington District from 1795 to 1797, when he was murdered on his way to court.[41]

Political Activity

Even though Greenville had become a county, the low country members who controlled the state legislature were not yet willing to give it representation in the General Assembly. Indeed, the battle for representation for Greenville was part of a larger struggle by up country voters, who outnumbered those in the low country, to secure equal representation. The struggle had begun with the Regulator movement in 1768 and only recessed during the War for Independence. The results were slow and uneven. In 1786 the up county secured the relocation of the state capital in Columbia, but the legislature had stoutly refused to reapportion itself the year before, in accordance with the provisions of the state constitution. On October 28, 1788, Judge Henry Pendleton, that perennial champion of the up country, arose in the state House of Representatives to report a bill granting representation to Greenville and Augusta Counties. On October 31 the bill passed second reading, and it went to the Senate where it died. Pendleton gave notice that during the next session of the General Assembly he would reintroduce the measure. Despite Pendleton's death in the meantime, the legislature ratified an act on March 7, 1789, which provided the county one senator and two members of the House of Representatives. Elections were held in May at the courthouse by Commissioners Robert Maxwell and James Harrison. The role of election commissioner was politically important, for the commissioners themselves were often elected to office. Indeed, James Harrison became the first senator to represent the new county, and Robert Maxwell and Lemuel Alston members of the House of Representatives.[42]

The citizens of Greenville took their newly won access to the legislature seriously. They sent petitions reflecting their concerns specifically and those of the up country generally. A petition from 313 persons urged debtor relief by amending the law to extend payment of debts over a longer period and requesting the reopening of the foreign slave trade. The low country, representing the interests of the merchants and large slaveholders, opposed such actions. But one petition did receive a favorable response. Greenville citizens joined those in Union, Spartanburg, Chester, and York to urge the establishment of a tobacco inspection warehouse in the northwest area of the state. In the years immediately following the Revolution, up country planters were searching for a major staple like rice and indigo in the low country, and tobacco seemed the likely crop. In 1792 the legislature, led by Colonel Thomas Brandon, established a warehouse in Union County at Fish Dam Ford. But within five years Eli Whitney invented the cotton gin, creating the possibility of an upland "cotton kingdom." Cotton, not tobacco, became a major staple in South Carolina in the nineteenth century, but it did not become a major factor in the Greenville economy until after the Civil War.[43]

Crucial to the hope of the up country for equal representation in the General Assembly was the revision of the state constitution, adopted as a war measure in 1778. In March 1789 the legislature provided for the election of delegates to a state convention. James Harrison and Robert Maxwell were appointed managers for the election on October 27–28. The polling place was set, not at the courthouse, but at the house of Lemuel James Alston. Perhaps there was already some dissatisfaction with the location of the county seat. Samuel Earle, John Thomas, Jr., Robert Maxwell, and James Tarrant represented Greenville when the convention assembled in the new State House in Columbia on May 10, 1790. Like the legislature, the convention was controlled by the low country. While the up country gained a majority in the House of Representatives in the new constitution, the low country still controlled the Senate. Only an amendment in 1808 would shift control of the Senate to the upstate. The 1790 constitution, which remained in force until 1865, created an "aristocratic republic" which was acceptable to both sections. It redefined the counties as election districts, and the Greenville District would be designated as such until it was reconstituted a county by the Reconstruction Constitution of 1868.[44]

Changes in the Court System

Another change which affected Greenville County citizens was the revision of the court system. Greenville continued to be a part of the Ninety Six Circuit Court District. In 1789 the circuit courts gained complete jurisdiction for the first time. Before reform, only the court in Charleston could issue writs and other processes. The circuit court convened twice each year at Cambridge, the renamed village of Ninety Six. The following year, in 1790, the legislature expanded the equity court system, providing for it to meet in Ninety Six, Columbia, and Charleston. Then in 1791 the legislature expanded the circuit courts to accommodate the growing population in the up country. The old Ninety Six District was divided, and Greenville and Pendleton became part of the Washington Circuit Court

District. Robert Maxwell, James Harrison, and John Ford of Greenville joined Andrew Pickens, Robert Anderson, John Brown, and John Hallum of Pendleton as commissioners to select a seat for the district and oversee the building of a jail and courthouse. The legislature confirmed the commissioners' choice of Pickensville—described as "the place or village in Pendleton County lately conveyed to the said commissioners by the Honorable Brigadier General Charles Cotesworth Pinckney." This arrangement proved temporary, however. In 1799 the legislature increased the number of courts. The county courts, created in 1785, had fallen into disrepute because of the ineptitude and, in some cases, the ignorance of lay judges. So the Circuit Court Act of 1800 abolished the county courts and created a circuit court in every election district in the state. The circuit court ceased to sit in Pickensville, and the village soon disappeared. The Greenville District became the seat of its own circuit court sessions.[45]

Enlarging the County

In 1792 the legislature enlarged Greenville County. On November 30 fifty-eight residents of upper Laurens County petitioned the General Assembly for incorporation into Greenville. According to the petition, they lived "between the Ancient Boundary Line and Enoree River which forms an Angle . . . twenty to thirty miles from Laurens Court House" and within "eight to fourteen miles of Greenville Court House." The legislature confirmed the change on December 21, and appointed Daniel Wright of Laurens and James Harrison of Greenville to survey the proposed line. At the next session, on August 21, 1793, they reported that they had run the line 13 miles southwest from Zaddock Ford's place on the Enoree River to the Widow Killet's. For their work they received £10 11s. 4p.[46]

Controversy Over the Courthouse Location

Just as the residents of upper Laurens County were being annexed to Greenville so as to be closer to the courthouse, residents of upper Greenville became increasingly disturbed that the courthouse was not located closer to them. As some of them argued in a petition to the legislature, "the Justices in the upper and other parts of the County [have found that] the friends of [the present courthouse] were receiving all the advantages and themselves and the rest of the Inhabitants, experiencing all the Inconveniences that would result from a permanent Establishment [in a more central location]." The disgruntled citizens demanded a survey of the county and discovered that the courthouse was 10 miles from its center. When the matter was appealed to Governor Charles Pinckney and the council, the governor proposed a referendum on the issue, and the current site on Ford's plantation carried the day.[47]

The losers complained that the election had been unfair: "When we consider the Influence which Interest has over the Human mind in all situations, and how Improperly votes are frequently obtained on Much more important occasions w[e] shall not be surprised to find that the Vigorous and united Exertions of a few particular characters soon Procured a Majority in favor of the first Establishment." Governor Pinckney proposed only a second hearing before the council. In the legislative delegation, Senator Ford and Representative Maxwell were residents of the southern part of the county, while only George Salmon lived in the north. The vocal residents of the upper part of the county continued their protest, and during the 1792 session of the legislature 331 residents petitioned the House of Representatives to overturn the council's decision. The petition was referred to a committee composed of Robert Anderson of Pendleton, Robert Maxwell, and George Salmon. Maxwell was from the south and Salmon from the north, but Anderson—the father-in-law of Maxwell—was hardly disinterested. The committee reported on December 12, but the journal failed to record the content of the report. The modern editor of the journal only notes that no further action was taken. Whatever legislative maneuvering occurred, the effort to move the courthouse failed once more.[48]

The proponents of relocation persisted. A year later, on December 5, 1793, another petition urged the move, and the same committee considered it. But this time they reported that the petition should be granted. On December 21 an act empowered Henry M. Wood, Larken Tarrant, John Thomas, Jr., and James Harrison Barret "to assemble and Consult on the most suitable and convenient place for holding the said court . . . having respect to the central situation of the same with regard to all the inhabitants." Further, the act ordered that court be held near the chosen location until a courthouse could be erected.[49]

In the meantime, the legislature directed that the forthcoming election for members of the General Assembly on October 13–14, 1794, be held at the house of Elias Earle, under the direction of Jesse Carter, James Seaborn, and John Thomas, Jr. Earle's plantation, the Poplars, was located near the center of the county just north of the Reedy River falls on what became Rutherford Road. A son of Samuel Earle, Elias had moved to Greenville in September 1787, where he began to accumulate property eventually including some 7,000 acres of land and thirty-three slaves. Elias Earle had signed the petition for moving the courthouse and was no doubt a major proponent of locating it near the falls.[50]

Lemuel Alston and the New Courthouse

The new courthouse was not located on Earle's property, but instead was placed on the property of Lemuel James Alston. The rivalry between the two men would enliven upstate politics for the first fifteen years of the nineteenth century. Alston, a native of northeastern North Carolina, moved to South Carolina after the Revolution, read law, and was admitted to the bar. Eventually he purchased 11,028 acres in Greenville, including 400 acres from Colonel Thomas Brandon of Union in 1788. The Brandon tract included the falls of the Reedy River and the site of Richard Pearis's plantation, Great Plains. On an eminence high over the Reedy River which he called Prospect Hill, Alston built a two-story mansion facing south. Edward Hooker, a Connecticut native and a tutor at the South Carolina College, visited Alston in September 1805, and pronounced the house "without exception the most beautiful that I have seen in [up country] South Carolina." At least, it rivaled Richard Harrison's house on Cripple Creek. Alston's house sat some 600 feet from the main road, which was still called Pearis's Wagon Road after the Revolution. Leading from the road to his house, Alston laid off a broad avenue shaded by sycamore trees planted 24 feet apart. The grounds of Prospect Hill stretched from the avenue to the banks of the Reedy River.[51]

The house itself was constructed of logs covered with clapboard. It sat on a brick basement which rose almost a story above the ground. On the front a flight of stone steps led to a square porch with two narrow wings. An upper porch corresponded to the middle section of the lower one. On the first floor a wide door led into a square reception hall with bedrooms on either side. Directly behind the front hall was a drawing room with a large fireplace and windows on either side that looked out toward the mountains. Through folding doors to the left was the dining room. From the reception hall winding stairs led to the hall on the second floor. There were four bedrooms upstairs.[52]

The first post office in the county was authorized for Greenville Courthouse on February 22, 1795, but it did not open for business until shortly before April 1. By this time it is likely that the new courthouse was completed. Clearly the courthouse was ready for use by December 12, when the legislature appointed it the polling place for the next election. The courthouse was a one-story log structure that stood halfway up the hill in the middle of the road on the east bank of the Reedy River. Down the hill to the south of the courthouse, near the spring which had once provided water for Richard Pearis's household, was the new jail—a two-story log structure with chimneys at each end.[53]

McBeth's Store on the White Horse Road

The growing importance of the central area of the county was indicated by the opening of a second store in Greenville County, in addition to Richard Harrison's. The new store was operated by Alexander McBeth, and it opened prior to January 1794, at least a year before the occupation of the second courthouse. McBeth was a wealthy landowner in Union County who had operated a mercantile business there since December 1789. Concurrently with his expansion into Greenville, he opened another branch of Alexander McBeth & Company in Spartanburg County. In Greenville he leased 8 acres west of the Reedy River from John Blassingame, whose father was sheriff of Union County, at the point where the Island Ford Road, once Pearis's Wagon Road, crossed the White Horse Road. It was a major intersection between two important thoroughfares. McBeth's store was a frame structure—30 feet by 18 feet—roofed with shingles.[54]

For four months—from January to April 1794—McBeth recorded his transactions in a daybook which still survives. His clientele came from a wide geographical area, including Waddy Thompson and James Williams in Pendleton County and Baylis Earle in Spartanburg County. Thompson purchased household goods such as paper, pins, ribbon, and shoes and osnaburgs to clothe his slaves. Lemuel Alston bought a punch bowl, three small mugs, a large glass tumbler, six tablespoons, ribbon, a pocket handkerchief, and two nutmegs. John Blassingame purchased a looking glass, a blue teapot, and six earthenware plates. By far the most common purchase was a half-pint of whiskey for 7s. 6p. A number of McBeth's customers purchased almanacs at the beginning of the new year, and William Jarvis bought a copy of the New Testament.[55]

McBeth secured goods from Charleston, and with little coinage in circulation, he took in exchange for purchases a large number of deerskins, pork, tallow, beeswax, whiskey, corn, wheat, and cotton. Besides the customary retail and banking services, he provided blacksmithing as well. In addition, he purchased a still from Charleston with which he may have stocked his store with whiskey. As yet, Greenville County had no urban center to form the focus of its economic and political life.[56]

The six years between the opening of Greenville land for settlement in 1784 and the taking of the first federal census in 1790 formed a period of rapid growth in the area. The land rush resulted in the development of farms and plantations out of the former Indian land and the creation of economic, political, religious, and cultural institutions. In less than a decade, the foundation of a new society had emerged in the rolling hills of the upper South Carolina Piedmont.[57]

Notes

1. *The Statutes at Large of South Carolina,* ed. Thomas Cooper and David J. McCord (Columbia, 1836–1840) 4: 410–13, 590.

2. David Duncan Wallace, *South Carolina, A Short History, 1520–1948* (Chapel Hill, N.C., 1951), 333; *Journals of the House of Representatives, 1783–1784, State Records of South Carolina,* ed. Theodora J. Thompson and Rosa S. Lumpkin (Columbia, 1977), February 7, 1783, 205; *S.C. House Journals, 1787–1788,* January 25, 1787, 15.

3. *S.C. House Journals, 1783–1784,* February 7, 1783, 105; "Henry Pendleton," *Biographical Directory of the South Carolina House of Representative,* ed. Walter B. Edgar and N. Louise Bailey (Columbia, 1974–1992) 3: 547.

4. *S.C. House Journals, 1783–1784,* 266, 275, 278, 401, 620; *Statutes at Large of S.C.* 4: 590–93; "John Thomas, Sr.," *House Biographical Directory* 3: 708–9.

5. *Statutes at Large of S.C.* 4: 590–93, 645–46; *S.C. House Journals, 1783–1784* 411–12 (Hite), 486 (Armstrong), 568 (Wilkinson and Pritchard), 578 (Earle).

6. Greenville County Register of Mesne Conveyance, Commissioner of Locations, Ninety Six District North Side of Saluda River, 1784–1785, 1788, 1793–1794. Plat Book A, S.C. Department of Archives and History, Columbia, S.C. (microfilm, Greenville County Library, Greenville, S.C.).

7. Plat Book A; James M. Richardson, *History of Greenville County, South Carolina* (Atlanta, Ga., 1930, 1980), 53–54; "Thomas Brandon," *House Biographical Dictionary* 3: 86–88.

8. Plat Book A; Richardson, *Greenville County,* 54–55; "Aedanus Burke" and Richard Winn," *House Biographical Dictionary* 3: 105–6, 779–81; Benjamin F. Perry in the Greenville *Enterprise,* August 30, 1871.

9. *Statutes at Large of S.C.* 4: 411, 647; Tony Draine and John Skinner, *Revolutionary War Bounty Land Grants in South Carolina* (Columbia, 1986), passim.

10. Plat Book A, 36, 116 (Richard Pearis), 21 (Robert Pearis), 29 and 31 (Hite), 17 (Stephen Ford), 40 (Sheril), 63 (Langston), 90 (Dill).

11. Ibid., 50 (Salmon), 71 (Clark), 57 (Brandon).

12. Ibid., 62 (Davis, Dunn).

13. *S.C. House Journals, 1791,* xvi; ibid., *1792–1794,* xxiv–xxv; *Statutes at Large of S.C.* 5: 233–35.

14. Wallace, *Short History,* 337; *Statutes at Large of S.C.* 7: 211.

15. *Statutes at Large of S.C.* 4: 661–68; 7: 211. The name, Hereford County, appears in *S.C. House Journals, 1785–1786,* 116.

16. *Spartanburgh County, South Carolina, Minutes of the County Court, 1785–1799,* ed. Brent H. Holcomb (Easley, 1980), 1–8.

17. "George Salmon," *House Biographical Dictionary* 4: 504–5; National Register of Historic Places Inventory Nomination Form, "George Salmon House," S.C. Department of Archives and History, Columbia, S.C.

18. Estate of Robert Maxwell, Inventory, Greenville County Will Book A, 80, cited in Greenville County Judge of Probate Inventories, Will Book A, 1787–1800, WPA transcripts, South Caroliniana Library, University of South Carolina, Columbia, S.C.

19. Ibid.

20. Ibid.

21. U.S. Bureau of the Census, *Heads of Families at the First Census . . . 1790, South Carolina* (Washington, D.C., 1908), 67–71.

22. Holcomb, *Spartanburgh County*, 4–7; Joseph E. Birnie, *The Earles and the Birnies* (Richmond, Va., 1974), 79, n.11.

23. Virginia Meynard, *The Venturers: The Hampton, Harrison, and Earle Families of Virginia, South Carolina and Texas* (Easley, 1981), 292; "James Harrison," *Biographical Dictionary of the South Carolina Senate, 1776–1985*, ed. N. Louise Bailey et al. (Columbia, 1986) 1: 678–79.

24. James Harrison Account Book, 1783–1793, Harrison Family Papers, South Caroliniana Library, University of South Carolina (microfilm, Greenville County Library, Greenville, S.C.). The involvement of Harrison with Wade Hampton I is discussed in Ronald E. Bridwell, "The South's Wealthiest Planter: Wade Hampton I of South Carolina" (Ph.D. diss., University of South Carolina, 1980), 81–83.

25. Meynard, *Venturers*, 295–99.

26. Harrison Account Book, passim.

27. Sara M. Nash, *Bicentennial History of Lebanon United Methodist Church, 1785–1984* (Fountain Inn, 1984), 1–4.

28. Mary Lou Stewart Garrett, *History of Fairview Presbyterian Church of Greenville County, South Carolina* (Greenville, 1986), 3, 5–6, 9–10, 35.

29. Leah Townsend, *South Carolina Baptists, 1670–1805* (Florence, 1935), 213–22.

30. S.C. Senate Journal, March 8–10, 1786, in *The Records of the States*, ed. William S. Jenkins (microfilm, Library of Congress), A.1a. Roll 7; *Statutes at Large of S.C.* 7: 245; *S.C. House Journals, 1785–1786*, 521–31, 534, 536. The spelling appears as "Greeneville" in the legislative journals and in S.C. Manuscript Acts, 1786, No. 1325, S.C. Department of Archives and History. The spelling was modernized in *Statutes at Large of S.C.* 7: 245.

31. *S.C. House Journals, 1787*, March 28, 1787, 296; "Nathanael Greene," *Dictionary of American Biography*, ed. Allen Johnson and Dumas Malone (New York, 1935) 7: 569–73; *Statutes at Large of S.C.* 4: 649–51.

32. Robert Mills, *Statistics of South Carolina* (Charleston, 1826, 1972), 572; Richardson, *Greenville County*, 14.

33. Alexander S. Salley, Jr., "Sources Whence the Counties of South Carolina Obtained Their Names," *S.C. Legislative Manual, 1946*, ed. James E. Hunter and Inez Watson (Columbia, 1946), 335; Richardson, *Greenville County*, 14.

34. *S.C. House Journals, 1785–1786*, March 20, 1786, 575, 594; Smith and Owens, *Patent Land Survey*, passim.

35. "John Ford," *Senate Biographical Directory* 1: 519.

36. Petition of George Foster et al., General Assembly Petitions, 1792, S.C. Department of Archives and History. See also Petitions, 1792, No. 159.

37. Chapman J. Milling, *Red Carolinians*, 2nd ed. (Columbia, 1969), 324–25; Clyde R. Ferguson, "General Andrew Pickens" (Ph.D. diss., Duke University, 1960), 372–85; "Henry Machen Wood," *Senate Biographical Directory* 3: 1779.

38. Ferguson, "Andrew Pickens."

39. Ibid.; Thomas Pinckney, Greeneville County, to Andrew Pickens, December 14, 1787, Thomas Pinckney Papers, Charleston Library Society, Charleston, S.C.

40. *Journal of the Convention of South Carolina Which Ratified the Constitution of the United States, May 23, 1788* (Atlanta, Ga., 1928, 1988), 20, 33, 46; Ferguson, "Andrew Pickens"; J. Franklin Jameson, ed., "Diary of Edward Hooker, 1805–1808," in *Annual Report of the American Historical Association, 1898* 1: 898. For the struggle over the Constitution in the South Carolina up country, see A. V. Huff, Jr., "Who Shall Rule at Home: The Role of the South Carolina Back Country in the Ratification of the Constitution," *With Liberty and Justice: Essays on the Ratification of the Constitution in South Carolina* (Columbia, 1989), 9–19.

41. "Robert Maxwell," *House Biographical Dictionary* 3: 487–88; A. Charles Cannon, "The Maxwells, A Pioneer Greenville Family," *The Proceedings and Papers of the Greenville County Historical Society* 8 (1984–1990): 187–92; *Statutes at Large of S.C.* 5: 60.

42. *S.C. House Journals, 1787–1788*, October 28, 29, 31; November 4, 1788, 601, 603, 610, 628; *Senate Biographical Directory* 3: 1814; *House Biographical Directory* 1: 224.

43. *S.C. House Journals, 1789–1790*, February 2, 1789, 98; January 30, 1789, 92; Allan D. Charles, *The Narrative History of Union County, South Carolina* (Spartanburg, 1987), 73–74.

44. *S.C. House Journals, 1789–1790*, March 6, 1789, 231; *Journal of the Constitutional Convention of South Carolina, May 10–June 3, 1790*, ed. Francis M. Hutson (Columbia, 1946), 6.

45. Wallace, *Short History*, 409–14; *Statutes at Large of S.C.* 7: 253–58; 5: 258–65, 310–11.

46. *S.C. House Journals, 1792–1794*, 36–37, 74, 245, 321, 441; *Statutes at Large of S.C.* 5: 220.

47. *S.C. House Journals, 1792–1794*, 132–33, 167; Petitions from rival groups can be found in General Assembly Petitions, December 10, 1792, 0010-003-1792-0015300 and 010-003-1792-0015400, S.C. Department of Archives and History.

48. Ibid.

49. Ibid., 312, 378, 567; *Statutes at Large of S.C.* 5: 230–31.

50. *S.C. House Journals, 1792–1794*, 446, 450–51; "Elias Earle," *House Biographical Directory* 4: 176–77.

51. "Lemuel James Alston," *House Biographical Directory* 3: 34–35, 46; Jameson, "Diary of Edward Hooker," 1: 197–98; Perry, *The Writings of Benjamin F. Perry*, ed. Stephen Meats and Edwin T. Arnold (Spartanburg, 1980) 3: 318.

52. Greenville (S.C.) *News*, February 4, 1934.

53. Dixon D. Davis and Dixon I. Durham, "The Greenville County Postal System, 1795–1967," *PPGCHS* 1 (1965–1968): 45; S.C. House Journal, December 12, 1795, 257, in Jenkins, *Records*, A.1b. Roll 23; Plat Book A, Plat of Pleasantburg.

54. Minnie L. Mabry, ed., *Union County Heritage 1981* (Winston-Salem, N.C., 1981), 45, 322; *Spartanburgh County Court*, 199, 209, 222, 225, 228, 231, 265–66; "John Blassingame," *House Biographical Directory* 3: 74–75; Stanley S. Crittenden, *The Greenville Century Book* (Greenville, 1903, 1970), 16–18; Greenville Deed Book C, 173, cited in Mary C. Simms Oliphant, "The Genesis of an Upcountry Town," *The Proceedings of the South Carolina Historical Association, 1933*, 54–56.

55. Alexander McBeth Daybook, 1794, Greenville County Library, Greenville, S.C.

56. McBeth Daybook; Benjamin F. Perry in the Greenville (S.C.) *Enterprise*, September 6, 1871.

57. Lacey K. Ford, Jr., distinguished between the upper and lower Piedmont in antebellum South Carolina. Greenville was part of the upper Piedmont, along with the Anderson, Pickens, Spartanburg, York, and Lancaster Districts. The upper Piedmont remained distinctive because the population was two-thirds white and occupied small- and medium-sized farms. Ford, *Origins of Southern Radicalism: The South Carolina Upcountry, 1800–1860* (New York, 1988), 46.

CHAPTER THREE

Laying the Foundations
for Antebellum Society

In the opening years of the nineteenth century the small planters, yeomen farmers, the few manufacturers, and the slaves and free blacks of the upper Piedmont, which included the Greenville District, gradually formed part of a distinctive society in antebellum South Carolina. Different from the great plantation economy of the low country and even the cotton-producing districts of the lower Piedmont, Greenville based its economy on diversified agriculture and the growth of small manufacturing companies. The district was further defined by developments in transportation, the creation of a courthouse village, the coming of the Second Great Awakening, the organization of militia units, the emergence of political factions allied with the national party system, and the patriotic fervor surrounding the War of 1812.

During this time, the population of Greenville continued to grow rapidly. In fact, the population grew faster after 1800 than it had from 1790 to 1800. (In 1810 the population had increased 87.6 percent over the previous ten years.) Though slavery was still peripheral to the district, the number of slaveholders grew from 314 (19 percent of the householders) to 443 (25 percent) in 1810. The number of slaves held by individuals also began to grow. The number of slaveholders who owned one slave dropped from 35 percent of the total slaveholders in 1790 to 28 percent in 1800 and remained constant (27.5 percent) in 1810. But the number of planters (those holding twenty or more slaves) grew from two in 1790, to fourteen in 1800, and seventeen in 1810.[1]

Agriculture and Manufacturing

Economically, wheat and corn dominated local agriculture. The price of flour rose from $5.55 a barrel in 1791 to $9.35 in 1795. These prices held until the end of the War of 1812. The price of tobacco, which was still being grown in the county, brought about seven cents a pound. The price was reasonable, but not high enough to make tobacco a staple crop.[2]

Greenville was never a part of the antebellum cotton kingdom. The farmers and few planters of the district were growing some cotton by 1801. Even though Eli Whitney invented the cotton gin in 1793, 1799 was the first year that short-staple cotton was widely grown in South Carolina. In 1802, when cotton was selling for seventeen cents a pound in Charleston, Methodist Bishop Francis Asbury commented on the high price of cotton during a visit to Greenville. But he made it clear in his *Journal* that James Douthit, a farmer near Table Rock, was planting cotton for domestic use only. In 1840, according to Benjamin F. Perry, only 275 bags of cotton were produced in the entire district.[3]

Manufacturing operated on a small scale in Greenville, but it was dependent on agriculture. In 1802 Governor John Drayton indicated that Lemuel Alston was operating a flour mill at the falls of the Reedy River that produced twelve to sixteen barrels a day, and there was a fulling mill on the river as well. Greenville also became a center of iron manufacturing. Henry and Joshua Benson operated a foundry on the Enoree River, 12 miles from the courthouse. A second foundry was owned by Lemuel Alston and Adam Carruth on the Reedy River, and Elias Earle operated a third on the north fork of the Saluda River. Just west of the line in the Pendleton District was Jesse Murphy's, located on George's Creek. These foundries produced the farming implements and building materials needed in an expanding agricultural society.[4]

The Wagon Road Over the Mountains

The Greenville District became the beneficiary of the efforts of the planters and merchants of the low country to revive the commercial importance of Charleston after the American Revolution. In 1786 the General Assembly chartered the Santee Canal Company to build a canal connecting the Santee and Cooper Rivers. Completed in 1800, the Santee Canal permitted produce from the up country to come directly into Charleston. At the same time, the legislature improved roads and ferries to form a wider transportation network. Thus goods from every area of the state could be funnelled into the port city.[5]

The road which proved a boon to the economy of Greenville was known as the "waggon road over the Western Mountains." On December 1, 1794, the state Senate approved the concept of such a road, and ordered a committee composed of Greenville Senator John Ford, Joshua Saxon of Pendleton, and Elias Earle to report on the expediency of building such a road. When the General Assembly met in November 1795, the committee proposed a road from Merritt's Mill on the North Fork of the Saluda River through the mountains to Green River Cove and on to Buncombe Courthouse in western North Carolina. From the French Broad River the road would cross the mountains to Knoxville. In his message to the General Assembly, Governor Arnoldus Vanderhorst made it clear that such a road would "open communications between Charleston and the Inhabitants of the Southwest Territory of the United States." The legislature appropriated two thousand dollars for the building of the road and stipulated that the road must be wide enough for four horses to pull a wagon with a load weighing one ton.[6]

The governor appointed Andrew Pickens, Henry Machen Wood, and Joshua Saxon as commissioners to oversee the construction of the road. These men signed a contract with Elias Earle and John William Gowen, a veteran of the Revolution and the son of Earle's niece Miriam. First of all, permission for the construction of the road had to be secured from both Governor William Blount of Tennessee and the Buncombe County Court in North Carolina. More problematical was a petition "from sundry Inhabitants of Greeneville County, praying that the $2,000 for making a Road over the Western Mountains, may not be appropriated for that purpose." The independent-minded inhabitants of the county were not about to achieve unanimity on even as important a matter as a road to enhance the economy, but the legislature failed to act on the petition. Finally, on November 29, 1797, the commissioners reported to the General Assembly that Earle and Gowen had completed the road and submitted a certificate from William W. Smith that he had driven his wagon over the road with a one-ton weight in it.[7]

On a journey through the up county in July 1810, William Ancrum of Charleston traveled over the road from Greenville to Knoxville. In his journal Ancrum noted that he left the village after breakfast on Saturday, July 21, and traveled on a very good road for about 12 miles. Ancrum enjoyed the view of some handsome farms before the terrain began to rise. Through Saluda Gap, the road was "so narrow that two waggons cannot pass each other, where sometimes is a tremendous precipice of upwards of 100 feet or more nearly perpendicular immediately at your feet." In the "Valleys or Coves of the Mountains" the land "appear[ed] to be very good, from the appearance of the Corn growing upon it. I am informed that the best produces from 45 to 50 bushels of Corn to the acre."[8]

The Droving Trade

In 1802 Governor John Drayton reported that the road opened a new source of wealth to the state. Large Conestoga, or covered wagons with narrow wheels drawn by four to six horses, traveled over the road in caravans of fifteen to twenty. "Hence," Drayton wrote, "where the roads are clayey, in wet weather, they are cut into deep ruts; and are sometimes rendered almost impassable." The wagoners, he wrote, were rough, rude, whooping, and cursing. They traveled about 24 miles a day and camped every evening in the woods near the road.[9]

Horses, mules, cattle, sheep, and hogs from Kentucky and Tennessee came over the road in large herds. An annual event was the passage of thousands of turkeys, driven in flocks of four hundred to six hundred. The birds were kept together by drovers carrying long whips with pieces of red flannel attached. By night the turkeys roosted in nearby trees, and by day they could travel about 8 miles. Both flocks and herds required large amounts of feed on the journey. The drives occurred every fall and continued until about 1885 when the railroads made them obsolete.[10]

The coming of these long drives to the Greenville District brought a number of changes. The county court and later a board of commissioners was responsible for maintaining the road. Landowners on either side were required by law to keep it in repair. In November 1802 the first of a series of petitions from the area went to the General Assembly requesting the creation of "a Turnpike on the Road leading from the Western Country across Saluda Mountain, at some convenient place between where the said road crosses the North fork of the Saluda River and the boundary between North and South Carolina." But evidently no action was taken on the proposal until the construction of the state road twenty years later.[11]

Meanwhile, taverns and stores grew up along the road where drovers established camp sites. William Bishop and his wife operated an inn just north of present-day Travelers Rest on Highway 25. The animals were herded into an enclosure nearby, while the drovers slept on the floor of the inn. Local markets for livestock and turkeys were held at these camp sites when the drovers arrived. Residents of the area later remembered that a local innkeeper had a barn where he kept the hogs overnight. The barn had a trap door in the floor and during the night the owner opened the trap door so that several hogs fell into a pit below. When the drovers moved on, the innkeeper rescued the hogs to feed his family.[12]

Even more colorful was the story told about the tavern owned by Susan Loftis, and later her daughter-in-law Sarah Loftis, in the Lima community. Near their tavern, the women operated a still where they made spirits and sold them to the drovers. According to Leonardo Andrea, a well-known genealogist who grew up near Jackson Grove, the drovers would drink at the tavern and often leave without any money. The daughter-in-law, "Old Sukey Loftis" as she came to be known, lived to the age of 103. In her later years she "got religion" and joined New Liberty Baptist Church. In order to be baptized, she had to be tied in a chair to be immersed.[13]

The Village of Greenville Courthouse

At the same time that Elias Earle was constructing the wagon road, Lemuel J. Alston was laying out a village around the courthouse at the falls of the Reedy River. In 1797 Alston filed with the clerk of court a plat for the village of Pleasantburg. The plat consisted of four blocks or squares on each side of Pearis's wagon road between the river and avenue leading to Prospect Hill, Alston's home. Only two streets were named. Present-day Main Street was designated "the Street," and the lane to Prospect Hill, present-day McBee Avenue, was named "The Avenue." In the eight blocks, Alston laid off fifty-two lots.[14]

There was no rush to purchase lots, since few Greenville County residents saw the need for building town houses or operating businesses in the village. The first sale of property in what was designated on the deed as "Greenville C.H. Village of Pleasantburg" took place on April 22, 1797, when Isaac Wickliffe purchased lots 11 and 12 on the northwest corner of the courthouse square for one hundred dollars. Over a year later, on September 5, 1798, John McBeth purchased the entire block of six lots on the southwest corner for six hundred dollars. A decade after the lots were first offered for sale, only twenty-six of the fifty-two had been sold. The name Pleasantburg had already dropped out of use—replaced by Greenville Courthouse, or simply Greenville.[15]

In September 1805, when Edward Hooker (a twenty-year-old Connecticut native, graduate of Yale College, and teacher in the academy at Cambridge) visited Lemuel Alston, he described the village in his diary. After dinner at Prospect Hill on September 22 he walked to the village with Mr. Henderson, a young lawyer who was a half-brother of Alston. Hooker met George Washington Earle, the clerk of court and son of Elias, and Jeremiah Cleveland, one of the local merchants. The village itself, he wrote, was "quite pretty and rural: the street covered with green grass and handsome trees growing here and there." Hooker counted some six dwelling houses, two or three shops, and several other log buildings.[16]

Hooker described the courthouse as "a decent two story building. The jail is three stories, large and handsome." Benjamin F. Perry later recalled that the courthouse was framed, sealed, weatherboarded, and covered with shingles. When it became too small, a more spacious courthouse was built, which stood until 1826. The older building was sold to Chancellor Waddy Thompson, who moved it to the present location of Springwood Cemetery and added two wings for a dwelling.[17]

Hooker reported that the local view was that the village was "as healthy as any part of the United States," but it was "not a seat of much business." The courts sat twice a year and often finished the session in two or three days. There was only one attorney, presumably Henderson, who reported that the "law business" was dull. One or two physicians lived nearby, but their practice was mainly at the Golden Grove—a settlement 10 miles away. A minister who lived within 6 or 7 miles preached at the courthouse every three or four weeks. In the village itself, by 1807, stood John Archer's blacksmith shop at lot 47 and a small store operated by Erwin, Patton, and Cleveland at lot 36. A few years later Jeremiah Cleveland bought out his partners and became the sole proprietor of the leading mercantile business in Greenville in the early nineteenth century. Jeremiah's father was Captain Robert Cleveland, a native of Virginia who settled in western North Carolina and fought beside his brother, Colonel Benjamin Cleveland, at the battle of King's Mountain in October 1780. After the Revolution, Robert Cleveland's sons, Jeremiah and Jesse, migrated to South Carolina. Jeremiah settled in Greenville in 1805, and Jesse in Spartanburg in 1810.[18]

The rhythm of village life was regulated by the sessions of court twice a year, the arrival of the drovers in the fall, and local events such as militia musters, the arrival of the mail and supply wagons at Cleveland's store, and the irregular visits of ministers who held services in the courthouse.

The Second Great Awakening

The religious climate of the up country began to change after 1800 with the coming of the Second Great Awakening—a widespread religious revival in the early nineteenth century that brought with it a redefinition of the whole society. Indeed, the influence of Protestant evangelical religion would continue into the late twentieth century and give rise to a sizeable fundamentalist Christian community. Prior to 1800 Greenville had been heir to the First Great Awakening of the 1740s and 1750s through the arrival of the Separate Baptists. The Second Great Awakening swept across the region in the wake of a series of camp meetings that began on the frontier. This Awakening consolidated the revivalistic spirit of the Separate Baptists, who embraced predestination, and the Methodists, who championed the doctrine of free will. The Awakening began in Virginia and North Carolina about 1790, but it burst forth in full power in August 1801 at a camp meeting at Cane Ridge, Kentucky. There between twelve thousand and twenty-five thousand people gathered to hear some thirty-six preachers exhort them day and night. From the West the revival swept back across the mountains into North and South Carolina.[19]

On Saturday, October 17, 1801, Methodist Bishop Francis Asbury crossed the Saluda River and entered the Greenville District on his annual episcopal visitation through the United States. While holding a quarterly meeting at Salem Church, near Staunton's Ferry, he spent the night with Henry Paris. At Paris's house Asbury received a letter containing an account of the revival of religion among Presbyterians and Methodists in the Cumberland region of Tennessee. Two days later, after conducting a service at Fairview Presbyterian Church, he stopped at Thomas Terry's house at Fork Shoals where he read "James M'Gready's narrative of the works of God in Logan county, Kentucky." Perhaps it was by comparison with the accounts he was reading that Asbury noted his impressions of religion in "Pendleton, Greeneville, Laurens, Spartanburg, and Newbury [sic] counties in South Carolina" at the end of the week. "I cannot record great things upon religion in this quarter," he wrote, "*but cotton sells high.* I fear there is more gold than grace—more of silver than of 'that wisdom that cometh from above.'"[20]

Asbury shared with his audience the glad tidings of revival as he traveled across the up country. Only six months later the Great Awakening reached South Carolina. In April 1802 near Lancaster, twelve thousand people gathered for a camp meeting. On July 2 Methodist, Baptist, and Presbyterian ministers led about five thousand people in a camp meeting on the Tyger River in the Spartanburg District. Shortly thereafter the first camp meeting was held in Greenville—the first time an event in the area had brought together thousands of people for any purpose. In December 1802 Asbury wrote to a colleague in Philadelphia: "The camp meetings in North and South Carolina and Georgia have been the equal if not superior to Cumberland and Kentucky, and must supply an addition of hundreds and thousands to the Methodists, Presbyterians, and Baptist Societies."[21]

The cooperative spirit of the camp meeting among the churches did not last. Within a year, the Presbyterians in the up country allied themselves with the Old School group in the denomination against the New School revivalists, and Presbyterian ministers began to withdraw from participation in the camp meetings. At the same time, the Baptists, in order to guard their Calvinist doctrine and church order, began to hold separate protracted meetings in their own churches and associations. The Methodists were left with the camp meetings, and they exploited them. In the Greenville District the Methodists held annual camp meetings at Bethel Church, between Mauldin and Simpsonville; at Ebenezer, near Batesville; and at Jackson Grove, near Travelers Rest. The last Methodist camp meeting in Greenville County was held at Bethel in 1897, though the tabernacle or stand for preaching was not demolished until 1943.[22]

The interracial nature of the antebellum Methodist camp meetings is reflected in a letter written by Bishop William Capers. Widely known as the founder of the Methodist mission to the plantation slaves, Capers commented that he was "struck with the appearance of the black portion of the congregation." At the camp meeting at Ebenezer, Capers observed them "all dressed very finely; most of them in silks or muslins or broadcloths. Their appearance indicates good treatment, contentment and happiness." The bishop noted that he had stayed with William Bates and dined with Major Alexander and Alexander McBee.[23]

An important dimension of evangelical Protestant life was the enforcement of church discipline. In an era when law enforcement was spotty at best, the churches provided a crucial element in the social structure. Not only did the churches police personal morality, but they created a standard for social behavior as well. The only power the churches held was that of disciplining wayward members. The accused member was called up on charges before the congregation, in the case of the Baptists, and before the session in the Presbyterian and the quarterly conference in the Methodist churches. After a trial, disciplinary action was imposed which consisted of a gradation of punishments. The first was probation until the guilty party confessed and asked for forgiveness. The second was denying some privilege of membership, such as participation in the Lord's Supper, and the third was exclusion—a last resort. In the Greenville District the churches tried to guard their members from sins such as drinking, dancing, fiddling, playing cards, and sexual misconduct. In June 1802 Brushy Creek Baptist Church placed Archibald Fowler on probation for drunkenness and other sins. The following month he publicly admitted his faults and was restored to fellowship. Two years later he was convicted of drunkenness a second time. Finally, on December 15, 1805, he was excluded from the church.[24]

In an agricultural society, truth and honesty were regarded as cornerstones of the growing economy. The churches preserved these social values in their disciplinary role. Brushy Creek Church found members guilty of forcing others to sell them goods at too low a price, dealing severely with creditors, and expressing the opinion that it was allowable to take a mortgage on one's lands. Perhaps the most celebrated case concerned Abraham Carney, who was accused of grinding meal on Sunday. On a Saturday Carney had placed corn in the hopper of his mill, intending to grind it when he returned from a trip to Greenville. He did not return until midnight and discovered that relatives from Rutherford County, North Carolina, had come to visit. There was no meal in the house, so he ground enough meal to use on the Sabbath. At the next meeting of the church, he was brought up on charges. He defended himself successfully before the congregation in a speech that entered the folklore of the community:

> You can turn me out of the meeting if you are amind to, but I am as sure as I am of God Almighty, that if Joseph, and remember that Jesus Christ, the son of God A'mighty was living with Joseph, that if Joseph had gone to Jerusalem and got back late and did not have his meal ground and found that he had a passel of North Caroliny hungry kinfolks come to his house a visiting late of a Saturday night, I am sure that Joseph would have gone to his grist mill and turned on the water and ground them some meal. . . . That is just what I did and I am not one bit ashamed of it, and if I had not done so, I am sure my old woman would have given me so much hell that I would have cursed a blue streak of real Irish oaths which would have been more of a sin than grinding a turn of meal. . . . Now turn me out of the meeting if you are of a mind to, and if you do, I had just as soon be outside of meeting with honest sinners than in with a passel of damn hypocrites.[25]

The rekindling of the Second Great Awakening decisively shaped the evangelical Protestantism of the region. Based on the individual experience of conversion (which was more emotional than rational), Southern evangelical Protestantism emphasized personal morality more than social reform. It provided a moral discipline for the community without questioning the social system and brought to the people who lived in relative isolation in a rural society a sense of community.[26]

The State Militia

Another important element in shaping the society of the Greenville District was the state militia. Not only did the militia include all white adult males, but it created a military organization that subdivided the district into community units and, in addition, served as a slave patrol. The first militia unit in the county was organized by General Andrew Pickens in 1787. In 1794 the General Assembly reorganized the militia to conform to the national structure created by Congress in 1792. All free white males between the ages of sixteen and forty-five were required to enroll and to muster periodically.[27]

In 1794 the Washington District, which included Greenville County until 1800, became a part of the Fourth Brigade of the First or Western Division of the state militia. There were two regiments in the Washington District: the Fifteenth, commanded by Colonel Lemuel J. Alston, and the Seventeenth, commanded by Colonel Henry M. Wood. Both were residents of Greenville County. The regiments were divided into two battalions, and each battalion was divided into four beat companies and one company of Light Infantry, or riflemen. Each division was required to have one company of cavalry, and each regiment could have an artillery company. The term, beat company, referred to the patrol service that each company provided within a fifteen-mile radius to regulate slave behavior.

When the state militia was reorganized once more in 1819, the Greenville District militia was placed in the First Brigade of the First Division. The First Regiment, known as the Upper Regiment, was composed of the Tyger Battalion and the Saluda Battalion. The Third Regiment, or the Lower Regiment, had similar battalions.

Every member of the militia was required to attend company muster four to six times a year and the regimental muster annually. Only the officers attended the brigade muster every two years. It lasted five to six days and was often held at Pickensville. In the early years of the nineteenth century the nearest newspaper was published in Pendleton which carried the regular muster notices. For example, on November 7, 1808, Lieutenant Colonel Thurston's regiment and the cavalry, under the command of Captain Goode and Captain Earle, were ordered to meet at Major Benson's near Travelers Rest. In 1818 the Seventeenth Regiment met at Benson's Old Field, and the Fifteenth Regiment met at William Toney's store near Fountain Inn.

Washington Taylor was an active participant in the militia. His daily diary gives a detailed account of his involvement from 1835 to 1845. He regularly attended company muster, which was held every two months from February to December, as well as the battalion and regimental musters. On April 1, 1837, when he was twenty-seven years old, Taylor was appointed first sergeant. That summer he joined the newly formed artillery company and was elected first lieutenant. In his capacity as an officer, Lieutenant Taylor attended the brigade muster at Pickensville, October 2–7. Upon his arrival at the camp muster, as he called it, Taylor noted in his diary that the "tents were arranged[, and] companies laid off which was about all that was done." Governor Pierce Mason Butler and Major General George McDuffie were present. On Tuesday, October 3, there were drills throughout the daylight hours. The following day Taylor was placed on guard duty and "sent out after night," he noted, "in pursuit of some disorderly members[.] I started [after] one and he[,] running the road[,] came to a hole or hog wallow and fell and I[,] close behind[,] came to the hole[,] fell and pierced my bayonet into the back of his thigh." On Friday the militia and the cavalry fought in a mock battle.[28]

The local militia groups did not always operate smoothly. In November 1837 the captain of Washington Taylor's beat company resigned. Taylor was then elected captain, and his brother Zion was elected second lieutenant in December. Before Washington Taylor resigned his commission in June 1838, he had to attend two regimental court martials. He reported on June 30 that fines of $125 and $130 were imposed on the regiment. Thereafter, Taylor simply recorded his attendance at various musters and took no active part.[29]

The Emergence of Party Politics

An important element which characterized Greenville society early in the nineteenth century was the emergence of political factions allied with national parties. Under the Constitution of 1790 which governed the state until 1865, voters elected only two groups of officials—members of the state legislature representing the Greenville District and the member of Congress from the congressional district in which Greenville was located. On the state level, the Greenville District allied itself with the other up country districts in an effort to secure equality with the low country parishes in the General Assembly. In national politics the low country was strongly Federalist, favoring strong government support of the economy. The leaders of the up country gravitated toward the Republican or Democratic Party of Thomas Jefferson, which championed the self-sufficient society of agriculture and small manufacturing already emergent there. By 1800 Republican sentiment was strong enough in the legislature to carry the state for Jefferson in the presidential election. Eight years later, the General Assembly adopted the Compromise of 1808, which insured a balance of representation between the up country and the low country. In 1810 South Carolina became the first state in the Union to give the vote to all free white males of twenty-one years of age.[30]

In typical eighteenth-century fashion, early elections in Greenville were contests between the gentry without the rough-and-tumble characteristics of later politics. In the congressional district in which Greenville was located, a series of highly respected men served for a single term. Only Thomas Tudor Tucker of Charleston represented the district for two terms (1789–1791). More typical was Samuel Earle of Greenville, who resigned his seat after one term. In fact, Samuel was one of three members of the Earle family who held the seat. His cousin, John Baylis Earle, served from 1803 to 1805, and their uncle, Elias Earle, served from 1805 to 1807.[31]

As politics in the nation began to break into Federalist and Republican factions, a similar division occurred in the South Carolina up country. Among the events that sparked the division were the arrival in Charleston of Citizen Edmond Genêt, the representative of the French Republic to the United States, and the negotiation of the Jay Treaty with England. All over the United States groups of citizens formed Democratic-Republican societies which supported the French Revolution and opposed the Jay Treaty. On July 4, 1794, the Madison Society of Greenville County met at the courthouse and adopted resolutions that were reprinted in newspapers as far away as Philadelphia. Without mentioning the Federalists by name, the resolutions decried the "thirst for power" which would lead any group to hold an undue proportion of political offices. Such action would tend to destroy the equality among the citizens, they maintained, which is a leading feature of republican government.[32]

After the text of the Jay Treaty became public in the fall of 1795, the militia units of the Washington District did not hide their displeasure. In Pendleton they erected a Liberty Tree containing a Liberty Cap, a United States flag, and an inscription at its base that expressed dissatisfaction with the treaty. The militia in Greenville must have concurred, for on September 28, the Franklin or Republican Society of Pendleton County met to express "the sense of the district." The resolutions adopted at that meeting denounced the "pusillanimity, stupidity, ingratitude, and TREACHERY" of the Jay Treaty which allowed Great Britain "to blast the rising grandeur of our common country—of our infant empire!"[33]

In the wake of the Jeffersonian Revolution of 1800, there were bitter contests for office among the elite in the Greenville District. In 1808 someone, who signed himself only "No Candidate" in the Pendleton *Messenger,* lamented the passage of the old politics: "That the progress of corruption may be forcibly impressed upon your mind, call to your recollection the representation of this district eight or ten years since; when the public mind was tranquil, and not agitated by *Electioneering intrigues;* when each man voted according to the dictation of his own mind; unbiased by threats or solicitations; and when each candidate depended on real merit for his success." In the present system, he wrote, "the public mind [is] agitated; tossed to and fro by malicious reports; promises are made without intention or ability to perform; your vanities are flattered, and your prejudices and passions kept on the wing."[34]

The new politics of the congressional election of 1806 was described by Edward Hooker on his trip through the area. After 1800 the Greenville and Pendleton Districts formed the Eighth Congressional District, and the incumbent was Elias Earle, who lived in Greenville but owned substantial lands in Pendleton. Only three residents of Greenville had occupied the congressional seat since the First Congress met in 1789—all members of the Earle family. The election of 1806 was a three-way contest among Elias Earle, Lemuel Alston, and William Hunter. Earle and Alston, whose lands adjoined one another north of the village of Greenville, were planters with more than twenty slaves, while Dr. William Hunter of Pendleton owned eighteen slaves. Hunter was the son-in-law of General Robert Anderson, who owned thirty slaves and more than 6,000 acres of land.[35]

On Sunday, September 21, 1806, Hooker encountered Lemuel Alston in the Oolenoy Valley in the mountains of the Pendleton District, where Alston was exerting all his energy in campaigning. The previous day he hosted a barbecue at Twelve Mile Creek and announced his intention of attending church in the area on Sunday. Hooker noted that "the expectation of the mountaineers was of course excited: for of the various candidates, [Alston] was one in whose favor they were considerably prejudiced." When Alston arrived, he was the center of attention. Men, women, and children gazed at him as if he were some strange sight. Hooker commented that a superficial observer might suppose Alston came to worship God, but he suspected that he came to worship the people. After church, the candidate spoke to everyone present. Alston, according to Hooker, "was perfect master of the art, and played his game with so much adroitness as almost to persuade one that nobody could have a more cordial attachment to him, or feel a greater interest in his welfare. . . . His whole demeanor . . . was marked by such easy civility, as to gain the good will of all." Later, Alston's half-brother confided to Hooker that the family Bible on the table in the keeping room at Prospect Hill was bought only after Alston became a candidate for Congress and was secured for the purpose of making a good impression on whomever might call.[36]

On Saturday, September 27, Hooker went with Lemuel Alston to the militia muster at Pickensville. He repeated in his diary the report that the troops were called out specifically for political purposes. The three congressional candidates distributed whiskey, hosted dinners, talked, and harangued while their supporters made similar exertions on their behalf. The scene Hooker described was emergent democracy at its best:

> I placed myself on a flight of stairs where I could have a good view of the multitude, and there stood for some time an astonished spectator of a scene, the resemblance of which I had never before witnessed: a scene, ludicrous indeed when superficially observed, but a scene highly alarming, when viewed by one who considers at the same time what inroads are made upon the sacred right of suffrage. Handbills containing accusations of federalism against one, of abuse of public trust against another—of fraudulent speculations against a third—and numerous reports of a slanderous and scurrilous nature were freely circulated. Much drinking, swearing, cursing and threatening—but I saw no fighting. The minds of uninformed people were much agitated—and many well-meaning people were made to believe the national welfare was at stake and would be determined by the issue of this back-woods election. Dr. Hunter conducted with most dignity, or rather with the least indignity on this disgraceful occasion—confining himself to a room in the tavern, and not mixing with the multitude in the street—Alston fought for proselytes and adherents in the street; but took them into the bar-room to treat them but Earle *who loved the people more than any of them,* had his grog bench in the middle of the street and presided over the whiskey jugs himself. Standing behind it like a shop boy behind his counter, and dealing out to any one who would honor him so much as to come up and partake of his *liberality.*[37]

Lemuel Alston won the seat in Congress and kept it for two terms, when Elias Earle recaptured it.

The War of 1812

Meanwhile, the citizens of the Greenville District, as well as the entire nation, became concerned about the efforts of Great Britain and France to draw the United States into the war between them. When the British navy stopped American ships to search for deserters, Jefferson responded by restricting the importation of British goods. On June 22, 1807, the British frigate *Leopard* confronted the American frigate *Chesapeake* as it sailed out of Chesapeake Bay. When the American commander refused to allow the British to search the *Chesapeake,* the *Leopard* fired warning shots that killed three men. The British then seized four suspected deserters.[38]

News of the *Chesapeake* affair reached the village of Greenville on July 7, in a newspaper brought from Washington. Two days later, the Pendleton *Messenger* announced the news to the entire area. On July 30 it printed Governor Charles Pinckney's call for volunteers to fill the secretary of war's quota for South Carolina of fifty-seven hundred men. On August 3 there was a public meeting at the Greenville courthouse to discuss the crisis, with Chancellor Waddy Thompson as chair and Joel Grace as secretary. The meeting adopted a series of resolutions which "announc[ed] to our Government, and Fellow Citizens generally, that, although not the first to address, we are willing to be the first in action to avenge our Nation for the Indignity committed on her Flag by the unwarrantable, unprovoked, and cowardly attack made on the United States frigate *Chesapeake.*" Despite "a variety of sentiments . . . with regard to our internal regulation, yet we are a firm, determined, and united people, against our insolent or invading foe; and will at any time, march to any point of the continent of America, to aid out brethren in their repulsion." The members of the resolutions committee who were officers of the militia used their military titles in signing the report: "Colonel Thurston, Colonel Alston, Colonel Austin, Major Blassingame, Major Alexander, John H. Harrison, Robert Anderson, and William Henderson, Esqs."[39]

The Fourth Brigade of the state militia in the Greenville and Pendleton Districts met by regiments to raise their proportion of the men requested of the state. The Pendleton *Messenger* reported that "when the drum beat for Volunteers, a much larger number than was called for immediately turned out. In Colonel Thurston's and Brown's regiment every man marched forward." But the martial spirit waned as diplomatic negotiations stretched out. In December 1807 the newspaper printed "A Letter from a Member of Congress to his Friend in Greenville" indicating that as yet there were no dispatches from the American envoys in England. In fact, it was not until six years later that the War of 1812 began.[40]

The war did not greatly affect the citizens of the Greenville District until the Creeks attacked American settlers in Alabama in the summer of 1813. On January 15, 1814, the *Messenger* printed the order "to detach 13 companies of Infantry and 1 of Artillery and 1 of Cavalry from the Quota of the First Division of the Militia of this state, for United States service . . . to rendezvous at Abbeville Court House on Tuesday the 25th Instant on their way to Fort Hawkins . . . to be joined by North Carolina detachments to fight the Creek Indians." On January 23 some five hundred volunteers marched from Pendleton to the Creek Nation. About one-fourth of the group was from the upper part of Greenville. On the march they were joined by a company from Pendleton, and at Abbeville another from Greenville joined them. Companies from Abbeville and Edgefield raised the number of volunteers to one thousand. The *Messenger* described the troops: "With them Captain Kelly's Troops of Cavalry, partly from there and partly from Greenville district, whose appearance and equipment does them credit, uniformed in black of their own manufacture, well mounted and bearskined up, they were a corpse [sic] 'Black, bold, and Terrible.'"[41]

On March 27, 1814, Andrew Jackson delivered a final blow to the Creeks at Horseshoe Bend, near present-day Montgomery, Alabama, and in August the Indians were forced to cede more than half their lands to the United States. The fighting ended on January 8, 1815, when Jackson stopped the British invasion of New Orleans, and a wave of national pride swept the Greenville District and the entire nation.[42]

During the early decades of the nineteenth century, the diversified agriculture and small manufacturing enterprises in the Greenville District created the foundation of a distinctive society in the upper Piedmont of South Carolina. The society in Greenville was defined further by the development of the road across the mountains, the establishment of the courthouse village, the Second Great Awakening, the establishment of militia units, the emergence of politics, and the fervor surrounding the War of 1812. In the decades leading to the Civil War, a mature antebellum society, still distinctive in many ways from the rest of South Carolina, emerged.

Notes

1. U.S. Second Census, 1800. South Carolina (microfilm, National Archives), Roll 47; U.S. Third Census, 1810. South Carolina, Roll 62.

2. Marjorie S. Mendenhall, "A History of Agriculture in South Carolina, 1790 to 1860: An Economic and Social Study" (Ph.D. diss., University of North Carolina, 1940), 37–38.

3. Ibid.; Francis Asbury, *The Journal and Letters of Francis Asbury*, ed. Elmer T. Clark, 3 vols. (New York, 1958) 2: 361; Perry in the Greenville *Enterprise,* October 11, 1871.

4. John Drayton, *A View of South Carolina* (Charleston, 1802, 1972), 139, 151, 153.

5. David Duncan Wallace, *South Carolina: A Short History, 1520–1945* (Chapel Hill, N.C., 1951), 373–74.

6. S.C. Senate Journal, December 1, 1794, December 13, 1796, in *The Records*

of the States, ed. William S. Jenkins (microfilm, Library of Congress) A.1a, Rolls 7–8; S.C. House Journal, November 23, December 8, 1795; November 27, December 1, 1797, A.1b, Rolls 23–23a.

7. Ibid., Drayton, *View of South Carolina,* 158. The identity of John William Gowen can be ascertained in Joseph E. Birnie, *The Earles and the Birnies* (Richmond, Va., 1974), 185, and G. Ronald Temples, comp., *South Carolina 1800 Census* (Provo, Utah, 1973), 211.

8. William Ancrum, Journal, July 4–August 5, 1810, William Ancrum Papers. South Caroliniana Library, University of South Carolina, Columbia, S.C.

9. Drayton, *View of South Carolina,* 158.

10. Thomas D. Clark, "Livestock Trade Between Kentucky and the South, 1840–1860," *The Register of the Kentucky Historical Society* 27: 569–81; Elizabeth L. Parr, "Kentucky's Overland Trade with the Ante-bellum South," *The Filson History Quarterly* 2: 71–81; Wilma Dykeman, *The French Broad* (Knoxville, Tenn., 1955), 137–51; Mildred W. Goodlett, *Travelers Rest at Mountain's Foot* (n.p., 1966), 4–6.

11. S.C. Senate Journal, November 27, 1802 December 3, 1804, and November 3, 1807, in Jenkins, *Records,* A.1a, Rolls 21–22.

12. Goodlett, *Travelers Rest,* 4–5.

13. Loftis Folder, Leonardo Andrea Genealogical Files (microfilm), South Caroliniana Library, University of South Carolina, Columbia, S.C.

14. James M. Richardson, *History of Greenville County, South Carolina* (Atlanta, 1930, 1980), 60–61. The plat is in the Greenville County Register of Mesne Conveyance. Commissioner of Locations, Ninety Six District North Side of Saluda River, 1784–1785, 1788, 1793–1794. S.C. Department of Archives and History, Columbia, S.C. (microfilm, Greenville County Library), Plat Book A.

15. Richardson, *History of Greenville County,* 60–64. The original landowners in the village were Isaac Wickliffe, lots 11, 12 (1797); John McBeth, lots 1, 2, 3, 16, 17, 18 (1798); Thomas Alexander, lot 36 and John W. Wood, lots 22, 37, 39, 40, 47, 48 (1799); Francis Wickliffe, lots 14, 15 and John Blackman, lots 5, 10, 13 and John McBeth, lots 33, 34, 35 (1800); Elias Earle, lot 6 (1801); John Taylor, lot 4 (1804); and John Archer, lot 46 (1807).

16. J. Franklin Jameson, ed., "Diary of Edward Hooker, 1805–1808," in *Annual Report of the American Historical Association . . . 1896,* 2 vols. (Washington, D.C., 1897) 1: 898.

17. Ibid.; Perry in Greenville *Enterprise,* September 6, 1871.

18. Jameson, "Diary of Edward Hooker," 1: 898; Stephen S. Crittenden, *The Greenville Century Book* (Greenville, 1903), 21; John B. O. Landrum, *History of Spartanburg County* (Atlanta, Ga., 1900), 353–54.

19. John B. Boles, *The Great Revival, 1787–1805: The Origins of the Southern Evangelical Mind* (Lexington, Ky., 1972), 54–67. William G. McLoughlin broadens the definition of the awakenings in *Revivals, Awakenings, and Reform* (Chicago, Ill., 1978), passim.

20. Asbury, *Journal,* 2: 309–11. Henry Paris is buried on the Easley Bridge Road just off the White Horse Road. An early nineteenth-century house, desig-

nated as the Owings House in honor of the donor, from the Paris tract is now part of the Pioneer Farm at Roper Mountain Science Center. Asbury's first visit to Greenville County occurred in 1799 when he went to Cox's Meeting House at the Golden Grove. He described it as "the best society we have in South Carolina: the land here is rich." Ibid., 212–13.

21. Asbury to Ezekiel Cooper, December 23, 1802, Ibid., 3: 253.

22. Boles, *Great Revival,* 94–100; Samuel M. Green, *An Historical Outline of Greenville Circuit, South Carolina Conference, M. E. Church, South* (Greenville, 1884, 1984), passim.

23. *Southern Patriot,* August 17, 1854.

24. G. B. Moore, "A Sketch of Brushy Creek Church from 1794 to 1901," in Greenville Baptist Association, *Minutes,* 1925, 55–56, S.C. Baptist Historical Collection, Furman University, Greenville, S.C.; Brushy Creek Church Book, June 19, July 17, 1802, and December 15, 1805, cited in Lacy K. Ford, Jr., *Origins of Southern Radicalism: The South Carolina Upcountry, 1800–1860* (New York, 1988), 34.

25. Camp-Kemp Folder, Andrea Files.

26. The best treatment of Southern evangelical religion in the antebellum South is Donald G. Mathews, *Religion in the Old South* (Chicago, Ill., 1977).

27. Jean Martin Flynn, "Musters and Old Muster Grounds in Greenville County," *The Proceedings and Papers of the Greenville County Historical Society, 1964–1965* 1: 22–24. Also see her more recent work, *The Militia in Antebellum South Carolina Society* (Spartanburg, 1991).

28. Washington Taylor, *A Diary of Transactions from 1835–1855 of Washington Taylor* (Frederick, Md., 1988), 18–34.

29. Ibid., 35, 40, 42, 44, 48, 60.

30. John Harold Wolfe, *Jeffersonian Democracy in South Carolina* (Chapel Hill, N.C., 1940), chaps. 6–8.

31. Kenneth C. Martin, *The Historical Atlas of United States Congressional Districts, 1789–1983* (New York, 1982), 267; Benjamin F. Perry in the Greenville *Enterprise,* August 30, 1871.

32. *American Daily Advertizer* (Philadelphia, Pa.), September 4, 1794, in Philip S. Foner, ed., *The Democratic-Republican Societies, 1790–1800; A Documentary Sourcebook of Constitutions, Declarations, Addresses, Resolutions, and Toasts* (Westport, Conn., 1976), 391.

33. Foner, *Democratic-Republican Societies,* 398–409.

34. Pendleton *Messenger,* September 10, 1808.

35. Ford, *Origins of Radicalism,* 102, 108–9.

36. Jameson, "Diary of Edward Hooker," 893, 896–97, 899.

37. Ibid., 900–1.

38. Reginald Horsman, *The War of 1812* (New York, 1969), 10–11.

39. Pendleton *Messenger,* August 20, 1807.

40. Ibid., September 24, December 3, 1807.

41. Ibid., January 29, 1814.

42. Horsman, *War of 1812,* 224–25, 244–49.

CHAPTER FOUR

Economic Growth
and Unionist Politics

The two and a half decades after the War of 1812 had a profound effect on the development of the Greenville District and the courthouse village. The events of those years which decisively shaped the society were the clear demarcation between blacks and whites, westward migration, the rise of industry, the internal improvements movement, the intensification of evangelical Protestantism, the growing importance of the village of Greenville, and the emergence of the district as a Unionist stronghold in the nullification era.

The population of the district, which increased rapidly from 1786 until 1810, began to grow at a much slower rate than South Carolina as a whole. Between 1810 and 1820 the district's population increased 9.6 percent, and in the 1820s grew 11.8 percent. Even more striking was the impact of western migration on the white population, which increased only 2.5 percent in the 1820s and 3.2 percent in the 1830s. Though the number of blacks was small, the black population increased much more rapidly than the white, from 9.5 percent of the population in 1790 to 30.9 percent in 1830.[1]

Execution of a Runaway Slave

Whatever informality in the relationship between blacks and whites which may have existed on the frontier in the Greenville District before the War of 1812, this relationship was now transformed into a caste system as the number of blacks increased. In South Carolina as a whole the number of blacks surpassed 50 percent in 1820 for the first time since 1708. As the numbers of blacks increased, white residents feared that the level of violence would grow. There were occasional insurrections in the early years of the nineteenth century, but the aborted Denmark Vesey plot in Charleston in 1822 confirmed the worst fears of whites. One estimate credits Vesey, a free black, with enlisting as many as six thousand blacks from Georgetown to Beaufort to throw off white control prior to the discovery of the insurrection. In reaction, the newly formed state Baptist Convention published a defense of slavery based on biblical evidence, and the state legislature tightened the laws governing slaves and free blacks.[2]

With a relatively small black population, whites in Greenville appeared to have little to fear. But they grew anxious that blacks from outside the district might import hostile words and feelings. The opportunity for whites in Greenville to send a powerful message to the black population came in 1825 when a runaway slave was executed by burning at the stake during the very week when the whites were celebrating Independence Day.

According to the story circulating in Pickensville at the time, and recorded in the diary of Caroline Laurens of Charleston, the slave "had made an attempt to kill his master, but not succeeding, he ran away and lodged in the barn of an old farmer." The farmer, who needed some grain, went out to the barn one night, not knowing anyone was there. The slave, according to Laurens, "who had just awoke out of a sound sleep and thinking he was pursued by his master[,] instantly jumped up and killed the old man and made his escape, but after a few weeks was caught and sentenced to be burned." Another account, written by John Campbell of Gowensville when he was seventy-two, recalled the events of fifty-seven years before. "It was circulated throughout the County, (that is, the lower part of it,) that there was a runaway negro in the County, breaking in milk-houses, smoke-houses and kitchens, and stealing provisions." Peter Garrison surprised the renegade in his barn, and the black killed Garrison by stabbing him with a stalk of polk. Campbell recalled that the runaway slave belonged to a man who lived in Georgia, whose name was Boone.[3]

According to Campbell's account, after the slave was convicted of murder and condemned to death, the sheriff hired John Stone to burn him at the stake. The place of execution was located on the Pendleton Road, about 1 mile from the courthouse, within the present limits of the city of Greenville. The slave, guarded by thirty men, was chained to a post and covered with tar. "Then they permitted the black people to come near him. There was one [who] spoke a few words with him. And then a white preacher, who went to the doomed man and prayed for him, and then the sheriff permitted him to pray."[4]

Impact of Westward Expansion

After the War of 1812 the rich cotton lands of North Georgia, Alabama, and Mississippi were opened to settlers from the older South, and there was a steady stream of migration westward. Benjamin F. Perry, writing in 1871, expressed the opinion "that the population of our county would have been double what it is, but for the emigration to the West. It is singular fact, that very few of the citizens of Greenville are now living on lands which belonged to their ancestors 70 or 80 years ago."[5]

Local newspapers carried the notices of sales by many who planned to move west. J. S. Edwards advertised in July 1831 that he intended to move westward and had for sale 571 acres of land, a cotton gin, saw mill, flour mill, distillery, hogs, corn crop, and twenty slaves. In January 1832 John McClanshaw advertised 2,083 acres, a nine-room house in the village, and nineteen slaves.[6]

The most prominent citizen the Greenville District lost to western migration was Lemuel J. Alston, the founder of the village of Greenville Courthouse. In 1815 Alston, at the age of fifty-five, sold his 11,028 acres in the Greenville District and moved to a plantation he named Alston Place, near Grove Hill in Clarke County, Alabama.[7]

The man to whom Alston sold his estate for $27,550 was Vardry McBee of Lincolnton, North Carolina. McBee would play a dominant role in the life of the Greenville District until his death in 1864. Born in 1775 in the Spartanburg District, McBee grew up at Limestone Farm, near the site of Gaffney. When he was six years old, he heard the firing at the Battle of Cowpens. When the elder McBee suffered financial problems after the Revolution, the twelve-year-old son dropped out of school and went to work in the fields. At eighteen McBee went to Lincolnton, North Carolina, to learn the saddle trade under the direction of his brother-in-law, Joseph Morris. McBee worked briefly in Charleston, Kentucky, and middle Tennessee before returning to Lincolnton. There he opened a store in partnership with James Campbell of Charleston. In 1804 he married Jane Alexander of Rutherford County, and the next year he purchased a large farm and began the practice of scientific agriculture. In 1812 McBee was elected clerk of court of Lincoln County, a position he held until 1832. When his associates in Lincolnton urged him not to purchase the Alston property, he cited in Greenville's favor its location on the wagon road across the mountains and its readily available waterpower.[8]

McBee was once described by his summer neighbor, Joel Roberts Poinsett, as "uneducated, but shrewd and intelligent." *DeBow's Review* in 1852 characterized McBee as "strictly temperate and methodical. He is a man of great industry and activity of life. . . . Having been crippled whilst a young man, by being thrown from his horse, he is not able to walk any distance." He consequently lived in his saddle during the day. He was small and had an even temperament, but when provoked, he unleashed his fierce anger. Vardry McBee continued to live in Lincolnton until 1836, but he visited regularly, and the village of Greenville Courthouse and the entire district began to feel his influence long before he moved to Prospect Hill.[9]

The Growth of Industry

Another major development in the Greenville District after the War of 1812 was the growth of industry. The demand for firearms increased, and both Adam Carruth and Elias Earle turned to the manufacture of muskets. Carruth, at his foundry on the Reedy River, produced five hundred muskets for the state and applied to the federal government for an even larger contract. Meanwhile Elias Earle had secured a contract to furnish ten thousand muskets for the ordnance department in 1815. But he was unable to complete them, and on November 14, 1816, he transferred his contract to Carruth. Under the terms of the agreement, Carruth agreed to deliver two thousand stands of arms with bayonets and ramrods to the state armory in Greenville by January 1, 1818. Each succeeding January he contracted to deliver an additional two thousand. Carruth was also required to assume the debt of more than twelve thousand dollars that Earle owed the federal government.[10]

On December 7, 1817, Carruth petitioned the state legislature for a loan of ten thousand dollars to complete the contract. He claimed that he had twenty thousand dollars in arms that he could not ship until they were inspected. Unfortunately Carruth was never able to make satisfactory delivery. For three years the legislature postponed collecting the debt. In 1822 Carruth's other creditors forced him into bankruptcy.[11]

The textile industry was more successful than the manufacture of firearms, and, more important, textiles laid the foundation for the post-Civil War industrial revolution in the up country. In 1812 Adam Carruth, planter Waddy Thompson, and several others petitioned the General Assembly for help in erecting a textile mill. The legislature appropriated ten thousand dollars for building a mill of not less than five hundred spindles. The mill was never built, and the development of the textile industry came only with the arrival of a group of experienced New Englanders.[12]

With the end of the war in 1815, the textile industry in New England was depressed because of competition from English mills. Finding the swift streams of the upper Piedmont and the growing supply of cotton from the plantations to the south, a group of Rhode Island textile entrepreneurs arrived in the Spartanburg District in 1816 and built the first mill in the region on the banks of the Tyger River. Soon they expanded into Greenville.[13]

One of the original members of the group from Rhode Island was Thomas Hutchings, who was not only a manufacturer but also a Methodist local (lay) preacher. By February 1820 he had left Spartanburg and purchased 300 acres of land in the Greenville District on the Enoree River, at what later became Pelham. In April he was operating a mill there with 144 spindles. The following year he purchased additional machinery with 720 spindles and opened a second mill on the Enoree. Before 1830 Hutchings's operation was purchased by Josiah Kilgore and Philip C. Lester. For many years the mills were known as Lester's Factory. Hutchings moved to a nearby creek and operated another mill for a brief period.[14]

About the time that Thomas Hutchings built his first mill on the Enoree, two other mills opened. Shubal F. Arnold built a mill at Fork Shoals on the Reedy River. He operated a single spinning frame with seventy-two spindles. Eventually the Fork Shoals mill came into the possession of a nearby planter, Hudson Berry, and his sons. The Berrys operated the mill until 1852. In 1820 or 1821 John Weaver moved to McCool's Shoal on Beaverdam Creek between the Middle and South Tyger Rivers. His three brothers—Philip, Lindsey, and Wilbur—were in the original Rhode Island group. John Weaver opened a mill with the financial assistance of Josiah Kilgore and later William Bates. Weaver operated the mill until the 1860s.[15]

Perhaps the most prominent mill owner in the Greenville District in this period was William Bates. He was born in Pawtucket, Rhode Island and was the son of John and Deborah Bates. He began working in a textile mill at the age of eight. In 1819 he came to South Carolina to work in the Weavers' factory in the Spartanburg District. He accumulated some capital and married Mary McCarley of Rutherford County, North Carolina. He worked in and then invested in various mills in the Spartanburg and Laurens Districts. In 1830 he bought John Weaver's mill at McCool's Shoal at a sheriff's sale for $1,235 and deeded a half interest in the mill to Weaver's son. Next, Bates moved to Lester's factory on the Enoree. In 1833 he bought 300 acres of land from Josiah Kilgore for $810 on nearby Rocky Creek. He built a cotton mill at what came to be known as Batesville and expanded it several times before the Civil War. In 1847 Thomas M. Cox became Bates's partner, and two years later William Pinckney Hammett, who had married Bates's daughter, became business manager of William Bates and Company. In 1860 the company was operating twelve hundred spindles and thirty-six looms with seventy operatives. The company was capitalized at fifty thousand dollars. Bates had become one of the most successful mill owners in the South Carolina up country.[16]

Nicholas Van Patten was a different sort of textile entrepreneur. A native of New York, he bought land on the Enoree River in 1852. He set up not only a cotton mill but also wool cards, a grist mill, a cotton gin, a machine shop, and a cabinet shop. He built a bridge across the river, a large house for himself, houses for his workers, and a store. When he offered the entire village for sale in 1838, he found a buyer for the textile machinery alone. Van Patten remained on the Enoree River until his death in 1889. He was something of an eccentric, though, and constructed numerous models of a perpetual motion machine as well as improvements for textile machinery which he claimed were stolen from him.[17]

Vardry McBee's textile mill at Conestee on the Reedy River was a small, but significant, part of his holdings in the Greenville District. He first built a yarn mill to which he added wool carding. At first McBee hired experienced superintendents to operate his mill. Colonel Leonard Allen was a skillful manager, but he died about 1843 and was replaced by "first one and then another incapable man," according to a young worker. Then in 1844 McBee enlisted his son, Alexander, to supervise the mill. Both father and son were unhappy with the arrangement. The elder McBee wrote to his son, Pinckney: "Alex is in trouble now & I am low sperited [as] it is now divulged that the factory has been loosing money & I suppose a goodeal." Alex McBee and John Adams, the overseer, had allowed the river to undermine the waterwheel. "All my children can subtract but none can add & continue to take from the mountain & you will remove the whole at last." The father refused to permit Alexander to build a house at Conestee in order to have his family nearby. "Surely after doing a very disagreeable business almost night and day for 13 years," Alex wrote his father, "I *am* entitled to *some* sort of house to *stay in*." According to the son, Vardry McBee did not believe his children could "do anything."[18]

The growth of the textile industry in the up country gave rise to a small but definable class of mill workers. One of these was the Reuben Reid family of Big Rabun Creek in the Laurens District. The father had been a surveyor, school teacher, and sometime ferry operator and tavern keeper before his death in 1837. He left a wife, aged thirty-seven, and five children—the oldest of whom was thirteen and the youngest eight months. According to a memoir written by the eldest son, Mrs. Reid "consulted with the neighbors as to what would be the best thing for her to do under the circumstances in which she was left." Already her thirteen-year-old son had some work experience in a nearby textile mill. "She was advised to go, if she could do so, to a cotton factory."[19]

The eldest son and his eleven-year-old sister "went to the Reedy River factory in Greenville, owned by Vardry McBee, and readily made arrangements . . . to move there immediately." The workers at Conestee had a "neat appearance," and the village was attractive and comfortable. The houses had ample gardens. A striking feature of the village was an octagonal brick church built by McBee's overseer, John Adams, for services conducted by the Methodist circuit riders. Octagonal churches had been popular in Britain in the eighteenth century and were favored by John Wesley as a design for his chapels.[20]

"When I first moved to Reedy River factory and for sometimes afterwards," young J. W. Reid later wrote, "the factory ran day and night, having two sets of hands, who relieved each other at mid-day and mid-night." The Reids were morning hands who went to work at midnight and worked until noon, and J. W. often fell asleep standing on his feet. The mother soon contracted a fever. Though she lived fourteen years longer, she was often unable to leave the house. When the eldest sister married within a year, the rest of the family moved to Hutchings's Factory on the South Tyger River. Eight months later the factory closed, and they moved back to Greenville to work in a paper mill owned by Andrew Patterson. Reid moved a number of times—twice back to Conestee—until 1848 when he left the textile industry. In 1846 he married, and the following year his only child, Washington Irving Reid, was born. At the age of twenty-four, J. W. Reid became a stonemason and gave up the life of a mill worker in the uncertain world of antebellum textiles.[21]

Internal Improvements

Another major development in the Greenville District after the War of 1812 was internal improvements. South Carolina was caught up in the national movement, and between 1817 and 1829 the legislature appropriated $1.9 million for a system of canals and roads. The most lasting project was the construction of the state road that connected Charleston with Saluda Gap in the upper Greenville District. Like the earlier wagon road which it replaced, this road was designed to bring trade to Charleston from western North Carolina and Tennessee. The new road bypassed the major towns and villages of the up country with the exception of Columbia. There is no evidence, however, that the state road interrupted the flow of traffic to the village of Greenville Courthouse. Drovers and traders traveled through the Saluda Gap on the new road and then turned down what had become known as the Buncombe Road toward Greenville and Augusta.[22]

In 1817 the General Assembly appointed John Wilson of Charleston as state civil and military engineer. His first report to the legislature in 1818 described the roads of South Carolina as "oppressive and ineffectual." He recommended the construction of a road from Charleston to 50 miles into the interior. From that point three branches would lead to Lancaster, Saluda Gap, and York. "The middle branch," he wrote, "ought to pass from Columbia along the ridge between the Tyger and Enoree rivers to the Saluda Gap. A good road over this passage of the Blue Ridge would doubtless attract a great portion of the trade of East Tennessee to this state."[23]

Not until 1820 was the road through the Greenville District laid out. By 1819 Wilson was ill, and Abram Blanding became acting commissioner of public works. Blanding was a native of Massachusetts and had graduated from what is now Brown University in 1797. Influenced by his roommate, later Governor David R. Williams of South Carolina, Blanding moved to Columbia where he studied law and became a successful attorney and planter. In 1822 he became chief superintendent of public works, a position he held until 1827. Closely associated with Blanding was Joel R. Poinsett, who served as president of the Board of Public Works from 1819 to 1821. A native of Charleston, Poinsett was educated in schools there, in England, and in Connecticut. He studied medicine briefly at the University of Edinburgh and read law with Chancellor Henry W. Desaussure. A well-read and widely traveled individual, he was appointed by President Madison in 1809 to negotiate trade treaties with Argentina and Chile. He returned to South Carolina in 1815 and was elected to the state legislature. As president of the Board of Public Works, Poinsett personally supervised the construction of the state road over Saluda Mountain.[24]

In May and June 1820 Blanding explored the passes of Saluda Mountain where, he reported, there were several roads already in use. None of them took the desired direction so he recommended the construction of a new road, stretching 11 miles southeast of Saluda Gap. A force of workers was hired, a camp was established, and actual construction began on July 17. But between forty and fifty of the workers became ill, and the weather was very rainy. According to Blanding, three of the members of the Board of Public Works visited the site and issued licenses for the selling of spirits to the workers. When one member of the work force became intemperate, he was discharged. Additional skilled laborers were not available, so the work progress slowed.[25]

The road was completed in October 1820 and was 17 feet wide, except on the steep mountainside where ten feet was cut through solid rock.

Forty-four small bridges were constructed as well as three arched bridges. The bridge at Hodges' Creek had one circular arch, was 12½ feet high, and was 50 feet long. The Saluda River bridge had two elliptical arches and was 60 feet long and extended fifteen feet above the water. The Gap Creek bridge contained a Gothic arch 15 feet high and 7 feet wide. Known today as the Poinsett Bridge, it stretches 130 feet across the stream and is still in good repair.[26]

At the foot of the mountains, the state road passed though a farm of 369 acres, which the Board of Public Works purchased for one thousand dollars. A toll house was constructed, and a Colonel Marony was employed as toll collector. His only compensation was the use of the farm, which contained about 50 acres of cultivated land. Blanding estimated that the annual amount required to keep the road in repair would be from one thousand to eighteen hundred dollars. "This expense," he wrote, "is a charge on the toll, which I believe will more than meet it."[27]

The lower section of the state road through the Greenville District was laid off through Woodruff. It passed over such favorable ground, Blanding reported to the legislature, that local labor would be adequate to keep it in repair.[28]

On October 4, 1820, a letter "from a gentleman in the back country, to his friend in Columbia" on the progress of the state road appeared in the Pendleton *Messenger*. "It is a noble undertaking," he wrote, "and admirably executed. The Difficulty of ascending the mountain is entirely removed; and a waggon may descend with the heaviest load that it can bring to the mountain, without locking a wheel." He praised the work of the commissioners: "It is a work equally honorable to the state, and the persons to whom the execution of it is entrusted. Messrs. Poinsett and Blanding have erected to themselves, a monument which will perpetuate their names as persons who have deserved well of their country."[29]

The internal improvements movement also resulted in the construction of two new public buildings in Greenville—a courthouse and jail. In December 1820 the state Board of Public Works appointed Robert Mills, a native of Charleston and a major American architect, as acting commissioner and later superintendent of public buildings. There followed a decade of public building in South Carolina that established a national standard of excellence.[30]

Within a year after his appointment, Mills had surveyed the district buildings of the state and reported that they were generally in a dilapidated state. He recommended the rebuilding of both the courthouse and the jail in Greenville. The "lot on which the court-house stands," Mills wrote, "is too small to admit of enclosure, and a small addition to it can be procured if provision were made for the purpose. . . . Some small repairs [are] to be made to the gaol to render it secure; but a thorough repair was thought inexpedient."[31]

The commissioners of public buildings for the Greenville District— Jeremiah Cleveland, Richard Thruston, and Alex Sloan—signed a contract in 1821 with Pond, Graham, and McCulloch for the erection of a new courthouse for ten thousand dollars. The first bricks made for the building were not suitable, and Mills reported to the legislature that there would be some delay in completing the work. The date set was April 30, 1822.[32]

The new Greenville District Courthouse was constructed according to prototype plans which Mills designed and used at least twelve times. The courthouse was rectangular and composed of two stories with a gabled roof and a portico with four Tuscan columns on the second level. The portico was raised on an arcade and framed by lateral stairs. The courtroom was on the main floor above a ground floor containing vaulted rooms for offices and storage. The ground floor had a barrel-vaulted central corridor and was designed to be fireproof. The courthouse was Palladian in style and was intended to match the dignity of the Exchange and the City Hall in Charleston.[33]

The new jail was also built according to a Mills prototype. Like the courthouse, the jail was two-stories high and of masonry construction. The upper floor was a single large room and was subdivided into cells by wooden partitions. The lower floor had a central corridor and was flanked by rooms for the jailer and for the confinement of debtors.[34]

Summer Resort for Low Country Planters

Another change that came to the Greenville District after the War of 1812 was the development of the area as a summer resort for low country planters. The custom of moving away from the plantations in the summer dated back to the Revolution. By 1790 outbreaks of malaria became frequent on the coast, so the planters at first moved their families to the beaches and pineland villages of the low country. Those who wished to venture farther afield began to travel to Pendleton, Spartanburg, and Greenville. They came in the late spring and remained until after the first frost in the fall. The coming of these summer residents brought a new dimension to life in the Greenville District.[35]

Two of the earliest planters to come to Greenville were governors of the state—Henry Middleton and Joseph Alston. A rice planter, Middleton was born in London in 1770, the son of Arthur Middleton who was one of the signers of the Declaration of Independence. In 1824 Middleton owned 15,224 acres of land, 420 slaves, and town property in Charleston. His home at Middleton Place on the Ashley River boasted one of the finest formal gardens in America. After completing his term as governor (1810–1812), Middleton built Whitehall on land he purchased from Elias Earle north of Greenville Courthouse in 1813. Middleton, his wife, eleven children, and their servants occupied Whitehall each summer until 1820, when he was appointed minister to Russia by President Monroe.[36]

Joseph Alston, like Middleton, was a wealthy rice planter. Born in 1779, the son of "King Billy" Alston of All Saints, Waccamaw, he was educated at the College of Charleston and Princeton. He read law with Edward Rutledge, but he devoted his life to rice planting. He lived at The Oaks on the Waccamaw River and eventually acquired 6,300 acres and 204 slaves. In 1801 Alston married Theodosia, the daughter of Aaron Burr, who was vice president of the United States. Alston served as governor of South Carolina from 1812 to 1814. Alston purchased 130 acres in the Greenville District on the Pendleton Road where he built a summer home and planted the land with a force of thirty slaves. His only son, Aaron Burr Alston, died of a fever in 1812, and his wife Theodosia died at sea the following year. A broken man, Alston died in 1816 at the age of thirty-eight.[37]

In 1815 Edmund Waddell rented Prospect Hill from Vardry McBee as a hotel for summer residents until McBee moved to Greenville in 1836. Squire Waddell and his wife were known as genial hosts. He was unable to read and could only sign his name with difficulty, but his malapropisms delighted generations of Greenvillians. "I am too much crowded," he said one day, "in fact I will have to build a condition to my house, that I may entertain my low country friends in a more hostile manner."[38]

Soon there were other boarding houses and hotels to accommodate the visitors. David Long opened a boarding house on what is now the corner of Main and Washington Streets; Blackmon Ligon operated another. In 1824 Colonel William Toney purchased lots 7 and 8 adjacent to the courthouse for a hotel. Toney bragged that his new hotel would "excel any house in the upper part of the State in appearance and accommodation for the traveling public." Samuel Crayton, the previous owner of the land, charged the colonel the extremely high price of five thousand dollars. The Mansion House, which Toney built, was an imposing edifice for the little village. A three-story, brick building, it was *L*-shaped around two sides of the courthouse square. The son of a later owner described it in glowing terms: "The floors were laid of heart pine, the roof of tin, and the circular stairs . . . [were] considered a rare piece of workmanship. The parlor, on the ground floor . . . extended the whole depth of the building, and was large as to require the unique feature of having two fire places."[39]

Dr. John Crittenden had a small hotel opposite the Mansion House, but in 1830 he purchased the larger hotel for ten thousand dollars. Five years later, in 1835, Crittenden sold the Mansion House to John T. Coleman for $10,500. Coleman later sold it to Swandale and Irwin. Another hotel, the Goodlett House, was operated by R. P. Goodlett and advertised fifty rooms in 1858.[40]

The summer residents did not always bring the elements of culture and refinement from the low country to the up country. Frederick A. Porcher indicated in his memoirs that Benjamin Allston, one of the richest rice planters on the Waccamaw River, spent his summers in Greenville. Allston's conversation, according to Porcher, appeared to be from one who was utterly uneducated. Porcher also described the demeanor of Major Warley, a planter from St. John's, Berkeley. Warley spent the days shifting his seat from one side of the street to the other to enjoy the shade. When he could find whist players, he would spend the whole day, and sometimes the night as well, playing cards. The site of many of these card games was known as the Fun Bank, which opened during the summers on the second floor of a building on Main Street known as "the war office."[41]

In August 1836 Benjamin F. Perry described the summer visitors in rather harsh terms in his diary. "We have had a good deal of company here this summer," he wrote, "but not much company as would interest a man of sense and reading." Rather "they all seem disposed to gratify their animal propensities without cultivating their interests at all, if they have any to cultivate—drinking, eating, gambling & whoreing is the summit of their ambition."[42]

Much more to Perry's liking was Joel R. Poinsett, who was a summer resident in the Greenville District from 1834 until a few years before his death in 1851. After Poinsett supervised the building of the state road in the summer and fall of 1820, he served in Congress (1821–1825) and then as ambassador to Mexico (1825–1830). Returning to South Carolina, Poinsett brought with him a number of botanical specimens, including the red Christmas flower that was later named the *Poinsettia pulcherrima* in his honor. At the time of his return, the state was in the midst of the nullification crisis. Poinsett became one of the leaders of the Unionist Party in support of his old friend, President Andrew Jackson. While serving in the state legislature, Poinsett first met Benjamin Perry, a strongly Unionist legislator from the Greenville District.[43]

In 1833 Poinsett married Mary Izard Pringle, and they moved to her rice plantation, White House, on the Waccamaw River. The following year he asked Perry to negotiate for him the purchase of a summer place in Greenville. Poinsett bought the two-hundred-acre farm of John Blassingame, Jr., on the Pendleton Road west of the village without ever having seen it. Almost every summer, except for the years from 1837 to 1841 while he served as secretary of war in Martin Van Buren's cabinet, the Poinsetts lived at their Greenville home—named the Homestead. He remodeled the house and laid out the grounds with hedges, a vineyard, an orchard, and flowers. A neighboring farmer planted the farm itself on shares. "I was on terms of great intimacy with Poinsett in the latter part of his life," Perry wrote. "I was a frequent visitor at his house. These visits were always pleasant and instructive. . . . He had traveled all over the civilized world, and had seen all the great men of Europe and America. He was a very observing man, and treasured up all he had seen and heard."[44]

Also a summer resident and a close friend of Perry was Judge John Belton O'Neall, chief justice of South Carolina. Unlike most summer visitors, O'Neall was a native of the up country—the Newberry District where he lived on his plantation, Springfield. In the Greenville District he occupied a house on the South Tyger River on land that had once belonged to Colonel John Thomas. O'Neall was speaker of the state House of Representatives from 1824 to 1828, when he was elected to the bench. He became chief justice in 1859. A staunch Baptist, O'Neall served as president of the state Baptist Convention and was a leader in the temperance movement. He was president of the State Temperance Society, and in 1852 he was elected Most Worthy Patron of the Sons of Temperance of North America. Perry wrote that O'Neall was "a strong Union man, and our political associations produced an intimacy and friendship which lasted as long as he lived. He was a warm-hearted, generous, noble gentleman ever ready to serve a friend or relieve anyone in distress."[45]

In the 1830s and 1840s a number of resort hotels opened at mineral springs in the up country where low country planters could "take the waters." Among the most well-known were Limestone Springs near Gaffney and Glenn Springs near Spartanburg. Rivaling them in the antebellum period was Chick Springs in the Greenville District.[46]

As early as 1802 Governor John Drayton had described a sulphur spring flowing from Paris Mountain. In 1838 Dr. Burwell Chick of the Charleston and Newberry Districts was hunting deer near the site of Taylors. He stopped at the home of Asa Crowder, who hired two or three Indians from their village on the Enoree River to guide Chick to Lick Spring where deer often gathered. The Indians told Chick that the ground around the spring would heal sores. In 1840 Chick opened a resort at Lick Spring, some 5 miles east of the village of Greenville.[47]

A large hotel at Chick Springs, as it came to be known, was ready for the summer season in July 1842. A later inventory listed twenty-five bedsteads and fifty mattresses, as well as crockery, four settees, cane and split bottom chairs, a piano, and a billiard table. Chick sold lots to individuals, such as Josiah Kilgore and Philip Lester, who built summer cottages.[48]

When Chick died in January 1847, his two sons purchased the property for three thousand dollars. They enhanced the resort by adding billiards and a tenpin alley on the lawn. There were dances in the ballroom, including one in honor of Governor John L. Manning who visited the hotel in August 1853. The Chicks sold the property to Franklin Talbird of Beaufort and his brother-in-law, John T. Henery of Charleston, in 1857. The new owners operated a daily stage from Greenville to the hotel and advertised that they would "spare no efforts to make the Springs all that can be desired, whether to the invalid seeking health or those in quest of pleasure." On the eve of the Civil War, Alfred Taylor, the hotel manager, indicated that there were over one hundred guests each day from August 7 to September 7, 1860, with 156 registered on August 17. No doubt the improved economy of the 1850s and the coming of the railroad to Greenville also improved the fortunes of the Chick Springs resort.[49]

Two permanent residents of Greenville who were attracted to the area by the climate were Dr. William Butler of Edgefield and Thomas O. Lowndes of Charleston. Butler had been a surgeon in the navy during the War of 1812. He married Jane Perry, the sister of Commodore Oliver Hazzard Perry who won fame in the Battle of Lake Erie. Butler was elected to Congress as a Whig in 1840 and later moved to Arkansas. His son, Matthew Calbraith Butler (later a Confederate general and U.S. senator), attended the Greenville Male Academy. The Butler and the Lowndes families settled on two adjoining hills east of the village. The Butlers lived at Chestnut Hill, on what is now Butler Springs Road, and the Lowndes family lived at Lowndes Hill in a house that is still standing.[50]

The most famous resident of the Greenville District in this period, but almost unknown at the time, was the future president, Andrew Johnson. Born in Raleigh, North Carolina, in 1808, Johnson was the son of a hotel porter. He was apprenticed to a tailor at the age of ten, but he left Raleigh and practiced his trade in Laurens for a number of years. About 1826, when he was eighteen, Johnson moved to Greenville and was employed by George Boyle, a tailor who had a small shop at the upper end of Main

Street. Soon afterwards Johnson left Greenville for Greeneville, Tennessee, where he prospered and eventually entered politics. When he succeeded Abraham Lincoln as president in 1865, Andrew Johnson appointed Benjamin Perry as provisional governor of South Carolina.[51]

Education

Another development in Greenville after the War of 1812 was the growth of schools. As early as 1785 the first school in what became the Greenville District was conducted by Mark Moore, a Methodist lay preacher. Before 1820 at least nine citizens of the district made provision for the education of their children in their wills. After the passage of the Free School Act of 1811, the legislature appropriated three hundred dollars per legislator per year for the maintenance of free schools. But preference was given to orphans and paupers, and people of means refused to send their children to the "pauper schools." Many poor people resented having to take the pauper's oath to become eligible for free tuition. Consequently, the most common school in the state became the private academy. Between 1820 and 1860 thirty-four private schools and academies were mentioned in the Greenville newspapers. Sixteen of these were located in the village and eighteen in rural areas.[52]

The most notable of the local schools was the Greenville Academy in the village, with separate branches for males and females. According to William Bullein Johnson, first principal of the Female Academy, the movement to establish the academy began at the suggestion of several summer visitors. In 1819 forty-nine citizens of the district subscribed some five thousand dollars for the construction of two brick buildings. The amounts ranged from five hundred dollars contributed by Jeremiah Cleveland, Francis MacLeod, Tandy Walker, and William Toney to five dollars donated by Peter Cauble. The leaders of the movement approached Vardry McBee with the request that he donate a site for the academy. He deeded 30 acres adjoining the village on the Buncombe Road to Cleveland, Toney, William Young, John Blassingame, Spartan Goodlett, and Baylis J. Earle in August 1820. The following year these seven, along with Thomas G. Walker, were named as trustees of the school in the state statute of incorporation.[53]

The trustees erected two brick buildings. The male academy was built on the present site of the Charles E. Daniel Theatre, and the female academy stood in the middle of present-day Academy Street. Out of cash by May 1822, the trustees petitioned the state legislature for one thousand dollars a year for five years. They received a one-time grant of five hundred

Bethel Camp Ground Arbor. Bethel Methodist Church, Simpsonville. Courtesy of Bethel United Methodist Church.

Portrait of Vardry McBee. Courtesy of Roper Mountain Science Center, Coxe Collection.

William Bates House, Batesville, Highway 14. Courtesy of Choice McCoin from the collection of Jon Price Ward.

Poinsett Bridge, near U.S. 25, 1820. Courtesy of Roper Mountain Science Center, Coxe Collection.

Mansion House, located on Main Street on the site of the Poinsett Hotel, 1824.
Courtesy of Choice McCoin from the collection of Henry B. McKoy.

Poinsett Spring, Main Street. Courtesy of Greenville
County Library.

Greenville County Courthouse, 1822 (later the Record Building). Chamber of Commerce, Greenville. Courtesy of Greenville News Piedmont.

Joshua Tucker, *Southeast View of Greenville, S.C.*, 1825. Courtesy of Abby Aldrich Rockefeller Folk Art Collection, Williamsburg, Virginia.

Greenville Baptist Church, 1826. Courtesy of Choice McCoin from the Furman University Library, Special Collections.

Portrait of Benjamin F. Perry.
Courtesy of Greenville County
Library.

Portrait of Mrs. Benjamin F. Perry.
Courtesy of Greenville County
Library.

Boyce Lawn, on Spartanburg Road (now East North Street). Courtesy of The Southern Baptist Theological Seminary, Louisville, Kentucky.

Gower, Cox, and Gower Carriage Factory. Courtesy of Greenville County Library.

College Station—Columbia and Greenville Railroad Depot, 1853–1937. Courtesy of Roper Mountain Science Center, Coxe Collection.

Furman University, University Ridge. Courtesy of Choice McCoin from the
Furman University Library, Special Collections.

Christ Church, Church Street, 1854. Courtesy of Roper Mountain Science Center, Coxe Collection.

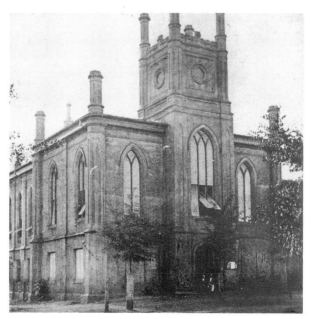

Greenville County Courthouse, 1854. Courtesy of Greenville County Library.

James Clement Furman. Courtesy of Furman University Library, Special
Collections.

dollars and the promise of the proceeds from the sale of escheated or abandoned lands in the district. From the beginning, the two schools were operated as separate institutions, and in 1836 the land was legally divided between them. Two years later the enrollment reached sixty-five young men and forty-four young women.[54]

The young men were prepared to enter the junior class at South Carolina College in Columbia or similar colleges, and the female academy provided a finishing school for young women. While the young men labored over the *Iliad,* mathematics, and natural philosophy, the principal of the Female Academy from 1823 to 1830, William Bullein Johnson, did not neglect the "solid branches of learning." In the studies of the fourth year, the young women were introduced to natural philosophy, chemistry, logic, moral philosophy, Latin, and Greek. In the 1830s modern languages and fancy needlework were added as electives.[55]

For many years the students at the academies enlivened the village with their celebrations of May Day. In 1839, for example, the queen of the May and her attendants gathered at an early hour at the academy. A group of local musicians entertained the court before they joined the students of the Male Academy and marched to the Baptist Church to hear an address by the Reverend E. T. Buist. In the evening the young women and their friends enjoyed music and dancing until ten o'clock.[56]

The Greenville academies continued to operate until the early 1850s. In 1852 Furman University opened in Greenville, and the Male Academy closed soon after the resignation of William Leary, once Robert E. Lee's tutor, as principal. The Female Academy closed in 1854, when the academy land and buildings were transferred to the state Baptist Convention for the establishment of a female college.[57]

The Continuing Impact of Evangelical Protestantism

A remarkable feature of Southern evangelical religion was its ability to regenerate itself. In 1830 another wave of revivalism swept though South Carolina, corresponding with the political upheaval of the nullification controversy.[58] In the Greenville District the institution which characterized the revival of the 1830s was shaped-note singing. The technique of teaching persons to sing using different shaped notes began in New England in the eighteenth century and spread through the South after Ananias Davison published the *Kentucky Harmony* in 1817. The technique came to the South Carolina Piedmont through the work of "Singing Billy" Walker, who was born in 1809 at Cross Keys in the Union District. At age eighteen

Walker moved with his family to Cedar Spring, near Spartanburg. He joined a Baptist church at an early age and devoted his life to compiling and writing hymns, as well as teaching them. In 1835 Walker published *Southern Harmony*, which sold six hundred thousand copies by 1854, when he published *Christian Harmony*.[59]

The importance of the singing convention in the Greenville District is reflected in the diary of Washington Taylor, who lived on Rutherford Road in O'Neal Township about a mile from Gilreath's Mill. Taylor listed singings, along with preaching, protracted meetings, and camp meetings as part of the regular round of religious activity. He first attended a singing at Edward Miller's on Sunday, February 22, 1835, and listed them regularly thereafter. On Friday, July 31, he noted that "Wm Walker commenced [a] singing school at Brush creek[;] Wm Walker tarried with me." The singings continued during the next two weeks and were quite eventful for Taylor, who proposed marriage to Nancy Cunningham, his future wife on Sunday, August 16. On Friday, the August 28, he "went to singing and home with Nancy and asked for her." On Saturday, December 19, he "went to Walkers singing at Brushy creek[.] Walkers books come." By February 7, 1836, Taylor and his brother Zion were organizing singing schools. He noted that they "went to Reedy river to see about making a singing school." By April 3, they enrolled twenty-six persons, and the school was held on two weekends, on April 9–10 and 23–24. Meanwhile, Zion Taylor organized another school at Pleasant Grove with sixty students enrolled.[60]

The revival fires were rekindled in the Greenville District in the decade before the Civil War as the nation was wrenched in the struggle over sectionalism and slavery. In the village of Greenville the Baptists experienced a revival in 1851. During the week of May 19–25, there were three services a day, with ten additional members added to the church. The following week there were eight more additions. By the summer, services were so crowded that the pew doors had to be removed so that more seats could be placed in the aisle and around the walls. Soon plans were under way to build a larger church structure.[61]

Brushy Creek Baptist Church reported a series of revivals throughout the decade of the 1850s. In July 1854, for example, a protracted meeting lasted for eleven days. Seven ministers gathered to preach. On Saturday, July 22, according to Washington Taylor's diary, "eleven persons joined the church." The next day "6 joined." On Monday "[I] went to Baptising 23 baptised[,] 6 Joined [by letter] . . . the meeting broke held 10 days & About 60 Joined." On Wednesday, July 26, Taylor noted: "Brushy creek 74 persons Joined the church by Experience and 4 by letter."[62]

Two additional elements were added to the evangelical Protestant culture of Greenville—the Sunday school and the temperance movement. In 1838 the Baptists in the village of Greenville organized a Sunday school with twenty-three students which met in a schoolhouse on West Coffee Street (because there was no heat in the church building). Evidently, the adults were more willing to endure the cold. In 1844 Washington Taylor attended Sunday school at Milford Church. On June 16 he wrote in his diary: "The sunday school agent came and we bought of him $10 worth of books." Two weeks later Taylor heard an address by C. J. Elford promoting the Sunday school at Brushy Creek Church. Then, in the 1830s William Bullein Johnson, the principal of the Greenville Female Academy, organized a temperance society at Brushy Creek Church. The temperance advocates began to refer to drinking as a "heinous crime."[63]

The periodic rekindling of the Second Great Awakening decisively shaped the religion of the district. In 1843 William Gilmore Simms reported that Presbyterians remained the most numerous denomination in the Greenville District, but the Methodists and Baptists were second and third, respectively. Perhaps the most lasting impact of the Second Great Awakening was the formation of local churches which institutionalized the revival through camp meetings, protracted meetings, and singing conventions. The churches, in turn, generated waves of revivalism which insured the future of the movement.[64]

The Village of Greenville

In 1826 Robert Mills published the *Statistics of South Carolina* which included a description of the village of Greenville—regularly laid out in squares. He proudly mentioned the public buildings: "a handsome brick court-house, (lately erected,) a jail, a Baptist meeting house, an Episcopal church, and two neat buildings for the male and female academy." The village consisted of about five hundred people who lived in some seventy houses.[65]

Benjamin F. Perry, who first came to the village to attend the Male Academy in 1823, gave a less flattering picture of his future home. He estimated the population at three to four hundred people and the limits of the village at not more than 200 to 300 yards in any direction from the courthouse. The citizens included two doctors and three lawyers. He counted five stores owned by Jeremiah Cleveland, William Toney, Samuel Crayton, John Brown, and Roger Loveland. The proprietors stocked their stores with goods from Charleston and Baltimore. According to Perry, the merchants "got on their horses and rode to Baltimore or Charleston to make their purchases." Their profits were enormous—100 or 150 percent was very common.[66]

The stores were well supplied with whiskey and rum which was sold to customers in great quantity. It was rare to go into a store without seeing someone either drunk or drinking. On his first evening in Greenville, Perry saw two drunk men on the public square quarreling, cursing, and throwing stones at each other. There was no police, and no one attempted to interfere. It was customary, he wrote, for "the gentlemen to meet in the piazzas of the stores on Main Street, and sometimes on the sidewalks, and play cards for hours, with their bowl or toddy in front of them. . . . There was very little business of any character to occupy the time of the citizens."[67]

There were no banks in Greenville, nor would there be any until after the Civil War. But, according to Perry, "there were wealthy men who kept a large capital to loan on long and easy terms. This practice supplied the means of procuring money without a bank." Jeremiah Cleveland was among the first of these bankers. He refused to purchase slaves to cultivate his land, believing that tenants were more profitable than slave labor. The capital he might have invested in slaves he lent out at 7 percent. The procedure for borrowing was quite direct. Colonel Crittenden remembered one occasion when Wesley Gilreath applied to Captain Cleveland for a loan. Cleveland's reply was simple: "I don't know much of your circumstances, but you can get the money. Any man who plows around his corn in the day time and breaks out the middles by moonlight I am not afraid to trust." Other "bankers" in Greenville were "Captain Choice, Colonel Hoke, William Jacobs, and Mr. Norton. . . . If you wished to borrow money or wished funds in New York or Charleston, you could be accommodated without going to a bank."[68]

The mail arrived in Greenville once a week on the route from Asheville to Columbia. According to Perry, the "post rider's trumpet always gave us warning of his approach." The postmaster "kept books and charged postage as a merchant did in selling goods." Later the Post Office Department established "a line of hacks by Greenville, and a two-horse stage carried four passengers from Greenville to Columbia in three days." But there were seldom any passengers to or from Greenville.[69]

Greenville in the 1820s had few of the niceties of life. Perry could remember only two carriages in the district. Colonel William Toney in the village owned one, and Chancellor Waddy Thompson, still living on Grove Creek in 1823, owned the other. Perry described Thompson's carriage as "an old vehicle, built somewhat after the style of Noah's Ark." Sofas were rarer than carriages; there was only one—in the Mansion House. There were two carpets—one at the Mansion House and another at Crittenden's Hotel. The three pianos in the village belonged to Colonel Toney, William B. Johnson, and Francis MacLeod. Silver spoons were almost as rare. The drawing room of Colonel Cleveland, one of the wealthiest men in the village, was sparsely furnished. He had several split bottom chairs, a table, and a bookcase with ten or twenty volumes in it. Women made their own dresses, and hoops and bustles were unknown.[70]

High excitement came to the village on sale days—the first Monday of every month—and court days in October. Perry remembered that "the country people would come into the village, and hitch their horses to the fences and trees along the streets." The courthouse square was crowded with ginger-cake wagons, where the rural people bought cider and beer and ginger cakes for dinner. Almost all of them also drank something stronger, and the streets were filled with drunken men. There was horse racing and horse trading. "Mounted on their steeds," Perry recalled, "the owners would ride about challenging the crowd for a swap."[71]

In the summer there were excursions into the mountains. When Perry was a student at the Male Academy, he remembered, "Professor Nott accompanied us" on a trip to Paris Mountain. The professor "drew fire from heaven and kindled a brush heap, over which some of the ladies made a cup of tea for each one of the party, which we drank with great zest." There were other trips to Table Rock. Governor John Lyde Wilson celebrated the Fourth of July on top of Table Rock during his administration [1823–1824]. A cannon was carried up, and a salute was fired to each of the original thirteen states. The romantic element was not incidental to these excursions. Perry remembered that one such trip "resulted in four engagements, and in due time to four weddings. It seemed as if the mountains inspired love."[72]

The greatest community event was the annual celebration of Independence Day on the Fourth of July. In 1831, for example, at a public meeting in May at the courthouse a committee was elected to plan the event—Perry E. Duncan, Elias D. Earle, and George F. Townes. On the glorious day itself, thirteen rounds of artillery fire woke the village at dawn. At eleven o'clock three companies of militia marched to the courthouse. There the parade marshal, Colonel Thomas P. Brockman, assisted by Colonel Barron, Colonel Greene, and Major Goodlett, formed a procession and marched to the Baptist Church where the Reverend Mr. Folkes offered a prayer, William J. Gantt read the Declaration of Independence, and Benjamin F. Perry delivered an oration. At three o'clock forty persons gathered for a sumptuous dinner at the Mansion House. Afterwards there were thirteen regular toasts and thirty volunteer toasts. The following evening there was a National Anniversary Ball at the Mansion House, and the ballroom was filled with dancers. At the same time there was a circus in the village, featuring "Tippo Sultan" the elephant and "Dandy Jack," a barebacked rider.[73]

In 1839 the English traveler James S. Buckingham reported a second celebration at the home of Guilford Eaves, in the upper part of the Greenville District, where between six and eight hundred persons were present. The marshal was William Walker, no doubt "Singing Billy," who presided over the usual prayer, the reading of the Declaration, and an oration. After the solemnities, Buckingham noted, a long table was spread, "laden with the good and choice productions of our mountainous region, high over which waved in majestic style the Star-spangled Banner." The dinner was followed by the usual toasts—thirteen regular ones and fifty-one volunteers.[74]

A major change in the economic life of the village and the surrounding area came with the arrival of Vardry McBee. He opened a store in Greenville in partnership with John Roberts. They were the first merchants in the village who sold goods for cash at moderate prices. According to Perry, "everyone went to these to purchase." Soon Cleveland, Toney, and Brown, "the oldest merchants of the place, seemed to be disgusted with the new order of business, and closed their stores." Newer merchants began to follow the example of McBee and Roberts.[75]

The village acquired a newspaper in 1826. The year before, John Hill Hewitt, a New York native who taught music at the Female Academy who later became famous as the composer of "All's Quiet Along the Potomac Tonight," persuaded W. C. Young, the local printer, to purchase a used Ramage press and a font of type to publish a literary magazine—the *Ladies' Literary Portfolio*. The magazine was superseded by the Greenville *Republican*, a weekly newspaper published by Young and Timme. The first issue appeared on July 12, 1826. Charles W. D'Oyley, formerly of Charleston, became the editor on October 27, and a year later O. H. Wells, a native of Massachusetts, became owner and publisher. Wells published the paper until August 30, 1828. Then he stopped publication for four months in order to acquire better equipment. On January 10, 1829, Wells resumed publication under a new name, the Greenville *Mountaineer*.[76]

Formation of Churches in the Village

The years after the War of 1812 also saw the formation of four churches in the village of Greenville, and Vardry McBee played a key role in their development. The first was St. James Mission of the Episcopal Church, which later became Christ Church. In the spring of 1820 the Reverend Rodolphus Dickinson, a native of Massachusetts and a graduate of Yale, established three missions—one in Greenville, one near Adam Carruth's factory, and one at Pendleton. The congregation in Greenville consisted of a few Episcopalians led by Mr. and Mrs. Edward Croft, whose families were spending their summers in the up country. This congregation worshipped in the courthouse from early spring until fall. On September 25, 1825, Vardry McBee deeded 4 acres of land and twenty-three poles to Edward Croft for an Episcopal church. A building committee was formed which included Croft, Joseph P. Labruce, and John Crittenden, and the cornerstone of a brick church, 55 feet by 30 feet, was laid. The church was first used for worship in 1826, but it was still incomplete in 1830.[77]

Two years after St. James Mission was established, William Bullein Johnson became principal of the Female Academy. He joined Brushy Creek Baptist Church, but was soon preaching in the courthouse and conducting a Sunday school. In 1824 Vardry McBee conveyed a lot 120 feet square, facing Avenue Street, to Baylis J. Earle, Jeremiah Cleveland, Sr., Richard Thruston, and George Fleming, as trustees. Johnson organized a building committee of citizens, and in 1826 a brick meeting house was erected. Not until 1831, however, was the Greenville Baptist Church organized. On November 2, at the conclusion of a three-day meeting, James Hyde, Elizabeth D. Sloan, Elizabeth Ligon, Emma McGregor, Sarah Cleveland, Dinah Hyde, Frances Rhodes, Elizabeth Rhodes, Emmala E. Thompson, and Mahala Fleming were received by profession of faith and constituted the Greenville Baptist Church of Christ. In March 1832 Samuel Gibson and Sanford Vandiver each were invited to preach once a month. Gibson was of English descent and worked as a blacksmith on Colonel William Toney's plantation; and Vandiver was a farmer in the Anderson District.[78]

Since 1825 Methodist circuit riders preached regularly at the courthouse. On October 11, 1832, Vardry McBee executed a deed for land in the village for the Methodists. To James Douthit, John Darby, William Saxon, Thomas Hutchings, and Richard Burdine, he gave a lot 100 feet by 120 feet near the Episcopal Church. Not until two years later did six people gather at the home of Mrs. Maria Turpin on Main Street to organize the Greenville Methodist Episcopal Church—Mr. and Mrs. John Darby, Mrs. Nancy Hoke, Mrs. Self, Mrs. Service, and Mrs. Turpin. These people constructed a two-story wooden church, and two years later, in 1836, organized a Methodist Sunday school.[79]

Colonel Crittenden later recalled that "Methodism flourished in the early days . . . [and] crowded audiences were attracted to the old church by the powerful sermons of 'Uncle Tommy Hutchings,' Mouzon, Moody, and others." There were additional attractions as well. "Particularly on Sunday nights," Crittenden wrote, "most of the school girls attending the Female Academy and boarding in the village attended that church, and as a natural consequence, the young men did also."[80]

The Presbyterians accounted for the largest denomination in the Greenville District, but they were the last to organize a church during the antebellum period. In 1847 Mrs. Sarah Gantt Stone, a devout Presbyterian and the daughter of Judge Richard Gantt who lived in Greenville, invited Dr. Benjamin Morgan Palmer, pastor of the Presbyterian Church in Columbia and one of the great Presbyterian preachers in the South, to spend the summer in Greenville and preach regularly. Mrs. Stone and a group of women requested the presbytery to consider the establishment of a church. By February 1848 the Presbyterian Church of Greenville Courthouse was formed and included Francis H. McLeod, his wife, Mary Ann, and daughter, Frances; John Adams, from Scotland, who Vardry McBee brought to Greenville from Lincolnton, and his wife, Mary Ann; Whitefoord Smith, Sr., and his daughter, Margaret; James McPherson; J. W. Montgomery; Margaret Cunningham Cline; Sarah A. Shaver; Sarah Gantt Stone; Jane Alexander McBee, the wife of Vardry McBee; Mariah S. Harrison; Sarah L. Butler; and Mary C. Speer. The first pastor was Savage S. Gaillard, former pastor of Mount Tabor Church at Bailey's Crossroads, about 2 miles south of present-day Greer. John Adams was a member of Fairview Church, and half of the new congregation were members of Mount Tabor. On July 24, 1850, Vardry McBee, who became a member of the church in 1861, presented the Presbyterians with a lot on the west side of Richardson Street. Within a year a brick church was built.[81]

The Development of Greenville as a Unionist Stronghold

Political life in the Greenville District was enlivened after 1815. Not only did it reflect local rivalries, but broader, national issues as well. Nationally, the Federalist Party had faded into oblivion, though the voters of Greenville had been staunchly Republican from the beginning. The Jeffersonians were divided into two factions, the Old Republicans who stoutly defended strict construction of the Constitution and states rights and the Young Republicans who supported a strong federal government, a large armed force, and internal improvements. In South Carolina in the 1820s the Old Republicans were led by U.S. Senator William Smith of York, and the Young Republicans by Congressman John C. Calhoun of Pendleton. Greenville was treated to a debate between the two factions in the columns of its new newspaper, the *Republican*.[82]

On July 26, 1826, Benjamin Perry, then a law clerk in the office of Baylis J. Earle, wrote the first of a series of letters he signed "Junius." Perry defended the views of the Young Republicans against William Smith's resolutions in the state legislature that attacked internal improvements and the tariff. Perry denounced the Old Republican view of states rights. Not the state legislatures, he argued, but only the people of the states could dictate to their representatives in Congress. Perry was answered by an adversary in the York District, William Smith's home, and by John Hill Hewitt in Greenville. Perry replied by proposing universal manhood suffrage and the right of every voter to select presidential electors. Already he was espousing solid Jacksonian principles.[83]

On September 29, 1826, the citizens of Greenville held a public dinner and ball at the Mansion House to honor John C. Calhoun, who had been elected vice president in 1824. Perry wrote the toast that was offered to the vice president: "*John C. Calhoun Vice President of the United States—* Alike distinguished for his great talents, and faithful political services. A nation's gratitude his just reward." The event was a harmonious occasion, with no hint of the bitter political battles over nullification soon to ensue both in the state and in the Greenville District.[84]

Greenville, along with the rice and Sea Island cotton planters of the low country districts, remained prosperous because of its diversified agriculture, dependence on trade from the western drovers, and summer visitors. But the planters of short-staple cotton in the low country and the lower Piedmont suffered from low prices resulting from the Panic of 1819. Increasingly, the political leadership of the state seized on the tariff as the source of their economic woes. But men in the Greenville District, like Baylis Earle and Jeremiah Cleveland, supported the Tariff of 1824. In the summer of 1827 the Greenville *Republican* editor D'Oyley denounced the critics of the tariff who were already hinting at disunion. "The wretch who would seriously wish for a separation of the States should be hunted down like a wild beast, or shot like a mad dog," he wrote.[85]

In 1828 after Congress adopted an even higher tariff, Vice President Calhoun joined the fray by proposing nullification as an ultimate remedy. He abandoned his Young Republican views in the *South Carolina Exposition and Protest*, which he wrote anonymously for the antitariff faction in the state. The Constitution, he argued, was a compact between the states, not the people, and a state convention could declare a federal law null and void within its boundaries. In Greenville an antitariff meeting gathered on September 15, 1828. Waddy Thompson, Jr., a member of the state legislature, denounced the tariff in no uncertain terms. He promised to "live on snow birds, and walk around the circuit on foot rather than eat Kentucky pork or ride Kentucky horses." (Kentucky, a major source of Greenville's drover trade, supported the tariff.) Editor O. H. Wells of the *Mountaineer* approved the *Exposition* as "an able state paper," but he wrote that it was "more ingenious than correct in the remedy it proposes."[86]

On January 30, 1830, Benjamin Perry became editor of the Greenville *Mountaineer,* and it soon became one of the leading Unionist newspapers in the state. But sentiment in the district did not unanimously support Perry. At a public dinner in Greenville on July 28, Congressman Warren R. Davis of Pendleton declared that he had no love for the Union. Dr. William Butler and Waddy Thompson, who were candidates for the state legislature, declared that they were Nullifiers. But in the election in October the incumbents—Nullifiers Thompson, Tandy Walker, and Butler—were decisively defeated by the Unionists—Wilson Cobb, Micajah Berry, and John H. Harrison. Perry's assessment of the sentiment in the Greenville District was vindicated. "We know that the mass of citizens in Greenville," he wrote, "the hardy yeomanry of the mountains, the bone and sinew of government, are far, very far, from being in a revolutionary state."[87]

Statewide, the Nullifiers had elected a majority in the state legislature, but not the two-thirds required to call a convention to nullify the tariff. So party lines were drawn tighter. In July 1831 the Nullifiers met in Charleston and formed the States Rights and Free Trade Party. In Greenville on September 5, the Nullifiers met to organize within the district. The Unionists countered with a rally on October 3 and denounced nullification as revolution. A meeting in the upper part of the district threatened secession from the state if South Carolina nullified the tariff.[88]

Feelings ran so high over nullification that the annual Fourth of July celebration in Greenville was canceled in 1832. No one's feelings ran higher than those of *Mountaineer* editor Benjamin Perry. He barely avoided duels with Waddy Thompson, the editor of the Pendleton *Messenger* Frederick W. Symmes, and former classmate Henry H. Townes. Perry and William Choice, a Nullifier candidate for the legislature in 1832, engaged in a series of fights, but they stopped short of a duel. Choice's spouse, Caroline Cleveland, who was Perry's former sweetheart, never spoke to the impetuous editor again. Finally, on August 16, 1832, Perry met Turner Bynum in a duel.[89]

Bynum had been persuaded by the Nullifiers to come to Greenville to edit a newspaper in opposition to the *Mountaineer.* The *Southern Sentinel* issued its first edition on June 23 and on August 4 Bynum attacked Perry in its columns. Perry challenged his opponent to a duel, and they met on an island in the Tugaloo River on August 16. Bynum was mortally wounded and died the next day. He was buried at midnight at the Old Stone Church near Pendleton.[90]

All the efforts of the Nullifiers in Greenville were unsuccessful. In the election in October 1832 the Unionists swept the district. Eighty-four percent of the eligible voters went to the polls. The Unionist incumbent, Banister Stone, was re-elected to the state Senate over the Nullifier candidate, Dr. William Butler—1,311 to 334. In the House, Cobb (1,293), Harrison (1,280), and Berry (1,279) were re-elected over Tandy Walker (500), Robert Maxwell (471), and William Choice (427). At Dickey's, one of the mountain precincts, the Nullifiers received only one vote out of 184. The Greenville District's vote against nullification was 72 percent. Spartanburg, with 69 percent, ran a close second among the up country districts.[91]

In the state as a whole, however, the Nullifiers won the day. The legislature met in special session and called an election for a convention to nullify the tariff. Predictably, the Unionists candidates in Greenville (Benjamin F. Perry, Silas R. Whitten, Thomas P. Brockman, and former Governor Henry Middleton) defeated the Nullifiers (Baylis Earle, William Butler, William Thruston, and Benjamin Arnold). At the convention the Greenville delegation voted against nullification and failed to sign the ordinance when it was adopted. They opposed the test oath that the convention required of all state officeholders. Back in Greenville, the Unionists erected a liberty pole in front of the courthouse, and at a public meeting they condemned the actions of the convention.[92]

In accordance with the directions of the state Unionist Party, six local Unionist societies organized in Greenville, denounced the test oath, and voted to support President Andrew Jackson's intention to use force if necessary to collect the tariff in South Carolina. When Governor Robert Y. Hayne called on the militia to defend the state, only 120 volunteers from the Greenville District responded, and hundreds of local militia members refused to take the test oath. On March 24, 1834, the Unionist Party held a state convention in Greenville in the Methodist church. The meeting was led by Daniel Elliott Huger of Charleston, Joel R. Poinsett, and Benjamin F. Perry.[93]

In the fall elections in 1834 Benjamin Perry opposed Nullifier Warren Davis for Congress. Perry carried Greenville easily, but he was defeated in Pickens and Anderson. When Davis died in office in 1835, Perry ran against Nullifier Waddy Thompson and lost once again. At the anniversary of the Battle of Cowpens in 1835, Perry expressed the views of the vast majority of the people of the Greenville District: "Look to this sacred Union—reared by the wisdom and cemented with the blood of your fathers—as the Bulwark of your Freedom—as the Palladium of your Liberty—as the *very existence* of your National Independence and your prosperity and happiness as a people." Unlike the state, the Greenville District emerged from the nullification controversy in the mainstream of the Union.[94]

The Seminole War

If the men of the Greenville District had missed an opportunity to fight during the nullification crisis, they were soon embroiled in another conflict. President Andrew Jackson was confronted with the presence of thousands of Indians east of the Mississippi River, who occupied millions of valuable acres of land. When Jackson ordered the removal of the Indians to west of the Mississippi, the Seminoles refused to leave Florida. Led by their young chief Osceola, they attacked federal troops sent to remove them, and from 1835 to 1838 the United States was engaged in the Seminole War. In the Greenville District on September 14, 1837, First Lieutenant Washington Taylor joined his artillery company, as he put it, "for the purpose of drafting or volunteering to go to Florida to fight the Seminoles." Eventually a company of Greenville and Laurens men served in the Seminole conflict.[95]

At the height of the nullification crisis, the state legislature recognized the growing importance of the village of Greenville and at the same time drew it more closely into the political and economic orbit of South Carolina. On December 17, 1831, Governor James Hamilton, Jr., the leader of the Nullification Party in the state, signed "An Act to Incorporate the Village of Greenville." The village limits extended 1 mile from the courthouse. The delegation to the state legislature was empowered to appoint an intendant and four wardens to serve until their successors could be elected the following year. Because municipal government was so rare in South Carolina, the authority of the village council was defined in terms of the powers delegated to the district court. The council, "vested with all the powers of justices of the quorum of this State, within the limits of the said village," was empowered to adopt ordinances, hold court, appoint constables, and exercise the powers granted to the commissioners of roads.[96]

A major section of the act of incorporation, in keeping with the demands of a society dependent on slavery, concerned the control of the slave population. Within the village, the council assumed the responsibility of patrol duty which the militia companies performed in the district. "The said intendant and wardens shall have power . . . to classify and arrange the inhabitants liable to do patrol duty," the statute read, "and to require them to perform such duty, as often as occasion may require, and enforce the performance thereof."[97]

The town clerk was empowered by the council to keep a roll of all persons liable for patrol duty. Two patrol companies were organized. The first patrolled on Monday, Wednesday, and Friday evenings from 9:00 P.M. to midnight and on the first, third, and fifth Sunday afternoons and evenings. The second company patrolled on Tuesday, Thursday, and Saturday evenings and on the second and fourth Sundays. All slaves beyond the premises of their masters and not accompanied by a white person over ten years of age were required to have a ticket. Slaves without such tickets were liable to arrest.[98]

Greenville might have been overwhelmingly Unionist in sentiment in the 1830s, but it was still a slaveholding society. Unionist views in a society that permitted slavery would be severely tested in the decades that followed. "Slavery," Benjamin Perry confided to his diary in 1835, "is the only thing that can produce a dissolution of the Union."[99]

Notes

1. Julian J. Petty, *The Growth and Distribution of Population in South Carolina* (Columbia, 1943, 1975), 226–27.

2. The most complete treatment of the Vesey insurrection is John Lofton, *Insurrection in South Carolina: The Turbulent World of Denmark Vesey* (Yellow Springs, Ohio, 1964). The insurrection's impact on the state is outlined in William W. Freehling, *Prelude to Civil War: The Nullification Controversy in South Carolina, 1816–1836* (New York, 1965).

3. Caroline Olivia Laurens, "Journal of a Visit to Greenville from Charleston in the Summer of 1825," *S.C. Historical Magazine* 72 (1971): 164–69, 220–33; Greenville *Enterprise,* July 17, 1882. Laurens indicates that the date of the execution was July 1, 1825; Campbell places it on July 7, 1824.

4. Greenville *Enterprise,* July 17, 1882.

5. Ibid., September 27, 1871.

6. Greenville *Mountaineer,* July 9, 1831, and January 7, 1832, cited in Albert N. Sanders, "Greenville in the 1830s," *The Proceedings and Papers of the Greenville County Historical Society* (cited hereafter as *PPGCHS*) 7 (1979–1983): 86.

7. "Lemuel J. Alston," *Biographical Dictionary of the S.C. House of Representatives,* ed. Walter B. Edgar and N. Louise Bailey (Columbia, 1974–1992) 3: 34–35.

8. *DeBow's Review* 13 (September 1852): 314–18; Marion M. Hewell, "Vardry McBee of South Carolina," *PPGCHS* 1(1962–1964): 37–42. Roy McBee Smith

has written and published a biography of his ancestor after an exhaustive search of available sources. Roy McBee Smith, *Vardry McBee, 1775–1864: Man of Reason in an Age of Extremes* (Columbia, 1992).

9. Poinsett to Gouverneur Kemble, June 12, 1847, in *Calendar of Joel R. Poinsett Papers* (Philadelphia, Pa., 1941), 214–15; Hewell, *PPGCHS* 1: 47.

10. Ernest M. Lander, Jr., "The Iron Industry in Ante-Bellum South Carolina," *Journal of Southern History* 20 (August 1954): 3, 340.

11. Lander, "Iron Industry," 341.

12. Ernest M. Lander, Jr., *The Textile Industry in Antebellum South Carolina* (Baton Rouge, La., 1969), 11–12.

13. Lander, *Textile Industry*, 13–14.

14. Ibid., 16–17.

15. Ibid., 18–20.

16. Ibid., 20–21, 27–28; Jon Price (Mrs. David) Ward, "William Bates and the Batesville Community," *PPGCHS* 7 (1979–1983): 118–24.

17. Lander, *Textile Industry*, 24.

18. Ibid., 23–24, 97, 83–84; J. W. Reid, *History of the Fourth Regiment of the S.C. Volunteers* (Greenville, 1892, 1986), 136–37.

19. Reid, *Fourth Regiment*, 131–35; Lander, *Textile Industry*, 97.

20. Reid, *Fourth Regiment*, 135–38; Laura S. Ebaugh, *Bridging the Gap to Greenville: A Guide to Early Greenville, S.C.* (Greenville, 1966, 1970), 92.

21. Reid, *Fourth Regiment*, 135–38.

22. David Kohn, ed., *Internal Improvements in South Carolina, 1817–1828* (Washington, D.C., 1938), 582; Daniel W. Hollis, "Costly Delusion: Inland Navigation in the South Carolina Piedmont," *Proceedings of the South Carolina Historical Association, 1968*, 28; David Duncan Wallace, *South Carolina: A Short History, 1520–1948* (Chapel Hill, N.C., 1951), 375.

23. Kohn, *Internal Improvement*, 600, A19.

24. "Abraham (Abram) Blanding," *Biographical Directory of the House* 4: 60–61; "Joel Roberts Poinsett," *Biographical Directory of the S.C. Senate*, ed. N. Louise Bailey et al. (Columbia, 1986) 2: 1286–87.

25. Kohn, *Internal Improvement*, 48–49.

26. Ibid., 49.

27. Ibid., 50.

28. Ibid.

29. Pendleton *Messenger*, October 4, 1820.

30. John M. Bryan, ed., *Robert Mills, Architect* (Washington, D.C., 1989), 75.

31. "Report of the Board of Public Works . . . for the Year, 1821, 1822," in David Kohn, ed., *Internal Improvement in South Carolina, 1817–1828* (Washington, D.C., 1938), 108, 111.

32. Ibid., 152, 154; "Report of the Commissioners of Public Buildings for Greenville to the Legislature of South Carolina, November 17, 1827," cited in Bryan, *Mills*, 103, n32.

33. Bryan, *Mills*, 79–80.

34. Ibid., 84.

35. Lawrence F. Brewster, *Summer Migrations and Resorts of South Carolina Low-Country Planters* (Durham, N.C., 1947), 51.

36. Brewster, *Summer Migrations*, 57; "Henry Middleton," *Directory of the S.C. House* 4: 394–96; Ebaugh, *Bridging the Gap*, 46–47. Whitehall still stands on Earle Street in the city of Greenville.

37. "Joseph Alston," *Biographical Directory of the House* 4: 32–35. Alston's house, according to Benjamin F. Perry, "was burned down thirty or forty years since." His nieces later lived on the Alston land. Greenville *Enterprise,* September 6, 1871.

38. Brewster, *Summer Migrations*, 59; Stephen S. Crittenden, *The Greenville Century Book* (Greenville, 1903), 28.

39. Brewster, *Summer Migrations*, 59–60; James M. Richardson, *History of Greenville County, South Carolina* (Atlanta, 1930, 1980) 63; Crittenden, *Century Book*, 27–28, 34. The definitive treatment of the Mansion House is Henry B. McKoy, "The Mansion House," *PPGCHS* 7 (1979–1983): 21–28.

40. Crittenden, *Century Book*, 27–28, 34; Greenville *Enterprise,* September 20, 1871.

41. Brewster, *Summer Migrations*, 61; Frederick A. Porcher, "Memoirs of Frederick Adolphus Porcher," *S.C. Historical Magazine* 47 (1946): 92–94; Greenville *Enterprise,* October 4, 1871.

42. Brewster, *Summer Migrations*, 61.

43. "Joel Roberts Poinsett," *Biographical Directory of the Senate* 2: 1286–90; J. Fred Rippy, *Joel R. Poinsett, Versatile American* (Durham, N.C., 1935), 205, 221.

44. Lillian A. Kibler, *Benjamin F. Perry, South Carolina Unionist* (Durham, N.C., 1946), 83; Perry, *The Writings of Benjamin F. Perry,* ed. Stephen Meats and Edwin T. Arnold (Spartanburg, 1980) 3: 204.

45. Perry, *Writings* 3: 131, 406; John Belton O'Neall, *Biographical Sketches of the Bench and Bar of South Carolina* (Charleston, 1859, 1975) 1: xxiii–iv.

46. Brewster, *Summer Migrations*, 77.

47. Jean Martin Flynn, *Chick Springs, Taylors, South Carolina* (Travelers Rest, S.C., 1972), 1; see also Flynn, "Chick Springs—1840 to 1941," *PPGCHS* 6 (1975–1979): 40–44.

48. Ibid., 1–2.

49. Ibid., 2.

50. Crittenden, *Century Book*, 54–55.

51. Greenville *Enterprise and Mountaineer,* August 4, 1875.

52. Marion T. Anderson, "Some Highlights in the History of Education in Greenville County," *PPGCHS* 5 (1971–1975): 12–14; Antoinette M. Williams, "Education in Greenville County Prior to 1860" (M.A. thesis, University of South Carolina, 1930), 24–26.

53. Marion M. Hewell, "The Academies," *PPGCHS* 5 (1971–1975): 99–100; William B. Johnson, "Reminiscences of William Bullein Johnson," *Journal of the S.C. Baptist Historical Society* 7 (1981): 4; Crittenden, *Century Book*, 28–29; Judith

T. Bainbridge, "History of the Greenville Woman's College" (manuscript in possession of the author) 1: 3–4.

54. Hewell, "Academies," 104; Bainbridge, "Woman's College," 5–6.

55. Hewell, "Academies," 102; Bainbridge, "Woman's College," 7

56. Greenville *Mountaineer,* May 3, 1839, cited in Hewell, "Academies," 105–6.

57. Hewell, "Academies," 106–9.

58. The continuing impact of the Second Great Awakening is treated in William G. McLoughlin, *Revivals, Awakenings, and Reform: Essay on Religion and Social Change in America, 1607–1970* (Chicago, 1978), 98–140.

59. George P. Jackson, *White Spirituals in the Southern Uplands* (Chapel Hill, N.C., 1933), 366–69; Curtis L. Check, "The Singing School and Shaped Note Tradition" (D.M.A. diss., University of Southern California, 1968), passim.

60. Washington Taylor, *A Diary of Transactions from 1835–1855 of Washington Taylor* (Frederick, Md., 1988), 2, 7–8, 12, 14, 16.

61. Robert N. Daniel, *A Century of Progress, being the History of the First Baptist Church, Greenville, South Carolina* (Greenville, 1959), 24, 32.

62. Moore, "Brushy Creek," 63–64; Taylor, *Diary of Transactions,* 235.

63. Daniel, *Century of Progress,* 19; Taylor, *Diary of Transactions,* 113–15, 150; G. B. Moore, "Brushy Creek Church," 60.

64. William Gilmore Simms, *The Geography of South Carolina* (Charleston, 1843), 84.

65. Mills, *Statistics,* 572–73.

66. Greenville *Enterprise,* September 20, 1871.

67. Ibid., September 13, 1871.

68. Ibid., October 4, 1871; Crittenden, *Century Book,* 51–52.

69. Greenville *Enterprise,* September 20, 1871.

70. Ibid., September 13, 1871.

71. Ibid.

72. Ibid., September 27, 1871.

73. Greenville *Mountaineer,* May 28, June 11, July 9, 1831, cited in Sanders, *PPGCHS* 7: 89–90.

74. J[ames]. S. Buckingham, *The Slave States of America* (London, 1842) 2: 180–82.

75. Greenville *Enterprise,* September 20, 1871.

76. J. Mauldin Lesesne, "The Nullification Controversy in an Up-Country District," *Proceedings of the S.C. Historical Association, 1939,* 13; John Hammond Moore, *South Carolina Newspapers* (Columbia, 1988), 123–24; Kibler, *Perry,* 48–49.

77. Robert C. Wood, *Parish in the Heart of the City: Christ Church, Greenville, S.C.* (Greenville, 1976), 13–14, 19–20.

78. Johnson, "Reminiscences," 7: 4–6; Robert N. Daniel, *A Century of Progress, Being the History of First Baptist Church, Greenville, South Carolina* (Greenville, 1957), 1–5, 9–11.

79. A. M. Moseley, *The Buncombe Street Methodist Story* (Greenville, 1965), 1–2, 4–5, 9.

80. Crittenden, *Century Book*, 41.

81. Henry B. McKoy, *A History of the First Presbyterian Church in Greenville, South Carolina* (Greenville, 1962), 7–20; F. T. McGill, *A Short History of the First Presbyterian Church of Greer, South Carolina, 1841–1941* (Greer, 1941), 3–5.

82. Lacy K. Ford, Jr., *Origins of Radicalism: The South Carolina Upcountry, 1800–1860* (New York, 1988), 113–14; Kibler, *Perry*, 50.

83. Kibler, *Perry*, 50–54.

84. Ibid., 56–57.

85. Lesesne, "Nullification Controversy," 13–14.

86. Ibid., 14–15.

87. Ibid., 15–17; Greenville *Mountaineer*, July 9, 1830, cited in Kibler, *Perry*, 97.

88. Lesesne, "Nullification Controversy," 17–18.

89. Kibler, *Perry*, 108–20.

90. Ibid., 124–34.

91. Lesesne, "Nullification Controversy," 19; Ford, *Southern Radicalism*, 139.

92. Lesesne, "Nullification Controversy," 19–20; Kibler, *Perry*, 143–44.

93. Lesesne, "Nullification Controversy," 22.

94. Ibid., 23–24.

95. Glyndon G. Van Deusen, *The Jacksonian Era, 1828–1848* (New York, 1959), 48–50; Washington Taylor, *A Diary of Transactions from 1835–1855 of Washington Taylor* (Frederick, Md., 1988), 33; Broadside, Church Museum, Fairview Presbyterian Church, Fountain Inn, S.C.

96. *Statutes at Large of S.C.* 6: 2540.

97. Ibid.

98. Greenville *Mountaineer*, October 24, 1845.

99. August 8, 1835, entry, cited in Ford, *Southern Radicalism*, 155.

CHAPTER FIVE

From Unionism
to Civil War

In the last two decades of the antebellum period—from 1840 to
1860—the Greenville District continued to prosper. The town itself flourished with the coming of the railroad and as a center of higher education.
Politically, in the heat of the controversy over slavery, the district shifted
from a Unionist majority to support for secession and civil war. After an
initial demonstration of Confederate loyalty, however, there was continuing division in Greenville over the war.

The population of the Greenville District continued to increase, but at
a rate parallel to the sluggish growth of the state. There was still considerable migration to the West. On October 5, 1854, the *Southern Patriot*
reported that in one neighborhood there were one hundred persons about
to set out for Texas. Seven or eight families in the upper part of the district
moved west under the leadership of Dr. Welborn Barton, who had practiced medicine for a year in Washington County, Texas. According to his
daughter's account, written in 1929, one hundred people left the Tigerville
area in covered wagons with all their belongings, including slaves; others
moved to Florida. "The spirit of emigration is rife amongst the people of
the mountains," wrote the editor of the *Southern Patriot*, "We shall loose
[sic] some of our best citizens."[1]

Agriculture

Agriculture remained the chief source of employment in the district.
In 1850 Greenville produced only 2,452 bales of cotton and 637,784 bushels of corn. In the up country only the Pickens District produced fewer
bales of cotton than Greenville. Ten years later, the production of cotton
in the Greenville District had risen somewhat to 2,984 bales, and corn had
dropped to 623,288 bushels. Greenville newspapers of the time mentioned
corn, wheat, and oats, but seldom cotton. In 1853 the *Southern Patriot*
reported that "the cotton crop is small, but in this crop we are not so much
interested." Washington Taylor, who farmed in the Milford section of the

Greenville District, wrote in his diary in 1841 that grain was his major crop. On April 30 he indicated that he had "made 1159 gallons whiskey in 4 months out of 650 bushels counting malt & has made use of some 5 or 6 bushels of rie[,] 10 bushels [of] brand[,] 6 or 7 bushels of oats." Taylor sold whiskey by peddling it through the countryside. On May 4 he wrote that "Geo[rge] Cunningham has got back & left 300 gallons whiskey not sold in Laurens." The following week Taylor himself set out and sold 350 gallons in two weeks. Taylor recorded that he first picked cotton in November 1852. A year later, on June 30, 1853, he helped construct a cotton gin.[2]

Strange as it may sound, the Greenville District was the site of a brief experiment in the growth of tea. In December 1848 Junius Smith, a native of Connecticut, who had failed in his efforts to promote the Atlantic steamship trade, planted a tea garden about a mile from town on land owned by Dr. Charles B. Stone. In August 1850 Smith purchased 269 acres on Golden Grove Creek where he cultivated tea. Among the local residents, only Benjamin F. Perry was intrigued by Smith's efforts. After Smith was severely beaten in December 1851 for suspected abolitionist leanings, his health declined rapidly. He returned to the north and died in January 1853. The tea farm was sold a year later.[3]

The distribution of wealth in the Greenville District was very uneven. The 1850 census indicated that there were 188 tenants (15 percent) in Greenville out of a total of 1,271 people engaged in agriculture, and there were 706 slaveholders out of a total of 2,351 heads of household (30 percent). The 1860 census showed that 33.2 percent of the farmers held from zero to 50 acres of farm land, 39.2 percent between 51 and 100 acres, 26.1 percent between 101 and 500 acres, and only 1.5 percent over 500 acres. The number of slaveholders had grown to 808 out of 2,698 heads of household, but the percentage of slaveholders remained constant at 30 percent.[4]

In 1850 eighty-two persons owned twenty or more slaves, thereby qualifying as planters. The planters comprised 3.4 percent of the heads of household. Ten years later, in 1860 there were seventy-six planters, who comprised 2.8 percent of the heads of household. Vardry McBee remained the largest landowner in the district at the end of the antebellum period. Because of his landholdings, farming interests, and business enterprises, McBee was in a class by himself. He owned thirty-seven slaves in 1850 and fifty-six a decade later. Only seven persons owned more in 1860, and only Colonel T. Edwin Ware owned more than one hundred slaves.[5]

Thomas Edwin Ware was the only Greenville resident listed by Chalmers Davidson as one of the "great planters" of South Carolina. He was born in

1806 in the Abbeville District and in 1834 married Mary Williams Jones, the only child of Adam and Jane Jones of Greenville who owned twenty slaves in 1850. The Wares moved to the Greenville District and lived with Jones on his plantation, later known as Ware Place. In 1854 Ware built a spacious home on Pendleton Road, on a hill overlooking the town of Greenville. The site had been the summer home of Mrs. Susan H. McCall of Charleston, the sister of U.S. Senator Robert Y. Hayne and the mother of Mrs. Benjamin F. Perry. The Ware house was surrounded by a grove of oaks set on a tract of some 30 acres. The 1860 census valued Ware's real property at seventy thousand dollars and his personal property at ninety thousand dollars. He owned 102 slaves in 1860. He served both in the state House of Representatives (1840–1847) and in the state Senate (1848–1864).[6]

Much more numerous than the planters were the large-acreage farmers, who owned between six and nineteen slaves, and their number was growing. In 1850 there were 282 large-acreage farmers in the Greenville District (11.9 percent of the heads of households), and by 1860 their number had increased to 331 (12.3 percent). Typical of this group was Thomas Taylor and his son Alfred, who lived near Chick Springs (now Taylors). Thomas Taylor's grandfather had come with twelve other families from Culpeper County, Virginia, in 1785. By 1850 Thomas and his wife Sarah lived in a two-story wooden farmhouse and owned 400 acres of land and fifteen slaves. Their son, Alfred, born in 1823, was educated in a local academy and in 1845 began operating a sawmill for his father. The mill, built for five hundred dollars, made seven hundred dollars the first year. Alfred also managed a country store where he sold a variety of cloth and foodstuffs such as sugar, coffee, salt, and homemade whiskey. He stocked nails, hand tools, guns, shoes, and a few miscellaneous items such as cologne, ribbons, and tea cups. Taylor did a large credit business and had connections with commission merchants in Charleston. In 1853 Alfred Taylor married Malinda Bowen, and they moved into their own house. In 1859 he became the manager of the hotel at Chick Springs.[7]

But Thomas and Alfred Taylor thought of themselves primarily as farmers. They planted corn, wheat, and sweet potatoes and raised cattle and hogs. Alfred Taylor, like his brother Washington in the Milford community, was an active churchgoer. He and his wife joined Brushy Creek Baptist Church in 1854 after he had a moving religious experience. "He felt a new creature," Alfred wrote in his diary in the third person, "the burden all rolled away." The Taylors enjoyed Sunday dinners with their neighbors, and the men spent many winter days hunting turkey, duck, and quail. They marked the year by the regular militia musters and community harvest gatherings, such as corn shuckings. Such was life for a large-acreage farmer in Greenville in the final decades of the antebellum period.[8]

Yeomen farmers, who owned from one to five slaves, held 72.4 percent of the farms in the Greenville District, but only 14.8 percent of the slaves. Typical of these yeomen was the family of Alsey Albert and Ann Pool Neves in the Mush Creek community, north of Travelers Rest. Alsey's father William immigrated from Ireland in 1789, landed in Charleston, and settled on 350 acres on the Tyger River in the Greenville District. Alsey Neves was born in 1814, and inherited the farm in 1844. About 1834 Alsey married Ann Pool who was five years older. In 1835 their first child, William Perry Zacharias Franklin, was born. He was the first of ten children born between 1835 and 1852.[9]

By 1860 Alsey Neves was bedridden with rheumatism, and W. P. Z. F. Neves, at age twenty-five, assumed direction of the farm and the five children at home (ranging in ages from eight to sixteen). He also operated a country store that served the Mush Creek community. Neves was a meticulous recordkeeper who entered crop yields and store accounts in a book with a red and green handstitched cover. The farm produced wheat and corn, and all the able-bodied family members did their share of the work. On occasion, Neves employed black laborers or white sharecroppers. The women were engaged in weaving and dying cloth for the family's use.[10]

Although they were not church members, the Neves family attended protracted and association meetings at nearby Baptist churches. The family gave parties, and W. P. Z. F., who was fair and handsome, was popular with the women. His cousin, Caroline Bailey, after seeing his picture, informed him that "your likeness I thought it was a very pretty one[.] I think if the girls was to see you they would eat you up." He also played the fiddle and the clarinet. During the Civil War the younger Neves men attended local boarding schools. From his penmanship and recordkeeping, it is likely that W. P. Z. F. Neves attended a similar school.[11]

The Town of Greenville

The town of Greenville prospered in the two decades before the Civil War. The population grew from 1,100 in 1843 to 1,750 in 1852. In 1860 the town contained 1,815 people. "Never before," reported the *Southern Patriot*, "have we known so much prosperity in our town. Everything seems to be thriving and business of every kind increasing and extending itself. All who work are doing well, and those who don't, make out to live!" The business district continued to center around the courthouse. On sale days the country people congregated in an open area known as "Sandy Flat" beyond North Street on the west side of Main. At the top of hill on Main Street, stood a grove of oak trees where cows, which belonged to the towns-people, grazed. Beyond the trees was the house occupied first by Chancellor Waddy Thompson and later by Francis H. McLeod. Adjacent to it was the village cemetery, Springwood, deeded to the district commissioners in 1829. The cemetery had once been the garden of the Thompson house where Mrs. Thompson's mother, Mrs. James Williams, widow of one of the commanders at the Battle of King's Mountain, was buried in 1812.[12]

In 1850 the merchants and professional people composed only 3.9 percent of the population in up country South Carolina, but they were an important element in society. The political rivals, Benjamin F. Perry and Waddy Thompson, Jr., were the most notable examples. To varying degrees, the two men demonstrated the way in which the entire society was dependent on agriculture.[13]

At the end of the nullification controversy, Benjamin Perry, still a bachelor, was living at the Mansion House. He resigned as editor of the *Mountaineer* in 1833, and after two unsuccessful congressional races, he concentrated on his law practice. But his retirement from politics was premature. In October 1836 he was elected to the state legislature and represented the Greenville District until after the Civil War, with the exception of five years. By 1836 he was in the midst of a whirlwind courtship with Elizabeth F. McCall of Charleston. They married in 1837, and the next year they moved into their new house on Main Street south of the courthouse. The house was built of wood and was two stories high with front porches upstairs and down. The roof was square and painted green. Oaks and cedars shaded the spacious lot. In the rear was a kitchen and flower and vegetable gardens.[14]

Perry purchased 201 acres of land in 1844, and by 1850 he owned twelve slaves. He found slaveholding very onerous. Slaves are "hard to manage and give me most of my trouble," he wrote, "they become idle and impudent. . . . I dislike whipping them & yet we cannot get on without it." When he was away from home practicing law on the circuit, he advised his wife: "It is better to pass over their idleness and impudence. . . . They are poor, ignorant, lazy creatures, who have very little motive or inducement to do well. We must make great allowance for them." Perry seemed to have little understanding of the way in which slaves exploited the system through work slowdowns.[15]

Perry was deeply religious, but he never joined a church. Before his marriage Perry generally attended the Baptist church, though he found the Methodists more liberal and rational. After 1837 he attended the Episcopal church with his wife, but he confided to his journal that "generally religious persons are less liberal, less kind, less social, more sordid & more selfish than others." Perry prospered as his reputation spread. In 1850 his property was valued at $31,840, and his annual income was $3,000. His library of twenty-five hundred volumes was the largest in the district.[16]

Waddy Thompson, Jr., was more typical of the professional class of the state who were also planters. Thompson was a leading Nullifier during the 1830s. Born in Pickensville in 1798, he was the son of Chancellor Waddy Thompson, who later moved to Greenville and established himself as a planter. Young Waddy graduated from South Carolina College in 1814 and read law in Edgefield. There he married Emmala Butler, the sister of Dr. William Butler, returned to Greenville, and from 1826 to 1830 served in the state legislature. Later he was solicitor of the Western District of South Carolina and for ten years was a brigadier general in the militia. In 1835 he defeated Benjamin Perry for U.S. Congress, and served until 1841. The next year President John Tyler appointed him minister to Mexico. When Thompson returned to Greenville in 1844, he began work on his *Recollections of Mexico*, which he published in 1846. Thompson developed a large law practice, much of it before the United States Supreme Court. He was a highly successful planter who owned thirty-three slaves in 1850. Until 1855 Thompson lived on the Spartanburg Road (now East North Street) near Christ Church. That year he sold his estate to Furman professor James Petigru Boyce and built a home on Paris Mountain where he housed his fine library, Mexican artifacts, and collection of portraits. Thompson's brother, Henry, lived at the foot of the mountain, and the two families communicated by semaphore. Henry Thompson's son, Hugh Smith Thompson, later state superintendent of education and governor, flagged messages up the mountain.[17]

The business and professional leaders of Greenville were quite homogeneous. Most of them were descendants of up country settlers who had lived in the region since the Revolution. There were a few exceptions. George Heldmann arrived in 1846 at the age of twenty-seven. A native of Hesse in Germany, he came with very little, opened a shop on Main Street as a saddler and harness maker, and accumulated considerable wealth. Heldmann married a local resident and was accepted into the community, though his heavy German accent and his pride at being the son of one of Blücher's troops at Waterloo set him apart. Less successful were several Jewish merchants. In 1859 Mrs. Abigail Levy and her husband L. L. Levy, who had operated a dry goods store in Charleston, moved to Greenville. She was described as "a contemptible Jew[,] a pest of the community," and by June

1860 the family left Greenville. About that same time, Morris Samuel, a Russian Jew and a "lager beer seller," was convicted "for retailing" and left in June 1861. David Lowenberg, equally unsuccessful, opened a small confectionery shop in September 1860. He was described as "one of those strangers no one knows," and by 1865 he too was gone. Greenville was clearly not hospitable to Jews.[18]

Among the most sensational events that occurred in Greenville in the antebellum period were murder trials involving two prominent citizens— the trial of William Lowndes Yancey for the murder of his wife's uncle, and the trial of state Senator T. Edwin Ware for the murder of his father-in-law.

Yancey had come to Greenville in 1833 to read law with Benjamin Perry. It was at the height of the nullification controversy, and Yancey shared Perry's Unionist views. Yancey became editor of the *Mountaineer* in December 1834, and the next year he married Sarah Caroline Earle, the daughter of George Washington Earle, and began planting on Earle land with thirty-five slaves. In 1836 the Yanceys moved to Alabama, where he grew cotton, but they spent the summers in Greenville.[19]

In September 1838 Yancey attended a militia muster at which Waddy Thompson and Joseph N. Whitner of Anderson, the candidates for Congress, spoke. Afterwards Yancey made a disparaging remark about Thompson, and Elias Earle, the seventeen-year-old nephew of Thompson and a cousin of Sarah Yancey, responded by calling Yancey a liar. Yancey slapped Elias Earle, and Earle hit the older man with his riding crop. The following day Yancey apologized to Dr. Robinson Earle, Elias's father and his wife's uncle, and the affair seemed over. Several days later Dr. Earle attacked Yancey on the porch of Crittenden's store with the handle of a grain cradle and a knife. Yancey drew a pistol and mortally wounded the doctor. On the spot, Dr. Earle declared that "had Yancey not fired I would have easily whipped him." Yancey was brought to trial and defended by Perry, Armistead Burt of Abbeville, and David L. Wardlaw of Edgefield. Yancey was found guilty of manslaughter, and Judge Josiah J. Evans indicated that the shooting seemed to be entirely accidental and not attributed to the angry and excited behavior of Earle. Yancey was fined fifteen hundred dollars and sentenced to twelve months in jail. Governor Patrick Noble remitted two-thirds of the fine and commuted the jail sentence. Yancey returned to Alabama, where he later served in Congress and became a champion of secession.[20]

The second murder trial involved state Senator T. Edwin Ware, the largest slaveholder in the Greenville District. On February 16, 1853, Ware was arrested for the murder of his wife's father, Adam Jones. Two years prior to the murder, Mrs. Jones died, and her husband began to keep company with several women, one of whom he intended to marry. His remarriage became a point of contention between the daughter and the father. They quarrelled constantly, and Jones eventually demanded that the Wares move out of his house. On the day of the murder Jones was drinking heavily. He was sixty-four-years-old, 6 feet tall, and a large man. After an argument, as Ware was leaving the room, Jones rose and struck him with a pair of fire tongs. Ware then shot Jones, who died instantly.[21]

The trial was held in Greenville on April 14, 1853. Benjamin Perry defended Ware, a fellow member of the legislature. The jury found Ware guilty of murder, and he was imprisoned in the district jail. A week later Governor John L. Manning pardoned Ware, but ordered him to pay a fine of five hundred dollars. The inscription on Adam Jones's tomb in the family cemetery at Ware Place concludes with these words: "Forgive us, Oh Lord."[22]

A new, thriving business—a wagon and carriage factory—opened in 1835. Ebenezer N. Gower, a native of Maine, formed a partnership with Thomas M. Cox, who would later become a partner of William Bates in the textile mill at Batesville. Gower and Cox located their business on the banks of the Reedy River, just above the falls, on land belonging to Vardry McBee. In 1841 Gower's younger brother, Thomas Claghorn, who was nineteen years old, arrived in Greenville and for two years was apprenticed as a carriage maker. After his marriage to Jane Williams, T. C. Gower established a successful factory south of the village in 1845. In fact, he was so successful that the older company offered him a partnership. The new firm was known as Gower, Cox and Gower, and the agent of R. G. Dun of New York reported that "Cox is the head man." The elder Gower was a good blacksmith, Cox a bookkeeper, and the younger Gower a woodworker—"all steady." In 1851 they added a dry goods store. Two years later, H. C. Markley joined the company and expanded its operations. In 1856 the Greenville Coach Factory, as it was then known, employed one hundred men and annually sold vehicles worth eighty thousand dollars. It was described as the largest carriage factory below the Potomac. The *Patriot and Mountaineer* reported that the business was "one of the most complete and extensive in the Southern States. . . . From the plain one-horse wagon to the splendid four horse chariot they can fill any order, at short notice, in the very best manner." Their work was considered equal to any Northern factory.[23]

An account of manufacturing in the Greenville District in 1853 listed two paper mills owned by McBee and Benajah Dunham; five or six cotton mills; two or three gun factories, including one owned by Boyd and another by Peden; several carriage works; two tinworks owned by Dunham and Westfield; numerous flour mills; a gold mine operated by Carson, McBee, and Randolph; and a broom factory owned by Kingsland.[24]

The Coming of the Railroad

Perhaps the greatest economic development in the two decades before the Civil War was the coming of the railroad. The initial impetus for railroad construction in South Carolina came from the business community in Charleston who wished to restore the declining prosperity of the city by attracting trade from the interior. In 1833 the South Carolina Railroad was completed to Hamburg on the Savannah River opposite Augusta. The economic impact of the railroad was not lost on the leaders of Greenville. When a scheme was launched in 1835 to connect Charleston with Louisville and Cincinnati, a public meeting at the courthouse, led by Benjamin Perry and Waddy Thompson, Jr., endorsed the enterprise. Perry indicated in his journal that "many of the people seem to be in the spirit of the grand enterprise & I hope they will persevere everywhere." Perry did see a possible political dimension of "railroad fever." It may be, he wrote, "the means of uniting political parties & giving a death blow to past differences & nullification." Perry and John T. Coleman became commissioners of the railroad company in order to receive individual stock subscriptions in Greenville. Perry's wife's uncle, Robert Y. Hayne of Charleston, was president of the railroad. After Hayne's death, Vardry McBee became president of the company. But the necessary investment was too vast for the state's limited resources. In 1840 the stockholders decided to build a branch line from the Charleston-Hamburg route to Columbia, not all the way to Louisville.[25]

Coleman conceived of a scheme to connect Columbia to Greenville. He interested Perry, Joel Poinsett, and Thompson to join him. On October 20, 1845, at a public meeting to discuss the railroad, Vardry McBee presided and resolutions were presented by Poinsett, Thompson, Coleman, Samuel M. Earle, Elias D. Earle, Dr. Andrew B. Crook, and T. Edwin Ware. A steering committee of thirty was appointed.[26]

In December 1845 Perry championed the chartering of the Greenville and Columbia Railroad in the legislature which required raising three hundred thousand dollars within one year. The original plan was to build the railroad through Newberry and Laurens on the east side of the Saluda River. But the total amount was not raised within the year, and a second campaign began. On May 11, 1847, the stockholders met in Columbia and elected Judge John Belton O'Neall of Newberry and Greenville president. That summer an effort was made by a rival group of stockholders to route the railroad through the Edgefield, Abbeville, and Anderson Districts on the west side of the Saluda River. At a meeting of the stockholders on November 19, the supporters of the Laurens route were defeated.[27]

Meanwhile, Vardry McBee went north in the summer of 1847 to gather information about railroads. Before he returned home, he had invested ten thousand dollars in the Seaboard and Roanoke line.[28]

In May 1848 the Greenville stockholders asked for a refund of their investment in the railroad, but the refund was refused, and they decided to build a branch road from Belton to Greenville. At a public meeting in August, O'Neall, Perry, and Thompson spoke in favor of the project, and Vardry McBee increased his investment from twelve thousand to fifty thousand dollars. At the stockholders meeting in October, the Anderson stockholders opposed the effort of Greenville—preferring to build the railroad first to Anderson and then on to Greenville. The debate was heated, but this time Greenville won.[29]

On December 8, 1853, the railroad was completed. The passenger depot was located in a former residence on the Augusta Road, near the present site of Greenville High School. The track was laid to the rear of the house, and the carriage drive up the front lawn from the Augusta Road was left intact. The rooms on the second floor became railroad offices. A brick freight depot was built on the street joining the Augusta and the Pendleton Roads. The first railroad agent was Captain Samuel Stradley. Before the end of the year, the *Southern Patriot* reported that "the omnibus, the hack, and the private carriage are daily seen moving with spirit towards the Depot. . . . Morning and evening the loud tones of the steam whistle are heard ringing in our ears." More important was the sight of "several wagons loaded with cotton, wending their way towards the Depot. . . . We look upon this circumstance as the opening of the trade that will be conveyed through this speedy and otherwise economical channel." The mail, too, began to arrive in Greenville by train.[30]

The building of the railroad strained the company to the point of bankruptcy. The roadbed was poorly constructed, and the annual report of 1855 referred to public opinion "that this is a rickety road, exposed constantly to the danger of being swept away by freshets." Even though the topography was hilly and the railroad had three river crossings, the road was built for less than fourteen thousand dollars a mile. Even so, a 20 percent assessment was made on the original stockholders, and the road was mortgaged for eight hundred thousand dollars. The legislature guaranteed the debt and took a lien in return.[31]

Prosperity and New Public Buildings

The railroad soon justified the expectation of its promoters. Between 1853 and 1860 the value of goods sold in Greenville increased 45 percent. For the first time, institutional banking services were available. Thomas M. Cox, a partner in the carriage factory, became the local agent for the Bank of Newberry, and Hamlin Beattie, the son of merchant Fountain F. Beattie, was agent for the Bank of Charleston.[32]

The prosperity of Greenville was reflected in the grand public buildings constructed in the 1850s—a new courthouse, three churches, Furman University, and the Greenville Baptist Female College. Benjamin Perry observed in the *Southern Patriot:* "When our College buildings, Church[es] and Court House are completed, the village of Greenville will have something to boast of in the way of architecture."[33]

In 1851 the General Assembly appropriated eight thousand dollars for a new courthouse. In February 1852 the Board of Commissioners of Public Buildings adopted plans for a building with a courtroom that would accommodate five hundred people. But it was over a year before the contract was awarded to Mr. Shackleford of North Carolina for $13,800. By September 1853 the contractor withdrew, and the commissioners undertook to build the courthouse themselves. The materials did not arrive on the site of the market opposite the old courthouse until August 1854. The officers of the Recovery Masonic Lodge laid the cornerstone in mid-September, and a year later the *Southern Patriot* announced that the courthouse would be ready for the next term. The courthouse was built of brick stucco in modified Gothic style, complete with a tower and crenelated battlements. The courtroom, the newspaper reported, "will accommodate half of the voters of the district." The windows were "large and lofty, giving light and air." Cocoa matting was ordered to muffle the sound in the room, and the ground floor contained offices separated by intersecting corridors 12 feet wide. But the commissioners overspent their funds, and the state legislature needed to appropriate an additional fourteen thousand dollars.[34]

In April 1845 the vestry of Christ Church proposed the building of a larger house of worship. Joel Poinsett, a member of the vestry, submitted plans, but they were too expensive. A building committee appointed in 1848 accepted the plans of John D. McCullough, the rector of the Church of the Advent in Spartanburg, who had designed a number of Episcopal churches in the up country. When it was completed in 1854, the building was described as a First Point Gothic brick structure, with a brick tower 130 feet high, and with fifty pews that could seat five hundred worshipers, though the congregation at that time numbered just over one hundred.[35]

The Presbyterian and Baptist churches adopted the older, more conservative neoclassical style for their buildings. The new Presbyterian church
faced Richardson Street on the corner of West Washington. The brick
structure, 32 feet by 62 feet, had a portico with four Doric columns and a
large steeple.[36]

In August 1853 the members of the Baptist church agreed to raise a
subscription for a new building. In June 1854 the building committee
took title to the property on what is now West McBee Avenue, and obtained plans from Sloan and Stewart, a firm of Philadelphia architects, for a
massive Greek Revival structure with a steeple. The sanctuary sat atop a tall
basement, and a high flight of steps rose in front to a portico with six Ionic
columns. Not until March 1857 was the lecture room in the basement
ready for use. On February 21, 1858, the new building was dedicated with
one honored guest being Dr. William Bullein Johnson, president of the
Southern Baptist Convention. These new public buildings gave a sense of
permanence and prosperity to the growing town.[37]

Cultural Life and Education

Greenville also began to enrich its cultural life during this period. A
new Lyceum Hall was opened in February 1842, and a local band played
for the dedication on Washington's birthday. By 1847 the Greenville Brass
Band was performing an original composition, "The Greenville Quickstep."
Touring musical companies presented concerts at the hotels, and the local
Thespian Society combined musical and dramatic presentations. There were
a number of dancing masters in town, and the Cotillion Club sponsored
frequent soirees. Visiting artists painted portraits of local notables such as
Vardry and Jane McBee, Chancellor Waddy, and Eliza Thompson. Among
the painters was William Harrison Scarborough, whose family spent the
summers in the nearby mountains. The local artists included C. H. Lanneau
and Thomas Stephen Powell.[38]

Antebellum Greenville became a center of higher education with the
establishment of Furman University, the Greenville Baptist Female College, and the Southern Baptist Theological Seminary. Furman, also Baptist
related, had its beginnings as an academy in Edgefield in 1827 and later
moved to the High Hills of Santee near Sumter. In 1836 the school was
relocated near Winnsboro and after 1840 it operated solely as a school for
training ministers. In December 1847 the Board of Trustees appointed a
committee to consider moving the institution once more and in 1849
agreed to add a liberal arts college to the theological school. In June 1850

Captain Wesley Brooks and Perry E. Duncan presented the advantages of Greenville to the state Baptist Convention, and on June 16 the convention voted to seek a charter for Furman University and locate it in Greenville.[39]

Furman opened in February 1851 in McBee Hall on the corner of Main Street and McBee Avenue. On June 18 the trustees purchased land from Vardry McBee on a high hill across the Reedy River west of town. A wooden cottage (now on the present Furman campus) and a large room in the Tiddman house, later occupied by Mrs. Mary Cleveland, were used as classrooms. The faculty, which consisted of James S. Mims, James Clement Furman, Peter C. Edwards, and Charles H. Judson, operated a classical school, a theological school, and a preparatory school.[40]

In 1852 the president's home was completed, and a committee appointed by the trustees employed Edward C. Jones of Charleston to design the main college building. Jones planned an Italianate structure with a bell tower on the axis of Main Street, facing Greenville across the river. Work on the building was completed in 1854, and that year enrollment increased from ninety-nine students to 206.[41]

The annual commencement became a social event for the town, with addresses and public examinations. The first such occasion in Greenville was held in August 1852. As Benjamin Perry wrote in the *Southern Patriot*: "If anyone had predicted thirty years ago, that we should have had a college commencement in Greenville in the summer, and a steam car [railroad] running here the next spring, from Charleston in fifteen hours, he would have been regarded as a fit subject for the Lunatic Asylum."[42]

A leading figure at Furman was the chair of the faculty and later president, James Clement Furman, who was destined to play a major role in the Greenville District in the events leading to the Civil War. Born in Charleston in 1809, the son of Richard Furman, one of the leaders of Baptists in the United States, James Furman graduated from the College of Charleston in 1826. Preparing to study medicine when he had a deeply moving religious experience, Furman was instead licensed to preach. He moved to the family plantation at the High Hills of Santee, and in 1830 enrolled in the Furman Theological Institution, which was located there at the time. Active in the revivals of 1830, he was ordained in 1832 to the ministry by the church in Charleston. He was married twice, both times to daughters of Jonathan Davis, a minister and planter of the Fairfield District. In 1845 he became senior professor at the Furman Institution that had moved to Fairfield. He was a leader in the transformation of the institution into a college and its movement to Greenville.[43]

Higher education for women was an important issue for the churches of South Carolina in the 1850s. The Associate Reformed Presbyterians opened a college for women in Due West, and South Carolina Methodists bravely planned three colleges. With discussion of a Baptist female college in the air, a public meeting was held at the courthouse on May 22, 1854, to discuss transferring the property of the Female Academy to the Baptists. Charles J. Elford, Perry E. Duncan, and Colonel E. P. Jones were appointed to raise a subscription and determine community interest. The local newspapers disagreed over the issue. The *Southern Patriot,* edited by Benjamin Perry, and the new *Enterprise,* edited by J. O. Bailey, supported the college. The *Mountaineer,* edited by George F. Townes, opposed it. At a second meeting on June 14, the committee reported that fifty-four hundred dollars had been subscribed and 126 signatures placed on a petition in favor of transferring the property. William Choice countered with a second petition with sixty names and spoke against education for women and the transfer of the Academy property. Perry, Choice's old nemesis from the nullification battles, rose to the attack. He denounced Choice's view of women and his interpretation of the law, and said that Choice, an Episcopalian, was only interested in "checkmating and neutralizing" the Baptists. Vardry McBee strongly supported the new college, and the Academy trustees voted to transfer the property.[44]

On July 22, 1854, the state Baptist Convention met in Greenville and debated the issue of a college for women and its possible location. When Greenville offered the Female Academy property, over five thousand dollars in cash, and a pledge to raise a total of twenty thousand dollars for the new college, the convention accepted the offer and placed the college under the control of the Furman trustees. The Greenville Baptist Female College opened on February 7, 1855, with seventy students in its primary, academic, and collegiate departments.[45]

A year later the new president, the Reverend Hansford A. Duncan, and a faculty of seven were in place. The college curriculum took three years to complete, and the first students graduated in 1858. The rules of conduct were few and direct. Boarding students were required to attend church and remain on the campus unless they had permission to leave; they could not open accounts at stores without their parents' permission; they could not attend public parties or receive visitors; all correspondence, except with their parents, was monitored; and all funds had to be deposited with the president.[46]

The third institution of higher learning established in Greenville was the Southern Baptist Theological Seminary. In 1845, when the Southern Baptist Convention was established, there was considerable discussion about a seminary. In Louisville in 1857 Furman professor James Petigru Boyce issued a challenge proposed by South Carolina Baptists: an endowment of one hundred thousand dollars for a seminary in Greenville if an equal amount could be raised elsewhere. At another meeting in Greenville in 1858, Boyce announced that he had raised sufficient funds. In October 1859 the seminary opened with twenty-six students and four faculty members—Boyce, John A. Broadus, Basil Manly, Jr., and William Williams. Classes were held in the old building of the Baptist church, and the students boarded with local families.[47]

Boyce, who became president of the seminary, was a resident of Greenville from 1855 until he moved to Louisville in 1872. Born in Charleston in 1827, he was the son of Ker Boyce, a wealthy commission merchant and president of the Bank of Charleston, the largest in the South. A Unionist in the nullification controversy, the elder Boyce named his son for James Louis Petigru, the Charleston Unionist leader. James Boyce was educated at Brown University and Princeton Theological Seminary. After serving as pastor of the Baptist church in Columbia, Boyce joined the Furman faculty. He purchased the Waddy Thompson place on the Spartanburg Road, which he renamed Boyce Lawn, and soon was raising wheat, rutabagas, and cattle.[48]

Like the other towns in the state, Greenville boasted its own military company, the Butler Guards, which was organized in the summer of 1855. The company's officers were Captain H. Lee Thruston and Lieutenant David Hoke, recent graduates of the Citadel. Unlike other militia companies in the district, they drilled several nights a week. At muster with the Lower Regiment at Toney's Old Field, they marched like army troops.[49]

War with Mexico

Though Greenville citizens continued to move west, there was little enthusiasm when Congress declared war against Mexico in May 1846. Four different musters were held to raise volunteers. By the time a company was organized, Governor William Aiken already had enough units to make up the Palmetto Regiment. The men of Greenville were left without their own company. As the *Mountaineer* put it, the volunteers "were disappointed, and many were absolutely mortified." Those who wished to serve had to join units from other districts.[50]

Henry H. Townes, a Greenville native who had married into the Calhoun family and who was living in the Abbeville District, wrote to a reluctant member of his family in Greenville: "Mother ought to have made you volunteer. I will always regret our family was not represented in the Army in Mexico." Samuel Townes wrote to George F. Townes about an in-law who did not volunteer: "[He] unfortunately is in perfect health and has not the remotest idea of going to Mexico to be shot. If it were possible to get the beast off I venture anything that all the cannons in Mexico discharged at once at him [from a distance of] ten steps would not hurt."[51]

Once the war began, the *Mountaineer* carried letters from Mexico written by Greenville soldiers. Robert A. Joyce wrote five letters before he was killed at Buena Vista in February 1847. A Greenville native, he had volunteered with the Mississippi regiment commanded by Colonel Jefferson Davis. The newspaper printed the letter from Davis, informing Waddy Thompson of Joyce's death, as well as letters from H. Judge Moore, William H. Goodlett, and two others in the company from the Fairfield District. Moore advocated the annexation of Mexico—"the object of our enlistment . . . and we are willing to battle for the honor of our flag until that desideratum shall have been obtained." Goodlett complained about the way in which the Carolinians were treated. "Notwithstanding that some of the privates are gentlemen when at home," he wrote, "they are hardly looked upon as human beings here." He reported that they did not receive the rations to which they were entitled nor the uniforms purchased by the state legislature.[52]

Despite Greenville's lack of volunteers, the town supported the war effort more enthusiastically than any community in the state. Governor David Johnson proclaimed May 6, 1847, as a day of thanksgiving. That evening at eight o'clock the entire town burst into light as a torchlight procession led by the band paraded through the streets. Every soldier from Greenville was honored by a transparency, as were the American generals. The following evening news arrived of the victory at Cerro Gordo, and there was a second procession, speeches, and hearty cheers.[53]

Sectionalism and Secession

Such enthusiasm for national issues was already being submerged in Greenville, as elsewhere in the South, because of the controversy over slavery. In 1846 Congressman David Wilmot of Pennsylvania introduced a proviso to the appropriations bill requiring that slavery be prohibited in any territory gained from Mexico. A public meeting in October 1847 protested the Wilmot Proviso. A series of resolutions drawn up by Benjamin Perry pledged resistance "at all hazards and to the last extremity." On May 7, 1849, another public meeting endorsed U.S. Senator John C. Calhoun's

Southern Address, which called on Southerners to stand up in defense of their property, prosperity, equality, liberty, and safety. At this meeting George F. Townes, editor of the *Mountaineer,* introduced a series of resolutions that denounced the Wilmot Proviso and "all kindred schemes of Abolition aggression." A Committee of Vigilance and Safety was appointed, according to the newspaper, to "submit such information to the people as may be deemed important to protect their interests against all Abolition movements."[54]

The slavery issue came to a head with the Compromise of 1850 which proposed to admit California to the Union as a free state. Calhoun opposed it, but he died in March. In his stead, South Carolina secessionists began calling for the state to withdraw from the Union if the Compromise were not defeated. Among the few voices raised in support of the Compromise were spokespersons from Greenville—Waddy Thompson and Benjamin Perry, as well as summer residents Joel Poinsett and John Belton O'Neall. Perry confided to his journal: "I love the Union, & am not willing to give it up—& still hope that there is good sense enough, North & South, to preserve it." When the Compromise became law, William H. Campbell, the young secessionist editor of the *Mountaineer,* demanded radical action. In the state elections in October the secessionists swept every district but Greenville. Unionists Perry, Thomas P. Brockman, and Perry E. Duncan were easily re-elected to the legislature.[55]

Every newspaper in South Carolina supported secession, so Perry proposed to Waddy Thompson that they begin a newspaper to rally the old Unionists of nullification days. On October 27, 1850, five citizens met to establish the *Southern Patriot*—Perry, Thompson, Wesley Brooks, Benajah Dunham, and C. J. Elford.[56]

Meanwhile the secessionists of Greenville held a public meeting at the courthouse on November 1 in order to form a chapter of the statewide Southern Rights Association. Christopher G. Memminger of Charleston spoke for nearly two hours in a fiery speech urging disunion. When Thompson and Perry attempted to speak, they were hissed, and a new Committee of Vigilance and Safety was formed under the leadership of Dr. Andrew B. Crook. The secessionists threatened to destroy the *Southern Patriot* office and tar and feather the Unionists. The next day a friend urged Perry to give up the paper. Replied Perry: "The *Southern Patriot* shall go on, if it sinks every cent of property I have in the world, and sacrifices my life into the bargain!"[57]

The vigilance committee did its work in secret. There were rumors that Junius Smith, who operated a tea farm on Golden Grove Creek, favored abolition and was a life member of the American Colonization Society. When he was severely beaten at his home in December 1851, some people accused the local slave patrol. Perry was fearful of its efforts to shape public opinion and denounced the patrol in the *Southern Patriot* as comparable to "the bloody inquisition of Spain, and the all-powerful and unknown police of the French Revolution."[58]

The Pendleton *Messenger* crowed over "the dethronement of the old dynasty" in the Greenville District. Elford wanted to withdraw from the new newspaper, but Perry persuaded him to stand firm: "I do not believe . . . that Greenville has yet gone over to disunion. The ballot Box will tell a different story." Even Vardry McBee was upset by the attacks on slavery from the North. He wrote his son, Vardry, that "these Abolition Fanaticks have set themselves never to cease until the Negroes are all free & regardless of the manner whether it is by cutting throats or any other manner never seem to enter their imagination or reflect on the consequence."[59]

There were only three Unionists in the legislature—Perry, Brockman, and Duncan of Greenville. But many secessionists abhorred the thought of precipitous, single-state secession. The Greenville delegation joined forces with these cooperationists to delay the meeting of a state convention to consider secession. When the election of delegates for the convention was held in February 1852 only Greenville elected Unionists—Perry, Duncan, Brockman, Vardry McBee, and Jesse Senter. Although they were Unionists, these men were not abolitionists, Perry reminded his readers in the *Southern Patriot:* "Southern people will defend the institution of African slavery at all hazards, to the last extremity. [But the radical secessionists] would weaken & destroy the institution of slavery & involve the country in civil war & ruinous taxation."[60]

Before the convention met, there were elections in the congressional districts for delegates to a Southern convention to consider secession. In the Second District, which included Greenville, the cooperationists proposed Colonel J. H. Irby of Laurens and Colonel James L. Orr of Anderson. These men garnered 73.6 percent of the vote, while Greenville gave them 86.4 percent. Only Pickens gave Irby and Orr a larger vote. The proposed Southern convention never met, but in South Carolina the cooperationists defeated the single-state secessionists 25,062 votes to 17,617. By the time the state convention met on April 26, 1852, it was clear that South Carolina would not secede. Perry wrote to the *Southern Patriot:* "The Union is safe . . . and peace restored to our State."[61]

In the years following the abortive convention of 1852, South Carolina was divided into two political factions—the National Democrats and the Southern Rights advocates. In the *Southern Patriot* Benjamin Perry supported James L. Orr's efforts to lead South Carolina into the National Democratic Party, while George F. Townes in the *Mountaineer* championed the cause of secession. The two editors attacked each other unmercifully in their newspapers. Townes had Perry arrested for libel, before friends of the two—Orr, W. H. Simpson, and James W. Harrison—brought about a reconciliation.[62]

Nationally, the sectional controversy remained calm until abolitionists began to attack the Kansas-Nebraska Bill. This legislation, proposed by U.S. Senator Stephen A. Douglas of Illinois, gave the western territories the right to decide whether they would be slave or free states. On May 20, 1856, Charles Sumner of Massachusetts arose in the U.S. Senate to attack the slave states that supported such a choice. He singled out South Carolina Senator Andrew P. Butler as an example of a Southern knight who had taken slavery as his mistress. Two days later Congressman Preston Brooks of Edgefield, a relative of Butler, caught Sumner at his desk and caned him into unconsciousness. Ironically, Brooks belonged to the National Democratic faction, not the extremist Southern Rights group. As a wave of indignation against Brooks's action swept the North, South Carolina rose to his defense.

Perry declared in the *Patriot and Mountaineer* that "Mr. Brooks's gallantry, spirit, and patriotic course in Congress, have made him a hero worthy of the respect and admiration of his State." On September 8, there was a Brooks Ball at the courthouse, preceded by dinner at the Mansion House. Several hundred persons attended the ball. At the supper table one of the pyramids of cake was decorated with a flag on which was painted a hand holding a cane. Greenvillians were ready to defend slavery and the honor of the South, but they were not yet ready to divide the Union.[63]

Southern leaders watched with alarm as the new Republican Party gained political power, but a crisis of fear swept South Carolina after John Brown's attack on the federal arsenal at Harper's Ferry in October 1859. Even Benjamin Perry was caught up in the excitement. He denounced Brown as a "notorious horse thief, assassin, and traitor [who] . . . had committed treason, murder, and robbery." In the state legislature he indicated that South Carolina was ready to act to defend its interests "in the Union or out of it." But he soon regained his balance. He wrote to his constituents at the end of the session: "I do not believe anything serious will grow out of our present excitement, neither disunion, civil war nor danger to slavery."[64]

But William P. Price, the editor of the *Southern Enterprise*, denounced the Republican Party whose goal was to destroy slavery and the Southern way of life. The growing atmosphere of panic was indicated by a resolution passed unanimously by a public meeting in March 1860 which condemned all Republicans for "stirring up a servile insurrection which was to murder the master." In the summer of 1860 the *Enterprise* published rumors of slave insurrections, and in September it warned the residents of Greenville "to keep a sharp look out . . . for everything of a suspicious character."[65]

In the fall, the vigilance committee investigated rumors of local abolitionist activities. Harold Wyllys, a native of the Greenville District, was accused of owning a copy of *The Impending Crisis of the South* by Hinton Rowan Helper of North Carolina. Published in 1857, *The Impending Crisis* attacked slavery alone for retarding the progress and prosperity of the South. Wyllys also was accused of distributing abolitionist tracts to local residents, including one literate black man. Dr. Crook, chair of the committee, wrote to Benjamin Perry that Wyllys had been arrested and was being held without bail. "I think," Crook wrote, "when you have examined the Book you will agree with me that no man who will give aid to its circulation should be permitted to go at large in our community." He should be "kept in a safe place until he can be tried and hung." Crook did not want Wyllys's case mentioned in the press. Only after the accused was found guilty and sentenced to one year in jail did the *Southern Enterprise* mention the matter.[66]

The National Democratic Convention convened in Charleston in April 1860, and Benjamin Perry was a member of the South Carolina delegation. When the convention refused to support the protection of slavery in the territories, William Lowndes Yancey, Perry's former law clerk, led delegates from five Southern states out of the meeting, thereby splitting the party. Perry was one of only two delegates from South Carolina who remained in the convention. The next day, amid hisses and boos from the gallery, Perry rose to declare himself: "I love the South, and it is because I love her, and would guard her against evils which no one can foresee or foretell, that I am a Union man and a follower of Washington's faith and creed. It was as a Democrat and a Union man that I came into this Convention, determined to do all that I could to preserve the Democratic party and the Union of the States."[67]

Southern Rights leaders denounced the National Democratic faction because they had been unable to secure the party's support for slavery in the territories. It was their turn to take charge. The leaders proposed the election of new delegates to a state convention. This group would in turn select a new delegation to attend a convention in Richmond called by the disaffected Southern delegates in Charleston. In the Greenville District the secessionists seized control of the process and dominated a public meeting on May 21. The chair was Dr. James C. Furman, the president of Furman University, who was also a planter and a slaveholder. The secretaries were the prosecession editors of the local newspapers, William P. Price of the *Southern Enterprise* and George E. Elford of the *Patriot and Mountaineer*. Together with a committee of five—William H. Campbell, H. Lee Thruston, William K. Easley, Dr. James Harrison, and S. G. McClanahan—they controlled the meeting. Delegates to the state convention were named by a committee of fifteen avowed secessionists. Perry commented that the process was repeated all over the state: "Conservative men stay at home and avoid those meetings, whilst fire-eaters and politicians attend them." But he was firm in his own views: "Whether mistaken or not in regard to public sentiment in this Congressional District, I never was more thoroughly convinced than I am now, of the correctness of my own course in remaining in the Charleston Convention."[68]

During the summer of 1860 the position of the secessionists was reinforced by two visiting speakers. On July 2 William Lowndes Yancey, who had supported the Unionist position during the nullification crisis, delivered a fiery secession speech. On July 4 T. S. Adams delivered an oration on "The Necessity of a Southern Confederacy," and at the fall term of court there were more speeches.[69]

Only Benjamin Perry spoke out against the secessionists. In a long letter to the Charleston *Courier* he accused the disunionists of rejoicing at the destruction of the National Democratic Party. "They saw in that movement . . . their defeat in the coming Presidential elections. They saw in the future the election of a Black Republican, and knew what a powerful lever it would be in their hands to wield against the Union." On the secessionists and abolitionists alike he vented his anger: "Well may it be said, we have fallen on evil times; and that 'those whom the gods intend to destroy, they first make mad.'" Perry did not run for re-election to the state legislature in October. But two ardent secessionists, William P. Price and William H. Campbell, were both defeated. T. Edwin Ware was re-elected to the state Senate; John W. Stokes, David Hoke, J. P. Hillhouse, and Dr. J. M. Sullivan were elected to the House.[70]

Two leaders in mobilizing the Greenville District for secession were H. Lee Thruston and William H. Campbell who were active members of the Association of 1860. The aim of the association was to unite the South, as one of the leaders put it, "through the publishing of strong and incendiary pamphlets that will stir the sleeping South out of the lethargy fostered by the poison called love of Union." Thruston and Campbell were also the officers of the local unit of the statewide Minute Men for the Defense of Southern Rights. Campbell, the editor of the *Mountaineer,* was captain and Thruston became first lieutenant. The Minute Men wore blue cockades to symbolize the unity of what they called the new "Revolution for Freedom" and the "Revolution of '76."[71]

As soon as the news that Abraham Lincoln had been elected president reached Columbia, the state legislature called for the election of a secession convention. In Greenville the secessionists were ready for action. Fifty citizens, including J. W. Brooks and G. E. Elford, Perry's former associates in founding the *Southern Patriot,* signed the call for a meeting to select a slate of delegates for the convention. On November 15 the Minute Men mustered at a newly erected Liberty Pole and raised a flag consisting of a single star above the word, secession, and the Palmetto tree. The Furman University Riflemen, established in 1856, saluted the flag with a volley and gave three cheers for "the New Republic."[72]

On November 17, the public meeting "to take into consideration matters of public interest now transpiring in the State growing out of the Election of a Black Republican to the Presidency of the United States" met in the courthouse. Benjamin Perry remained in his law office across the street, describing the "crowd of persons rushing in, composed of college boys, and their professors, merchants, mechanics, doctors, lawyers and idlers from the hotel, with a sprinkling of farmers and planters." J. Wesley Brooks was chair of the meeting, and William K. Easley and James Clement Furman gave the major addresses. Brief remarks were made by Dr. Andrew B. Crook, George F. Townes, Perry E. Duncan, Vardry McBee, Charles J. Elford, and William P. Price.[73]

The meeting unanimously adopted a resolution endorsing the forthcoming convention. Their words made it clear that the secessionists of Greenville regarded slavery as the cause of their action. "*Abraham Lincoln* and *Hannibal Hamlin* have been elected President and Vice President of the United States," they resolved, "and it is well known that they regard the institution of slavery as a *moral, social* and *political evil,* and do not accede to the decision of the Supreme Court on the Dred Scott case."[74]

Perry supported slavery, to be sure, but he could not bring himself to endorse secession. When he heard the applause from the meeting in the courthouse, he later wrote, "I repeated in my heart the memorable words of Christ: 'Father, forgive them, they know not what they do!' My mind was filled with the worst forebodings as to the future." But he could do nothing. "My political influence was gone, and my voice was powerless to stay the angry and excited feelings of my fellow citizens."[75]

The secessionists kept Greenville at fever pitch before the election of convention delegates. On November 19 a crowd of citizens gathered at the Mansion House to serenade state Representative Henry Buist of Charleston, who had written the bill calling for the convention. On November 21 Christopher G. Memminger, no stranger to Greenville audiences, delivered a rousing speech. A meeting in the courthouse on November 27 was addressed by Judge Andrew G. Magrath, who had dramatically resigned from the federal bench in open court after Lincoln's election. The *Southern Enterprise* carried a letter signed by a committee which James C. Furman chaired. "If you are tame enough to submit," the letter warned, "Abolition preachers will be at hand to consummate the marriage of your daughters to black husbands!"[76]

A week before the election, the *Southern Enterprise* called attention to a meeting to select a cooperation ticket. The candidates selected were Benjamin Perry, Judge O'Neall, Dr. W. A. Mooney, T. C. Bolling, and James Petigru Boyce. O'Neall and Boyce withdrew their names; the others ran without campaigning. On election day the secessionist candidates won by a large majority, each one receiving over thirteen hundred votes. The cooperationists had only token support; Perry received 225 votes, Mooney 196, and Bolling 190. A majority of the voters did not go to the polls. Perry wrote later: "The Union men thought it was a foregone conclusion that the State would secede, & it was not worth their while to go to the polls." Perhaps those who did not participate in the events leading to secession were represented by Alfred Taylor who jotted only two references in his diary. First, he recorded: "Lincoln is elected[;] times is dull." Then, he wrote with more concern: "Great excitement in reference to the State[']s seceding[. E]verybody appears to be on the lookout for an insurrection."[77]

The delegation that represented the Greenville District in the Secession Convention in December 1860 was composed of James C. Furman, William K. Easley, Perry E. Duncan, William H. Campbell, and Dr. James P. Harrison. They were all slaveholders, and two of the five—Furman and Campbell—were not natives of the Greenville District. Four were involved in agriculture—Easley planted in the Pickens District, Duncan, Furman, and Harrison in Greenville. Duncan owned fifty-nine slaves, Harrison fifty-two, Furman forty-one, and Easley eighteen. Four were professionals—Furman was a minister and college professor, Easley and Campbell were attorneys, and Harrison was a physician. Campbell was also a newspaper editor.[78]

The Secession Convention convened in Columbia on December 17. On the first ballot, Furman received six votes for president. The following day, after the convention moved to Charleston, he delivered the invocation in the Institute Hall. On Thursday, December 20, the Greenville delegation, along with the other members of the convention, unanimously approved the Ordinance of Secession. That evening they placed their signatures on the document. When Benjamin Perry heard the news, he wrote his fellow Unionist, James L. Petigru: "I have been trying for the last thirty years to save the State from the horrors of disunion. They are now all going to the devil, and I will go with them." James Petigru Boyce reconciled himself to secession, but he feared its consequences: "I believe I see in all of this the end of slavery. I believe we are cutting its throat, curtailing its domain. And I have been, and am, an ultra-proslavery man."[79]

Preparing for Civil War

As the convention assembled, the legislature directed the governor to call for volunteers from the militia and to resort to a draft where the quotas were not filled. Subsequent acts of the convention and the legislature provided for regular army troops. Once the Confederate States of America was established and the fighting began, the state troops were mustered into the Confederate army.[80]

The Greenville Guards, organized in December 1860, later became Company K of the Sixteenth Regiment. Their flag, designed by Miss Mamie Cleveland, was a white banner trimmed in red that contained a green palmetto tree and a single star. In one corner were the words "We Conquer or We Die," and above the tree was the date: December 20, 1860. A similar flag was raised by George E. Elford over his printing office.[81]

By May 1861 three companies of volunteers had left Greenville, and three more were ready. The Butler Guards left for Virginia on May 6 and became Company B of the Second Regiment, South Carolina Volunteers. Their muster roll of May 1, 1862, indicates that they were at Camp Greenville near Manassas Junction. They took part in the battles of Antietam and Fredericksburg before being transferred to the Army of Tennessee, in which they fought at Chickamauga. Company F of the Fourth Regiment was mustered into Confederate service in Columbia on June 7.[82]

On May 20, a public meeting was held at the courthouse to raise money to outfit a new group, the Brooks Cavalry, which intended to serve in the Hampton Legion under the command of Colonel Wade Hampton III. Hampton, whose roots were deep in the up country, joined James C. Furman, Waddy Thompson, and Benjamin Perry in an appeal for public support. "As an old Union man," Perry said, "I give to this Brooks Cavalry my son [William Hayne], two horses and a Negro boy, and fifty dollars. . . . I hope no secessionist, who wore in peace his blue cockade, ready to march at a moment's warning, will refuse to do less, now that war has come upon us."[83]

Professor John F. Lanneau resigned from the Furman faculty to command the Brooks Cavalry, and the University Riflemen volunteered. Lanneau requested Furman to allow him to take Jacob, one of Furman's slaves, as a body servant. Furman agreed, but Gower, Cox, and Markley, to whom Jacob was hired out, was so shorthanded the firm refused to part with him. Furman's son, Charles Manning, was already in Virginia as a member of the Second Regiment. Another son, James, would go in August. Dr. W. L. Manning Austin, who owned twenty slaves, raised a second company which Hampton accepted for service. Yet the town of Greenville never gave the war unanimous, unqualified support. As late as July 1862 Benjamin Perry confided to his journal that he "had no respect for any able bodied man who was a Secessionist & is now at home safe. . . . There are such men here now in this Village who even refuse to give money to supply the wants of the soldiers! Infamous in all time to come shall be their name & remembrance!"[84]

At first there were few volunteers from the upper part of the Greenville District, which had always been strongly Unionist. Perry addressed the Upper Regiment at their regular muster and encouraged them to defend the state. They formed two volunteer companies, two-thirds of whom were former Unionists. In August Perry went to Pine Mountain with Samuel Townes to encourage volunteers. A few weeks later he went to the Dark Corner, still a Unionist stronghold. According to James C. Furman, "few Dark Corner men . . . volunteered. . . . It is to be hoped that some light will yet break upon their darkness."[85]

In the fall of 1861 there was an additional call for volunteers, and Charles J. Elford was authorized to raise the Sixteenth Regiment. Ten companies were formed, and he was elected colonel of the regiment. Professor Boyce agreed to serve as chaplain. In April of that year Elford was succeeded by Colonel James McCullough, a planter in the southern part of the district who owned thirty-three slaves who remained in command until February 1865 when the regiment was consolidated with other troops. The Sixteenth served at first in the coastal area of North and South Carolina. In May 1863 the regiment was transferred to Mississippi for the defense of Vicksburg. Many men returned home rather than go west, but those who went served in General States Rights Gist's brigade. They fought in the Atlanta campaign and at Franklin, where they lost fifty-six men. After the Battle of Nashville they joined General Joseph E. Johnston at

Bentonville in North Carolina and surrendered at Greensboro in April 1865.[86]

In all, the Greenville District furnished the Confederacy with fifteen companies, and the highest-ranking officer from Greenville was Matthew Calbraith Butler, the son of Dr. William Butler and Jane Perry Butler. He was born in Greenville in 1836, attended the Male Academy, and went with his father to Fort Gibson, Arkansas, where the elder Butler served as a Cherokee agent. After his father's death, Butler moved to the Edgefield District to live with his grandmother, Behethland Butler, and his uncle, U.S. Senator Andrew P. Butler. He graduated from South Carolina College and married the daughter of Governor Francis W. Pickens. Butler and six of his brothers served in the Confederate Army. An officer in Hampton's Legion, Matthew Butler lost a foot at Brandy Station in Virginia in 1862, and by the end of the war he had risen to the rank of major general.[87]

Life in Confederate Greenville

The rhythm of life in Confederate Greenville began to change even as the soldiers marched off to war. The textile mills began to manufacture goods for the army. The Batesville Mill, consisting of sixteen hundred spindles and forty looms, produced shirting. The mill was commandeered by the Confederate government, but William Bates was permitted to sell one day's output per week to the civilian population. In 1863 the mill was purchased for three hundred thousand dollars by George W. Williams, one of the wealthiest business people in Charleston. Gower, Cox & Gower furnished its entire output of wagons to the Confederacy, and by 1865 the carriage factory had supplied war material in the amount of $140,000. When T. C. Gower was mustered into the Hampton Legion in June 1861, he left his business in charge of his wife and his eldest daughter, Cordelia, a recent graduate of the Laurensville Female College. Such changes in the role of women occurred all across the South. In March 1862 the state Department of Manufacture and Construction established the State Military Works in Greenville because it was an inland town and because Vardry McBee offered 20 acres of land near the railroad. David Lopez became superintendent and secured machinery and skilled workers from Nashville and Charleston. They repaired small arms and manufactured various kinds of weapons, including a few cannon, shells, cannon balls, and pikes. The most famous weapon produced at the State Military Works was the Morse carbine—a breech-loading rifle invented by George W. Morse for cavalry use. Governor Milledge L. Bonham declared that it was the best gun in the world at the time. But the State Military Works proved unprofitable, and the legislature attempted to close it or move it to Columbia. Neither effort was successful, and the facility remained in Greenville.[88]

At Furman so many students volunteered for army service that commencement exercises were cancelled in 1861. When the college reopened in August, no students appeared, and Furman closed until the war was over. The faculty sought other employment, and James C. Furman became president of the Female College. The seminary fared little better. The number of students declined to eight during the first year of the war. When Boyce failed to get theological students exempted from the draft, the school closed. After serving as chaplain to the Sixteenth Regiment, Boyce was elected to the state House of Representatives. Other members of the seminary faculty supplied nearby churches. In the summer of 1863 Professor John A. Broadus became a missionary to the Army of Northern Virginia, and at the same time a correspondent for the Charleston *News and Courier*.[89]

During the war Professor Basil Manly, Jr., persuaded the Southern Baptist Convention to create a Sunday School Board, which opened its office in Greenville in 1863. Manly and his colleague, John Broadus, produced hymnbooks, children's catechisms, and class books for teachers and pupils. Their most enduring work was the creation of a small monthly paper entitled *Kind Words for the Sunday School Children*.[90]

In Greenville one of the major concerns of the people was news from the war front. With no local telegraph or daily paper available, crowds gathered at the railroad depot in the afternoons to await the arrival of newspapers from Charleston. Dr. Edward T. Buist, pastor of the Presbyterian church, stood on the depot platform and read the casualty list in a loud voice. Near him the pine coffins of war dead were often piled, waiting to be claimed.[91]

As in towns all over the South, the women of Greenville were engaged in relief work. On July 19, 1861, a group formed the Greenville Ladies Association in Aid of the Volunteers of the Confederate Army. The group elected Mary Ann Wilks Duncan, the wife of Perry E. Duncan (one of the delegates to the Secession Convention), as president. Described as "deeply religious, well read, full of life and fun, and the mainspring of her life was to help those with whom she came in contact." Duncan built Duncan Chapel, a Methodist church, in 1847 on the Duncan place on the Buncombe Road. When a minister was not available, Duncan entered the pulpit, lined out the hymns, and preached. Three of her sons joined the Confederate army, and she became president of the Confederate Hospital Relief Corps which collected and distributed supplies east of the Mississippi River. She made several inspection tours of the military hospitals in Virginia.[92]

The object of the Ladies Association, according to its constitution, was "firstly, to relieve the sick and wounded among the soldiers, by forwarding to them linen, underclothing, cordials, bed ticks, &c., &c., secondly, To make winter clothing for the Volunteers in the Confederate Army." The roll listed 211 female members and forty-nine men as honorary members. Soon boxes of goods were being sent to the front in Virginia. An example of a typical box sent to the Virginia front contained "2 comforts 19 pillow slips—10 sheets—16 new shirts-phd. kerchiefs—2 pr. socks— 5 old shirts 4 pr. draws.—linen & cotton rags lint. soap—6 bundles tracts. dried fruit, crackers, cocoa—tea—arrow root. 4 bottles 6 b. cordial. 2 bottles peppermint. 1 bottle honey—pine apple jam—sage."[93]

As casualties mounted and the wounded arrived in Greenville by train, the Ladies Association became involved in hospital work. By February 1, 1862, the group was providing board and lodging for the wounded at E. F. Latimer's Hotel, as well as a dispensary. A Depot Committee carried daily supplies of provisions and clothing to the station for arriving soldiers. When Latimer refused to care for the wounded any longer, the town council offered the association the old Academy building for a Solders' Rest.[94]

The Soldiers' Rest continued to operate, even though the Confederate government established a Wayside Hospital in Greenville at the Goodlett House in May 1864 under the direction of Dr. George S. Trezevant of Columbia. The association contributed to the work of the Confederate hospital, and when the Female College requested the return of its facilities, the association moved to the Goodlett House.[95]

In November 1861 a U.S. Naval squadron under the command of Samuel M. DuPont sailed into Port Royal on the coast and seized control of a great part of the Beaufort District. Overnight the families of low country planters and town residents became refugees. The flood of migrants increased when Charleston was besieged. Among the most popular destinations for these refugees was Greenville. In 1864 Cornelius Burckmyer wrote from Greenville to his wife, the sister of James Petigru Boyce, that "the town is full of refugees from Charleston." He listed "Tom Smith's family, Arthur Huger (who married Miss King), Gadsden King, Julius Smith, Robert Chisholm (Lynch Bachman's husband), Dr. Whitridge, Sam Black and all the Axsons, Mrs. Gilman with her daughters, Mrs. Frank Porcher and Mrs. Jervey, Mrs. Dr. Porcher (the Dr. died a year or two ago) with her mother and sister, and some others whom I do not remember now." They "fill the place pretty full and there is not much room to spare."[96]

Perhaps the most widely known of the refugees in Greenville was Caroline Howard Gilman, the widow of the longtime minister of the Unitarian Church in Charleston. Born in Boston in 1794, she moved with her husband to Charleston where she began to publish the *Rose-Bud, or Youth's Gazette,* one of the earliest children's magazines in the country. After Dr. Gilman died in 1858, she remained in Charleston. In March 1862 Mrs. Gilman, two daughters, and several grandchildren arrived in the up country and rented suitable quarters. The bedroom, she commented, was "lovely . . . all curtained and carpeted, with the clearest glass you ever saw made from rosin."[97]

Caroline Gilman spent her time in relief work, reading, and playing with her grandchildren. There was also time for socializing. In a letter of August 21, 1863, she recounted a visit she and her daughter made to the home of Waddy Thompson on Paris Mountain. Gilman marveled at the house, his collection of Mexican artifacts, and an ivory carving of his first wife. She went on: "General Thompson, you may be aware, is a great spiritualist. His second wife is his medium, and keeps up a constant communication with the first. He recited to us two little poems, from the Spirit world, with great tenderness of manner, purporting to be from the latter."[98]

Family news was of great importance to the refugees, especially to Mrs. Gilman, since her two younger daughters were living in New England. To one relative she sent a letter through the lines, with the aid of son-in-law, Lewis Jervey, who was in Nassau engaged in the "import-export" business (a euphemism for blockade-running). Gilman's letters thus went to Nassau by way of Charleston and then were placed on a Union vessel. In October 1864 she informed her daughters: "Three packages, containing dates through June and July, have just come to hand, completing, I fancy, your entire series. They have followed Lewis Jervey about[,] being directed to him. Hereafter direct to me, care of the firm at Nassau."[99]

Life in the rural areas of the Greenville District also focused on the war. Alsey and Ann Neves lived at Mush Creek, with five of their ten children ranging in age from eleven to twenty-six when the war began. For several years the oldest son, William Perry Zacharias Franklin Neves, had been operating the family farm because his father was bedridden at times with severe rheumatism. He also operated a store and took charge of the younger children.[100] On August 27, 1861, Neves and his brother John volunteered as privates. George Washington Neves, a younger brother, joined the army on January 9, 1862.[101]

Meanwhile, the two younger brothers attended local boarding schools and worked on the farm, while the women were busy weaving wool cloth for themselves and their soldier relatives. They did not join the Mush Creek

Ladies Aid Society, but worked at home, dyeing the cloth they had woven for uniforms pale blue and washing it until it was gray. They sent the uniforms, fruit, and other items to their brothers at the front by relatives or soldiers from the community who were in transit. In return, W. P. Z. F. Neves sent items such as paper, pins, needles, and thread which were not available at home.[102]

Despite his rheumatism, Alsey Neves resumed the direction of the farm. The growing seasons from 1862 to 1865 were unusually wet which resulted in poor harvests. Ann Neves wrote to her sons in April 1862 that "there is nothing here but rain[.] we plowed Thursday after dinner till Saturday evening and it commenced raining again[.] next morning the water was all over the bottoms." In June Alsey wrote that the bottom land near the Tyger River had produced only ten bushels of grain at harvest and that he had hauled the crop to Washington Neves's house to stack it. In July he predicted that only half the crop would produce corn and the other half would surely fail. With three sons in the army, Alsey Neves hired black farmhands and parceled out small plots of land to sharecroppers. Yet Neves did not blame the Confederacy for the crisis. The South "must expect to lose a great many men God only knows how many but we have to whip the yankees, let it cost what it may in men or money."[103]

In camp near Charleston, W. P. Z. F. Neves found a way to improve his family's financial situation. Salt was a precious commodity in the upper Greenville District, and he became the commission merchant for a salt cartel organized by A. Barrett of Mush Creek. On June 14, 1863, Barrett sent Neves $315 for the purchase of twenty-five bushels of salt. Alsey Neves informed his son that salt sold at market for from fifty to ninety cents per pound, and the barter of salt could obtain needed farm supplies when cash was not available. With the profit from the salt trade, the Neves family purchased food for themselves and the men in camp. In September 1863 they used the cash to send a box of food—containing fresh peaches, apples, watermelons, and potatoes—to Charleston.[104]

Alfred Taylor at Chick Springs willingly sawed lumber for the construction of gun carriages and wagons, but he was unwilling to serve in the army. When he was conscripted in 1864, he attempted to find a substitute but was drafted into the Army of Northern Virginia and served the final four months of the war. In her husband's absence, Malinda Taylor directed the family farm. In January she oversaw the butchering of eight hogs, followed by plowing in March and planting potatoes. By the time Alfred Taylor arrived from Appomattox Courthouse, she also had fields of corn and sugar cane.[105]

By 1863 many former Unionists in the upper Greenville District, along with residents in the other mountainous areas of South Carolina, were reappraising their loyalty to the Confederacy. When the Sixteenth Regiment moved from Charleston to Jackson, Mississippi, many of the men returned home. As Major John D. Ashmore, the local conscript officer put it: "The order to go forward to the west was the signal for a general desertion." In February 1864 a large part of the Fourth South Carolina and three companies of the Third Regiment had also deserted.[106]

In August 1863 Ashmore, the chief enrolling officer for the Pickens, Greenville, and Spartanburg Districts, informed the Confederate superintendent of conscripts that deserters in the area were daily increasing in numbers. Even deserters from North Carolina were crossing the border into the state. Few would volunteer information, and groups of ten or more set out guards while the others worked on their farms. Ashmore reported that the deserters had even erected a log stockade at Gowensville and requested a swivel or a six-pounder to destroy the fortification. The chief gathering points for deserters were, he reported, Caesar's Head, Potts' Cove, Solomon Jones' Turnpike, Saluda Gap, on the headwaters of the Tyger, Howard's Gap, and Hogback Mountain. Later Ashmore reported another rendezvous near Lester's Factory on the Enoree River. Governor Milledge Bonham responded by sending Boykin's Rangers, but they met with little success in restoring order.[107]

Some residents aided escaping Union officers who were imprisoned at Camp Sorghum near Columbia late in the war. One example was W. H. Shelton, an officer in the First New York Artillery, who was captured in Virginia at the Battle of the Wilderness. In December 1864 he escaped by one of the usual routes—traveling either along the Saluda River or by the Greenville Road into North Carolina. He was recaptured in Cashiers, North Carolina, and returned to jail in Greenville. There, he reported, the jailer was a Unionist who kept his position to escape miliary service. This man supplied him with rations, directions, and then released him. Shelton first followed the North Fork of the Saluda and spent the night with a Unionist woman. At Caesar's Head he stayed with a man whose name was Pink Bishop. He also stayed with the Case family whose two sons had shot Confederate conscription officers. Eventually Shelton made his way to Knoxville, Tennessee, which was in Union hands.[108]

Even before the Confederate defeats at Vicksburg and Gettysburg in 1863, Benjamin Perry was apprehensive about the future. "My heart is so full of my country's distress & ruin that I cannot enjoy life," he wrote in his journal. To be sure, Perry was a loyal Confederate. In March 1862 he was appointed Confederate district attorney, and in the fall he was elected to the state legislature. Then in January 1865 he was appointed a Confederate district judge by President Jefferson Davis. But Perry was worried: "I cannot read & study as I once did. . . . My mind is constantly preoccupied with the painful news of battles in which thousands and tens of thousands are slain! . . . Taxes [are] enormous to pay the Confederate Government. The necessaries of life at fabulous prices! Provisions can not be purchased even at those prices!" Perry told his wife that his heart was broken and that he could write no more in his journal and he put it aside.[109]

By the end of 1863 the rate of inflation was so high and the suffering among the many families of soldiers was so great that the state legislature passed a tax in kind on food, cloth, and salt for their relief. In Greenville on Sale Day—the first Monday of each month—rations were distributed to the needy. Sale Day became Draw Day, and hundreds of people appeared for the distribution of corn.[110]

The end of the war proved more devastating than Perry had imagined. Sherman's army entered the state in January 1865 and cut a path 40 miles wide from the Savannah River northeast to the Great Pee Dee River at Cheraw. One-third of the city of Columbia was burned. Governor Andrew G. Magrath called a special session of the legislature to meet in Greenville on April 25, but only a few legislators arrived. The governor addressed them bravely before they adjourned.[111]

The Union invasion of South Carolina brought more refugees. "We have a constant succession of Frank [Porcher]'s relatives and friends here," Caroline Gilman wrote. "He is so hospitable that he will share his last with others. Not a week passes but we have an improvised bed, what the soldiers call a 'shake-down' in the parlor." But the trip to Greenville became more difficult after Sherman destroyed the railroad tracks as far north as Alston. "We are living in a strange way now," Mrs. Gilman reported. "Isolated by the cutting off of the R.R.s we have only accidental communication with the outer world, no stores for two years open; without currency; no post-office, that is, no paid P[ost] M[aster] and a future dependent on the strangest combination of affairs."[112]

Stoneman's Raid

The fighting finally came to Greenville in the last weeks of the war. In April 1865 Union Major General George Stoneman, the commander of the District of East Tennessee, made a final raid into southwestern Virginia and western North Carolina. Returning to Tennessee, he left his cavalry east of the mountains to obtain forage and to intercept any bands going south. During the last week of April, Stoneman received word that Jefferson Davis had abandoned Richmond and was headed through South Carolina, and he ordered the cavalry to pursue Davis "to the ends of the earth" if necessary. Two brigades left Hendersonville on April 29 and rode through Jones Gap toward Pickensville. A third rode through Spartanburg and the Golden Grove. In Asheville Brigadier General Davis Tillson ordered 150 additional cavalry, under the command of Major James Lawson, to join in the pursuit. Lawson crossed the mountains, and on May 2, he rode down the Buncombe Road and into Greenville.[113]

As she described the scene in a letter, Caroline Gilman and her family had just seated themselves "at the table, with some pleasant jests on the subject of a roast pig, which Lou had provided." They heard the servants shouting: "The yankees are coming!" Rushing to the piazza, they saw "a negro man, in a cart, whipping his horse to a full gallop. . . . A dozen of the enemy's cavalry came after him and fired. In an instant, almost, his horse was unharnessed and taken possession of." The troops began to search the houses for arms and horses. They broke into empty shops on Main Street where the refugees had stored their belongings. "Everything was rifled," Mrs. Gilman wrote. "Books, costly plate, wines, pictures, bed linens thrown into the street to be picked up by any passerby. All the afternoon we saw white and black, laden with goods, passing by the house." She reported that one of the soldiers, a Mr. Simpson, was wearing Professor Boyce's cloak and "lighted one of [his] segars." Only Captain Wesley Brooks's house was set on fire, "but it was not burned." The cavalry found thirty thousand dollars in cash from the Bank of Charleston that was hidden at Hamlin Beattie's store. A white resident wounded a raider and was shot instantly. A former slave was killed later. By evening the cavalry rode on toward Anderson. "So ends the history of the Greenville Raid," wrote Caroline Gilman.[114]

And so ended the Civil War in the Greenville District. For thirty years Greenville had struggled with the question of loyalty to the federal government. At first unionist sentiment prevailed, but in 1860 the district cast its lot with the Confederacy. In the ordeal of war, however, the people of Greenville remained divided until the Southern cause was finally lost.

Notes

1. *Southern Patriot,* October 5, 1854; Greenville *News,* June 26, 1962.

2. Lacy K. Ford, Jr., *Origins of Southern Radicalism: The South Carolina Upcountry, 1800–1860* (New York, 1988), 48–49; Greenville *Southern Patriot,* June

26, 1853, June 14, 1855; Washington Taylor, *A Diary of Transactions from 1835–1855 of Washington Taylor* (Frederick, Md., 1988), 76–77, 215–16, 220–22.

3. J. C. Carbough, "The Golden Grove Tea Farm of Junius Smith: Preliminary Findings," *The Proceedings and Papers of the Greenville County Historical Society* (cited hereafter as *PPGCHS*) 8 (1984–1990): 144–51.

4. Ford, *Southern Radicalism*, 250–51; U.S. Seventh Census, 1850. Agriculture, South Carolina (microfilm, National Archives), Roll 853; Slave Schedule, Roll 865; U.S. Eighth Census, 1860, Slave Schedule, Roll 1220.

5. U.S. Seventh Census, 1850. Slave Schedule, S.C., Reel 865; U.S. Eighth Census, 1860. Slave Schedule, S.C., Reel 1231.

6. "Thomas Edwin Ware," *Biographical Directory of the South Carolina Senate, 1776–1985*, ed. N. Louise Bailey et al. (Columbia, 1986) 3: 1677; Greenville *Southern Patriot*, April 21, 1853, October 12, 1854; Chalmers G. Davidson, *The Last Foray, The South Carolina Planters of 1860: A Sociological Study* (Columbia, 1971), 259; Stanley S. Crittenden, *The Greenville Century Book* (Greenville, 1903), 43.

7. Ford, *Southern Radicalism*, 71; David Salmon, "Alfred Taylor: Community, Class, and Industry in an Antebellum Upstate South Carolina Farmer" *Furman Humanities Review* 3 (May 1990): 1–8.

8. Salmon, "Alfred Taylor," 3: 8–12.

9. The percentage of farms is derived from the 0–100 acres columns in Table 2.4 in Ford, *Southern Radicalism*, 48. The use I have made of the percentage is suspect because the total, based on acreage and not slaveholding, includes some middling planters. Information on the Neves family is taken from Marion Neves Hawkins, "Genealogical Survey: Neves Family" (Greenville, 1972), manuscript in possession of Daisy Neves (Mrs. Earl) Jones, Travelers Rest, S.C.; 1860 Census. South Carolina. Greenville District. Roll 1220; Mrs. Beverly T. (Mildred E.) Whitmire, *The Presence of the Past: Epitaphs . . . in Greenville County, S.C.* (Baltimore, Md., 1976), Cemeteries 75, 150, cited in Thomas M. (Buck) Wall III, "The Neves Family: The Upcountry During the Civil War, 1861–1865" (Directed Study, Furman University 1990), in possession of the author.

10. Wall, "Neves Family."

11. Ibid.; Caroline Pool Bailey to W. P. Z. F. Neves, March 25, 1862, W. P. Z. F. Neves Papers (microfilm), Library, North Greenville College, Tigerville, S.C.

12. Crittenden, *Century Book*, 65; William Gilmore Simms, *The Geography of South Carolina* (Charleston, 1843), 84; *Southern Patriot*, November 16, 1854; Lillian A. Kibler, *Benjamin F. Perry: South Carolina Unionist* (Durham, N.C., 1946), 195.

13. Ford, *Southern Radicalism*, Table 2.5, 50.

14. Kibler, *Perry*, 157–84, 225. The Perry house remained standing until 1928. Greenville *News*, February 17, April 15, 1928.

15. Kibler, *Perry*, 184–85.

16. Ibid., 192–93, 196–97, 201–3.

17. Helen Kohn Hennig, *Great South Carolinians of a Later Date* (Chapel Hill, N.C., 1949), 158–67; *Patriot and Mountaineer*, October 4, 1855.

18. *Historical and Descriptive Review of the State of South Carolina* (Charleston, 1884) 3: 108–9; Whitmire, *Presence of the Past,* Cemetery 22; R. G. Dun and Company, Credit Ledgers, South Carolina, Greenville County, 132C (Levy), 132C/2 (Lowenberg), 132M (Samuel), Baker Library, Harvard School of Business Administration, Cambridge, Mass.

19. "William Lowndes Yancey," *Dictionary of American Biography* (New York, 1936) 20: 592–95; John W. DuBose, *The Life and Times of William Lowndes Yancey* (New York, 1892, 1942) 2: 70.

20. Kibler, *Perry,* 198–99; DuBose, *Yancey,* 1: 74–75. There is a full account of the trial in the Greenville *Mountaineer,* November 9, 1838. Yancey's young son died in Greenville and is buried in the Earle Family Cemetery on the Old Buncombe Road near Morgan Memorial Baptist Church in Sans Souci.

21. *Southern Patriot,* April 21, 1853.

22. Ibid., April 21, 28, 1853; Whitmire, *Presence of the Past,* Cemetery 90.

23. *Historical and Descriptive Review* 3: 72; "Thomas Claghorn Gower" in James M. Richardson, *History of Greenville County, South Carolina* (Atlanta, 1930, 1980), 153; R. G. Dun and Company, Credit Ledgers, South Carolina; Greenville *Patriot and Mountaineer,* January 31, 1856. A detailed description of the Carriage Factory complex is found in Felicia Furman Dryden, "Guidelines for the Preservation of the Reedy River Commercial and Industrial District" (M.S. thesis, Columbia University, 1979).

24. *Southern Patriot,* September 2, 1853.

25. Kibler, *Perry,* 211–12; Roy McBee Smith, *A McBee Genealogy* (Spartanburg, 1983), 95–96. A general account of local railroads in the nineteenth century is William P. Barton, "The Railroad Comes to Greenville," *PPGCHS* 5 (1971–1975): 54–64.

26. Kibler, *Perry,* 213; Greenville *Mountaineer,* October 24, 1845; Ulrich B. Phillips, *A History of Transportation in the Eastern Cotton Belt to 1860* (New York, 1908, 1968), 337. The committee of thirty, whose names appeared in the newspaper on October 24, provides a list of the major promoters of Greenville in the closing decades of the antebellum period: Poinsett, E. D. Earle, McBee, Tandy Walker, Perry, Benajah Dunham, Crook, George F. Townes, William Choice, Fountain F. Beattie, E. P. Jones, Coleman, J. H. Joyce, Ware, Perry E. Duncan, Henry Smith, Thomas P. Brockman, Josiah Kilgore, Robert Cox, Harvey Cleveland, William Butler, M. T. Hudson, T. B. Williams, Wilson Batson, Silas H. Whitten, and David Blythe.

27. Phillips, *History of Transportation,* 340–42; Kibler, *Perry,* 214–15.

28. Smith, *McBee Genealogy,* 97–98; Roy McBee Smith, *Vardry McBee, 1775–1864: Man of Reason in an Age of Extremes* (Columbia, 1992), 193–97.

29. Phillips, *History of Transportation,* 342–43; Kibler, *Perry,* 215–16.

30. Greenville *Southern Patriot,* February 19, 1852; December 8, 15, 1853; Crittenden, *Century Book,* 42–43.

31. Francis B. Simkins and Robert H. Woody, *South Carolina During Reconstruction* (Chapel Hill, N.C., 1932, 1966), 200–1.

32. Ford, *Southern Radicalism*, 237, 242.

33. Greenville *Southern Patriot*, June 16, 1853.

34. Ebaugh, *Bridging the Gap*, 38; Greenville *Southern Patriot*, February 19, 1852; June 16, September 8, 1853; August 10, September 21, 1854; September 13, 1855; Greenville *Patriot and Mountaineer*, June 19, 1856.

35. Robert C. Wood, *Parish in the Heart of the City: Christ Church, Greenville, S.C.* (Greenville, 1976), 24–27.

36. Henry B. McKoy, *A History of the First Presbyterian Church in Greenville, South Carolina* (Greenville, 1962), 19.

37. Robert N. Daniel, *A Century of Progress being the History of the First Baptist Church, Greenville, South Carolina* (Greenville, 1957), 29–32.

38. Lennie Lusby, "Music," 31–32; Lila E. Earle and Evelyn P. Daniel, "Art: Architecture and Painting," 65–68; Dorothy Richey, "Theatre Arts," 75–77; all in Alfred S. Reid, ed., *The Arts in Greenville, 1800–1960* (Greenville, 1960).

39. William J. McGlothlin, *Baptist Beginnings in Education: A History of Furman University* (Nashville, Tenn., 1926), 96–101.

40. Ibid., 101–8.

41. Ibid., 110–11, 235.

42. *Southern Patriot*, August 19, 1852.

43. Harvey T. Cook, *The Life Work of James Clement Furman* (Greenville, 1926), 3–143.

44. Judith T. Bainbridge, "History of the Greenville Woman's College," 27–31 (manuscript in the author's possession); Kibler, *Perry*, 309–12.

45. Bainbridge, "Woman's College," 42–50.

46. Ibid., 52–55.

47. John R. Sampey, *Southern Baptist Theological Seminary: The First Thirty Years, 1859–1889* (Baltimore, Md., 1890), 5–11.

48. John A. Broadus, *Memoir of James Petigru Boyce, D.D., LL.D.* (New York, 1893), 1–110.

49. *Southern Patriot*, September 5, 1855.

50. James W. Gettys, "To Conquer a Peace: South Carolina and the Mexican War" (Ph.D. diss., University of South Carolina, 1974), 175. The most recent treatment of the role of the state and its most prominent political leader in the conflict is Ernest M. Lander, Jr., *Reluctant Imperialists: Calhoun, the South Carolinians, and the Mexican War* (Baton Rouge, La., 1980).

51. Henry Townes to ———, December 4, 1846, and Samuel A. Townes to George F. Townes, November 24, 1847, Townes Family Papers, South Caroliniana Library, University of South Carolina, Columbia, S.C., cited in Gettys, "Mexican War," 355–56.

52. Ibid., 185–88.

53. Ibid., 202–3.

54. Kibler, *Perry*, 221–22, 240; Ford, *Southern Radicalism*, 186–87; Gettys, "Mobilization for Secession in Greenville District," *PPGCHS* 6 (1975–1979): 58.

55. Kibler, *Perry,* 244–46. The most recent treatment of the first secession crisis in South Carolina is John Barnwell, *Love of Order: South Carolina's First Secession Crisis* (Chapel Hill, N.C., 1982).

56. Kibler, *Perry,* 248–49.

57. Ibid., 249–50.

58. Gettys, "Mobilization for Secession," 58; Carbough, "The Golden Grove Tea Farm," *PPGCHS* 8: 149.

59. Kibler, *Perry,* 250; McBee to Vardry A. McBee, November 26, 1850, cited in Steven A. Channing, *Crisis of Fear: Secession in South Carolina* (New York, 1970), 62.

60. Kibler, *Perry,* 257, 270.

61. Ibid., 271–72; 274–76; Barnwell, *Love of Order,* 198–99.

62. Gettys, "Mobilization for Secession," 59–60.

63. *Patriot and Mountaineer,* September 4, 15, 1856.

64. Kibler, *Perry,* 296; Gettys, "Mobilization for Secession," 60–61.

65. Gettys, "Mobilization for Secession," 61–62.

66. Ibid., 62; Harvey Wish, ed., *Antebellum: Writings of George Fitzhugh and Hinton Rowan Helper on Slavery* (New York, 1960), 27.

67. Kibler, *Perry,* 3–6.

68. Gettys, "Mobilization for Secession," 63–64; Kibler, *Perry,* 319.

69. *Southern Enterprise,* June 14, July 5, 1860, cited in Gettys, "Mobilization for Secession," 64.

70. Charleston *Courier,* August 13, 20, 1860, cited in Kibler, *Perry,* 327. The election results are cited in Kibler, *Perry,* 331.

71. *Southern Enterprise,* November 1, 8, 1860; Gettys, "Mobilization for Secession," 65; Channing, *Crisis of Fear,* 261–62, 269–70.

72. Kibler, *Perry,* 335, 337: Gettys, "Mobilization for Secession," 65.

73. *Patriot and Mountaineer,* November 22, 1860; Kibler, *Perry,* 337–38.

74. *Southern Enterprise,* November 22, 1860, cited in Kibler, *Perry,* 338–39.

75. Kibler, *Perry,* 339.

76. *Southern Enterprise,* November 22, 1860; Kibler, *Perry,* 341–42.

77. Kibler, *Perry,* 342–43; Alfred Taylor, Diary, 2: November 10, 1860, cited in Salmon, "Alfred Taylor," 11–12.

78. John A. May and Joan R. Faunt, *South Carolina Secedes* (Columbia, 1960), 103, 122, 137, 140–41, 146–47, 157; *1860 Census, Slave Schedule, Pickens District* (Central, S.C., 1991), 64.

79. May and Faunt, *South Carolina Secedes,* 7, 16; Kibler, *Perry,* 248; Broadus, *Boyce,* 185.

80. Charles E. Cauthen, *South Carolina Goes to War, 1860–1865* (Chapel Hill, N.C., 1950), 113–15.

81. Undated newspaper clipping, Cleveland Scrap Book, in possession of Harriet Cleveland (Mrs. Richard) Dobbins.

82. *South Carolina Troops in Confederate Service,* Alexander S. Salley, comp. (Columbia, 1914) 2: 35–37; J. W. Reid, *History of the Fourth Regiment of the S.C. Volunteers* (Greenville, 1892, 1986).

83. Kibler, *Perry*, 348–50; Cook, *Furman*, 203–4.

84. Cook, *Furman*, 203–4; John S. Taylor, *Sixteenth South Carolina Regiment from Greenville County, S.C.* (Greenville, 1964), 6; Kibler, *Perry*, 363–64.

85. Kibler, *Perry*, 351–52; Cook, *Furman*, 206.

86. Taylor, *Sixteenth Regiment*, 10–15; Broadus, *Boyce*, 187–89.

87. "Matthew Calbraith Butler," *Dictionary of American Biography* (New York, 1930) 3: 263–64.

88. Dun Credit Ledgers, 132X; Richardson, *Greenville County* (Atlanta, 1930, 1980), 85–86; Greenville *Mountaineer*, October 31, 1894; Cauthen, *South Carolina Goes to War*, 150; David Duncan Wallace, *South Carolina: A Short History, 1520–1948* (Chapel Hill, N.C., 1951, 1966), 544; *Report of the Chief of the Department of the Military*, August 30, 1862 and *S.C. Reports and Resolutions, 1863*, 156, cited in Joab Mauldin Lesesne, "The State Military Works at Greenville," an address delivered at the dedication of the marker at the State Military Works, 1949 (copy in possession of the author). After the Civil War the arsenal was "turned over to Governor [James L.] Orr. . . . All finished and unfinished arms and ammunition to be taken by the United States authorities." In 1866 the building was sold to Dr. Samuel S. Marshall for use as a cotton factory. In 1872 it was purchased at auction by Alexander McBee. *Southern Enterprise*, March 29, 1866; Greenville *Mountaineer*, November 22, 1866; March 13, 1872.

89. Archibald T. Robertson, *Life and Letters of John Albert Broadus* (Philadelphia, Pa., 1901), 189, 196–98.

90. Robert A. Baker, *The Southern Baptist Convention and Its People, 1607–1972* (Nashville, Tenn., 1974), 231–32.

91. Kibler, *Perry*, 367.

92. *Minutes of the Proceedings of the Greenville Ladies' Association in Aid of Volunteers of the Confederate Army*. Historical Papers of the Trinity College Historical Society, Series 21 (Durham, N.C., 1937): 15, 115–16; May and Faunt, *South Carolina Secedes*, 137. See also Jane Carson Brunson, "A Sketch of the Work at Greenville," in Mrs. Thomas Taylor et al., eds., *South Carolina Women in the Confederacy* (Columbia, 1903), 26–28.

93. *Ladies' Association*, 15, 98, 107–11.

94. Ibid., 40–41.

95. Ibid., 61–62, 65, 67, 69.

96. Charlotte R. Holmes, ed., *The Burckmyer Letters, March 1863–June 1865* (Columbia, 1926), 446. See my "Caroline Howard Gilman and Confederate Refugee Life in Greenville," *PPGCHS* 6 (1975–1979): 67–77.

97. "Caroline Howard Gilman," *Dictionary of American Biography*, ed. Allen Johnson and Dumas Malone (New York, 1935) 7: 298–99; Edward T. James, ed., *Notable American Women* (Cambridge, Mass., 1971) 2: 37–39. Caroline Gilman to children, March 12, 1862, in "Letters of a Confederate Mother: Charleston in the Sixties," *Atlantic Monthly* 137 (April 1926): 505; Gilman to children, October 31, 1865, Carolina Gilman Papers, S.C. Historical Society, Charleston, S.C.

98. Gilman to children, August 21, 1863, S.C. Historical Society.

99. Ibid., March 27, August 21, 1863; October 13, 1864, S.C. Historical Society.

100. Wall, "Neves Family."

101. Compiled Service Records of Confederates in Organizations from South Carolina, Third Battalion Palmetto Light Artillery (microfilm, National Archives), Microcopy 267, Cards, 8944, 49258288, 49329265.

102. Emily Neves to W. P. Z. F. Neves, February 9, May 28, 1862; September 14, 1863; Martha Cox to W. P. Z. F. Neves, November 9, 1861, William P. Z. F. Neves Papers (microfilm), Library, North Greenville College, Tigerville, S.C.

103. Ann Pool Neves to W. P. Z. F. Neves, April 27, 1862; Frances Neves to W. P. Z. F. Neves, February 9, 1862; Alsey Neves to W. P. Z. F. Neves, January 20, June 20, 1862, W. P. Z. F. Neves Papers.

104. A. Barrett to W. P. Z. F. Neves, June 14, 1863; Alsey Neves to W. P. Z. F. Neves, October 11, 1863; Frances Neves to W. P. Z. F. Neves, September 4, 1863, W. P. Z. F. Neves Papers.

105. Rosser H. Taylor, "Some Comments on the Diary of Alfred Taylor" *Furman University Bulletin, Faculty Studies,* N.S. 11: 1, 13–16.

106. James T. Otten, "Disloyalty in the Upper Districts of South Carolina During the Civil War," *S.C. Historical Magazine* 75 (1976): 100–101; *The War of the Rebellion: A Compilation of the Official Records in the Union and Confederate Armies* (Washington, D.C., 1880–1901), Series 4, 2: 769 (hereafter cited as *O.R.*).

107. *O.R.,* Serial 4, 2: 769–74; Otten, "Disloyalty," 103.

108. W. H. Shelton, "A Hard Road to Travel Out of Dixie," *Century Magazine* 40: 942–44, cited in Otten, "Disloyalty," 107–8.

109. Kibler, *Perry,* 353–54, 359, 369, 370.

110. Cauthen, *S.C. Goes to War,* 193–94; John William DeForest, *A Union Officer in the Reconstruction* (New Haven, Conn., 1948), 54.

111. Cauthen, *S.C. Goes to War,* 228.

112. Caroline Gilman to Annie, n.d., in "Letters of a Confederate Mother," 509.

113. Ina W. Van Noppen, *Stoneman's Last Raid* (Raleigh, N.C., 1961), 99–112; *O.R.,* series I, 49, pt. 2: 407; 49, pt. 1: 546–48; 49, pt. 2: 555. See also Thomas B. Keys, "The Federal Pillage of Anderson, South Carolina: Brown's Raid," *SCHM* 76 (1975): 80–86.

114. Caroline Gilman to Eliza, June 2, 1865, S.C. Historical Society, and Mrs. Arthur Huger to Mrs. William Mason Smith, May 8, 1865, in *Mason Smith Family Letters, 1860–1868,* ed. Daniel E. Huger Smith et al. (Columbia, 1950), 206–7; *Mountaineer,* May 14, 1884.

CHAPTER SIX

The Reconstruction of Greenville

As in the South generally, the years after 1865 brought great changes to the Greenville District, or Greenville County as it was designated in 1868. The close of the Civil War ushered in economic dislocation, an end to slavery, and a new role for the freedmen. During Reconstruction there was a brief period of military occupation and the operation of the Freedmen's Bureau. By 1872, however, the old white power structure had regained political control of the county, and in 1876 the white Democrats in Greenville joined forces with the state Democratic leadership to "redeem" the government of South Carolina from Republican control.

Economic Dislocation

The Civil War resulted in serious economic problems for the South and for the Greenville District. John William DeForest, chief of the Freedmen's Bureau in Greenville from 1866 to 1868, wrote of the "suffering people" in all classes. His description of the district itself indicated that in many ways it had not changed from the antebellum period. The district was, he wrote, "an upland region, a country of corn rather than of cotton, cultivated by small farmers and middling planters." Since Greenville had "few slaves . . . only a moderate proportion of its capital had been destroyed by emancipation." Local poverty, in DeForest's opinion, resulted "from the leanness of the soil, the imperfection of agriculture, the loss of hundreds of young men in battle, the exhaustion of stock and capital during the war, the lack of intelligent and zealous labor, and the thriftless habits incident on slavery." Besides these general conditions, there was a severe drought during the growing season of 1866, and the resulting harvest was poor. The price of corn rose to two dollars a bushel and bacon to forty cents a pound. As a result, he conceded there was "widespread want."[1]

Indeed, DeForest described the Greenville District in one word—bankrupt: "The great majority of planters owed to the full extent of their property." When he left Greenville in January 1868, DeForest estimated that "there was something like a thousand executions [or foreclosures for debt] awaiting action; and, had the commanding general allowed their collection, another thousand would have been added to the docket." Land which had brought seven or eight dollars an acre in 1860 was sold for $1.12 an acre. "Labor was equally depreciated, able-bodied men hiring out at seventy-five cents a day if they found [food and housing] themselves; at twenty-five cents if found by their employers." But most farmers could not pay even these low wages and were forced to plant on shares. So much, DeForest asserted, "for the political economy and, in one word, so much for slavery."[2]

The census figures for 1870 present an equally gloomy picture. In the decade from 1860 to 1870 the population of Greenville grew only 1.7 percent, from 21,892 to 22,262. While the white population grew 3.3 percent, the black population declined 1.7 percent. In 1867 the editor of the *Southern Enterprise* reported that "from every part of the State, accounts reach us of the emigration of large numbers of negroes to other States." He indicated that "during Christmas times, [there was] a great falling off in the number of negroes about the streets of Greenville from what they were in years past. A large number of them are still going off, induced by higher wages, and the hard times that afflict both white and black in this State."[3]

Among the white citizens who left Greenville were both large and middling planters. Waddy Thompson, Jr., former minister to Mexico, sold his home and 900 acres on Paris Mountain in 1867 and moved to Madison, Florida, where he raised cotton until his death in 1868. J. H. Arnold, the son-in-law of Colonel T. Edwin Ware, the largest planter in the district in 1860, once owned seven slaves and a store in the upper Laurens District. But by November 1865 he was deeply in debt, and his plantation was estimated to be worth only two to three thousand dollars. In June 1869 he was in bankruptcy, and in January 1871 he left Greenville for Mississippi.[4]

Peter Cauble was typical of those planters who remained in Greenville but who lost a fortune during the war years. He was described in 1860 by the R. G. Dun Company as an "eccentric moneylender, blacksmith, planter with $100,000 in money, negroes and land." By October 1865 Dun estimated that his land was worth between three and four thousand dollars, and he had considerable debts. By 1870 his financial condition was described simply as insolvent. Even so, DeForest reported that Cauble "was one of the men to whom the poor and outcast of his district chiefly resorted for help. White or black, good or bad, Peter Cauble gave them food, found them shelter, and went bail for them."[5]

Emancipation

The changes that were in store for Greenville in the postwar period became apparent even before the Union cavalry departed on May 2, 1865. The presence of Union troops signified emancipation to the slaves. In their enthusiasm for their new status, a number of blacks seized goods stored in David's warehouse in West Greenville—items Union troops had spurned. Among the treasures taken were six Rutledge family portraits, including one of Charles Cotesworth Pinckney. The portraits were later recovered by Louisa Porcher, Caroline Gilman's daughter. Cloth from local textile mills stored at the railroad depot was given away.[6]

Twenty years later G. W. Taylor, a mechanic in the State Military Works during the war, recalled the new air of freedom among the blacks the day the troops arrived. "In the presence of the Yankees," he said, "some of the negroes were exceedingly impudent." A freedman who Taylor thought belonged to Vardry McBee's estate shot at him from a distance of several hundred yards. Taylor remembered that "the Yankees themselves killed this same negro, from impudence, in the woods near the Foundry." Not all blacks in Greenville gained a sense of their new freedom so quickly and tragically as the shooting victim. "Our servants," Mrs. Porcher wrote at the time, "all behaved well." At Chick Springs, Alfred Taylor's slaves remained to harvest the crop which they had planted. On June 29, 1865, Taylor's slaves were formally freed.[7]

Presidential Reconstruction

Within a month Governor Andrew G. Magrath was arrested, and General Quincy A. Gillmore, the army commander at Hilton Head, divided the state into military subdistricts and established martial law. Louisa Porcher wrote in July 1865 that "the Yankee garrison are here, & although it is galling in the extreme to see them, yet they are very quiet and orderly, & I have heard of their putting down the complaints of the negroes in a very summary manner." Porcher's defiant spirit was evident in these remarks: "The General is here too, Van Wyke, but of course no one that we know, fraternizes with either him or his officers." Perhaps Porcher overstated the case. On Sunday, July 23, 1865, "six Yankees" were "present at Sunday School" at the Methodist church, according to the superintendent.[8]

With no stores open in Greenville and railroad traffic to Columbia disrupted, Frank Porcher took steps to supply the town. In June 1865 he borrowed two hundred dollars and drove his wagon to Charleston. There, according to his wife's letter of July 29, he "bought a cargo of goods, coffee, herring, soap, dry goods, two dozen round hats trimmed with deep blue & magenta, some of them called 'the fall of Charleston.'" Back in Greenville, Porcher "hired Mr. Ketchum's store, which is empty, set up shop, with Wilson Glover for clerk, and has been fortunate, so much so that he returns to Charleston next week to purchase more!" Willy Glover, she noted, made "an admirable shopman, & praises his goods & is quite a favorite with his lady customers."[9]

The low country refugees began the journey home in the fall of 1865. After Joseph E. Johnston's Confederate Army surrendered in April, D. E. Huger Smith was mustered out. Smith came to Greenville in October to dispose of his family's possessions which could not be moved. He reminded his mother on October 31, that "you have a valuable piece of property quarantined in Slow-Hole, as this place may most deservedly be called." He advertised the family piano for sale and was offered $150 by "the Misses De Choisel . . . in Greenbacks . . . half paid now & the other half in six months." He sent the family carriage to Cox and Gower, but they give him little hope of selling it immediately. Smith also had to dispose of carpets, bedding, and books. "Mr. Porcher," he observed, "sold out the remnant of his stock of goods at auction yesterday. He has gone down, but the family & Glover still remain."[10]

The white leaders, eager for the military officials to restore civil government, held a series of public meetings throughout the state to petition President Andrew Johnson to act quickly. On July 3, at the meeting in Greenville, Benjamin Perry pled with his fellow former Confederates to "abandon at once and forever all notions of Secession, Nullification and Disunion, determined to live, and to teach your children to live, as true American citizens." Even as he spoke, but unknown to him, Perry had been appointed provisional governor of South Carolina by the president.[11]

On June 24 a committee from Charleston had called on Johnson who asked them to submit a list of persons for provisional governor. On the list was Perry's name. "Is that Ben Perry?" the president asked. "I know him well, but is he not too much of a people's man to be acceptable to the city of Charleston?" No, was the reply, "he has always been a good Union man and a gentleman of strict integrity." On June 30 the president issued the proclamation appointing Perry. Not until a week after the meeting in Greenville did a messenger from the president overtake Perry and a committee from Greenville on their way to Washington to intercede with Johnson. The group continued on their journey, and on July 19 the president met with them at the White House. Immediately Governor Perry issued a proclamation urging the white citizens to take the oath of allegiance to the United States and calling an election for delegates to a state constitutional convention.[12]

Since the state had never provided a home for the governor, Perry returned to Greenville where he restored civil officials to office and received between two thousand and three thousand individual applications for pardons from persons owning taxable property of twenty thousand dollars or more. Perry proposed to Charles J. Elford that he become the agent for those applicants whose petitions had been slowed down in the bureaucracy of Washington. Perry also spent a great deal of time attempting to adjudicate matters between large landowners, army officers, and the Freedmen's Bureau.[13]

Voting for delegates to the state convention of 1865 was very light, since many eligible voters had not taken the oath of allegiance prior to the election. In the Greenville District only 850 voters went to the polls and elected the governor's son and private secretary, William Hayne Perry; James Petigru Boyce; T. C. Bolling; and Dr. J. P. Latimer to represent the Greenville District. The convention met in Columbia in the Baptist Church—the site of the first meetings of the Secession Convention. The delegates quickly repealed the Ordinance of Secession and recognized the abolition of slavery. In his message to the convention, Governor Perry urged a more democratic state government. But Perry was clear about the limited role freedmen should have, and his views were echoed by Dr. Boyce: "This is a white man's government." Perry urged the legislature to "protect" the freedmen by adopting a "Black Code" that was little better than bondage.[14]

On October 18, 1865, white South Carolinians went to the polls for the first time to elect a governor and members of the legislature. Only about one-third of those who were eligible voted. James L. Orr of Anderson was narrowly elected over former Confederate General Wade Hampton III, and Greenville elected George F. Townes as its state senator. Townes, who had advocated secession as editor of the Greenville *Mountaineer*, had given up his law practice and turned to planting full time on his 5,214 acres. The House members elected were William Hayne Perry, John H. Goodwin, Henry P. Hammett, and William P. Price, who later resigned and was replaced by Alexander McBee. On October 28 the legislature elected Benjamin Perry as a U.S. senator on the first ballot. The antebellum power structure was still in place—at least, for a while.[15]

The Greenville District's first encounter with the federal government during Reconstruction came when a garrison of troops was stationed in the town. On September 26, 1866, Company H of the Sixth Regiment of

Infantry under the command of Brevet Captain Thomas Britton arrived. They pitched their tents near the Academy Spring at the rear of the Female College, and quickly established the routine of camp life. The day began with reveille at sunrise, breakfast at 7:00 A.M., and ended with tattoo at 8:00 P.M. and taps at 8:30 P.M. On Sunday morning there was inspection at 10:00 A.M. According to their orders of the day, enlisted men were forbidden to leave the camp to visit the town without passes. Those who did go to town were required to wear dress uniforms with coats buttoned and shoes nicely polished. On October 8 daily drill began for everyday except Saturday and Sunday. The orders also specified that "Field Music will practice during the drill hour at a sufficient distance in the woods not to be heard at the drill ground."[16]

The garrison had orders to assist the federal marshal. On December 20, 1866, for example "2nd LT Godman with a detachment of 1 non-commissioned officer and 5 privates" was ordered to "proceed to the premises of James Taylor on what is known as the Buncom [sic] Road to search for 1 horse and equipment, property of Oliver Holt and of which he has been defrauded by James Taylor and Daniel Noe." The troops also aided with the black population. On April 16, 1867, T. L. Bozeman, a local marshal, asked for assistance "in arresting one Foncy Walker, who is reported to be a man of violent and dangerous character and who has repeatedly resisted the civil authority." Sergeant Warren Secord with four men was ordered to the Plain Post Office on the Laurens and Greenville Road to lend assistance. On November 3, 1866, the commander reported that "as far as my observation extends, the law now makes no distinction on account of color, and justice is honestly administered for Whites against Blacks, and Blacks against Whites." On the whole, the troops seldom engaged in any military operation other than the usual routine of garrison duty. In May 1867 the post of Greenville closed and the garrison transferred to Newberry. The post in Newberry was closed on December 30 and the troops ordered to Charleston.[17]

The operation of the Freedmen's Bureau office had a longer duration in Greenville. On March 3, 1865, Congress created within the War Department the Bureau of Refugees, Freedmen, and Abandoned Lands to promote the well-being of both the freedmen and white refugees. The bureau was authorized to provide food, fuel, clothing, medical care, education, and abandoned lands held by the government for the poor. The state was divided into six bureau districts, one of which was northwestern South Carolina. It included the subdistrict of Greenville, which was composed of the Greenville and Pickens Districts until August 1867, when the

Anderson subdistrict was abolished and Anderson was added to Greenville. The headquarters of the subdistrict was located in Greenville on the ground floor of the old courthouse. The first officer in charge was Brevet Lieutenant A. E. Niles. On September 30, 1866, the military commander in Greenville reported that Niles "ably manages the affairs of this Department and the Freedmen are generally well-disposed." He indicated that there was perhaps better feeling between the whites and blacks of Greenville, than in any other part of the state. Niles was succeeded on October 2, 1866, by Brevet Major John William DeForest, who remained in Greenville until he retired from Army service and was replaced by W. T. Hoyt.[18]

According to DeForest, who later published an account of his experiences in *Harper's New Monthly Magazine,* life as a bureau officer was leisurely and pleasant. He lived in the Mansion House, where his customary breakfast consisted of "beefsteak, bacon, eggs, and hominy." At first DeForest went to work at eight o'clock in the morning, but later the hour became nine, and eventually ten. As he smoked his after-breakfast pipe and read the Charleston papers which had arrived the previous day by train, DeForest kept an eye out for his constituents. "The appearance of one or more freedmen, sitting on the stone steps or leaning against the brick columns . . . was the signal for me [to] lay down my *Courier,* pick up such official documents as I might have received by mail, and repair to my various though not often ponderous duties." He closed the office at two in the afternoon "after from three to five hours of labor or lounging." After a substantial dinner, he took an afternoon constitutional and returned to the Mansion House for tea.[19]

Neither DeForest nor the members of the military garrison were the villainous Yankees of later lore who forced their will on the defenseless white South. DeForest did complain that "no young man would like to be seen much in my company," but he did not think "that the hatred of Northerners was seriously bitter." I "could not personally complain," he wrote, "of inhospitality on the part of the elder soldier citizens. Yankee, military officer, and Bureau agent as I am, I was invited to breakfasts, dinners, teas, and picnics." Indeed, DeForest believed "that, if I had set my heart upon it, I could have made a footing in Greenville society." The major did become a member of "a literary club in Greenville; it had weekly essays and discussions and provided the public with lectures; it had a reading room also and a list of some thirty American and English periodicals." DeForest observed, contrary to many earlier and subsequent critics, that "Southern society has a considerable element which is bookish, if not literary." When DeForest left Greenville, the *Southern Enterprise* "cheerfully testif[ied] to his ability, impartiality and fidelity in discharging the perplexing duties of his office. . . . He has our personal good wishes and esteem." The friendly reception DeForest received was similar to the experiences of many Army officers stationed in the South during Reconstruction.[20]

DeForest himself complained of other federal officials in the area. There were the revenue officers, one of whom, he said, "stayed drunk from morning till night, falsified his returns, and solicited bribes." Another, a German of military bearing, "acted with energy and courage, even to the point of exceeding his instructions." With a mounted detail from Anderson, "he swept over Greenville and Pickens districts like a whirlwind of honest severity, confiscating stills by the hundred." He did "incalculable good," according to DeForest, "to a region in which whiskey was ruinously plentiful and corn at famine scarcity." But the man was also a "peculator, gobbling up horses and cattle for his own profit and pocketing considerations." Both men eventually were arrested, tried, and convicted.[21]

A major task of the Freedmen's Bureau was the negotiation of labor contracts between freedmen and white landowners. In 1867 DeForest approved 151 contracts for the labor of 322 people. At first, he proposed a system of weekly wages, but "this policy was above the general reach of Southern capital and beyond the usual circle of Southern ideas." Eventually the contracts evolved into a system of tenancy, already familiar to up country farmers. The workers agreed to furnish their labor for one-third of the crop, while the landowners furnished housing, seed, tools, and farm animals for two-thirds of the crop. The terms changed from time to time, but the system of sharecropping remained the same.[22]

Much more time consuming for DeForest was his role as ombudsman for the freedmen with the white population. If the complaint were minor, the major "usually persuaded the Negro, if possible, to drop it or to 'leave it out' to referees. Without a soldier under my command, and for months together having no garrison within forty miles, I could not execute judgment even if I could see to pronounce it." The civil courts had been restored in October 1866, and DeForest had no authority to act in property matters. Besides, he had a rather high opinion of local judges: "New York City would be fortunate if it could have justice dealt out as honestly and fairly as it was dealt out by the plain, homespun farmers who filled the squire-archates of Greenville, Pickens, and Anderson."[23]

The distribution of public welfare in Greenville was at first avoided by Major DeForest on the advice of Lieutenant Niles. "My predecessor," he wrote, "had counseled me against it, assuring me that I would be surrounded by hundreds of claimants and that I would be unable to distin-

guish between really needy persons and sturdy beggars." But the crop failure in 1866 made a bad situation even worse. The winter of 1867–1868
was unusually cold, and DeForest requisitioned clothes from the Bureau
office in Charleston. He received thirty greatcoats, forty blankets, thirty
pairs of trousers, seventy pairs of brogans, twenty women's skirts, and twenty
dresses, but the supply was soon exhausted. On March 30 Congress appropriated $1 million for poor relief in the South. With the help of local citi-
zens, DeForest eventually issued 1,325 bushels of corn and 1,000 pounds
of bacon to 1,666 individuals—813 whites, 853 blacks; 193 men, 411
women, and 1,062 children. He was quite aware of the problems of such
relief. "It alleviated a considerable amount of suffering," he wrote, "prevented possibly a few cases of starvation, seduced many thousands of people
from work, and fostered a spirit of idleness and beggary."[24]

One of the major duties of the bureau was the creation of schools. In
South Carolina, Reuben Tomlinson, the state superintendent of education
for the bureau, listed sixty-nine schools in operation in 1867 with forty
more for which he had no reports. Among these was the Elementary School
of Greenville. The leader in establishing the local school was Charles T.
Hopkins, whom DeForest described as "a full-blooded black from the low
country, for many years a voluntary exhorter among his people and eventually an ordained preacher of the Methodist [Episcopal] Church." A slave
for fifty years, Hopkins had nevertheless gained an education. He was "a
meek, amiable, judicious, virtuous, godly man, zealous for the good of the
freedmen."[25]

With the help of two assistants, Hopkins taught the first classes in the
summer of 1866 in the Goodlett House on Main Street that had been
seized by the federal government. They taught reading and spelling lessons
to between sixty and seventy pupils. The teachers received a modest salary
from the New York Freedmen's Union Association. When the hotel was
restored to its owner, Hopkins raised funds for a school building. He was
"so thoroughly trusted by the whites," wrote DeForest, "that he was able
to raise a subscription of two hundred and sixty dollars among the impov-
erished [white] citizens of Greenville."[26]

Hopkins purchased a wooden storehouse that had belonged to the
State Military Works, adjacent to the railroad on what is now Green Avenue, and secured a three-year lease on a lot belonging to Randall Croft on
Laurens Street. A mass meeting of freedmen moved the storehouse 2 miles
to the new location. Carpenters, masons, and plasterers went to work to
remodel the building. The entire cost was $560, and the Freedmen's Bu-
reau paid for the land and the building. There was no money left for sala-

ries, and the two assistants left. Hopkins eventually secured twenty-five dollars a month from the Methodist Freedmen's Aid Society. When the school reopened, two white teachers from the North had arrived to teach the higher classes.[27]

In 1866 the Bureau reported three teachers and 186 pupils. There were fifteen pupils up to the age of six and 170 between the ages of six and sixteen. The report listed sixteen of the pupils as free before the war; forty were of mixed blood and sixty were black. Most students were enrolled in the initial three grades; others were taught specialized subjects such as mental and practical arithmetic, geography, and writing. A second report listed two hundred pupils enrolled. DeForest reported that books were "gratuitously supplied by a leading New York publishing house. The discipline was admirable; the monotony of study was relieved by gleesome singing." Most of "the leading scholars were from one family, a dozen or so brothers, sisters, and cousins—all of mixed blood and mostly handsome."[28]

The school became a center of social life for the freedmen. Major DeForest attended an evening concert that consisted of tableaux performed on a stage at one end of the room "with a curtain of calico and an inner curtain of white gauze to assist the illusion." Among the scenes were "Pocahontas saving the life of Captain John Smith, the Goddess of Liberty, and a French family scene." A May Day celebration was organized at the school in 1867. The children, led by Postmaster James M. Allen and the teachers, formed a procession in the morning and marched down Falls Street and up Main Street to the army encampment. After a picnic, they returned to the school, accompanied by the military band. That evening the black citizens attended a supper and a dance at the Goodlett House.[29]

DeForest noted that within a year after the end of the Civil War the freedmen in Greenville, as in many other places, divided into two factions. "There was deep and abiding jealousy between the blacks and mulattoes," who formed distinct groups that crystallized into separate churches. When the mulattoes had a program to support their church, "the far more numerous blacks kept at a distance and made the show a pecuniary failure." When the mulattoes requested the use of the school for a fair to support their church, "some of the blacks intrigued against the request and were annoyed at my granting it." But when DeForest attended the fair, he noted that "the room was crowded, for the blacks had been unable to resist the temptations of a spectacle and had forgotten temporarily their jealousy of the mixed race." Still, the two groups vied for superiority, and the mulatto group, according to DeForest, had "more than its share of intelligence and of those qualities which go to the acquisition of property."[30]

Thomas C. Gower in
Confederate Uniform.
Courtesy of Blake Praytor.

Wilson Cooke, South Carolina
Photographic Collection,
Radical Legislature of 1868.
Courtesy of S.C. Department
of Archives and History.

The Reverend James R. Rosemond. Courtesy of the South Caroliniana Library, University of South Carolina.

Air Line Railroad Depot, West Washington Street, 1873. Courtesy of Greenville County Library.

Huguenot Cotton Mills, Greenville, 1895. Courtesy of Oscar Landing.

Henry P. Hammett. Courtesy of Joe
F. Jordan.

Ellison Adger Smyth. Courtesy
of E. Smyth McKissick III.

Mary Camilla Judson. Courtesy of
Furman University Library, Special
Collections.

Sheriff Perry Gilreath. Courtesy of
Greenville County Sheriff's Office.

Main Street, Greenville, 1890–1900. Courtesy of Oscar Landing.

Confederate Monument, shown in front of the Ottaray Hotel. Courtesy of Oscar Landing.

Chicora College, 1893–1915. Courtesy of Richard Sawyer.

Greenville Cotton Fields (undated). Courtesy of Richard Sawyer.

Load of Raw Cotton (undated). Courtesy of C. L. Baley Collection, Schomberg Institute, New York Public Library.

American Spinning Mill, 1894. Courtesy of Oscar Landing.

Poe Mill, 1895. Courtesy of Oscar Landing.

Mary Putnam Gridley. Courtesy of Choice McCoin from the collection of Mr. and Mrs. John Baker Cleveland.

Monaghan YMCA. Courtesy of Oscar Landing.

Confederate Hospital/Goodlett House. Courtesy of Southern Baptist Theological Seminary, Louisville, Kentucky.

View of Early Mill Village at American Spinning Mill. Courtesy of Roper
Mountain Science Center, Coxe Collection.

"Blease, the Working Man's Friend." Courtesy of Roper Mountain Science
Center, Coxe Collection.

Congressional Reconstruction

Meanwhile the radical Republicans in Congress were increasingly unhappy with the course of Reconstruction in the South. They opposed Andrew Johnson's lenient policy toward the Southern states and the attitudes of former Confederates who expected to rebuild the antebellum power structure. As a result, Congress refused to seat the Southern congressional delegations, including Benjamin Perry, a new senator from South Carolina. In March 1867 Congress passed its own Reconstruction plan over the president's veto: the new state governments were suspended, and the Southern states were divided into military districts, governed by the army. New constitutional conventions were called, freedmen were granted the right to vote, and whites who had held office prior to the war and supported the Confederacy were disfranchised.[31]

On March 21, 1867, Major General Daniel E. Sickles, commander of the Second Military District which included North and South Carolina, divided the state into eleven subdistricts. Post Number 8 included the Greenville, Pickens, and Anderson Districts. The headquarters was established at Anderson Courthouse with Lieutenant Colonel A. T. Smith in command.[32]

In preparation for the election of delegates to the 1868 state constitutional convention, the South Carolina Union Republican Party was organized. It was immediately clear that the party was in the hands of Northern whites and blacks who became known as carpetbaggers, Southern whites known as scalawags, and freedmen divided along color lines—mulattoes and blacks. At the meeting of the state Republican Party in Columbia on July 24, 1867, the Greenville District was represented by Wiley A. Bishop, identified in the press as a "Southern white man"; James M. Allen, a "Northern white man"; and Wilson Cooke. Cooke represented the district on the state Central Committee. All of them would play important roles in Greenville during the Reconstruction period.[33]

James M. Allen, born about 1823 in New York, was a stonecutter who moved to Greenville several years prior to the Civil War. A Republican, he served as postmaster of Greenville from 1866 to 1871 and as county treasurer from 1872 to 1873. Allen was also a state senator from 1868 to 1872. As a business person, he was awarded contracts to repair the State House, enlarge the state Lunatic Asylum, and construct the Columbia City Hall. Allen received the State House contract, though his was the highest bid. A suit was brought against him for inflating costs on the city hall. In 1873, as county treasurer, he defaulted on money due the state. He was convicted, sentenced to a year in the state penitentiary, and fined two thousand dollars. Benjamin Perry claimed Allen was unjustly convicted and wrote an open letter to Governor Franklin J. Moses, Jr., requesting a pardon. Allen was subsequently pardoned and he returned to the North.[34]

Wilson Cooke, a native of North Carolina, was "a very genteel mulatto" who said that he was the son of a former owner. Brought to Greenville by Vardry McBee, Cooke became a tanner and saved fifteen hundred dollars by working after hours. When McBee refused to allow Cooke to buy his freedom, he kept the money and eventually used it to begin life as a freedman. DeForest described Cooke as "the most notable colored man in his district, a person of remarkable intellect, information and high character." He owned a general merchandise store, a tannery, and considerable property. The 1870 census listed his wealth as five thousand dollars, and R. G. Dun and Company of New York indicated his wealth in 1876 as six thousand dollars. In 1881 Cooke was the largest black taxpayer in the county. He was a member of the state Constitutional Convention in 1868 and served in the state legislature from 1868 to 1870. In the legislature Cooke was described as "a quiet but efficient member." He was later appointed a jury commissioner by Governor Robert Scott and was a presidential elector in 1876 on the Republican ticket. He was one of the founders of the Methodist Episcopal Church in Greenville and later represented the South Carolina Conference in the 1880 General Conference of the denomination.[35]

An important arm of the Republican Party was the Union League of America, or the Loyal League, which had been organized in the North during the Civil War to support the Union cause. It spread to the Southern states following the war as a training ground for citizenship and to encourage membership in the Republican Party among freedmen. Meetings were held at night and consisted of a secret ritual and formal debates. Blacks traveled 10 or 20 miles to attend the meetings in Greenville. Former Confederates complained that officers of the Freedmen's Bureau were unduly involved in the activities of the league. DeForest did not agree: "As an officer, I wanted to see reconstruction furthered, and as a Republican I desired that the great party which had saved the Union should prosper." But in order to "prevent famine in my district, I felt it necessary to discourage the zeal of the freedmen for political gatherings." In Greenville the league met in the Bureau schoolhouse, and "there, too, were the great men and eloquent orators of the party and the secret insignia of the League. I remonstrated strenuously against the abuse and reduced the number of meetings in the schoolhouse to once a week."[36]

The *Southern Enterprise* reported a meeting of the Greenville District Union League Association in Marietta on July 20, 1867. J. M. Runion, a white Baptist minister, addressed the league on the proper relationship between the races. "You must never become proud and exalted under these great privileges [of citizenship]," he said. "They were never intended to elevate you above the white man. They were only intended to give you political rights equal with the whites, not *social.*"[37]

After the Civil War the Fourth of July became a holiday solely for freedmen. White citizens who had directed the celebrations in the antebellum period did not participate. In 1870, for example, the Greenville *Enterprise* reported that "a large procession of colored citizens marched through Main Street . . . preceded by the Neptune Fire Company in their neat uniforms, the colored band discoursing music for the occasion." After the parade, there was a celebration at the Academy Spring where a number of Republican officeholders spoke including the state comptroller-general, the governor's private secretary, Wilson Cooke, and James M. Allen. The assembly enjoyed a barbecue, and that night there was a public meeting in the courthouse. The "speakers exhibited a good deal of party bitterness, more than on any occasion for a year or two past in Greenville."[38]

The registration of voters and the election of delegates to the state Constitutional Convention took place in the summer and fall of 1867. On August 1 General Sickles designated the board of registrars for Greenville, and by the middle of October they had enrolled 2,253 whites and 1,310 blacks. The Republican Party held a meeting in the public square in front of the old courthouse on August 9. Wilson Cooke addressed the assembly of Freedmen and white citizens. He "avowed himself a Republican, with kind feelings for all, white and colored; advised all who voted, to vote for the best man, even if such were a former master," and said "he had been raised amongst respectable people, and had, while a slave, always tried to be an honest man."[39]

Benjamin Perry urged white citizens to vote against the calling of a constitutional convention, and on October 21 leaders representing "the white people of South Carolina" met in Columbia. Perry was elected one of the vice presidents of the group. To no avail, the members denounced the Reconstruction acts and urged citizens to vote against a state convention. Only 4,628 whites of 46,882 persons who had registered in the state voted, and a majority of those voted for a convention. In Greenville, Perry and George F. Townes spoke at a meeting at the courthouse on October 29 against the convention. The vote in the Greenville District was 319 against the convention and 1,211 for it.[40]

When the state Constitutional Convention of 1868 assembled in Charleston on January 14, the Greenville delegation consisted of James M. Allen, W. B. Johnson, and J. M. Runion (all white), and Wilson Cooke (who was black). Cooke had received the smallest number of votes of the four. The resulting constitution was an experiment in democracy for the Palmetto State. Universal manhood suffrage was adopted, property qualifications for office-holding were removed, and representation in the lower house of the General Assembly was apportioned on the basis of population alone. A single system of universal public education was provided, and militia units were not segregated by race. Divorce became legal in South Carolina for the first time. To satisfy the freedmen's desire for land, a commission was established to purchase land and resell it in small tracts. Local government was reformed. Henceforth judicial and election districts were called counties, and Greenville returned to its original designation as Greenville County. In each county there was a board of commissioners to care for the roads and disburse public funds. A probate court was also established in each county. Most county officers were elected by popular vote, and the counties were divided into school districts and townships.[41]

By March 17, 1869, the survey of the county into townships had been completed by William A. Hudson and published in the *Southern Enterprise*. There were sixteen townships of fairly equal size. From south to north they were Dunklin, Oak Lawn, Fairview, Grove, Austin, Gantt, Butler, Greenville, Chick Springs, Paris Mountain, O'Neall, Bates, Highland, Glassy Mountain, Saluda, and Cleveland.

The first divorce cases in Greenville under the new Constitution of 1868 came before Judge James L. Orr on May 21, 1869. Mary E. Cameron of Charleston, who was represented by Perry and Perry, was granted a divorce from Robert Cameron, whose "cruelty caused the separation and who went and married a lady in Philadelphia saying he was a widower." Two other cases were represented by Sullivan and Stokes. Amanda C. Linderman divorced Francis C. Linderman because he "had cruelly treated her and had married or taken up with another woman," and John W. Walker sued for divorce from Mary J. Walker "on the allegation of her desertion some six or eight years ago, and her violent temper and abuse which occasioned it, and the hopelessness of a reunion." Judge Orr "was not satisfied that he ought to grant the husband a divorce, but intimated to the counsel that he would further consider the case." He later "ruled against the divorce."[42]

The Constitution of 1868 created a state system of public schools. Dr. James Harrison was elected first commissioner of education for Greenville

County. One of his duties was to preside over the meetings of the Board of Examiners, which was entrusted with certifying teachers for the schools. In 1870 Greenville County reported seventy-eight schools with an enrollment of 2,060 white students and 597 black students. There were eighty-six teachers, of whom fifty-seven were men and twenty-nine women. Three years later there were ninety-one schools valued at $2,870, including forty-nine log buildings, forty-one frame, and one brick.[43]

The freedmen's school continued to operate in the town of Greenville. The *Southern Enterprise* reported on June 24, 1868, that the school enrolled 430 students. A recent public examination "was very creditable to both teachers and scholars," and Dr. Harrison "was present during a great part" of the proceedings. The newspaper indicated that the future of the school was in doubt once the Freedmen's Bureau was abolished, but it continued under the new state system. In a special ceremony on June 5, 1869, the school was renamed the Allen School, in honor of state Senator James M. Allen. Allen introduced the guests, including Justus K. Jillson, the state superintendent of education.[44]

The "Reverend Dr. Sears" of the George Peabody Fund arrived in Greenville on March 18, 1868, "to discuss a donation to help [the] education [of whites] in Greenville." On March 23 at a public meeting in the courthouse to discuss the proposal, Benjamin Perry presided, and A. A. Foster and Hamlin Beattie served as secretaries. The people present agreed to establish a primary school for young white men and women in the Old Male Academy, an academic department for young men at the Gaillard School, and one for young women at the Female College. The Peabody Fund agreed to contribute one thousand dollars, if the citizens of Greenville raised twenty-five hundred.[45]

The town council appointed a board of commissioners of public education with Ellison Capers, rector of Christ Church, as chair; Hamlin Beattie as secretary-treasurer; Basil Manly, Jr., Thomas Steen, W. H. Hovey, Henry C. Markley, J. A. David, E. T. Buist, and Leonard Williams as members. The matching funds were raised by April 15, 1868, and the primary school opened on April 13 in the old Male Academy building with ninety students. The teachers were Sophie C. Smith, Eliza Powell, and Eliza Bailey. The academic department opened in August. The young men attended Professor J. B. Patrick's School, which also served as the preparatory department of Furman University, located in the Gaillard School in West Greenville. The young women attended Professor Charles H. Judson's Female College. Unfortunately, the Peabody Fund suspended its grants to Greenville after two years.[46]

White Efforts at Redemption

Meanwhile, white Democrats began to organize throughout the state to stem the tide of Republican political control. A Greenville County Democratic Club was organized on March 24, 1868, with George F. Townes as chair and Benjamin F. Perry as the main speaker. Local clubs were organized in the antebellum militia beats. The Republicans countered with county-wide meetings in Greenville and invited candidates for state offices to speak. Republicans carried the new state constitution by a vote of 1,607 to 774. The editor of the *Southern Enterprise* estimated "that 1200 voters failed to vote and that most of these were whites."[47]

Both parties nominated slates for the state legislature. James Petigru Boyce was the Democratic candidate for the Senate, and A. C. Stepp, Absalom Blythe, J. K. Dickson, and Alexander McBee were candidates for the House. The entire Republican slate was elected—James M. Allen, state senator, and Samuel Tinsley, John B. Hyde, Wilson Cooke, and Wiley Bishop, members of the House. A. C. Stepp, a Baptist minister and a leading Democrat, complained that the reason "why Radicals aren't defeated" is that the Democrats "have too many conflicting interests and prejudices . . . to secure unity of action."[48]

Whatever differences existed among the local Democrats, they united before the election of county officials in June 1868. The Democrats were able to muster 1,471 votes to 1,307 for the Republicans. Of the eighteen precincts in Greenville County, the Democrats carried ten, and the Republicans eight. The victors in the county elections were S. J. Douthit, judge of probate; W. A. McDaniel, clerk of court; A. B. Vickers, sheriff; H. M. Smith, coroner; Dr. James Harrison, school commissioner; and Alexander McBee, J. H. Goodwin, and J. Dunklin Sullivan, county commissioners. On June 27 the Fairview Democratic Club met "and adopted a resolution thanking God for the Democratic victory in the county election." The club further declared that it "will rely on God's help in helping the National Democratic Party." Local Republicans, however, relied on the Republican governor to appoint certain officers of his own political persuasion—W. W. Robertson, county treasurer; James M. Runion, county auditor; and John Carman and W. C. Kellett, county assessors. In the Fourth Congressional District election in November, William D. Simpson of Laurens, the Democratic candidate, won in nine up country counties. Even though Congress refused to seat him, Greenville gave Simpson a Democratic majority of 273. Only Chester and Fairfield Counties in the district had Republican majorities. Republican domination of Greenville was not off to an auspicious beginning.[49]

The state legislature instituted a unique program of land reform by creating the South Carolina Land Commission. Through the issuing of state bonds, the commission purchased plantations, subdivided them into small tracts, and resold them to settlers. The state retained the title to the land until the full amount had been paid. According to the law, land was available to both races, but few whites participated in the program. In some instances the land office became a source of fraud. Benjamin F. Bates, a scalawag who was the grandson of William Bates, the Greenville textile pioneer, and a nephew of Mrs. Henry P. Hammett, sold the commission poor-quality land in Spartanburg County and used the high sale price to bribe the commissioner. In Greenville County the land commission purchased the Cleveland tract of 1,766 acres. In 1872 thirty-two persons held deeds or certificates of purchase for this land, but by 1880 only twenty-one of these were in residence. What made the situation in Greenville unique, however, was that in 1880 fourteen of the settlers were white and seven were black, the only occurrence of a white majority in a sample of fourteen counties throughout the state.[50]

More successful as a community of freedmen was the Kingdom of the Happy Land located in part in Greenville County. According to local tradition, a group of freedmen left Mississippi or Alabama after the Civil War in search of a new place to settle. They formed a wagon train and elected one of their own, Robert Montgomery, as king. They secured a tract near the town of Tuxedo, North Carolina, on the border of North and South Carolina, where Montgomery and his wife Luella lived in two cabins—one on either side of the property. The freedmen cleared the land, built homes, and planted crops of mostly corn and sweet potatoes. They raised hogs and wove their own cloth. The kingdom survived until after the death of Montgomery, when the community began to disintegrate. The land was sold in 1907.[51]

In the election of 1870 there was a statewide effort by Democrats and a group of reform Republicans to unite as the Union Reform Party. Regular Republicans denounced the effort as a Democratic ruse to seize political control. While fusion did not succeed on the state level, the white Democrats in Greenville made substantial gains in the election. At the county Republican Convention in Greenville on August 13, 1870, there was a serious split between a group led by white House member John B. Hyde and another led by black member Wilson Cooke. Hyde, who was chair of the convention, withdrew from the meeting with the delegation from his township. He reported to the *Southern Enterprise* that he would "take the stump against Wilson Cook[e]." By the time of the election in October there were two Republican tickets—the regular Republican ticket, which included Hyde for the legislature, and a Union Republican ticket, which included Cooke. While regular Republican James M. Allen was re-elected to the state Senate, the Union Reform candidates for the House were victorious—Leonard Williams, Stephen S. Crittenden, Washington Taylor, and Hewlitt Sullivan, all white Democrats. Two years later, in the election of 1872, a Democrat, Thomas Quinton Donaldson, was elected to the state Senate. Political Reconstruction was short-lived in Greenville County.[52]

Ku Klux Klan Activity

Greenville also escaped widespread terrorism by the Ku Klux Klan. Established in 1865 in Tennessee as a secret social club for white males, the Klan spread over the South as an instrument used by whites to terrorize freedmen. In March 1868 the Greenville *Southern Enterprise* took notice of the Klan as "something new" that was "striking terror into the Loyal Legions. Its object is announced to be Conservative and hostile to extreme Radicalism." The editor wrote that he "would not be surprised if the 'Ku Klux Klan' has a great run." On April 1 the newspaper carried this cryptic announcement: "Ku Klux Klan/MEET at the accustomed ground, at the usual hour, on Saturday night, April 4th, to administer justice. G. S. K. K. K." No such other notice appeared in the Greenville newspapers.[53]

There were reports of Klan activity in ten South Carolina counties during the election of 1870, and numerous incidents of terrorism occurred nearby in Spartanburg and Union. On September 2, 1871, the New York *Herald* reported that "the Ku Klux has been active in Spartanburg and Greenville and that near Greenville a lot of negroes had been whipped." The *Enterprise* took exception to the report: "We are satisfied that . . . inexcusable outrages and crime have occurred in some places in the State. . . . As to Greenville, it has been her boast that she is as quiet and orderly as any county in any State, North or South." Certainly no evidence of Klan activity in Greenville was submitted to the Joint Congressional Committee which held hearings in South Carolina in July 1871, nor was Greenville among the nine counties in the state in which President Ulysses S. Grant suspended the writ of habeas corpus because of Klan outrages.[54]

On April 28, 1875, the *Enterprise and Mountaineer* identified Walter Jackson and Ed Watson as "two more of the Clan [sic] . . . that infect this section of the county" who were arrested in Newberry and returned to jail in Greenville by "Capt. Green, who has exerted great vigilance in bringing these desperados to justice." Alexander McBee "has also been very active in the matter, and deserves much praise for his efforts to have these fellows brought to Greenville" for trial.[55]

Election of 1876

When antebellum white leaders sought to end Republican control of state government once and for all in 1876, Greenville County was in the forefront of the movement. The executive committee of the county Democratic Party met to establish its plans on January 11, under the leadership of attorney John W. Stokes. The committee resolved "to rout from position those who, by ignorance and corruption, have beggared the people and paralyzed their energies" and appointed committees in each township "whose duty it shall be to organize Democratic township clubs." The county convention on February 12 issued an appeal for support in the old Unionist and Republican areas of the county: "The reformation of the State Government and the expulsion of rogues from office, rise above all party considerations. In uniting for such a purpose, the Republicans may still adhere to their Republicanism . . . and the Democrats to their Democracy."[56]

After months of committee and convention meetings, the state Democratic Party nominated former Confederate General Wade Hampton III for governor. One Greenvillian was on the state ticket: Hugh Smith Thompson as a candidate for state superintendent of education. Former Confederate General Martin W. Gary of Edgefield organized a statewide campaign of terrorism and intimidation of Republican voters based on the Mississippi Plan of the previous year. Democratic rifle clubs organized all over the state, including the Independent Riflemen of Greenville which had forty-eight to fifty members. The officers were J. W. Gray, captain; Vardry McBee, Jr., first lieutenant; Samuel Mauldin, second lieutenant; Richard Thruston, third lieutenant; Dr. J. W. Vance, surgeon; and Ellison Capers, chaplain. The company ordered a stock of Enfield rifles, but they were never used, according to McBee.[57]

John P. Scruggs, the deputy federal marshal in Greenville, reported that the rifle club rode into Republican meetings and forced the leaders to divide the time with Democratic speakers. Scruggs himself attended a meeting at Poplar Springs, now Mauldin, where the rifle club demanded a division of the time. Republican Governor Daniel H. Chamberlain ordered the clubs to disband, but they reorganized under other names.[58]

White landowners applied economic pressure to their tenants to vote Democratic. On September 23, 1876, a Labor Reform Society formed in Paris Mountain Township with eighty members, led by William Choice. The group agreed that "we will not hereafter patronize, or employ, or rent our lands to those who vote the radical or Republican ticket." They further resolved "to act fairly and honestly with all our tenants, laborers and employees."[59]

The climax of the Democratic campaign in Greenville occurred on Thursday, September 7, 1876, with the visit of Wade Hampton III. From the fairground, near the present Park Place, a procession escorted Hampton to University Grove. Bands played, and military companies marched in order. The general shared his carriage with William D. Simpson of Laurens, the candidate for lieutenant governor, and former Governor Benjamin Perry. In the evening there was a torchlight procession and illumination. According to the *Enterprise and Mountaineer,* "mounted men pass in seemingly endless procession, and as they go, a thousand shouts at one time rend the air—sky rockets flying, Roman candles shooting, fire crackers bursting, and the city shaken with the loud mouthed cannon! To add to these, a thousand Chinese lanterns beautified every square."[60]

Prior to election day, Governor Chamberlain ordered a detachment of troops to Greenville to keep order. The night before the election Democratic supporters broke the stillness by anvil shooting all over the county. (Firing at anvils produced a sound like a cannon firing, according to Deputy Federal Marshal Scruggs.) There are two divergent accounts of what happened in Greenville on election day itself. One was given by Scruggs; the other by Vardry McBee, Jr. When the polls opened "in Greenville City," Scruggs reported that he saw "a great many democrats coming with the colored people up to vote. They would walk up beside them and take them by the arm, and tell them that they must vote the democratic ticket; and would say, 'If you don't vote this ticket' (showing the ticket to them) 'we can't give you any employment; you will have to look out for new homes; you will have to go to your republican friends and get homes.'" He named Vardry McBee, Jr., as one of those involved. Scruggs also reported that merchants, such as Thomas Davis, threatened them: "We can't supply you with any more provisions as we have done heretofore [under the lien law]."[61]

On the ground floor of the courthouse, where the polling place was located, whites crowded into the room so that Republican voters could not get in. When a known Democrat appeared, he was placed on a box at the window and was allowed to vote over the crowd. When black voters complained to Scruggs, he attempted to clear the polling place. Knives and pistols were drawn by whites and blacks. Scruggs then asked the federal troops to intervene, and the polling place was cleared. But "a great many of the colored people left" without voting.[62]

McBee, on the other hand, recounted that there was no fraud nor force used to get blacks to vote the Democratic ticket. The election "went off very quietly—perfectly so until about ten o'clock. Then there was some little disturbance, which was caused by a negro trying to get up to the polls or rushing in and catching hold of some colored man who was standing by the polls." Then, McBee said, he summoned the troops: "I wanted them to be there and see exactly what was going on."[63]

When the votes were counted, Greenville County went for Hampton and the Democratic ticket by a majority of 2,446 votes. On Friday, November 10, 1876, word reached Greenville from the state Democratic chair that Hampton was victorious. From five to seven o'clock in the evening, according to the *Enterprise and Mountaineer,* "old men and boys, colored men and youth, men on horse-back, little boys in wagons, each one shouting at the top of his voice, or ringing a bell, or beating a tin pan or drum, or hallooing for Hampton—presented a scene to the eye which is very hard to describe." There was a procession and cannon fire, and from a platform in front of the Mansion House Dr. James C. Furman, former Confederate General Ellison Capers, the rector of Christ Church, and Dr. James A. Broadus spoke to the assembled crowd.[64]

But the celebration was premature. Because of the widespread fraud, the outcome of the election was in doubt. Indeed, the election in South Carolina became crucial to the presidential race between Democrat Samuel J. Tilden and Republican Rutherford B. Hayes. Eventually a bargain was struck in Washington between Northern Republicans and Southern Democrats that resulted in Hayes's election to the White House and Wade Hampton's election as governor of the state. Wilson Cooke of Greenville, one of South Carolina's Republican presidential electors, cast his ballot for Hayes. In April 1877 the new president ordered the removal of the last federal troops in South Carolina. On April 11 the troops withdrew from the State House in Columbia, and Wade Hampton occupied the governor's office. In Greenville, according to the report in the *Enterprise and Mountaineer,* a crowd gathered "on the piazza of the Greenville Hotel" in West Greenville to celebrate. Several "stirring speeches" were delivered, the first by Dr. James C. Furman. The houses and stores on Pendleton and Augusta Streets were illuminated. A cannon was fired, rockets set off, and firecrackers exploded. "Thus was celebrated the reception of the news that Hampton was the acknowledged governor of South Carolina."[65]

Formation of Black Churches

Much more lasting than political power in the hands of the freedmen was the formation of black churches. The leading spirit in establishing black Methodism in Greenville was the Reverend James R. Rosemond. Known only as Jim when he was born on February 1, 1820, he was the son of

Abraham and Peggy, who were slaves of Waddy Thompson, Jr. When Jim was six, his parents were sent to Alabama with one of Thompson's sons. Jim remained in Greenville and went to live with a family of Methodists under whose influence he was baptized in 1844. The following year he became a class leader. In 1851 Jim gained permission of the church to travel with the black Baptist preacher, Gabriel Poole. On September 12, 1854, Osgood A. Darby, pastor of the Greenville Methodist Church, recommended Jim as a "Colored preacher." The next Sunday he preached his first sermon at Salem Church near the Saluda River. He preached regularly at Sharon Church in the Anderson District, and the congregation collected funds to purchase his freedom. His owner, Vardry McBee, agreed to the price of eight hundred dollars, but the church raised only five hundred dollars before the Civil War. According to his biographer, Jim received his "freedom without pay" through emancipation. A note in the church records of the Greenville Methodist Church in 1862 indicates that "among the colored people you will find a person, Jim McBee, who has been allowed to preach for the last ten or eleven years."[66]

After the Civil War Jim took the name James R. Rosemond, and he soon gathered a group of black Methodists in Greenville to establish a church—Frank Williamson, Wilson Cooke, Alexander Maxwell, and Wiley Pool. According to one account, the group first met at Cooke's house and agreed to pay the trustees of the Greenville Methodist Church one hundred dollars a year to meet there weekly. When Charles Hopkins arrived and opened the Freedmen's Bureau School, the black congregation began to meet at the schoolhouse. In 1866 T. Willard Lewis, one of the white leaders sent to South Carolina by the Methodist Episcopal Church, purchased for $225 a lot from Alexander McBee on the hill west of the residence of William Choice. According to the local newspaper, McBee "sold them the land for $50 less than it was worth," and by February 1869 a building seating five hundred people had been constructed by Cline & Gibbs. The church had three hundred members and held three services on Sundays and a prayer meeting on Thursday nights. Frank Williamson served as superintendent of the Sunday school. At first the church was known as Silver Hill, but in 1902 the name was changed to John Wesley Church.[67]

In January 1867 Rosemond entered the Baker Theological Institute in Charleston, a forerunner of Claflin College, and after one term he was ordained a deacon under the missionary rule. Rosemond returned to Greenville and began to establish churches—first St. Matthew near Chick Springs, and then St. Mark near Travelers Rest, where a camp meeting was held every year. Later he organized Wesley Chapel and Golden Grove and began to travel more widely into neighboring counties where he established more churches. In 1868 he was ordained an elder, and before his death in 1902 he established fifty churches from York to Oconee.[68]

Prior to the Civil War Rosemond had traveled with Gabriel Poole, who played a leading role in organizing black Baptist churches in Greenville. On February 1, 1842, the black members of the Greenville Baptist Church selected Gabriel, as he was then known, who was a slave belonging to the Cleveland family, to assist "Isaac, a servant of Dr. Thos. B. Williams" in overseeing the black members and to serve them communion. After refusing one black member a license to preach, the church granted a license to Gabriel on October 24, 1847.[69]

The ambiguous status of the black membership in the Greenville Baptist Church after the Civil War was indicated in November 25, 1867, when the congregation voted "to have the slaves (Negroes) put up in the body of the Church." Five months later, on April 21, 1868, Dr. James P. Boyce reported that sixty-five black members requested dismissal from the church to establish a separate congregation. Among those listed in the minutes, with family names for the first time, was Gabriel Poole. Perhaps the wealthiest member of the group was Dudley Talley, a drayman, whose wealth was listed in the 1870 census as $1,050. A month later sixteen other members joined the group.[70]

For five years the new congregation met in the basement of the Greenville Baptist Church and held services on Friday evenings and Sunday afternoons. In May 1867 Gabriel Poole was ordained "a regular Minister by the Elders of the Greenville Baptist Church" along with four black deacons. Dr. Basil Manly, Sr., "on a visit to Greenville, took part in the ordination." On Sunday, September 10, 1871, the first service was held in the new Springfield Baptist Church on McBee Avenue. According to the newspaper account, "some whites attended," and James P. Boyce preached the first sermon in the new house of worship. By October 1875 the Springfield church had about five hundred members.[71]

Black churches of other denominations were formed in Greenville in succeeding years. The *Enterprise* reported on June 15, 1870, that a black woman preacher from Virginia had delivered a sermon in the courthouse, "endeavoring to raise funds in the interest of the African Methodist Episcopal Church." Her efforts were not immediately successful, and in 1879 Allen Temple AME Church was organized by R. W. Sinclair. In January 1881 the congregation purchased the former Gaillard School in West Greenville for two thousand dollars. James T. Baker was pastor, and the trustees were J. M. Chiles, Joseph Plumer, E. G. Griffin, Sr., C. Ward, and

Dercy Watt. The stewards were William Brown, June Hanes, Henry Down, and James H. Chiles. S. Mattoon organized the Mattoon Presbyterian Church with seven members in 1878, and the Israel Metropolitan Colored (now Christian) Methodist Episcopal Church was founded in 1891 by A. J. Stinson.[72]

With the end of political Reconstruction in Greenville, the black schools and churches survived as the most tangible results of the effort of blacks to maintain their freedom and improve their status in the New South.

Notes

1. John William DeForest, *A Union Officer in the Reconstruction*, ed. James H. Croushore and David M. Potter (New Haven, Conn., 1948), 65, 73, 75.

2. Ibid., 199, 201.

3. Julian J. Petty, *The Growth and Distribution of Population in South Carolina* (Columbia, 1943, 1975), 227–28; *Southern Enterprise*, January 10, 1867.

4. Helen K. Hennig, *Great South Carolinians of a Later Date* (Chapel Hill, N.C., 1949), 167; Deed of Waddy Thompson to Caroline C. Jones, Waddy Thompson Papers, Library of Congress, Washington, D.C.; R. G. Dun Credit Ledgers, S.C., Greenville County, 132F, Baker Library, Harvard Graduate School of Business Administration, Cambridge, Mass.

5. R. G. Dun Ledgers, South Carolina, Greenville County, 132N; DeForest, *Union Officer*, 35.

6. *Mason Smith Family Letters, 1860–1868,* ed. Daniel E. Huger Smith et al. (Columbia, 1950), 207, 227; Greenville *Mountaineer*, May 14, 1884.

7. Greenville, *Mountaineer*, May 14, 1884; *Mason Smith Family Letters*, 207; Rosser H. Taylor, "Some Comments on the Diary of Alfred Taylor," *Furman University Bulletin* N.S. 11: 1, 16–17.

8. Francis B. Simkins and Robert H. Woody, *South Carolina During Reconstruction* (Chapel Hill, N.C., 1932, 1966), 29; *Mason Smith Family Letters*, 228; A. M. Moseley, *The Buncombe Street Story* (Greenville, 1965), 27.

9. *Mason Smith Family Letters*, 227.

10. Ibid., 242–43.

11. Lillian A. Kibler, *Benjamin F. Perry: South Carolina Unionist* (Durham, N.C., 1946), 379–81.

12. Ibid., 377–78, 384–86.

13. Ibid., 395–404.

14. Ibid., 405–10, 414–16.

15. Ibid., 420, 426; *Biographical Directory of the S.C. Senate, 1776–1985*, ed. N. Louise Bailey et al. (Columbia, 1986) 3: 1627–1628; *Biographical Directory of the S.C. House of Representatives*, ed. Walter B. Edgar and N. Louise Bailey (Columbia, 1974–1992) 1: 399.

16. RG 393. Pt. 4. 520. 1; 522. 4, 8. National Archives, Washington, D.C. The location of the camp is indicated in the *Southern Enterprise,* May 2, 1867.

17. RG 393. Pt. 4. 522, 31, 16; 520, 23.

18. Martin Abbott, *The Freedmen's Bureau in South Carolina, 1865–1872* (Chapel Hill, N.C., 1967), 4; RG 393. Pt. 4. 520, 4; DeForest, *Union Officer,* xix, 25, 49; *Southern Enterprise,* August 15, 1867; January 22, 1868. A recent assessment of DeForest is found in James F. Light, *John William DeForest* (New York, 1965).

19. DeForest, *Union Officer,* 25, 44.

20. Ibid., 46–47; *Southern Enterprise,* January 22, 1868. For the experience of the army in the South as a whole, see James E. Sefton, *The United States Army and Reconstruction, 1865–1877* (Baton Rouge, La., 1967).

21. DeForest, *Union Officer,* 43–44.

22. Ibid., 28–28. Typical labor contracts are reprinted in Abbott, *Freedmen's Bureau,* 141–43.

23. DeForest, *Union Officer,* 28–31.

24. Ibid., 69, 83, 88, 90.

25. Abbott, *Freedmen's Bureau,* 85–86; DeForest, *Union Officer,* 118.

26. DeForest, *Union Officer,* 119.

27. Ibid., 119–20.

28. Joseph D. Mathis, "Race Relations in Greenville, South Carolina, From 1865 Through 1900" (M.A. thesis, Atlanta University, 1971), 13 (copy in the S.C. Room, Greenville County Library); DeForest, *Union Officer,* 121.

29. *Southern Enterprise,* May 2, 1867.

30. DeForest, *Union Officer,* 124–6. In his study of leadership in Reconstruction, Thomas Holt discovered the same division in South Carolina as a whole; see Holt, *Black Over White: Negro Political Leadership in South Carolina* (Urbana, Ill., 1977).

31. Simkins and Woody, *S.C. During Reconstruction,* 64–71.

32. John S. Reynolds, *Reconstruction in South Carolina, 1865–1877* (Columbia, 1905, 1969), 64–65; *Southern Enterprise,* April 25, 1867.

33. Reynolds, *Reconstruction,* 59–60.

34. *Biographical Directory of the S.C. Senate* 1: 47–48; *Southern Enterprise,* June 18, 1873.

35. Charleston *Daily Republican,* February 7, 1870, cited in Holt, *White Over Black,* 48; A. V. Huff, Jr., "A History of South Carolina United Methodism" in *United Methodist Ministers in South Carolina,* ed. Morgan David Arant, Jr., and Nancy McCracken Arant (Columbia, 1984), 397–98; R. G. Dun and Co., 132P; Mathis, "Race Relations," 54, 56–57.

36. Simkins and Woody, *S.C. During Reconstruction,* 74–75; DeForest, *Union Officer,* 99–100.

37. *Southern Enterprise,* August 22, 1867.

38. Ibid., July 6, 1870. See also July 5, 1871.

39. The Greenville registrars were Solomon Jones, Absolom Johnson, William Robertson, John Dill, Samuel Tinsley, Henry Raines, A. W. Folger, William C. Kellett, James M. Allen, R. W. Goodard, John T. Cureton, and A. Cobb. *Southern Enterprise,* August 1, 15, October 9, 1867.

40. Kibler, *Perry,* 450, 460–61; *Southern Enterprise,* October 30, November 27, 1867.

41. Simkins and Woody, *S.C. During Reconstruction,* 97–102; *Southern Enterprise,* November 27, 1867; January 1, 1868. In the 1868 convention Cooke served on the Committee on the Legislative Part of the Constitution, Runion on the Executive Part, and Allen on the Miscellaneous Provisions. Allen also served on a special committee to investigate the financial condition of the state. *Southern Enterprise,* November 27, 1867; January 29, 1868.

42. *Southern Enterprise,* May 26, August 18, 1869.

43. Marion T. Anderson, "Some Highlights in the History of Education in Greenville County," *Proceedings and Papers of the Greenville County Historical Society* 5 (1971–1975): 18–19.

44. *Southern Enterprise,* June 24, 1868; June 9, 1869.

45. Ibid., March 25, 1868.

46. Ibid., April 1, 15, 29, July 8, August 5, 1868.

47. Ibid., April 22, 1, 8, 1868,

48. Ibid., April 1, May 13, 1868.

49. Ibid., June 10, July 1, November 11, 18, 1868.

50. Carol R. Bleser, *The Promised Land: The History of the South Carolina Land Commission, 1869–1890* (Columbia, 1969), 27–29, 48–53, 162, 167.

51. Sadie Smathers Patton, *The Kingdom of the Happy Land* (Hendersonville, N.C., n.d.); "The Kingdom of Happy Land" in *Echoes: Reflections of the Past,* Walt Cottingham, ed. (Travelers Rest, 1985–) 1 (1985): 15–24.

52. Greenville *Enterprise,* October 5, 26, 1870.

53. *Southern Enterprise,* March 18, April 1, 1868.

54. *Enterprise,* September 6, 1871; David Duncan Wallace, *South Carolina: A Short History, 1520–1948* (Chapel Hill, N.C., 1951, 1962), 580–82; 42d Congress, 2d Session, Report of the Joint Select Committee to Inquire into the Condition of Affairs in the Late Insurrectionary States. House Report 22: 1, 22.

55. *Enterprise and Mountaineer,* April 28, 1875.

56. Ibid., January 5, 12, 1876.

57. 44th Congress, 2d Session. South Carolina in 1876. Testimony as to the Denial of the Elective Franchise in South Carolina at the Elections of 1875 and 1876. Senate Misc. Doc. 48: 1, 556–57.

58. Senate Misc. Doc. 48: 1, 368.

59. *Enterprise and Mountaineer,* September 27, 1876.

60. Ibid., September 13, 1876.

61. Senate Misc. Doc. 48: 1, 370.

62. Ibid., 369–71.

63. Ibid., 1, 556–58; see also *Enterprise and Mountaineer,* November 8, 1876.

64. *Enterprise and Mountaineer,* November 15, 1876.

65. Ibid., April 4, 1877.

66. James A. Tolbert, *Christ in Black; or the Life and Times of Rev. James R. Rosemond* (Greenville, 1902), 3–25; A. M. Moseley, *The Buncombe Street Methodist Story* (Greenville, 1965), 27.

67. Tolbert, *Christ in Black,* 25–27; Mathis, "Race Relations," 38–40; *Southern Enterprise,* February 17, 1869.

68. Tolbert, *Christ in Black,* 28–32, 48.

69. Robert N. Daniel, *A Century of Progress, being the History of the First Baptist Church, Greenville, South Carolina* (Greenville, 1957), 12; *Southern Enterprise,* May 23, 1867.

70. Daniel, *Century,* 44–45; Mathis, "Race Relations," 35–36, 57.

71. *Enterprise,* September 13, 1871; Mathis, "Race Relations," 37; *History of Springfield Baptist Church* (Greenville, 1970); *Enterprise and Mountaineer,* October 6, 1875.

72. *Enterprise,* June 15, 1870; Crittenden, *Century Book,* 62; *Enterprise and Mountaineer,* January 5, 1881.

CHAPTER SEVEN

The Stirrings
of the New South

While the experience of Greenville during Reconstruction was fairly typical of much of the South, the region underwent a series of major economic shifts in the twenty-five years after the Civil War that basically altered life in the Southern Piedmont and set the region on a new course. Agriculturally, Greenville moved into the postbellum cotton kingdom, and the arrival of new railroad systems spawned both a growing urban center and a series of smaller towns. The textile industry brought even more wealth to Greenville and deeply affected the society and its culture.

The Coming of the Cotton Kingdom

Before the Civil War Greenville County grew primarily grain and subsistence crops. In 1860 the county produced only 2,682 bales of cotton, and in 1865 production declined 44 percent to 1,864. But by 1880 cotton production in Greenville had risen to 17,064 bales, and it increased to 28,482 bales in 1890. Since Greenville had been primarily a grain-producing region in the antebellum period, the cotton-corn ratio indicates what was happening even more graphically: 1:7 in 1850, 1:9 in 1870, and 20:3 in 1890. Clearly Greenville was becoming a part of the cotton kingdom in the postbellum period.[1]

By March 1868 the Greenville *Southern Enterprise* found it "strange . . . [that] there was never, as we believe, any regular cotton trade in Greenville, till the past Fall and Winter." Colonel John D. Ashmore "if we mistake not, is the first merchant who ever really advertised to deal in the article; and he is entitled to the credit of inaugurating a business in the Town, which has been of great advantage to it and to the country." In October 1870 the *Enterprise* noted that "our farmers are bringing their cotton to market, to a much greater extent than we expected." The next year Benjamin F. Perry commented on the change that was taking place: "For thirty years I never saw a bag of cotton brought here for sale. But thousands of bags have been sold during the past few years." The reasons that Greenville farmers were turning to cotton were not hard to find. The traditional market for grain was the droving trade, and that, according to Perry "in great measure, ceased" with the building of railroads. "The uplands are very much exhausted. Until recently, no farmer thought of manuring his lands." However, both guano and the new phosphate fertilizers were widely used. And there was a profit to be made in cotton. In August 1873 the *Rural Carolinian* showed how larger profits could be made from cotton than from corn: "Spite of old complications; spite of fraud, corruptions, unequal, unjust and burdensome taxation, and in spite of the inefficiency of labor, the farmers have prospered by and through the cotton plant." Alfred Taylor, for example, sold 1,225 pounds of cotton in Greenville in January 1871 for $153. By 1880 forty thousand bales of cotton were sold in the town. An agricultural revolution had occurred.[2]

The Immigration Effort

But agriculture required labor, and the population of Greenville County was not growing. Between 1860 and 1870 the total population had only grown 1.7 percent, and the black population had actually declined 1.7 percent. With many freedmen leaving, the answer to the labor shortage seemed to lie with European immigration. In 1865 the legislature created the office of commissioner of immigration, and John A. Wagener, a native of Germany who had established a German colony at Walhalla prior to the Civil War and later served as mayor of Charleston, was appointed to the position. He published an attractive pamphlet, *South Carolina: A Home for the Industrious Immigrant,* in English, German, and the Scandinavian languages. Greenville native and former Confederate General Matthew C. Butler made it very clear that European immigration would replace blacks with "an intelligent, thrifty, white population." The *Southern Enterprise* promised that "a good class of emigrants from the Northern States or Europe, can find wealth and happiness among us," especially Northern "men of improved ideas in farming and in the mechanic arts—the effect on our progress would be magical."[3]

On Sale Day in June 1868 a public meeting in Greenville promoted the cause of immigration, and two years later E. S. Irvine, Dr. Samuel S. Marshall, Leonard Williams, and Julius C. Smith represented Greenville at a state Immigration Convention in Charleston. By 1875 Greenville had its own Immigration Board composed of Samuel Stradley, T. C. Gower, James C. Furman, A. Miller, J. H. Whitner, William E. Earle, William Beattie, J. K. Vance, Samuel M. Green, George Heldman, and J. C. Hicks. Tilman R.

Gaines, a New York agent, opened an office in Greenville to promote immigration, but the effort yielded little. In 1880 there were only 7,686 people in South Carolina who were foreign-born, and by 1900 the number had dropped to 5,528.[4]

Furnishing Merchants and Towns

An important element of the new cotton economy was the furnishing merchant who operated a store in addition to farming or practicing a profession. Stores, operated by individuals such as Alfred Taylor at Chick Springs and W. P. Z. F. Neves at Mush Creek, were common in the antebellum period. But in 1866 the state legislature passed the first lien law in South Carolina which permitted any individual who advanced credit to a farmer for supplies to secure a prior lien on the resulting crop to the extent of the advances, provided that the lien was duly recorded. Many of the antebellum stores closed by the end of the Civil War, but others took their place. James H. Traynham, a farmer at Live Creek, was typical of the smaller general store owners. He was described in 1869 in the credit ratings of R. G. Dun and Company of New York as "an energetic young man of good character and highly deserving of credit in a small way." In April 1874 he had been "in business about eighteen months . . . now steady." James Anderson & Son had operated a general store at Pliny before the war, characterized by Dun as "good as gold," and their total worth in 1859 had been estimated at thirty-five thousand dollars. In 1865 it was calculated to be five thousand dollars; nevertheless, in 1866 the firm was characterized as "shrewd and businesslike." By 1873 it had bought out another store, Woodside & Anderson, and was "doing well." In 1883 Greenville County had twenty-six "towns and trading settlements." Alba, Batesville, Chick Springs, Fountain Inn, Gowensville, Lickville, Mush Creek, Pelham, Pliny and Hart had one store each. Bellvue, Fork Shoals, Lima, O'Neal, Plain, Sterling Grove, Taylors, and Highland Grove had two stores each. Huntersville, Marietta, Merrittsville, and Sandy Flat had three each, and Fairview had five stores.[5]

The rural merchants did not prosper as greatly as those in the towns. Though the total number of stores in the up country increased from 780 in 1854 to 1,693 in 1880, the number of business sites increased only 38 percent. After the Civil War, the town of Greenville resumed its position as the mercantile center of the county, and in 1869 it was officially incorporated as a city by the state legislature. By 1883 it boasted 149 stores. In a category all its own was William Beattie & Company. Originally F. F. Beattie

& Company, the firm had a total worth of "$75,000 at least" in 1859 and was rated by R. G. Dun "as good . . . as the Charleston Bank." After the Civil War Hamlin Beattie had two partners, William Holland and Charles D'Oyley, and Beattie himself was worth "at least $20,000." By 1875 the firm's estimated worth was between thirty and forty thousand dollars, and it had "a very heavy business." In 1878 Dun rated the company as "A No. 1."[6]

The Growth of Railroads

Crucial to the development of the city of Greenville and to the growth of towns in the county was the coming of new railroad lines. The Greenville and Columbia Railroad was in dreadful straits. The depot and office building in Columbia, 12 miles of track, five bridges, and several engines were all victims of war. In January 1866 a freshet had washed away some forty additional miles of track. When the railroad reopened on September 1, 1866, the federal government seized it but failed to reimburse the company. Then the railroad fell victim to the greed of a group of state officials. The railroad ring, as it was called, was led by "Honest John" Patterson, a Pennsylvania native who eventually bought one of South Carolina's seats in the U.S. Senate for forty thousand dollars. The ring hired former Governor James L. Orr to buy up the private holdings of stock, and in 1870 persuaded the legislature to create the Sinking Fund Commission to which they were appointed. The commission then sold to the ring the state's stock in the railroad, and the legislature transformed its lien on the company into a second mortgage. Then the company began to sell first mortgage bonds in New York. The ring had swindled the state out of its stock and its lien on the railroad, but it could not make a profit. In 1872 the Greenville and Columbia Railroad went into bankruptcy and in 1878 into receivership.[7]

By far the most important railroad construction in the postwar period was the building of the Atlanta and Charlotte Air Line Railway through the city and county of Greenville. In November 1868 the *Southern Enterprise* informed its readers that "the most favorable route strikes this State at a point which places Greenville precisely in the 'Air-Line' to Charlotte, North Carolina." On May 11, 1869, a public meeting at the courthouse considered the importance of the railroad to Greenville. The keynote speaker was W. P. Price, a member of the Georgia legislature who was interested in the Greenville route, and this committee was appointed to work with the officers of the railroad: William K. Easley (chair), Henry P. Hammett, Benjamin Perry, Alexander McBee, and William T. Shumate.[8]

After a flurry of meetings of various local groups the next year, the county commissioners agreed to issue two hundred thousand dollars in bonds "provided . . . that the railroad be constructed through the corporate limits of the City of Greenville." On June 25, 1870, a referendum approved the bond issue—1,618 votes to 324. Predictably, Greenville Township was overwhelmingly in favor (869 votes to 2) while the four townships that opposed the bond issue—Dunklin, Saluda, Highland, and Glassy Mountain—were far away from the proposed route. On July 2 the stockholders decided to build the railroad through Greenville. William K. Easley and Gabriel Cannon of Spartanburg were elected directors of the railroad, and Easley was named to the executive committee.[9]

The initial section of the railroad included Greenville and was constructed southwest from Charlotte. T. C. Gower and Otis P. Mills were awarded the contract to prepare the grade from Greenville to Enoree. According to the *Enterprise*, "W. T. Shumate and others have a big contract" as well. The site of the depot was located "in the Old Race Track, a little over three fourths of a mile from the public square." The Air Line Railroad was completed the week of April 16, 1873, and the city entertained guests from Charlotte and Spartanburg who rode the train into Greenville. A ball was held at the courthouse and "an Entertainment in the rooms of the Greenville City Club." On June 29 there was an excursion for the citizens of Greenville and Spartanburg to Charlotte. "Fully two hundred persons left Greenville, embracing all classes of citizens, including a number of ladies, who went to participate in the enjoyment and recreation of the occasion." In the summer of 1873 the new depot opened. Captain J. J. Roberson, who built similar depots in Charlotte and Spartanburg, constructed a building 30 feet by 60 feet, with a covered platform 8 feet wide surrounding it. W. T. Shumate became depot agent for the new railroad. John Westfield, who had purchased Prospect Hill and the surrounding land from the McBee family, extended Washington Street from the Presbyterian Church to the depot across what had once been Vardry McBee's corn field.[10]

When the gauge of the old North Carolina tracks from Charlotte to Greensboro was widened to that of the Air Line in the spring of 1875, the *Enterprise and Mountaineer* reported that "cars can now run through from Richmond, and beyond Richmond to New Orleans. . . . All the points along the Great Piedmont Air-Line route, are rejoicing at the establishment of the unbroken current of trade and travel. Greenville partakes in the rejoicing, and must, with other places, share largely in the benefits of the change. More travel and cheaper freights must be the consequences." A month later the newspaper was trumpeting the "destiny" of the railroad as "the thoroughfare of travel between the great cities of New York, Philadelphia, Baltimore, Washington, Richmond and New Orleans. . . . The travel and traffic on the road must now increase rapidly and become permanently large."[11]

The building of the Air Line stimulated interest in further rail connections. In September 1871 the *Enterprise* encouraged "a Railroad between Greenville and Asheville, for it would connect Greenville to Western North Carolina, East Tennessee, Kentucky, and the Northwest." On May 9, 1873, the incorporators of the Laurens and Asheville Railroad elected T. C. Gower as president, and William E. Earle, James P. Moore, James Birnie, and J. Mims Sullivan as local directors. But the Panic of 1873 discouraged further railroad construction. In 1881 William L. Mauldin of Greenville was elected president of the company and when the economy began to revive, the railroad prospered. On September 8, 1886, a year after Mauldin became lieutenant governor, the Laurens and Greenville Railroad made its first run.[12]

Though the railroads in Greenville did, in fact, provide the impetus for economic development after the Civil War, their survival was constantly in doubt. The economic base of the postwar South was too weak, and the nationwide Panic of 1873, caused by wild speculation in railroads and overexpansion in industry and agriculture, took its toll on Southern railroads. The Greenville *Enterprise and Mountaineer* was concerned about the future of the Air Line Railroad: "If the sale of the road can be staved off, the stock may become remunerative. Greenville and other places which have contributed to build it, will receive dividends. The bond creditors, however, may default all this, and hurry up a sale, if in their power, that they may secure a better bargain."[13]

In September 1873 the Atlanta and Richmond Air Line defaulted, and three years later the bondholders purchased the railroad at public auction in Atlanta and reorganized it as the Atlanta and Charlotte Air Line. In 1880 the Columbia and Greenville Railroad was acquired by the Richmond Terminal Company, and the next year the railroad was leased to the Richmond and Danville. Then, in 1882, the two Virginia companies merged. But the relative prosperity of the 1880s in the South attracted Northern capital, and by 1893 Greenville's two major railroads became part of the Southern Railway system controlled by J. P. Morgan of New York. Meanwhile, in the decade that followed, the Laurens and Greenville became part of yet another system—the Atlantic Coast Line Company formed in Connecticut in 1889. Railroads in the South had thus passed out of local ownership and were controlled by northeastern financiers. The economic reconstruction of the South, unlike its political equivalent, left the region a colony of the North.[14]

Yet the dream of a railroad connecting Greenville with Asheville did not die. In 1887 the Carolina, Knoxville, and Western Railway Company was formed. Public meetings were held at the Reedy River Baptist Church, Marietta, Merrittsville, Dickey, Sandy Flat, Ware Place, Fountain Inn, Walkersville, and Greenville to arouse interest in the new line. Only a little money was raised, and track was laid from Greenville north along the banks of the Reedy River. In 1892 the railroad reached Marietta, and in 1908 it reached Potts' Cove, which was renamed River Falls—but, it went no further. The short line was soon nicknamed the Swamp Rabbit.[15]

Towns Along the Railroads

The building of the railroads gave rise to a number of new towns in Greenville County. Twelve miles east of the city of Greenville the Air Line Railroad established a flag station on the two-hundred-acre farm Manning Greer had purchased from William Thackston in 1868. Once the railroad route had been surveyed and the station established, Greer sold his property to William T. Shumate. The new landowner laid off town lots, but the name of the station remained Greer. The town of Greer was incorporated in 1875, and Hughes and Bomar soon opened a general store, followed by D. D. Davenport. Dr. H. V. Westmoreland had already established a practice in the community about 1870, and in 1883 Dr. Benjamin F. Few opened an office as well. The first school in the village was taught by Sallie Cannon, and in 1900 the Bank of Greer opened its doors.[16]

Fountain Inn, Simpsonville, and Mauldin were located on the road from Greenville to Laurens, sometimes called the Old Stage Road. Prior to the Civil War, Fountain Inn was a stagecoach stop, and a post office opened there in 1832. After the war Noah Cannon purchased the present site of the town and opened a store. His son, James A. Cannon, became a partner until his father moved to Greer and left the son to operate it. In 1884 a railroad station was established on the Greenville and Laurens line, and James I. West purchased a half interest in the Cannon property. Cannon and West divided the land near the station into sixty-five lots, and the new town of Fountain Inn was chartered. A Baptist congregation had been organized in 1880, and Methodist and Presbyterian churches were founded in 1887. In 1897 a group of local business people established the Fountain Inn Cotton mill which began operation the next year, and the growth of the town was insured.[17]

Simpsonville took its name from Peter Simpson who moved into the area from the Laurens District in 1836. Before his death in 1847 he operated a blacksmith shop, as well as a farm. Prior to the Civil War Silas Gilbert operated a store at the fork of the Old Stage and the Georgia roads. The first post office in the area was known as Plain. About 1879 S. J. Wilson purchased 200 acres and operated a farm and a store. When the railroad was built in 1886, Wilson divided his land along the railroad into lots and built a brick store. The town began to grow after 1907 when Edward F. Woodside organized the Simpsonville Cotton Mill.[18]

Mauldin was known originally as Butler's Crossroads. It was named for Willis Butler who bought the site of the present town in 1853 from James McDaniel, who had served as quartermaster-general in the War of 1812 and later as sheriff of the Greenville District. In 1869 Jacob B. Hyde donated a tract of land near the crossroads to the Methodists for the Poplar Springs Church and School. Surveyor Paul B. Kyzer laid off twenty-one lots near the proposed railroad depot in 1884. When the railroad was built in 1886, the name of the community was changed to Mauldin in honor of William L. Mauldin—president of the railroad from 1881 to 1885 and then lieutenant governor of South Carolina. The Mauldin post office opened the following year. Riley E. Cox served as postmaster, as well as depot agent.[19]

The Transformation of the Textile Industry

A major component of the postwar economy of Greenville was the textile industry, which had its roots in the antebellum period. At the end of the Civil War there were only three mills in operation in the Greenville District. In 1865 Lester and Brothers operated a yarn mill with one thousand spindles on the Enoree River. The partners, according to R. G. Dun and Company, were worth one hundred thousand dollars. In 1868 they were "making money," but by the end of 1872 the company was insolvent, and the mill was purchased by E. H. Bobo and Company. Meanwhile, in 1870, the Lesters had bought the Buena Vista Mill at Batesville, which manufactured shirting, sheeting, and yarn. The mill's stock increased in value from twenty thousand dollars in 1870 to thirty-five thousand dollars in 1876. The McBee Mill at Conestee was operating fifteen hundred spindles and twenty-four looms and made jeans and shirting. The mill, originally built by Vardry McBee, was worth one hundred thousand dollars and was owned by John W. Grady, O. Hawthorne, and William H. Perry. By 1870 the mill was in the hands of Alexander and Vardry McBee, Jr. An additional yarn mill was built at Fork Shoals by the Sullivan Manufacturing Company in 1870 with Dr. James M. W. Sullivan of Laurens as president and William Perry and Captain G. Sullivan of Laurens as directors.[20]

But the major promoter of the post-Civil War textile movement in Greenville was Henry Pinckney Hammett. Born in 1822 on the family farm on Hammett's Bridge Road, 12 miles east of the village of Greenville, he became a teacher and later a partner in a country store. In 1848, after his marriage to Jane Bates, the daughter of textile mill owner William Bates, Hammett became a partner in the Batesville Mill. In 1862 the Batesville Company, with an eye toward relocation and modernization, purchased 225 acres of land at Garrison's Shoals on the Saluda River near the Greenville and Columbia Railroad. The following year the Batesville Mill was sold to the George W. Williams Company of Charleston, and Hammett moved to Greenville. After the Civil War Hammett was elected to the state legislature, and in 1866 he became president of the Greenville and Columbia Railroad. Hammett had a commanding presence. He was a man of huge size, with a bald head and a smooth-shaven face. He rode in a buggy especially made to hold him. By February 1873 Hammett gathered a group of local business leaders interested in building "a Cotton Factory and Wheat and Corn Mills" on the Saluda River. The group was composed of Hamlin Beattie, James Birnie, Alexander McBee, and T. C. Gower.[21]

Within a month Hammett had secured one hundred thousand dollars in subscriptions for the stock of his proposed company, and on April 30, 1873, the subscribers met at the courthouse to organize the Piedmont Manufacturing Company. Hammett was elected president, and the directors included J. Eli Gregg, Wesley C. Norwood, J. N. Martin, Hamlin Beattie, James Birnie, T. C. Gower, and Alexander McBee. In May 1873 Hammett wrote George C. Whiten of the Whiten Machine Company in Massachusetts for an estimate on the price of textile machinery. Receiving a figure of forty-one thousand dollars, Hammett placed an order, but the Panic of 1873 intervened. According to Colonel James L. Orr in his history of the mill, "scarcely had the work commenced when the panic of 1873 came on which crushed all hope, strangled all enterprise, and work was suspended. Many of the subscribers refused to pay the installments and others sold out at any price they could get for the stock." Hammett canceled the order for the Whiten machinery.[22]

In February 1875 the *Enterprise and Mountaineer* announced joyfully that there were "large additional subscriptions" for stock, including "the well known firm of Pelzer, Rodgers & Company, of Charleston." By spring Hammett was able to reorder the textile machinery at the reduced price of thirty-one thousand dollars. Construction resumed, and the mill machinery was shipped to Greenville in August. It consisted of five thousand spindles and 112 looms. Local workers were hired by mill Superintendent J. W. Rounds, and the machinery was started on March 20, 1876. According to Colonel Orr, "everyone from the superintendent down were born in this Piedmont section and learned his business in this mill." Hammett had not paid for the machinery, and in July 1877 he paid Whiten twenty-five thousand dollars in cash and offered him sixteen thousand dollars in stock for which Whiten paid eight thousand dollars. Hammett immediately ordered seventy-eight hundred additional spindles and 112 more looms.[23]

The Piedmont Manufacturing Company not only built the mill, but it also created the surrounding mill village. In 1883 Piedmont was described as "a flourishing manufacturing town" with a population of 1,150. The company constructed a two-story schoolhouse that would accommodate one hundred students; the upper floor was used as a town hall and meeting place. A Union Church seating four hundred people was built for eighteen hundred dollars. The town also boasted a hotel. When Henry Hammett died in 1892, Piedmont was one of the leading mills in the region—operating forty-seven thousand spindles and thirteen hundred looms. The mill purchased twenty-five thousand bales of cotton that year. Three thousand people lived in the mill village, thirteen hundred of whom worked in the mill.[24]

Northern capital was drawn into Greenville textiles through machinery sales and marketing, although Whiten became a stockholder in the Piedmont company somewhat unwillingly. Woodward, Baldwin and Company of Baltimore and New York was a leading commission house and became the selling agent for the Piedmont Manufacturing Company. Soon after 1900 the company did the marketing for twenty-one mills in South Carolina. More directly, Oscar H. Sampson, George L. Hall, and George Putnam, who operated a cotton commission house in Boston, built the Camperdown Mill on the Reedy River within the city of Greenville.[25]

On January 9, 1874, Vardry and Alexander McBee leased to Sampson, Hall & Company the old McBee Mill on the Reedy River and its waterpower. The McBees agreed to build a new floor in the lower story of the building and remove the mill stones and grinding equipment. Sampson, Hall & Company purchased waterpowered spinning machinery from Fales and Jenks of Philadelphia, the same company from which William Gregg had purchased equipment for the Graniteville Mill prior to the Civil War. A factory house was constructed near the dam at the Main Street ford of the river where presumably a number of workers lived. George Putnam became the mill's superintendent.[26]

On May 7, 1875, Sampson, Hall & Company contracted with the McBees for an extension of their lease, and the McBees agreed to build a brick mill (225 feet by 64 feet) on the site of the Cagle Planing Mill across the Reedy. The new mill would be two stories, each 15 feet high, with a tower for staircases. The McBees also agreed to build a picker house (40 feet by 50 feet). The agreement was made "in contemplation of the formation of a joint stock company."[27]

The Camperdown Mills Company was organized in January 1876 at the county courthouse. The officers were Oscar H. Sampson, president; Hamlin Beattie, vice president; George L. Hall, treasurer; and Alexander McBee, secretary. The board of directors was composed of Sampson, Hall, Thomas M. Cox, H. C. Markley, Beattie, George Putnam, and McBee. The initial stock subscription totaled $150,000, and by the end of the year it increased to $168,000. But the Camperdown Mills suffered two fires within a year. On April 28, 1875, the *Enterprise and Mountaineer* reported that a fire had started in the picker room and did damage estimated at between five hundred and six hundred dollars. On March 8, 1876, a second fire damaged cotton and the batting worth eight hundred dollars. The future of the Camperdown Mills did not seem bright. George Putnam left the company and purchased the Batesville Mill at auction in 1879. By 1885 the company was insolvent, and in August it was sold to Henry P. Hammett who reorganized it as the Camperdown Cotton Mills.[28]

Another source of capital for the textile industry lay in the South Carolina low country. After the Civil War, Charleston became a commercial backwater. Even the phosphate fertilizer boom did not substantially improve its economy. By 1880 business leaders were beginning to invest heavily in the textile industry in the up country. Among them was Ellison Adger Smyth who was born in Charleston in 1847, the son of a Presbyterian minister. As a child his ambition was "to be a rich man." He served in the Confederate army, and after the war he went to work with his uncle in the family wholesale hardware business—J. E. Adger & Company. But the business closed, and Smyth decided to move to the Piedmont and try his hand at textiles. His associate was Francis J. Pelzer, a partner in Charleston's leading factorage firm and a phosphate producer. Originally Smyth proposed to Pelzer that they purchase the yarn mill at Fork Shoals, but Pelzer warned that it was too far from the railroad. So in 1880 Smyth, Pelzer, and William Lebby organized the Pelzer Manufacturing Company; Smyth became president and treasurer. He held both offices until the mill was sold forty-three years later. The initial issue of stock amounted to four hundred thousand dollars. The mill they built at Pelzer in Anderson County on the Saluda River was waterpowered and operated ten thousand spindles. In 1881 Smyth moved to Pelzer so he could oversee the construction, but in 1886 he relocated to Greenville, where he remained, except for a brief period, until he retired to Flat Rock, North Carolina, in 1925.[29]

The speed with which "mill fever" resulted in the formation of a cotton mill is exemplified by the Huguenot Mill, built in 1882. According to the Baltimore *Journal of Commerce and Manufacturing Record*, "the company that erected the Huguenot Mill at Greenville formed February 10, 1881; a charter was obtained March 13; a lot bought in the heart of the city and the first brick laid March 23, the last June 2; by July 22 the machinery was in place and the mill weaving cloth."[30]

The Huguenot Mill was also an example of advanced planning and design. Organized by Charles E. Graham and Charles H. Lanneau, the company had a capital of $150,000. Lanneau, the superintendent, was a self-taught miller who had been treasurer of the Reedy River Mill at Conestee. The Huguenot Mill, a two-story brick building incorporating the latest fireproof techniques, was located on the Reedy River adjacent to the carriage factory. But its two hundred looms, built by Wood of Philadelphia, were not driven by waterpower but by an eighty horsepower engine. The mill manufactured plaids, cottonades, and gingham—the only such mill in South Carolina. It originally employed 120 operatives. By 1893 the mill had 2,750 spindles and employed 175 people.[31]

In 1882 Greenville County had seven textile mills in operation, one more than Spartanburg—its nearest competitor in the state. The largest mill was Piedmont, then capitalized at five hundred thousand dollars, with 550 employees. The second largest mill was the Camperdown Mill which was capitalized at $168,500 with 350 employees. The third was the Huguenot Mill which was capitalized at sixty thousand dollars with 130 employees. Reedy River at Conestee, Fork Shoals, Pelham, and Batesville were smaller operations, with capital ranging from forty thousand to fifty thousand dollars and between thirty and seventy-five workers. Piedmont, Reedy River, and Pelham operated solely with the use of waterpower, while Huguenot was the first mill that operated totally by steam. Camperdown, Fork Shoals, and Batesville used both water and steam. To be sure, the textile industry in Greenville was still in its infancy, with $906,000 in total capital and employing 1,225 people. However, in the seventeen years after 1865—with the development of cotton, the growth of the railroad, and the rise of textiles—Greenville County had catapulted into the New South.[32]

The New South

The emergence of the New South economy did not escape the notice of the editor of the *Enterprise and Mountaineer*. "Under the old system," he wrote in 1875, "the South could afford to devote its resources to agriculture and the raising of slaves, and grow rich and powerful. . . . But our present condition forces the necessity of manufacturing so strongly upon the judgment, that no business man will deny its advantages." Manufacturing will "bring capital, population and wealth into the country, and infuse a new life and energy into our people, which they have never before experienced."[33]

There could be no mistake about the primary motive of industrialization. In 1881 Henry P. Hammett made an address on "Southern Cotton Mills" to the joint meeting of the state Agricultural and Mechanical Society and the Grange. "The main object in building a mill by those who put their money into it," he told his audience, "is the prospective profits upon the investments; there may be laudable desire to give employment to the people and benefit the community—the latter is always incidental and secondary, if at all." Even among members of the press who wrote of "philanthropic" motives, Hammett said, they know that "nobody is going to invest money, as he pays taxes, for the public benefit."[34]

The Emergence of the Mill Worker

Industrialization did not come without a price. By 1882 South Carolina had the beginnings of a new social and economic class—the mill worker. Already the state Department of Agriculture reported 4,467 mill hands. There were 1,245 in Greenville County alone, 28 percent of the total. Caught in the poverty of the tenant system, these white farmers flocked with their families into the new mills to work eleven to twelve hours a day, six days a week. Disciplined by the mill whistle, men, women, and children worked side by side in the mills and lived in boarding houses or villages isolated from the rest of society. Wages were low. In 1890 male loom fixers averaged 13.3 cents an hour; female spinners, 3 cents; male weavers, 6.9 cents; and female weavers, 6.2 cents. But at the end of the week they had something they had never known before—payment in cash or scrip. Some mill workers realized their new status and attempted to improve their lot by unionization. Their efforts were met by an immediate and hostile response from the mill owners. This angry reaction set the attitude of Southern mill executives toward organized labor for the next century.[35]

The first labor union to appear in the mills was the Knights of Labor. In 1886 this national union began to recruit mill workers in the upper Piedmont whose wages had been cut in the aftermath of the depression of 1883. In April 1886 Ellison Smyth informed Henry Hammett of signs of labor organization at Pelzer. Smyth was alarmed and proposed the formation of a manufacturers' group to challenge the union. Hammett urged caution, but in March he had already ordered his mill superintendents at Piedmont and Camperdown to "nip in the bud" the "Yankee inspired" unions by firing any operatives involved. Hammett's fear of unions was irrational. When the Knights of Labor ordered a strike in the mills in Augusta, Georgia, Hammett offered the mill executives there his support. He advised them to "crush the Knights beyond resurrection." They were a greater threat to the mills, he said, than "the depression of the last two or three years, or any threat in the last twenty years." Ironically, the union organizer was the son of the Reverend E. J. Meynardie, Hammett's pastor at the Methodist Church in Greenville.[36]

In October 1886 the Knights began to organize the workers at Piedmont and Pelzer. Hammett ordered the Piedmont superintendent to discharge and not to rehire anyone who joined the Knights. The mill was to be closed, if there were any further disturbance. When a local union was formed at Pelzer, Smyth reported that the organizer "got frightened and ran away." In 1888 the Knights stirred up a small disturbance in Greenville, but they left the county and never returned. Despite the failure of the Knights of Labor in Greenville, they had proved that mill workers would respond. Management, on the other hand, became convinced that a strong anti-union stand was quite effective. They would take strong action again, if the occasion demanded it.[37]

The townspeople in Greenville were well aware of the threat of radicalism that unionization might bring. At a meeting in the Baptist church in 1888, W. J. Thackston warned that in "the great northwest with millions of gold and its brilliant cities . . . [is] dimly outlined in the gathering mists that enshroud the future the blood-dyed form of Anarchy, ready at any moment to swoop down and destroy all that this nation holds dear." In the East "under the very statue of Liberty, thriving, growing, increasing, is found a spirit of communism that unless checked will destroy this government." But in "the sunny Palmetto groves of Carolina," there is "no anarchy; no communism. Scan the horizon east and west. Surely you will not find any grim threat[e]ner of the nation." The South was free from such upheaval and intended to maintain that freedom.[38]

In 1890 the specter of unionization lifted its head again briefly, this time in the city of Greenville. A carpenters' union was organized, and in June and July carpenters working at Jacob W. Cagle's fertilizer factory went on strike. They demanded a ten-hour day at their current wages, and "the demand was conceded." Business person William T. Shumate announced that he wanted no workers who belonged to the union, and they should seek work elsewhere. According to the *Enterprise and Mountaineer,* "more building and repairing is going on in Greenville than for years past. Workmen can get all the work they want." Two weeks later the same newspaper observed that "colored waiters seem[ed] to be on a strike. The Exchange Hotel and the Hotel Altamont have recently been inconvenienced by a suspension of labor."[39]

The City of Greenville

The three and a half decades between 1865 and 1900 saw the transformation of the town of Greenville into a city. Legally, the charter of the town was amended in 1869 to make Greenville "a city, with the usual powers, rights and corporate privileges appertaining." The population had tripled between 1820 and 1860. It grew from five hundred inhabitants to 1,518. But from 1860 to 1900 the population grew from 1,518 to 11,857. By 1883 there was a building boom under way. A description published by the state Department of Agriculture reported that "there were in the course of erection sixteen residences, seven stores, one warehouse, one stable, one large church, and a musical conservatory three stories high, and including twenty-one rooms." Symbolizing the growth of the city was the construction of a City Hall in 1879 under the leadership of Mayor Samuel A. Townes. Located on the corner of Laurens and McBee Avenues, its tower rose three or four stories with an alarm bell at the top.[40]

Banking

Central to the development of a modern urban center were banking services which had been provided in antebellum Greenville first by merchants, such as Jeremiah Cleveland, and later by local agents of banks in other towns, such as Newberry and Charleston. In December 1871 Hamlin Beattie, who had been the agent of the Bank of Charleston prior to the Civil War, filed a request with the U.S. comptroller of the currency to establish a national bank in Greenville with a guaranteed capital of forty thousand dollars. On January 30, 1872, the application was approved, and Greenville became the site of the first national bank in South Carolina. Hamlin Beattie was president, and the board of directors included M. J. Bearden, Henry P. Hammett, James Birnie, Alexander McBee, A. B. Stephens, William Beattie, James Petigru Boyce, J. J. Blackwood, James Sullivan, and R. L. Oates of Charlotte. On March 23 the *Enterprise and Mountaineer* announced that "the National Bank, Hamlin Beattie, president, is open for the transaction of business in its office in the Goodlett

House, at the corner of Washington and Main Street." By the end of the year the capital stock had been increased to one hundred thousand dollars.[41]

Soon the National Bank of Greenville was joined by two other banks. The People's Bank opened in 1887 in the Ferguson and Miller Building at Main and Washington Streets. Frank Hammond was president, and the board included James L. Orr, Jr., James A. Hoyt, E. H. Fulenweider, Otis P. Mills, H. F. Means, W. M. Hagood, and Francis W. Poe. The Greenville Savings Bank opened in 1888 with J. Wilkins Norwood, president, and directors H. C. Markley, James L. Orr, Jr., Theodore B. Hayne, William C. Cleveland, Thomas Q. Donaldson, James H. Maxwell, Julius H. Heyward, and John Slattery. In one year its capitalization grew from twenty-five thousand to fifty thousand dollars.[42]

The Board of Trade and Cotton Exchange

In 1879 the business elite of Greenville created the Board of Trade and Cotton Exchange to promote the city as a center of commerce. On October 6 a "large assemblage" of business leaders gathered in the old courthouse, where they elected William Beattie as president, and a board of directors consisting of Samuel Stradley, Otis P. Mills, Julius C. Smith, A. S. Duncan, T. W. Davis, and Mayor Samuel A. Townes. The aim of the Board of Trade, Beattie said, was to make Greenville a big city. In order to achieve that goal, the board needed to secure lower freight rates on Southern railroads, encourage residents to patronize local businesses, and establish cotton brokerage firms in the city. From the beginning, the board was known locally as the Chamber of Commerce. After Beattie's death in 1882, the chamber languished, but it was revived by his nephew in 1886 and survived until 1893. When local farmers complained that the mills in Greenville paid less for cotton than those in Easley, Pelham, and Greer, the chamber raised thirty-five hundred dollars in 1890 to buy cotton from the farmers at a higher price and arranged better prices with local mill owners. A new generation of leadership organized the Young Business Men's League in 1894, led by Lewis W. Parker and Alester G. Furman. Not until 1901 was a new chamber organized.[43]

A Bridge Over the Reedy River and the Street Railways

Before 1870 there had been only a foot bridge across the Reedy River. That year T. C. Gower ran for mayor on a platform promoting the construction of a bridge. He was elected, and the city council awarded the contract for the construction of a bridge below McBee's old saw mill to L. W. Watson and Thomas H. Paris for $450. It was known as the Gower Bridge and survived until 1890 when it was replaced by "a new iron bridge" constructed by the Southern Bridge Company.[44]

When the Air Line Railroad was constructed in 1873, Gower saw the need for connecting the two depots in Greenville with a street railway system. There were no paved streets, and in wet weather heavily loaded wagons mired in the mud. On August 2, 1876, the *Enterprise and Mountaineer* reported that the city council had granted to the Street Railway Company of Greenville the "exclusive privilege of using the streets of Greenville for the purpose of running street cars." The officers of the company were Gower, president; William L. Mauldin, secretary-treasurer; and William C. Cleveland, William T. Shumate, W. A. Hudson, J. T. Steele, and J. C. Sage, directors. The tracks for the horse-drawn railway ran from the Greenville and Columbia depot on Augusta Street, across the Reedy River bridge, and up Main Street to Washington. The tracks turned west on Washington Street and ended at the Air Line depot. Gower purchased two passenger cars, three flat cars for freight, and a "tallaho" for special excursions. Gower & Reilly and a number of other firms used the street railway to deliver goods from their warehouses to local merchants. In 1890 the street railway extended its tracks to the fertilizer factory and the Laurens depot.[45]

In 1881 the Richmond and Danville Railroad purchased both the Greenville and Columbia and the Air Line railroads and connected the two older lines. The depot on West Washington Street became the principal freight terminal. After T. C. Gower's death in 1894, his son, Arthur, leased the Gower warehouse to the railroad and hauled freight from the depot by means of the street railway. In 1897 the Southern Railway built a depot on River Street, and Gower dismantled the old street railway system. The next year the city council granted George M. Bunting and Associates of Philadelphia a franchise for an electric street railway. By 1900 tracks were laid from the Southern Depot to the city limits on Pendleton Street and within a block of the city limits on Augusta Street; from Main and Washington Streets up Main to College and Buncombe Streets and on to Poe Mill; and on North Street to Manly, then to McBee Avenue, and back to Main and Washington Streets.[46]

Suburban Developments

The coming of the railroads and the streetcar opened the way for new suburban developments. The West End, across the Reedy River from the city of Greenville, had begun to develop in the 1850s with the building of the Furman University campus and the Greenville and Columbia Railroad. After the Civil War construction in the area increased. By 1867 a black volunteer fire company, the Neptune Company, was serving the West End, and in 1870 the company promoted the successful candidacy of T. C. Gower for mayor. By the late 1870s there were warehouses to accommodate the new trade in fertilizer and cotton. New residences were built in the French Second Empire style. William Wilkins's house was constructed in 1877 on Augusta Street, and Charles H. Lanneau built his house on what is now Belmont Avenue in 1878. Churches were established to serve the West End. Allen Temple AME Church located there in 1881. Pendleton Street Baptist Church was organized in 1890, St. Paul Methodist Church in 1891, and Second Presbyterian Church in 1892. St. Andrew's Episcopal Church began as a mission in 1900.[47]

Two other suburbs began to flourish as well. In 1884 William Goldsmith formed a real estate company, and among his first purchases was Boyce Lawn, the former estate of James Petigru Boyce. To Boyce Lawn, Goldsmith added the lands of the Rowley family. The streets in the new suburb were named for the professors of the Baptist seminary—Boyce, Broadus, Manly, Williams, Toy, Whitsett, and Petigru. The land of the McBee family between West Washington and Buncombe Streets was subdivided about 1890, and soon Queen Anne and the newly popular revival houses were rising along West Avenue, renamed Highland and later Hampton Avenue.[48]

New City Services

As the city began to grow, there were efforts to provide greater services to its residents. The campaign to bring the telegraph to Greenville prior to the Civil War had failed. In May 1870 the *Enterprise* announced that "Northern contractors" proposed to the officials of the Greenville and Columbia Railroad that they could "construct a line of Telegraph along the Railroad from this point to Columbia." The cost was sixteen thousand dollars, and the line could be completed in two months. In December Alexander McBee, Jr., became the agent for stock in the telegraph line. In September 1871 the *Enterprise* reported that "Mr. Lamb [was] in charge of the Telegraph Office."[49]

After Alexander Graham Bell secured the first patent on the telephone in 1876, the Southern Bell Telephone Company established an exchange in Charleston in 1879 and in Columbia in 1880. Two years later, on May

16, 1882, Southern Bell opened a switchboard in Greenville located over a livery stable on the corner of Laurens and West Washington Streets. The first manager was Arthur G. Gower, and there were sixteen subscribers. Only two of the telephones were in private homes—the residences of Ellison Smyth and Jeff M. Richardson. At the end of the first year there were fifty telephones in use. In 1883 Henry Hammett built a telephone line to Piedmont to connect his office in Greenville with the mill. In 1889 telephone lines extended to Travelers Rest, Batesville, and Pelham, and the next year they reached Chick Springs and Greer. In the 1890s the Home Telephone Company inaugurated a separate service in Greenville, and some businesses kept a telephone supplied by each company. Eventually Southern Bell bought out its competitor. In 1907 there were one thousand telephones in Greenville.[50]

Prior to 1883 there were no paved streets in Greenville and few paved sidewalks. There were 600 yards of granite sidewalks, 1,200 yards of other rock, and 1,200 yards of brick. In February 1883 the city council began paving Main Street, beginning near Broad. A paved street brought a new dimension to the city by the Reedy River.[51]

In 1887 John Ferguson and Jacob Miller piped water from the Gaol Spring on Spring Street into a wooden tank on the roof of their store on Main Street. Soon a group of business people encouraged A. A. Gates, the proprietor of the Mansion House, to visit the American Pipe Manufacturing Company in Philadelphia to investigate the possibility of a water system. They formed the Paris Mountain Water Company, which built two reservoirs on Paris Mountain and installed a pipeline and pressure and filter pumps on Richland Creek. The first water from Paris Mountain reached Greenville in 1888. The pressure and filter pumps were moved to Paris Mountain, and in 1901 a standpipe with a capacity of 460 thousand gallons was erected at Pendleton and Leach Streets. In 1904 two more reservoirs were constructed on Paris Mountain.[52]

Just prior to the Civil War a gas plant had been built in Greenville, and gas lights illuminated Main Street for the first time on December 20, 1860—the day South Carolina seceded from the Union. During the war, gas production was suspended, but in November 1866 J. B. Sherman reopened the plant. It shut down once more and was operated only briefly in 1870 and 1873. Finally in September 1875 the city council signed a contract with Reuben R. Asbury of Talladega, Alabama, to provide gas lights. On Saturday night, September 4, according to the *Enterprise and Mountaineer,* "the bright lights burned brilliantly from one end of the city to the other. . . . Three lamps will soon be placed in the western portion of the city—one at the end of the Gower bridge, one on top of the hill, and at the fork of Augusta and Pendleton Streets."[53]

Thomas A. Edison built the first electric generating plant for the city of New York in 1882, and six years later the Greenville City Council voted to bring electric lighting to Greenville. In May 1888 the city acquired Brush arc generators to power eleven arc lights from the Brush Electric Company of Cleveland, Ohio, and a coal-fueled, steampowered engine for driving the generators. A powerhouse was built on Broad Street. In 1890 the city sold the plant to Reuben Asbury and his son, Abner D. Asbury. The contract with the city called for forty arc lights to operate on "moon schedule." In full moonlight they were not turned on. If clouds obscured the moon, the mayor, through the chief of police, notified Asbury and Son, and the company had one hour to turn on the lights. The following year, in 1891, Asbury and Son became a stock company—the Greenville Gas, Electric Light and Power Company.[54]

Cultural and Social Life

The growing cities of the New South boasted opera houses in which traveling companies presented cultural performances of various sorts. In 1879 Jacob Cagle, William Wilkins, Frank Coxe, and James T. Williams built an opera house on the corner of Main Street and McBee Avenue on the site of McBee's Hall which had burned in 1866. Cagle's daughter named the new structure the Academy of Music. The opera house burned on December 7, 1879, after only a few performances. Five black men were arrested for arson, and three of them were eventually hanged. In 1880 the Gilreath Opera House, seating eight hundred, was opened on Main and Coffee Streets. Under the management of B. T. Whitmire, the opera house flourished.[55]

A daily newspaper also signaled the coming of age of Greenville. The *Mountaineer,* founded in 1824, and the *Enterprise,* established in 1854, were consolidated into a weekly newspaper, the *Enterprise and Mountaineer* in 1873. But that same year A. M. Speights founded the Greenville *Daily News,* which became the voice of the New South in the Piedmont. By 1889 the *Daily News* was controlled by a board of directors representing the business elite: James L. Orr, Jr., (president), Henry P. Hammett, Alfred B. Williams, Ellison A. Smyth, William H. Perry, John Ferguson, William Wilkins, J. H. Morgan, and P. H. Reilly.[56]

Greenville was gradually acquiring other accoutrements of a growing city. In May 1870 the business leaders established the Greenville City Club for the "promotion of sociability and good feeling . . . [and] a kind and cordial reception and entertainment of strangers." The initiation fee was five dollars, the monthly dues one dollar, and the membership limited to thirty. The club occupied rooms over Ferguson and Miller's Store. The officers were Frank Coxe, president; Abraham Isaacs, vice president; and William L. Mauldin, secretary-treasurer. Among its members were three Beatties, three McBees, two Perrys, and two Coxes, as well as William K. Easley, William E. Earle, James P. Moore, Samuel A. Townes, T. Q. Donaldson, and Absalom Blythe. The club was succeeded in 1876 by the Mountain City Club.[57]

The business elite also did not neglect its formal social life. As early as 1873 a Cotillion Club held a dance on June 10. William E. Beattie was president, and Isaac M. Bryan secretary. But in 1888 Ellison Smyth formed a permanent Cotillion Club based on the pattern of the St. Cecelia Society in Charleston; he insisted on the same formality and strict code of dress and behavior. Smyth was the first president and James L. Orr, Jr., was vice president. Other early presidents were Orr and Francis W. Poe, but Smyth served longer than any other. His daughter, Margaret, made her debut at the first dance at Ferguson and Miller's Hall on Main Street in 1888. There were three dances a year—one at Christmas and two more in January and February. Each began with a Grand March at 9:00 or 9:30 P.M., followed by fifteen to twenty card dances. Supper was served at midnight or 1:00 A.M. The supper at the dance on January 10, 1895 consisted of stewed oysters, croquettes, salad, potato chips, and olives, with punch and coffee afterward.[58]

Cultural activities were not they left entirely to visiting performances in the opera house. The Greenville Musical Association was founded about 1888. In 1890 the association had sixty-five members, and the officers were Ellison A. Smyth, president; R. G. McPherson, vice president; J. W. Hewell, secretary-treasurer; and Mrs. R. H. Kennedy, musical director. The Excelsior Reading Club had twenty-six members in 1867, half men and half women. Each month the members selected a book, and at the meetings a critic addressed comments to the readers. Seminary Professor John A. Broadus was apparently the leading spirit of the club. The Literary Club of Greenville, organized in January 1867 by a group of twenty-five to thirty men, established a library of "the best English reviews and periodicals—the best Northern and the best Southern—they are literary, religious, humorous." The club joined town and gown with members such as Broadus, James Clement Furman, and Benjamin F. Perry. In the closing years of the nineteenth century, two new literary groups were formed—one for women and one for men. On March 7, 1889, twelve women formed a group for serious study and discussion, which they named the Thursday Club. The officers were Frances Perry Beattie, president; Mary Putnam Gridley, vice president; and Martha Orr Patterson, secretary. The club met every two weeks, and the members presented papers on assigned subjects. In 1898 the Thursday Club became a charter member of the South Carolina Federation of Women's Clubs. The Thirty-Nine Club, a study club for men, was organized by Furman Professor Gordon Beverly Moore in 1897. The name was chosen as a "triple defiance to the common superstition that thirteen is an unlucky number."[59]

As early as 1868 a group of women organized the Greenville Circulating Library. Two years later it had over thirty members and had purchased 170 "novels, travels, history and poetry." The library arranged with two or three "northern publishing houses to send their most popular works as soon as published." Nearly three decades later, on February 27, 1897, the Neblett Free Library was incorporated by a group of eleven men and women. Mrs. A. Viola Neblett transferred a house on East McBee Avenue, across Westfield Street from Central School, to the association. The library began with a collection of one thousand volumes, and by 1900 had grown to more than three thousand. It charged a small subscription fee, but most of its books were acquired by donation.[60]

In the 1870s there was a movement in Greenville to establish a Young Men's Christian Association (YMCA), and a meeting was held in the Methodist Church on Buncombe Street on Sunday afternoon, April 16, 1876. Julius C. Smith proposed that an interdenominational committee "be appointed to take into consideration the establishing of a" YMCA with O. A. Pickle as chair. The committee consisted of George W. Sirrine and Charles A. David representing the Methodists; T. B. Ferguson and John C. Bailey, the Presbyterians; and Pickle and P. Henry Reilly, the Baptists. The following officers were elected: S. C. Clyde, president; Pickle, vice president; and David, secretary. By 1889 the YMCA had rooms in the old courthouse, which by that time was known as the Record Building. They were described by the Charleston *News and Courier* as "unquestionably the finest and best arranged in the State." Besides parlors, the YMCA boasted a gymnasium, bath rooms, and recreation rooms."[61]

Health Care

The health care of Greenville was in the hands of physicians who met on February 5, 1866, in the courthouse to organize the Greenville Medical Society. W. A. Harrison presided at the first meeting, and W. R. Jones served as secretary. A committee was appointed to draw up a constitution and bylaws consisting of J. H. Dean, W. R. Jones, M. B. Earle, W. H. Austin, and J. H. Hewell.[62]

Hospital care was more difficult to provide. In 1877 two physicians, George E. Trescott and John H. Maxwell, opened the Greenville Infirmary at Main and Coffee Streets over the Earle and Wilkes Drugstore, but it closed after a short time. Two decades later, in 1895, two cases of typhoid were reported in Greenville among traveling workers. The Rowena Lodge of the Knights of Pythias asked every organization in the city to appoint a delegate to a central committee. The committee, which met on February 5, 1896, formed the Greenville Hospital Association, with George W. Sirrine as president. A month later the Ladies Auxiliary Board of the Hospital Association was formed. At its first meeting on March 18, 1896, Mrs. E. B. L. Taylor became president; Mrs. James L. Orr, Jr., vice president; and Mrs. J. C. Woodside, secretary-treasurer. These women began to raise funds immediately, but by the end of the decade they had only $2,238.26 in hand, and it would be another decade and a new century before a permanent hospital became a reality.[63]

Education

The leaders of Greenville sought with greater success to improve public school education for their children. In 1885 T. C. Gower was the leader in securing a special act of the state legislature to create the City School District of Greenville. The first school board, appointed in May 1886, was composed of T. Q. Donaldson, chair, F. W. Marshall, T. C. Gower, H. T. Cook, and S. S. Thompson. The following September they secured the services of Professor W. S. Morrison as superintendent. He had organized the city schools in Spartanburg and served there for two years. By 1888 the city passed a bond issue for eighteen thousand dollars to build two new schools for whites. Central School was built adjacent to Prospect Hill at the head of McBee Avenue, and Oaklawn was built on Pendleton Street in the West End. Allen School continued to serve the black population. In 1890 the Greenville City schools had an enrollment of 1,071. The following year Professor Morrison resigned to become professor of history at the newly opened Clemson College, and Professor E. L. Hughes replaced him.[64]

Greenville's institutions of higher learning reopened after the Civil War, but had a very difficult time. The Southern Baptist Theological Seminary, which had only seven students in the fall of 1865, acquired the Goodlett House as a student residence hall two years later. Among the new faculty after the Civil War were Crawford H. Toy and William H. Whitsett, both graduates of the seminary who had studied in German universities. Toy became one of the leading scholars of ancient Near Eastern languages in America. After the seminary moved to Louisville, he was dismissed from the faculty because he embraced the theories of biblical higher criticism. He went on to the faculty of Harvard University. Whitsett eventually became president of the seminary in Louisville, but he too was forced to resign because he examined the early history of Baptists in England and concluded that they had only gradually adopted the practice of baptism by immersion.

In addition, faculty salaries were often in arrears. The question of removing the seminary to a more favorable location was raised, and Louisville, Kentucky, was selected as the new site in 1872. Dr. James Petigru Boyce moved there to raise funds for a new campus, and in the fall of 1877 the seminary moved to Kentucky. This left only the names of faculty on the streets of Boyce Lawn in Greenville and the seminary burial plot in Springwood Cemetery.[65]

At Furman, the faculty, rather than the trustees or the state Baptist Convention, took the initiative to reopen the institution in February 1866 with 140 students. The number declined, and the college closed in 1868. Nevertheless, President James C. Furman refused to give up. He told the Reedy River Baptist Association: "I have been urged to abandon the university and seek a field of labor more certain. But I have resolved, if the university should go down, to sink with it." Classes resumed in February 1869, and an endowment fund of two hundred thousand dollars was pledged to allow students free tuition. But by 1879 many of the bondholders defaulted on their payments, and most of the faculty resigned. In 1881 Dr. Charles Manly, former pastor of the First Baptist Church of Greenville, became president. The prospects of Furman began to improve, and by the time Manly resigned as president in 1898, the future of the institution was secure. Manly was succeeded by Dr. Andrew P. Montague, professor of Latin at Columbian College, now George Washington University. He was a layperson, not a minister as his predecessors had been, and a professional educator. He was the first member of the faculty to hold the new Ph.D. degree. A new era for Furman was about to begin.[66]

Although both the seminary and Furman had closed during the Civil War, the Female College remained opened, and in 1864 Charles H. Judson replaced James C. Furman as president. Judson, a native of Connecticut who was educated at the University of Virginia, had come to Furman in 1851 when the school moved to Greenville. A man of vigor and vision and deeply committed to his Baptist faith, Judson remained president until 1878, though he continued to teach at Furman and also serve as the school's treasurer. Judson extended the college curriculum to four years, but financial problems plagued the college. The only possible solution was to sell land owned by the college. Of the original 22.5 acres, 17.5 were sold. The college became debt free, but without a science laboratory or a library the education of the students suffered.[67]

Charles Judson's greatest gift to the struggling college was to secure the services of his sister, Mary Camilla Judson. Born in 1828, she was educated in private schools. When the family moved to New Haven, Mary Judson was allowed to study in the Yale College Library, though it was a men's college and she could not attend classes. Committed to women's education, she moved to South Carolina and taught in several female academies and for a brief period at the Female College. After returning to the North in 1868, she came back to Greenville in 1874 and remained for the rest of her life. In 1876 Mary Judson was appointed lady principal of the Female College. Two years later Charles Judson returned to Furman and was succeeded as president by Alexander S. Townes. The son of George Townes and the grandson of William Bullein Johnson, the first principal of the Greenville Female Academy, Townes served until 1894. At his suggestion Miss Judson formed a literary society, but it was criticized both by Furman students and Baptist leaders who did not believe that women should be encouraged to speak in public. Miss Judson ignored them and informed the Thursday Afternoon Club in 1897 that she hoped the members of the society would return home after graduation and establish similar groups. The Greenville Female College, as it had come to be known, awarded the first Bachelor of Arts degree in 1893.[68]

A new Presbyterian college for women, Chicora College, was established in Greenville in 1893. At a meeting of the session of the First Presbyterian Church on August 7, a special committee chaired by John A. Russell recommended the formation of a college for women. A fund of one thousand was raised, and a house was rented on McBee Avenue. Ellison A. Smyth became president of the Board of Trustees, and the Reverend S. R. Preston was elected president. The college purchased McBee Hill (or McBee Terrace) on the west bank of the Reedy River overlooking the city of Greenville as a permanent campus and erected a series of buildings there. Every Sunday morning the Chicora students marched up Main Street to Washington and then to the Presbyterian church for services. At the same time, the students of the Greenville Female College marched past the Presbyterian church to services at the Baptist church. In 1906 Chicora College came under the control of the Enoree, Bethel, and South Carolina Presbyteries of the South Carolina Synod.[69]

City Churches

The improving economy permitted the white Methodists and Presbyterians to build handsome new churches equal to those constructed by the Episcopalians and Baptists during the 1850s. In August 1870 the *Enterprise* reported that "the [Greenville] Methodist Church has bought T. Henry Stokes' house and land on Buncombe St. for thirty-two hundred dollars. The house will be a parsonage." The following year work was begun on the new church by J. Franklin Carpenter and Cline & Gibbs. The building, 50 feet wide and 85 feet long, was constructed in the older Classical Revival style, rather than the newer Gothic Revival. A spire was planned, but a less-expensive belfry was built, and the organ from the old church was moved into the balcony of the new. According to the *Enterprise,* "the pulpit, chandelier, furniture for pulpit and chancel, were chiefly procured from the North. . . . The altar is a beautiful piece of workmanship, upon which Mr. C. Hahn has devoted his most careful attention." The cost of the building was twelve thousand dollars.[70]

The church was dedicated by Bishop D. S. Doggett on February 9, 1873. The congregations of the white Presbyterian and Baptist churches joined the Methodists, and their ministers participated in the service, along with James C. Furman of Furman University and Crawford H. Toy of the seminary. After the bishop's hour-long sermon, the pastor, E. J. Meynardie, asked the trustees to lock the doors and announced that twenty-five hundred dollars had to be raised before the building could be dedicated debt-free. The minister and church members Henry P. Hammett, J. A. David, John W. Stokes, and Mrs. Charlotte Norton, along with visiting ministers Furman and Toy, agreed to give one hundred dollars each. Within another hour the total amount was pledged, the service was completed, and the doors were unlocked.[71]

Washington Street Presbyterian Church, as the Greenville church had been renamed, had outgrown its building by the early 1880s. Robert H. Nall became pastor in January 1878 and he enlisted the support of Elders Logan B. Cline and T. C. Gower in building a new church. Arthur Gower later remembered that "the conservative, pessimistic, and ultra-cautious fought hard for slower going . . . , but the optimistic and wide visioned of the membership prevailed, though the adoption of their ideas created a debt that hung for a long time over the Church." In 1882 Joshua W. Nichols, a member of the congregation, was awarded the contract for the new building for $24,596.71. The old church was demolished, and a new Gothic Revival structure was built on the same site. The new church was constructed of brick with bands of ornamental concrete, and on the corner rose a tower with large, arched openings. The first service in the new building was held in the Lecture Room on December 2, 1883. The debt was not paid and the building dedicated until August 1890. Seven years later the women of the church raised funds to stucco the exterior of the building and install stained glass windows.[72]

In the Protestant churches of the South after the Civil War, women became involved in the formation of foreign and domestic missionary societies. In the Greenville Baptist Church, for example, a number of women formed a Sewing Society to finance church projects and to aid the poor. But in the 1870s women ceased to attend church conferences, and two professors in the seminary became involved in a disagreement about the role of women in the church. In 1871 James Petigru Boyce strongly supported a motion at a church conference that women no longer be allowed to vote. He was opposed by Basil Manly, Jr., and the motion lost.[73]

In 1872 two members of the church, Lula Whilden and her sister, Mrs. Edwards, sailed to China as foreign missionaries, and three years later the Central Committee of the Baptist Woman's Mission Societies was established at a meeting in Society Hill, South Carolina. On March 17, 1875, the pastor of the Greenville church, James C. Furman, called a meeting of seventeen women and read them an article from the Central Committee. They organized a Woman's Missionary Society and elected Harriet McBee, president; Caroline Mauldin, treasurer; and Annie Broadus, secretary. Their object was "to assist in providing homes and other appliances of usefulness for those pious women who, from among ourselves, have given themselves to the work of making the Saviour known among the Chinese." The members placed their offerings in mite boxes, and monthly they sent what they had collected to the Central Committee. In 1880 the women organized the children into a missionary society, the Willing Workers, at the home of Mrs. Charles M. Furman.[74]

The founding of St. Mary's Catholic Church in 1876 caused a great deal of controversy. It became clear to the leaders of the community who supported European immigration that a Catholic church was an important element in their campaign. As early as 1868 Father T. C. McMahon, who was stationed in northwestern South Carolina, had written to the *Southern Enterprise* that he was attempting "to induce others of his co-religionists to come and partake of all the advantages to be derived from agricultural pursuits here, and enjoy this salubrious climate." The *Enterprise and Mountaineer* made it clear that "from our observation of the followers of the Roman Catholic faith, we think the rearing of a church for them in the community will have the effect of bringing many to the place who could otherwise go elsewhere."[75]

The first mass in the county had been said in the home of John Keenan on Main and Elford Streets in 1852. The Keenans, the brothers John and Peter King, John O'Gora (or Love), and James Galligan were the only Catholics in the area at that time. On December 21, 1870, Bishop Patrick Lynch visited Greenville and preached at the Mansion House. His visit provoked the *Enterprise* to voice a view of the Roman Catholic Church typical of much of Southern evangelical Protestantism: "Whilst we regard Romanism . . . as having been a great curse to mankind by its perversion of the plain and simple teachings of Christ, its intolerance to Jew and Gentile Protestant Christians, and all who do not bow to the *infallible* Pope, we have no unkind feeling or want of respect for sincere individuals of that faith, be they bishops, priest, monk or layman."[76]

In 1875 Bishop Lynch appointed Father A. M. Folchi, a native of Rome who had served as a professor of theology at the University of Innsbruck, to build a church in Greenville. Vardry McBee, Jr., and another local business person agreed to help raise the funds. In two days they collected two thousand dollars and McBee contributed 1 acre of land on the corner of Hampton Avenue and Lloyd Street for the building. This positive response provoked a war of letters for six months in the local newspaper. Leading the attack against building the church was Allen C. Stepp—a Baptist minister, a leader in the local Democratic Party, and a state legislator. In one letter he exposed his anti-Catholic feelings: "Now as a test of the spirit of liberality, I make the following proposition: If the Roman Catholics in South Carolina will, by order of Pope Pius, pay $1,000 toward the building a Baptist Church in Rome, I will be one of a number of Baptists in South Carolina who will pay the same amount towards building a Roman Catholic Church in Greenville. We will further obligate ourselves never to '*hoot*' or hiss a Catholic in the streets of Greenville."[77]

Not surprisingly, the individual who stepped forward to defend the Catholic effort was former Governor Benjamin F. Perry. "The Scriptures teach us," Perry wrote, "that we must obey God in all things. This is the doctrine of all Protestants, and the Roman Catholics teach no more. How one christian can look upon another as an enemy, and the building up a church for him, is the erection of a fortification for the troops of an enemy is beyond my comprehension." These views came from Perry who fourteen years before had allowed Captain William Fitzgerald, a Catholic who had died with no burial lot, a space in his family plot at Christ Church.[78]

Despite the anti-Catholic feelings of many Greenvillians, others proved very helpful. William Choice permitted the Catholic congregation to hold services in his unoccupied house. In July 1876 Jacob W. Cagle began building the wooden Gothic Revival church according to the plans of G. L.

Norrman, a Charleston architect. The building was 88 feet wide and 67 feet long, and the arched ceiling was 27 feet high. On the roof was an open belfry with a cross at the top. On October 15, 1876, Bishop Lynch dedicated the new church to Our Lady of the Sacred Heart of Jesus. According to the *Enterprise and Mountaineer*, two services were filled with "Catholics, Baptists, Presbyterians, Episcopalians, and 'Nothings.'" Gradually the church came to be known as St. Mary's, proof that the horizons of the community had been widened somewhat by the New South spirit.[79]

Christ Church had undergone its own agonizing Reconstruction at the close of the Civil War, but it emerged with strong leadership. In 1866 Thomas S. Arthur had been rector of the parish for twenty years. He had led the construction of the new church building, founded the Dehon School for the Poor in 1851, and remained through the trying war years. On February 7, 1866, Arthur submitted a bitter letter of resignation to the vestry: "This flock and this fold have been my constant care for nearly a quarter of a century. . . . Some of them, it is true, have stoned me to my present attitude. . . . I may shortly be called upon to submit to the annoyance of an Ecclesiastical Trial. If this trouble should come upon me, let me beseech you, brethren, not to withdraw your arm from around me." The vestry did not accept Arthur's resignation, but the trial came anyway.[80]

William H. Campbell of Greenville, Arthur's brother-in-law, leveled serious charges of sexual misconduct against the rector. The parish was divided, and Bishop Thomas Davis appointed two clergy, Paul Trapier and J. S. Hanckel, to investigate the matter. In June 1866 Trapier arrived in Greenville and was joined by Hanckel. They gathered depositions, and on October 3 Arthur submitted a second letter of resignation. This time it was accepted. The bishop convened a trial court the following year with former rector of the parish, Charles Cotesworth Pinckney, as judge. Two attorneys participated in the proceedings. Armistead Burt of Abbeville represented the diocese, and former Confederate General Matthew C. Butler, himself once a member of the parish, represented the accused. Arthur was apparently acquitted on the major charges, but was found guilty on two minor counts and was suspended from parish work for five years. He continued to live in Greenville, and on May 11, 1867, Elizabeth McCall Perry wrote to Mrs. Armistead Burt that Arthur was studying law and would likely be admitted to the bar.[81]

Christ Church faced an uncertain future until the church secured the services of Ellison Capers as lay reader. Born in 1837 in Charleston, the son of Methodist Bishop William Capers, the younger Capers was a graduate of the Citadel and taught mathematics prior to joining the Confederate army. At the end of the war, after the Battle of Franklin, Tennessee, he was promoted to the rank of brigadier general. During the fighting Capers had decided to enter the ministry, and though he became South Carolina's secretary of state in 1865, he began to read the orders under the direction of Bishop Davis. He served as lay reader at Christ Church until he was ordained deacon and priest in 1867. He then resigned as secretary of state and became rector of the parish, a post which he held, with the exception of one year, until 1887. In 1893 Capers was elected bishop coadjutor of the diocese and, after the death of Bishop W. B. W. Howe, became bishop of South Carolina.[82]

For twenty years Ellison Capers lived and served in Greenville. Early in his tenure he decided to appeal to a number of wealthy parishes in the North for financial aid. One day in New York City Capers met James Petigru Boyce, his Greenville neighbor, on the street. When Boyce inquired about Capers's success, Capers replied that after his last sermon only one five-dollar bill appeared in the collection plate. To which Boyce replied: "And I your neighbor put that in." In addition to his ministry at Christ Church, Capers taught mathematics at the Female College, at Furman University, and at the Greenville Military Academy. He actively participated in many facets of the life of the city, such as the Literary Club and the Independent Riflemen during the election of 1876. Because of his service as a general officer in the Confederate Army, he was a living reminder in the community of the Lost Cause.[83]

The Cult of the Lost Cause

As the Civil War began to recede into the past, there was a concerted effort on the part of the former Confederates to keep the memory of the Lost Cause alive. On June 16, 1866, the Ladies' Memorial Association of Charleston held the first Confederate Memorial Day observance in the state. The next year, since so many white Charleston residents spent the summer in the mountains, they selected May 10 for the observance—the anniversary of General Stonewall Jackson's death. Similar services soon spread all over the state. On November 12, 1869, a meeting of Confederate veterans in Greenville formed a local chapter of the Survivors' Association with Ellison Capers presiding and James T. Williams as secretary. Capers appointed six delegates to the meeting of the State Survivors' Association in Charleston on November 18—Captain William E. Earle, Lieutenant E. H. Bates, William L. Mauldin, John Ferguson, and W. C. Bailey. Another committee was appointed to write a constitution and call a second meeting.[84]

When news arrived in Greenville of the death of Robert E. Lee on October 12, 1870, Mayor T. C. Gower asked that church bells toll for two hours before noon the following day and that all businesses close out of respect. That evening there was a large assembly at the courthouse. A choir sang funeral hymns, James Petigru Boyce offered a series of resolutions, and Basil Manly, Jr., William K. Easley, Benjamin F. Perry, and James C. Furman spoke. "The memory of Robert E. Lee," Perry intoned, "will live in the hearts of his countrymen as proudly and as affectionately as if success had crowned all his efforts and sacrifices. His wisdom, his heroism, his unselfish ambition, and patriotic devotion to his country, have gained the admiration of the world, and endeared him to foe and friends." When Jefferson Davis died in 1889, a similar service was held in the opera house.[85]

As in many Southern towns, a group of women in Greenville established a Ladies Memorial Association whose goal was the erection of a monument to the Lost Cause. In 1875 the association performed an oratorio based on the story of Queen Esther to raise funds for the state monument in Columbia. This "brilliant success," which raised $170, encouraged the association to erect its own memorial. On September 19, 1891, the cornerstone was laid for a monument in the center of North Main Street. Ellison Capers delivered the address. A year later, on September 27, 1892, the monument, described by the Columbia *State* as "one of the handsomest and costliest in the South," was unveiled. The railroads gave reduced rates, and military companies from all over the state came for the dedication.[86]

After a parade with bands playing, the crowd assembled at the monument where young women dressed in uniforms represented each of the Confederate states. Newspaper editor James A. Hoyt memorialized the Lost Cause: "Let these shafts tower to the skies, represented the cause so dearly loved and which men of valor died to save. Let them shadow forth the respect due to every soldier's grave, and tell the world that once there lived 'the man who wore the grey.'" Sue Harris then unveiled the monument.[87]

Atop the towering shaft was the statue of a common soldier. Police Chief James B. Ligon was the model for the sculptor, C. F. Kohlrus of Augusta, Georgia. Ligon had been the first man to volunteer in Company G of the Fourth Regiment. The inscription was simple and straightforward: "Erected in honor and memory of the Confederate Dead of the County and City of Greenville by the Ladies Memorial Association, Sept. 1892."[88]

Summer Resorts

One dimension of life in the antebellum South which the business elite of the New South attempted to perpetuate was the summer migration. But Greenville never recovered its position as a major resort for low country residents after the Civil War. Some returned, but many more were attracted to the mountains of North Carolina. The effort to revive Chick Springs was not immediately successful. The hotel had burned in November 1862, and in 1868 the two sons of Burwell Chick regained possession of the property. Not until 1885, after the death of Reuben Chick, was the property bought by George Westmoreland, an Atlanta attorney who built a small hotel and several cottages. He advertised "Summer Health Resort, Chick Springs, Taylors Station, Greenville County, S.C., on the Southern Railway." But by 1903 he sold the property to a group of local investors.[89]

More successful than Chick Springs was the hotel operated after 1873 by Robert W. Anderson on the Buncombe Road in Travelers Rest. Anderson and his wife, Mary McCullough, purchased the fourteen-room house built by Chevis Montgomery in 1851 and entertained visitors who came for several weeks or the entire summer season. The Charleston *News and Courier* reported that "the house of Col. R. W. Anderson is filled with boarders and they have already put up the 'standing room only' sign. Col. Anderson and his wife are untiring in their attention to the guests and everyone is made to feel entirely at home."[90]

In 1898 Anderson's daughter, Minnie Anderson Hillhouse, inherited the house, enlarged it, and named it the Spring Park Inn. The tracks of the Carolina, Knoxville, and Western Railroad passed nearby, and the train stopped there briefly. A pavilion in the park near the inn became the scene of outings and political meetings.[91]

In 1883 the Paris Mountain Hotel Company was incorporated, and in 1890 the Altamont Hotel, sometimes called the Paris Mountain Hotel, was built. A large three-story structure, it had twenty-three rooms and porches on all four sides. A mule-drawn coach made the two-hour trip from Greenville every day. John Marchbanks, the coach driver from 1894 to 1896, stopped at the foot of the mountain and blew a series of blasts on his horn—one for each passenger. The manager of the hotel would know how many guests were coming. But the hotel did not prosper and was sold in 1898.[92]

The construction of the Carolina, Knoxville, and Western Railroad promoted two resorts farther north. The antebellum hotel at Caesar's Head in the northern tip of Greenville County became more accessible, and the cool breezes of Caesar's Head and the panoramic view of the Dismal Valley attracted a number of visitors. Just over the line in North Carolina at Cedar Mountain, Ellison Capers bought a small house he named "Camp Cottage." T. C. Gower built the Hotel de Gower close by to accommodate summer residents. As Cedar Mountain became popular, Capers dreamed of building a chapel for summer services, and in 1894 he built a small place of worship he called Faith Chapel.[93]

New South Statesman: Hugh Smith Thompson

A individual with Greenville roots, widely known in the closing decades of the nineteenth century, was Hugh Smith Thompson. Typical of the New South leadership that emerged in South Carolina, he was the grandson of Chancellor Waddy Thompson and the nephew of Waddy Thompson, Jr. He grew up on the farm of his father, Henry Tazewell Thompson, at the foot of Paris Mountain. He was born in Charleston, because his mother, Agnes Smith Thompson, insisted on returning to her home for his birth. Thompson graduated from the Citadel in 1856 and taught French and literature at the Arsenal Academy in Columbia until the outbreak of the Civil War. In 1861 he commanded a company of Arsenal cadets in Charleston. After the war he became principal of the Columbia Male Academy and served in that position until he was elected state superintendent of education in 1876. From 1876 to 1882 he lay the foundation for the state's public school system. In 1882 Thompson was elected governor and served until he was appointed assistant secretary of the treasury by President Grover Cleveland in 1886. In May 1889 he was appointed to the Civil Service Commission; he resigned in 1892 to become comptroller of the New York Life Insurance Company. He remained in that position until his death in 1904.[94]

By the decade of the 1890s the future of Greenville was set for the next century. The county was still predominantly rural—a part of the cotton kingdom, but dotted with small towns and crisscrossed with railroads. Along the railroads and rivers were the recently constructed textile mills, surrounded by mill villages. At the junction of the railroads was the burgeoning city of Greenville. A small group of interrelated business elite controlled the mills, banks, and growing retail businesses and were committed to the rising spirit of the New South. That spirit was aptly caught in the words of Ambrose E. Gonzales, writing of Greenville in the Charleston *News and Courier* on July 8, 1889: "With such a splendid commercial and industrial exhibit, with her magnificent location, fine climate, perfect health, powerful and intelligent press, sound financial institutions, splendid schools, colleges, and churches, there is no height in the social, industrial, and commercial world to which [Greenville's] hopeful, thrifty, and energetic people may not elevate the Pearl of the Piedmont."[95]

Notes

1. Lacy K. Ford, "Rednecks and Merchants: Economic Development and Social Tensions in the South Carolina Upcountry, 1865–1900," *Journal of American History* 71: 2, 301.

2. *Southern Enterprise,* March 11, 1868; *Enterprise,* October 19, September 27, 1871; Francis B. Simkins and Robert H. Woody, *South Carolina During Reconstruction* (Chapel Hill, N.C., 1932, 1966), 261; Rosser H. Taylor, "Some Comments on the Diary of Alfred Taylor," *Furman University Bulletin. Faculty Studies,* N.S. 11: 1, 17.

3. Julian J. Petty, *The Growth and Distribution of Population in South Carolina* (Columbia, 1943, 1975), 227–28; Simkins and Woody, *S.C. During Reconstruction,* 244–45; Butler, cited in Eric Foner, *Reconstruction: America's Unfinished Revolution, 1863–1877* (New York, 1988), 419; Greenville *Southern Enterprise,* November 6, 1867.

4. *Southern Enterprise,* July 15, 1868; *Enterprise,* May 11, 1870; *Enterprise and Mountaineer,* March 3, June 30, 1875; Charleston County School District, *The Ethnic History of South Carolina* (Charleston, 1975), 192.

5. Ford, "Rednecks and Merchants," 310–11; R. G. Dun, S.C.: Greenville County, 132E, 132F, 132H, 132R, 132O, Baker Library, Harvard Graduate School of Business Administration, Cambridge, Mass.; State Board of Agriculture of South Carolina, *South Carolina, Resources and Population, Institutions and Industries* (Charleston, 1883), 708–9.

6. *Southern Enterprise,* May 5, 1869; R. G. Dun, S.C.: Greenville County, 132E–33, 132F, 132H; Ford, "Rednecks and Merchants," 310–11.

7. John F. Stover, *The Railroads of the South, 1865–1900* (Chapel Hill, N.C., 1955), 76–77, 145; Simkins and Woody, *S.C. During Reconstruction,* 203–8.

8. *Southern Enterprise,* November 11, 1868; May 12, 1869.

9. *Enterprise,* June 1, 29, July 6, 1870.

10. Ibid., April 5, June 28, October 4, 1871; April 16, June 4, 18, 25, 1873.

11. *Enterprise and Mountaineer,* March 24, April 7, 1875.

12. *Enterprise,* September 20, 1871; May 21, 1873; William P. Barton, "The Coming of the Railroad to Greenville," *Proceedings and Papers of the Greenville County Historical Society* (cited hereafter as PPGCHS) 5 (1971–1975): 61; "William Lawrence Mauldin," *Biographical Directory of the S.C. Senate,* ed. N. Louise Bailey et al. (Columbia, 1986) 2: 1077–79.

13. *Enterprise and Mountaineer,* April 7, 1875.

14. Stover, *Railroads,* 145–46, 233–53.

15. Mrs. Robert N. Daniel, "The 'Swamp Rabbit,'" *PPGCHS* 1 (1962–1964): 23–28.

16. James M. Richardson, *History of Greenville County, South Carolina* (Atlanta, Ga., 1930, 1980), 119–20.

17. *Enterprise and Mountaineer,* March 26, 1884; *Greenville County,* 123; Caroline S. Coleman and B. C. Givens, *History of Fountain Inn* (Fountain Inn, n.d.), 5–9, 15.

18. Richardson, *Greenville County,* 121–22.

19. Mildred C. Hart, "Mauldin," *PPGCHS* 8 (1984–1990): 45–51; *Enterprise and Mountaineer,* March 26, 1884; "Mauldin," *Biographical Directory* 2: 10-77-79.

20. *Enterprise,* June 29, 1870; R. G. Dun Ledgers, S.C.: Greenville County, 132O, 132U, 132X.

21. "Henry P. Hammett," *Cyclopedia of Eminent and Representative Men of the Carolinas of the Nineteenth Century* (Madison, Wis., 1892, 1972) 1: 471–72; "Henry Pinckney Hammett," *Dictionary of American Biography* (New York, 1935) 8: 201; *Enterprise,* February 19, 1873.

22. Stephen S. Crittenden, *The Greenville Century Book* (Greenville, 1903), 66; Thomas R. Navin, *The Whiten Machine Works Since 1831: A Textile Machinery Company in an Industrial Village* (Cambridge, Mass., 1950), passim.

23. *Enterprise and Mountaineer,* February 10, 1875; *Cyclopedia* 1: 472–73; Navin, *Whiten Machine Works.*

24. State Board of Agriculture, *S.C. Population and Resources,* 710; *Cyclopedia* 1: 472–73.

25. David L. Carlton, *Mill and Town in South Carolina, 1880–1920* (Baton Rouge, La., 1982), 57; *Enterprise and Mountaineer,* January 26, 1876; L. L. Arnold, "A Story of Textile Greenville," *Cotton* 80 (October 1915), 503; Nell B. Adams, "Four Sisters From Boston," *PPGCHS* 6 (1975–1979): 14–15.

26. Letter of Mrs. Beverly T. (Mildred E.) Whitmire in "Camperdown Mill" folder in the vertical file, S.C. Room, Greenville County Library; *Enterprise and Mountaineer,* April 28, 1875; November 5, 1879.

27. Whitmire letter; *Enterprise and Mountaineer,* May 19, 1875.

28. *Enterprise and Mountaineer,* April 28, 1875; January 26, March 8, 1876; November 5, 1879; *Cyclopedia,* 473.

29. Carlton, *Mill and Town,* 43–45; *Cyclopedia* 1: 468–70; William P. Jacobs II, *The Pioneer* (Clinton, S.C., 1934), 21–33; Choice McCoin, "Captain Ellison Adger Smyth," *PPGCHS* 8 (1984–1990): 25–31.

30. Cited in Broadus Mitchell, *The Rise of the Cotton Mills in the South* (Baltimore, Md., 1921), 6.

31. *Historical and Descriptive Review of the State of South Carolina* (Charleston, 1884) 3: 77–78; Felicia Furman Dryden, "Guidelines for the Preservation of the Reedy River Commercial and Industrial District" (M.S. thesis, Columbia University, 1979), 20–24.

32. *S.C. Resources and Population,* 582.

33. *Enterprise and Mountaineer,* June 2, 1875.

34. Charleston *News and Courier,* July 29, 1881, cited in Carlton, *Mill and Town,* 60.

35. *South Carolina, Resources and Population,* 576; Melton A. McLaurin, *Paternalism and Protest: Southern Cotton Mill Workers and Organized Labor, 1875–1905* (Westport, Conn., 1971), 24–30; "Early Labor Union Organizational Efforts in South Carolina Cotton Mills, 1880–1905," *South Carolina Historical Magazine* 72 (1971): 44–45.

36. McLaurin, "Early Labor Union," 46–47.

37. Ibid., 48–49, 59.

38. *South Carolina Baptist Courier,* September 6, 1888, cited in Carlton, *Mill and Town,* 87–88.

39. *Enterprise and Mountaineer,* June 25, July 2, 16, 1890.

40. *Southern Enterprise,* February 24, 1869; Richardson, *History of Greenville County,* 91; *South Carolina. Resources and Population,* 709. The amendments to the charter of Greenville are printed in the *Southern Enterprise,* May 5, 1869. There is a description of the City Hall in the Greenville *News,* December 30, 1923.

41. Judith T. Bainbridge, "Greenville's National Bank: A Brief History," *Cornerstone* (Greenville, n.d.).

42. Charleston *News and Courier,* July 8, 1889, reprinted in John Hammond Moore, ed., *South Carolina in the 1880s: A Gazetteer* (Orangeburg, S.C., 1989), 138.

43. Judith T. Bainbridge, *Centennial: The Chamber in Retrospect* (Greenville, 1988), 1–2.

44. *Cyclopedia* 1: 557; *Enterprise,* November 2, 1870; *Enterprise and Mountaineer,* November 27, 1889; June 11, 1890.

45. Thomas Charles Gower, "Greenville's First Street Railway System," *PPGCHS* 1 (1962–1964): 33–35; *Historical and Descriptive Review of S.C.* 3: 61–63; *Enterprise and Mountaineer,* August 2, 1876; April 9, 1890.

46. Gower, "First Street Railway," 37.

47. Judith T. Bainbridge, "Greenville's West End: A Brief History" (manuscript in the author's possession); Crittenden, *Century Book,* 60; Henry B. McKoy, *History of the First Presbyterian Church of Greenville South Carolina* (Greenville, 1962), 169.

48. Loulie Latimer Owens Pettigrew, *The Thursday Club, Greenville, S.C., 1889–1989* (Greenville, 1988), 116; Building Conservation Technology, *The Historic Resources of Greenville, South Carolina* (Nashville, Tenn., 1981), 33, 61.

49. *Enterprise,* June 1, 1870; September 27, 1871.

50. Greenville *News,* June 26, 1962, cited in Linda Friddle, ed., *Famous Greenville Firsts* (Greenville, 1986), 84; *Enterprise and Mountaineer,* November 21, 1883; October 16, November 27, 1889; April 23, 1890.

51. State Board of Agriculture, *S.C. Resources and Population,* 709; *Enterprise and Mountaineer,* February 21, 1883.

52. John L. Hawkins, "A History of Greenville Water Supply From Its Inception to January 1, 1981," *PPGCHS* 7 (1979–1983): 14–15.

53. *Mountaineer,* November 22, 1866; *Enterprise,* May 4, June 8, 1870; May 7, 21, 1873; *Enterprise and Mountaineer,* February 17, September 8, 1875; Blanche Marsh, *Hitch Up the Buggy* (Greenville, 1977), 30.

54. Thomas B. Smith, Jr., "The History of Power Generation and Distribution in the Greenville Area," *PPGCHS* 8 (1984–1990): 34; Marsh, *Hitch Up the Buggy,* 30–31.

55. Frank Barnes, *The Greenville Story* (Greenville, 1956), 214–15; Crittenden, *Century Book,* 45; Joseph D. Mathis, "Race Relations in Greenville, South Carolina, From 1865 Through 1900" (M.A. thesis, Atlanta University, 1971), 43; Alfred S. Reid, *The Arts in Greenville, 1800–1960* (Greenville, 1960), 78; John Hammond Moore, ed., *South Carolina in the 1880s: A Gazetteer* (Orangeburg, S.C., 1989), 141.

56. Crittenden, *Century Book,* 57; Moore, *S.C. in the 1880s,* 143–44.

57. *Enterprise,* May 25, 1870; *Enterprise and Mountaineer,* January 19, 1876.

58. Moore, ed., *South Carolina in the 1880s: A Gazetter,* 140; A. Charles Cannon, Jr., *The First Hundred Years, 1888–1988: A Portrait of the Cotillion Club of Greenville, South Carolina* (Greenville, 1988), 11–18; The *Mountaineer,* January 10, 1895, gives an account of an early dance.

59. *Southern Enterprise,* January 31, February 21, 1867; Reid, *Arts in Greenville,* 34–35, 22, 117; Pettigrew, *Thursday Club,* 14–17, 32–33. The role of clubs in the emerging status of women is traced in Karen J. Blair, *The Clubwoman as Feminist: True Womanhood Redefined, 1868–1914* (New York, 1980).

60. *Enterprise,* December 21, 1870; Crittenden, *Century Book,* 63; Reid, *Arts in Greenville,* 22; Ellen Perry, "The Story of the Greenville Library," *PPGCHS* 5 (1971–1975): 134–35.

61. *Enterprise and Mountaineer,* April 19, 1876, cited in Moore, *S.C. in the 1880s,* 139.

62. *Enterprise,* February 8, 1866.

63. *Enterprise and Mountaineer,* June 20, 1877; Dave Partridge, "A Brief, Highlight History of the Greenville Hospital System" *PPGCHS* 8 (1984–1990): 176–78. There are some discrepancies between the newspaper account and Partridge. A more complete account of the Greenville Hospital is found in Partridge, *The First 80 Years: Greenville Hospital System, Its History Through 1992* (Greenville, 1992).

64. Anderson, "History of Education," 20–21.

65. John R. Sampey, *Southern Baptist Theological Seminary: The First Thirty Years, 1859–1889* (Baltimore, Md., 1890), 14–16; Robert A. Baker, *The Southern Baptist Convention and Its People, 1607–1972* (Nashville, Tenn., 1974), 281, 302; John A. Broadus, *Memoir of James Petigru Boyce, D.D., LL.D.* (New York, 1893), 222–24, 249–50.

66. William J. McGlothlin, *Baptist Beginnings in Education: A History of Furman University* (Nashville, Tenn., 1926), 130–172.

67. Judith T. Bainbridge, "History of the Greenville Woman's College," chapter 2 (manuscript in the author's possession).

68. Ibid., chapter 3.

69. Henry B. McKoy, *History of the First Presbyterian Church of Greenville, South Carolina* (Greenville, 1962), 49, 54–55. Chicora College moved to Columbia in 1915 and in 1930 it was merged with Queens College and moved to Charlotte, N.C. Greenville *News*, March 25, 1930.

70. *Enterprise*, August 10, 1870; January 22, 1873; A. M. Moseley, *The Buncombe Street Story* (Greenville, 1965), 36–38.

71. *Enterprise*, February 13, 1873; Moseley, *Buncombe Street*, 38–40.

72. McKoy, *First Presbyterian Church*, 37–39, 57.

73. Robert N. Daniel, *A Century of Progress Being the History of the First Baptist Church, Greenville, S.C.* (Greenville, 1957), 46–47, 50.

74. Ibid., 49–51.

75. *Southern Enterprise*, July 22, 1868; *Enterprise and Mountaineer*, October 18, 1876; Timothy E. Hicks, "The History of St. Mary's Catholic Church, Greenville, South Carolina: A Study of Its Beginnings and Growth" (Directed Study, Furman University, 1990; manuscript in possession of the author).

76. Hicks, "St. Mary's Catholic Church," 2–4, 17–18; *Enterprise*, December 21, 1870.

77. Hicks, "St. Mary's Catholic Church," 21–24; *Enterprise and Mountaineer*, August 4, 1875. There is a biographical sketch of Stepp in T. H. Garrett, *A History of the Saluda Baptist Association* (Richmond, Va., 1896), 326–31.

78. *Enterprise and Mountaineer*, July 14, 1875; Hicks, "St. Mary's Catholic Church," 24–25.

79. Hicks, "St. Mary's Catholic Church," 28–29; *Enterprise and Mountaineer*, July 5, September 6, October 18, 1876.

80. Robert C. Wood, *Parish in the Heart of the City: Christ Church, Greenville, S.C.* (Greenville, 1976), 24–25.

81. Investigation of Paul Trapier into allegations against T. S. Arthur, June 1866, and related papers; Elizabeth McCall Perry to Mrs. Armistead Burt, May 11, 1867, all in the Armistead Burt Papers, Manuscript Department, William R. Perkins Library, Duke University, Durham, N.C.

82. Wood, *Parish*, 37–38; Frances Saterlee Alexander, "The Rt. Rev. Ellison Capers, D.D." in *Fifty-First Year—1989. Faith Memorial Chapel, Cedar Mountain, N.C.* (Greenville, 1989); Walter B. Capers, *The Soldier-Bishop, Ellison Capers* (New York, 1912), 123–51.

83. Greenville *News*, May 24, 1931; Wood, *Parish*, 40.

84. *History of the Confederated Memorial Association of the South* (New Orleans, La., 1904), 1: 241–42. The committee on the constitution and bylaws was composed of William T. Shumate, Joseph M. Carson, Lieutenant William H. Perry, Colonel James McCullough, and Dr. James McClanahan. *Southern Enterprise*, November 17, 1869.

85. *Enterprise*, October 19, 1870; *Enterprise and Mountaineer*, December 11, 18, 1889.

86. A. V. Huff, Jr., "The Democratization of Art: Memorializing the Confederate Dead in South Carolina, 1866–1914," in David Moltke-Hansen, ed., *Art in*

the *Lives of South Carolinians: Nineteenth Century Chapters* (Charleston, 1978) 1: AVH1–8; *Enterprise and Mountaineer,* April 28, May 5, 1875; Greenville *News,* June 26, 1962.

87. Greenville *News,* June 26, 1962.

88. Ibid.

89. Jean Martin Flynn, "Chick Springs—1840 to 1941," *PPGCHS* 6 (1975–1979): 45–46.

90. Mildred W. Goodlett, *Travelers Rest at Mountain's Foot: The History of Travelers Rest* (Travelers Rest, 1966), 14–15.

91. Ibid., 16.

92. Robert C. Tucker, "A History of Paris Mountain," *PPGCHS* 7 (1979–1983): 115–16.

93. Nancy Vance Ashmore, *Greenville: Woven From the Past* (Northridge, Calf., 1986), 106; *Mountaineer,* October 31, 1894; *Fifty-First Year—1989: Faith Memorial Chapel, Cedar Mountain, N.C.* (Greenville, 1989).

94. *Cyclopedia* 1: 531–36; Helen K. Hennig, *Great South Carolinians of a Later Date* (Chapel Hill, N.C., 1949), 167–79. William J. Cooper, Jr., has studied the white conservative leadership in *The Conservative Regime: South Carolina, 1877–1890* (Baltimore, Md., 1968), 39–44, 208–13.

95. Cited in Moore, *S.C. in the 1880s,* 149.

CHAPTER EIGHT

Farms and Mills
at the Turn of the Century

In the late nineteenth and early twentieth centuries three great movements swept across the United States. Confronted with a serious decline in
agricultural prices, farmers joined in a series of efforts—collectively known
as Populism—to improve their plight. Meanwhile, the continued growth
of big business produced a true Industrial Revolution in America. Faced
with a new set of problems created by industrialization, the Progressives, a
network of groups from the rising middle class, launched a series of reforms to improve the new urban society. In the South, and in Greenville
County in particular, agriculture remained dominant, and the farmers, to
the disgust of the business elite, embraced the Tillman movement in South
Carolina politics. But in Greenville, the textile industry expanded and modernized and created a large class of mill workers that developed a distinctive
society—shaped by the necessities of work in the mill, the rural heritage of
the workers themselves, and Progressive programs fostered by the mill
owners.[1]

Religion

Despite the growth of the textile mills, Greenville County remained
largely rural with its culture dominated by Protestant evangelical churches
that were in the midst of a revival in the late nineteenth century. In 1890
some 37 percent of the population were church members, but by 1916
church membership had grown to 52 percent. The vast majority of the
people were Baptists, Methodists, and Presbyterians, but the relative standing
of the denominations had shifted since William Gilmore Simms's assessment in 1843. In the antebellum period the Presbyterians predominated in
the Greenville District, and the Methodists and Baptists were second and
third, respectively. Fifty years later, in 1890, Southern Baptists formed the
largest group among the whites with 8,029 members; the Methodist Episcopal Church, South was second with 2,429, and the Presbyterian Church,
U.S. was third with 730. There were 262 Episcopalians, 94 Disciples of
Christ, and 85 Roman Catholics.[2]

Black church membership in Greenville County differed only slightly from whites. In 1890 black Methodist churches, which had been so active on behalf of the freedmen after the Civil War, accounted for 2,991 members divided among the Methodist Episcopal Church (1,754), the Colored Methodist Episcopal Church (26), the African Methodist Episcopal Church (425), and the African Methodist Episcopal Church, Zion (768). Black Baptist churches affiliated with the National Baptist Convention had a membership of 1,702, and Northern Presbyterians claimed 65 members. By 1916 black Baptists were in the majority with 7,575 members, while the Methodist churches were in second place with 1,806 members.[3]

Possum Kingdom and Dark Corner

Large areas of Greenville County remained isolated. The southern part of the county had few towns and mills, and the rich farming community in that area was known as Possum Kingdom. Its chief economic and social institution, outside the churches, was the annual Fairview Stock and Agricultural Show which began in October 1886. The northern area of the county had a comparable show at Locust Hill, and the area around Glassy Mountain, known as Dark Corner, experienced none of the modernization that was occurring in the city of Greenville. Typical of the families who lived in Dark Corner were David and Jane Crain. Five of their children lived beyond infancy—Shade, Emma, Dean, Buford, and Elizabeth. Dean, the middle child, who was born in 1881, become a distinguished Baptist minister. The family lived in a log house on a subsistence farm, as had many of the people in the area for a century. The crops were corn, wheat, and a patch of cotton; a large garden provided beans, okra, turnips, tomatoes, and potatoes. Pumpkins and peas were planted "in the corn middles" in late summer. There were fruit trees, and cattle, hogs, and chickens provided meat.[4]

Cooking was done in the open fireplace in cast-iron kettles resting on the coals or three-legged skillets, known as spiders, with long handles and heavy iron covers. Everyone in the family joined in the chores. Cabbage was shredded and packed into crocks with salt and vinegar to make sauerkraut. Corn was soaked in a solution of lye to make big hominy, and pork was salt cured or made into sausage, stored in corn shucks, and hung in the smoke house.

The day began at four o'clock in the morning, and lasted until sundown. After dark there was the light of the fire and small brass oil lamps. A passage from the Bible was read every night. The father could not read, so the mother read to the family. Years later Dean Crain remembered: "We did not need much light because we went to bed with the chickens and got up with the crowing of the same."[5]

Life was tedious and routine, but there was time for fun. Buford Crain remembered that on wash day, after the clothes were hung out to dry, "we children would crawl up under the sheets and 'play-like' it was our house or wig-wam." Families gathered for popcorn poppings, potato roastings, and corn shuckings. A favorite was the corn shucking in the early fall. The men and young people gathered to work around large piles of corn, while the women prepared supper and refreshments.[6]

The community was served by itinerant preachers, mostly Baptist. Services were held in local churches once a month, and Sunday schools assembled on afternoons during the summer months. Protracted meetings were held in the summer as well. The Reverend A. D. Bowers preached in the area for forty years, but never received a salary. Dean and Buford Crain remembered going to "preaching" about four times a year. Their mother, Jane, was converted after her marriage and rode with her husband on a mule 5 miles to be baptized in the creek near Glassy Mountain Baptist Church.[7]

While the Crain family had no still, distilling whiskey or making moonshine was one of the few sources of cash for residents of Dark Corner. Dean Crain later wrote that he "could make three gallons of corn whiskey from a bushel of corn and sell it for one or two dollars per gallon when he could only get sixty cents for his corn." He knew of "as many as twenty distilleries in two miles of each other." He himself gained a wide reputation for his ability to break up more mash at the stills of neighbors and relatives than most people could with a mash stick. Whiskey was sold nearby in Hendersonville, Campobello, Greenville, and particularly Woodruff.[8]

Since moonshining was a violation of federal law, revenue officers often invaded Dark Corner or stopped the wagons filled with whiskey on their way to market. Dean Crain remembered one cold, wintry day when word came that the officers had left Greenville on their way into the area. He was posted at the top of a hill to watch for them, but he was so cold that he left his post to get a dram of whiskey. "All of a sudden there came a shout from up the branch, 'Hold up your hands, boys.' I looked and began to get up the hill. We held up to the bushes as we ran, but that was all the holding up we did. . . . I did not wait to see further results. I was rather in a hurry just at that time."[9]

Another element of life in Dark Corner was the family feud. Children learned a rigid code of loyalty, and the slightest insult sometimes led to violence. Dean Crain remembered that "I went with a friend one night to shoot some boys who had gotten me out one night and 'run' me as far as they could see me. . . . There was scarcely a boy in the neighborhood above twelve years old who did not carry a pistol." Buford Crain later said that "in my early life several people buried here in Glassy Mountain, Highland, Oak Grove, Gowensville, Ebenezer-Welcome, and Mountain Hill Cemeteries died with their shoes on." When the killers were apprehended, they sometimes went free. "Sometimes when some of the mean men in the country were killed," according to Buford Crain, "the people were glad, and the man who did the killing would 'come clear' on a plea of self-defense."[10]

There were few schools, and Dean Crain remembered that the first school opened in 1891 in a one-room building constructed by the men of the community near Ebenezer-Welcome Church. A long, narrow bench around the wall served as seats for the pupils, and the blackboard was a painted rectangle on the wall. Each child had a slate and pencil with which he or she learned to write and to figure. There was a special dunce bench at the front of the room for students who misbehaved. The school session lasted only a few weeks each summer.[11]

The dream of a high school in northern Greenville County began with John Ballenger of the Tigerville community in 1891. At a union meeting at Double Springs Baptist Church on September 30, he proposed that "the question of establishing in the bounds of the [North Greenville Baptist] Association a high school" be discussed at the next meeting of the association. On October 14 at the Marietta Baptist Church, Dr. M. L. West of Travelers Rest urged the creation of the high school: "As we value the happiness of our dear children for life and for eternity, let us rise in our might, now that this opportunity is offered, and let us establish and maintain a High School within our borders that will be a blessing to our children and a monument of glory to the North Greenville Association."[12]

The articles of organization were drawn up by Dr. Benjamin Perry Robertson, later one of the founders of Limestone College and the New Orleans Baptist Theological Seminary. Benjamin Franklin Neves, the son of Alsey A. Neves and the younger brother of W. P. Z. F. Neves of Mush Creek, who operated a farm and a country store at Tigerville, gave the school five hundred dollars and 10 acres of land. The original building of three rooms stood on the knoll of the hill on the new campus, and the faculty consisted of Professor Hugh L. Brock (principal), Cancie Hill, and Pearl Power.[13]

North Greenville High School opened on January 16, 1893, with eighty students. The Greenville *News* called it "the finest institution of learning in the county outside the city of Greenville." Dr. Jesse Bailey, who was the honor graduate at the end of the first year, remembered: "The school had three rooms, two porches, a piano and a bell. I thought it was the grandest place I had ever seen, and it was." Dean Crain and his brother Buford later attended the school. Dean Crain served as principal from 1910 to 1912, and Buford became pastor of the Tigerville Baptist Church. Buford Crain once spoke of the impact that the school had on the area: "In overcoming the power of darkness, North Greenville has done more good than all the revenue officers and sheriffs combined for a hundred years. In instilling a love for Christ, it has changed the streams once used for whiskey into rivers of baptism."[14]

Perry Duncan Gilreath

From 1876 to 1900, law enforcement in Dark Corner—and in Greenville County—was in the hands of Perry Duncan (P. D.) Gilreath. Born in 1836 near Milford Baptist Church, he married Mary Emily Taylor, the daughter of Washington Taylor, in 1855. During the Civil War, P. D. Gilreath served as captain of Company F in the Sixteenth Regiment, the Hampton Legion Mounted Infantry, and Gary's Cavalry. After the war, he farmed near Greenville until 1876, when he ran for sheriff on the Hampton ticket and was handily elected over his Republican opponent. As sheriff for twenty-four years, he seldom carried a gun and generally enforced the law by the respect of the people.[15]

In 1885 a revenue agent named Springs was killed in Dark Corner, and Hub Garmany, who lived on Gap Creek, was accused of the crime. Sheriff Gilreath went to arrest him, but Garmany was in hiding. After a talk with the sheriff, John Garmany, the father of the accused, gave Gilreath directions to his son's hideout. Unarmed, P. D. Gilreath found Hub Garmany, who drew a gun. After a long talk, the younger Garmany surrendered to the sheriff and went with him to Greenville. It was late, and Garmany ate supper and spent the night at Gilreath's home on Buncombe Street. The next morning Garmany walked with Gilreath to the county jail. Garmany was tried at the next session of court and acquitted. This story was duplicated many times in the course of Sheriff Gilreath's career.[16]

Life of Cotton Farmers

The major crop in the county was cotton. In 1890 Greenville produced 28,485 bales of cotton, and between 1901 and 1906 production rose to an average of 32,505 bales. Cotton production reached an all-time high of 48,000 bales in 1920. By 1915 Greenville was the third largest cotton-producing county in the state—only Orangeburg and Anderson Counties surpassed it. As the size of the crop increased, the price fell. The average market price between 1874 and 1877 was 11.1 cents a pound; however, between 1894 and 1897 it fell to 5.8 cents a pound. But statistics did not tell the whole story. Most farmers sold their crop before December 1 when the market price was recorded. In 1894, for example, the actual farm price was 4.6 cents a pound. The common wisdom was that cotton could not be raised at a profit for less than eight cents. Consequently, by the 1880s Greenville cotton farmers were working twice as hard for the same pay and still operating at a loss.[17]

Typical of the large cotton farms in Greenville County was the one owned by James Edward and Ella Hawkins Thackston on Roe Ford Road, on the present site of Furman University. Besides his farm, Thackston operated a cotton gin and a country store. There were eleven children in the family—eight girls and three boys. J. Ford Thackston remembered that the rhythm of life on the farm was defined by the cotton crop. "There was cotton all around then. It was the main crop." Protracted meetings at the nearby Reedy River Baptist Church were held in August during "lay-by" season, after the cotton had been hoed for the last time. School did not begin at Duncan Chapel School until October, when cotton picking was over.[18]

Besides cotton to pick, there was fodder to pull and cows to milk. "We grew everything we had to eat," Thackston remembered. "We butchered a hog or killed a cow. When you killed a cow or a neighbor would, you'd divide it into quarters in a wagon and swap with your neighbors. Then when they butchered they'd do the same thing." Electricity was a luxury of city life in Greenville. "The only lights" the Thackstons had "were kerosene lamps. We had aladdin lamps, a wick with netting. We trimmed the wicks and washed the lamp chimneys everyday so they'd be good and bright. We had one on the wall in front of a reflector to reflect on the cooking stove. That was a big old iron stove with about six eyes you put pots on. . . . The only heat we had beside the cookstove was in the fireplace. You burned on one side and froze on the other."[19]

The Rise of Farmer Movements

As many farmers in Greenville struggled to survive after the Civil War, the Greenville Agricultural Society was founded in August 1868 to promote "the Agricultural interest of the country." The group's leadership, however, reflected the white antebellum farming interest that also had a substantial stake in the growing city of Greenville. The officers of the society were Alexander McBee, president; Joseph A. David, vice president; and James P. Moore, secretary-treasurer. Two years later the local group was succeeded by the Greenville County Agricultural and Mechanical Association. In 1873 the association secured 30 acres of land on the west side of Rutherford Road, just beyond the city limits, as a fairground. The association published premium lists for the annual county fair.[20]

Farmers also had an advocate in the pages of the *Rural Carolinian,* published in Charleston beginning in 1869. The newspaper urged farmers to support the National Grange of the Patrons of Husbandry, generally known as the Grange. The first chapter in South Carolina was established in Charleston County in 1871, and it spread rapidly under the leadership of D. Wyatt Aiken, a planter at Cokesbury in Abbeville County. By 1875 there were 350 local groups in South Carolina. When a Grange was organized in Greenville in August 1872, Aiken was present. The officers, like those of the agricultural society, reflected town as well as farming interests. Alexander McBee was master; Milton L. Donaldson, overseer; William H. Perry, lecturer; George Heldman, steward; and James C. Furman, chaplain. Soon, however, chapters of the Grange formed in the rural areas. On August 25, 1875, for example, the *Enterprise and Mountaineer* carried the notice that the Grangers had a picnic at Taylor's Turnout.[21]

The program of the Grange was educational, social, and political, and included lectures on agricultural topics and family social events to relieve the boredom of life in the country. In some counties there were efforts at cooperative buying, but not in Greenville. Not until the conservative whites gained control of state government after 1876 was the legislature responsive to Grange concerns. In 1879 a state Department of Agriculture was established, and in Congress Aiken was the chief sponsor of the bill to give the federal Bureau of Agriculture cabinet rank. By 1880, however, the Grange had practically ceased to exist—its program was too ambitious; its accomplishments too few; and the concern of white conservatives to end Reconstruction in the state was too overwhelming. What was left of the Grange joined forces with the conservative-dominated state Agricultural and Mechanical Society.[22]

Increasingly, however, many farmers felt alienated from the town and manufacturing interests. The Grange had taught them a new class consciousness and regard for the government as a source of help for their troubles. The farmers did not oppose urban and industrial economic development, but they would not support it at their own expense. In 1882 Greenville County voters narrowly approved a special tax to raise fifty thousand dollars for the building of the Greenville and Laurens Railroad. The voters in the city of Greenville, where property values had increased ten times since the building of the Air Line Railroad, approved the tax more than twelve to one. But the rural townships defeated the tax, three to one. In neighboring Spartanburg County J. B. Davis, an angry farmer, wrote that "the present power of railroad corporations to tax the public" had developed "a monied aristocracy in this country such as the world had never seen."[23]

In 1887 over a million acres of land in the state was sold for nonpayment of taxes. Between 1875 and 1885 the price of cotton fell six cents a pound. This decline was the difference between a comfortable life and the threat of poverty. More aggressive than the Grange was the Farmers' Alliance—a new national organization that came to South Carolina in the 1880s to voice the discontent of the farmers with the New South oligarchy of the towns. The Alliance, unlike the Grange, focused almost exclusively on cooperative efforts by farmers to better their economic situation. The Alliance entered the Pee Dee region of South Carolina in the fall of 1887, and the State Alliance was organized in July 1888.[24]

A Farmers' Alliance was organized in Greenville County, and the Alliance newspaper, the *Cotton Plant,* established in Marion in 1883, was published in Greenville in two periods: from 1887 to 1890 and again from 1899 to 1904, when it merged with the *Progressive Farmer.* The county alliance met quarterly in the courthouse. In April 1890 Dr. H. V. Westmoreland presided over a meeting of some two hundred delegates representing forty-two suballiances. The Alliance voted to establish a Farmers' Warehouse and Storage Company "to do a general warehouse and banking business." The capital was set at twenty thousand dollars with shares priced at ten dollars each. There were also half-shares and quarter-shares. A two-story brick warehouse was planned at the intersection of South Main and Augusta Streets with offices for the manager, assistants, and the headquarters of the State Alliance Exchange. According to the newspaper account, "advances will be made on cotton stored in the warehouse, and money will be loaned to Alliance members." There was also discussion of building a cotton seed oil mill and opening an Alliance store. The idea of the store was defeated, but the cotton seed oil mill was referred to a committee which made a favorable report. When the Greenville warehouse opened, the state exchange was located there for several years, until it moved to Columbia. Milton L. Donaldson was state business agent of the Alliance, and John R. Harrison was a member of the board of directors of the state exchange.[25]

A pioneer in the diversification of agriculture in the upper South Carolina Piedmont was Jefferson Verne Smith, born near Greer in 1875 and a descendant of the Scotch-Irish Presbyterians that had settled Greenville just after the American Revolution. Smith went to work initially for the Bank of Greer and later opened the Greer Furniture Company. In 1901, at the age of twenty-six, Smith planted peaches on 50 acres of land he named the Mount Vernon Orchard. Three years later he harvested the first crop. Smith worked in the orchard day after day, experimenting with insecticides and eventually irrigation. When the coming of the railroad and the refrigerator car made peach production profitable, Smith expanded his own operation into Georgia, where he developed the Alto Orchard. Meanwhile, he became a champion of peach production throughout the region. By 1924, when the South Carolina Peach Growers' Association was established, Smith was shipping twice the number of peaches shipped by growers in Spartanburg County. At his death in October 1933, he was serving as president of the state Peach Growers' Association.[26]

The Rise of Tillman

Meanwhile the Farmers' Alliance in South Carolina was coopted by the state Farmers' Association founded by Benjamin R. Tillman of Edgefield as an overtly political group. Tillman had initially declared war against the state conservative leadership in a speech before a joint meeting of the Grange and the Agricultural Society in August 1885. He blamed the plight of the farmers on "the polluted atmosphere" of the State House, which was controlled by "General This and Judge That and Colonel Something Else." The following year he established the Farmers' Association to wrest control of the state Democratic Party from the conservatives. On April 29, 1886, a Farmers' Convention met in Columbia. The Greenville delegation was composed of A. M. Howell, Milton Donaldson, T. J. Austin, George L. Blakeley, James L. McCullough, and H. P. Edwards. Conspicuously absent were the business leaders of Greenville. With high hopes, Tillman's supporters demanded a state-supported agricultural college, repeal of the lien law, abolition of the Citadel (which they called "that military dude factory"), an industrial college for women, and a new state constitution.[27]

For four years Tillman failed in an effort to elect sympathetic conservative leaders. In the meantime, Thomas Green Clemson left a bequest of money and the Calhoun estate to South Carolina for an agricultural college, but the bill to establish the Clemson Agricultural and Mechanical College passed the state Senate in December 1888 only by the vote of Lieutenant Governor William L. Mauldin of Greenville. This slim victory led Tillman to adopt a more aggressive political strategy.[28]

On March 27, 1890, the Farmers' Convention met to nominate Benjamin R. Tillman for governor. There were ten members of the Greenville delegation—John R. Harrison, H. B. Buist, J. P. Goodwin, Arthur Eubanks, Dr. H. P. Goodwin, J. I. Austin, J. M. Whitmire, J. J. Mackey, W. P. Addison, and A. W. McDavid. In the words of Alfred B. Williams, the editor of the Greenville *News* who was once a friend of Tillman but who became one of his severest critics, "the Farmers' Movement, for the farmers, of the farmers, and by the farmers, has been twisted into a Tillman Movement, for Tillman, and by Tillman."[29]

One of Tillman's chief lieutenants in Greenville was Milton Lafayette Donaldson, brother of T. Q. Donaldson, former state senator (1872–1876) and active promoter of local mills, railroads, and banks. Milton Donaldson was born in the Greenville District on July 29, 1844. He left school to enlist in the Confederate army and after the war became a farmer in Laurens and Greenville Counties. In 1866 he married Margaret Louisa Ware. He was considered one of the leading agriculturists in the state and regularly published articles in farm journals. He served in the state House of Representatives from 1878 to 1885 and in the state Senate from 1888 to 1891. He was a delegate to the Bennettsville convention in 1885 when Tillman launched his political campaign. A life trustee of Clemson College from 1888 until his death in 1924, Donaldson served as president of both the Greenville County Farmers Alliance and the state alliance (1892–1893). He was manager of the state Farmers Alliance Exchange from 1889 to 1891, national Democratic executive committee member from South Carolina from 1892 to 1896, and also served as a deacon of Pendleton Street Baptist Church.[30]

Tillman quickly won his first victory over the state Democratic machinery. On May 8, 1890, the state executive committee, whose chair was James A. Hoyt of Greenville, was determined to hold a series of stump meetings in every county seat in the state to allow the candidates for governor to present their cases to the voters. The meetings began in the up country, and the debate in Greenville was set for Tuesday, June 10. This precedent set the form of statewide politics in South Carolina until the advent of television after World War II.[31]

There were three candidates for governor in 1890—Tillman; state Attorney General Joseph H. Earle, a native of Greenville and the choice of the conservative leadership; and John Bratton, a conservative planter from York County. They arrived in Greenville on June 9 and stayed at the Mansion House. Anticipating a crowd too large for the courthouse, the traditional location of public meetings, the county Democratic Executive Committee set the site in the new City Park on North Main Street and erected a speakers' stand for the occasion.[32]

According to the Charleston *News and Courier,* "long before sunrise buggies, wagons, and all kinds of vehicles began to pour into Greenville filled with the sturdy yeomen of the Piedmont country. . . . All classes were there, from the dapper young lawyer of the city to the political seer of the country crossroads." There were "a number of ladies in carriages on the outskirts of the crowd." A few minutes before 11:00 A.M., the Greenville Brass Band began playing outside the Mansion House as a procession of carriages waited to carry the candidates to the park. "The carriage in which Captain Tillman rode was decorated with clover blossoms, sheaves of oats and wheat, ears of golden corn and other products of the fields."[33]

The county Democratic chair, Benjamin F. Perry, Jr., called the meeting to order and introduced Tillman, the first speaker. In a high, rasping voice, the Edgefield farmer began by saying that "he was the most maligned man in the State, and he wanted the people to see him and know what he looked like." He declared that "we are on the eve of a revolution. Some old things are to be done away with. . . . I am a mere instrument in the hands of a higher power. . . . Why are the people from Charleston to the mountains rising in their might? They want self-government." Elected officials "have arranged for their successors in office. We common people have demanded the primary, but we couldn't get it." When Tillman sat down, there were "storms of applause and cries of 'Go on!' 'Give us some more!' 'Don't stop yet!'"[34]

Next, Joseph H. Earle spoke after identifying himself as a Greenville native. But the crowd was clearly for Tillman. "I have no need of an introduction to a Greenville audience," Earle said, "as I am upon my native heath." He took issue with Tillman by saying that "we now have control of the government. . . . All is not rotten in the state of Denmark." He asked rhetorically: "What is all this fuss about?" And a voice from the crowd answered: "Tillman, and we are going to have him." Earle responded that "other citizens" besides farmers "have rights. Farmers pay taxes, but others pay even more. . . . I belong to no ring, and I never intend to act with any ring." Bratton followed Earle, but the crowd shouted even louder for Tillman.[35]

The Charleston *News and Courier* and the Greenville *News*—both anti-Tillman newspapers—attacked Tillman and his supporters at the Greenville rally. "The attempt of the shouters for Tillman," the Charleston newspaper said, "to convert into a Tillman rally a meeting regularly called by the State Democratic authorities . . . is not calculated to make a good impression upon the public mind or to gain any strength for Captain Tillman." A. B. Williams of the Greenville *News* questioned Tillman's integrity. "Tillman and his supporters are sworn to support a primary, but they have not made an effort in any county to choose delegates to the State [Democratic] Convention by primary. In Abbeville where they are in the majority on the executive committee, they voted down a resolution for a primary."[36]

But the stump meetings of 1890 grew even more raucous. Tillman was hissed at in Columbia, and U.S. Senator Wade Hampton, the hero of the conservatives, was shouted down at Aiken. It became increasingly clear that Tillman was sweeping the state. Throughout the weeks of June and July, the Democratic clubs in the rural townships of Greenville County met and endorsed Tillman. The resolution of the Batesville club on June 7 was typical: "Resolved, That the Batesville Democratic Club do heartily endorse the action of the March Convention in the nomination of B. R. Tillman for Governor, and that we pledge our hearty support to secure his nomination at the September convention." Conspicuous by its contrary action was the "enthusiastic meeting" of the East Piedmont Democratic Club "held in the office of the Piedmont Manufacturing Company" which nominated James L. Orr, Jr.—conservative political leader, president of the Greenville *News,* son-in-law of Piedmont Mill President Henry P. Hammett, and Hammett's heir apparent—for governor. Clearly, the manufacturing interests and the majority of the city leadership in Greenville did not support Tillman.[37]

Tillman captured both the state Democratic Convention and the nomination for governor. Diehard conservatives split the party by holding a rump convention that nominated Alexander C. Haskell of Columbia. Most conservatives, including those from Greenville County, refused to join the diehards and open the door for a Republican resurgence. The Greenville *Enterprise and Mountaineer* had made its position clear after the March convention: "'Tillmanism' may be ridiculed by the opponents of Col. [sic] Tillman, but, for all that it is our opinion that since his name has been brought forward in the manner it has, it and the Farmers' movement have become synonymous—they stand or fall together. This is a contest to be waged within the Democratic party. . . . [T]he Democratic party will stand together as a unit."[38]

Prominent on the statewide Tillman ticket was Greenville attorney William David Mayfield, the candidate for state superintendent of education. Born in 1854 in Polk County, Tennessee, the son of South Carolina natives William and Lillian Blythe Mayfield, he returned to South Carolina soon after the Civil War. Following graduation from Tennessee's Hiwassee College in 1875, Mayfield taught school for several years, and in 1878 he was elected a school commissioner of Greenville County, where he served four terms. He was admitted to the bar in 1880, and in 1881 entered a partnership with his uncle, Absalom Blythe, the circuit solicitor and later a U.S. marshal. He was elected state superintendent of education in 1890 and served four terms, retiring in 1898 to practice law in Columbia.[39]

Textile Legislation under Tillman

The hostility of the town elite to Tillman seemed justified when petitions came to the General Assembly in 1890 seeking child labor legislation. A bill abolishing child labor until sixteen and limiting women's work to ten hours a day was introduced in November, and immediately "the Big Four" mill presidents—Henry Hammett and Ellison Smyth of Greenville and John H. Montgomery and Dexter E. Converse of Spartanburg—headed for Columbia. They reached an agreement with the Tillmanites that dropped any reference to child labor and set the limitation on the hours that women and children could work at eleven. The House passed the bill, but it was defeated in the Senate under the leadership of Augustine T. Smythe of Charleston, the brother of Ellison. Milton Donaldson supported the measure since "there was now a chance to settle a matter that cropped up annually." He declared that "it [was] unjust that the Senate should now try to undo an agreement in the absence of those who had come to the agreement."[40]

In March 1892 the conservatives of Greenville sent a delegation to a Peace and Harmony Convention in Columbia to nominate candidates to oppose the Tillmanites. The delegation was composed of former Lieutenant Governor William L. Mauldin, Piedmont Mill President James L. Orr, Jr., Greenville *News* editor A. B. Williams, S. G. Smith, John W. Baker, C. O. Allen, T. B. Cunningham, T. K. Earle, Silas Trowbridge, Philemon D. Huff, John W. McCullough, and D. R. Anderson. The convention nominated former governor and Furman alumnus John C. Sheppard, an Edgefield banker, for governor and James L. Orr, Jr., for lieutenant governor.[41]

In 1892 Tillman injected a new issue into the campaign. He declared that the "issue is . . . whether people or corporations shall rule." He blasted Sheppard and Orr as "representatives of corporate power," controlled by railroads such as the Air Line. At the stump meeting in Greenville, Tillman charged that Orr was "president of a factory that is making men and women work thirteen hours a day." Orr replied that the governor did not know "what he is talking about" and was trying to arouse prejudice against cotton mills as he had against banks and railroads.[42]

Though Tillman was mainly a spokesperson for the farmers and was accused of referring to millworkers as "that damned factory class," his supporters tried to organize the mill vote. They accused the mill owners of political intimidation. In his speech in Greenville the governor read an affidavit from W. L. Snipes, an employee at the Pelzer Mill, claiming that he was discharged for attending a Tillman rally. Ellison Smyth promptly sent a telegram to the governor: "The statement of Snipes is false. . . . He voluntarily left the employ of the company." At the same time Smyth told the press that he had discharged other employees, but for "non-political reasons." The workers at Pelzer held a mass meeting to protest Tillman's charge that operatives were "tyrannically treated" and to express their affection for Ellison Smyth. In the end, Tillman's success with the mill workers was mixed. He carried the Pelham Mill box, but Pelzer supported the conservative ticket by four votes, and Piedmont, where Orr was president, went for the conservatives more than two to one.[43]

In the newly elected legislature in 1892, Tillman reigned supreme, and a maximum hours bill was quickly introduced in the House, supported by Benjamin F. Perry, Jr., of Greenville, son of the former governor. The "Big Four" once against descended on Columbia, this time including Orr. A stormy session produced a compromise limiting hours to eleven per day and sixty-six per week. But the mill presidents were able to avoid their worst nightmare—child labor legislation. In September 1892 Orr had written the president of the Newberry Mill that "I do not dread the labor law for hours as much as I do for ages. A law prohibiting the working of children under 16 yrs. old, would increase the cost of production about 25%, and if the age were fixed at 14 the cost would be increased at least 10%." It was Orr's view that "from 12 to 16 they make the best spinners and doffers and I don't see how we could get along in the Spinning room without that class." Orr had little to fear; there was no more labor legislation until 1903.[44]

Prohibition and the Dispensary

One of Tillman's major innovations in state government was the creation of the dispensary—his effort to control the sale of alcoholic beverages in South Carolina. The postbellum temperance crusade had begun in the state in the 1870s, and the Greenville Division of the Sons of Temperance was organized in October 1872 at the courthouse, under the leadership of E. J. Meynardie, pastor of the Methodist Church. Concurrently, the Greenville Lodge of Good Templars was established. On March 26, 1873, the *Enterprise* indicated that the movement was organized in almost every town in South Carolina and was growing in influence. A decade later Frances Willard formed groups of the Women's Christian Temperance Union (WCTU), and in February 1884 the Greenville WCTU opened a reading room adjacent to the post office. The library was the gift of Paul Trapier Hayne, a local business person, school trustee, and a member of the city council. In 1890 the state legislature outlawed the sale of liquor in rural areas, and by 1891 seventy-eight communities had exercised local option to secure prohibition. A state Prohibition Party supported statewide legislation. The proposal passed the House; but failed in the Senate, and a referendum on prohibition was placed on the ballot in 1892. Statewide, the measure passed by 15,558 votes. In Greenville County the vote was 1,545 for prohibition and 1,016 against. But only 53 percent of those voting for political candidates cast ballots for or against the referendum.[45]

Fearing that his supporters might become divided on the temperance question, Tillman proposed state monopoly of liquor sales, and on July 1, 1893, the offices of the state dispensary opened in every county of the state. In Greenville the saloons on Main Street did a brisk business on June 30, the last day they were open. The Columbia *State* reported: "Corn and rye sold at cost. . . . Main Street was dignified by the man and jug, laying in a supply for the rainy day. Saloon keepers have sold out closely, having on hand remnants of peach and apple brandy, short in rye and no corn."[46]

Tillman proposed to enforce the dispensary law by the use of constables especially appointed for the purpose. But local law enforcement officials often failed to support the new law. On October 4, 1894, state Constable W. B. Workman arrested the black driver of a wagon who was delivering a supply of export beer from the home of Sol Edel on North Street to the Mansion House. The constable secured a search warrant for Edel's home, but Sheriff P. D. Gilreath refused to execute it. "You are going too far," the sheriff told Workman, "when you undertake to search people's private houses before the constitutionality of the law has been passed on." Informed of the sheriff's refusal, Tillman wired him from Columbia: "If you do not execute search warrant . . . will have to report it to the General Assembly and ask your removal." But the old sheriff was not cowed. Edel appeared on his porch and, according to the Greenville *News,* declared "time after time he would blow out the brains of any man who entered his house without permission." A crowd of some two hundred people gathered in the street and greeted his threats with rebel yells. When another constable drew a pistol, people in the crowd began to draw theirs. The Greenville chief of police quickly arrested the constable. When the governor asked Mayor James T. Williams for police support, the mayor refused. The following day the *News* reported that "there is an evident determination among all classes of people that [the constables] shall not search private houses in Greenville." The dispensary was eventually abolished during the administration of Greenville Governor Martin F. Ansel in 1907 and replaced by local option permitting communities to allow or prohibit liquor sales.[47]

The Age of Segregation

A more enduring legacy of Tillman, which survived in Greenville County for more than fifty years, was the legal system of segregation. Since the end of Reconstruction the pattern of race relations had not been defined legally. The public schools were segregated, as were the churches. Personal relations were seldom, if ever, on the basis of equality. But the state civil rights laws of 1869 and 1870 had not been repealed.[48]

In the city of Greenville blacks lived on almost every street and in every section. Black-owned businesses were quite common—dominating the hacking and drayage business, as well as the bakeries, blacksmith shops, and catering. As late as 1899 there were six black-owned barbershops on Main Street with fifteen barbers, three retail stores, one meat market, and three restaurants.[49]

But the mood of the nation as well as the South had begun to change. In 1882 the South Carolina legislature passed the Eight Box Law that disfranchised enough black voters to remove the threat of a Republican resurgence in the state. The next year the United States Supreme Court declared provisions of the federal Civil Rights Law of 1875 unconstitutional. In 1888 a young Tillman lieutenant, John Gary Evans, introduced a bill in the state legislature to separate white and black passengers on the railroad; it did not pass, but the die was cast. In 1890 Tillman in his inaugural address announced without equivocation: "The whites have absolute control of the State Government, and we intend at any and all hazards to retain it."[50]

In subsequent years, Tillman regarded the state Constitution of 1895 as his crowning achievement, since, in his opinion, he disfranchised blacks and removed the threat of the Republican Party in South Carolina. The Greenville County delegation to the constitutional convention consisted of J. Walter Gray, a Greenville attorney; J. Thomas Austin, the register of mesne conveyance and a farmer; Hugh M. Barton, a farmer from Chick Springs; and Hugh B. Buist, Harry J. Haynsworth, and G. G. Wells, all Greenville attorneys. Haynsworth served on the all-important Committee on Rights and Suffrage, of which Tillman himself was chair. The committee proposed a poll tax and residence requirements for voting that discriminated against many blacks.[51]

The Suffrage Committee recommended that voters be able to read and interpret any section of the constitution the county registrar required or pay taxes on property assessed at three hundred dollars or more. These provisions, overwhelmingly approved by the convention, disfranchised most black voters, and as a result the Republican Party was radically reduced in numbers. The next year, in 1896, the state Democratic Party adopted a statewide primary that allowed only blacks who had supported Hampton in 1876 to vote. Tillman had fulfilled his promise to maintain white supremacy in state and local governments.[52]

But the Tillmanites did not stop there. The constitution required that the state operate separate schools for white and black students. In 1898 the legislature passed a law requiring railroads to provide separate coaches for the two races. In 1904 segregation was required on steam ferries, and the next year the law was extended to trolley cars. Whites were to be seated from the front, and blacks from the rear. In 1902 only qualified voters were allowed to serve on juries. The Factory Law of 1915 prohibited textile mills from employing workers of different races in the same room. Legal segregation became a fact of life in South Carolina.[53]

The coming of segregation in Greenville County paralleled the change in the growth of the black population. In 1870 there were only 7,141 blacks, a decline of 1.7 percent since 1860. But in the following decade the black population jumped 103.2 percent to 14,511. In 1880 38.7 percent of the population of Greenville County was black, but the percentage began to decline. By 1910 there were 20,861 blacks in Greenville County, down to 30.1 percent.[54]

County Government

The Tillman legacy not only inscribed white supremacy in the fundamental law of South Carolina, but it changed county government as well. In 1894 the position of county supervisor was created by the legislature with "general jurisdiction over all public highways, roads, bridges and ferries, and over paupers, and in all matters relating to taxes and disbursements of public funds for county purposes." There was also a county board of commissioners established with one representative from each township. The County Government Act of 1899 shifted real power in the county to the legislative delegation. The supervisor and a new board of two commissioners were appointed by the governor on recommendation of the delegation. The county budget, or the supply bill, was to be adopted annually by the state legislature, which accepted the recommendation of the delegation. Since there was only one county senator, and the supply bill had to pass the Senate, he quickly became the single most powerful figure in county government. Little could be done without his initiative or approval. As James M. Richardson, a later state senator, put it, the county delegation "assumed what amounts to dictatorial powers over all county officials and county affairs. In state matters they are legislators, but in their county they are executives."[55]

If Tillman had anticipated that the state senators would insure the perpetuation of Tillmanism on the county level, such was not the case in counties with growing urban and industrial areas. Greenville County elected only two Tillman lieutenants to the state Senate—Milton L. Donaldson, who served one two-year term from 1890 to 1891, and John R. Harrison, who served two terms from 1892 to 1896. Both were farmers. Harrison was born in 1845 near Fountain Inn and had served in the Confederate Army. He lived on the family farm until 1900, when he moved to Laurens for two years and then to Fountain Inn. An elder of Fairview Presbyterian Church, Harrison served in the state House of Representatives at three different times—1880–1882, 1888–1891, and 1905–1912. During his second term in the state Senate (1894–1896), Harrison was elected president pro tem. He was active in the Farmers' movement, the Alliance, and unsuccessfully ran for secretary of state in 1894 and for governor in 1896.[56]

After the adoption of the Constitution of 1895, however, four persons served as state senator from Greenville County until after World War I, and all were residents of the city of Greenville—Alvin Henry Dean, William Lawrence Mauldin, Wilton Haynsworth Earle, and Procter Aldrich Bonham. Only Mauldin, a pharmacist, was not an attorney. All had attended college—Dean, Mauldin, and Earle at Furman, and Bonham at Georgetown University and the College of Charleston. Earle had a law degree from the University of Michigan; Dean had studied law for two years at Vanderbilt, and Bonham briefly at the University of North Carolina. Mauldin and Dean were both mayors of Greenville; Earle was city attorney. Bonham served as circuit solicitor from 1909 to 1916. (Under the Tillman constitution, incumbencies were longer: from 1876 to 1891 the average term was 2.8 years; after 1891 the average term lengthened to 6.6 years.)[57]

The New Shape of the Textile Industry

While Tillman personally dominated state politics through the Convention of 1895, he had moved on to a seat in the U.S. Senate in 1894, and his influence began to wane locally. At the same time, the textile industry, which had developed slowly through the Panics of 1873 and 1893, began to accelerate its growth in 1895. "Prior to 1894," according to Alester G. Furman, a key figure in the new generation of business leaders in Greenville, "our industrial enterprises did not represent a very large invested capital." The new mills, built in the two decades before another brief slump in the Southern economy in 1914, were patterned on the larger New England model adopted by Henry P. Hammett at Piedmont and Ellison Smyth at Pelzer rather than the smaller mills, such as Camperdown and Reedy River. Indeed, a publication of the Massachusetts Bureau of Statistics of Labor in 1905 indicated that "a large proportion of the mills (Southern) built and started between 1890 and 1900 are thoroughly up-to-date in all respects; in fact some improvements in mill construction are to be found in that section which are not yet introduced in the manufacturing regions of the North."[58]

The new textile industry began to take shape in 1894 when the Camperdown Mills closed. Oscar H. Sampson, one of the major investors in the Camperdown company, purchased the company by paying nine thousand dollars for an eighty-seven-thousand-dollar mortgage. He built the Sampson Mill near the Air Line Railroad outside the city limits, and the machinery from Camperdown was moved into the new structure. Sampson Mill was reorganized as the American Spinning Company, and by 1903 it had a capital of six hundred thousand dollars and operated thirty-five thousand spindles. Between 750 and 800 operatives were employed in the mill. James H. Morgan, a native of Greenville County who had been a merchant in the city of Greenville since 1871, became president. James L. Orr, Jr., was vice president, and W. B. Boyd was secretary.[59]

In 1895 Francis W. Poe organized the F. W. Poe Manufacturing Company, which was located across the Air Line railroad from the American Spinning Mill. Poe was born in Montgomery, Alabama, in 1855 and grew up near Pendleton. He opened a clothing store in Greenville in 1880. Although highly successful, at the age of forty he left the mercantile business so as to enter cotton textile manufacturing. Francis Poe served as president and treasurer of the company, and his brother, Nelson, who was in the hardware business, became vice president. The company was initially capitalized at $250,000 in order to construct a mill with ten thousand spindles. In two years five thousand spindles were added, and in 1903 Poe Mill was operating sixty thousand spindles, and the capital had increased to five hundred thousand dollars. The plant employed between nine hundred and one thousand persons who lived in the adjacent mill village which had a population of some twenty-five hundred.[60]

A third cotton mill, the Mills Manufacturing Company, was organized in 1895 by Captain Otis Prentiss Mills. Born in Henderson County, North Carolina, Mills served in the Confederate army and later moved to Greenville, where he entered the mercantile firm of Miller, Mills & Patton on Augusta Street. He married Susan Cordelia Gower, the daughter of T. C. Gower, in 1867. After organizing a successful dairy business and a fertilizer company, he organized Mills Mill in the mid-1890s with capital of $371,000 and five thousand spindles. By 1903 the capital had grown to more than six hundred thousand dollars, and the company operated twenty-seven thousand spindles and 740 looms. O. P. Mills was president and treasurer, and his son-in-law, W. B. Moore, was secretary and general manager.[61]

The continuing interest of low country business people in up country textiles was represented by J. Irving Westervelt, a native of Pinopolis. In 1880 he entered the firm of Arthur Barnwell & Company and soon became secretary and treasurer of the Charleston Cotton Mill. When Barnwell became president of the Pelham Mill, Westervelt became its treasurer. In 1900 Westervelt organized Brandon Mill and served as president and treasurer. The other directors included Ellison Smyth, Frank Hammond, Summerfield Baldwin, Jr., J. Ross Hanahan, T. Q. Donaldson, and William E. Beattie. Begun with a capital of $220,000 and ten thousand spindles, Brandon increased its capital to $450,000 and spindles to forty-one thousand in 1903.[62]

Two cousins, Thomas Fleming Parker and Lewis Wardlaw Parker, became cotton manufacturers by 1900. The elder, Thomas Parker, was born in Charleston in 1860 and came to Greenville from North Carolina, where he had been involved in the Linville Land Improvement Company. The younger cousin, Lewis Parker, was born in Abbeville in 1865 and came to Greenville to practice law in 1889. In 1897 he was attorney for the Victor Mill in Greer, which was in financial difficulties. The directors requested that Parker reorganize the business, which he did. Meanwhile, in February 1900, the Parkers organized Monaghan Mill, which they located on Cedar Lane Road just beyond the Poe and American Spinning mills. Thomas Parker became president of the company, and Lewis Parker treasurer. The original stock subscription was $450,000, which was increased to $700,000 by 1903. The number of spindles increased during the same period from twenty-five thousand to sixty thousand.[63]

The Woodside Empire

Typical of the new generation of textile entrepreneurs who turned the industry into big business in South Carolina was John T. Woodside. Born in 1865 on his father's farm in lower Greenville County, Woodside was one of twelve children of Dr. John Lawrence Woodside (a country doctor, farmer, and cotton gin, saw mill, and tannery owner) and Ellen Charles Woodside (an exemplar of Presbyterian piety and fortitude). The family attended Fairview Church until Ellen Woodside founded Lickville Presbyterian Church closer to their home in 1882. After completing the local school, nineteen-year-old John Woodside taught school for a year in Greer and then went to work for three years at the Reedy River Mill at Conestee, where his uncle Joseph D. Charles was secretary and treasurer.[64]

In 1887 Woodside left Greenville to work in Birmingham, Alabama, but he stayed there briefly, returning to the Reedy River Mill where he worked until 1891. Having accumulated several thousand dollars, Woodside invested in a mercantile business at Pelzer, where there was no company store, in partnership with his brother-in-law, James W. Williams, and another individual. In April 1893 Woodside married Lou Carpenter, sold his interest in the Pelzer store, and moved to Greenville. Soon he was the proprietor of a grocery store on Main Street near the courthouse; but, as the boom years of the textile industry began, Woodside became restless. First, he joined his younger brother, J. D., in building a cottonseed oil mill in Gainesville, Georgia. In 1902 they decided to build a cotton mill in Greenville, and riding in a bright new buggy, John Woodside set out to sell stock in his new enterprise. In thirteen days the brothers raised more than eighty-five thousand dollars. With that sum, plus money borrowed from Northern investors and the profits from his grocery business, Woodside began to build a mill west of Monaghan which would run eleven thousand spindles.[65]

The Woodside Mill quickly became the cornerstone of a business empire. In 1904 the Woodsides enlarged their mill to thirty-three thousand spindles; in 1906 they bought the controlling stock in the Fountain Inn Manufacturing Company, which operated ten thousand spindles and added seven thousand more; and in 1908 another brother, Edward F. Woodside, who was working at Pelzer, joined the dynasty to build an eight-thousand-spindle mill in Simpsonville. This mill subsequently expanded to twenty-five thousand spindles. Soon, John Woodside consolidated the three mills into a single corporation. He became president; his brother, Edward, vice president and operating manager; and his brother, J. D., vice president and treasurer. In September 1912 Woodside announced his most ambitious improvement. The Woodside Mill would expand to 112,000 spindles. The Greenville *Daily News* said that the addition would make Woodside "the largest complete cotton mill in the United States under one roof, and one of the largest in the world."[66]

Meanwhile, in 1907 John Woodside had entered the banking business. He brought another brother, Robert I. Woodside, into the group to establish the Farmers and Merchants Bank. He referred to the brothers as "the big four." Within ten more years, the Woodsides had added the Woodside National Bank, the Bank of Woodville, the Citizens Bank of Taylors, and the Farmers Loan and Trust Company to their financial empire. By his own reckoning, John Woodside accounted himself the richest man in Greenville County prior to World War I.[67]

Lewis W. Parker

In that period Lewis W. Parker became the master of mill consolidation. Descended from the distinguished Wardlaw family of the up country and the Parker family of Charleston, he was born in Abbeville on July 11, 1865—the same year as John T. Woodside. He attended school in Abbeville until the age of fifteen, when he went to work as a store clerk. Following graduation from South Carolina College in 1885, Parker studied law, taught school, and then began the practice of law in Greenville. First, he was a partner of Joseph A. McCullough and, later, of Harry J. Haynsworth. In 1891 he organized the Piedmont Savings & Investment Company and subsequently became president of the Bank of Greer. During this same decade, Parker began to invest in cotton mills. He became president of Victor Manufacturing Company in Greer and joined his cousin, Thomas F. Parker, in establishing Monaghan Mill. Meanwhile, W. B. Smith Whaley of Columbia had organized a group of four mills there and the Appalache Mill in Greer. When "the Whaley group" was reorganized, Parker became president and treasurer of the company, which was capitalized at $5 million dollars and operated 340,000 spindles. With this base, in December 1910, Lewis Parker organized the Parker Cotton Mills Company, which owned sixteen mills, had a combined capital of $15 million dollars and operated more than a million spindles. As president and treasurer, Parker controlled more spindles than any individual in the country.[68]

Smaller Mills

Meanwhile, other mills had been established—the Carolina Mill which later became Poinsett, the Franklin Mill of Greer, and the McGhee Mill. In 1910 Dunean Mill and Westervelt Mill, which became Judson Mil, were opened. The Huguenot Mill purchased the old Camperdown building on the east bank of the Reedy River, installed three hundred looms, and began operations there. A new departure was the construction of the Union Bleaching and Finishing Company in 1902. The company was financed by Benjamin N. Duke and James Buchanan Duke of North Carolina. With the opening of Union Bleachery, large quantities of "grey goods" could be bleached, dyed, and finished in Greenville rather than shipped to Northern mills for the finishing process. The Union Bleachery opened with a capacity of 125,000 yards per day, but the building was constructed so that its output could be easily doubled. The impact of the rapidly expanding textile industry in the Southern Piedmont was evident by April 1906 when the Southern Railway issued $200 million dollars in bonds to begin constructing double tracks.[69]

A few small, independent mills were still operating in Greenville County. Notable for its management was the Batesville Mill on Rocky Creek. After the closing of the original Camperdown Mills in 1879, George Putnam purchased the Batesville Mill. His oldest daughter, Mary Putnam Gridley, kept books for her father at Batesville, and when George Putnam died in 1890, she became president—perhaps the first woman mill president in the South. According to family tradition, she signed her name "M. P. Gridley" because women were not generally believed capable of conducting such an extensive business. She remained president until 1912, when the mill was sold.[70]

A New Class: The Mill Worker

The growth and consolidation of the textile industry in Greenville County between 1895 and 1914 created a large market for labor, and thousands of people flooded into the area to work. The census indicated that in the thirty years between 1890 and 1920 the white population of Greenville County grew 42 percent. The "great migration," as the movement of workers from the farms to the cotton mills is sometimes called, came in two waves. As cotton prices fell in the 1880s and 1890s, farm laborers—both men and women—moved to the mills. The women included widows, heads of households, and single women. Then, as credit became tighter and prices fell even lower, landowning families and tenant families headed by men began to migrate. After 1900 cotton prices began to rise. As the number of mills increased, mill owners began to recruit labor actively.[71]

Some families came from the farms of Greenville County; more came from North Carolina, east Tennessee, and north Georgia. For example, Whildon Batson Anderson's father and mother were tenant farmers near Travelers Rest. "When they came to the [Camperdown] mill cotton sold at three cents a pound," she recalled, "so farmers just couldn't make it. . . . Seed and fertilizer cost more than they made." In 1905 agents from the Brandon Mill arrived in Newport, Tennessee. They persuaded the grandfather, father, and uncles of Jessie Lee Carter to move to Greenville. The mill supplied horse-drawn wagons, in which the family packed their belongings. With a milk cow tied to one wagon, the little caravan crossed the mountains and arrived in Greenville a week later.[72]

An important aspect of recruitment was often a family member or a friend who had already made the transition to the mill. Grover Hardin remembered that his mother tried to operate the family farm in east Tennessee after her husband died, leaving her with three children. A friend in Greenville "wrote and told my mother that if she'd come down she could get a job, you know, and make a living for us." Hardin cared for the younger children, while his mother went to work in the mill. When he was eleven, he began work as a sweeper. Ernest Hickum's brother left the family farm in western North Carolina and went to work at Woodside Mill. Later the rest of the family followed.[73]

The Textile Manufacturing Process

With the exception of a few smaller mills like Batesville, which employed only forty-seven workers in 1907, the newer, integrated cotton mills transformed raw cotton into yarn and then into cloth. The process began in the opening room, where the cotton was removed from the bales, and the fiber torn apart and cleaned by the opening machine. Huge vacuum tubes conveyed the lint into the picker room, where pickers cleaned it and smoothed it into sheets. The sheets of cotton were fed into carding machines, which further cleaned them and twisted them into loose roping. The cotton roping or slivers were fed into a drawing frame that combined and thinned them. The yarn was twisted and spun into thread. As the bobbins filled with thread, the doffers removed them, while the spinners repaired breaks and snags in the thread. Then, a spooling frame combined the threads from a number of bobbins to make it stronger and larger.

In the weave room, the thread was mounted on a loom beam, and draw-in hands laced each thread through metal eyes on the harness. The beam and harness were mounted on a loom, and the shuttle began to weave warp and weft into cloth, as the loom raised and lowered the harnesses. A reed beat the newly woven threads against the cloth. The woven cloth was wound around a cloth beam and taken into the cloth room. There the cloth was inspected and prepared for shipment.[74]

The Work Force in the Mills

The mills were operated by superintendents, who were self-taught and had been promoted through the ranks. Each department had its overseer, who had second hands to enforce discipline and section men to keep the machinery in operation. Colonel James L. Orr compared Piedmont Mill to a university: "As a university points with pride to its graduates, so Piedmont refers to the . . . superintendents who have taken their 'degrees' in the mechanical college. . . . There are thirty-eight superintendents [in 1903] who have gone out from Piedmont controlling more than 550,000 spindles in this state, Georgia and North Carolina." Orr defined work, character, and energy as the three characteristics necessary for the success of any superintendent. "Any cotton mill man possessing them," Orr wrote, "can attain such a position."[75]

In the mills themselves the owners and managers depended on the family labor system of men, women, and children. To be sure, most mill families had once worked together on the farm, but in the mill they were subject to the discipline of the machine. Whildon Anderson recalled that she "went to work at the mill when [she] was thirteen. You worked from a quarter to six in the morning to quitting time at a quarter to six in the evening." The pounding of the leather belts and the clacking of the machinery were ever present. Cotton lint swirled through the air and settled on the hair and clothes of the operatives and marked them as "lintheads." They inhaled cotton dust, and their lungs became clogged with it. Working conditions varied from mill to mill. Anderson remembered that "the mill was clean; Camperdown kept their place clean." John Heath in City View remembered "how dirty the mills were. So many women dipped snuff, and the men chewed tobacco. They'd spit right on the floor! There were no health laws then." Heath's father went to work as a young man at Woodside Mill when it opened. The discipline of children was sometimes severe. "He said if there was anybody he hated in his life it was the boss, the foreman. He held a boy by his feet and dangled him out of the window; that was to make him work. They did that to kids."[76]

Mill workers took pride in the jobs they had learned at an early age. Naomi Trammell went to work in the Victor Mill at Greer and "didn't know hardly about mill work." She remembered how she "had to crawl up on the frame, because I wasn't tall enough. I was a little old spindly thing. I wasn't the only one, there's a whole place like that. And they had mothers and daddies [but they] wasn't no better off than I was. They had to learn us, but it didn't take me long to learn. They'd put us with one of the spinners and they'd show us how. It was easy to learn—all we had to do was just put that bobbin in there and put it up."[77]

Almost all mill workers were white. Slaves had worked in the spinning and weave rooms of some of the antebellum factories, but after the Civil War production jobs were customarily reserved for whites. Custom was written into law in South Carolina by the Segregation Law of 1915. It became illegal for anyone "engaged in the business of cotton textile manufacturing" to allow persons "of different races to labor and work together within the same room." The law did permit blacks to work in nonmachine jobs, so black men were hired to unload cotton bales and load finished goods. Later, when health laws were enacted, black women were employed to scrub the floors and clean the bathrooms in the mills.[78]

Despite the long hours and poor working conditions, the mills offered their workers something they had never had on the farm—a pay envelope. "The mill always paid in cash," John Heath remembered; "nickels and dimes and quarters in little manilla envelopes." Adult white males received the highest wages, followed by women and children. Blacks earned slightly more than children. In 1904 white men were earning between about $4.50 and $5.50 a week. When Martin Lowe began working at Poe Mill at the age of twenty-one in 1912, he recalled, he was paid "a dollar a day, ten cents an hour. Sixty hours and six dollars, that's what we made." Several months later he moved to American Spinning for $1.25 a day. A few years later he received $2.25. Payment was based on the number of machines a worker could operate. After a worker passed his thirties, his wages began to decline. Wages in Southern textile mills were about 60 percent lower than those in the North, while the cost of living was only slightly lower in the South. On the whole, Southern mill owners retained a higher share of the profits than owners in the North.[79]

Life in the Mill Village

Greenville mill owners had provided housing for their operatives since the antebellum period. In the late nineteenth century mill owners built houses for their workers in the style of nearby farm houses. They were rented to workers for twenty-five cents, later fifty cents, per room per month. In 1899 Daniel Augustus Tompkins, a native of Edgefield who became a leading textile manufacturer and engineer, published a handbook for mill owners entitled *Cotton Mill, Commercial Features*. He included plans for three- and four-room mill houses. Most mill houses built after 1900 reflected Tompkins's designs. The smaller villages, according to a report by federal investigators in 1907–1908, "are often primitive in the extreme. The streets are mere wagon roads and there are no sidewalks. Frequently the yards are not fenced off, and chickens, pigs, and cows run at large." Larger villages had graded roads, cinder paths, and pens for livestock."[80]

T. Charles Gower, writing in 1962, recalled that Poe Mill village had "no sewage system, but running water was furnished. Coal was sold at cost, about $2 a ton. Most of the cooking was done with wood, which sold for about $2 a cord. . . . Kerosene lamps were about the only source of light. Community stables were provided for workers at the Piedmont Mill, and a shallow steam tank and hot water was furnished near the boiler room for 'hog killing time.'" Woodside Mill village had no running water until 1930. John Heath remembered that "we drew water out of a well on our back porch. Every family had its own well. . . . The toilets were out-door backhouses." When the Camperdown Mill was electrified, power was added to the mill houses as well. "We had electricity at night," Whildon Anderson remembered. "They turned it on once a week in the day time to let you iron; that was Wednesday. The electricity was turned on at seven o'clock at night and turned off at seven in the morning. The lights were connected to the mill; they had control."[81]

More than one-third of the mills in the South operated stores in 1900. Not only did the companies provide wood and coal for their operatives, but mill stores did a general merchandise business. The Monaghan store, for example, was located across the street from the mill. "You could buy anything you wanted," according to Robert Campbell, "clothes, shoes, groceries." Credit was available at the store against the next pay period. According to John Heath, "what you bought was deducted from your pay even before you were paid. Many people didn't get one penny out of their pay ticket. Everything went to the store." At times the mills did not pay in cash, but in paper scrip or brass "looneys," which had to be redeemed at the store.[82]

Another aspect of life in the mill village was the elementary school operated sometimes independently of the city and county systems already in place. Schools were held in buildings provided by the mill, and teachers were carried on the mill payroll. Each of the mills in the Textile Crescent on the west side of the city of Greenville had its own school. According to August Kohn, the Brandon School building "cost $2,500, erected by the mill corporation. The company pays $700 a year towards the salary of three teachers and supplies the fuel. The county funds are used to the extent of $450." But as workers flooded into the mill villages, the schools were "over-crowded and in poor physical condition." The nearest high school was in the city of Greenville, and one mill parent complained that he had to pay $5 a month in tuition and 12.5 cents a day for transportation. As Victoria Hunter described the situation in 1924, "nearly every boy and girl thought that his education would end with the sixth grade. Many have already gone to work in the mills."[83]

Religion in the Mill Villages

Mill owners provided churches for their workers in the village. Usually these were Union church buildings in which Baptists and Methodists, and sometimes Presbyterians, met. Later the mills contributed the land and a significant part of the building cost for separate churches. Often the mills contributed to the support of the ministers. In the Camperdown Mill village, for example, there were Baptist and Methodist churches. According to August Kohn writing in the Charleston *News and Courier*, "the buildings were put up entirely by the corporation, and the company provides one-fourth of the salary of each of the pastors." The ministers often reciprocated by preaching a gospel of hard work, gratitude, and patience in adversity. Occasionally, however, a minister did not cooperate. Mack Duncan, concerning Preacher Anderson at Poe Baptist Church, recalled that "some of the officials of the company did not like some of the things he preached. They ordered him out of the church, [but] he didn't go too freely. So the church was locked up by the company." When the pastor insisted on preaching from his front porch, the company evicted him from his house in the village and found a new minister.[84]

More independent-minded mill workers joined denominations such as the Wesleyan Methodist Church, the Pentecostal Holiness Church, or the Church of God that operated at the edge of mill villages, beyond the control of the owners. The Wesleyan Methodist Church, for example, appeared in the upper Piedmont of South Carolina as early as 1887 and flourished initially in the counties east and west of Greenville. Wesleyans emphasized the "second blessing" of sanctification; the renunciation of tobacco, alcohol, and jewelry; and refusal to join "secret orders." The declaration of "the Farmers' Union" as a secret society in 1906 may have confirmed an attitude that restricted Wesleyan growth in rural areas during the Populist era.[85]

When the Wesleyans organized the South Carolina Conference in November 1893, one of the eleven churches was located at Pelzer, and Piedmont was listed as a "preaching point." In 1894 Flat Rock Church, later Golden Grove, was organized, followed by Bethany Church in Greer in 1896. By 1900 there were twenty-four churches with 1,131 members in the state. A church was established in Conestee in 1902, and churches were formed in Greenville, Poe Mill, and Camperdown Mill in 1906. The Fountain Inn Church was organized in 1916, and the annual camp meeting was located permanently in Greer in 1918.[86]

The Pentecostal movement burst upon upstate South Carolina in November 1896 when Wesleyan Methodist leaders invited Benjamin Harden Irwin, a flamboyant holiness preacher from Nebraska, to conduct a series of revivals. At the Wesleyan Church in Piedmont his preaching was like a bombshell. Not only did he proclaim the usual "second blessing" of holiness but also a "third blessing"—the baptism of fire that was accompanied by emotional outbursts such as speaking in tongues. Subsequent blessings—dynamite, lyddite, and oxidite—were more problematical. Out of Irwin's work emerged the Fire-Baptized Holiness Church, which he formed at a meeting in Anderson in 1898. In 1911 it united with the Pentecostal Holiness Church, which had emerged in North Carolina and Tennessee. Meanwhile the Church of God formed in the same area.[87]

Progressivism in the Mill Village: Parker and Hollis

Early in the twentieth century the mill companies inaugurated a number of Progressive programs known as welfare work. They included YMCA and YWCA programs, libraries, and kindergartens. One of the pioneers of welfare work was Thomas F. Parker, whose aim was to inspire each employee to do his best in a helpful environment. He employed a landscape architect to lay out the village at Monaghan, including space for playgrounds, a medical clinic, and the first industrial YMCA in the South.[88]

The first secretary of the Monaghan YMCA was I. E. Umger, a native of Iowa and former missionary to India. The work grew so rapidly that in the summer of 1905 Umger employed an assistant secretary, Lawrence Peter Hollis. When Umger left Greenville in the fall, L. P. Hollis became secretary. For the next three-quarters of a century Hollis was a prime mover in the educational and cultural life of Greenville. Born in 1883 in Chester County, South Carolina, he was the son of Victoria Gaston and Peter Hollis, a farmer. Following graduation from the University of South Carolina in 1905, Hollis became secretary at Monaghan at the age of twenty-one, and for four summers he attended YMCA training sessions at Lake George, New York. At an early training session, Hollis met Dr. James Naismith, the inventor of basketball, and decided to introduce basketball at Monaghan. On his way home Hollis stopped in New York City and purchased a basketball and a rulebook. On that same trip he met Lord Robert Baden-Powell, the founder of the Boy Scout movement. As a result, Hollis organized the first Boy Scout troop in South Carolina.[89]

The printed "programme" of the Monaghan YMCA for 1907 indicates the variety of activities over which Hollis presided. "It is written," he said, "for the young men who have good red blood in their veins, and are looking for some means of bettering their conditions spiritually, socially, mentally, or physically, or all of them." The physical department offered classes for men and boys on Tuesday and Thursday nights. In addition to basketball, there were bowling alleys, pool tables, skating, volleyball, and cross country runs. A Ramblers' Club took occasional trips, and at Christmas the gym classes sponsored a country circus.[90]

The educational department showed movies every two weeks during the winter. The Textile Club took "up the practical problems which they have to meet in the mill and work them out." Specialists, including a Clemson professor, met with the group. There were regularly scheduled health talks by local physicians, such as Dr. E. W. Carpenter who gave a lecture on consumption. The religious department sponsored Bible classes. A class for men met weekly to study "Main Lines in the Bible," and five cottage classes, taught by five different persons in different parts of the village on Monday nights, studied characters of the Bible. A leaders' class was taught by Hollis himself. A Dramatic Club presented two plays a year. There was a meeting for men every Sunday afternoon except the last Sunday of the month when a joint meeting was held with the YWCA.[91]

The social department held joint socials with the YWCA, including a potato roast at the tennis court. A Married Men's Club met every two weeks on Friday night, and all men in the village were invited to join. The themes of social uplift and progress were evident in the topics for the meetings—civic improvement, investments, and best plans of saving money. The meetings for November included a debate and the inevitable social with the Married Women's Club.[92]

The statistics that L. P. Hollis gave Thomas Parker on the welfare work at Monaghan were astounding. The mill employed over five hundred operatives, and the village population was over sixteen hundred. In a twelve-month period there were 47,168 visits to the YMCA and YWCA.[93]

In 1911 after the formation of the Parker Cotton Mills Company, Hollis became director of welfare activities for the sixteen-mill company. Then from 1916 to 1923, he was superintendent of the Victor-Monaghan Elementary Schools. After World War I Hollis became a nationally known educational figure. But in the early years in Monaghan, he got to know every man, woman, and child in the village. Not only a friend, he pledged his money and credit to people in trouble. Years later his secretary would complain: "He never has a dime because he is always lending people money. Everybody owes him from $10 to $50." Robert L. Campbell remembered the community spirit of Monaghan: "Everybody was happy. . . . L. P. Hollis was a wonderful person to help the mill people; he did much for the people!"[94]

Mill owners were not always disinterested reformers. Thomas Parker, in an address at Trinity College, now Duke University, on October 3, 1910, was clear about the economic motivations of welfare work. "If mills could afford a yearly average expenditure of 1 percent of their capital for adequate buildings and competent welfare workers with active support by the presidents," he said, "the villagers would quickly be revolutionized, and not only would they retain a true friendliness towards the management, which is decreasing, but would escape the future control of demagogues and labor agitators."[95]

A number of mill owners gained a reputation for their paternalism. Everette Padgett remembered an occasion when Richard Arrington, president of Union Bleachery, rescued him from financial difficulty. The company doctor had charged Padgett $150 for an operation for his wife. Company regulations forbid an employee from withdrawing more than one hundred dollars from the "sick benefits" program. According to Padgett, Arrington "picked up the phone, and he called Dr. Parker. He said, 'Now look here, this boy and girl just started out. . . . They can't stand no kind of bill like that. Couldn't you do something about it?' Padgett never knew what the doctor said; but, as he relates, Arrington "made out a check to me and Dr. Parker for fifty dollars. Now that's the kind of people they were."[96]

The paternalistic system did not imply social familiarity. Thomas Parker wrote that "it is undeniable that South Carolina mill managements, owing to various causes, come into closer personal touch with their individual operatives, and feel more interest in them as a body, than do Eastern cotton manufacturers." They were "of the same stock as they themselves." But they were "composed as a class of the less successful." The town people in Greenville called mill workers "factory crackers and lint heads." According to John Heath, they "would walk on the other side of the street from you or on the edge of the sidewalk! That was because we had lint in our hair from the mills. Many of the people were consumptive; they were sallow complected." Segregation in Greenville County was based on economic class as well as race.[97]

Vast changes transformed Greenville County in the last decade of the nineteenth and the early decades of the twentieth century. Rural life changed least, but the Tillman movement swept into power bringing hostility between farm and town. Tillman reforms included the dispensary system, enforced racial segregation, and a new structure for county government. Meanwhile, the textile industry created large integrated mills, along with a new class of mill workers and a distinctive culture in the mill villages. Greenville County had thus become a major center of New South industrialization.

Notes

1. For three decades the definitive treatment of Southern populism and progressivism was C. Vann Woodward, *Origins of the New South, 1877–1913* (Baton Rouge, La., 1951). This treatment has been supplemented by Edward L. Ayers, *The Promise of the New South; Life After Reconstruction* (New York, 1992). The farmers' revolt in South Carolina centered on the career of Benjamin R. Tillman. The definitive work remains Francis B. Simkins, *Pitchfork Ben Tillman, South Carolinian* (Baton Rouge, La., 1944, 1964). For progressivism, a more detailed, if less interpretive, treatment is Dewey W. Grantham, *Southern Progressivism: The Reconciliation of Progress and Tradition* (Knoxville, Tenn., 1983).

2. William Gilmore Simms, *The Geography of South Carolina* (Charleston, 1843), 84; Bureau of the Census, Department of the Interior. *Report of the State of Churches in the United States . . . 1890* (Washington, D.C., 1894), 164–717; *Census of Religious Bodies, 1916* (Washington, D.C., 1919), 1: 306.

3. Bureau of the Census, *Churches in the United States . . . 1890*, 175, 517, 549, 562, 606, 642; *Census of Religious Bodies* 1: 306.

4. In regard to Possum Kingdom, see Nancy Vance Ashmore, *Greenville: Woven From the Past* (Northridge, Calf., 1986), 101–2. Attorney J. Frank Eppes traced the name to his ancestor, Thomas Chapman, about 1790. Greenville *News,* June 8, 1934. Lillie B. Westmoreland, *J. Dean Crain, A Biography* (Greenville, 1959), 1–5. Crain told his own story in *A Mountain Boy's Life Story* (Greenville, 1914).

5. Westmoreland, *Crain*, 5–7.

6. Ibid., 7.

7. Ibid., 13–14.

8. Ibid., 8.

9. Ibid., 9.

10. Ibid., 11.

11. Ibid., 18–20.

12. Jean Martin Flynn, *A History of North Greenville Junior College* (Tigerville, 1953), 6–7.

13. Ibid., 8–11.

14. Ibid., 11–12, 54–58, 60.

15. John H. Gilreath, *Biographical Sketch of Perry Duncan Gilreath, High Sheriff of Greenville County, South Carolina, 1876–1900* (Greenville, 1968), 1–27.

16. Ibid., 29–30.

17. Lacy K. Ford, Jr., "Rednecks and Merchants: Economic Development and Social Tensions in the South Carolina Upcountry, 1865–1900," *Journal of American History* 71 (September 1984): 2, 301; S.C. Department of Agriculture, *Handbook of South Carolina, 1907* (Columbia, 1907), 269; Guy A. Gullick, *Greenville County, Economic and Social* (Columbia, 1921), 57; Greenville *News*, April 10, 1917; Woodward, *Origins of the New South* (Baton Rouge, La., 1951), 185–86.

18. Mrs. Beverly T. (Mildred E.) Whitmire, ed., *The Presence of the Past; Epitaphs . . . in Greenville County, South Carolina* (Baltimore, Md., 1976), Cemetery No. 82; Blanche Marsh, *Hitch Up the Buggy* (Greenville, 1977), 78–79, 4.

19. Marsh, *Hitch Up the Buggy*, 77.

20. *Southern Enterprise*, August 19, 26, 1868; April 14, 1869; *Enterprise*, February 9, March 9, 1870; December 25, 1872; February 12, 26, 1873; *Enterprise and Mountaineer*, April 7, August 25, December 22, 1875.

21. J. Harold Easterby, "The Granger Movement in South Carolina," South Carolina Historical Association *Proceedings*, 1931, 23–25; *Enterprise*, August 28, 1872; *Enterprise and Mountaineer*, August 25, 1875.

22. Easterby, "Granger Movement," 29–30; Harry A. Chapman, "The Historical Development of the Grange in South Carolina" (M.A. thesis, Furman University, 1951), 43; Simkins, *Ben Tillman*, 77.

23. Ford, "Rednecks and Merchants," 313–14; Simkins, *Ben Tillman*, 77.

24. Simkins, *Ben Tillman*, 77–78; Robert C. McMath, Jr., *Populist Vanguard: A History of the Southern Farmers' Alliance* (Chapel Hill, N.C., 1975), 151–54, 40.

25. John Hammond Moore, ed., *South Carolina Newspapers* (Columbia, 1988), 119; *Enterprise and Mountaineer*, April 9, June 25, 1890; McMath, *Populist Vanguard*, 51.

26. Greenville *News*, October 21, 1933; "S.C. Peach Festival Association Dedicates the 1959 Festival to the Memory of J. Verne Smith, Sr., 1875–1933" in the possession of Senator and Mrs. J. Verne Smith, Greer, S.C.

27. Simkins, *Ben Tillman*, 92–94, 100–1, 104–5; Charleston *News and Courier*, April 30, 1886.

28. Simkins, *Ben Tillman*, 134–35.

29. Ibid., 138–39; *News and Courier*, March 27, 1890.

30. "Milton Lafayette Donaldson," *Biographical Directory* 1: 400–1.

31. *News and Courier*, May 9, 1890.

32. Simkins, *Ben Tillman*, 148–49; *News and Courier*, June 1, 1890.

33. *News and Courier*, June 11, 1890.

34. Ibid.

35. Ibid.

36. Ibid.

37. Simkins, *Tillman*, 152–61; *Enterprise and Mountaineer*, June 11, 25, July 2, 10, 1890; "Colonel James Lawrence Orr," *Cyclopedia of Eminent and Representative Men of the Carolinas of the Nineteenth Century* (Madison, Wis., 1892, 1972) 1: 107–9.

38. Simkins, *Tillman*, 161–68; *Enterprise and Mountaineer*, April 2, 1890.

39. Simkins, *Tillman*, 147; J. C. Garlington, *Men of the Time* (Spartanburg, S.C., 1902, 1972), 304; *Historical and Descriptive Review of the State of South Carolina* (Charleston, S.C., 1884) 3: 109.

40. Gustavus G. Williamson, Jr., "South Carolina Cotton Mills and the Tillman Movement," S.C. Historical Association *Proceedings*, 1949, 38–40. The Charleston branch of the Smyth family had changed the spelling to Smythe.

41. Simkins, *Ben Tillman*, 198; Columbia *State*, March 25, 1892.

42. Williamson, "Cotton Mills," 38.

43. David L. Carlton, *Mill and Town in South Carolina, 1880–1920* (Baton Rouge, La., 1982), 162; Williamson, "Cotton Mills," 46–47.

44. Williamson, "Cotton Mills," 41–42, 49.

45. Simkins, *Tillman*, 235; Greenville *Enterprise*, August 7, October 6, 23, November 13, 1872; March 26, 1873; *Enterprise and Mountaineer*, February 6, 1884; *State*, September 2, 8, 1892.

46. *State*, July 1, 1893.

47. *News*, October 4, 8, 1894, cited in Gilreath, *P. D. Gilreath*, 49–57.

48. George B. Tindall, *South Carolina Negroes, 1877–1900* (Columbia, 1952, 1966), 291–92.

49. Joseph D. Mathis, "Race Relations in Greenville, South Carolina, From 1865 Through 1900" (M.A. thesis, Atlanta University, 1971), 60–62.

50. Tindall, *Negroes*, 292–93; Albert N. Sanders, "Jim Crow Comes to South Carolina," S.C. Historical Association *Proceedings* 1966: 33–37.

51. *Journal of the Constitutional Convention of the State of South Carolina* (Columbia, 1895), 5, 22, 738.

52. Sanders, "Jim Crow," 36–37; Idus A. Newby, *Black Carolinians: A History of Blacks in South Carolina from 1895 to 1968* (Columbia, 1973), 42–43.

53. Sanders, "Jim Crow," 38–39.

54. Julian J. Petty, *The Growth and Distribution of Population in South Carolina* (Columbia, 1943, 1975), 228–29.

55. Columbus Andrews, *Administrative County Government in South Carolina* (Chapel Hill, N.C., 1933), 33–37; G. Wayne King, *Rise Up So Early: A History of Florence County, South Carolina* (Spartanburg, 1981), 247–48; James M. Richardson, *History of Greenville County* (Atlanta, Ga., 1930, 1980), 125.

56. "John Ramsey Harrison," *Biographical Directory* 1: 680–81.

57. "Alvin Henry Dean," *Biographical Directory* 1: 370–71; "William Lawrence Mauldin," 2: 1077–79; Wilton Haynsworth Earle," 2: 452–53; "Procter Aldrich Bonham," 1: 155–56.

58. Alester G. Furman, cited in Stephen S. Crittenden, *The Greenville Century Book* (Greenville, 1903), 68; Thomas F. Parker, "The South Carolina Cotton Mill— A Manufacturer's View," *South Atlantic Quarterly* 8 (1909): 333.

59. Greenville *Mountaineer*, November 7, 1894; Crittenden, *Century Book*, 68, 101; *Historical and Descriptive Review*, 102; L. L. Arnold, "A Story of Textile Greenville," *Cotton* 80 (October 1915), 504ff.

60. Crittenden, *Century Book*, 68–69; Richardson, *Greenville County*, 312–13.

61. Crittenden, *Century Book*, 69; Richardson, *Greenville County*, 147–48.

62. J. C. Garlington, *Men of the Time* (Spartanburg, 1902, 1972), 444; Crittenden, *Century Book*, 69, 91.

63. Crittenden, *Century Book*, 69; Garlington, *Men of the Time*, 340–42.

64. James A. Dunlap, "Victim of Neglect: The Career and Creations of John T. Woodside, 1865–1986" (M.A. thesis, University of South Carolina, 1986), 6–21.

65. Ibid., 30–32.

66. Greenville *Daily News*, September 11, 1912; Dunlap, "Woodside," 34–38.

67. Dunlap, "Woodside," 38–39, 34.

68. Richardson, *Greenville County*, 249–50; William P. Jacobs, *The Pioneer* (Clinton, n.d.), 40–41, 47; Frank Barnes, *The Greenville Story* (Greenville, 1956), 133.

69. Crittenden, *Century Book* 71–72, 113; Richardson, *Greenville County*, 98–99; Barnes, *Greenville Story*, 107.

70. Loulie Latimer Owens Pettigrew, *The Thursday Club, Greenville, South Carolina, 1889–1989* (Greenville, 1988), 106–7; Nell B. Adams, "Four Sisters from Boston," *Papers and Proceedings of the Greenville County Historical Society* 6 (1975–1979): 23–24.

71. Julian J. Petty, *The Growth and Distribution of Population in South Carolina* (Columbia, 1943, 1975), 228–29; Jacquelyn Dowd Hall, James Leloudis, Robert Korstadt, Mary Murphy, Lu Ann Jones, Christopher B. Daly, *Like A Family: The Making of a Southern Cotton Mill World* (Chapel Hill, N.C., 1987), 33–34, 36.

72. Marsh, *Hitch Up the Buggy*, 56–57; Hall, *Like A Family*, 36.

73. Hall, *Like A Family*, 36–39.

74. The manufacturing process is described in detail in Hall, *Like A Family*, 49–51.

75. Cited in Crittenden, *Century Book*, 67.

76. Marsh, *Hitch Up the Buggy*, 57, 48–49.

77. Hall, *Like A Family*, 64–65.

78. Ibid., 66–67; Marsh, *Hitch Up the Buggy*, 49.

79. Marsh, *Hitch Up the Buggy*, 49; Hall, *Like a Family*, 78–81.

80. Hall, *Like a Family*, 114–19.

81. Marsh, *Hitch Up the Buggy*, 45–46, 50, 57.

82. Hall, *Like a Family*, 130–31; Marsh, *Hitch Up the Buggy*, 54, 49.

83. Hall, *Like a Family*, 127–29; Kohn, *Cotton Mills*, 155; Mary G. Ariail and Nancy J. Smith, *Weaver of Dreams: A History of Parker District* (Columbia, 1977), 28.

84. Hall, *Like a Family*, 124–25; August Kohn, *The Cotton Mills of South Carolina* (Columbia, 1907, 1975), 155.

85. James B. Hilson, *History of the South Carolina Conference of the Wesleyan Methodist Church of America* (Winona Lake, Ind., 1950), 11–19.

86. Hilson, *History of the S.C. Conference*, 58–62, 78, 88, 103.

87. Robert F. Martin, "The Holiness-Pentecostal Revival in the Carolinas, 1896–1940," S.C. Historical Association *Proceedings* 1979, 59–78.

88. Thomas F. Parker, "The South Carolina Cotton Mill Village—A Manufacturer's View," *South Atlantic Quarterly* 9 (1910): 353; Ariail and Smith, *Weaver of Dreams*, 11.

89. Ariail and Smith, *Weaver of Dreams*, 23–27.

90. Kohn, *Cotton Mills*, 144.

91. Ibid., 144–45.

92. Ibid., *Cotton Mills*, 146.

93. Parker, "Mill Villages," 355.

94. Ariail and Smith, *Weaver of Dreams*, 26–27; George Kent, "Mill Town Miracle," *School and Society* 54 (August 9, 1941): 1389, 81; Marsh, *Hitch Up the Buggy*, 54.

95. Parker, "Mill Villages," 352–53.

96. Hall, *Like a Family*, 122.

97. Parker, "Mill Village," 349; Marsh, *Hitch Up the Buggy*, 52.

CHAPTER NINE

The Progressive Era
and World War I

In the cities and states of America on the eve of the twentieth century, networks of Progressive business leaders and reformers emerged from the rising middle class to improve the new industrial and urban society. Nationally, progressivism reached its climax during the administration of Woodrow Wilson. In the South, Progressives tended to be business and professional people imbued with the "New South" spirit and committed both to efficiency and fair play—within the limitations of a racially segregated society.[1]

During the Progressive era the city of Greenville grew rapidly on an expanding economic base of textiles and related businesses. In the thirty years between 1890 and 1920 the population shot up by 169 percent. In 1890 the census listed 8,605 people in the city limits; by the end of the era the population totaled 23,127.[2]

Progressive Leadership: Sirrine and Furman

Leading this vibrant city was a generation of young business leaders typified by Joseph Emory Sirrine and Alester Garden Furman. J. E. Sirrine was born in Americus, Georgia, in 1872. His father, George W. Sirrine, was engaged in the manufacturing of wagons and buggies in Americus and later in Charlotte, North Carolina. In January 1876 he moved to Greenville and became superintendent of the Gower and Cox Carriage Factory. He was subsequently president of the successor firm, Markley Hardware and Manufacturing Company. George Sirrine retired in 1910 and in 1914 became a member of the Board of Trustees of the Greenville City Schools. In 1921 he was elected chair of the board and served until his death in 1927. His older son, William G. Sirrine, was born in 1870, attended Furman and the University of South Carolina, and became a newspaper reporter. In 1895 he was admitted to the bar, served as city attorney, and from 1920 to 1950 was president of Textile Hall. The younger son, J. E. Sirrine, became the most widely influential member of the family. He graduated from Furman in 1890 and began an engineering career that would bring him considerable renown. In 1895 he was employed by Lockwood, Greene and Company as resident engineer in the construction of Poe Mill. He later became Southern representative of the firm and earned a reputation as one of the leading engineering consultants in the cotton textile industry. In 1902 he established the J. E. Sirrine Company, which continued to be one of the major textile engineering firms in the South even after the founder's death in August 1947.[3]

In 1956 Frank Barnes wrote that Alester Garden Furman came "nearer being the ideal citizen any community would be proud of." Furman was born in 1867 in Sumter County and was the grandson of James C. Furman, the first president of Furman University. The younger Furman moved with his family to Greenville in 1877, attended Furman, and studied law in his father's office. Though Furman passed the bar, he never practiced law but chose a business career instead. He began selling insurance and was soon involved in real estate. In 1888, at age twenty-one, he founded the firm which eventually bore his name. Dealing in real estate, insurance, and investment securities, Furman was deeply involved in almost every aspect of Greenville's development. He remained a powerful presence until his death at age ninety-four in 1962.[4]

Among Alester Furman's first ventures was the Mountain City Land and Improvement Company, a suburban development enterprise. In this capacity, he located sites for numerous textile mills—including Poe, Monaghan, and Westervelt Mills. He served on the boards of directors of a number of mills, banks, and insurance companies. In 1903 he organized the Carolina Power Company with Lewis W. Parker, J. Irving Westervelt, and Harry J. Haynsworth. That same year Furman constructed the second hydroelectric plant in the state on the Saluda River and furnished electric power both to Brandon Mill and the city of Greenville. In 1910 the company was sold to the Southern Power Company, later known as Duke Power. One of Furman's earliest civic efforts was obtaining a training camp for troops in Greenville during the Spanish-American War.[5]

The Spanish-American War

War fever began in earnest with the sinking of the battleship *Maine* in Havana harbor on February 15, 1898, and Congress declared war with Spain on April 25. At that time, the Butler Guards, the only active military company in Greenville, were part of the South Carolina National Guard. Oscar K. Mauldin was captain, Wade H. Ligon was first lieutenant, and

Thomas B. Ferguson was second lieutenant. Within a few days, a second company, known both as the Greenville Guards and the Greenville Volunteers, was organized by Captain Augustus D. Hoke, First Lieutenant James W. Gray, Jr., and Second Lieutenant William D. Whitmire.[6]

On May 3 the two companies assembled at the City Armory where they were addressed by Captain J. W. Cagle, the commanding officer of the Butler Guards at the close of the Civil War. Afterwards Captain Mauldin presented "the old bullet scarred battle flag of the Butler Guards," declaring that "this company would always keep this flag and its memory unsullied." The next day the troops left for Columbia by train. The schools were dismissed, and a crowd assembled to bid them farewell. A large number of the volunteers failed the physical examination, but the ranks were simply filled by others. The Greenville troops became Companies F and H of the First South Carolina Volunteer Infantry. However, the volunteers went only as far as Camp Cuba Libre, Florida, when the war ended. The volunteers were mustered out in Columbia on November 10, 1898. Wade Hampton Parker, a member of Company H, who died in Columbia on August 18, was buried in Springwood Cemetery with military honors.[7]

There were efforts to organize two additional units before the war ended. On July 10, 1898, the *Daily News* carried the notice of the recruitment of the Mountain City Volunteers—"a colored company, being organized by J. C. Hill." The unit evidently never materialized. The Home Guards and those rejected for the Butler Guards formed a new unit under the command of Captain Frank B. McBee, First Lieutenant S. F. Burgess, and Second Lieutenant A. Parkins.[8]

The establishment of Camp Wetherill, an army training camp, had a much greater impact on the city. On June 15, 1898, the *Mountaineer* carried a notice that there was an excellent chance that Greenville might be selected for a camp the army intended to establish in the South. Mayor James T. Williams, Alderman James F. Richardson, and Alester Furman immediately set out by train to Columbia to meet with the site selection committee. In Columbia they discovered that the committee had left for Augusta, and they followed the committee only to find they had returned to Columbia. Eventually the group from Greenville met the committee and invited them for a site visit, which occurred in September, even though the protocol ending hostilities was signed in August. The United States was still involved in Cuba and the Philippines, and the future was uncertain.[9]

On October 1, 1898, a public meeting in Beattie's Hall endorsed the work of the local committee. Former Lieutenant Governor Mauldin presided, and Alester Furman was secretary. The Greenville committee went to Washington, where they called on President McKinley. They were assured that a camp would be established in Greenville with two brigades of about ten thousand men. The local newspaper informed its readers that a "division headquarters will be in Greenville which gives us a set of officers of high rank and these as a rule are gentlemen of good social standing, whose families will accompany them." There were assurances that no black troops would be stationed at the installation.[10]

The camp was named in memory of Captain Alexander M. Wetherill, one of the first persons killed at San Juan Hill, and consisted of two sections. The First Brigade was located north of Earle Street between Buncombe Street and the present Wade Hampton Boulevard. The only house on the property was Whitehall, the former home of the Middleton family, which was used as a nurses' home for the Hospital Corps. The Second Brigade was located south and east of Anderson Street, stretching beyond Mills Mill, and the Second Division headquarters was located on the site of Greenville General Hospital. Wooden buildings were erected for the headquarters, the hospital, and the mess, but the soldiers lived in tents.[11]

The first troops arrived in Greenville from Camp George G. Meade in Pennsylvania during the first week of November 1898. The *Mountaineer* announced that "Greenville already has assumed a livelier look. With the soldiers the town began to look brighter and there is a perceptive increase in hurry and bustle. It has been extremely cold and one soldier remarked that Greenville was not the 'Sunny-South he had heard about.'" Indeed, the winter of 1898–1899 was one of the most severe that the region had ever experienced. Only a few of the tents had wooden floors, but they provided some respite from the snow and mud outside.[12]

Business was bustling, and the Christmas season was the greatest in living memory. Cards and gifts were impossible to find. Before Camp Wetherill closed in March 1899, the installation made a lasting impact on Greenville. The pace of life quickened, and a considerable amount of money passed through the hands of local merchants.[13]

Suburban Development

The growth of the economy and the increase in the population of the city resulted in suburban expansion. The site of the First Brigade camp on Earle Street became a real estate development. Alester Furman employed an auctioneer and led a brass band from Main Street to the property, where lots were sold in the course of one day for the tremendous total of fifteen thousand dollars. But the most prestigious neighborhood was Boyce Lawn, and William Goldsmith was selling lots there to wealthy mill owners and business leaders by 1907. In 1914 over one-fourth of the state's spindleage was controlled by sixteen mill presidents living in Boyce Lawn. Only the presidents of two small rural mills lived near their operations. To accommodate the working population outside the mill villages, a West Virginia company purchased the old fairgrounds property on Rutherford Street and opened the Park Place subdivision.[14]

Black citizens joined the movement to the suburbs. The section of Camp Wetherill occupied by the Second Brigade along Dunbar Street became a center of this movement. Eventually this area became the location of Sterling High School, the major black institution (except for churches) in Greenville until it closed in 1970.[15]

Though blacks faced increasing discrimination in the age of segregation, they responded by establishing the Greenville Academy in 1896 under the direction of D. M. Minus, the pastor of John Wesley Methodist Episcopal Church. For eleven years he was president of the school and received the sum of eighty dollars a month. After the closing of Camp Wetherill, the school moved to a small farm outside of the city on what became the corner of Jenkins and Malloy Streets. Nearby, Minus Chapel was built. In 1902 the name of the school was changed to the Sterling Industrial College, perhaps reflecting the emphasis on vocational education made by Booker T. Washington, then the major spokesperson for blacks. The school's purpose was "the intellectual, industrial and religious training of the boys and girls of the negro race." In 1907 Sterling had two hundred students and six teachers. Minus was succeeded for a brief time by Casey Jones, and after his departure, Sterling closed. Several years later, the Enoree Baptist Association, under the leadership of E. C. Murray, reopened the school with the name changed to Enoree High School—with E. E. Riley as principal. In 1929 the school came under the control of the city board of education, and its name was changed to Sterling High School.[16]

Business Progressivism

The reviving economy encouraged the new generation of business leadership to reorganize the Board of Trade after its collapse during the Panic of 1893. In 1894 Lewis W. Parker and Alester Furman formed the Young Men's Business League, which soon boasted a membership of almost two hundred professional men. By October 1901 the leaders were determined to reestablish the board itself. With A. A. Bristow, a leading merchant, as president and Alester Furman as secretary, the group opened an office in the Beattie Building on the corner of Main and Washington Streets. In 1906 John Wood became the first staff member, and he was followed by A. S. Johnston in 1909. In the years before World War I, the board elected a series of Progressive-minded presidents—Frank F. Capers, Harry J. Haynsworth, Furman, Sirrine, David W. Ebaugh, and Charles S. Webb. When the South Carolina Chamber of Commerce was chartered in 1912, the board reorganized itself into a local chamber.[17]

Progressivism also gave rise to national civic clubs. In March 1916 twenty-five business leaders organized the first Rotary Club in South Carolina. By 1920 the club had sixty-two members, and the roll of early presidents included Sirrine, YMCA Secretary John M. Holmes, John H. Williams, D. E. McCuen, E. M. Blythe, and W. Lindsay Smith. In 1920 the Kiwanis Club organized and soon had a membership of seventy-two.[18]

The new spirit of boosterism was reflected in the publication in 1903 of *The Greenville Century Book*—a history of the county through the eyes of former state Senator Stephen S. Crittenden. "What have we to offer the homeseekers of the world," he wrote, "those seeking a healthful climate, a delightful place of residence, educational advantages, exemption from mosquito and other insect nuisances, opportunities for business, and employment for all disposed to work? To each of these we can say Greenville fulfills today the promise of all of these conditions." In 1911 the Board of Trade published an illustrated guide to the city entitled *The Pearl of the Piedmont,* and the *Daily News* published a special souvenir number: *The Gateway to Get There—Greenville, 1911.*[19]

The Effort to Diversify Industry

While the Board of Trade, and later the Chamber of Commerce, did concern itself with reform, its primary task was economic development. The first major effort was the diversification of local industry. In 1903 members raised funds to construct a building for the American Cigar Factory on the site of Richard Pearis's home. Colonel Crittenden reported that "Messrs. Ebaugh and Ebaugh have just completed the cigar factory near the public square, one of the largest brick buildings in the city. Its dimensions are 137 x 60 feet, 4 stories high, and was completed in about 100 days from commencement." The factory employed "150, or more, girls and young women, while the capacity of the factory will require 900 or 1,000 employees." The factory, he said, "expect[ed], in three months, to be turning out half a million cigars per week." The Board did not neglect agricultural development. The secretary arranged farmers' rallies and organized Boys' Corn Clubs and Men's Pig Clubs to encourage better methods of farm production.[20]

The business leadership also began to cultivate a new source of capital as Greenville became the headquarters for three insurance companies. The Southeastern Life Insurance Company was formed in Spartanburg in 1905, but problems forced reorganization. In 1910 T. Oregon Lawton, Jr., conceived the idea of bringing the company to Greenville. A thirty-five-year-old native of Barnwell, Lawton was a graduate of Erskine College and a staunch Baptist. He taught school briefly, and in 1903 opened the Lawton Lumber Company in Greenville. He went door-to-door to secure investors for Southeastern Life Insurance and received the backing of such men as William Sirrine, Lewis Parker, J. Irving Westervelt, Ellison Smyth, Eugene A. Gilfillin, Harry J. Haynsworth, Frank F. Capers, W. A. Lawton, and Frank Hammond. By March 1910 the Greenville group gained control of the company, with Capers as president, followed in less than a month by Westervelt. But Lawton was chief executive officer, and local directors included Gilfillin, Dr. Curran B. Earle, Haynsworth, Lewis Parker, Thomas F. Parker, Smyth, and Alester Furman. In 1910 there was $3.3 million in insurance in force. In 1914 Lawton became president, and a year later the company had agents in twenty-five towns and communities in the state. By 1920 the company boasted $18 million of insurance in force, including some of the first group policies in the South. From 1915 to 1942 Southeastern occupied its own building on the corner of Main and Broad Streets—the present site of the Peace Center. The three-story building became a landmark, easily seen by the large, illuminated statue of a gladiator on top. Southeastern built its business on the proposition that "the public at large is waking up to the mistake of sending their cash capital out of South Carolina in the form of Insurance Premiums."[21]

The American Home Fire Insurance Company was organized in 1909 and opened its home office in the new six-story Masonic Temple on Main Street, on the site of the present City Hall. Charles F. Hard was president, and the local directors included Smyth, the Parkers, Henry P. McGee, John W. Norwood, A. A. Bristow, J. B. Bruce, Westervelt, William Goldsmith, Jr., J. M. Geer, Haynsworth, and D. D. Davenport of Greer.[22]

Destined to become the most successful of the three was the Liberty Life Insurance Company, founded in 1919 by William Franklin Hipp. Born in 1889 in Greenwood County and reared in Newberry, Hipp was a devoted Lutheran. After graduating from Newberry College, he entered the insurance business, and in 1912 attracted the attention of T. O. Lawton, who offered him the position of general agent of the Southeastern Life Insurance Company in Spartanburg. After a bout with tuberculosis, Hipp moved to Greenville in 1918 and entered the textile securities business. Meanwhile, convinced it was time that South Carolina had its own weekly premium insurance company, he secured one hundred thousand dollars in capital, and on October 13, 1919, he announced the creation of Liberty Life with offices in the Mansion House. Hipp was president; E. Roy Stone was vice president and general manager; and Henry E. Vogel was secretary. Local members of the board included B. A. Morgan, William B. Smith, J. R. Fulmer, and J. P. Carlisle. The appeal of the company, in Frank Hipp's view, was the two-cents-a-week life insurance policy sold door-to-door to lower and average income South Carolinians. In 1920 the company sold $1.7 million in new insurance alone.[23]

But some leaders of the company wanted to add ordinary premium policies and expand into nearby states. Hipp was dead set against modifying his vision, and those who disagreed soon departed. Henry Vogel remained firmly committed to the original course, and by 1922 Liberty Life challenged Life of Virginia for first place in weekly premium insurance sales in the textile belt. That same year Hipp acquired Home Life and Accident Insurance Company of Charleston. In 1923 Liberty Life wrote its first ordinary life policy, becoming a combination company. With almost $6 million of insurance in force in 1926, the staff consisted of Hipp, Vogel, Paul Agnew, two stenographers, and six clerks. The company moved its headquarters to the Blue Building on Main Street.[24]

City Planning

Thomas F. Parker, president of the Municipal League, was the prime mover in bringing the nationwide City Beautiful movement to the attention of local leaders. The League employed Kelsey and Guild of Boston, national leaders in the movement, to develop a city plan. The result was *Beautifying and Improving Greenville, South Carolina*, published in January 1907. The plan proposed a series of boulevards encircling the city, the creation of gateways, a civic center, public art, and a park along the Reedy River.[25]

The plan made the leadership of Greenville more conscious of the community's appearance. Early in 1910, according to the *News*, the city began to demolish the buildings along Court Street, "where for years the glimmer of lurid red lights have flashed offering temptation to the weak." In place of these "buildings of the underworld" rose "handsome railroad buildings." In the spring of 1914 the cesspools beneath the Main Street bridge were filled with oil to kill mosquitos and relieve the odor arising from the river. The county jail installed modern sewer connections which carried waste water into the street rather than emptying it into the yard.[26]

Downtown Building Boom

In the summer of 1917 the *News* reported that a "building boom is on. . . . On almost every street in the city, residential or business, construction work is in progress." In the business district the installation of modern store fronts improved its appearance, and in September 1917 the *Tradesman*, the national hardware magazine, carried a five-page story describing Greenville as a "city . . . lined with modern buildings and well-lighted shop windows."[27]

Prominent among the new buildings rising in Greenville were two new hotels. The Ottaray Hotel was built on Main Street in the shadow of the Confederate Monument in 1908–1909 by a group of business people— including Alester Furman, Harry Haynsworth, A. A. Bristow, and Jesse R. Smith. Five stories high with eighty-six rooms, the building was leased by Minnie Quinn of Portsmouth, Virginia. The *News* noted that the Ottaray was furnished with eleven carloads of furniture, including a piano purchased from K. S. Conrad for one thousand dollars. Within a year Quinn married Walter L. Gassaway, president of the textile mill in Central. She continued to operate the Ottaray until 1919 when it was leased by J. L. Alexander, whose son, J. Mason Alexander, became manager. The Mansion House, built in 1824 and closed in March 1910, was remodeled into offices and stores and was renamed the Swandale Building. In 1912 a new hotel, the seven-story Imperial, was opened on West Washington Street opposite the Presbyterian Church. In the fall of 1917 the Imperial added a seven-story annex. That same year the need for hotel rooms was so great that the Mansion House reopened under the ownership of A. D. L. Barksdale, Edward L. Ayers, and D. E. Massey.[28]

As early as 1907 there was a movement to build a new county courthouse and jail, and a commission was named to oversee construction: Alester Furman (chair), Benjamin F. Neves, and John D. Harris. On May 11, 1915, Furman and a group of associates purchased one hundred thousand dollars in bonds issued by the county for the project. (The old jail was a "dungeon-like" building on Broad and Falls Streets known as "Little Siberia.") On May 15, 1915, Jamison and Morris began to build a new jail on the site of the old one for thirty thousand dollars, which was completed in January

1916. The architects for the courthouse were F. Thornton Mayre of Atlanta and H. Olin Jones of Greenville. The building was designed in two sections. The front consisted of three stories, and the rear seven stories. The new concrete structure, erected by J. A. Jones of Charlotte, was faced with cream-colored brick and ornamented with terra cotta.[29]

There were delays in construction, but the probate judge and register of mesne conveyance moved into the building in late January 1918. On April 1 the first term of court opened in the new courtroom as Judge John S. Wilson complimented Greenville County on the building of one of the finest courthouses in the country. Clerk of Court Harry A. Dargan called the list of jurors, headed by W. J. Mullinax. The first case called was *Davenport v. Hawkins*, represented by Cothran, Dean, and Cothran and Haynsworth and Haynsworth.[30]

The Changing Role of Women

Women of the middle class were employed in the stores and offices of Main Street for the first time in the early twentieth century. For twenty years women had worked in the textile mills and in the American Cigar Factory. When Eli Alston Wilkes, a Methodist minister who had grown up in Greenville, returned, he observed the new trend: "One thing I noticed in this thriving town that has progressed and prospered so . . . is the employment of ladies in stores, offices and big business places—a fact, however, now rather conspicuous in many other intelligent communities. Rustling skirts stand behind counters and work at office desks." One of these women was Beulah Cunningham, who came to Greenville in 1902 at the age of eighteen. She worked on Main Street and lived in one of the boarding houses for young ladies kept by the "better people" in the city. She lived at first on Broadus Street in Boyce Lawn and later with the Westervelts on East North Street. Even though Irving Westervelt was president of Brandon Mill, he had put all of his capital into the business, and the family was happy to have boarders. Cunningham ate three meals a day with the Westervelts. The offices on Main Street closed at noon, and people walked home for lunch.[31]

E. A. Wilkes was not entirely pleased with the changing role of women. "Woman is being commercialized," he noted, "and the tendency seems to make a business being of her. Her dress is narrowing down and getting shorter and the corset is made longer than formerly." The fashion seemed "to compress hips, arrest such development, and ere long, alas—maybe she will discard skirt and chemise and get into some sort of bloomer at last."[32]

Wilkes would have been more pleased with the lecture at the Bijou Theater on a Sunday afternoon in May 1914 on the topic, "Give the Girls a Square Deal." The *Daily News* indicated that "this lecture is for the purpose of agitating and building up a higher moral standard between sexes among the oncoming generation. This strikes direct to the home and the nation and the thing that every man ought to be thoroughly interested in." But two weeks later, Lavinia Engle, a field-worker for the National Equal Suffrage League, presided at the organization of a local league at the YWCA. Leagues were established at the same time in Spartanburg, Columbia, and Charleston, and were associated with the National American Woman Suffrage Association (NAWSA) led by Susan B. Anthony and Elizabeth Cady Stanton.[33]

The Equal Suffrage Club met every two weeks at the YMCA, and Ellen Perry, or in her absence Mary P. Gridley, presided over the spirited discussions. Two Greenville women became field-workers for NAWSA—Eleanor Furman, the daughter of Alester Furman, worked in Washington and Maryland; and Eudora Ramsay, the daughter of President David Ramsay of the Greenville Woman's College, worked in New York. In November 1915 the South Carolina branch of the more militant Congressional Union, later the National Woman's Party (NWP), was organized in Charleston by Alice Paul, the national president. On October 15, 1917, a committee of local suffragists sponsored an address in Greenville by Maud Younger of the NWP. She spoke in the Colonial Theater, which was decorated in the party colors—purple, white, and gold. Helen E. Vaughan, chair of the state NWP branch, presided, and Younger was introduced by Judge Joseph A. McCullough. The Greenville Equal Suffrage League was the only local group in the state to shift its affiliation from the moderate NAWSA to the NWP.[34]

In March 1918, when the U.S. Senate was heatedly debating the woman's suffrage amendment, Helen Vaughan wrote an open letter to Senator Benjamin R. Tillman, taking issue with his speech on the floor in which he said that he had been asked to support the amendment by "pretty college girls." Vaughan expressed her indignation that Tillman did not choose to refer to the letters and petitions that he had received "from all parts of the state." After Tillman's death in 1918, Vaughan and her associates organized a campaign to persuade his successor, William Pollock of Cheraw, to support the suffrage amendment. The Greenville *Piedmont,* along with the Charleston *Evening Post,* published numerous editorials in support. Pollock eventually spoke favorably on the floor of the Senate and voted for the amendment.[35]

Working women in local offices shared in the spirit of business progressivism and in April 1918 organized the Business Women's Club. The club's membership was at first restricted to forty, but early in 1920 the limitation was removed and the roll increased to one hundred members.[36]

Perhaps the most visible individual in Greenville who exemplified the "new woman" was attorney "Miss Jim" Perry. Born about 1895, she was the daughter of James M. Perry, a professor at the Greenville Woman's College. Determined that his third daughter should bear his name, Perry named the child James Margrave. In 1913, after graduating from the Woman's College, Miss Jim entered the University of California at Berkeley, received an accredited bachelor's degree, and was accepted into the law school. In 1917, after receiving a degree and passing the California bar, she returned to Greenville to work for the firm of Haynsworth and Haynsworth in the Masonic Temple. In 1918 the South Carolina legislature opened bar examinations to women, and on May 3, 1918, James M. Perry became the first women attorney in the state. She later was a partner in the Haynsworth firm and a civic leader until her death in 1963.[37]

The Development of Racial Segregation

Though business progressivism in the South included women, as C. Vann Woodward pointed out in *Origins of the New South*, it was "for whites only." In 1898 the Mansion House Barbershop advertised "all white tonsorial artists" for the first time. By 1900 the number of black businesses on Main and adjoining streets began to decline. Whites replaced blacks in the baking, hauling, and drayage trades. A threat to the peace of the community erupted in the summer of 1899 when a race riot broke out between the workers at Poe Mill and the residents of a nearby black settlement who worked in the fertilizer factory. According to the newspaper account, there was considerable firing of weapons, and six men were wounded.[38]

The Kelsey and Guild report on the beautification of Greenville in 1907 added its weight to the segregation movement. The first difficulty listed in the proposed plan for the city was "the large negro population. Greenville's 'negro quarters' adjoin the best and the poorest residence districts, and are scattered likewise throughout the business sections." The report proposed "encourag[ing] the tendency towards segregation to the extent of having *fairly large units* of both white and colored population, with no residence encroachments by either."[39]

In 1912 segregation was written into a city ordinance when B. D. Goldsmith and W. H. Goldsmith, two black business people, signed a contract to buy a lot on the corner of Main and Elford Streets for a hotel for blacks. There was an immediate outcry among the white business leadership, and the contract was withdrawn. On February 12 the City Council adopted "an ordinance for preserving peace, preventing conflict and ill-feeling between the white and colored races of the city of Greenville . . . so far as practicable for the use of separate blocks for residences, restaurants, places of public amusement, stores, and places of business of all kinds." The ordinance was modeled after one adopted in Baltimore the preceding year. No whites could live in any part of a house occupied by blacks, or vice versa. Nor could blacks and whites occupy the same church, school, restaurant, or store. The penalty for breaking the ordinance was a one hundred dollar fine or thirty days in jail. The difficulty of enforcing the ordinance quickly became apparent, and in 1913 the council amended the law to conform to the two-thirds rule by making it illegal for anyone of one race to move into an area that was two-thirds occupied by members of another race.[40]

Among the Greenvillians lost to the city in this era of segregation was William Wilson Cooke, whose father had been a prominent leader in business, political, and church affairs during Reconstruction. The younger Cooke, born in Greenville in 1871, was a student at Claflin University in Orangeburg and eventually earned a bachelor of science degree in technology from Columbia University in 1902. He worked as an architect for the Freedmen's Aid Society and the Woman's Home Missionary Society of the Methodist Episcopal Church, and about 1906 established himself in Greenville as a contractor, builder, and architect. However, in 1907 Cooke passed the civil service examination and entered the office of the supervising architect of the Treasury Department in Washington as a senior architectural designer. He was the first black to hold this office. Before his death about 1945, Cooke had worked in a variety of government agencies and in private practice.[41]

Although the white leadership did not condone violence, their position was similar to that found elsewhere in South Carolina. On April 2, 1912, the *Piedmont* reported two lynchings of blacks in South Carolina and the near death of a white man accused of rape. But even the editorial against lynching in the same paper had racist overtones: "What a horrible blot upon the State it would have been if this innocent [white] man had suffered. Yet if this wholesale lynching continues, not only will a negro [sic] possibly suffer but it is even possible that an innocent white man might also. . . . Something must be done about it." Even those white Progressives who decried racial prejudice did so within the framework of the segregated society. Edwin L. Hughes, superintendent of the city schools, wrote in the Columbia *State:* "We need to educate our people, white and black, up from race prejudice to race pride. That would make possible civic, economic, legal and even political justice without any sort of racial intermingling."[42]

Even popular culture reflected the theme of white supremacy. In December 1905 the stage version of Thomas Dixon's novel *The Clansman* was performed at the Grand Opera House, and in August 1907 it returned for another run. In February 1916 after D. W. Griffith had transformed the novel into the first full-length feature moving picture, *The Birth of a Nation*, the movie played at the opera house for three days and was "heavily patronized." Accompanying the silent film was a symphony orchestra with thirty members. The film was a sensation all over the nation, and when it returned to Greenville in December 1918, it played four times in the Colonial Theater in the remodeled Chicora College auditorium, complete with symphony.[43]

The Jewish Community

The white, segregated society in Greenville did make room for the organization of a Jewish congregation and the beginnings of a Greek community during the Progressive era. A few Jewish individuals and families had lived in antebellum Greenville, and I. W. Hirsch had served in the Butler Guards during the Civil War. The first city directory for the year 1876–1877 listed two businesses operated by Jewish merchants. Harris C. Mark was a clothier and Israel Gittleson was a general merchandiser on Main Street. Levy and Philip Epstein were clerks in Mark's clothing store, and Daniel Aaron was a clerk at Gittleson's. By 1912 there were some sixty-one Jews listed in the city directory.[44]

In 1910 about twenty-five families met to organize a conservative synagogue. They elected officers and chose Charles Zaglin of Asheville as the resident rabbi of the new Beth Israel congregation. At first, they rented quarters for the high holy days in the Bank of Commerce building on Main and Coffee Streets and the Woodmen of the World building on Laurens Street. The congregation received a charter from the state on June 13, 1914, and in 1929 they secured a lot on Townes Street, where a synagogue was built the following year.[45]

During the same decade a Jewish Reform congregation also appeared. In 1911 these eight men met at the home of Lee Rothschild on East North Street to establish the Temple of Israel—Rothschild, Hyman Endel, Morris

Lurey, George J. Reisenfeld, Manas Myers, Alexander B. Myers, Isaac W. Jacobi, and David Kohn. Rothschild was first president; Endel, vice president; Jacobi, secretary; and Reisenfeld, treasurer. Jacobi was Reader for the congregation, and the first services were held above a store on McBee Avenue. In 1927 the temple received a charter of incorporation, and the following year a building was constructed on Buist Avenue. The 1926 religious census listed 195 Jews living in Greenville County.[46]

The Arrival of Greek Immigrants

George Condouros and Sotirios Maurogiannis, the first Greeks in Greenville, arrived from Sparta about 1898—a time when the only sizeable Greek community in South Carolina was in Charleston. The two men opened a candy store on Main Street, and by 1904 their wives had joined them. Among the Greeks coming to Greenville in the next decade was Andrew J. Theodore, also a native of Sparta. Like so many others, Theodore, who left Greece in 1914, settled first in New York where he became a fruit seller. However, within six months a friend convinced him to come south. Several years later he returned to Greece and brought back his intended wife, Lula Merns. They were married in Greenville. One of their five children, Nick Andrew Theodore, served in the state House of Representatives and the state Senate, and in 1982 he was elected lieutenant governor of South Carolina.[47]

By 1921 there were five Greek families in Greenville. A Greek Orthodox priest from Augusta visited regularly and performed the Divine Liturgy. In 1929 the women of the growing community organized and employed Katina Efstration as the teacher of a Greek school, and in 1931 forty-two members met to constitute St. George's Greek Orthodox Church. A house was purchased on DeCamp Street and transformed into a church building.[48]

Religion: Pentecostalism

As a part of what has become known as the Third Great Awakening in American Protestantism from 1890 to 1920, the Holiness and Pentecostal movements made an impact on the city through the work of a Presbyterian minister, Nickels J. Holmes. Born in Spartanburg in 1847, he was the son of the Reverend Zelotes Lee Holmes and Catherine Nickels, a member of the Simpson family of Laurens County planters and political leaders. As a child, Holmes moved with his family to Laurens, where his father was a pastor and president of the Female Academy. After serving in the Confederate army, Holmes studied at the University of Edinburgh and returned to Laurens to read law and practice with the firm of Simpson and Simpson. In 1876 he married Lucy Simpson, the daughter of lieutenant governor and later Governor William D. Simpson. After announcing his candidacy for solicitor in 1888, Laurens felt called to enter the ministry and became an evangelist for the Enoree Presbytery.[49]

Holmes was intrigued by the Holiness movement, and in 1891 he attended the Northfield Conference founded by the nationally known evangelist, Dwight L. Moody. Under Moody's influence, Holmes began to preach the doctrine of sanctification, and in March 1892 he assisted in the organization of the Second Presbyterian Church in Greenville and became its first pastor. But Holmes's enthusiasm for the Holiness movement led him far beyond the confines of Southern Presbyterianism. In November 1895 Holmes resigned as pastor of his church and resumed evangelistic work, and, after being accused of heresy, he resigned from the Southern Presbyterian Church. In November 1898 he opened the Altamont Bible and Missionary Institute in the old hotel on Paris Mountain. The school moved briefly to Atlanta and Columbia, but returned to Greenville in 1905. The following year Holmes became involved in the Pentecostal movement. When a young woman began speaking in tongues in class, Holmes himself, at the age of sixty, joined in. In May 1909 he opened a tabernacle on Buncombe Street that became the permanent site of Holmes Bible College, where thousands of Pentecostal ministers and missionaries have received their training.[50]

Many black Greenvillians also were caught up in the Pentecostal movement. In 1898 the Fire-Baptized Holiness Church, a precursor of the Pentecostal Holiness denomination, was established in Anderson, and W. E. Fuller, a minister of the AME Church, was present. Fuller, who had received the baptism of fire the previous year, joined the new denomination. There was no racial tension in the denomination itself, but outsiders often threw rocks and wrote threatening letters because the services were integrated. In 1904, for example, some young white men collapsed the tent in which a Fire-Baptized Holiness revival meeting was in progress in Greenville. Four years later, in November 1908, the black members of the denomination met in Greer and organized the Fire-Baptized Church of God of the Americas, and chose W. E. Fuller as their bishop. This group, which became one of the largest American denominations of black Pentecostals, established its headquarters in Greenville, where members opened the Fuller Normal and Industrial Institute.[51]

Trolleys and Automobiles

As the city continued to expand physically, the trolley lines tied the new suburban areas together. In 1911 the Board of Trade described the system as "modern and up-to-date in plant and equipment. The track covers fifteen miles of city streets connecting all parts of the city and outlying districts and villages." The fare was five cents, and children rode free. The "belt" extended down Pendleton Street through West Greenville past all the mills and back to College and Main Streets. When Overbrook was developed by the Woodside brothers, the trolley line was extended out East North Street to Richland Creek and across the bridge that reached the new development. Service was informal and helpful. A. D. Asbury recalled that "several school teachers lived on North Street and rode the trolley regularly to school. If they were not ready when [the trolley] came, [the driver] would stop the trolley and clang the foot bell until they came out." Ava McBee remembered that "women along the line would ask the conductor to do shopping for them like a spool of thread. If it was the wrong color, he had to take it back."[52]

The automobile made its first appearance in Greenville early in the century, and by 1904 there were five automobiles in the county. That year six more motor cars were ordered from Detroit, making eleven total. Among the earliest owners of automobiles were local physicians J. B. Earle, J. Wilkinson Jervey, and Curran B. Earle. Lewis W. Parker purchased one about the same time. An automobile was also used by the Chick Springs Hotel, which had reopened, and on June 12, 1904, Alfred Taylor noted in his diary that he "had [his] first ride in [an] automobile. Met many friends new and old. Spent the day and returned." In April 1909 the first automobile race was held in Greenville, the Main Street Hill Climb, which began on Park Avenue and ended at the old courthouse. Eugene Smith, driving Dr. Joseph B. Earle's Buick, won the race. The following month the City Council adopted a speed limit of 15 miles an hour for automobiles, but the Hill Climb continued annually until 1911. Jesse R. Smith's son, Alfred, later recalled that "in the most memorable race, Frank Koneleb and Frank Poe lost control of their car and plummeted off the fifty-foot embankment at Park and Main and crashed into the City Park below. Neither [was] killed but both were seriously injured." In 1914 there were 1,038 automobiles in Greenville County, the largest number in any county of the state.[53]

The arrival of the automobile spurred the Good Roads movement that had been organized in South Carolina as early as 1894. As a result, improvements to roads and streets were made in the county and city of

Greenville simultaneously. In September 1910 a modern route to Asheville was surveyed to replace the Old Buncombe Road, and in 1913 the Jones Gap Road to Caesar's Head and on to Transylvania County, North Carolina, became a toll-free, state road. In January 1915 the county legislative delegation proposed a bond issue of $950,000 for road construction. Once it was approved, John W. Norwood, chair of the county Highway Commission, began to build the finest system of county roads in South Carolina using the "million dollar bond issue," as it was called. On August 11, 1917, the new Greenville-Hendersonville Highway formally opened.[54]

In 1910 the city approved a three-hundred-thousand-dollar bond issue for permanent improvements. In September of that year work began on a new concrete bridge over the Reedy River on Main Street, a contract was let for a second bridge on River Street, and eighty-nine new arc street lights were purchased. By January 1912 Main Street and all the side streets leading into it were paved. Two months later the City Council authorized the borrowing of fifteen thousand dollars to pave Augusta Street, and in May an additional bond issue for one hundred thousand dollars for more paving was overwhelmingly approved. By 1918 two national highway systems passed through the city and county—the east-west Bankhead Highway and the north-south Dixie Highway.[55]

Health Care

The fast-paced years before World War I finally saw a city hospital open in Greenville. In 1901 the Women's Hospital Board was concentrating on "outdoor relief work" by working with churches, drugstores, and grocery stores to provide medicine and food to needy people. The board raised money through charity events such as teas, rummage sales, and bazaars. By the spring of 1905 the members had a balance of four thousand dollars and pledges from several doctors for the building of a hospital. An Emergency Hospital was opened in 1910 at the Salvation Army Citadel on East Broad Street. Meanwhile, three physicians—Adams Hayne, J. R. Rutledge, and L. G. Corbett—opened a private sanitorium on Arlington Avenue which treated alcoholics and mental patients. The sanitorium was not a financial success, and they offered the facility for a city hospital for twenty thousand dollars. The Hospital Association and the women's board agreed to raise the necessary funds. On January 10, 1912, the new hospital opened with eighty-four beds. Martin F. Ansel was chair of the Board of Governors, which included George W. Quick, Mr. and Mrs. Charles F. Hard, W. A. Marrott, Milton G. Smith, Mrs. C. F. Dill, Mrs. J. T. Woodside,

Mrs. Lewis W. Parker, Mrs. John Slattery, and Mrs. Mary Carey. In the first month the hospital admitted forty-six patients, and by August patients had to be turned away for lack of room. The first nursing students entered training on January 13, and two graduated in 1915—Jessie Greer and Myra Mary Young. In 1917 the city of Greenville purchased the hospital and within four years added a building and moved the entrance to Memminger Street.[56]

The YMCA and YWCA Movements

The white evangelical Protestant establishment of Greenville eagerly supported the YMCA and YWCA movement. A downtown YMCA was organized in 1910, when a whirlwind campaign raised fifty-one thousand dollars, and a lot was secured on East Coffee Street. The building was completed in 1912, and the dedication service was held at the First Baptist Church. Charles J. Kilbourne, the first general secretary, organized a full schedule of activities including a summer camp at Cedar Mountain in August. In 1914 the camp moved to Blythe Shoals and remained there until 1924. Meanwhile Kilbourne resigned, and Charles Dusham served for a short period, succeeded by John M. Holmes who remained until his retirement in 1944.[57]

"Uncle Johnny" Holmes, as he was known to generations of young Greenville men, was born in Newark, New Jersey, in 1884, as the son of a Methodist minister. Preparing for missionary work in China, he attended Johns Hopkins University. But his wife became ill and died, and Holmes became the religious work secretary of the Baltimore YMCA until coming to Greenville in the spring of 1914. Holmes represented the finest of the social gospel tradition. He combined warm-hearted piety with social uplift. Holmes accepted the findings of biblical higher criticism and defined the essence of religion as "living a good life" in accordance with the teachings of Jesus.[58]

After an initial effort to establish a YWCA in the city in 1904 failed, a permanent group formed in 1917. On May 17 Miss Skinner, a YWCA field-worker, addressed the Business Girls' Bible Class which met weekly at the Chamber of Commerce rooms. The class was taught by Dr. B. D. Hahn, pastor of the Pendleton Street Baptist Church. On June 5 an open meeting was held to gauge public interest, and by the end of the month a board of directors was in place and 150 members were enrolled. Mrs. Harry J. Haynsworth was elected president, and the board included Mrs. Walter L. Gassaway, Mrs. Charles F. Hard, Mrs. W. J. Thackston, Mrs. Martin F.

Ansel, Mrs. William C. Cleveland, Mrs. J. M. Charlotte, Dr. Lou Ellie Johnson, and Miss Edna Marchbanks.[59]

At first the activities were held in borrowed quarters. On Tuesday and Friday afternoons the pool of the Greenville Woman's College was open to YWCA members under the supervision of Laura Ebaugh and Frances Marshall. On September 5 Gertrude Owens, the first secretary, arrived in Greenville, and a suite of six rooms was opened on the second floor of the Cleveland Building on Main Street.[60]

Cultural Life

A series of annual events enriched the cultural life of the city. One such event was the weeklong visit of Redpath's Chatauqua in May of each year, patterned on the summer program at Chatauqua, New York (once a Methodist camp meeting). In April 1917 the Greenville *News* reminded citizens that "in a little more than a month the great tent of the annual Chatauqua will be spread" in the City Park. Along with twenty million Americans— one-fifth of the population—in three thousand cities, Greenvillians thrilled to a variety of cultural events. The 1917 program included a daily Children's Hour, concerts, lectures, moving pictures, and a performance of Gilbert and Sullivan's *The Mikado*.[61]

In addition to the Chatauqua was the visit of the circus, which had been a staple of Greenville life since the antebellum period. The circus train unloaded the animals at the depot on Augusta Street, and there was a parade up Main Street. Before the Gower bridge across the Reedy River was replaced, the elephants had to ford the river for fear they were too heavy for the bridge. Dr. Thomas Goldsmith remembered that "it took all day to come in from Cedrus, see the parade, and go home. . . . It cost too much to see the circus. Negroes would have food stands along the street to the circus. They cooked fish and sold it to the people." The circus and the accompanying carnival set up on Main Street. Alfred Smith remembered that "the Ferris wheel was always located at the corner of Main and Washington, while the popular merry-go-round always whirled at the intersection of Main and McBee."[62]

For those Greenvillians who were nostalgic for the old-time religion of the camp meeting, there was the citywide revival. Billy Sunday had succeeded Dwight L. Moody as America's premier urban evangelist, and the Greenville *News* carried regular excerpts of Sunday's sermons from places like Madison Square Garden in New York City. Greenville itself had to be content with regional imitators of the Sunday style. In October 1916 Baxter

Alester G. Furman. Courtesy of Roper Mountain Science Center, Coxe Collection.

203rd New York on Parade Ground at Camp Wetherill, 1898. Courtesy of C. L. Baley Collection, Schomberg Institute, New York Public Library.

W. Frank Hipp. Courtesy of Roper
Mountain Science Center, Coxe
Collection.

Thomas F. Parker. Courtesy of
Greenville County Library.

Miss Jim Perry. Courtesy of Betty
Dendy, The Haynsworth Law Firm.

John M. Holmes. Courtesy of
Buncombe Street United Methodist
Church and Greenville County YMCA.

Greenville County Courthouse, 1918. Courtesy of Roper Mountain Science Center, Coxe Collection.

Greenville City Park. Courtesy of Oscar Landing.

Circus (undated). Courtesy of Oscar Landing.

John Broadus Watson. Courtesy of Furman University Library, Special Collections.

Southern Textile Exhibition at Textile Hall. Courtesy of Choice McCoin from the collection of Textile Hall Corporation; photographic reproduction by Joe F. Jordan.

Camp Sevier: 105th Ammunition Train in front of YMCA Building, ca. 1917.
Courtesy of Oscar Landing.

Parker High School, 1924. Courtesy of Joe F. Jordan.

L. P. Hollis. Courtesy of Choice McCoin from the collection of Juliet Hollis McAfee.

"Shoeless Joe" Jackson. Courtesy of Roper Mountain Science Center, Coxe Collection.

Poinsett Hotel, 1925. Courtesy of Choice McCoin from the collection of the
Greenville County Library.

Woodside Building on Main Street, looking South, 1923. Courtesy of Choice
McCoin from the collection of the Greenville County Library.

Phillis Wheatley Association, Broad Street, 1924. Courtesy of Greenville County
Library, Laura Ebaugh Collection.

Peg Leg Bates. Courtesy of
The Greenville Cultural
Exchange Center.

Josh White. Courtesy of The
Greenville Cultural Exchange Center.

Grading the Caesar's Head–Greenville Road (Buncombe Road and Geer Highway). Courtesy of South Carolina Highway Department.

F. McLendon of Bennettsville, a Methodist-turned-Baptist preacher, pitched his revival tent on Augusta Road. "Cyclone Mac" urged sinners to repent and make their way down the sawdust trail in his tabernacle as a public witness to their change of life.[63]

Education

Meanwhile, Furman University, high on University Ridge overlooking the Reedy River, became a greater center of intellectual inquiry under the leadership of two presidents between 1897 and 1918—Andrew P. Montague and Edwin McNeill Poteat. Montague, who took advantage of the improving Southern economy and constructed a series of new buildings on the campus, was the first president of Furman to hold the relatively new Ph.D. degree and brought to the Greenville campus scholars who were conducting creative research and teaching. For the first time, the Furman faculty had only one minister. Chemist William Franklin Watson was an expert in photomicrography and produced a textbook in experimental chemistry, and Gordon B. Moore was an exciting and probing teacher of philosophy.[64]

But the coming of such individuals caused stress for a college that had all too often simply passed on "the best that has been thought and written" without critical examination. Professor Watson led the growing discontent within the faculty with what some perceived to be a laxness toward academic standards. In June 1900 Watson was censured by the Board of Trustees. More serious were the reports of Gordon Moore's biting classroom manner and his alleged skepticism of the doctrine of the atonement and the biblical miracles. Though Moore was the only minister on the faculty, he was questioned by the trustees, initially vindicated, and eventually dismissed in June 1903. The strain of these controversies caused President Montague to resign in the midst of the Moore crisis. Such incidents that questioned the prevailing orthodoxy periodically disrupted life at Furman for the next half-century.[65]

To succeed Montague as president of Furman, the trustees chose Edwin McNeill Poteat, a member of a distinguished Southern Baptist family that championed the liberal views and missionary zeal of mainstream American Protestantism. A native of North Carolina, Poteat had been the pastor of churches in Baltimore, New Haven, and Philadelphia. His aim at Furman, he said, was to avoid narrow sectarianism, yet define the college's distinctive Christian spirit and build a strong academic community. Poteat, who continued the building program initiated by his predecessor, laid the foundation of a strong emphasis on science by creating separate departments of biology and chemistry and establishing the bachelor of science degree. He regularly appointed to the faculty individuals with Ph.D. degrees from some of the finest graduate schools of the time such as Chicago, Cornell, Virginia, and Vanderbilt. None did original research, but the faculty formed a strong community of scholars and teachers. True to his own commitments, Poteat resigned from the presidency in 1918 to go to China as a missionary.[66]

During the Progressive era Furman graduates brought national recognition to Greenville. John Matthews Manly was the son of former Furman President Charles Manly. Born in 1865, he received a master's degree from Furman in 1883 and the Ph.D. degree from Harvard in 1890. After teaching at Brown, he was appointed first head of the English department at the University of Chicago, where he remained until his retirement in 1933. He won international acclaim as a scholar of *Piers Plowman* and Chaucer's *Canterbury Tales*. When he died in 1940, he was buried in the family plot in Springwood Cemetery. Manly's brother, Charles Matthews Manly, was born in 1876 and graduated from Furman in 1896. He received a master's degree in engineering from Cornell in 1898 and immediately joined Samuel P. Langley, secretary of the Smithsonian Institution, in his aviation experiments. Though Manly was nearly drowned in Langley's final effort, he invented a water-cooled radial gasoline engine—the first modern aircraft engine.[67]

More controversial was John Broadus Watson, the father of behaviorist psychology. Born near Travelers Rest in 1878, Watson attended the Reedy River, White Horse, and Travelers Rest Schools before enrolling at Furman, where he came under the influence of Gordon Moore who challenged his already rebellious student to probe more deeply into the conventional explanations of things. Watson took a master's degree at Furman in 1899 and went on to the University of Chicago, where he received the Ph.D. degree in psychology in 1903. Ten years later, as a professor at Johns Hopkins University, Watson published "Psychology as a Behaviorist Views It" in the *Psychological Review*—a manifesto for a new scientific approach to psychology using animal research and not depending on consciousness in the experimental subject. In 1915 Watson served as president of the American Psychological Association.[68]

Months after Furman awarded Watson an honorary degree in 1919, he was involved in a widely publicized divorce. The day after the divorce was granted, Watson married a former graduate assistant. Shut out of the academic world, he entered advertising and served as a vice president of

both J. Walter Thompson and William Esty and Company before his retirement in 1958.[69]

Social Life for the Elite

The business elite of Greenville, in their growing affluence, did not
neglect their own social life. In the early months of 1903 there was talk of
forming a country club in Greenville, especially when Sans Souci, the former
estate of Governor Benjamin F. Perry (for many years a fashionable school
for young women), became available for the purpose. In 1905 a group of
business leaders, headed by Ellison A. Smyth, purchased the estate and
opened it as the Sans Souci Country Club. The French Second Empire
house was surrounded by gardens, a nine-hole golf course, and clay tennis
courts. The country club remained at Sans Souci until 1923, when it moved
to its present location on Byrd Boulevard. The business leadership also had
increasing need for a downtown club, after the Greenville City Club closed.
On January 1, 1909, the Greenville *News* reported that there was talk of
organizing a social club in the Coxe home adjacent to Ottaray Hotel. Shortly
thereafter the Poinsett Club was formed with Ellison A. Smyth as president, William Choice Cleveland as vice president, and T. R. Riley as secretary. By May the renovation of the building was complete, and the formal
opening was held. In 1926 the original Poinsett Club moved to the Marshall
house on West Washington Street, and closed in 1929.[70]

Southern Textile Exposition

Greenville attained national recognition as the site of the Southern
Textile Exposition, which began in 1915. Earlier in the century, members
of the Southern Textile Association (STA) discussed the possibility of staging such an affair. In 1914 the STA invited exhibitors to hold an exposition
in Atlanta the following year. But World War I began in Europe in August
1914 and those plans floundered. When fears about war subsided, local
members of the STA urged the business leaders of Greenville to make a bid
for the show. On December 12, 1914, fifty individuals met for dinner at
the Chamber of Commerce with T. B. Wallace, the superintendent of
Dunean Mill, presiding, and the group agreed to proceed.[71]

The Greenville group incorporated as the Southern Textile Exposition
and formed a series of committees to handle the details—headed by Milton
Smith, education and welfare; David Kohn, publicity; James H. Maxwell,
transportation and hotels; J. E. Sirrine, hall and buildings; J. H. Spencer,

machinery and supply department; and G. G. Slaughter, mill products. The Southern Textile Association eagerly gave its sponsorship, and November 2–6, 1915, was set for the exposition.[72]

Sirrine secured the new warehouse of the Piedmont and Northern Railway on West Washington Street as the site, and 169 exhibitors took every available space. Eventually forty thousand people flocked to see the exhibits. The Southern Textile Association convened at the Ottaray Hotel, where the members heard Mayor C. S. Webb, Governor Richard I. Manning, Ellison A. Smyth, and Congressman James F. Byrnes.[73]

The exposition was an overwhelming success, and the Greenville group immediately planned for future shows and a permanent Textile Hall. The Southern Textile Exposition, Inc., elected new officers for the task—Bennette E. Geer became president, Ellison A. Smyth became vice president, G. G. Slaughter became secretary, and Edwin Howard became treasurer. The directors were W. P. Anderson, A. B. Carter, F. Gordon Cobb, John A. McPherson, J. E. Sirrine, and T. B. Wallace of Greenville and J. M. Davis and Zach F. Wright of Newberry. The executive committee met weekly to make plans for a Textile Hall on the north side of West Washington Street.[74]

Plans for the massive hall were drawn by the J. E. Sirrine Company, and the cost was projected at $130,000. With $49,500 in cash and a mortgage for the remainder, construction began in 1916 and was rushed for the opening of the second exposition on December 10, 1917. The building was ready, although the back wall was not finished and a tarpaulin did not keep out the cold winds. *Cotton* magazine saluted "the Greenville boys": they "have completed a building that is a fitting monument to their industry—mute evidence of what the proper cooperative spirit can accomplish when suitably inspired." The city was making its bid to become known as the Textile Capital of the South.[75]

Greenville's increasing importance in South Carolina politics was recognized when Martin Frederick Ansel, a Progressive reformer, was elected governor in 1907 and served until 1911. He was born in Charleston on December 12, 1850, to German immigrant parents. A few years later the Ansels moved to Walhalla, where young Martin was educated in the local schools. Financially unable to attend college, he read law, was admitted to the bar in 1870, and moved to Greenville in 1876. He became a member and later an elder of the First Presbyterian Church. In 1882 he was elected to the state House of Representatives and served in that body until he became solicitor of the Eighth Judicial Circuit. In 1902 he ran for governor in the Democratic primary as a Progressive candidate against the dispensary, opposing Ben Tillman's nephew, James H. Tillman. Both Ansel and Tillman lost, but the former was victorious in 1906. Though personally a prohibitionist, as governor he proposed the county option plan to the legislature, and it was adopted. Within a short time only six counties maintained the dispensary system. An advocate of educational reform, he supported the establishment of 150 additional high schools during his administration. He attended the first Governors' Conference called by President Theodore Roosevelt in 1908 and served on the executive committee. After his service as governor, Ansel returned to Greenville to practice law. In 1912 and again in 1916 he campaigned for Woodrow Wilson's election to the presidency in the North and Midwest.[76]

Progressive Politics

Politics also became the arena in which a large segment of the mill population of Greenville County could express its discontent with industrialization and efforts of Progressive reformers to change their lives. Though Ben Tillman had initially denounced mill workers as "that damned factory class," his followers attempted to woo them. Tillman's nephew, Jim, made a special appeal to the mill workers in his campaign for lieutenant governor in 1900. He did the same in 1902 when he ran for governor against Martin Ansel. But Ansel was a favorite son in the up country, and he defeated Tillman in the textile precincts in Greenville and the northwestern counties of the state. In 1908 Coleman L. Blease, who had been a Tillman lieutenant since 1890, was the lone challenger to the incumbent (Martin Ansel) in the governor's race. Though he appealed for the mill vote, Blease did not succeed in Greenville. In Piedmont and Monaghan, for example, Ansel received 58.4 percent of the vote to Blease's 20.5 percent.[77]

But by 1910 when Blease ran for governor and won, the mill vote in Greenville County had changed. In the mill precincts Blease took 63.7 percent of the vote, and in 1912, when Blease was re-elected, the Greenville County mill boxes went for the incumbent by 70 percent. By contrast, the town precincts were adamantly opposed to Blease and supported his opponents two to one. Mill owners Lewis and Thomas Parker, Ellison Smyth, and J. I. Westervelt publicly supported Blease's opposition. While Blease was denounced by Progressives as a demagogue, his appeal to the mill workers was clear. He attacked Lewis W. Parker by name and his creation of the Parker Cotton Mill Company as an effort to depress wages and control workers. Blease accused Parker, as well as other mill owners, of bribing and trying to intimidate voters. At the same time, Blease embraced the mill workers. "These people," he said in his inaugural address in 1911, "are our people; they are our kindred; they are our friends, and in my opinion they should be let alone, and allowed to manage their own children and allowed to manage their own affairs."[78]

Blease blasted much of the welfare work in the mill villages and the Progressive legislation supported by the business elite. He denounced the commission form of government adopted in Spartanburg and Columbia as a way of diluting the mill vote (which was true). He opposed compulsory education and the use of schools as laboratories for social experiments. He particularly denounced programs of medical inspection of children—a stance that horrified the Progressives of the towns. Blease attacked women's clubs as groups of arrogant busybodies who refused to stay at home and look after their own children. For all the bluster, Blease and the mill people agreed on one simple truth: many of the "do-good" programs advocated by Progressives were designed to benefit, first of all, the reformers themselves and, second, perhaps, those being reformed.[79]

When Blease was succeeded as governor by Progressive Richard I. Manning in 1915, the mill workers no longer felt they had a champion in the governor's mansion, despite Manning's support of labor's right to organize and his willingness to arbitrate labor disputes. When a strike was called in the Brogdon Mill in Anderson in September 1915, Manning wrote J. Rion McKissick, the editor of the Greenville *Piedmont,* to broach the idea of the governor's mediation of the strike with Ellison Smyth. McKissick replied that "it would be impossible for you to effect any real mediation here, that both sides are determined to stand their ground, that there is nothing to arbitrate. . . . There is considerable . . . sentiment that you ventured into this hazardous field unnecessarily."[80]

Nevertheless, Manning entered the fray. When Bennette E. Geer, the president of Judson Mill, heard that his workers were attempting to form a union, he called representatives of the workers together to show them that they were in error. He argued that they were allying themselves with their enemies—the textile workers of the North. He appealed to their loyalty as Southerners. Geer announced his determination to fire those who had joined the union, which he did. A committee of the union met with Geer and urged that those who had been discharged be reinstated. The president refused, the union called a strike, and the mill closed.[81]

After a few days, a majority of the operatives petitioned Geer to reopen the mill. Their representatives asked Greenville Sheriff Hendrix Rector to protect them. Geer indicated his willingness to reopen the mill, and Governor Manning conferred with the sheriff to insure the safety of those who returned to work. Eventually Geer called on Sheriff Rector to eject the families of the strikers from their houses in the mill village.[82]

Despite Manning's efforts on behalf of the workers, they failed to support his campaign for re-election in 1916 and stood by Blease and his followers. The mill presidents were not enthusiastic about Manning's re-election. Of six polled by Greenville banker John W. Norwood, three refused to vote at all, and two supported Manning as the lesser of two evils. Ellison Smyth replied that he was holding his nose and voting for Blease. The progressivism of the business leaders of Greenville was not only racist but anti-union as well.[83]

Economic Uncertainty on the Eve of War

The prosperity of the Progressive era in the South received a jolt in August 1914 when World War I broke out in Europe. Cotton had been bringing thirteen cents a pound, and a bumper crop of sixteen million bales—the largest in American history—was beginning to mature. On August 3 the major cotton exchanges failed to open and, in fact, remained closed for three months. Ten cents a pound was considered the break-even price, and cotton fell to eight and then to five cents. Some $5 million, half the value of the crop, was lost. Cotton remained in the fields unpicked. The price failure affected the farmers, the business people, the textile mills, and eventually the entire Southern economy.[84]

The Greenville *News* listed the price of cotton at 7.95 cents on January 4, 1915, and three days later the newspaper announced the failure of the Parker Cotton Mill Company. Lewis Parker, who was already suffering from the cancer that would end his life, indicated that he would reopen his law practice. The Parker board of directors reorganized, and William E. Beattie became president. Eventually the Parker mills went into receivership, and Greenville's largest textile empire collapsed.[85]

By the end of 1915 the cotton exchanges had reopened, and the price of cotton rose to nine cents. But with the sinking of the *Lusitania* by German submarines and the loss of American life, the United States began to prepare for possible entry into World War I. Whatever happened, Greenville, like the rest of the South, was solidly committed to the leadership of President Woodrow Wilson. The *News* had supported his nomination in 1912 for predictable reasons: "He is a man of scholarly attainments, of wide breadth and knowledge, of unimpeachable character—a high-toned Christian gentleman, sprung from the sturdiest stock of the South, born in Virginia, reared in South Carolina and Georgia." He was touted as the embodiment of the Progressive spirit who had fought as governor of New Jersey for "the purification of politics, the dethronement of bossism and the general betterment of the State."[86]

Two years later, when Alester G. Furman, Jr., graduated from Furman University, he submitted "Woodrow Wilson" as the topic for his senior essay. "The people," he wrote, "are generally satisfied with the way the President has handled his administration, and although it is but a year old we are entering into a very prosperous era. The President has a peculiar sense of responsibility to all parties and parts of the country and possibly feels his obligations more than any other President has ever done."[87]

As American entrance into the European war seemed more certain, the nation was suddenly plunged into fighting on the Mexican border. Mexican General Pancho Villa, angry at the policy of the United States toward the Mexican Revolution, massacred American citizens and raided the town of Columbus, New Mexico. Wilson ordered a punitive expedition to assemble in Texas under the command of General John J. Pershing. In the summer of 1916 the Butler Guards in Greenville were mobilized as part of the First Regiment of the South Carolina National Guard. Colonel Edgeworth M. Blythe, the son of Absolom Blythe, was regimental commander. The Butler Guards first went to Camp Styx in Lexington County and then to El Paso, Texas, where they were placed on border patrol. After several months, the Guards returned and Colonel Blythe resigned his commission.[88]

Meanwhile, the Chamber of Commerce conducted a campaign among the school children to raise some six hundred dollars for an electric sign that would tower over Main Street. The sign contained an American flag and the slogan: "Our Country First—Then Greenville." The Atlanta *Tradesman* commented that the sign was "proof of both the progressivism and patriotism of the community."[89]

World War I

When President Wilson asked Congress to declare war against Germany on April 2, 1917, the Greenville *News* carried a banner headline: "For Liberty and Humanity." Editorially, the paper affirmed Wilson's position: "In words that will live until Doomsday, the President has set forth the position of the United States, making it clear that this country will not permit Germany unmolested to sink its ships, murder its citizens and conspire against its sovereignty and that it must make common cause with the forces of mankind that wars upon the common enemy of civilization and liberty." The following night the speakers in the oratorical contest at Greenville High School delivered their addresses under a large American flag. Louis Carter recited Patrick Henry's "Liberty or Death" speech, Walker Holland spoke on the "National Crisis," and James Allen spoke on "A Vision of War." Carlisle Holler delivered an oration on "Woodrow Wilson," and Mac Wells recited the 1912 nominating speech for Wilson.[90]

Overnight the Furman students who resided in Montague Hall organized a fifty-person company who pledged to go as a unit if called. Every male student at Greenville High School joined one of two companies. The younger students formed Company A with William Rivers, captain, and Melton McManaway, first lieutenant; the older students formed Company B with Harry Martin, captain, and Carlisle Holler, first lieutenant. Benjamin F. Neves of Tigerville wrote to Governor Manning: "It is high time now to defend ourselves, and to that end I wish to tender to President Wilson, through you, myself, three sons and every dollar I possess in defense of our country. South Carolina must and will do her duty."[91]

The black community also joined in the enthusiastic support of the war. On Friday night, April 6, the Dunbar Lodge No. 60 of the Knights of Pythias staged a display of patriotism as J. A. Brier introduced a formal resolution of support that was adopted unanimously. The entire group rose to their feet and sang "My Country, 'Tis Of Thee," while William Bullard, an Army veteran, marched around the room with the United States flag.[92]

In less than two weeks after the declaration of war, Captain G. Heyward Mahon, Jr., regimental adjutant, received a telegram from Governor Manning calling into federal service the First Regiment of the Guard. Shortly before midnight on April 12, 1917, the Butler Guards were notified to report to the armory. They were commanded by Captain William D. Workman, First Lieutenant William T. Adams, and Second Lieutenant Samuel D. Willis. On April 16 the 147 men left by train for Camp Styx in Lexington County. According to the newspaper account, "a grey headed Confederate veteran . . . said that it reminded him of another morning more than half a century ago when Greenville's gallant youth in gay spirits waved farewell to home and dear ones."[93]

By the end of April Congress passed a draft law, and Greenville was assigned three companies as its quota. Colonel Blythe, Clerk of Court Harry A. Dargan, and Probate Judge Walter Scott were appointed to the county registration commission. A number of men volunteered to attend the Officers' Training Camp at Fort Oglethorpe, Georgia; others enlisted in various branches of the service. One Greenville man, Francis J. Beatty, did not wait for the declaration of war but volunteered as an ambulance driver on the French front. In May 1917 he returned home to secure his place in the National Guard.[94]

On the home front, forty-five members of the Pelzer company of the National Guard returned to Greenville "for relief duties and emergencies." They were stationed at Camp Blythe in the City Park. Fifty others were ordered to guard the Southern Railway bridges from Westminster to Duncan. A countywide Civic Preparedness Rally was held in the Grand Opera House on April 21 with Governor Manning in attendance and music provided by the Greenville Concert Band. The governor appointed three Greenvillians to the State Council of Defense—J. E. Sirrine, E. M. Blythe, and J. B. Wassum (division superintendent of the Southern Railway). A home guard, the Greenville Rifle Club, was organized on May 16 with Dr. J. L. Mann, superintendent of the city schools, as president. P. A. McDavid, a Civil War veteran, was among the eighty-one persons to sign up. By November service flags indicating the number of persons in the armed forces were being displayed by local churches and organizations.[95]

During these hectic years there was a series of efforts to raise funds to support the war—among them, three Liberty Loan bond drives. Joseph A. McCullough was chair of the first, which began in June 1917; F. F. Beattie headed the second in October; and John W. Arrington, the third in April 1918. The textile mills were thoroughly canvassed. In the first Liberty Loan drive, for example, more than half of Greenville's goal of $750,000 was subscribed by the special mill drive headed by Ellison A. Smyth.[96]

Black citizens generously responded to the call for funds. In support of the Red Cross, blacks held a massive parade on May 26, 1917, that marched from the American Bank on South Main Street to the City Park. Black schools, churches, and lodges participated. From four until six in the afternoon the "park was turned over to the colored people." The committee that planned the event included J. A. Brier (chair), Professor J. C. Martin, E. W. Biggs, W. B. Sewell, J. N. Dolley, E. D. Holloway, Lou Willis, Professor A. P. Allison, and R. C. Daids. During the third Liberty Loan drive, a large group of black leaders formed a Colored Committee that met at Springfield Baptist Church on April 23, 1918, under the leadership of Charles F. Gandy, the pastor of the church for forty-two years.[97]

By 1918 the war began to bring some hardships to Greenville. The most minor of these hardships was a lack of Coca-Cola because of the sugar shortage. In January 1918 there was a severe shortage of coal. Beginning on January 21 all manufacturing plants closed for five days and for ten Mondays thereafter. Mill workers received half-pay for the enforced holidays. Almost every store was closed on what came to be called "Heatless Days," though employees received full pay.[98]

Other changes in 1918 were permanent. The new federal income tax went into effect and former governor Duncan C. Heyward, the state collector of internal revenue, reported in a letter to the newspaper that "Greenville citizens are not making their Federal income tax returns. . . . Other counties are making a better showing." He warned that "the internal revenue service is determined to see that all who are due taxes pay them." If returns "are not made . . . steps will be taken." On Sunday, March 31 daylight savings time went into effect. Christ Episcopal Church advertised that it "will observe the new government time, and its service will begin this morning at 11:30 on that time."[99]

The Greenville *News* began to print letters from those in the service in Europe. On May 13, 1918, there was a letter from "somewhere in France" written by Joe Duncan. He was serving with the black engineers known as "the Black Boys in Brown." This letter, he wrote, is "from one who is now fighting over here for a cause which is a good one and one that is to defend the Nation and to keep Old Glory on top, now and forever. I answered the call from Ohio, but you will remember I am one of Greenville's true sons." He recalled that his grandfather, Bob Duncan, was well known and a long-time employee of the H. C. Markley Coach Factory. "In fact, I was reared in and about the old coach factory." Duncan ended his letter with a plea for contributions to the Liberty Loan drive.[100]

Not until after the war was Major G. Heyward Mahon's chance encounter with the king of Belgium widely known. Mahon was a battalion commander in the 118th Infantry of the Thirtieth Division. One day as he was pecking on a typewriter in a dugout, a tall officer entered, and Mahon rose and saluted. The stranger identified himself: "I am Albert." Mahon thought "it was someone trying to be smart," and he replied: "I am Heyward." Then he learned it was King Albert. "Smiles and explanations followed, and the king departed."[101]

While Confederate Memorial Day was observed in Greenville during the war, the Fourth of July took on increasing significance. According to the editor of the *News*, J. Rion McKissick, in July 1917, "that slow-dying resentment has in late years dwindled fast away. . . . The South now regards itself as the most important segment of the nation. . . . It is natural therefore that the Fourth of July is being restored to its former place in the Southern calendar. All over what was once the proud domain of the Confederacy the supreme national holiday is being more and more observed on a large scale." Banks and stores were closed, and there were "picnics, auto rides, ball games, fishing parties, movies, courting parties, and excursions." The Piedmont and Northern Railroad offered excursion rates to all points, and the Greenville and Western round-trip ticket to River Falls was only seventy-five cents. There were special attractions at Chick Springs, and at Dukeland Park the activities included a "Kaiser sinking." The mill and black baseball teams played double headers.[102]

Camp Sevier

The War Department had no camps of the size needed to train the large expeditionary force for the battle front in France, so large, temporary cantonments were established in the southeast. Aware of the success of Camp Wetherill during the Spanish-American War, a group of local business leaders began to explore the possibility of bringing a cantonment to Greenville even before the declaration of war. In late March 1917 Mayor Charles S. Webb, W. F. Robertson, John B. Marshall, and A. L. Mills visited the War Department in Washington and returned home assured that Greenville had an equal chance with Columbia for securing a cantonment. Alester G. Furman, William G. Sirrine, and Oscar K. Mauldin took options on 1,000 acres of land northeast of the city. The Chamber of Commerce invited General Leonard Wood, commander of the Department of the Southeast, to inspect the site. He arrived on June 22, 1917, and addressed a large crowd in the City Park. Greenville was selected, and 2,000 acres of land was leased for from eight to ten dollars an acre from the Finley, Greene, Black, Edwards, and Ballenger families primarily. Both the Southern and the Piedmont and Northern railroads passed through the property.[103]

On July 16 Major Alex C. Doyle, constructing Army quartermaster, arrived in Greenville. He consulted with J. E. Sirrine, James F. Gallivan, and the Fiske-Carter Construction Company, as well as Allen Bedell, Sirrine's site engineer. Army engineers were ordered to clear the land and lay out the camp. Henry B. McKoy of Wilmington, later a resident of Greenville for seventy years, was a member of the 105th North Carolina Engineers that helped saw the trees, level drill fields, construct wooden floors, and pitch tents.[104]

National Guard units from North Carolina, South Carolina, and Tennessee were ordered to Greenville. The units became part of the Thirtieth Division—nicknamed "Old Hickory" in honor of Andrew Jackson who was claimed by all three states. Perhaps the most famous individual stationed in Greenville was Grantland Rice, the sports broadcaster, who was a second lieutenant in the 115th Field Artillery. On August 2 the canton-ment was officially named Camp Sevier, in honor of John Sevier, militia commander in the American Revolution and governor of Tennessee when it was admitted to the union. By the end of August 1917 some thirty thou-sand troops were stationed at Camp Sevier. Alfred Taylor noted in his diary that the "roads [were] crowded and dusty and aeroplanes [were] flying over the camp and surrounding country."[105]

On April 30, 1918, the first group of soldiers left Sevier for Camp Mills on Long Island for embarkation to France. The next day the entire division departed. According to Frances Withington, "they moved by rail, leaving at daybreak which was supposed to be a secret, but every girl in town was on hand to tell them goodby and wish them well, solemnly prom-ising to wait till the war was over!" The Eighty-second Division was trans-ferred from Camp Jackson in Columbia to Sevier. The Twentieth Division was formed in August 1918 and remained at Sevier until February 1919. In all, one hundred thousand men were stationed in Greenville.[106]

Meanwhile, the city of Greenville cooperated with the War Camp Com-munity Service to provide programs and activities for the troops. A Com-munity Club for Enlisted Men opened at Coffee and Laurens Streets, opposite the Grand Opera House. The Colored Soldiers' Club was located at 113 East Washington Street, and the Poinsett Club was opened to offic-ers. The YWCA supervised dances on the third floor of the Cleveland Build-ing.[107]

Mrs. Harry C. Duke, who lived in an apartment on Manly Street, pre-pared sandwiches for the canteens at Camp Sevier using her own recipe for mayonnaise. Her daughter Martha was called "the Sandwich Queen" by her friends because she entertained them while spreading sandwiches. Af-ter the war the Duke Sandwich Company continued to operate. Mrs. Duke perfected her mayonnaise recipe and in 1923 began to produce it, along with relish, in one of the old Carriage Factory Buildings on the Reedy River under the name of the Duke Products Company. In 1929 C. F. Sauer of Richmond, Virginia, purchased Duke's recipes and began to oper-ate the Greenville factory.[108]

In the fall of 1918 the soldiers at Camp Sevier and the citizens of Greenville fell victim to the epidemic of the Spanish influenza that was sweeping the nation. Camp Sevier was put under quarantine. Frances Withington recalled that "never a day passed that one or more funeral corteges did not wend their way down West Washington Street (where we lived) en route to the Southern depot where caskets were stacked like cord wood awaiting transportation home to loved ones." The Greenville *News* carried the frightening statistics: "Tuesday, October 8: new cases 300, new pneumonia cases 29, deaths 2; Wednesday October 9: new cases 328, new pneumonia cases 40, deaths 7; Thursday October 10: new cases 300, new pneumonia cases 29, deaths 5." On East Park Avenue, Joseph G. Cunningham lay ill with influenza in his second-story bedroom. He became impatient and wanted to get up and return to work. But each day his wife Beulah pointed out to him the funeral processions driving into Springwood Cemetery, and he was content to lie abed one more day. He survived the epidemic.[109]

The Armistice and the End of the Progressive Era

The war in Europe came to an end by an armistice agreement on the eleventh hour of the eleventh day of the eleventh month—November 11, 1918. The Greenville *News* reported on the local celebration: "It seemed that every device that human genius could devise was brought into use to make a noise." The mills "closed down at noon, and soldiers from Camp Sevier were in town by the thousands. Many stores closed for several hours and their employees joined in the general celebration." That night Textile Hall was jammed, and the band of the Thirtieth Infantry furnished music for the occasion. The speakers included Mayor H. C. Harvley, Brigadier General Switzer (acting commander of the Twentieth Division, Camp Sevier) and Colonel Lewis VanShaick (commander of trains and the military police). Outside Textile Hall, "several thousands were in the streets, having a good time—ringing bells, waving flags, shooting fireworks and throwing talcum powder (the stock of confetti in the city having been exhausted)."[110]

As the veterans came home from the war, the era of Progressive reform in the nation ended with the defeat of the Versailles Treaty and Wilson's dream of American leadership in the League of Nations. But the South supported the League, and there the Progressive spirit continued. "The South is heart and soul for the Treaty," the Greenville *Piedmont* declared. "It hasn't read it, but it has read some of the speeches of them darned Republicans." Just as the Spanish-American War brought Greenville into the Progressive mainstream, so World War I broadened the horizons of its citizens. "With the war of 1914–1918," wrote the Southern poet Allen Tate, "the South re-entered the world." But the twentieth-century world would prove to be an era of even greater change for the piedmont South.[111]

Notes

1. Since 1951 the standard treatment of Southern progressivism has been C. Vann Woodward, *Origins of the New South, 1877–1913* (Baton Rouge, La., 1951). A more recent and detailed, if less interpretive, account is Dewey W. Grantham, *Southern Progressivism: The Reconciliation of Progress and Tradition* (Knoxville, Tenn., 1983).

2. James M. Richardson, *History of Greenville County, South Carolina* (Atlanta, Ga., 1930, 1980), 91; S.C. Department of Agriculture, Commerce and Industries, *South Carolina: A Handbook* (Columbia, 1927), 274.

3. Richardson, *Greenville County*, 253–54; Frank Barnes, *The Greenville Story* (Greenville, 1956), 261–62; Greenville *News*, October 2, 1960.

4. Barnes, *Greenville Story*, 223–24; Robert Smeltzer, "Alester G. Furman: He Helped Build Greenville," *South Carolina Magazine* 19 (November 1954): 11, 14–15, 18; Greenville *News*, March 7, 1962.

5. Smeltzer, "Furman," 15; Barnes, Greenville *News*, March 3, 1905, cited in *Greenville Story*, 94.

6. Henry Bacon McKoy, "The Spanish American War and Greenville," *Proceedings and Papers of the Greenville County Historical Society* (cited hereafter as *PPGCHS*) 2 (1965–1968): 89–90. This article is reprinted in McKoy, *Greenville, S.C. As Seen Through the Eyes of Henry Bacon McKoy* (Greenville, 1989), 24–37.

7. McKoy, "Spanish American War," 91–93.

8. Ibid., 93.

9. Ibid., 94–95; Greenville *News*, March 7, 1962.

10. McKoy, "Spanish American War," 95–96.

11. Ibid., 96–97.

12. Ibid.

13. Ibid., 103; Greenville *News*, March 7, 1962.

14. McKoy, "Spanish American War," 103; David L. Carlton, *Mill and Town in South Carolina, 1880–1920* (Baton Rouge, La., 1982), 106–7; Greenville *News*, January 1906, cited in Barnes, *Greenville Story*, 103.

15. Samuel L. Zimmerman, *Negroes in Greenville, 1970: An Exploratory Approach* (Greenville, 1970), 10).

16. Zimmerman, *Negroes in Greenville*, 10; S.C. Dept. of Agriculture, *Handbook of South Carolina* (Columbia, 1907), 219–20.

17. Judith G. Bainbridge, *Centennial: The Chamber in Retrospect* (Greenville, 1988), 2–3, 17.

18. Guy A. Gullick, *Greenville County, Economic and Social* (Columbia, 1921), 16–17.

19. Crittenden, *Century Book*, 71; *The Gateway to Get There—Greenville, 1911*, Greenville *Daily News*, 1911, rpt. 1966; Bainbridge, *Centennial*, 3–4.

20. Bainbridge, *Centennial*, 3–4; Crittenden, *Century Book*, 71.

21. *Gateway to Get There*, 13; Doyle Boggs, *The Liberty Spirit: History of the Liberty Corporation* (Greenville, 1986), 9–14.

22. *Gateway to Get There*, 26.

23. Richardson, *Greenville County*, 235–36; Boggs, *Liberty Spirit*, 21–23.

24. Boggs, *Liberty Spirit*, 23–25.

25. Kelsey and Guild, *Beautifying and Improving Greenville* (Boston, Mass., 1907, 1975), passim. The role of city planning and the City Beautiful movement is treated in Roy Lubove, *The Urban Community: Housing and Planning in the Progressive Era* (Engelwood Cliffs, N.J., 1967).

26. Greenville *News*, January 10, 1910; May 29, 1914.

27. Ibid., July 29, 31, September 11, 1917.

28. Barnes, *Greenville Story*, 115, 122, 149; Alfred T. Smith, Reminiscence, 1970 (manuscript in possession of the author); Greenville *News*, August 22, October 21, December 5, 1917; October 26, 1970.

29. Barnes, *Greenville Story*, 114, 164, 171–72; McKoy, *Greenville, S.C.* (Greenville, 1989), 61, 109–10.

30. Greenville *News*, January 27, March 30, April 2, 3, 1918.

31. Eli Alston Wilkes, *Echoes and Etchings* (Columbia, n.d.), 123; Interview with Beulah (Mrs. Joseph G.) Cunningham in 1989 at age 106.

32. Wilkes, *Echoes and Etchings*, 123.

33. Greenville *News*, May 2, 17, 1914; Sidney R. Bland, "Fighting the Odds: Militant Suffragists in South Carolina" *S.C. Historical Magazine* 82 (1981): 32.

34. Greenville *News*, April 8, May 7, August 16, October 15, 16, November 14, 1917; Bland, "Fighting the Odds," 38–43.

35. Greenville *News*, March 22, 1918; Bland, "Fighting the Odds," 41–42.

36. Gullick, *Greenville County*, 15.

37. Nancy Vance Ashmore, *Greenville: Woven From the Past* (Northridge, Calif., 1986), 136–37; Greenville *News*, May 3, 6, 1918.

38. Joseph D. Mathis, "Race Relations in Greenville, South Carolina from 1865 through 1900" (M.A. thesis, Atlanta University, 1971), 60–62; David Carlton, *Mill and Town in South Carolina, 1880–1920* (Baton Rouge, La., 1982), 150.

39. *Beautifying and Improving Greenville*, 12.

40. Mathis, "Race Relations," 49–50; Robert B. Everett, "Race Relations in South Carolina, 1900–1932" (Ph.D. disser., University of Georgia, 1969), 241.

41. John E. Wells and Robert E. Dalton, *The S.C. Architects, 1885–1935: A Biographical Dictionary* (Richmond, Va., 1992), 33–34.

42. Greenville *Piedmont*, April 2, 1912; Columbia *State*, April 7, 1912.

43. Woodward, *Origins*, 369; Greenville *News*, April 27, 1912, cited in Barnes, *Greenville Story*, 146; *News*, December 15, 1917. See Barnes, *Greenville Story*, 101, 110, and 172 for references to "The Clansman."

44. Barnett A. Elzas, *The Jews of South Carolina* (Philadelphia, 1905, 1972), 229; Notes of Sol Zaglin, copies in possession of Jack L. Bloom.

45. Greenville *News*, January 26, 1947; Notes of Jack R. Bloom; Friddle, *Greenville Firsts*, 106.

46. Greenville *Piedmont*, February 4, 1929; Notes of Jack R. Bloom; Bureau of the Census, Department of Commerce, *Religious Bodies, 1926* (Washington, D.C., 1930) 1: 670–71.

47. Charleston County, S.C., School District, *The Ethnic History of South Carolina* (Charleston, 1975), 199, 276–77; "Nick Andrew Theodore," *Biographical Dictionary of the S.C. Senate, 1776–1985* (Columbia, 1986) 3: 1589–91.

48. Friddle, *Famous Greenville Firsts,* 106.

49. William G. McLoughlin, *Revivals, Awakenings, and Reform* (Chicago, Ill., 1978), 141–78; Laurens County Historical Society, *The Scrapbook: A Compilation of Historical Facts About Places and Events of Laurens County, S.C.* (Laurens, 1982), 219–20, 222–23.

50. *Scrapbook,* 220; Henry B. McKoy, *History of the First Presbyterian Church of Greenville, South Carolina* (Greenville, 1962), 169–70; David Morgan, "N. J. Holmes and the Origins of Pentecostalism," *S.C. Historical Magazine* 84 (1983): 136–51.

51. Morgan, "N. J. Holmes," 145–46, 150–51.

52. Blanche Marsh, *Hitch Up the Buggy* (Greenville, 1977), 111–13.

53. Alfred T. Smith in his 1970 reminiscence recalled that "the race began up at Stone Avenue and the cars had to get up enough speed to make it up the big hill leading to the finish line at Elford Street." Greenville *News,* December 30, 1923; *News,* March 4, 1904, cited in Jean Martin Flynn, *History of the First Baptist Church of Taylors, S.C.* (Greenville, 1953), 33; Barnes, *Greenville Story,* 117–18; Greenville *News,* June 2, 1914.

54. Richardson, *Greenville County,* 106; Barnes, *Greenville Story,* 129, 157.

55. Barnes, *Greenville Story,* 122, 130, 141, 144, 147; Greenville *News,* May 17, 1918.

56. Dave Partridge, "A Brief, Highlight History of the Greenville Hospital System," *PPGCHS* 8 (1990): 178–81. Also see Partridge, *The First 80 Years: Greenville Hospital System, Its History Through 1992* (Greenville, 1992).

57. Barnes, *Greenville Story,* 119–20; Sudie M. Mulligan, "The History of Camp Greenville," *PPGCHS* 7 (1984): 29–32.

58. John M. Holmes, *Jesus and the Young Man of Today* (New York, 1920), cited in Alfred S. Reid, ed., *The Arts in Greenville, 1800–1960* (Greenville, 1960), 121–22.

59. Greenville *News,* May 17, June 5, 29, July 22, 1917.

60. Ibid., September 5, 1917.

61. Ibid., April 9, May 6, 1917.

62. Marsh, *Hitch Up the Buggy,* 72–74; Smith, Reminiscences (in possession of the author).

63. Greenville *News,* September 3, October 5, 1916.

64. Alfred S. Reid, *Furman University: Toward A New Identity, 1925–1975* (Durham, N.C., 1976), 22, 30; William J. McGlothlin, *Baptist Beginnings in Education: A History of Furman University* (Nashville, Tenn.), 171–72.

65. Reid, *Furman University,* 24.

66. Ibid., 30–31.

67. "John Matthews Manly," *Dictionary of American Biography* (New York, 1958), Supplement 2: 427–28 (hereafter *DAB*) "Charles Matthews Manly," *DAB* 13: 239.

68. "John Broadus Watson, *DAB* Supplement 6, 670–73.

69. *DAB;* Mary Wyche Burgess, "John Broadus Watson: Psychologist from Travelers Rest," *PPGCHS* 5 (1980): 65–73.

70. Greenville *News,* January–June, 1903; June 1905; January 1, 26, May 19, 1909, cited in Barnes, *Greenville Story,* 92, 98, 114, 118; Romayne A. Barnes, "Benjamin F. Perry, Unionist of Greenville District and South Carolina," *PPGCHS* 5 (1980): 34–35. Speaker Bankhead, the great-grandson of T. P. Brockman spoke in Greenville in March 1939. *News,* March 26, April 23, 1939. Henry B. McKoy, *Sketch of the Poinsett Club of Greenville, South Carolina* (Greenville, 1971).

71. Yancey S. Gilkerson, "Textile Hall's First Sixty Years," *PPGCHS* 5 (1980): 74.

72. Ibid., 74–75.

73. Ibid., 75–76.

74. Ibid., 76.

75. Ibid.

76. David Duncan Wallace, *The History of South Carolina* (New York, 1934) 4: 83–84.

77. Carlton, *Mill and Town,* 165–66, 216–17.

78. Ibid., 217–21, 233–34, 240, 254.

79. Ibid., 227–39.

80. Robert M. Burts, *Richard Irvine Manning and the Progressive Movement in South Carolina* (Columbia, 1974), 110–111.

81. Ibid., 112.

82. Ibid.; Barnes, *Greenville Story,* 170.

83. Burts, *Manning,* 112–13; Carlton, *Mill and Town,* 254.

84. George B. Tindall, *The Emergence of the New South, 1913–1945* (Baton Rouge, La., 1967), 33–34; William J. Cooper, Jr., and Thomas E. Terrill, *The American South: A History* (New York, 1991), 604.

85. Greenville *News,* January 4, 7, 10, March 17, 1915; May 11, June 10, 16, 1916, cited in Barnes, *Greenville Story,* 159, 162, 175–76.

86. Tindall, *Emergence,* 37–38; Greenville *News,* July 3, 1912.

87. Graduation Essays, Furman University, 1914, Furman University Archives, Greenville, S.C.

88. Greenville *News,* April 14, 1917; Richardson, *Greenville County,* 293.

89. Greenville *News,* September 11, 1917; November 15, 1931.

90. Ibid., April 3, 4, 1917.

91. Ibid., April 4, 9, 10, 1917.

92. Ibid., April 10, 1917.

93. Ibid., April 13, 14, 17, 1917.

94. Ibid., April 29, May 6, 18, 1917.

95. Ibid., April 22, May 19, 25, November 16, 1917.

96. Ibid., June 14, October 28, 1917; April 6, 1918.

97. Ibid., May 27, 1917; April 24, 1918.

98. Ibid., January 17, 21, 22, 1918.

99. Ibid., March 24, 30, 31, 1918.

100. Ibid., May 13, 1918.

101. Ibid., December 25, 1932.

102. Ibid., July 1, 3, 5, 1917.

103. Frances M. Withington, "Camp Sevier, 1917–1918," *PPGCHS* 4 (1971): 76–78; Greenville *News,* April 2, 1917.

104. Withington, "Camp Sevier," 78–79. More detailed information is contained in Alex C. Doyle, Major, QMC, USNG, "Completion Report of Camp Sevier, Greenville, S.C., December 1917" (copy in the S.C. Room, Greenville County Library, Greenville, S.C.).

105. Withington, "Camp Sevier," 79; Greenville *News,* December 10, 28, 1917.

106. Withington, "Camp Sevier," 83–84.

107. Ibid., 81.

108. Ibid., 83; A. F. Waldrop, "The C. F. Sauer Company Where Duke's Mayonnaise is Made," *Trucking,* January 1952, cited in Linda Friddle, ed., *Famous Greenville Firsts* (Greenville, 1986), 47.

109. Greenville *News,* October 15, 1918; Withington, "Camp Sevier," 79–80; Interview with Beulah (Mrs. Joseph G.) Cunningham.

110. Greenville *News,* November 12, 1918.

111. Cited in Tindall, *Emergence of the New South,* 68–69.

CHAPTER TEN

The Decade of
the 1920s

In 1920 the census indicated that 85.9 percent of the population in Greenville County was rural. This figure is misleading because it included the towns of Fountain Inn, Simpsonville, Greer, Piedmont, and the mill villages outside the city of Greenville. A more accurate index is the growth of the rural and urban segments of the population. Between 1910 and 1920 the rural population increased only 24.2 percent, while the urban population increased 46.9 percent. There were actual decreases in three rural townships in the northern part of the county—Saluda, Cleveland, and Glassy Mountain—and Dunklin Township had an increase of only twenty-five persons.[1]

The Problems of Agriculture

The high price of cotton after 1915 encouraged that industry's growth. In 1920 Greenville produced forty-eight thousand bales of cotton—the seventh highest production of any county in the state. But the end of World War I, the recovery of European farms, and the decreased demand for cotton created a depression in 1921. Cotton brought 40 cents a pound in the spring of 1920; by the end of the year, the price had dropped to 13.5 cents. Banker John W. Norwood wrote that "I do not expect to live to see upland cotton sell at twenty-five cents a pound again."[2]

Boll weevils arrived in South Carolina in 1917 and threatened the cotton crop with extinction in the early 1920s. In January 1922 the Greenville *Piedmont* carried the proposal of the American Cotton Association that $1 million be offered for a successful method of control. Various methods of crop dusting and poisoning were used, and a black farmer near Greer invented a compound that he said killed the boll weevils outright.[3]

But the price of cotton continued to drop—from a high of 28 cents in 1923 to 9.96 cents in 1930. The Great Depression, beginning in 1929, brought more stress to the cotton farmers. According to Clemson Professor W. C. Jensen in the *News* on January 4, 1932, "farmers are facing, in fact, are already in, a new era—an era of low prices and costs such as some of them have never seen and even the older operators have not witnessed for about fifteen to twenty years."⁴

After passage of the Smith-Lever Act of 1914 and the Smith-Hughes Act of 1917, Greenville County employed a farm agent through the Clemson Extension Service. By the end of 1923 W. R. Gray, the county agent, lauded the progress that farmers had made by using cover crops and commercial fertilizers. Prior to World War I, he wrote, only a half-dozen farmers planted crimson clover, and almost none planted winter cover crops. By 1923 nearly one thousand farmers utilized cover crops. The growth of corn was revolutionized by the use of new growing methods and commercial fertilizer, and there was widespread production of pure-bred hogs and other livestock.⁵

The peach industry continued to flourish in the post-World War I period. In 1919 there were 92,972 trees in Greenville County. By 1924 there were 157,853 trees producing 117,963 bushels of peaches. The leading growers were Verne Smith, W. T. Adams, Greenville Mayor Richard F. Watson, D. L. Johnson, and Mills Hunter in the Lowndes Hill section on Pelham Road; Arthur S. Agnew on Piney Mountain; W. H. Canada at Chick Springs; and E. R. Taylor, J. T. Taylor, and W. W. Burgess in Greer.⁶

One of the farmers who refused to abandon cotton and fought the boll weevils was Bernice Edward Greer. He was born in 1882 near Pelham, the son of W. H. Greer, who was a farmer before him. In 1904 Greer purchased a sixty-acre farm near Mauldin with the help of his family, built a small house, and married Florie Verdin. The first year they planted 15 acres of cotton producing eight to ten bales. The husband and wife did all the work themselves—arising before daylight and working near the house by the light of a lantern. At dawn they were in the fields and both worked until dark.⁷

As land became available, Greer purchased more acreage. In 1915 the Greers produced a bale an acre. In 1920 they produced 190 bales of cotton on 200 acres. In 1923 they owned 340 acres and had acquired a tractor with plows and harrows. When the price fell below ten cents, the Greers stored the cotton until the price rose to twenty-five cents. When the boll weevils appeared, the Greers reduced their acreage and began crop rotation. Not only was the crop attacked by the weevils but also by the red spider and army worm. The Greers planted 100 acres of cotton and rotated the land every three years. In the intervening years the Greers planted crimson clover and then peas, both of which were turned under. In the fields where cotton grew, the Greers planted winter rye to stop soil erosion. To combat the boll weevils, Greer fertilized the fields heavily, cultivated them intensively, and used poison. He applied a mixture of calcium arsenic and molasses with mops and sprinkled the plants with buckets in which he made holes. Using these improved methods, the Greers produced 120 bales on 100 acres.[8]

Tenant Farming

One of the major characteristics of agriculture in Greenville County—and the South generally—was tenant farming. In South Carolina 63 percent of all farms were operated by tenants, and in Greenville County the figure stood at 60 percent. With a population that was 69.5 percent white, 59.3 percent of the tenants were white. In Greenville 75.3 percent of the tenants were sharecroppers, and 21.3 were renters or cash tenants. White tenants preferred sharecropping to black tenants.[9]

Typical of the white sharecroppers was Charles Grogan, whose daughter Alice Grogan Hardin was interviewed by researcher Allen Tullos in 1980. Grogan, his wife Lydia Jane (Janie), their five sons, and three daughters lived on what Alice called "a pretty good size" farm and raised cotton and corn. Alice's grandfather, a furniture maker, and her grandmother lived with the family. Charles Grogan owned his own mules, plows, and hoes, and had a hired man who lived with the family. At the end of the year Grogan paid the landowner a third of his profit. The father and sons plowed in the fields; the mother and daughters hoed and picked cotton.[10]

The Grogans moved to two other farms, and the children regularly attended school for the four months that it was in session. The Grogans raised all their food—wheat for bread, hogs, fruits, and vegetables. They canned vegetables and fruits such as dried apples and peaches. Corn was taken to the mill and ground for meal. Times were hard, Alice Hardin remembered, and in 1926 the Grogans followed thousands of farmers to the textile mills.

Sociology Professor G. Croft Williams of the University of South Carolina praised the state's farmers for their "self-reliance, conservatism, stolidity, and an adverseness to organization." But these characteristics were also their undoing. In 1927 the U.S. Department of Agriculture reported that the average workday was 11.4 hours, yet between 1921 and 1931 the average farmer earned only $784 a year.[11]

Expansion of Textiles

The textile industry emerged from World War I operating at full speed. The older mills were expanding, and new diversified mills were being constructed. In August 1923 the *News* reported that there were textile projects costing $10 million under way within a twenty-mile radius of the city—including Southern Bleachery near Taylors, Southern Worsted at Paris, and additions to Dunean Mill, Judson Mill, and Union Bleachery. The Southern Weaving Company was organized in 1924 with F. L. Murdock as president, and in September 1925 Piedmont Plush Mills began building a plant on the Easley Bridge Road near Judson. It was touted as the first mill in the South to produce upholstery and drapery fabrics. The next year Judson added a silk mill in Greenville.[12]

In the 1920s the Southern textile industry began to overtake Northern mills. Faced with higher wages and fewer hours, Northern companies began to buy out Southern mills. In July 1923 there were rumors in Greenville of "eastern interests interested in Victor-Monaghan Mills." Not until August 9 did the officers of Victor-Monaghan announce the sale of three plants—none of them in Greenville. The day before, on August 8, Lockwood, Greene and Company of Boston purchased the controlling interest in the Pelzer Manufacturing Company from Ellison Smyth and the Pelzer family for three hundred dollars a share—a total of nearly $9 million. The following year, on August 23, 1924, Edwin F. Greene addressed a joint luncheon of the Chamber of Commerce and the Civitan Club as "fellow businessmen of Greenville."[13]

Nationally, the textile industry was hurt by the business slump of 1920–1921, though there was a partial recovery in 1923. But in 1924 profits were low and remained low until even greater losses were posted during the Great Depression. Meanwhile, the local earmarks of the late 1920s were additional reorganization and expansion of the textile industry. Early in 1927 John W. Norwood, acting president of the American Spinning Company, sold the plant to the Florence Mill of Forest City, North Carolina. Later in the year, Samuel Slater and Sons of Massachusetts began building a mill north of Travelers Rest in what became the town of Slater. Symbolically, the cornerstone of Samuel Slater's original mill in Rhode Island was brought from the Smithsonian Institution and incorporated into the new building. Judson Mills was sold to Deering, Milliken of New York, though B. E. Geer continued to serve as president. In 1928 the Brandon Corporation was formed, under the presidency of Aug W. Smith, as a $9.5 million business consolidating the Brandon Mill, Brandon Duck Mill, Poinsett Mills, Woodruff Mill, and Renfrew Finishing plant. That same year Fred Symmes sold his controlling interest in the Nuckasee Mill in Greenville to Hampshire Underwear and Hosiery Company, and in 1929 the plant was acquired by Union-Buffalo Mills. Nevertheless, Symmes remained as head of the mill.[14]

Mill Paternalism

The mill paternalism of earlier decades continued in the postwar era. Not only were villages expanded, but special features were added. In 1925 Judson Mills opened a hotel for the use of single employees. Judson President Bennette Geer used the formal opening as an occasion to talk about the absolute necessity of cooperation and complimented the Judson community on its spirit. The pastor of the local Methodist mill church, W. F. Gault, responded with a speech on the value of homes and declared that the people of Judson were fortunate in having excellent places to live.[15]

During the same period that many of the city elite were enjoying vacations in the mountains, John T. Woodside created Wildwood consisting of 1,500 acres of mountain land 25 miles north of Greenville on the Buncombe Highway. There Woodside constructed a lodge and twenty-five houses. In 1925 over twenty-five hundred employees spent at least one night, and some as much as a week. W. M. Grier, secretary of the Woodside Community House, and his wife directed the program at Wildwood.[16]

The Parker District Schools

The climax of mill paternalism was the creation of a separate school district for the textile crescent west of Greenville. At the close of World War I, each mill maintained its own elementary school, but there was no high school in the area. Some mill families paid five dollars a month in tuition to send their children to Greenville High School. In an essay written in 1924, Victoria Hunter, a student at Brandon School, indicated that many "parents were afraid to let young children go off to school. If they went to the city schools it was expensive, and people could not pay to have the children go." Most children expected to go to work as soon as they finished the sixth grade.[17]

In 1922 the mill executives petitioned the state legislature to create the Parker School District—named for Thomas F. Parker, who had been closely associated with mill welfare work since the beginning of the twentieth century. The new district contained 12 square miles in which twenty-five thousand operatives and their families lived. The district had about $9 million of taxable property which made it the wealthiest school district in the state. Initially, the Parker District included thirteen elementary schools and a new high school. The superintendent of the new district was Lawrence Peter Hollis—former director of the Monaghan YMCA, the director of welfare activities of the Parker Cotton Mill Company, and since 1916 the head of the Victor-Monaghan elementary schools. Local funding would be provided by a self-imposed tax on mill property. The first year the Parker District enrolled about six thousand students and employed 130 teachers.[18]

Under Hollis's leadership, the school district became a unifying element in the lives of the residents of the mill villages. The Parker District published a newspaper, *The Joy Maker,* from October 1923 to April 1924 that included school news, student essays, and articles boosting district spirit. On March 6, 1925, the paper was superseded by a weekly paper, *The Parker Progress.*[19]

The centerpiece of the school district was the Parker High School, whose first principal was Ellison M. Smith. The new high school building, which cost $120,000, was designed by the J. E. Sirrine Company and was located on a hill just west of the Parker District gymnasium in the Woodside Mill village. The cornerstone was laid with appropriate ceremonies on April 18, 1924. Despite bad weather, one thousand people gathered to hear the main address by Francis Pendleton Gaines, a Furman English professor and later president of Wake Forest College and Washington and Lee University. He spoke on "The Ideal of the School" and proclaimed it "the gateway of youth, the fortress of democracy, and the temple of the spirit."[20]

On May 26, 1924, the high school honored its first graduating class. All seventeen names appeared in the Greenville *News*—Kathryn James Long, Margaret Alice Mosby, Sam A. Henson, Hazel L. Gregory, Lorene League, Edith Jane Ashmore, Allen Lawrence LaFoy, Herbert Nichols, Hester [sic], Thelma O. League, Olfrin Elizabeth Langston, Ellen Frances Jameson, Mila Russell Mauldin, Lee Coleman, Wealthy L. Hamby, John Herbert White, Irene Jones, and Fred D. Moody. Professor E. H. Henderson of Furman delivered the commencement address. E. Buford Crain, pastor of City View Baptist Church and native of Dark Corner, preached the baccalaureate sermon.[21]

Hollis was no professional educator, but he created a vision of progressive education built on his own career of welfare work, his warm evangelical faith, and the idea of education as social amelioration from the American philosopher, John Dewey. Hollis believed that the school should fit the individual, not the individual the school. He wanted experience at the center of learning and envisioned science classes studying the environment outdoors and displaying the results at a "science fair." He enlisted the cooperation of parents in the learning process. Citizenship, music, and vocational education were essential elements of Hollis's curriculum, and he never forgot the mill culture that called the Parker District into existence. A reporter indicated that "'book larnin' is not unduly stressed in Parker district. More emphasis is placed upon fitting the student for some trade." *Textile World* praised Hollis for "trying to infuse into his school district an impulse which, for want of a better term, we shall call industrial consciousness." Hollis knows that "a Ford car, movies and a radio do not compensate for the loss of the thrill which comes from doing a good job." Nevertheless, the ambitions of Parker students grew beyond the mills. As early as 1925 nearly half of the Parker graduates planned to go to college.[22]

Hollis gathered a talented cadre of administrators and teachers. As the assistant superintendent of the elementary schools, for example, he employed Sadie Goggins. "I liked her," he said, "and I needed someone who knew about schools, so I could go around and meet the people." Lawrence G. Nilson became director of music and attracted wide attention with the Thousand Voice Choir, which sang in Textile Hall. In addition to her English classes, Mrs. Grace Heriot coached the high school Debate Club that won state and regional honors. Mrs. A. F. Geiger took great pride when a member of her civics class was chosen as a page by U.S. Senator Ellison D. Smith. The student, Wayne Oates, later became a renowned pastoral psychologist and a professor at the Southern Baptist Theological Seminary.[23]

Hollis was a strong advocate of adult literacy. In the Parker District, there were an estimated fourteen hundred people over the age of ten who could not write their names. He challenged each of the 140 teachers to teach ten persons in a single week in November 1923. Adult schools became a regular feature in the Parker District. On March 15, 1924, for example, Hollis presided over the closing banquet of the adult schools at Brandon Methodist Church. The main speakers were Brown Mahon, vice president of Judson Mills, and Wil Lou Gray, state supervisor of adult schools. The following year, in the 1925–1926 session, Greenville County led the state in adult school work.[24]

The program of progressive education in the Parker District brought widespread recognition to Greenville. Educators and journalists from across the United States came to observe in the schools, as well as visitors from Europe, South America, and New Zealand. In August 1941 George Kent's article, "Mill Town Miracle," appeared in the educational journal, *School and Society,* and was reprinted in *The Readers' Digest.* In 1949 Hollis was the only individual from the southeast included in a survey of one hundred outstanding educators by *Look Magazine.*[25]

"Shoeless Joe" Jackson and Nigel League

The increased opportunity for education also gave the talented and ambitious children of textile workers hope for a way out of the cycle of textile employment, just as the mills had provided an opportunity for people caught in rural poverty. The doors education opened are demonstrated by two individuals from successive generations—baseball star, "Shoeless Joe" Jackson, and political hopeful, Nigel League. Though both Jackson's and League's careers ended tragically, their stories illustrate the opportunities available to the two men.

Joseph Jefferson Jackson, like many thousands in the South Carolina Piedmont, was the son of a tenant farmer who found his way into the textile mill. Born in 1888 in Pickens County, Jackson moved with his parents and their nine children to Brandon Mill, where Joe went to work at age thirteen. Unable to read or write, he showed promise as a baseball player and joined the Brandon team—first as catcher, then pitcher, and eventually as an outfielder. In 1907 Jackson was spotted by Tom Stouch, who soon became manager of the Greenville Spinners. Stouch hired Jackson for the handsome salary of seventy-five dollars a month, almost double his pay at Brandon.[26]

Playing for the Spinners, Jackson made his reputation as a hitter and gained a nickname. Wearing a new pair of spiked shoes that hurt his feet, he decided to play in his stocking feet. No one noticed until the seventh inning when Jackson hit a triple. Someone called him "Shoeless Joe," and the name stuck. Near the end of the season Connie Mack gave Jackson a major league contract for $325, and his reputation as a hitter soared. Washington pitcher Walter Johnson once said that he considered Jackson the greatest natural ballplayer he had ever seen. In 1915 Charles Comiskey secured him for the Chicago White Sox for sixty-five thousand dollars.[27]

Jackson became part of a fast, new culture accustomed to money and flashy clothes. He purchased a pool hall and a farm in Greenville, as well as a house for his parents in Brandon. But his salary was never more than six thousand dollars. During the 1919 World Series, Jackson and seven of his teammates agreed to throw the series as their only defense against Comiskey. On September 28, 1920, Jackson appeared before the grand jury in Chicago and testified that he had received only five thousand dollars for his part in the conspiracy. According to the Chicago *Herald and Examiner*, "as Jackson departed from the Grand Jury room, a small boy clutched at his sleeve and tagged along after him. 'Say it ain't so, Joe,' he pleaded. 'Say it ain't so.'" Jackson was reported to have replied: "Yes, kid, I'm afraid it is."[28]

The Black Sox case did not come to trial until 1921. On August 2 the jury found Jackson and the others not guilty. But the baseball commissioner, Judge Kennesaw Mountain Landis, ended the celebration. "Regardless of the verdict of juries," he said, "no player who throws a ballgame . . . will ever play professional baseball."[29]

"Shoeless Joe" Jackson returned to Savannah where he and his wife Katie lived in the off-seasons, and played semiprofessional baseball. In 1929 the Jacksons moved to Greenville, and Joe opened a dry-cleaning business and continued to play semiprofessional baseball in the summers. In 1933 the Greenville club rejoined organized baseball and offered Jackson the position of player-manager, but Judge Landis refused to alter his ruling. In his last years, Jackson operated a liquor store and played baseball with the neighborhood children. He died on December 5, 1951, at the age of sixty-three. His funeral was held in the Baptist church in Brandon where he had lived as a young man.[30]

Nigel League, like "Shoeless Joe," attempted to move from the mill village into prominence, but by way of education and political office. League was born in 1909, the seventh of sixteen children of D. W. and Mary Odum League. D. W. League eventually became the overseer of the Number One and Number Two weave rooms at Poe Mill. He insisted that his children finish high school, though the young men began to work in the mill during the summers when they were twelve.

Nigel, whose name rhymed with vigil, was ambitious. As a young man he scrubbed floors for the neighbors and showed silent films. At Parker High School Nigel worked part-time at a local mortuary, and on the weekends he sold hot dogs at the mill. Likewise, in school he was known as an achiever. He was a cheerleader, president of the student body, and won the state declamation contest.[31]

In 1926 Nigel League entered the University of South Carolina. He worked at a series of jobs and joined the National Guard to earn the one dollar it paid for drill sessions. At the university League was a member of debating team, an officer in the Clariosophic Literary Society, and president of the junior class. In 1928 he announced his plan to run for governor of South Carolina in 1948. The story was picked up by the Associated Press and printed on the front page of the New York *Times*.[32]

After he graduated, League attended law school, returned to Greenville, and opened an office. In 1932 Hubert Nolin, a close friend and fellow Parker student who became county solicitor, persuaded League to run for the state legislature. Since League had no car, he had to walk to the stump meetings.[33]

League campaigned as a young mill hand who had made good. His platform included lower taxes, an eight-hour-maximum-hours law for mill workers, the consolidation of some state agencies, and the betterment of "my people." The enthusiasm and charisma of the candidate attracted wide attention, and he was expected to lead the ticket. On the night of August 22 League spoke at Simpsonville with unusual vigor, but minutes later he collapsed and died on the platform.[34]

Nigel League's effort to transcend the world of the textile mill, like that of Joe Jackson, was unsuccessful. The newspaper called him a victim of his own enthusiasm. Yet his failure touched countless mill families. Five hundred people crowded into Bethel Methodist Church near the family farm at Simpsonville for the funeral. Some twenty-five hundred more listened by loudspeaker outside. Dean Crain, the pastor of the Pendleton Street Baptist Church, intoned: "Every single move of this young man's life should be written and read throughout the country. . . . He reminds us of Joseph, who went from difficulty to difficulty, from pit to pit, yet who, at 30, was in control of Egypt." In Greenville in 1932 the promise of Joseph went unfulfilled.[35]

Modernization and the Stretch Out

In the textile mills during the 1920s and early 1930s, dramatic changes occurred in both machinery and management. To a new generation of Progressive mill owners, reduction of production costs seemed the only answer in the search for profits. One solution was to install machinery that operated faster with fewer hands. New spoolers and warpers could run at high speeds and eliminate much of the manual labor. The J. E. Sirrine Company began to make time and motion studies of local operations based on the theories of Frederick W. Taylor. Sirrine recommended the use of fewer employees and greater tasks. These improvements were centered in the weave room, where the most independent and best paid operatives worked.[36]

Mill workers had a simple word for the change—the stretch-out. At first, the operatives responded to the changes with stoicism and individual frustration. In November 1928 the superintendent at Poe Mill ordered D. W. League to increase the workload of the weavers from twenty to forty looms. League quit his job and moved to the Chesnee Mill in Spartanburg County as an overseer. There the superintendent asked him to work on Sunday. Again, he quit and moved to Judson Mill as a weaver. Later he became an overseer in Anderson, but he had to work almost twenty-four hours a day when the mill ran two shifts. In March 1931 D. W. League returned to the family farm and died at the age of fifty-one.[37]

The Strikes of the 1920s

In 1929 this private anguish gave way to a wave of strikes unprecedented in the South. The strikes began in Tennessee in March 1929 and spread to Gastonia and Marion—both in North Carolina. Especially threatening was the activity of the Communist-led National Textile Workers Union (NTWU) in Gastonia.[38]

Trouble moved closer to Greenville on March 15, 1929, when twelve hundred workers walked out at Ware Shoals. On March 25, in Pelzer, 1,250 employees went out on strike. The committee of workers demanded a "restoration of conditions prior to the installation some time ago of the 'classification' or 'stretch-out' system." When the president of Lockwood, Greene, quickly concurred, a mass meeting of workers gathered to ratify the agreement, and the four mills resumed operation.[39]

Much more serious was the walkout at Brandon Mill on March 27. Twelve hundred workers struck, leaving only fifty-five operatives in the cloth room. The secretary of the mill, C. E. Hatch, reported that the workers had demanded an end to the stretch-out. When no agreement was reached, the strike began. On March 29 five hundred workers at the Poinsett and Brandon Duck Mills joined the strike; on April 1 about one thousand workers at the Brandon plant at Woodruff walked out.[40]

South Carolina was the only state to respond to the strikes by appointing a legislative committee to investigate working conditions. The members reported "that we find conditions deplorable in many mill villages both as to pay and to living conditions. . . . [There are] families actually in need though members of those families are working regularly."[41]

Greenville's reaction to the strikes was mixed. The American Red Cross and the Salvation Army, the only relief organizations in the county, announced that they were not furnishing aid to any strikers, though they were prepared "to take measures . . . in case suffering is noted." Malcolm S. Taylor, the rector of Christ Church, preached a sermon on "The Relation of the Church to Industrial Disputes," and John N. Wrenn, former pastor of Brandon Baptist Church and later pastor of the West Greenville Baptist Tabernacle, was active in urging a settlement. Roland Hudgens, chair of the workers relief committee, noted that mill workers and a number of businesses had contributed to a relief fund. J. B. Childs, who headed the relief committee at the Poinsett Mill, indicated that employees in several mills were dismissed for contributing to the relief fund, while in other cases the mill management extended every courtesy to those asking for contributions.[42]

Governor James P. Richards dispatched his secretary, J. Austin Latimer, to assist in the negotiations, and he was joined by a representative of the U.S. secretary of labor. On May 15 the Greenville *News* reported that an organizer of the anti-Communist United Textile Workers of America (UTWA) was in Greenville and that fifteen hundred persons had filled out applications for membership. One day later the workers committee—composed of Vernon B. Allen, Charlie Dill, and Dave Owens—announced a compromise settlement.[43]

Unrest reached a new level at Mills Mill on May 31 when a member of the grievance committee was allegedly dismissed for membership in a union. About five hundred workers walked out and demanded an end to the stretchout, a 20 percent raise in pay, and the promise of nondiscrimination for union members. When mill President H. Arthur Ligon of Spartanburg refused the demands and closed the mill, the workers declared a lockout and voted unanimously to join the UTWA. George L. Googe, the regional representative of the American Federation of Labor (AFL), expressed the dismay of the workers at the changing conditions in the industry. Twenty years ago, he said, local owners lived in the same community as the mill. Now New York and eastern capitalists were in control and were encouraged by the Chamber of Commerce because labor was cheap, docile, illiterate, and unorganized, and there were few state laws regulating working conditions.[44]

The strike at Mills Mill did not end until July 18. In the meantime, the threat of the Communist-led NTWU loomed over South Carolina. The old champion of the mill workers, U.S. Senator Cole Blease, appeared at Anderson. "You ought to organize," he told them, "you should have organized long ago." But Coley warned them in the nativist, racist terms that appealed them:

> I am heartily in favor of any legal organization of the cotton mill people of my state, as long as it does not preach lawlessness, communism or IWWism and is not the product of a lot of Yankee trash running around down here stirring up devilment. I would be a traitor to the mill operatives of my state not to call their attention to the dangers of communism that places all laborers, white or black, on the same equality. You should organize yourself among yourselves.[45]

By the middle of August, the NTWU organizers were holding public meetings in Greenville. Sam Phifer, the state representative, announced a meeting would be held on August 30 at 560 Honour Street in West Greenville. He promised that several defendants in the strike at Gastonia would speak.[46]

Meanwhile, the NTWA began a statewide membership campaign, and on September 2, 1929, it sponsored the first Labor Day meeting in Greenville at the City Park. Mayor A. C. Mann addressed the crowd of about one thousand. "We must work together," the mayor said, "toward honest dealing between capital and labor. You mill people are only trying to better your condition for your own sake, for the sake for your families, and for the sake of your communities." He sounded the themes of nativism and racial solidarity: "In this section the percentage of native born Anglo-Saxon citizens [is] higher than in any other portion of the country."[47]

At rival meetings, the NTWU could not avoid talk of violence and revolution. When George Saul spoke at Poe Mill, he said: "We do not plan to use guns in our fight, not at this stage of the game." Asked to clarify his statement, Saul only made matters worse: "We do not contemplate using the force of arms now, or even in case of a strike; but should a general revolution break out and drastic methods become necessary, we will not fail to employ them."[48]

Consequently, when AFL President William Green came to Greenville, he was cordially received by the business elite. He stayed at the Poinsett Hotel and spoke at the courthouse. Brown Mahon, vice president of Judson Mills, gave him a tour of the plant prior to the meeting, and business and civic leaders, as well as mill executives, heard Green speak on "American Economic Issues and the Philosophy of the American Federation of Labor." In July the state Federation of Labor held its annual convention in Greenville.[49]

Three months later the Cotton Textile Institute pledged to eliminate night work for women and minors under the age of eighteen. Thomas M. Marchant, the president of Victor-Monaghan Mills, was the southern vice president of the Institute. Also present at the meeting were Robert E. Henry of Dunean, John T. Woodside of Woodside, and H. A. Ligon of Mills Mill. By November market conditions had improved so that the larger mills in Greenville were operating on a fifty-five-hour schedule, and night work was eliminated entirely. The union movement began to wane.[50]

Nevertheless, the NTWU threat ended in violence. A group of hooded men searched the tourist home where Clara Holden, the local organizer, was staying. Several weeks later, she was abducted by five men, taken across the Pickens County line near the Saluda Dam, robbed, and beaten. In a letter to the Greenville *News*, Alfred E. Whitman thanked "God the Communist bunch has not got a hold here. . . . Thanks to the police department and the Ku Klux Klan they have not made any headway. . . . Every red-blooded American citizen should fight against these Communist people. . . . When the AFL starts a strike, the Communist bunch come in to do the dirty work."[51]

The Growing City

The growth of the city of Greenville continued in the 1920s, but it did not match the boom years of the early twentieth century. The metropolitan area boasted a population of 63,668 in 1930, an increase of 20 percent over 1920; the city itself grew by 26 percent. Although the economy was still based primarily on farm and factory, the textile industry began to attract related businesses. In 1923 Steel Heddle of Philadelphia began building a plant on East McBee Avenue to manufacture the heddles that held strands of yarn for the weaving process. In 1930 the company began to manufacture loom shuttles in Greenville.[52]

One local business that developed an international reputation was Cooper and Griffin, Inc.—a cotton merchandizing operation. The president of the firm, Walter S. Griffin, was born in Greenville in 1875; entered the cotton business in Rome, Georgia, in 1891; and later moved to Atlanta. In 1904 he returned to Greenville and established Cooper and Griffin, of which he became sole owner in 1910. With branch offices in every major Southern city, the company became one of the six largest cotton merchandising firms in the world. In one year it handled six hundred thousand bales of cotton. Walter Griffin originated the term "call cotton," which was soon universally used by cotton brokers. In 1920 he cornered the July cotton market and sent the price to 43.75 cents per pound on the futures market—the highest price since the Civil War. Griffin repeated his achievement in 1924 and 1926 and brought millions of dollars into the South. Millions of bales of cotton a day were handled by cotton firms in Greenville, and the city became the second largest cotton market in the United States.[53]

There was a continued effort, however, to diversify the economic base. Highly successful was the meat packing business of William Hampton Balentine. Balentine moved to Greenville in 1888 and opened a meat market with his brother-in-law, Thomas L. Gilreath, in the West End. Later Balentine purchased Shreever's Market on Main Street and in 1905 moved to West Coffee Street. When America entered World War I, Balentine envisioned a meat packing plant that could serve the army training camps in South Carolina. In 1917 he closed his retail business and organized the Balentine Packing Company. Located on East Court Street, the plant could handle 125 hogs an hour and was the only complete meat packing plant in the state—producing lard, bacon, hams, and sausage. Before Balentine died in 1927, his Palmetto Brand products were well known all over South Carolina.[54]

Chamber of Commerce Tours

Perhaps as a result of slower economic growth after World War I, the New South spirit of deliverance through industry intensified. Under the leadership of William R. Timmons, secretary from 1920 to 1928, the Chamber of Commerce grew from 1,000 members in 1920 to 2,009 in 1923. In 1921 he launched a monthly magazine, *Greenville: A Civic and Commercial Journal,* which touted the virtues of the commercial climate and the programs of the chamber. Hundreds of local business people joined the national movement of Chamber acquaintance tours. By train they visited other cities from Florida to Canada to spread the economic gospel of Greenville. Local newspapers were filled with glowing reports of these economic missionaries. In April 1924, for example, J. Rutledge McGhee, a former reporter for the *News* who had moved to Florida, wrote: "The people of Greenville may well feel proud of the excellent impression left by their representatives who visited St. Petersburg, Florida a few weeks ago."[55]

There were also local and state tours. The Fountain Inn Chamber sponsored a tour of lower Greenville County. Smyth's Concert Band led a caravan of forty cars to Mauldin, Gray Court, and smaller communities. Even in the depths of the Great Depression, the chamber sponsored a three-day train tour to Charleston, Florence, Rock Hill, and points between.[56]

Greenville achieved national prominence at the Southern Exposition at the Grand Central Palace in New York City, May 11–23, 1925, with its exhibit of local wares. The exposition was the work of William G. Sirrine, president of Textile Hall. Only one other city from the region displayed textile products. Besides the exhibit mounted by the chamber, Judson and Victor-Monaghan Mills had displays as well. Concurrently, a story on Mrs. Harry C. Duke and the Duke Products Company appeared nationally in over two hundred newspapers. The exposition was, according to the *Manufacturers' Record,* "an unequalled opportunity for drawing capital to the South."[57]

Downtown Building Boom

About the same time, a building boom began that changed the skyline of the city. In March 1924 the *News* pronounced that "1924 promises to become the greatest building year in Greenville's history. Already business and residential construction worth about $810,000 is underway." That figure did not include the Poinsett Hotel and the Chamber of Commerce Building, whose projected costs were $1.25 million.[58]

The Poinsett Hotel, which was planned to replace the century-old Mansion House, was the brainchild of John T. Woodside and William Goldsmith who formed the Community Hotel Corporation to build a "million dollar hotel."[59] The Mansion House was razed, and the ground breaking for the new twelve-story hotel took place on May 30, 1924. W. L. Stoddard of New York was the architect, and Hunkin and Conkey of Cleveland, Ohio, was the contractor for the hotel. The Poinsett eventually cost $1.5 million and opened one hundred rooms in June 1925. An arcade led into the building from Main Street, and a half-flight of marble stairs rose to the lobby, which was paneled in walnut. The ballroom, according to the *News*, was "a thing of wondrous beauty." The first manager of the Poinsett was Charles G. Day, the former manager of the DeSoto Hotel in Savannah, and the chef, Felix Altman, presided over the kitchen with a staff of eight or nine cooks and a complete bakery.[60]

Built with much more difficulty was the Chamber of Commerce Building on the site of the 1822 courthouse on Main Street. This building resulted from the vision of John A. Russell, the president of the chamber in 1922. First, there were a few determined preservationists, like Mrs. P. A. McDavid, who wished to keep the historic building. Then, there were legal problems with the title which had to be cleared by an act of the legislature and a decree of the state supreme court. The building committee, chaired by Russell, employed Beacham and LeGrand as architects and the J. E. Sirrine Company as engineers. The new building was a ten-story structure of brick and steel construction with over one hundred offices, two fast Otis elevators, and in every office there were wash basins and outlets for an electric fan. The projected cost was $250,000 to be paid for by the sale of life insurance. The chamber set up a thirty-year policy on the life of each of its members, and the premiums would be paid by the office rentals.[61]

The contract for the building was awarded on August 20, 1924, to the Minter Homes Company—a builder of prefabricated mill houses that had moved to Greenville in 1921. The cornerstone was laid on January 12, 1925. Before the building was completed, however, Minter Homes went into receivership. The Maryland Casualty Company of Baltimore, the construction guarantor, offered security, and the chamber negotiated a new contract with the Potter and Shackleford Construction Company.[62]

The building opened on November 2, 1925, and all but five of the offices were rented. The chamber occupied the second floor, and Haynsworth and Haynsworth took up almost all of the tenth floor, which was especially tailored for the firm's use. The *News* called the building a "thing of beauty, slender, graceful and tall, a monument to engineering genius." Several thousand people attended the opening ceremonies, and the new tenants held an open house in their offices.[63]

To dominate Main Street as a symbol of his own financial empire, John T. Woodside planned the seventeen-story Woodside Building at a cost of $1.5 million. When it was completed in 1923, the tower, with its white marble exterior, was the tallest building in the two Carolinas. The lobby boasted marble, French plate mirrors, Ionic columns, and a large skylight. Atop the building was a roof garden with an extraordinary view.[64]

The hoopla on opening day in June 1923 included a speech by Woodside ("a day of community celebration over the completion of a great structure") and a concert featuring Handel's *Largo*. In August the roof garden opened with a private party for twenty couples of the business elite who danced atop the skyscraper beneath Japanese lanterns and soft moonlight. Servers attired in Japanese garb served ice cream, punch, and cake; music was provided by the Atlanta Footwarmers.[65]

Other new businesses, such as modern department stores, were beginning to reshape Main Street. Prior to World War I, Manas and Alex Meyers from Newport News, Virginia, bought the dry goods business of J. Thomas Arnold and reopened it under the name of the Meyers-Arnold Company. They were joined by two other brothers, L. A. and Nolin Meyers, and soon were specializing in ladies' and childrens' clothing. In 1916 Belk-Kirkpatrick, a Charlotte-based company, opened a small store on South Main Street with a local partner. In 1923 Dr. William D. Simpson of Abbeville, the half-brother of William Henry Belk of Charlotte, bought out the local interest in the Greenville store, and on March 1, 1924, the Belk-Simpson Company opened. Meanwhile, Colonel William Henry Keith had moved to Greenville from Timmonsville in 1920 and purchased most of the west side of the 200 block of North Main Street, which was dominated by the large castle-like residence of Hyman Endel. Keith began to develop the area, and in 1925 he purchased the firm of C. D. Stradley Company, a leading merchant. On July 2 Keith opened a department store—Keith's, Incorporated.[66]

Movies had become so popular that Greenville soon boasted several cinemas. The Bijou, which opened in 1908, had facilities for both stage and screen performances, but it was too small for new films such as "The Ten Commandments," directed by Cecil B. DeMille. This film was shown twice at Textile Hall in December 1924. The Greenville Hotel Corporation, which owned the Ottaray Hotel, opened the Carolina Theater with capabilities for stage and screen in June 1925. W. H. Keith announced plans to build "the finest exclusive silver screen palace in the Carolinas." Designed by Beacham and LeGrand, the theater contained 750 seats and opened on September 7, 1925, as the Rivoli Theater.[67]

A series of tragedies struck the Ottaray Hotel in the mid-1920s. On December 14, 1924, fire destroyed the roof and portions of the fourth and fifth floors. The eighty-five guests escaped without injury, but the entire building was damaged by water and had to be closed. It reopened on May 1, 1925, and did a flourishing business. A year later the hotel company announced plans to add twenty rooms, but on July 9 the Ottaray operator, J. L. Alexander, a native of Walhalla, was burned to death in an automobile accident near Columbia. Months later Bobby Goodyear was killed when he lost his footing and was crushed by the hotel elevator. The symbol of the Ottaray Hotel remained, however. Jack, a sixty-five-pound bulldog owned by the hotel bookkeeper P. M. Hilly, was known as the official mascot of the hotel and stayed at his post until his death in 1931.[68]

The 200 block of North Main Street became the center of a thriving business district during the 1920s. By 1931 only one residence, that of Jesse Smith, was left. Craig-Rush, Montgomery Ward, Sears Roebuck, and the Rivoli Theater had opened in five years. But already business was moving farther north. In July 1926 the Mackey Mortuary, which had been in the funeral business since 1882, announced the construction of a modern facility designed by J. E. Sirrine in the 300 block, adjacent to Springwood Cemetery. At the same time, business was extending east along Washington Street as far as Church Street and west to Butler Avenue.[69]

In the 1920s Christmas in Greenville, as in urban America generally, became an annual celebration of civic pride and retail marketing. On the evening of December 6, 1926, the city held its first Christmas parade sponsored by the Retail Merchants Bureau of the chamber. Main Street between the Poinsett and the Ottaray Hotels became "a veritable fairy land." At a cost of between four thousand dollars and five thousand dollars, thirty-four Christmas trees were placed on each side of the street and ropes of red and green electric lights extended from the street lights. Santa Claus arrived by a special train, illuminated by red torches, at the Piedmont and

Northern depot at 6:00 P.M. where he was met by Mayor R. F. Watson and escorted to Main and Broad Streets. There Santa led a parade of police escorts; the 327th Infantry Band; state, city, and chamber officials; the Furman University Band; and children from the local Greenacre and Bruner Homes. Thousands of lights came on as the parade was cheered by hundreds of spectators. At the Ottaray Hotel, Santa left the parade and greeted the crowd from the balcony.[70]

The role of Greenville as an insurance center was enhanced in 1925 with the formation of a new company, the Pioneer Life Insurance Company. T. Oregon Lawton, president of Southeastern Life for fifteen years, had retired the year before, but on February 11, 1925, he became president of the new company, along with Holmes B. Springs as vice president and secretary and M. R. Wilkes as vice president and treasurer. John T. Woodside was chair of the board. In less than four years, Pioneer became one of the leaders of the industry in South Carolina and increased its capital stock from $100,000 to $1 million. The company had in force over $17 million in insurance.[71]

Banking also expanded in the mid-1920s. In September 1925 the Norwood National Bank was sold to the Bank of Charleston. The combined resources of the new bank—soon to become South Carolina National—was over $19 million, and the board had twenty-five directors from Greenville and six from Charleston. The next year the Peoples State Bank, in business since 1887, secured a national charter under the leadership of its president, William C. Beacham.[72]

In the expansive spirit of the early 1920s, the historical consciousness of Greenville dimmed. Not only was the 1822 courthouse razed, but the Confederate Monument itself—the local shrine of the Lost Cause—gave way to progress. Since 1891 the monument had stood in the middle of Main Street flanked by two cannons and surrounded by an iron fence. In June 1922 the city council voted to move the monument to the front of the courthouse. In October the removal began. Then, in the middle of the night, the Confederate soldier was removed from the top of the monument. After a search, the statue was discovered in storage on a farm on Paris Mountain Road. The local camp of the United Confederate Veterans sought an injunction against the city council. The city appealed the case to the state supreme court, and the court ruled in favor of the city. On June 19, 1924, the city council announced that the monument would be moved to Springwood Cemetery.[73]

With their growing wealth, the business elite enriched their lifestyle. In 1923 J. E. Sirrine led a movement to relocate the country club from

Sans Souci, northwest of the city, to the Augusta Street area. The new club house and an eighteen-hole golf course were opened on July 4. Bennette E. Geer purchased the old Sans Souci Club for forty-five thousand dollars and remodeled the former home of Governor Benjamin F. Perry for his own use. In the summer of 1924 a group of Greenvillians were enjoying a moonlight picnic at the foot of the road to Caesar's Head when their conversation turned to the formation of a new colony of summer homes, and before the year was out twenty-four investors agreed to purchase 740 acres of land on that spot for the Mountain Lake Colony, which is now off of Highway 276.[74]

Expansion of the City

In its effort to expand, the city was hemmed in by the mill villages on the west side, so new suburbs developed in other areas. The former dairy farm of Otis P. Mills on Augusta Street had been subdivided earlier into Millsdale. Additional houses were built in Millsdale and farther south along Augusta Street. New homes were also constructed in Sans Souci. J. F. Gallivan formed the North Main Street Development Company, which laid out a fifty-acre tract into lots. By October 1926 North Main Street Extension was being paved as far as the intersection with Rutherford Road. A few months later the John W. Norwood estate facing McDaniel Avenue became the Alta Vista subdivision. In the fall of 1928 31 acres of the W. B. McDaniel estate became McDaniel Heights, and within two years McDaniel Avenue was paved from the railroad overpass on Broad Street to Cleveland Street to make the new area easily accessible to downtown.[75]

In 1927 the growth of these areas led the city council to create a City Extension Committee that recommended the incorporation of areas within a radius of $2\frac{1}{2}$ miles of the courthouse. Although the referendum was defeated by the suburban voters, city council did not give up the effort. Two years later, the council and the Chamber of Commerce announced the formation of a Greater Greenville Extension Committee, which included not only the suburban areas, but the mill villages as well. But the stock market crash in October postponed plans for expansion indefinitely.[76]

In 1913 the city council had established the Park and Tree Commission, which in the 1920s led to creation of both playgrounds and parks. The commission was headed by John A. McPherson, who became known as the father of Greenville playgrounds. At first, there was a small annual appropriation for shrubbery and playground equipment, and the only park owned by the city was the City Park on North Main Street. Organized playground work began in 1920 when the Kiwanis Club pledged six thousand dollars for one year to pay the salaries of two workers. A bond issue that included funds for improvements and additions was approved in 1922. Playgrounds on Donaldson Street and Anderson Street were opened, and in 1925 a park on Hudson Street was created for black citizens. Athletic activities, clubs, and scout groups were organized for youths.[77]

On December 31, 1924, William Choice Cleveland gave Greenville 110 acres of land in a great crescent on the southeast side of the city for a park and playground—developed into Cleveland Park. In November 1930 the Greenville Garden Club undertook the beautification of the old rock quarry on the edge of the new park.[78]

Peg Leg Bates and Josh White

Blacks in Greenville were still enmeshed in the age of segregation. "The Birth of a Nation," which had played in Greenville in the old Opera House, now returned to the Bijou as a gripping film with its message of white supremacy. In Greenville, as in other parts of the South, blacks joined the Great Migration to northern cities. The black population in the county dropped from 30.1 percent of the total in 1910 to 26.5 percent in 1920, and to 23.8 percent in 1930. Two Greenville emigrants who gained national reputations were Peg Leg Bates and Josh White.[79]

Born in 1906 in Fountain Inn, Clayton Bates learned to dance on the street corners at the age of five. His mother, Emma Stewart Bates, was deserted by her husband when Clayton was three. Clayton went to work in the local cotton seed oil mill, and in 1918, when he was twelve, his leg was mangled when he slipped into the augur. The leg was amputated (the operation performed on his mother's kitchen table). Once he recovered, young Bates began to dance with broomsticks—using them as crutches until his uncle, Whitt Stewart made him a peg leg. Two years later Bates dropped out of school and began work as a shoeshiner in an alley off Spring Street in Greenville near the black Liberty Theater. The manager of the theater discovered Bates making rhythms with his shoeshine rag, his peg leg, and his good foot. With this man's help, Bates began to win prizes in local amateur shows, and in 1924 he joined Eddie Lemon's Dashing Diner Review. In 1929 Lon Leslie saw Bates at the Lafayette Theater in New York and put him into the "Black Birds of 1929" with Bojangles Robinson. Peg Leg Bates (as he was called) soon was dancing in the top night clubs, including the Cotton Club in Harlem. In 1951 he bought land in the Catskill Mountains and opened the first resort there for blacks.[80]

Younger than Bates, Josh White was born in Greenville in 1914, the son of the Reverend Dennis and Daisy Elizabeth White who lived in Sullivan's Alley. Josh White dropped out of school after the sixth grade. Meanwhile, he met Blind Man Arnold, a traveling beggar and street singer, and soon became his lead man. The two men went to Chicago in 1924, and White left Arnold for Joel Taggart, another blind man from Greenville. Taggart and White began recording for Paramount Records in Chicago. White was then discovered by scouts of the American Recording Company. He subsequently went to New York in 1931 where he began recording spirituals, later moving on to blues. In 1933 he recorded "Howling Wolf Blues," "Black and Evil Blues," "Baby, Won't You Doodle-Doo-Doo," "Depression Blues," and "Greenville Sheik." He began to appear in night clubs, and at the time of his last engagement in 1947, he was making $750 a week as the voice of the "black folk song."[81]

The Black Middle Class

In Greenville there continued to be a small, but influential, black middle class. The white business elite always consulted E. W. Biggs, the black funeral director, as the representative of this group. Biggs had an impressive home on the corner of Brown and Elford Streets, was a member of Springfield Baptist Church, and was active in the Republican Party. When Biggs died in 1932, Mayor A. C. Mann, former Mayor H. C. Harvley, and U.S. District Attorney J. A. Tolbert spoke at his funeral. Biggs's estate was valued at $19,802.92. Perhaps more typical of the black middle class were Mr. and Mrs. Elias B. Holloway. He was a mail carrier for thirty-five years, and she was a graduate of Clark College in Atlanta. They were active members of John Wesley Methodist Episcopal Church, and Holloway was a delegate to the General Conference of the denomination, which met in Baltimore in 1908. In 1925 the Holloways' nine children were either graduates or students in college. Cornelius and Bronetta, the oldest children, were graduates of Clark. Cornelius was pastor of a Baptist church in Wytheville, Virginia, and Bronetta was assistant superintendent of the Phillis Wheatley Center in Greenville. Frieda was a graduate of Bennett College in Greensboro and a nurse for the city health department. Lillie, a graduate of Cheyne Training School in Pennsylvania, was a teacher. Elias Jr. was a senior at Tuskegee Institute, and Mabel was a senior at Howard University. The three youngest children were also college students—Roselle at Clark, and Lenelle and Georgia at Morgan State in Baltimore.[82]

The black middle class led in the vision to improve the life of their community in Greenville. One of these leaders was Hattie Logan Duckett.

Born in 1885, the oldest of the eight children of a Methodist minister, Duckett grew up in Greenville and attended the local schools. She received a bachelor of arts degree from Claflin College and returned to Greenville to teach first grade at Union School, on the corner of Markley and Calhoun Streets. She married Gilbert Duckett and moved to Florida, but after his death Duckett returned to Greenville. She dreamed of a social service agency for blacks and attended schools for social work in New York and Chicago.[83]

Her sister, Mae, later remembered: "I used to call our house the house of refuge." One night a woman with a small baby came to the door. Her husband, who was drunk, followed her. Hattie Duckett "answered the door. . . . She made him sit down on the sofa and when she finished talking to him, they left arm in arm. Sister had a way with everybody." When black travelers were stranded, she always took them in. Finally, in 1919 Duckett formed the Phillis Wheatley Association to develop a social center for young women. Black citizens contributed about thirty-five hundred dollars, and the association purchased a small house at the corner of E. McBee Avenue and Hellman Street for five thousand dollars. Soon there were programs for everyone. Duckett taught school in the mornings and directed the center in the afternoons and evenings.[84]

But the resources of the black community could not support the program, and Duckett approached Thomas F. Parker for help. For several years there had been an Interracial Committee in Greenville, but it had accomplished little. In 1922 the Chamber of Commerce appointed a second committee which proposed the reorganization of the Phillis Wheatley Association. In October 1923 a biracial board was created—composed of Parker, president; the Reverend Frank A. Juhan, vice president; Floyd Hughes, treasurer; Mrs. Frances Montgomery; Mrs. C. W. Crosby; J. P. Chappelle; E. B. Holloway, secretary; Mary L. Fisher; and Mrs. Eva Fitchett.[85]

Initially, twenty-seven thousand dollars was raised for the purchase of a lot on East Broad Street and the construction of a three-story building. By December 7, 1924, when the building was dedicated, twenty thousand dollars had been raised by blacks and forty-five thousand dollars by whites. The success of the center was phenomenal. By 1939 the annual attendance at all activities was 20,568.[86]

The social vision of Hattie Duckett and Thomas Parker was clear—uplift the black community while mounting no challenge to the segregated society. "What will it mean to Greenville County to have 20,000 industrious and capable citizens?" Parker asked. "If they know a trade, understand how to improve their living conditions, how to prevent the spread of disease and are, in addition, healthy and contented, they will be one of Greenville County's most valuable assets." And Parker was not afraid to work with the black community in the face of criticism from whites. There is a tendency, he said, "because of pressure from other matters and from fear of demagogues to let the less thoughtful views in this community concerning the negro question go unchallenged." Leaders must "work to bring about much needed improvements in the general living conditions and environment of negroes; to save them as far as possible from those who prey on them, or carelessly mistreat them."[87]

Thomas Parker's death on December 31, 1926, ended an era of Progressive concern led by a single individual. His spirit was summed up by contemporaries at his death. Parker was "deeply religious," one said, but "he did not talk glibly or familiarly about sacred matters." When he was once asked why he did not own an expensive automobile, "his reply was that as long as there was so much need in the world, he would never have an expensive car."[88]

There was an undercurrent in the black community of concern about civil rights. Elias B. Holloway was unhappy with the position blacks occupied. "The amendments to the constitution," he said, "conferred on them the rights of citizenship." Blacks pay taxes and support the government, but they must be given an opportunity to show responsibility. "To know what the city council has to do and how it is done he should be one of them. He should be represented on the boards of school trustees. When he becomes conversant by contact with the privileges and duties of citizenship he then will become a power against the forces of evil in any community." Holloway recalled the black volunteer fire companies of the late nineteenth century. "They were proud of the opportunity to show their love for Greenville by defending the homes of the citizens. . . . Now they pay taxes but they have no say in its distribution." Such views were seldom expressed in Greenville.[89]

Meanwhile blacks gained new visibility when major black figures appeared in the city. On November 19, 1923, Dr. George Washington Carver spoke to the Furman student body. In 1932 Roland Hayes, the operatic star, sang in Textile Hall, and separate entrances and seats were set aside for blacks and whites.[90]

Highway Construction

The demand for highway construction in Greenville County continued unabated in the 1920s. The "million-dollar" bond issue had made

Greenville County a leader in road building in South Carolina after 1915. The General Assembly created the state highway department in 1917 and a system of state highways the next year. But World War I intervened and not until 1920 did road construction began in earnest on the state level. That year Greenville and Pickens were connected by a topsoil road—the first connecting two county seats in the state. A survey of highways in 1924 found that, of the twelve most heavily traveled roads in South Carolina, five were in Greenville County. First was the Greenville-Spartanburg highway with 1,522 cars in twelve hours; second, the route from Greenville to Hendersonville with 1,346 cars; fifth was the Greenville-Anderson highway with 947 cars; and tied for ninth place were the Greenville-Fountain Inn and the Greenville-Princeton highways with 784 cars each. By 1926 Greenville had more automobiles per capita than any other county in South Carolina—one for every 1.3 persons. Spartanburg was second with 7.1.[91]

By 1924 there was a demand for paved highways across the state, and the General Assembly adopted a "pay-as-you-go" program to construct 4,000 miles of roads. Among the first highways designated for paving was the Mountains to the Sea Highway through Greenville County. Through a loophole in the 1924 law, the county delegation the following year proposed legislation permitting it to issue bonds for immediate paving of all state highways in the county. The annual estimated receipts under the "pay-as-you-go" law were pledged as security for the bonds. Greenville launched its second program of road building that began with the paving of the road between Mauldin and Laurens in June 1925. By March 1926 the Buncombe Road from Greenville to the North Carolina line was completely paved, and in July 1927 the new hard-surfaced highway to Spartanburg opened.[92]

Meanwhile, in 1927, the county delegation approved another bond issue for the paving of cross-country roads not included in the state system, and by 1930 Greenville County had some 225 miles of paved roads. In November 1931 the paved highway from Greenville to Atlanta was completed, and a motorcade of 338 persons from Atlanta arrived in Greenville on November 3 for a celebration. The Geer Highway to Brevard by way of Caesar's Head, planned since 1923 to replace the old Jones Gap Road, was finally completed in December 1931.[93]

Municipal Airport

The use of aircraft in World War I had focused public attention on flight. In March 1926 Knox Haynsworth, W. H. Allen, and Sam J. Taylor formed the Alhayor Company—the first commercial aviation firm in the state. From its field on Cedar Lane Road, the company made aerial photographs for the use of real estate developers. At the same time Federal Airways became interested in making Greenville an airmail stop between Atlanta and Greensboro, but the city council failed to appropriate funds for an airport, and Spartanburg became the official stopover.[94]

George Barr, who had served in the Army Air Corps and had a reserve commission as a pilot, and Errett Williams, a local "barnstormer," began to lobby for a local airport. Gradually they won the support of city council and the county delegation, and in 1928 the legislature created the Greenville Airport Commission. Land was purchased near the Laurens Road, and on September 9 the formal dedication took place. More than forty planes landed in perfect weather, and F. Trubie Davison, the assistant secretary of war, addressed the crowd of five thousand people.[95]

When Eastern Air Transport began passenger operations on December 10, 1930, Eugene Stone was the first general traffic representative. The Curtiss Condor plane landed on its inaugural flight from Atlanta to Newark. Earlier in the day Mildred Edwards and Beverly T. (Bevo) Whitmire of the Greenville *Piedmont* staff had been married at Christ Church. They boarded the plane and became "Greenville's first aerial honeymoon couple." The ticket to New York from Greenville was $66.85—25 percent higher than the train.[96]

Health Care

Another earmark of the 1920s was expansion of health care facilities. Soon after World War I a group of local textile executives opened a clinic for mill workers on Vardry Heights west of the City Hospital. In 1924 the Salvation Army assumed control of the clinic and renamed it the Emma Moss Booth Hospital. The mission of the hospital was enlarged to care for girls and young women. But Booth Hospital began to operate at a deficit, and the advisory board, chaired by Mrs. A. Foster McKissick, and the Salvation Army authorities agreed to close the hospital in 1931.[97]

Fortunately the Catholic Diocese of Charleston was planning to open an upstate hospital, and the Little Sisters of the Poor of St. Francis purchased the Booth Hospital and completely remodeled the building. When it opened, the St. Francis Infirmary contained sixty beds and eight bassinets. The formal dedication services were held at St. Mary's School on July 12, 1932. Monsignor A. K. Gwynne, pastor of St. Mary's Church, and Bishop E. M. Walsh of Charleston presided. Dr. W. S. Rankin, director of the hospital section of the Duke Endowment, spoke on "The Ministry of Healing."[98]

On May 2, 1925, the Greenville *News* announced that W. W. Burgess, a native of Greer and a promoter of the Victor and Franklin Mills, had created W. W. Burgiss Charities with an endowment of between $1.2 and $1.25 millions from his real estate investments in South Carolina and Florida. Burgess's chief interests were a home for delinquent children, scholarships at Furman University and the Greenville Woman's College, and a hospital for crippled children.[99]

Burgess was neither a Mason nor a Shriner, but he had become interested in the crippled children's work carried on by the Shriners. In November 1925 Burgiss Charities purchased land on Camp Road about 1 mile from the site of Camp Sevier, and plans were drawn for a fifty-bed hospital. Dr. J. Warren White, a famed orthopedic surgeon and brother of the heart surgeon, Paul Dudley White, became surgeon-in-chief of the new Shriners Hospital. The superintendent of nurses was Byrd Boehringer, who later married John M. Holmes, the secretary of the Greenville YMCA and chair of the hospital board.[100]

The Shriners Hospital received its first patients in September 1927 and on September 26 the dedication was held. Greenville was decked with flags and bunting, and a parade of Shriners was followed by simultaneous luncheons at the Imperial and Poinsett hotels. At 2:30 that afternoon, four thousand people attended the dedication.[101]

Prior to World War I, South Carolina women were active in the movement to care for the victims of tuberculosis. In 1915 Mrs. Harry J. Haynsworth and Mrs. Mary P. Gridley formed the Hopewell Tuberculosis Association in Greenville. That year it opened one of the pioneer tuberculosis camps in the state in a tent at the county home. For six years the Hopewell Association also operated a clinic at the City Hospital. In 1927 the county adopted a bond issue for $150,000 to build a permanent hospital on Piney Mountain. The main building, with a separate structure for black patients, opened in 1930 with Dr. S. E. Lee as superintendent.[102]

A Public Library

At the end of World War I, the Neblett Library remained the only such facility in Greenville. That year John W. Norwood invited Federal Judge Charles A. Woods to address the issue before a group of leading citizens, but it was not until May 1921 that Thomas F. Parker organized the Greenville Public Library Association.[103] The association raised five thousand dollars, employed Annie Porter as librarian, and opened a small rented building on East Coffee Street that contained five hundred books. In 1922 a public referendum approved a two-mill tax, and a free public library was established. The following year the library undertook to offer library services in the new Parker District, and the first bookmobile was purchased. In 1925 this service was extended to the rural schools. Meanwhile a branch library was established for black patrons at the Phillis Wheatley Center.[104]

Newspapers and Radio

A new era in communications began in 1919 when Bony Hampton Peace acquired control of the Greenville *News*. Born in northern Greenville County near Tigerville, Peace became a printer first in Spartanburg, and several years later in Greenville. In 1916 he became business manager of the *News*, and in 1919 he purchased the controlling stock interest from Captain Ellison Smyth. Within a decade the *News* was the leading newspaper in the state in circulation and advertising. In 1927 Peace acquired the Greenville *Piedmont*, which soon had the largest circulation of any afternoon newspaper in South Carolina. The three Peace sons—Roger, Charlie, and B. H. Jr.—went to work with the newspapers, and they quickly enlivened the community with their shrewd business acumen and Progressive spirit.[105]

At the end of World War I, the *Piedmont* began to publish a daily column written by the editor of the Fountain Inn *Tribune*, Robert Quillen. His columns caught the attention of George Horace Lorimer, the editor of the *Literary Digest*, and within a few years Quillen's work was syndicated in some four hundred newspapers. Hailed as "the Mark Twain of his time," Quillen was a native of Kansas, but left home at sixteen and eventually made his way to Fountain Inn. When he was syndicated, people all over the nation began reading about "Little Willie," the advice of "Aunt Het," and "Letters from a Bald-Headed Daddy [Quillen] to His Red-Head Daughter [Louise]."[106]

Quillen's popularity grew even greater in 1925 when he erected a monument to Eve at his home in Fountain Inn. In the *Tribune*, with characteristic tongue in cheek, Quillen protested: "They prophesied plagues upon me; they accused me of an unbecoming levity toward things that are sacred. . . . But this is purely a family affair. . . . Eve was a distant relative of mine, on my mother's side." Reporters in Greenville put the story on the Associated Press wire, and newspapers across the United States reprinted it.[107]

Radio was invented before World War I, but the production of equipment on a large scale did not begin until the 1920s. The first radio message was received in Greenville in 1921 by Claude E. Well, and the earliest radio set was constructed by Well, James Rutledge, and John Sitton. Later G. W. Fischback built the first broadcasting station in South Carolina, which he called WQAV—we quit at five. In 1925 he donated the equipment to Furman, and the university secured a license to operate WGBT. Brief broadcasts occurred on Tuesday and Friday nights at 8:00 P.M. In June 1926 WHBL, a fifty-watt station, was operated jointly by the Greenville *News* and the Carolina Theater for a two-week period, enabling moviegoers to watch the live broadcasts. In May 1927 the Chatauqua set up a portable station for four days in the Poinsett Hotel.[108]

Greenville still had no permanent radio station. By 1928 Furman had surrendered its license, and there were only two stations in South Carolina—at Clemson College and in Charleston. On March 14 the *News* reported that several local business people, led by Louis D. Chisholm, the president of the Battery and Electric Company, were seeking a license. Meanwhile, a Greenville program was aired on February 12, 1930, on WBT, the Charlotte station. The program carried the song, "We Are From Greenville," rendered by the Chamber of Commerce quartet composed of J. Mac Rabb, William R. Timmons, Douglas Poteat, and Thomas W. Barfield. By August the Spartanburg station, WSPA, was broadcasting an hour each morning and afternoon from the Imperial Hotel.[109]

In October 1930 B. H. Peace applied to the Federal Radio Commission for a thousand-watt station to be called WGNP. Objections were registered by WSPA in Spartanburg, and stations in Toccoa, Georgia and Miami, Florida. In May 1931 the application was denied because the Greenville area had a station only 30 miles away. The city did not have its own radio station until 1933.[110]

The Popularity of Football

Intercollegiate football had its beginnings in South Carolina on December 14, 1889, in a game between Furman and Wofford in Spartanburg. But not until after World War I did the game achieve wide popularity. In 1919 the Furman team, coached by William L. Laval, began to dominate football statewide. In 1927, after victories over Duke, North Carolina State, Clemson, and South Carolina, Furman was invited to Coral Gables to play in what later became the Orange Bowl. Students, alumni, and townspeople became fanatical in their support of the "Purple Hurricane."[111]

Perhaps the ultimate in team devotion occurred the previous year when Furman faced the University of Georgia in Athens on October 16, 1926. Several weeks before the game, Norwood Cleveland of Marietta vowed to walk the 101 miles from Athens to Greenville if Furman won the game. When Furman prevailed, 14–7, Cleveland made good on his promise. Four days later, on Wednesday, October 20, Cleveland walked onto Manly Field. Almost the entire Furman student body and two hundred to three hundred townspeople cheered Norwood and proclaimed him a great sport.[112]

Prohibition

Despite the pranks of the "roaring Twenties," much of the nation soon abandoned the optimism of the pre-World War I era. Just as the buoyant economy was replaced with uncertainty, the Progressive vision was replaced by a defensiveness against new ideas and a perceived breakdown in moral standards. The wide-ranging reform spirit of the early twentieth century, reinforced by the social gospel of the Protestant churches, narrowed to a single crusade—prohibition. South Carolina anticipated the adoption of the Eighteenth Amendment by the passage of statewide prohibition in 1914. Thereafter, pulpit and law enforcement officials in Greenville joined to maintain the "noble experiment." Typically, on Sunday morning, March 7, 1926, Dr. George W. Quick delivered a sermon from the pulpit of the First Baptist Church of Greenville demanding unqualified enforcement of the Eighteenth Amendment. Efforts to modify Prohibition, he said, were suspect as propaganda of the liquor power in the United States.[113]

Citizens in Travelers Rest formed a Law and Order League at a Fourth of July picnic at Spring Park in 1923. W. M. Hodgens was elected president, and the speaker Lieutenant-Governor Edmund B. Jackson, declared that the greatest problem of the day was enforcement of the law. Ninety percent of all violations in the state, he said, were related to the handling, selling, or drinking of whiskey.[114]

Throughout the decade—as they had for many years—county, state, and federal officers conducted raids on local stills. In November 1928, for example, Sheriff Carlos Rector and state Constable Joe Robinson destroyed a sixty-gallon still and fifteen hundred gallons of mash in the Talley Bridge section of lower Greenville County. The *News* reported in December 1932 that the largest amount of illegal whiskey in the county had been seized in an abandoned store on Paris Mountain Road. Fruit jars containing 363 gallons were transported to the sheriff's office in the courthouse, and it took deputies one and a half hours to empty the jars into the street at the rear of the building.[115]

The stories that circulated during the Prohibition era were not all serious. The *News* carried the tale of "a man at work in an office" near the city jail. He called his favorite bootlegger for a pint of whiskey and paid in advance. The bootlegger promised to return in a few minutes. But the supplier was arrested with the pint, placed in jail, and eventually sentenced to six months on the chain gang by Judge Martin Ansel. After three months the bootlegger escaped, stole $6, bought a pint of whiskey for $2.50, and delivered it to his customer. "Here's your pint you paid me for three months ago," the bootlegger said apologetically. "I'm sorry I was late. I got pinched on the way back." Needless to point out, the great moral crusade soon lost much of its initial fervor in many quarters in Greenville.[116]

Controversy over Sunday Closing Laws

In February 1927 Governor James P. Richards announced a campaign to restore the observance of Sunday in South Carolina. He ordered law officers to begin the enforcement of the long-dormant Sunday "blue laws" or closing laws. Drug stores, for example, could remain open only to dispense medicines. Four prominent Greenvillians—Proctor A. Bonham, David Ferguson, John W. Cushman, and W. G. Perry, Jr.—were arrested for playing golf on Sunday at the Greenville Country Club.[117]

The crusade was supported by church groups, such as the five small Methodist churches of northern Greenville County. On April 1 the churches published a resolution in the *News* on behalf of their six hundred members—signed by T. A. Inabinet (pastor), J. R. Anderson of Travelers Rest, A. W. Neves of Mountain View, W. T. Forrester of Few's Chapel, W. A. Neves of Jackson Grove, and J. W. Coleman of Marietta.

But a year later the Sunday observance crusade had languished. Justice Thomas P. Cothran of Greenville, an associate justice of the state supreme court, granted a restraining order allowing drug stores in Greenville to sell any article on Sunday. The *News* reported that with druggists permitted to sell anything in their stores and filling stations dispensing gasoline on the statement of their customers that their needs were cases of emergency, blue law enforcement in Greenville had effectively ended.[118]

Crime in Greenville

Nationally, gangsters and racketeers, such as Scarface Al Capone, seized the headlines. Although Greenville County had no comparable crime wave, there were a series of sensational murders in the years following World War I. The first occurred on July 4, 1919, when Sheriff Hendrix Rector was killed in Briscoe's Garage near the courthouse by Jake Gosnell, the deputy Internal Revenue collector. Both men were natives of northern Greenville

County and had been friends since childhood. Rector hired Gosnell as a deputy, but friendship soon gave way to rivalry and hatred. The court proceedings ended in a mistrial.[119]

Even more sensational was the murder of Sheriff Samuel D. Willis, who was appointed to complete Hendrix Rector's term. In 1920 he was defeated by Carlos Rector, Hendrix Rector's younger brother. Carlos Rector was, in turn, defeated by Willis in 1924 and served until Willis was ambushed on June 11, 1927, in his garage at 219 East Stone Avenue. Carlos Rector was then named to complete Willis's term. Meanwhile, state investigators arrested the wife of the former sheriff, Ethel Willis, and Deputy Henry S. Townsend for murder in a lovers' triangle. But in the subsequent trial the jury acquitted them after an hour's deliberation.[120]

By the next election in 1929 Sheriff Carlos Rector had not solved Willis's murder, and he was defeated for re-election by former Deputy Cliff Bramlett, who promised to find the killer. A year later a black man, Blair Rook, was arrested for Willis's murder. Rook confessed and led Bramlett to the murder weapon. However, Rook said he had been paid five hundred dollars by two white men to kill Willis—Sheriff Carlos Rector and Deputy J. Harmon Moore. Rook was sentenced to life imprisonment, and Rector and Harmon received ten-year terms. On January 2, 1939, Rector and Moore were pardoned by Governor Olin D. Johnston. Rector ran for sheriff in 1940, but he was overwhelmingly defeated.[121]

Prominent farmer and business person James Edward Thackston was murdered on the night of December 20, 1924, at his store near Travelers Rest at the present site of Furman University. Four persons were arrested: Jerry Hester and his two sons, Charlie and Claude (neighbors of the Thackstons), and J. C. Floyd (who was employed on the Thackston farm). Charlie Hester had been released from jail several days before Thackston's murder after serving five months for transporting illegal whiskey, and Thackston served on the jury that convicted him. Eventually Charlie and Claude Hester were acquitted, Floyd was sentenced to twenty years on the chain gang for manslaughter, and Jerry Hester was given life imprisonment.[122]

Ku Klux Klan

In an effort to preserve the purity of white, Protestant, American society, the Ku Klux Klan was revived nationally in a dramatic ceremony at Stone Mountain, Georgia, in November 1915. Eight years later, on June 28, 1923, the Klan reappeared in Greenville County, when a group of one hundred men paraded in full regalia down Trade Street in Greer. Yet in November the *News* quoted the New York *Times* report of a very small membership in South Carolina, perhaps no more than five thousand. This was the only state without a grand dragon.[123]

But in the spring of 1924 the situation began to change. On April 1 an organizational meeting of the Klan was held in Greenville at Cleveland Hall. A field agent from Ohio had been working in the area, and the *News* estimated that there were some 750 Klan members in the Greenville vicinity. The following year the Klan became more visible. A state grand dragon's headquarters was established in Spartanburg, and in Greenville the Klan occupied the entire third floor of two large buildings at $104\frac{1}{2}$ West North Street.[124]

On April 2, 1925, Greenville was the scene of a gathering of the Klan from the counties of upper South Carolina. Approximately three hundred persons in full regalia marched on Main Street, watched by twenty to twenty-five thousand. The parade was led by mounted Klan members bearing a fiery cross. According to the *News,* the ceremonies were the first of their kind in Greenville since the 1870s.[125]

A year later, on May 6, 1926, Dr. Hiram Wesley Evans of Atlanta, the Imperial Wizard of the Klan, spoke at a gathering of some four to five thousand Klan members at the City Park. Special trains brought Klan members from Georgia and North Carolina. Highways into the city were patrolled by mounted Klan members who greeted visitors. During the ceremonies a flaming cross was brightly burning. "I come to South Carolina not to defend the Ku Klux Klan," Evans said, "for it needs no defense in a state where so many thousands of men in every walk of life are within its ranks and where it is doing great things."[126]

The respectability the Klan enjoyed in the community is indicated by its activities in the mid-1920s. The Greenville Klavern held a family picnic at Looper's farm on the Easley Bridge Road on June 25, 1925. Some 250 people attended, and B. D. Hahn, pastor of the Pendleton Street Baptist Church, told the audience that the security of the world demanded that the United States forever maintain its independence of Europe. Congressman J. J. McSwain spoke on the "Victories of Americanism" and stressed the necessity of selective immigration to keep out the undesirables of Europe and Asia. Churches in mill communities often held special services during revivals for Klan members. In June 1926 the Poinsett Klan No. 16 endorsed the revival at Morgan Memorial Baptist Church in Sans Souci. In September members of the Klan presented Brandon Baptist Church with a statement of support for its revival and a gift. Eighty Klan members gathered at the Grove Station Baptist Church in May 1931 to hear the pastor, Fred V. Johnson, preach on "Americanism." He denounced the enemies of America—communism, Roman Catholicism, divorce, the crime wave, and social evils—and praised the ideals of the Klan.[127]

A more sinister dimension of the Klan's activity appeared on October 7, 1926, when a parade marched through the black business district along East Broad and Spring Streets. Only 168 members took part, but a cross, 35 feet high, was burned on the hill in nearby Cleveland Park. In December 1931 the Poinsett Klavern began conducting undercover work for the police—investigating prostitution and the sale of liquor. Seven black bellhops in small hotels were convicted of soliciting and selling whiskey. Chief of Detectives L. W. Hammond stated in the *News:* "We are grateful to the Klan for this work." But the Klan did not stop at investigation. Two bellhops were abducted and beaten, and local attorney J. Robert Martin appeared before city council demanding an investigation.[128]

Conservative Attack on Main Line Protestantism

The role of the church as the ultimate keeper of the faith and morals of the community was shaken in the 1920s as the threat of modernism seemed to question the tenets of Southern evangelical Protestantism. Yet in the spring and summer of 1924 the community seemed safe enough. The *News* carried the Weekly Bible Talk of William Jennings Bryan, three-time presidential candidate and latter-day defender of Christian orthodoxy. A new, brick home for the Holmes Bible Church replaced the old Pentecostal Tabernacle on Buncombe Street. And Baxter ("Cyclone Mac") McLendon was in Greenville for a six-week revival in a tent on Perry Avenue in Sans Souci.[129]

But a storm of controversy broke when McLendon began to attack local bulwarks of orthodoxy. First, he announced that modernism was being preached in the Furman University chapel. Then, he unleashed an attack on that symbol of mainstream Protestantism in Greenville—"Uncle Johnny" Holmes, devout Methodist layperson and secretary of the central YMCA. In 1919 Holmes had written for the national YMCA a study guide for the Gospel of Mark entitled *Jesus and the Young Man of Today.* In a warm, evangelical tone, the book made use of critical biblical scholarship. Describing the baptism of Jesus, Holmes said: "The writer does not believe that an actual dove descended or that an audible voice spoke. These are parts of the parable with which Jesus clothed this experience." In regard to the Virgin Birth, Holmes said that for him "it makes no difference as to the origin of His physical body. It is the origin of His spiritual life . . . that we wish to know about."[130]

The attack on Holmes by McLendon was followed by an editorial in the *Baptist Courier*. The editor, Z. T. Cody, wrote that it would be better to have an infidel at the YMCA. He vowed that never had he been so shocked by any books of Thomas Paine or Robert Ingersoll. In a series of sermons, B. D. Hahn, pastor of the Pendleton Street Baptist Church, confidently forecast "that the printed attacks on the great principles of Christianity would end in victory for the cause of the Master." Pendleton Street and Riverside Baptist Churches repudiated Holmes's work, and the Greenville Baptist Association voted to sever relations with the YMCA. At the next meeting of the North Greenville Baptist Association, E. Buford Crain denounced members of the Furman Board of Trustees who were supporters of Holmes and the YMCA.[131]

Meanwhile, the YMCA Board of Directors met and reaffirmed its support of John Holmes. Of his critics, they asked: "If the statements in Mr. Holmes's book, which was published five or more years ago, and is now out of print, established the fact in the minds of Christian leaders in this community that he is an unsuitable person . . . why have they waited five years or more to bring this to the attention of the community?" A group of young men who had been under Holmes's tutelage at the YMCA signed an open letter in his behalf in the *News:* "We have never known him to express any doctrinal beliefs that were inconsistent with the teachings of the orthodox churches; nor has he . . . endeavored to change the theology of anyone." The members of the Men's Bible Class at Christ Church, which Holmes had taught for three years, also came to his support.[132]

On Sunday afternoon, July 6, 1924, Holmes spoke at a meeting at the public library. For two hours Holmes explained his theological perspective. "I have felt," he said, "that as long as I accepted Jesus Christ as Savior and Lord and worshipped Him as God, and then tried to apply the truth He taught to my life and to get others to do the same, that I could hold whatever theories were most satisfying to my reason regarding the historical setting in which the truth was set forth." His statement was printed by the YMCA board in a pamphlet entitled *My Christ* and was promptly attacked by his detractors.[133]

The Evolution Controversy

The year 1925 focused national attention on the fundamentalist controversy through the Scopes Trial in Dayton, Tennessee. John Scopes, a Tennessee schoolteacher, was tried in July for teaching evolution in his biology class. He was defended by the Chicago attorney Clarence Darrow and opposed by William Jennings Bryan. The *News* conducted a survey of the opinions of educational leaders and the ministers of the downtown churches with little result. Only B. D. Hahn said that he was a fundamentalist. But he indicated that the state of Tennessee ought to decide its own affairs without outside interference. President David Ramsay of the Greenville Woman's College took a moderate position. "Religionists and scientists may have quarrelled," he said; "but science and religion have not done so. They seem to be willing to lie down in peace together. Most of us do not like to have ourselves labeled and nicknamed. It seems to me that we should get better results if we allowed both religion and science to pursue the even tenor of their ways in an earnest and reverent search for truth." At the Baptist Assembly at Furman in the summer of 1925, President William J. McGlothlin discussed the relationship of science and religion. He indicated that both were mutually dependent and assured his audience that there was no need to worry if they approached the question with open minds and an unwavering faith in God.[134]

Optimism at the End of the Decade

By the end of the decade there was little warning of the severe economic depression that lay ahead. On New Year's Day 1929 the editorial page of the *News* exuded hope: "Greenville and the Piedmont section of South Carolina, as well as the country as a whole, have good reason to look forward to the coming twelve months with satisfaction and optimism. . . . There have been no disastrous occurrences to check the general march of progress." Such optimism was scarcely warranted, as the nation sank into the Great Depression.[135]

Notes

1. Guy A. Gullick, *Greenville County, Economic and Social* (Greenville, 1921), 44–45.

2. Ibid., 57; Mary Katherine Davis Cann, "The Morning After: South Carolina in the Jazz Age" (Ph.D. diss., University of South Carolina, 1970), 12–14, 24–25, 31.

3. Gullick, *Greenville County*, 57; Cann, "Morning After," 12–14, 24–25, 31.

4. Cann, "Morning After," 20; Greenville *News*, January 4, 1932.

5. Greenville *News*, December, 30, 1923.

6. Greenville *News*, June 7, July 4, 1925. W. W. Burgess, according to his nephew, Greenville attorney Alfred F. Burgess, adopted the spelling Burgiss for his

Burgiss Charities to distinguish his philanthropies from the family name.

7. Ibid., December 30, 1923.

8. Ibid.

9. These figures are based on the 1910 census. Gullick, *Greenville County,* 52–53.

10. The interview with Hardin is reported in Allen Tullos, *Habits of Industry: White Culture and the Transformation of the Carolina Piedmont* (Chapel Hill, N.C., 1989), 256–63.

11. Cann, "Morning After," 52–53.

12. George B. Tindall, *The Emergence of the New South, 1913–1945* (Baton Rouge, La., 1967), 75–76; Greenville *News,* August 19, 1923; May 6, 1924; September 1, 1925, [n.m., n.d.] 1926.

13. Jacquelyn Dowd Hall et al., *Like a Family; The Making of a Southern Cotton Mill World* (Chapel Hill, N.C., 1987), 196–97; Greenville *News,* July 1, August 9, 10, 1923; August 24, 1924.

14. Tindall, *Emergence,* 76–77; Greenville *News,* February 10, April 27, October 13, July 9, 1927; March 10, June 2, 1928; April 6, 1929.

15. Greenville *News,* [n.m., n.d.] 1926; April 2, 1925.

16. James A. Dunlap III, "Victims of Neglect: The Career and Creations of John T. Woodside, 1865–1986" (M.A. thesis, University of South Carolina, 1986), 83–84; Greenville *News,* March 7, 1926. The site of Wildwood is part of the North Saluda Reservoir of the Greenville Water System.

17. Mary G. Ariail and Nancy J. Smith, *Weaver of Dreams: A History of Parker District* (Columbia, 1977), 28.

18. Ibid., 30; Tullos, *Habits of Industry,* 180–81.

19. Ariail and Smith, *Weaver of Dreams,* 73–76.

20. Tullos, *Habits of Industry,* 181; Greenville *News,* March 13, April 19, 1924.

21. Greenville *News,* May 26, 1924.

22. Ariail and Smith, *Weaver of Dreams,* 30–35; Tullos, *Habits of Industry,* 181, 185.

23. Ariail and Smith, *Weaver of Dreams,* 32, 36–37, 39–40; Greenville *News,* July 24, 1932.

24. Greenville *News,* November 21, 1923; March 16, 1924; December 19, 1926.

25. Ariail and Smith, *Weaver of Dreams,* 32–33; George Kent, "Mill Town Miracle," *School and Society* 54 (1941): 81–85.

26. Eliot Asinof, *Eight Men Out: The Black Sox and the 1919 World Series* (New York, 1963), 54–55.

27. Ibid., 55–57.

28. Ibid., 121, 152, 175–78.

29. Ibid., 232, 260, 272–73.

30. Ibid., 286–93.

31. Tullos, *Habits of Industry,* 180, 184–85; Ariail and Smith, *Weaver of Dreams,* 91.

32. Tullos, *Habits of Industry,* 185–87.

33. Ibid., 187, 191.

34. Ibid.; Greenville *News*, August 23, 1932.

35. Tullos, *Habits of Industry*, 193–95; Greenville *News*, August 25, 1932.

36. Jacquelyn Dowd Hall et al. *Like a Family: The Making of a Southern Cotton Mill World* (Chapel Hill, N.C., 1987), 197–206.

37. Tullos, *Habits of Industry*, 187–91.

38. Dowd, *Like a Family*, 212–17; Tindall, *Emergence*, 341–49; Greenville *News*, April 3, 1929.

39. Greenville *News*, March 26, 1929.

40. Ibid., March 28, 30, April 2, 1929

41. Tindall, *Emergence*, 350; Greenville *News*, April 5, 1929.

42. Greenville *News*, May 12, April 7, May 21, 1929.

43. Ibid., April 10, May 15, 17, 1929, June 29, 1932.

44. Ibid., June 1, 1929.

45. Ibid., June 29, 1929.

46. Ibid., August 29, 1929.

47. Ibid., September 3, 1929.

48. Ibid., September 9, 1929.

49. Ibid., February 28, July 1, 1930.

50. Ibid., October 16, November 4, 1930; March 2, 1931.

51. Ibid., September 2, 27, 1931.

52. The figures are cited in James M. Richardson, *History of Greenville County, South Carolina* (Atlanta, Ga., 1930), 116, 317–18; Greenville *News*, July 4, 1923; Nancy Vance Ashmore, *Greenville, Woven From the Past* (Northridge, Calif., 1986), 238.

53. Richardson, *History*, 327–28; Greenville *News*, February 23, 1926; February 14, 1939; Notes of William N. Cruikshank in possession of the author.

54. Greenville *News*, May 28, 1972; April 27, August 31, 1930.

55. Tindall, *Emergence*, 95–96; Judith G. Bainbridge, *Centennial: The Chamber in Retrospect* (Greenville, 1988), 7–9; Greenville *News*, April 4, 1924.

56. Greenville *News*, April 1, 1924; October 4, 1932.

57. Tindall, *Emergence*, 97; Greenville *News*, September 21, 1924; May 14, 18, 1925.

58. Greenville *News*, March 23, 1924.

59. Ibid., July 4, November 28, 1923.

60. Ibid., September 28, 1923; May 30, June 14, 21, 1925.

61. Ibid., September 26, December 11, 1923; May 27, 1924; Bainbridge, *Centennial*, 10; Bainbridge, "The Old Chamber Building" (manuscript in possession of the author).

62. Greenville *News*, May 26, 1925; Bainbridge, "Chamber Building."

63. Greenville *News*, November 3, 1925.

64. James A. Dunlap, III, "Victims of Neglect: The Career and Creations of John T. Woodside, 1865–1986" (M.A. thesis, University of South Carolina, 1986), 39–40, 68.

65. Greenville *News*, June 13, 17, August 15, 1924.

66. Richardson, *History,* 233–336; Ashmore, *Greenville,* 263.

67. Greenville *News,* November 8, 9, December 18, 1924; June 28, September 6, 1925.

68. Ibid., December 15, 1924; May 1, 1925; May 25, July 10, 1926; July 6, 1931. The Goodyear story was furnished by William N. Cruikshank.

69. Greenville *News,* July 31, 1931; July 30, 1926; August 7, 1931.

70. Ibid., November 10–11, 18, 23, 30, December 7, 1926.

71. Ibid., August 13, 1924; February 12, 1925; May 14, 1929.

72. Ibid., September 13, October 15, 1925; September 16, 1926; Richardson, *Greenville County,* 200.

73. Greenville *News,* June 10–11, 19, 1924; Blanche March, *Hitch Up the Buggy* (Greenville, 1977), 149–52.

74. Greenville *News,* July 14, 15, 1923; Martha Stewart Scott, *Before Paved Roads,* cited in Greenville *News,* June 22, 1986.

75. Greenville *News,* October 14, May 3, March 3, August 1, 1925; August 12, 1928; June 11, October 17, 1930.

76. Ibid., February 14, 17, April 19, 20, November 15, 1927; August 8, 22, 24, 1929.

77. Ibid., December 30, 1923; August 15, 1925. Prior to World War II, city council renamed the city park McPherson Park in honor of John A. McPherson.

78. Ibid., January 1, 1925; November 6, 1930.

79. Ibid., April 16, 1926.

80. Greenville *Piedmont,* November 24, 1973; August 24, 1989.

81. Joshua Daniel White, *The Josh White Songbook* (Chicago, Ill., 1963), 15–44.

82. Greenville *News,* September 8, November 26, 1932; December 20, 1925.

83. "Hattie Logan Duckett, 1885–1956," Biographical File, Greenville County Library, Greenville, S.C.

84. Ibid.; Greenville *News,* February 14, 1975.

85. "Phillis Wheatley Association—Memorandum," Historical File, S.C. Room, Greenville County Library, Greenville, S.C.

86. Greenville *News,* March 23, December, 4, 1924; October 20, 1939. A favorable account of the center was included in Edwin Mims, *The Advancing South* (New York, 1926), 275.

87. Greenville *News,* April 12, 1925; December 30, 1923.

88. Ibid., January 1, 1927.

89. Joseph T. Drake, "The Negro in Greenville, South Carolina" (M.A. thesis, University of North Carolina, 1940), 173.

90. Greenville *News,* November 23, 1923; November 6, 1932.

91. The story of highway construction from the state perspective is skillfully told in John Hammond Moore, *The South Carolina Highway Department, 1917–1987* (Columbia, S.C., 1987); Richardson, *History,* 106; Greenville *News,* September 20, 1924; March 20, 1926.

92. Moore, *Highway Department,* 61–62; Greenville *News,* June 3, 1925; March 20, 1926; July 14, 1927.

93. Richardson, *History,* 107; Greenville *News,* November 1, 1931; July 1, 1923; December 16, 22, 1931.

94. Greenville *News,* March 26, 1926; George D. Barr, "The Greenville (South Carolina) Municipal Airport Story," *Proceedings and Papers of the Greenville County Historical Society* 5 (1971–1975): 49–51.

95. Barr, "Airport," 54–55; Greenville *News,* September 8–10, 1928.

96. Greenville *News,* November 18, December 11, 1930.

97. Ibid., July 26, 1924; September 15, 1931.

98. Ibid., June 14, July 6, 13, 1932.

99. Ibid., May 2, 10, 1925.

100. Ibid., November 6, 1925; May 12, October 31, 1926; July 9, 1930.

101. Ibid., September 4, 25, 27, 1927.

102. Cann, "The Morning After," 239–40; Loulie Latimer Owens Pettigrew, *The Thursday Club, Greenville, South Carolina, 1889–1989* (Greenville, 1988), 36–37; Greenville *News,* February 27, October 9, 1927; June 15, 1928; April 6, July 27, 1930; May 4, 1992.

103. Ellen Perry, *Free Reading for Everybody: The Story of the Greenville Library* (Greenville, 1973), 3–6.

104. Ibid., 6–14.

105. Richardson, *History,* 324–25.

106. Ibid., 143–47; Lois Woods, "Robert Quillen, 1887–1948," *PPGCHS* 6 (1975–1979): 89–94.

107. Greenville *News,* December 19, 24, 1925. On November 2, 1927, the *News* reported that John P. Brady had erected a monument to Adam on his estate in Baltimore in 1909.

108. Ibid., March 1, 1936; April 7, 10, 1925; June 12, 13, 15, 16, 20, 1926; May 4, 1927.

109. Ibid., March 14, 1928; February 4, 13, 14, 1930; August 16, 1930.

110. Ibid., February 12, April 12, May 24, 1931.

111. Alfred S. Reid, *Furman University: Toward a New Identity, 1925–1975* (Durham, N.C., 1976), 21, 37–38; "Football," in *Encyclopedia of Southern Culture,* ed. Charles R. Wilson and William Ferris (Chapel Hill, N.C., 1989), 1221.

112. Greenville *News,* October 17, 21, 1926.

113. Ibid., March 8, 1926.

114. Ibid., July 5, 1923.

115. Ibid., December 1, 1928; December 10, 11, 1932.

116. Ibid., July 23, 1923.

117. Ibid., February 25, 28, March 5, 1927.

118. Ibid., February 19, 20, 1928.

119. Detailed reports of the murder and the subsequent trial appear in the Greenville *News.* A summary of the events appears in Johnny Mack Brown, "The Greenville County Sheriff's Office: Origins and History," unpublished manuscript in possession of the author, excerpted in *PPGCHS* 8 (1984–1990): 119–23.

120. Ibid.

121. Ibid.

122. Greenville *News,* December 21, 1924; January 5, 6, 13, March 14, 15, 20, 21, 24, 1925.

123. Ibid., July 1, November 22, 1923.

124. Ibid., July 1, November 22, 1923; April 1, 1924.

125. Ibid., March 15, April 2, 3, 1925.

126. Ibid., May 2, 6, 1926.

127. Ibid., June 26, 1925; June 8, September 14, 1926; May 18, 1931.

128. Ibid., October 8, 1926; December 27, 1931, January 20, 1932.

129. Ibid., June 28, December 13, May 4, 1924.

130. Ibid., May 10, June 20, 1924; John M. Holmes, *Jesus and the Young Man of Today* (New York, 1920), 13, 167.

131. Greenville *News,* June 20, 27, 30, July 11, August 10, 14, 1924.

132. Ibid., June 25, July 3, 4, 1924. The members of the YMCA board who signed the statement were D. L. Norris, president; George Wrigley, secretary; Alester G. Furman, Aug W. Smith, Thomas F. Parker, Henry T. Mills, D. E. McCuen, F. K. Spratt, R. W. Arrington, Luther McBee, Jr., W. A. Merritt, Thomas L. Lewis, and Louis Sherfree. Out-of-town signers were J. R. McKinney and A. H. Cottingham.

133. Ibid., July 3, 4, 10, August 20, December 29, 1924.

134. Ibid., May 31, July 25, 1925.

135. Ibid., January 1, 1929.

CHAPTER ELEVEN

The Depression
and the New Deal

Greenville entered the year 1929 with great expectations. On its editorial page on January 1, the Greenville *News* assured readers that "there have been no disastrous occurrences to check the general march of progress. . . . We have reason to hail the New Year with cheer and satisfaction." By the end of June, however, Major G. Heyward Mahon, Jr., lamented the loss of "the old Greenville spirit." In an address to the Kiwanis Club on June 27, Mahon reported that "there are many of our leading citizens who have lost faith in our city. It must be restored and the old time spirit revived."[1]

Major Mahon was correct—the old Progressive boosterism was gone, and economic uncertainty was giving way to depression. The Great Depression brought with it bank failures and textile cutbacks. Local relief efforts were unsuccessful, and Greenville had to depend on increasing federal aid culminating in the New Deal. By the end of the 1930s economic revival was in sight, but war in Europe clouded the horizon. Between 1930 and 1940 the population figures reflected the economic decline. In the 1930s the total population of Greenville County increased from 117,009 to 136,580. But the percentage of growth dropped from 32.22 percent in the 1920s to 16.7 percent in the 1930s.[2]

Financial Failures

The uncertain economy took its toll on the banking system. In 1926 the first bank failure occurred when the Bank of Commerce closed its doors. After several weeks of rumors and subsequent withdrawals, the president, B. A. Morgan, called the board of directors to meet with a state bank examiner. Morgan reported that the depositors would be paid in full, and George Norwood of the South Carolina National Bank, W. C. Beacham of the Peoples National Bank, and Robert I. Woodside of the Woodside National Bank assured their customers that "the financial soundness of Greenville" was not shaken by the bank's closing.[3]

In June 1929 the Chamber of Commerce itself received a major set-back. The Southeastern Life Insurance Company initiated proceedings against the chamber for failure to make interest payments on the Chamber of Commerce Building. In December 1931 the building was purchased by the Independence Life Insurance Company—a new venture associated with Liberty Life.[4]

In October 1929 the Woodside National Bank faced serious withdrawals. Overnight a large amount of cash was brought to Greenville by American Railway Express, and the next morning, on October 10, John W. Norwood, chair of the board of the South Carolina National Bank, appeared in the lobby of the Woodside Bank to discourage withdrawals. But the damage had been done. On October 19 the Peoples State Bank of South Carolina in Charleston announced that it had purchased the Woodside Bank. President R. Goodwyn Rhett, Jr., announced that Alester G. Furman, Jr., had been elected vice president in charge of the Greenville office. Three years later, in January 1932, the Peoples State Bank closed and was placed in the hands of bank examiners who predicted that patrons would receive 18 percent of their savings. Finally, in March 1934 the Reconstruction Finance Corporation (RFC) approved a loan of $2,838,000, which enabled the bank to pay a 20 percent dividend to the seventy thousand depositors.[5]

Textile mills continued to operate through the summer of 1929, but profits dropped steadily. In an address before the Southern Textile Association in Asheville, Thomas M. Marchant, president of the Victor-Monaghan Company, charged that "overproduction is the root of all the troubles in the textile industry today." He proposed that manufacturers stop using women and children for nightwork and raise the minimum age from fourteen to sixteen. By September virtually every mill in the Greenville area had curtailed production. Some operated alternate weeks for several months; others announced a three-day week for an indefinite period.[6]

The stock market crashed in October in what the *News* called "the most terrifying stampede of selling ever experienced on the New York Stock Exchange and other leading security markets." Prices crumbled, and the ticker recording the transactions fell five hours behind. October 29 was the single most devastating day in the market. Some 16.4 million shares were sold at a time when 3 million was considered a busy day. The crash revealed that the economic structure of the country was unsound, and local business failures accelerated.[7]

In October 1930 the American Cigar Company closed its factory on East Court Street, and two hundred employees, primarily women, were put out of work. The old hand-making method of cigar production was outdated, and the company transferred operations to its modern Charleston plant. T. Charles Gower and Alester G. Furman, on behalf of the Chamber of Commerce, negotiated with the company for the creation of a relief fund, and a committee of former employees, assisted by a citizens' committee headed by Fred W. Symmes, administered the fund.[8]

The most wide-ranging failure in Greenville was that of John T. Woodside. In the late 1920s Woodside had launched a new venture—speculation in beach property. In 1926 Woodside purchased 66,000 acres in Horry County for $1 million. The land surrounded a tiny resort community known as Myrtle Beach. His chief lieutenant was Colonel Holmes B. Springs, an Horry County native, who served as vice president of the Woodside National Bank from 1924 to 1928. Woodside directed the building of roads, hotels, and a championship golf course at Myrtle Beach. In 1927 he announced the construction of the million-dollar Ocean Forest Hotel, and in 1929 he unveiled plans for the Arcady development, an exclusive resort. The stock market crash, though, devastated the Woodside empire.[9]

In February 1931 the *News* announced that Woodside had been ousted from the presidency of the Woodside Cotton Mills. Heading the new board of directors were Floyd Jefferson and Oliver Iselin—officers of William Iselin and Company, a major commission sales company based in New York. A group of Myrtle Beach business people, who had originally sold the land to Woodside, and the Iselin Company purchased land at bargain prices that had millions of dollars of improvements. Woodside also lost his home on Crescent Avenue in Greenville, and he moved into a small house on East Washington Street. As these words reveal, only Woodside's stern Presbyterian faith sustained him in his last years:

> Money had to be raised to save the mills. Thus sacrificing my personal fortune and position to save the interest of others, I had not a penny on earth left that I could call my own. . . . Tragedy of tragedies, but the greatest tragedy of all . . . is the disloyalty and ungratefulness of friends. . . . I have an idea that in the world to come such are segregated in order that Satan himself may not be contaminated. . . . I will never try to get even with anyone. . . . Our maker is the great unerring evener.[10]

Local Cutbacks and Relief Efforts

As hard times increased, local agencies slashed salaries and services. In February 1931 the library announced cuts in salaries, rents, and gasoline;

county government could not always meet payrolls on time; and teachers were paid in scrip. The 1932–1933 school year was reduced to eight months, and Furman cut tuition by 10 percent. In July 1932 federal employees were notified that they would be required to take a one-month leave.[11]

The relief facilities in Greenville, as in most communities, were overwhelmed. In the first quarter of 1930 relief work increased by 102 percent, and in the second quarter the increase was 108 percent. The local Red Cross chapter and the Salvation Army were the only agencies equipped to handle such emergencies, and by July 1930 Margaret Laing, the executive secretary of the Red Cross, announced that her account with the Community Chest was overdrawn. The Salvation Army was overwhelmed by the demands and Laing appealed to local bakeries for day-old bread to feed the hungry.[12]

Mrs. William G. Sirrine agreed to head a general social service committee for the Red Cross with a subgroup in each township. In November 1930 the Red Cross listed 144 city and county families with some employment, but seeking relief; 117 families generally unemployed, with some work such as picking cotton and cleaning yards; 91 families of farm tenants with no work and without food or fuel; and 19 families not yet investigated.[13]

Meanwhile Governor James P. Richards advised each county to form a committee under the supervision of the state extension department to set up relief measures. Fifty citizens met at the library on December 4 and selected the Greenville County committee: J. J. McDevitt, director of the Federal Employment Bureau, chair; Frank O. Hamblen, vice chair; Eugene Bryant, secretary-treasurer; Malcolm S. Taylor; O. K. Owens; Brown Mahon; J. E. Mears; Mrs. William G. Sirrine; Mrs. A. D. Tanner; and Mrs. E. Y. Hillhouse. The committee requested a joint meeting with the trustees of the Community Chest on December 10. At that session, R. W. Hudgens, the acting chair of the Red Cross board, and J. V. Brezeale, the commandant of the Salvation Army, presented their needs. After discussion Aug W. Smith, president of the Brandon Corporation, moved that a campaign for ten thousand dollars be inaugurated immediately.[14]

When this drive failed to raise the needed amount, a community rally in Textile Hall called for additional funds, and the Greenville Elks opened a dining room for the poor on East North Street in cooperation with the Red Cross. But the Red Cross was overwhelmed by the crisis. Without funds and with more than five hundred cases which needed immediate relief, the local chapter closed its doors in September 1931. When it reopened a month later, the directors abandoned the Bureau of Family Service for lack of financial support.[15]

In October a committee of citizens established the Greenville Welfare Service under the leadership of John M. Holmes (chair), Robert E. Henry, and T. Charles Gower. The committee created an employment exchange under the supervision of J. H. Huff, Wyllis Taylor, and W. Ben Smith. Mrs. Mark Ellis became executive secretary.[16]

The Welfare Service opened its office in a store on McBee Avenue at the rear of the Belk-Simpson Company, donated by Nelson Poe. The rules for employment were simple and direct. If a person applied for work and a job was secured, the individual could refuse to work, but the committee would terminate aid. If the person went begging from door to door, the committee would report him to the police. Employment opportunities for whites included a sewing room for women at the YWCA and a wood yard on East Broad Street for men. A mountain wood detail brought logs into the city that were cut and split at the wood yard. Donated clothing and wood were sold to the public, and a municipal cannery opened at the curb market on East Court Street.[17]

Black men were employed digging ditches for the Greater Greenville Sewer Commission for fifty cents a day, with payment made in groceries. Applicants reported to the Phillis Wheatley Center each morning, but so many came that it was necessary to limit each person to one day's work a week. Some twenty persons a day were employed by end of July 1932.[18]

Funds for the Welfare Service came from the Penny-A-Meal campaign. Six thousand boxes were distributed house-to-house and through the churches, and five hundred were placed in businesses. Citizens were asked to contribute a penny at each meal. By the end of November, however, the boxes yielded only $1,635.47. Nevertheless, by February 1932 some 1,152 families had been helped. A special drive at Christmas resulted in 7,227 pounds of food distributed to the five hundred families most in need. In April 1932 the Welfare Service was taken over by the Community Chest amid praise that it was one of the most successful charitable enterprises ever sponsored by the city and county, chiefly because of its policy of self-help.[19]

The textile mills provided their own relief services. At Dunean, for example, Leonard Howard, the director of the Community House, was in charge of relief. If a family were in need, he sent an order for groceries at the Dunean store or two other designated stores that agreed to sell groceries at wholesale prices. A family of four to six people was given two dollars in groceries each week. Employees promised to repay at the rate of one dollar per week when the mill resumed work. The two dollars provided 4 pounds of fat bacon, 5 pounds of dry beans, 6 pounds of sugar, five cans of evaporated milk, 1 pound of cocoa, one dozen eggs, 4 pounds of grits, two tall cans of salmon, 5 pounds of potatoes, 2 pounds of lard, two gallons of meal, 3 pounds of cabbage, two cakes of soap, and 1 pound of rice.[20]

Despite such efforts, unrest surfaced from time to time. In June 1931 the Southeastern Compress and Warehouse Company advertised for workers. A crew of fifty black men were employed, and a number of enraged whites tried to oust the blacks from their jobs. A race riot ensued, and the sheriff intervened. Eventually the company hired both black and white workers.[21]

To raise the spirits of the community, various groups promoted activities. A Halloween parade was held in Greenville for the first time in 1930. The following year some two thousand witches, goblins, ghosts, and clowns marched down Main Street, and the Shrine Band and the American Legion Drum and Bugle Corps joined the parade. According to the *News,* "no shade of color was left out."[22] During the summer of 1932 L. P. Hollis promoted a series of concerts at the City Park and "anti-depression meetings" in the mill villages. At the park various groups performed with the finale by an all-black program arranged by Charles F. Gandy, pastor of the Springfield Baptist Church. Ten choirs, quartets, and orchestras provided music. At Judson, Hollis arranged for a performance that included a hundred-piece orchestra, a chorus, and a black-face minstrel show.[23]

Churches provided spiritual sustenance, as well as relief, depending on their theological perspectives. At Buncombe Street Methodist Church, for example, B. Rhett Turnipseed preached a sermon entitled "Facing the Future with Confidence" in January 1932. "We can put our Lord to the test," he said, "and when the journey is over, we will find that He has led us safely home." More conservative church leaders held a service at the City Park in July 1932 to pray for a revival of New Testament Christianity. E. Buford Crain, pastor of the City View Baptist Church, preached, and J. H. Viser, pastor of the Third Presbyterian Church, said they were convinced that the hope of civilization and the return of prosperity rested not in legislation or in business stimulation but in a revival of spiritual life.[24]

Unrest in Local Politics

The Great Depression put considerable stress on the business elite that controlled politics in the city and county. A sizeable number of the "Main Street crowd" organized to demand stringent government economy from their business associates and erstwhile friends. Prior to the organization of the South Carolina Farmers and Taxpayers League, 270 delegates from the sixty precincts in Greenville County met on October 31 at the courthouse.

Letters were mailed out with the signatures of Marshal Moore and Alester G. Furman, and Captain W. P. Conyers, the principal speaker, demanded that local governments operate on a sound financial basis.[25]

In response, the county legislative delegation proposed reducing taxes by 2 mills on a tax base of 13.5 mills, but the league was not satisfied. The county sheriff declared in no uncertain terms that he could not operate with a further reduction. When all the telephones were removed from the courthouse, the bar association demanded that at least four be replaced. When the league presented a fourteen-part questionnaire to the city school trustees, Chairman E. M. Blythe complained that it took him three-and-a-half hours to answer it. And when Conyers, on behalf of the league, proposed a reduction of $102,905 in the school budget, Blythe resigned in protest after a decade of service.[26]

Stung by these tactics, supporters of the schools began to speak out. L. P. Hollis called for a public meeting of the "friends of education" on February 29, 1932, to arouse concern for the payment of teachers's salaries. Those in attendance supported a resolution made by Lewis E. Brookshire, president of the S.C. Federation of Labor, urging the county delegation to issue short-term notes to pay teachers for the current session. A county-wide rally in behalf of public education was held in Textile Hall on March 7 at which J. L. Mann spoke.[27]

In December 1932 the taxpayers league demanded cuts in city expenditures beyond a proposed two-mill reduction. When attorney Henry K. Townes presented a petition signed by 285 citizens, Marshall Prevost declared: "We have carried on just about as far as we can. We must have relief. Governments will not stand under present taxation." Mayor A. C. Mann defended the city's record: "We appreciate times are hard and conditions are not what they need to be . . . [but] only four cities in the United States operate at a smaller per capita cost than Greenville."[28]

Federal Relief Efforts

When state and local efforts proved inadequate, President Herbert Hoover reluctantly moved toward the creation of federal relief programs. First, Congress established the Reconstruction Finance Corporation (RFC) in January 1932 to make loans to corporations. Then in July the president signed the Emergency Relief and Construction Act, providing RFC funds for relief loans to the states and money for public works.[29]

In the spring of 1932 surplus flour and garden seeds from the Department of Agriculture reached Greenville and were distributed by the Red

Cross, the Welfare Service, and the Salvation Army. By May 443 Greenville County farmers had received fifty-five thousand dollars in federal loans. The maximum loan was $400, but the majority applied for amounts from $50 to $125. A local committee composed of Frank H. Earle of Greenville, John L. Hawkins of Greer, and T. W. Stansell of Pelzer reviewed the loan applications. Free milk was distributed by the city health department to some eight hundred children, and each afternoon a bread line of five hundred people formed at the Salvation Army Citadel where day-old bread from local bakeries was distributed. The *News* reported that the recipients wrapped their loaves in flour sacks, newspapers, and old rags.[30]

An infusion of twelve thousand dollars in RFC money for Greenville was announced on December 22, 1932. This money was directed toward improvements at the airport and in park and sewer facilities; at the Boy Scout camp; and at the fish hatchery. Work payments ranged from fifty to seventy-five cents a day. Within a week 360 people had applied for work, and 188 were assigned to the projects.[31]

FDR, Prohibition, and the Election of 1932

Increasingly, the nation looked toward the presidential election of 1932 for a solution to its problems. Republicans were duty-bound to renominate Hoover, and the Democrats turned to Governor Franklin D. Roosevelt of New York as their standard-bearer. As a part-time resident of Warm Springs, Georgia, Roosevelt was an attractive candidate in Greenville. His private railroad car regularly passed through the county on its way from New York to Warm Springs.[32]

Prohibition, an issue which had divided Greenville County four years earlier, was still important, and the Allied Forces for Prohibition held four rallies. More than one thousand people attended the rally in the First Baptist Church on February 17. Allied Youth was led by Francis T. Cunningham, a Furman student from Greenville, and Allied Citizens was led by attorney J. Wilbur Hicks. Working in favor of repeal were William G. Sirrine, a member of the National Committee of Lawyers, and James D. Poag and Stephen Nettles, members of the state committee. In March 1932 the *Liberty Digest* published a poll showing 1,093 local citizens for repeal and 653 against.[33]

In the Republican camp, Herbert Hoover had abandoned the traditional state Republican Party composed of blacks and white officeholders known as the Tolbert faction (for the family that had controlled it since the late nineteenth century). The new "lily-white" group, supported by Hoover,

was known as the Hambright faction. When the Republican Party organized in Greenville County in March 1932, seventy-five persons attended
the meeting at the Coca-Cola plant. They were addressed by Major Silas
Williams, the son of former Mayor James T. Williams and a descendant of
Vardry McBee. He praised Hoover for serving the country during the worst
financial crisis in history. Postmaster Charles C. Withington presided, and
Ted Adams, the federal marshal for the Western District of South Carolina,
was elected chair. Among the delegates to the state convention was Federal
District Attorney Joseph A. Tolbert, nephew of the leader of the Tolbert
faction.[34]

Prior to the Democratic National Convention, Franklin D. Roosevelt
stopped in Greenville on May 25 at the depot on West Washington Street.
He was welcomed by Mayor A. C. Mann and County Chair Henry K.
Townes, who had to force their way through the crowd of thirty-five hundred. Looking tanned and vigorous, Roosevelt spoke confidently: "As I
see it the prospects are extremely bright for a Democratic administration at
Washington during the next four years."[35]

Three delegates from Greenville attended the National Democratic
Convention: Wilton H. Earle, Dr. R. M. Dacus, and C. G. Wyche. Wyche
and Roger Peace, who covered the convention for the *News,* drove to Chicago, while the others went by train. On the issue of prohibition, the three
local delegates favored repeal, though on the final vote Wyche sided with
the minority to resubmit the question to the states. About Roosevelt's
nomination, Wyche was clear: "The party presents a solid front against the
enemy. If we get busy now and let the people know the truth about the
Hoover administration, Roosevelt will be elected by a vast majority next
November."[36]

After the Democratic Convention there was still considerable rancor in
Greenville over prohibition. President William J. McGlothlin of Furman
declared that the "delegates [in Chicago] . . . must have been stampeded
by hoodlums or they would not have adopted such a platform." Wyche
shot back a reply: "If the president of Furman University desires to join the
ranks of the Republican party, as his statement would indicate, he has that
right and privilege. . . . The Republicans straddled the fence as usual and
the Democrats spoke in plain English." The local chapter of the Women's
Christian Temperance Union denounced both parties. The president, Mrs.
Alester G. Furman, delivered a call to arms on the state level: "Women can
show their true colors by voting for drys for local and state positions."[37]

The county political campaign was filled with the usual excitement.
The most colorful candidate was Clarence E. ("Mountain Lion") Sloan

whose successful campaign for the House of Representatives in 1924 had featured attacks on bathing suits and Sunday swimming. In 1932 Sloan ran for the state Senate against incumbent Joseph R. Bryson and won. But in the process Sloan had a fist fight with Representative J. Harvey Cleveland at the stump meeting at Travelers Rest. Sloan celebrated his victory, along with his seven brothers, at a "South Carolina feast" featuring veal, pork, chicken, and lamb—barbecued, fried, and stewed. The guest list included Governor Blackwood and Chief Justice Eugene B. Gary.[38]

The 1932 campaign included an effort by the Central Trades and Labor Council to boost local candidates who supported labor. Likewise, the Farmers and Taxpayers League sought support for government economy. Greenville County had an active Young Democrats organization—headed by Dr. Jack Jervey, president; Mendel S. Fletcher and Constance Furman, vice presidents; Bevo Arnold and Hallie McCuen, secretaries; and Larue Hinson, treasurer. More than one thousand people greeted Eleanor Roosevelt at a rally at the municipal airport in October.[39]

In the general election in November, the vote in Greenville County was unusually heavy, according to the *News*. Roosevelt swept the presidential vote 7,768 to 95 for Hoover, whose vote had declined from 270 in 1928. Hoover's greatest support came from Ward 1 in the city of Greenville, where he garnered sixteen votes, while Greer only received twelve votes. Norman Thomas, the Socialist candidate, received one vote.[40]

The Beginning of the New Deal

Two local men, J. D. Poag and Henry K. Townes, were Democratic presidential electors, and Roosevelt invited them to the inauguration with their fellow electors. Townes could not go, and James H. Price attended in his place. The local Drum and Bugle Corps marched in the inaugural parade. Others present included Mr. and Mrs. Roger Peace, Dr. and Mrs. R. M. Dacus, B. F. Rush, Mrs. H. H. Harris, J. B. Steinsprings, F. F. Beattie, Mr. and Mrs. G. C. Williams, and Mr. and Mrs. T. G. Wall. Poag reported: "The magnificent reception given Mr. Roosevelt's inaugural address impressed me most. . . . [The audience] did not become enthusiastic until the address."[41]

In Greenville the inauguration was acted out on a platform at the rear of the courthouse. As the ceremonies were broadcast, local citizens represented the national figures. C. G. Wyche played the part of Roosevelt; T. E. Christenberry, the clerk of court, played Chief Justice Charles Evans Hughes; and Joseph A. Tolbert, the Republican federal district attorney, played Hoover. Between one thousand and fifteen hundred people watched, and that night the Young Democrats held an Inaugural Ball at the Poinsett Hotel.[42]

Immediately after the inauguration, President Roosevelt began a rapid-fire series of relief actions in his first hundred days. On his second day in office, Roosevelt called a special session of Congress and declared a "bank holiday" which closed all the national banks for ten days to examine their strength. Greenville *News* reporter, Dan Crosland, surveyed the local populace and found that "FDR yesterday became truly a half-god to Greenville, so extraordinary was the omniscience given him by the trusting democracy." Already Roosevelt "had become beglamoured in their minds, because of his prompt decisions." One man exclaimed: "Boy! we've got a man."[43]

But the impact of Franklin Roosevelt and the New Deal on Greenville was far greater than a restoration of the old order. Together with the outbreak of World War II, the New Deal began to remold the foundations of the aging New South into a modern South after 1945 that few could have imagined.

Governor Blackwood followed Roosevelt's lead and declared a state bank holiday. The banks in Greenville remained open to change money, but no checks were cashed. Twenty-five businesses took a full-page advertisement in the newspaper: "We have faith in our banks. You might as well try to move Gibraltar as to shake the sound banking system of Greenville and the nation when backed by our united faith. [The] present crisis, from which we are already triumphantly emerging under the leadership of Franklin D. Roosevelt, merely calls for common sense." Only the South Carolina National Bank remained closed longer than the ten-day period. But it reopened in July, assuring customers that it was 100 percent safe.[44]

During the bank holiday the textile mills paid wages in scrip, and Frank Hamblen, president of the Chamber of Commerce, urged merchants to accept it at full value. Once the ten-day holiday was over, the *News* reported that "thousands of shoppers from the city and surrounding territory thronged here. . . . A flood of currency was loosed."[45]

Agricultural Reform

After the banking crisis, the administration turned to the problems of the farmer. Roosevelt created the Farm Credit Administration which refinanced farm loans at low interest rates. W. R. Gray, county farm agent, announced that 1,740 farmers had filed loan applications for $191,400.

The previous year there were four hundred applications for some fifty thousand dollars. Gray expected some nineteen hundred applications for two hundred thousand dollars in 1933.[46]

Roosevelt attacked the problem of farm surpluses with acreage reduction. In January 1933, prior to the inauguration, a group of local mill executives traveled to Washington to oppose farm allotments including Thomas M. Marchant, president of the American Cotton Manufacturers Association; D. E. McCuen, president of the American Cotton Shippers Association; Samuel M. Beattie, president of the Piedmont Manufacturing Company; W. P. Conyers, farmer and business person; R. E. Henry, president of Dunean Mills; Fred W. Symmes, president of the Nuckasee Mill; and Walter F. White, president of Acme Industrial Company. Nevertheless, the Agricultural Adjustment Act became law, and farming entered a new era.[47]

In South Carolina the Clemson Extension Department led the campaign to reduce crop acreage. In Greenville County, Farm Agent W. R. Gray was in charge of the program. The amount of cotton by which the local crop was to be reduced in 1933 was 20,500 acres. A meeting of farmers was held at Textile Hall on June 28, and some thirty-five hundred farmers, including several hundred blacks who were seated in the balcony, heard a fiery address by U.S. Senator "Cotton Ed" Smith, chair of the Senate Agriculture Committee. The crop had already been planted, Smith told the audience, but if you do not plow up your cotton now, it will plow you up in the fall. By July 20 four-fifths of the acreage was subscribed which gave farmers payments totaling $31,689.[48] But there was not unanimity among the farmers, and a wave of terrorism swept sections of the county where farmers did not sign up initially. Threats were made against them, and cotton stalks were pulled up.[49]

The goal of the program was to restore farm prices to parity—the level they had reached between 1909 and 1914. On August 6 the *News* carried a picture of Dave Burns, a Travelers Rest farmer, with his two sons plowing up his cotton with a team of mules. The program was so successful in Greenville that in 1934, the second year of operation, the farmers voted for controls ten to one, while the national vote was nine to one.[50]

By 1939 the New Deal farm program included not only parity payments, but payments for conservation and soil building as well. In all, Greenville County farmers qualified for payments of $704,000. In an effort to end the cycle of farm tenancy, in 1937 the Farm Security Administration began to make long-term loans to tenant farmers to purchase land, and Greenville was one of three hundred counties in the nation eligible for the program. In November 1940 Lewis M. Verdin, county rural rehabilitation supervisor, announced that twenty-seven farms, ranging in size from 50 to 150 acres had been purchased and resold to tenants.[51]

The combination of government assistance and farmer initiative led to the kind of success in Greenville that could be touted in the press by the county farm agent. In September 1935 Gray reported on the efforts of C. B. Loftis of Taylors who had planted the 5 acres of cotton allotted to him and produced a bale an acre from Coker's Farm Relief seed. His rule for success was "plant early, fertilize well and get a crop ahead of the boll weevil." In addition, Loftis planted 4 to 5 acres of corn that yielded 150 bushels. Along with small grains, the corn provided food for his stock, dairy herd, and poultry. He also planted 3 to 4 acres of sweet potatoes for market and Austrian peas as a cover crop.[52]

Loftis owned jointly with his father-in-law, H. W. M. McCauley, an orchard that contained 35 acres of peach trees and 1.5 acres of grape vines. Their annual yield was eight to ten cars of peaches, 3,000 bushels of apples, and grapes that sold for $102. Loftis also produced between five hundred and six hundred thousand potato, tomato, and pepper plants and had thirteen stands of bees that yielded several hundred pounds of honey.

Mrs. Loftis had a flock of fifty Rhode Island Red hens and sold three to four hundred fryers each year. She also supervised the canning of some one thousand cans of vegetables and the production of butter. Loftis and McCauley had built a two-acre fish pond, which provided water for spraying the orchard, as well as work for farm tenants. For the county farm agent, the Loftis farm illustrated the kind of diversified farming the agricultural extension service sought to promote.

The New Deal and the Textile Industry

The New Deal counterpart to the Agricultural Adjustment Act for industry was the National Industrial Recovery Act (NIRA). This act created the National Recovery Administration (NRA) which set up codes to regulate each industry to define labor standards and raise wages. But prior to the creation of the NRA, on March 3, there was a mass meeting of workers at Union Bleachery and Piedmont Print Works to protest the rumored reduction of the workday to eight hours. South Carolina mills could not compete, they said, if they were forced to pay as much for eight hours as they did for the ten-to eleven-hour schedule. They foresaw a cut in wages as inevitable. A similar meeting was held at Renfrew.[53]

As the NIRA moved through Congress, local textile owners joined in support of the forty-hour week. Victor-Monaghan President Thomas M. Marchant, who was also president of the American Cotton Manufacturers

Association, said in a speech in Charlotte on May 27 that "destructive competition" would be "eliminated by the newly developed policy of self-regulation under federal supervision." Eventually Marchant; Robert E. Henry, president of Dunean Mills; and Harry R. Stephenson, president of Southern Bleachery and Printworks, served on the committee of the Cotton Textile Institute that drew up the NRA textile code. Not only was the work week reduced, but the minimum wage for Southern workers was raised to twelve dollars a week—two dollars higher than the former pay scale. Bennette E. Geer, president of Judson Mills, was named one of three members of the National Industrial Relations Board for cotton textiles. J. E. Sirrine was a technical advisor to the board, and its national headquarters opened in the Federal Building in Greenville.[54]

Relief Agencies At Work

A most urgent need when Roosevelt took office in 1933 was the relief of personal distress. In Greenville local relief measures were inadequate, and the RFC had only limited resources. In May 1933 Congress created the Federal Emergency Relief Administration (FERA), which expanded the RFC program. In the winter of 1933–1934 the Civil Works Administration (CWA) was established to provide work on a wage basis. The Civilian Conservation Corps (CCC) employed thousands of young men in forests and in the creation of parks, and the Public Works Administration (PWA) made grants to state and local agencies for public improvements. The Works Progress Administration (WPA) replaced the CWA after the winter of 1934. Each of these agencies had a direct impact on the life of Greenville.[55]

FERA funds supported the Greenville County Emergency Relief Administration, which continued the work of the Welfare Service. Albert M. Rickman became the local administrator, and E. E. Hill was treasurer. Rickman operated the sewing room for women, the wood yard, and the community gardens established earlier. When the CWA came into existence, Rickman and Hill administered that program as well. They reported that 1,126 people were employed by the County Emergency Relief Administration, and in December 1933 the CWA funded sixteen projects in the amount of $356,295.[56]

Four CCC camps were established in Greenville County during the New Deal period. The first opened at Blythe Shoals near Cleveland in May 1933 when the 212 men of the 440th Company arrived for their first six months of service. Captain Ashley S. Legette from Fort Moultrie was in change of the camp, assisted by three reserve officers and three noncom missioned officers. The men were almost all from the South Carolina low country. The company's primary mission was to secure the forest against fire. In addition, the work included developing 118 miles of fire trails, 34 miles of sand gravel roads, and stringing 46 miles of telephone wires. On July 22 the camp was formally named Camp Palmetto.[57]

By 1935 the men at Camp Palmetto began construction of Paris Mountain State Park, the first such facility in Greenville County. On December 20, 1934, the Greenville City Council, the Chamber of Commerce, the Water Commission, and the Park and Tree Commission reached an agreement to deed 1,000 acres of the former watershed on Paris Mountain for a park. The county delegation agreed to seek the purchase of up to 150 acres to make the land contiguous. The lake on the property was drained and turned into a swimming pool, roads were surfaced, and brush was cleared. In December 1936 the camp at Blythe Shoals was moved to Paris Mountain, and the bathhouse and the caretaker's home were completed.[58]

Finally, on July 15, 1937, Paris Mountain State Park was dedicated. H. W. Lindsay, the new park superintendent, welcomed some five hundred people to the ceremonies. County Senator Ben T. Leppard delivered the main address, and the Greenville Municipal Band provided the music. That evening four thousand people gathered for a water pageant.[59]

Two additional CCC camps were constructed in Greenville County as part of the soil erosion demonstration project in the valley of the South Tyger River. The project, located in both Spartanburg and Greenville, was directed by Dr. T. S. Buie; the chief engineer was J. T. McAlister. One camp was built 2 miles north of Greer in the spring of 1934, and another was located near Tigerville on the farm of J. L. Lindsay. In addition to the filling of gulleys, some 35 feet deep, four million trees were planted to stabilize the soil.[60]

Work on the Reedy River within the city began in July 1933 with a grant from the RFC. Four hundred workers under the direction of City Engineer Dan Hulick modified the channel of the river for several miles. The meadows above Hudson Street were drained, and a new bed was dug in Cleveland Park. Bedrock was blasted from the shoals between Furman and the River Street bridge. After two years of work, five times as much water ran through the new channel, and the traditional smell associated with the Reedy began to diminish. On May 2, 1939, Congress approved a flood control project on the river above and below Greenville. A public hearing was convened in the city hall on July 26. George Anderson, president of the Virginia Manufacturing Company at Fork Shoals, described the flood of 1908 which caused fifty thousand dollars damage at Conestee

Mills and closed the plant for four years. L. Mell Glenn, secretary of the Chamber of Commerce, described the 1918 flood and the damage caused by the river in the city of Greenville in 1938.[61]

Major building renovations and additions were also made in Greenville with grants from New Deal agencies. Wings were constructed at both the City and St. Francis Hospitals. The municipal airport, which had been condemned by the Department of Commerce as a regular stop for mail in 1935, was completely overhauled and enlarged. Three major construction projects were Sirrine Stadium, a post office, and the new Greenville Senior High School.[62]

In September 1933 the Greenville City Council heard a request for a municipal stadium from a committee of the Park and Tree Commission composed of John A. McPherson (chair), Furman Coach A. P. "Dizzy" McLeod, and R. A. Jolly, president of the then-defunct Greenville baseball club. The council authorized the commission to proceed with plans for a twenty-thousand-seat stadium and to seek federal funds for construction. Not until the fall of 1935 did WPA Director Harry Hopkins submit the funding proposal to President Roosevelt. Finally, on Saturday, November 7, 1936, Greenville contractor Henry B. McKoy completed construction, and Sirrine Stadium, named in honor of J. E. Sirrine, was dedicated in the presence of U.S. Senator James F. Byrnes, Congressman G. Heyward Mahon, Governor Olin D. Johnston. The crowd then assembled for the Furman homecoming football game against the University of South Carolina.[63]

A year later, on September 27, 1937, the new post office building on the corner of East Washington and Church Streets (now the Clement F. Haynsworth, Jr., Federal Building) was dedicated. In March 1933 the city had begun negotiating for a new federal building to replace the grand, old post office built in 1892 in Victorian Romanesque style on South Main Street. Senator Byrnes and Congressman John J. McSwain secured an allocation of a half million dollars for the project. In February 1935 negotiations were concluded to allow the city to exchange the site of the old city hall, in use since the 1870s, on the corner of Laurens and West McBee Avenue, for the property on East Washington Street. In return, the city deeded that property to the federal government, and the federal government transferred the old post office on South Main Street to the city for use as a city hall.[64]

The cornerstone for the new post office was laid on November 7, 1936, and on September 27, 1937, a crowd of three thousand people gathered outside the handsome limestone structure to hear Postmaster General James A. Farley give major credit for the building to the recently deceased Congressman John J. McSwain. But Farley did not miss the opportunity to garner proper support for the Roosevelt administration: "I am glad to come to a state that gave [Roosevelt] the largest pro rata vote in both elections and into the county which I understand had the largest vote of any county."[65]

The new million-dollar high school on Augusta and Vardry Streets was made possible by a WPA grant of $488,000. Bids were opened on April 12, 1937, for the three-story, square, yellow brick building—designed by the J. E. Sirrine Company. The cornerstone was laid on July 27 with J. Rion McKissick, president of the University of South Carolina and former editor of the Greenville *News*, delivering the major address. At the same time, the College Place depot, at the foot of the hill near the new high school, was razed. Gone was Greenville's last visible link with the old Greenville and Columbia Railroad, stretching back to the 1850s.[66]

The New Deal on Main Street

The New Deal reached the Main Street business community in Greenville with the creation of the National Recovery Administration. On Friday night, July 29, 1933, local retailers met in the Library Hall to consider adoption of the NRA Code. They voted 100 percent in favor of the forty-hour week, a fourteen dollars weekly minimum wage, and daily store hours of 9:00 A.M. to 5:30 P.M., with late closing on Saturday at 6:30 P.M. The meeting enthusiastically voted to sponsor a "New Deal" parade, and the stores of Greenville soon displayed the NRA Blue Eagle of code compliance.[67]

A committee of citizens headed by R. W. (Pete) Hudgins agreed to solicit every business not represented at the meeting. The local Ku Klux Klan announced it would take action against businesses not subscribing to the code.[68]

The "New Deal" parade on August 1, 1933, wound along Augusta Street, up Main Street, and ended at the City Park. There Mayor Mann and Congressman Mahon delivered patriotic speeches. A mock trial of "Old Man Depression" followed with Clerk of Court T. E. Christenberry playing the "Old Man"; C. G. Wyche playing the prosecutor; and Lionel E. Wooten playing the defense attorney. Eventually "Old Man Depression" was convicted of causing untold misery for almost four years. He was hanged in effigy and burned in a bonfire.[69]

Nevertheless, an undercurrent of discontent with the code was explicit in an editorial in the *News* that same day: "One of the greatest problems which had faced employees is that of negro [sic] help." Locally, wages for blacks ranged from three dollars to ten dollars a week. When merchants inquired whether the minimum wage applied to black workers, the administration said it would not discriminate. The economic conditions for change in the racial orthodoxy of the South began to appear.[70]

Even the efforts of the New Deal did not relieve the needs of many people. On December 29, 1935, in the midst of a severe cold wave, 11 inches of snow fell on 3 inches already on the ground, the heaviest snowfall since 1930. The winter of 1935–1936 was the coldest since 1917–1918, and by February 1936 the Community Chest cut its funds by 10 percent. The Relief Committee of the Greenville Ministerial Union, chaired by Robert T. Phillips, the rector of Christ Church, called for the organization of a new county relief organization. The board of the Community Chest, whose president was Charles H. Nabors, the pastor of the First Presbyterian Church, supported the effort.[71]

On February 21, 1936, twenty-one leaders of Greenville formed the board of the Greenville County Relief Organization. Frank G. Hamblen was elected president, and J. Edgar Stockman, the pastor of Trinity Lutheran Church, secretary. The executive committee included Robert E. Henry, Fred W. Symmes, J. E. Sirrine, and Roger C. Peace. Hamblen appointed Nabors as chair of a committee to investigate what was being done.[72]

The General Textile Strike of 1934

The most serious unrest in Greenville during this period was the General Textile Strike of September 1934. Discontent over the stretch-out had smoldered since 1929, but the passage of the NIRA in 1933 brought the union movement back to life. Section 7(a) of the NIRA required the codes to include the right of workers to collective bargaining. A thousand workers at Poe Mill went out on strike in May 1933 charging that the mill had instituted the stretch-out. By June the UTWA claimed more than a thousand members in the Greenville area, the largest number in history.[73]

United States Senator James F. Byrnes called the stretch-out "a running sore which is the constant source of controversy between worker and manufacturer," and on June 20 asked for a nationwide investigation by the industrial relations board with a view toward eliminating the practice. A series of hearings were held before a three-person panel, including Bennette E. Geer, who represented the textile manufacturers. Geer indicated his hope that a regulation could be written into the textile code dealing with the machine load of employees.[74]

On July 14 the panel heard testimony in Greenville's federal courtroom. Senator Byrnes attended and questioned the witnesses. Samuel M. Beattie, president of the S.C. Cotton Manufacturers Association, testified that "if evils existed in the system, they would be properly and promptly corrected." But he "decried a set per-employee machine load." Mill owners and workers from Piedmont, Poe, Brandon, Poinsett, Monaghan, and Judson No. 2 mills testified privately. The workers indicated that the stretch-out was in force. C. W. Roe, a retired minister who described himself as a former mill hand and a present employee of the Reconstruction Finance Corporation at one dollar a day, said that Poe Mill stretched-out the work after giving a 10 percent pay increase. He added that they had laid off sixty-one men and cut wages 55 percent since 1929.[75]

On August 1, 1933, General Hugh S. Johnson, director of the NRA, approved an amendment to the Textile Code that banned the stretch-out. Geer and the other members of the panel were appointed to the Cotton Textile National Industrial Relations Board. This body was directed to hear complaints and mediate disputes, but it lacked the power to enforce the numerous violations.[76]

When temporary curtailments occurred at some mills in December 1933, local dissatisfaction reappeared. Lewis E. Brookshire obtained a leave of absence from the Greenville *News* and became the local organizer for the American Federation of Labor. In March 1934 Francis J. Gorman, the vice president of the UTWA, threatened a general strike "owing to alleged exploitation by mill owners." Thomas Marchant, president of the American Cotton Manufacturers Association, challenged Gorman to prove such an allegation.[77]

On April 21 nearly seven hundred textile workers from all over the state met at the library to organize the South Carolina Federation of Textile Workers. Thomas F. McMahon of New York, president of the UTWA, was present. The group endorsed the Wagner bill, pending before Congress, which guaranteed the right to collective bargaining. Further, the group demanded government enforcement of the stretch-out amendment. If the government can do nothing, the group declared, then the workers will ask the UTWA for permission to settle the matter in our own way.[78]

On August 15, 1934, the national convention of the UTWA voted for a general strike to begin on September 4, the day after Labor Day. A week later John A. Peel, the southern UTWA organizer, announced that Greenville would be the headquarters for the strike. There were, Peel reported, about forty-five thousand operatives in the state who had become members. He was optimistic that South Carolina's sixty-eight local unions would lend their support.[79]

By August 31, however, the *News* reported that in eight local mills overwhelming majorities were opposed. At Woodside Mill 523 out of 525 workers signed a statement protesting the strike; at Monaghan 795 out of

800 workers signed. Poe Mill, with sixteen, and Brandon, with eighteen, had the largest number of people supporting the strike. At a meeting in West Greenville, UTW organizer George W. Smith was greeted with rotten eggs, overripe tomatoes, and soft watermelon rinds. He told the workers: "You might not strike at first, but you will later on." To which many replied: "We don't want to strike. We want to work."[80]

Nevertheless, Francis Gorman laid plans for the strike with appropriate flourishes by sending "sealed orders" to local unions and making appropriate use of the telegraph, newspapers, and radio. He devised the "flying squadron"—a caravan of strikers who drove from mill to mill in an attempt to persuade workers to close down those mills that remained open. But Gorman had no war chest and no broad-based labor support. He faced hostility from the mill owners and growing animosity from the NRA. Nevertheless, as Southern historian and Greenville native George Tindall wrote, "it was the largest strike in American history to that time, its scope a new experience for Southern mills."[81]

On Labor Day, the day before the strike began, there was a parade on Main Street that concluded with a rally at the City Park. A crowd of four thousand heard from two North Carolina labor leaders. Council M. Fox, a young UTW organizer who represented labor on the Textile Industrial Relations Board, told the workers: "Do your part, and you will win." Meanwhile Governor Blackwood ordered national guard troops into the Piedmont. Thirty-four men of Company E, 105th Engineers, commanded by Captain Ray Page, went to Victor Mill in Greer. Shortly before midnight, fifty-three men of Company F, 118th Infantry, under the command of Captain James L. Rogers, arrived at Dunean, while labor picket squads took up positions around the mill.[82]

All the mills in Greenville opened as usual the following day, though American Spinning and Dunean closed for lack of personnel. At American Spinning, handbills announced "The Strike is On" and "Don't Be a Scab." Strips of red flannel were tied to the mill gates. At Dunean, workers had to walk through lines of pickets, and at Poe Mill workers were on guard. At the Poinsett Mill only male operatives arrived at 6:00 A.M.; the women came an hour later. The *News* estimated that thirteen thousand workers (37 percent of the mill workers in the South Carolina Piedmont) were on strike. Greenville County accounted for about 11.5 percent of the thirteen thousand workers, and almost all of those were from American Spinning, Dunean, and Conestee, where a strike had been in progress for several weeks.[83]

At Dunean, Sheriff B. B. Smith asked for no violence. O. T. Hopkins, the leader of the strike squad, assured him there would be none, but he was

Greenville Airport, 1928. Courtesy of Greenville County Library.

Shriners Hospital, 1927. Courtesy of Dr. Frank H. Stelling.

KKK March (undated). Courtesy of Joe F. Jordan.

Relief Agencies, Ladies with Quilt, late 1930s. Courtesy of Roper Mountain
Science Center, Coxe Collection.

Franklin D. Roosevelt with Mayor A. C. Mann, May 25, 1932. Courtesy of
Choice McCoin from the collection of Mr. and Mrs. John P. Mann.

CWA—Cleveland Park. Courtesy of Roper Mountain Science Center, Coxe Collection.

Dedication of Greenville Post Office, 1937. Courtesy of Roper Mountain Science Center, Coxe Collection.

Greenville High School, 1937. Courtesy of Oscar Landing.

Greenville Army Air Base. Courtesy of Choice McCoin from the collection of
Greenville County Library.

War Bond or Red Cross Drive. Courtesy of Choice McCoin from the collection of Greenville County Library.

Max Heller. Courtesy of Max Heller.

Alester G. Furman, Jr. Courtesy of
Roper Mountain Science Center,
Coxe Collection.

Peace Center Complex and downtown Greenville. Courtesy of Joe F. Jordan.

March on the Airport, January 1, 1960. Courtesy of James G. Wilson.

Charles E. Daniel. Courtesy of
Furman University, Special Collections.

bitter about the presence of troops. "We have done nothing to deserve having those troops sent here," a strike spokesperson said, "we have been as orderly as any group of persons could possibly be. . . . Everything has been so sweet you would think it was sugar-coated."[84]

The outward calm was shattered on the afternoon of September 4 when the first flying squadron arrived in Greer. About five hundred strikers from Spartanburg arrived in a caravan of two large trucks and a forty or more automobiles. The men, armed with oak clubs, were accompanied by a number of women and children. They forced the Victor Mill to close at 3:45 P.M. and then moved on to the Franklin and Apalache mills.[85]

By the next day Governor Blackwood had dispatched four additional national guard units to Greenville, bringing the total to some seven hundred troops. Colonel Harry O. Withington of Charleston was in direct command. The police stationed motorcycle officers at every highway leading into the city. When the flying squadron appeared, it had grown to a caravan of 105 trucks and cars, led by an automobile bearing a huge American flag. At the city limits the caravan was escorted by officers to the west side of Greenville, directly to Dunean Mill.[86]

At Dunean, Morris Campbell, the vice president of the S.C. Federation of Textile Workers, addressed the workers from the steps of the mill office declaring that the union was determined to close every mill in Greenville. Captain Harry Arthur, commander of the national guard unit from Union, which he proudly called the "strong arm" group, instructed his men to "shoot to kill" only in case of extreme necessity. Members of the flying squadron, aided by strikers from Dunean, shouted to the workers to come out. The guard members held their ground, and the squadron moved on to Judson.[87]

The first death occurred in Greenville a few minutes after Dunean Mill opened. Mill Deputy R. L. Putman shot and killed John Black, as Black advanced on him with a knife. Shortly thereafter a rumor circulated that the Duke Power substation at Monaghan was about to be dynamited. Captain Arthur rushed to Monaghan with a detachment of troops, but there was no sign of a threat. Mayor McHardy Mauldin called Governor Blackwood and requested a declaration of martial law.[88]

The flying squadron arrived at Judson at three o'clock in the afternoon. For an hour about twenty-five hundred strikers stormed the mill gates. Five persons were injured, including Deputy Sheriff Charlie Batson, who was disarmed. When the mill continued to operate, the caravan moved on to Woodside and then to Monaghan mills. At Woodside, several hundred strikers attempted to rush the troops and reach the mill workers who were drawing their pay envelopes at the office. The guard members fired tear gas into the strikers who then dispersed. All the mills in Greenville continued to operate, though some with reduced work forces.[89]

Some 40 miles away at Honea Path, the violence reached a bloody climax when police and deputized workers killed seven strikers on Thursday, September 6. The next day the governor issued a proclamation urging all persons to return to their homes by noon on Saturday. This was a preliminary step to a declaration of martial law, which the governor issued on Sunday, September 9. On Tuesday, September 11, John Peel, from his UTW office in Greenville, ordered the flying squadrons in South Carolina to disperse. President Roosevelt appointed a mediation board which called for additional study of wages, hours, and workloads. Thomas Marchant and Robert Henry were among those who spoke before the board. On September 13 the Greenville *News* reported that every mill in Greenville County operated with a full force yesterday for the first time in a week. There were picket lines at several mills, but the strike was effectively over.[90]

By the time Francis Gorman officially halted the strike in October, the union was badly beaten. According to the *News,* scores of strikers reported that they were refused employment when they returned to work. The UTW provided them with no recourse. By 1937 the union had only 726 members in South Carolina, and only one local union remained in Greenville. Nonunion workers felt betrayed by the general strike, and sometimes they attacked those who had supported the strike. Mill owners no longer felt the necessity of giving lip-service to collective bargaining. The new key words were efficiency, coordination, and profits.[91]

The division in Greenville between mill workers and mill owners was clearly shown in the state gubernatorial election held at the height of the strike. The two candidates were former governor and U.S. Senator Coleman L. Blease, once the darling of the textile mill workers, and Olin D. Johnston, the son of Anderson County tenant farmers and himself a former mill worker. Johnston swept the state, and in Greenville the mill precincts went overwhelmingly for "the cotton mill boy." In Dunean, for example, Johnston led Blease by 447 votes to 163. But in Ward 1, Box 1 in the city of Greenville, Blease led Johnston by 604 votes to 290.[92]

The old, paternalistic world of the mill village was passing. As early as 1933 Senator Byrnes argued that "a mill-owned village is repugnant to every true American principle." He called on the textile industry "to bring its workers into a house owning class." A "large mill owner in South Carolina," unidentified by name in the Greenville *News,* was convinced that textile workers, with a shortened work week, "would want to own their own homes." In August 1939 Judson Mill offered fifty-four houses for sale to their employees for an average price of one thousand dollars. The old order was beginning to change.[93]

Changing Race Relations

Few Greenvillians, white or black, in the 1930s could have imagined that the age of racial segregation was not permanent. Metropolitan Greenville was divided into distinct white and black neighborhoods. The black business district continued to occupy the area east of South Main Street and included East McBee Avenue, East Court, and East Broad Streets. Some five or six blocks east were the six black residential communities, which almost touched one another: Little Texas, Bucknertown, Southernside, Meadow Bottom, the Union School section, and Haynie Street. Insulating these communities from the white residential areas were small businesses and deteriorating rental property occupied by whites. On paved or unpaved side streets were large and medium houses owned or rented by black families. Behind the side streets were narrow, unpaved alleys lined with small houses, many in poor condition. The centers of these communities were black churches and schools, while small grocery stores served as informal gathering places.[94]

Less distinct were four other black communities within the city— Greenline, Newtown, Gower-Birnie Street, and Washington Heights. Even less well defined was an area known as "out toward Washington Heights," of which Sullivan Street was a subdivision. Outside the city were Nicholtown, Sterling Annex, Brutontown, and the black sections of Union Bleachery, Monaghan, West Greenville, and Freetown.[95]

In 1930 the city of Greenville had a small professional class of 251 black citizens. Most were teachers and ministers. There were four doctors, three dentists, and a veterinarian, as well as librarians, funeral directors, and tailors. There were very few skilled laborers, and most black workers were domestic or personal servants, with a smaller number in transportation and various trades. Those working in textile mills were odd-jobbers or cleaners.[96]

One black citizen interviewed by sociologist Joseph Drake in the late 1930s said that "times are better now for the Negro than they used to be." But the statement was relative to the era of the Great Depression. Another assured Drake that "a white employer would not hire Negroes on jobs that paid as much as five dollars a day, but would hire a white man regardless of his ability."[97]

What was described as "a reign of terror" by the Greenville *News* occurred in March 1933 among the black residents of the Princeton section of Greenville, Laurens, Anderson, and Greenwood Counties. After a black man was charged with assaulting a white woman and sent to the state penitentiary for safekeeping, unmasked mobs of whites appeared by night, seized several blacks, beat them, and ordered them to leave the country. White landowners offered some protection to their tenants, allowing them to sleep in buildings nearby. On March 18 Greenville Sheriff B. B. Smith mobilized deputies and the highway patrol to guard the area in cooperation with the Laurens sheriff.[98]

On November 16, 1933, the first lynching occurred in Greenville County in twenty-four years. Of the four previous lynchings in the twentieth century, two occurred in 1905 and two in 1909.[99] About eight o'clock in the evening, a black man and woman were taken from a house near Greer, stripped to the waist, and beaten by about twelve robed and masked men. Two hours later, a mob of nineteen arrived at the home of George Green near Taylors. They broke into the house and shot through the bedroom door. Green was hit in the chest and killed. Mrs. Green was pulled out of bed, but she was not harmed.[100]

Eventually, eighteen white men were arrested for murder—ten were indicted, and seven came to trial in November 1934. Once it was revealed that the defendants were Ku Klux Klan members from the Poinsett Klavern in Greenville, a large crowd filled the courtroom. Andrew Monk, a former Klan member, testified that he carried a message from Green's landlord, the late C. F. James of Taylors, to the Klan. The message indicated that James "desired to have the darkey moved out of his house." Monk praised the Christian character of James and reported that the Klan often consulted the chief of police or the sheriff before taking any action. After the jury deliberated for two hours, the defendants were set free.[101]

Despite segregation and terrorism, there were signs of a new spirit in the black community. By 1930 a local branch of the National Association for the Advancement of Colored People (NAACP) had been organized in Greenville, and two years later NAACP executive Robert Bagnall found "a decided revolt from . . . complacency on the part of young Negroes."[102]

This spirit of activism suddenly appeared on July 5, 1939, when fifty-seven blacks, mostly women, registered to vote in the forthcoming municipal general election. The *News* reported that some of the leading black citizens of Greenville were among the registrants. Several weeks before, the city council had turned down the request of the local housing authority to match a federal grant of eight hundred thousand dollars for a housing project, and J. A. Brier, president of the local NAACP, had appointed a committee to organize a voters' club. Assisting the black citizens to register were William Anderson, assistant secretary of the Greenville NAACP and president of the Negro Youth Council, and several men who wore badges of the Workers Alliance, an organization of WPA workers. Anderson told a Greenville *News* reporter that he expected that one thousand blacks would register by 1940 and perhaps as many as five thousand.[103]

Revival of Klan Activity

The Ku Klux Klan immediately responded to the voter registration effort. Fred V. Johnson, who was identified as the Klan "chief of staff in South Carolina," announced that the Klan would ride again in South Carolina and in the nation and preserve white supremacy. He called attention to a classified advertisement in the Greenville *News:* "FIERY SUMMONS.— All Klansmen are called to action regarding white supremacy. Read article in News of sixth concerning registration of negroes for city election. Write P.O. Box 1511, Greenville." Johnson attacked the NAACP and the Negro Youth movement, both of which met at the Phillis Wheatley Center that was supported by the Community Chest. He also attacked the Workers Alliance as the "WPA union" which was connected with the CIO. The CIO, he pointed out, had high officials that were Communists.[104]

Prior to the September municipal election, the Klan became highly visible in Greenville. On August 17 eight automobiles filled with Klan members paraded through the city. Despite the intimidation, 34 of the 230 registered blacks voted. On September 24 some fifty hooded men rode through Simpsonville and Fountain Inn. Fifteen to twenty blacks were beaten. Two months later, on November 15, five cars filled with thirty Klan members gathered in Sterling Annex in Greenville. One of the Klan members said they were seeking "a dangerous negro"; another announced they planned to ride all night. On November 22 the city council requested that J. E. Smith, the chief of police, ask the Klan "not to parade 'too much' in negro districts of the city." When Mayor C. Fred McCullough was asked what might happen if the Klan did not desist, he replied: "The law will be enforced." He did not elaborate.[105]

Klan membership in the nation as a whole dwindled in the 1930s to no more than fifty thousand. In April 1940 the state Grand Dragon Ben E. Adams of Columbia announced that two hundred members of the Klan in Greenville had been dropped from the rolls. He also indicated that the order of the Imperial Wizard dispensing with masks and ending night-riding would be enforced. However, the Klan conducted an initiation ceremony in the City Park on July 25 before a fifteen-foot burning cross, preceded by a parade of between 150 and 200 Klan members.[106]

The attitudes of many blacks about the Klan had begun to change. However, when the Klan rode, some still ran for shelter. Others, of the middle class, sat at home hoping they would not be harmed, but were prepared to resist. One black citizen told Joseph Drake: "Yesterday they ran when the klan rode, today they just stand to see what is going to happen. Tomorrow they will not stand, they will fight if given any provocation." A growing number of young blacks were "determined to meet the klan more than half way if trouble threatens."[107]

By 1940 many blacks in Greenville were willing to speak at least privately about their desires for a greater role in the community. These Greenvillians wanted the right to vote on the same basis as whites; wanted equal pay for equal work and a fair deal in the courts; wanted equality in education, housing, and recreational facilities; and wanted to be free from intimidation and the right to be treated as human beings, not animals.[108]

Political Reaction to the New Deal

The economic and social unrest that shook Greenville during this period had an impact on the political system. In September 1935 the Southern Committee to Uphold the Constitution was formed in Washington with the avowed purpose of campaigning against the renomination of Franklin Roosevelt. Retired banker John W. Norwood lead a delegation of four from Greenville to a meeting of the committee in Macon, Georgia, in January 1936. The group included J. W. Norwood, Jr., a member of the city council; E. W. Montgomery, a cotton broker; and George R. Koester, editor of a weekly newspaper.[109]

There was increasing local dissatisfaction with the Democratic Party when a black minister was invited to pray at the national convention in Philadelphia in 1936. South Carolina Senator "Cotton Ed" Smith and Charleston Mayor Burnet R. Maybank walked out of the convention. In a letter to the *News,* J. S. Goodwin complained that "Roosevelt [had] out-Lincolned Lincoln. . . . What is the big idea of this departure from the old democratic traditional practices? Have the democrats turned over a new leaf, or are they fishing for a big catch?" Such dissatisfaction did not impede a sweeping Democratic victory for Roosevelt over Governor Alfred Landon of Kansas. In Greenville County, the vote in November 1936 was 8,310 for Roosevelt and 92 for Landon.[110]

South Carolina Republicans offered little solace to dissatisfied whites. They were still divided between the Tolbert faction, which included black voters, and the Hambright "lily-white" group. In February 1936 the two factions organized rival Greenville County conventions. J. D. Langford was elected county chair of the Hambright faction, and Joseph A. Tolbert was elected chair of the Tolbert faction. At the national Republican convention the Tolbert faction replaced the Hambright faction as the official state Republican Party. On July 4 Joseph Tolbert addressed a small, local Republican rally in Cleveland Hall, warning the black members of the audience against deserting the GOP: "The colored citizens of the United States know the Democratic Party kept them in human bondage as long as it could do so; they know it is still keeping them in economic and commercial slavery."[111]

But white Democrats in South Carolina were not afraid of standing up to the national party—or to a popular president like Roosevelt—if need be. "Cotton Ed" Smith and other conservative Southern Democratic senators had become increasingly disillusioned with the New Deal. Roosevelt chose the primary elections of 1938 to attempt to purge these senators. In a speech from a train in Greenville Roosevelt called on South Carolina voters to defeat "Cotton Ed" and elect Governor Olin D. Johnston to the Senate. With the support of Roger Peace and the *News*, Smith was overwhelmingly re-elected, and one wag remarked that Roosevelt's Greenville speech may have been the only thing that saved Smith.[112]

In 1940 Roosevelt ran for an unprecedented third term. The county Democratic convention, chaired by attorney Alfred F. Burgess, endorsed FDR's candidacy, and C. Granville Wyche, keynote speaker for the state convention in Columbia, as well as Burgess's law partner and father-in-law, praised the achievements of the Roosevelt administration. Greenville County continued to support Roosevelt, but the Republican vote was larger—7,143 for Roosevelt; 517 for Wendell Willkie. Less than a year later, on August 7, 1941, Roger Peace, president of the Greenville News-Piedmont Company, one of Wyche's chief clients, was sworn in as a U.S. senator to complete the term of James F. Byrnes, who had been appointed to the U.S. Supreme Court.[113]

But the New Deal did little to unify the business elite in Greenville, which had split over reductions in the early 1930s. When the local Taxpayers' League continued to press for reduction of municipal salaries, city employees organized a boycott of local business people who supported what they called "the Conyers petition." William G. Sirrine, attorney and president of Textile Hall, expressed confidence in both the city council and the Taxpayers group in a letter to the *News*, although he expected no reduction of expenses for 1933.[114]

On January 18, 1933, the finance committee of the city council—Kerr

Wilson, James M. Richardson, and W. E. Freeman—met with the citizens committee, composed of C. Benjamin Martin, James F. Gallivan, and Marshall Prevost. The finance committee indicated the reduction of the deficit from $158,248.12 in 1930 to $76,876.78 in 1933. The deliberations resulted in a proposed reduction of salaries, some by as much as 50 percent.[115]

As a result, the race for mayor in the city Democratic primary became a contest between the two factions. John McHardy Mauldin, the son of former Lieutenant-Governor William L. Mauldin and a one-term member of city council, denounced Mayor A. C. Mann and "all but one alderman" as a political ring. Mann, who had been mayor for two terms, refused to run for re-election. In a statement he declared that "we have encountered many unexpected obstacles and difficulties, but in spite of these there has been no curtailment of service on the part of the various city operations and departments."[116]

For mayor, Mauldin faced James M. Richardson, former state senator (1925–1928), alderman (1931–1933), and member of the city council's finance committee. Prior to the election, the police department campaigned strenuously for Richardson; nevertheless, McHardy Mauldin was elected by fifty-five votes in what he called "the fiercest political battle in the history of Greenville." The mayor-elect then denounced the "pernicious activity of the police department"—assuring the citizenry that "merit will be recognized wherever found, but treachery I will not abide."[117]

A. C. Mann returned to his law practice with John L. Plyler, and Mann's supporters elected him president of the Chamber of Commerce. In December 1935 Mann attacked McHardy Mauldin for supporting a pay raise for the mayor. After serving two contentious terms, Mauldin refused to run again. "I have been constantly opposed," he said, "by people whose motives I could not then and do not yet understand. . . . Doctors have told me I could not stand the strain of another political campaign." C. Fred McCullough was elected to succeed Mauldin in 1937, and Mann returned to public office as city attorney.[118]

County government entered a new era when Ollie Southern Farnsworth announced her candidacy for register of mesne conveyance (RMC) in 1936. Born in Tigerville, the daughter of George and Nannie Southern, she attended North Greenville Academy, moved to Greenville in 1919, and began work in the RMC office. She later married Wallace Farnsworth, a native of Kentucky. Ollie Farnsworth won the Democratic primary and thus began a new career as Greenville's first woman elected official.[119]

Unsettling Social Issues

Prohibition remained a political issue in Greenville even after the election of Franklin Roosevelt. In 1932 Mrs. J. W. Jervey became Greenville County chair of the Woman's Organization for National Prohibition Reform—a group dedicated to the repeal of the Eighteenth Amendment and the establishment of better laws for the regulation of saloons. When repeal came, South Carolina reverted to the 1915 statute that allowed the sale of beer and wine, but not whiskey. The first sale of beer in Greenville after repeal occurred on April 14, 1933, at a local roadhouse where one hundred bottles were sold for twenty cents a bottle. By April 17 a limited supply went on sale, according to the *News,* in the dining room of a local hotel. The availability of beer caused the demand for bootleg whiskey to drop precipitously. The price in the mountains was one dollar a gallon, and in the city the price dropped in a week from twenty to twenty-five cents a bottle to ten cents.[120]

Meanwhile, Prohibition forces fought for a state referendum. Sergeant Alvin York, one of the heroes of World War I, appeared in Greenville on Sunday, October 15, 1933, to speak in favor of prohibition at Parker High School and the First Baptist Church. In November 1933 the voters of Greenville County supported prohibition, but a year later the wet forces triumphed. Legal sales of whiskey began in Greenville on May 27, 1935, for the first time in twenty-seven years. In July the First Baptist Church condemned the sale of whiskey as immoral and pled with members to abstain, and four months later the Central Baptist Church withdrew fellowship from two members because they worked in liquor stores.[121]

Furman and Community Development

Furman University and the Greenville Woman's College were swept up in community involvement and social reform during the 1930s. Furman's president, William J. McGlothlin, gratefully accepted James Buchanan Duke's inclusion of the university in the Duke Endowment and presided over coordination with the Woman's College. His career, however, was cut short by a fatal automobile accident in May 1933 and he was succeeded by Bennette E. Geer, the president of Judson Mills and a trustee of the Duke Endowment.[122]

In May 1936 Geer informed the Furman board that the two colleges had received a grant of eighty thousand dollars from the General Education Board to fund a five-year project of community development. This undertaking, he said, would be a cooperative effort involving the colleges, the city of Greenville, the Greenville and Parker District schools, the public library, and a number of government agencies. Coordinator of the project was the Greenville County Council for Community Development, chaired by Geer. L. P. Hollis became chair of the executive committee.[123]

The social science professors were enthusiastic about the program as a "way to social reform." Soon students were at work on surveys of local social service agencies, rural school buildings, and recreational facilities. Faculty members, such as sociologist Laura Ebaugh, served as consultants for various welfare organizations. An interracial committee, under the leadership of Hollis, brought black and white Greenvillians together to work on community problems. An investigation of black housing by students of Professor Gordon W. Blackwell was incorporated into a request by the local housing authority for federal funds for public housing. The federal grant was approved, but the city council rejected the request for matching funds.[124]

In 1938 the Negro Council for Community Development was created as a part of the larger group. R. O. Johnson became director of the council, and the officers were Dr. E. A. E. Huggins, president; J. E. Beck, vice president; R. E. Lipscomb, secretary; and E. C. Murray, treasurer.[125]

The community development program attracted national attention. Edmund de S. Brunner, professor of education at Teachers College of Columbia University, became advisor to the project in 1938 and prepared the final report to the General Education Board. In 1939 and 1940 Columbia University selected Greenville as the site of a field course to study Southern conditions in agriculture, labor, health, education, and race relations. In 1941 the American Council on Education and the General Education Board brought fifty leaders from the southeastern states to Greenville to evaluate the project. If some local residents were alarmed by the Progressive and interracial aspects of the program, Furman was still considered to be in the mainstream of American reform thought.[126]

Less acceptable to religious conservatives and fundamentalists was the growing perception of Furman as a haven for the modern scholarly study of the Bible and the theology of the social gospel. A storm of protest broke over the university following Religious Emphasis Week in February 1938. The principal speaker was Gordon Poteat, professor of social ethics at Crozer Theological Seminary and the son of former President Edwin McNeill Poteat. He antagonized conservative students by minimizing doctrine and emphasizing the relevance of faith to life. When Poteat's position was defended by Professor Herbert Gezork, J. Dean Crain, a Furman trustee, mobilized the ministers of the local Baptist associations. In July 1938 a special session of the Furman Board of Trustees fired Gezork, who went on to teach at Wellesley College and Andover-Newton Seminary (where he served as president from 1950 to 1965). Furman faculty members responded by forming a campus chapter of the American Association of University Professors. President Geer, who was already in difficulty with the trustees over fiscal and athletic policies, resigned before the Gezork affair was concluded. Clearly the winds of change were blowing across University Ridge.[127]

A Local Radio Station

The residents of Greenville were even more closely tied to the current thought of both nation and world when a local radio station finally went on the air. The *News* reported on April 30, 1933, that the efforts of B. H. Peace and his sons to secure a station had finally been successful. B. H. Peace, Jr., became station manager of WFBC, the call letters of the new station, and Charles H. Crutchfield became the program director. Studios were constructed on the second floor of the Imperial Hotel, and transmitting towers were erected on West Faris Road. WFBC began to operate with twenty-five watts during the day and one hundred watts at night.[128]

The radio station aired its first program on May 16 when George W. Quick, pastor of the First Baptist Church, and B. Rhett Turnipseed, pastor of Buncombe Street Methodist Church, offered prayers. B. H. Peace made a brief statement which was a climax to his career in communications. At a luncheon for the Chamber of Commerce following the broadcast, Roger and B. H. Peace, Jr., spoke, representing a change in generations. In October 1935 the Federal Communications Commission authorized the station to increase its power to five thousand watts, and in March 1936 WFBC became an affiliate of the National Broadcasting System.[129]

Already a Greenville native was at work on the next stage of development in communications. Dr. Thomas T. Goldsmith, Jr., a grandson of Furman President Charles Manly and an alumnus of Furman, was director of research for Allen B. DuMont Laboratories in New Jersey. Goldsmith developed a number of refinements on DuMont's work and held a number of patents on the early development of television. Eventually WTTG in Washington, a station of the DuMont network, carried Goldsmith's initials.[130]

Historical Awareness in the Community

The search for stability in a changing era led a group of Greenvillians to raise the historical consciousness of the community that in a more prosperous time had removed the Confederate Monument from Main Street and razed its century-old courthouse. On January 17, 1927, J. Rion McKissick, soon to become dean of the School of Journalism at the University of South Carolina, began a series of popular lectures on the history of South Carolina at Furman. In May 1928, mainly through the efforts of Mrs. Albert D. Oliphant, forty charter members organized the Upper South Carolina Historical Society.[131]

Mary C. Simms Oliphant, born in 1891 in Barnwell, was the granddaughter of antebellum author William Gilmore Simms. In 1917 Mrs. Oliphant revised Simms's *History of South Carolina* for use in the public schools, and in 1927 she published an elementary textbook, *The South Carolina Reader*. In the 1930s she had already begun her greatest scholarly achievement in cooperation with Furman Professor A. T. Odell—the collection and eventual publication of *The Letters of William Gilmore Simms* in six volumes.[132]

The historical society met at the public library and presented scholarly papers by local historians and invited lecturers such as Alexander S. Salley, Jr., secretary of the S.C. Historical Commission, and Wofford Professor David Duncan Wallace. The society began to mark historic sites in the upstate, and eventually joined the state Historical Commission in a statewide program funded by the WPA. The first county marker under the state program was erected on the site of the Mills Courthouse on Main Street. Other patriotic groups joined the effort: the Daughters of the American Revolution (DAR) marking the site of the William Butler plantation on Pelham Road, and the United Daughters of the Confederacy (UDC) marking the Soldiers' Rest at the Woman's College.[133]

The centennial of the incorporation of Greenville as a town was celebrated by a pageant at Textile Hall on November 19, 1931. The celebration was coordinated by John S. Taylor, then president of the historical society, which sponsored the event in cooperation with the local DAR and UDC chapters, the American Legion Auxiliary, the Boy Scouts, and the Girl Scouts. There were fifty speaking roles and six hundred persons in the cast. The sixteen episodes began with Cherokee dancers and concluded with farmers, spinners, and weavers before the throne of King Cotton. E. M. Blythe played John C. Calhoun, and C. G. Wyche portrayed Benjamin F. Perry.[134]

Social and Cultural Life

The rhythm of life for the families of the business elite changed very little in the 1930s. During the summer months they closed their homes in the city and moved to mountain resorts such as Mountain Lake Colony, Caesar's Head, and Cedar Mountain. In 1936 Dr. Alexander R. Mitchell, who had first come to Greenville in 1900 as rector of Christ Church and had established three mission churches, became concerned about the lack of worship services for the summer migrants. He held a service at Cedar Mountain that summer, and plans were made to build Faith Memorial Chapel, named in honor of the structure built by Bishop Ellison Capers in 1894.[135]

The 1930s saw the formation of local cultural institutions that enhanced Greenville's role in the arts. When the Greenville Woman's College orchestra, composed of students and townspeople, disbanded during World War I, the women members formed an ensemble that continued to perform. In 1938 Lennie Lusby suggested to Guy Hutchins, the director of music at Greenville High School, that the high school group merge with the college group and the townspeople to form a symphony. Hutchins agreed to become the director, and the Greenville Symphony Orchestra played its first concert on April 14, 1938. The orchestra was sponsored by the Music Forum consisting of Mrs. Richard Watson, president; Mrs. Robert I. Woodside, vice president; Mrs. Milton Smith, secretary; Mrs. Edward Mears, treasurer; Mrs. Charles Lee; and Mrs. C. C. Withington.[136]

The renewed interested in music was paralleled by a rising interest in the visual arts. The first effort to establish an art museum was made by the Greenville Lions Club in the fall of 1927 under the leadership of Dr. T. W. Sloan, pastor of the First Presbyterian Church. Sloan was elected president of the museum Board of Trustees, whose first purchase consisted of plaster casts of the Apollo Belvedere, Diana, and Venus de Milo. The statues were placed in Library Hall in the city library, but a storm of protest broke out over the public display of nudity. J. D. Gilbert introduced a resolution at a meeting of the Community Chest board calling for the removal of the "so called art." In response, there was a sudden rush of art patrons to view the statues. On March 22, 1928, Apollo received a pair of pink knickers with light green trim, which came by special delivery mail addressed to "Mr. Apollo." On November 3, 1935, the *News* noted that Apollo, Diana, and Venus had been banished to the third floor of the library.[137]

In the fall of 1932 Anna Tibbetts, president of the Thursday Afternoon Club, appointed a committee chaired by Mrs. Hiden T. Cox to survey the art of Greenville. On March 2, 1933, the club sponsored a tour of the private collections of Wilkins Norwood and Marshall Prevost, as well the studio of local artist, Margaret Moore Walker. In the fall of 1934 Walker and Prevost invited local artists to participate in a show in the hall of the public library. Interest was overwhelming both in showing paintings and viewing them.[138]

A permanent organization followed on May 11, 1935, when seventeen artists met at the home of Marshall Prevost on Washington Place to organize the Fine Arts League. The League sponsored not only showings of its own work but also public lectures, demonstrations, and outside exhibits. The first exhibit opened on November 4, 1935, in the library.[139]

A permanent gallery was funded by the WPA on the Furman campus and sponsored by the Fine Arts League. Eventually the gallery moved to the city hall, where it remained until after World War II. A series of WPA traveling exhibits exposed Greenville citizens to a wide variety of contemporary art. When the WPA ended its funding for the gallery, the Art League, then chaired by Mrs. L. O. Patterson, attempted to raise the funds to keep the gallery open. The city and county governments pledged nine hundred dollars each to pay the salary of Mrs. Sue Ferguson, the director, and friends of the League pledged an additional sum.[140]

The "little theater" movement had reached Greenville prior to the 1930s. In the spring of 1926 the local branch of the American Association of University Women invited Daniel Reid, the director of the Columbia Town Theatre, to bring his troupe for a performance of *The Circle* at the Woman's College. The following day Reid spoke to a group of seventy-five persons who then organized the Greenville Artists' Guild. The initial officers of the group were John W. Arrington, president; Mrs. W. L. Gassaway, first vice-president; Jack Mullan, second vice-president; Mrs. Frances Dahl, secretary; and William Henderson, treasurer. Soon local directors were producing plays starring prominent citizens.[141]

In December 1930 the Artists' Guild became the Little Theatre of Greenville. Mrs. J. W. Jervey was president, and Arthur Coe Gray, of Furman, and the Woman's College was director. The number of plays increased, and the Little Theatre also sponsored Sunday afternoon musicals under the direction of Wendell Keeney of Furman. Mrs. A. Foster McKissick served as chair of the entertainment committee, and Mrs. H. T. Crigler was chair of the play-reading committee. The Little Theatre flourished with the support of Furman and the Woman's College until the outbreak of World War II.[142]

The Greenville Public Library, which had become a major cultural center, improved its services during the New Deal era. In 1934 the library opened on Sunday afternoons, and fifteen WPA workers were assigned to the library staff. The lease on the library building on Main Street expired at the end of 1936, and temporary quarters were rented on the corner of Laurens and College Streets. Mrs. Caroline Coleman of Fountain Inn summed up the predicament of the library: "The splendid, efficient library staff is courageously carrying on under great difficulties, in a building that is inadequate, out of date and about as unsuitable for a library as a building could be." In 1939 the library board purchased the Park School building on North Main Street for $32,500, and the community raised ten thousand dollars for remodeling, with the assistance of the WPA. The new library opened its doors on February 10, 1940.[143]

Meanwhile the branch library in Greer, which had opened in temporary quarters in 1926, moved into the Davenport Memorial Library on September 23, 1938. The family of Clara Marchant Davenport gave the land and five thousand dollars for construction, while the town contributed fifteen hundred dollars, and the WPA furnished the labor.[144]

A Reviving Economy and the Threat of War

By the end of the decade of the 1930s the economy of Greenville had revived substantially. In four and a half years the WPA alone had expended $3,885,822 on projects, which was matched with $1,175,292 in state and local funds. In August 1939 the WPA announced a boost in wages. Unskilled workers would be raised from $26 to $35 a month; the wages of skilled workers would rise from $40 to $50.70. The number of workers decreased by 31.8 percent and employment in the private sector increased 43 percent in the city.[145]

New construction and new businesses were in evidence. The McDaniel Heights Apartments, with sixty-two units in five buildings, were completed in April 1939 at a cost of three hundred thousand dollars by the J. A. Jones Construction Company of Charlotte. On Main Street, Fletcher and Odus Stone and Prince Childress, Jr., opened Stone Brothers—advertised as "Greenville's newest clothing store." The era also brought a new way of burial to the community. Memorial parks were sweeping the country, and Woodlawn Memorial Park opened on the Superhighway in January 1939. Officers of the new enterprise included Clyde Gaffney, president; E. M. Blythe, Jr., vice president; and L. L. McGirt, Jr., secretary-treasurer.[146]

The city transportation system was modernized in February 1937 when Duke Power Company announced that the old streetcars would be replaced with trackless trolleys and buses. The new system cost between $125,000 and $150,000 and took six months to install. Service was extended to Union Bleachery and farther out Park Place, East McBee Avenue, and East Washington Street.[147]

The National Cotton Festival, a celebration of the local economy which occurred on October 9–14, 1939, emphasized Greenville's position as the Textile Center of the South. This event, the brainchild of Chamber of Commerce President G. Heyward Mahon, included a parade, a "Romance of Cotton" pageant with a cast of seven hundred people, and a visit by film star Ann Rutherford. A cotton nickel, designed and produced of durable cotton fabric, was redeemable in cash at the chamber office. The old "Greenville spirit" that Major Mahon had longed for in 1929 seemed to have been reborn.[148]

But there were clouds on the horizon. The nationwide epidemic of infantile paralysis, or poliomyelitis, reached Greenville in the summer of 1939. Sixteen cases were reported in the county before August 15. The *News* reflected the fear in the community: "Next to war, which falls ruthlessly on a country, this polio scare is causing more genuine anxiety in Greenville than anything else in a long time." The county was put under quarantine by the county health department. Sunday schools, movies, swimming pools, and summer camps were closed to children. Carter Stover, the daughter of Mr. and Mrs. Dakyns Stover, complained that "we ought to have two or three extra weeks vacation before school opens." Her activities were limited to playing cards with friends and visiting where there were no crowds. To her, summer days seemed to go on and on.[149]

Greenville General Hospital leased a Drinker respirator, known as the iron lung, for Catherine Robinson, a fourteen-year-old from Berea. Attorney J. D. Todd, Jr., president of the Junior Chamber of Commerce, announced the formation of a fund to purchase an iron lung for Greenville. The quarantine for children under twelve in Greenville County was lifted the first week in August, and schools with lay-by sessions were permitted to open on August 14.[150]

Even more ominous for the future were the signs of impending conflict overseas and the threat of American involvement in a second world war. In August 1939 the Greenville *News* reflected the changing mood of the region: "There can be no question of the wisdom of carrying forward our own program of a more aggressive defense of America as rapidly as possible. The lesson of current world events is certainly clear—that we should lose no time in being fully prepared to defend ourselves." The impending conflict bode greater change for Greenville than any armed conflict since the Civil War.[151]

Notes

1. Greenville *News,* January 1, June 28, 1929.
2. Julian J. Petty, *The Growth and Distribution of Population in South Carolina* (Columbia, S.C., 1943, 1975), 228–29.
3. Greenville *News,* December 3, 4, 18, 1926.
4. Ibid., June 30, 1929; December 25, 1931.
5. Ibid., October 11, 19, November 26, 1929; January 2, 3, June 11, 1932; January 19, 1933; March 31, 1934.
6. George B. Tindall, *The Emergence of the New South, 1913–1945* (Baton Rouge, 1967), 361; Greenville *News,* July 9, 1929; January 29, April 24, 1930.
7. Greenville *News,* October 25, 29, 1929.
8. Ibid., October 19, November 26, 1930.
9. James A. Dunlap, III, "Victims of Neglect: The Career and Creations of John T. Woodside, 1865–1986" (M.A. thesis, University of South Carolina, 1986), 46–55.
10. Ibid., 55–64.
11. Greenville *News,* February 16, 1931; May 8, 1932; May 7, June 8, 3, 16, July 4, 1932.
12. Ibid., July 9, 12, December 7, 1930.
13. Ibid., December 2, 1930.
14. Ibid., December 2, 10, 28, 1930.
15. Ibid., December 20, 1930; March 20, 28, September 30, October 7, 1931.
16. Ibid., October 17, 24, 1931.
17. Ibid., October 17, 1931; April 1, 3, 1932.
18. Ibid., August 3, 1932.
19. Ibid., October 18, 19, 22, November 29, December 21, 24, 1931; February 16, April 1, 1932.
20. Ibid., August 7, 1932.
21. Ibid., June 16, 1931.
22. Ibid., November 1, 1931.
23. Ibid., August 4, 7, 1932.
24. Ibid., January 4, July 17, 1932.
25. Ibid., October 31, November 25, 1931.
26. Ibid., January 1, 10, 21, 24, February 9, 24, 1932.
27. Ibid., February 25, March 6, 1932.
28. Ibid., December 21, 1932. Petitioners represented a sizeable number of the local business elite of the older and younger generations including Romayne Barnes, W. P. Conyers, T. C. Gower, Sam R. Zimmerman, Townes, William Goldsmith, Robert I. Woodside, J. M. Perry, J. A. McPherson, B. H. Peace, Prevost, J. W. Norwood, W. E. Beattie, J. I. Westervelt, W. W. Burgess, and Marion M. Hewell.
29. Tindall, *Emergence,* 373–74.
30. Greenville *News,* March 19, 27, May 5, July 1, 6, August 2, 1932.

31. Ibid., December 22, 28, 1932.

32. Tindall, *Emergence*, 385–86; Greenville *News,* October 3, 1932.

33. Greenville *News,* February 18, April 1, 1932.

34. Ibid., March 27, April 13, 1932.

35. Ibid., May 26, 1932.

36. Ibid., June 24, 30, July 2, 1930.

37. Ibid., July 7, 8, 12, 1932.

38. *Biographical Dictionary of the S.C. Senate,* ed. N. Louise Bailey et al. (Columbia, 1986), 3: 1478–79; Greenville *News,* July 27, September 14, 28, 1932.

39. Greenville *News,* July 31, September 2, 3, August 23, October 26, 24, 1932.

40. Ibid., November 9, 10, 1932.

41. Ibid., February 4, March 2, 3, 7, 1933.

42. Ibid., February 21, 26, 28, March 5, 1933.

43. Ibid., March 7, 1933.

44. Ibid., March 6, 8, 10, July 16, 1933.

45. Ibid., March 11, 16, 19, 27, 1933.

46. Ibid., April 9, 1933.

47. Ibid., January 22, 1933; Tindall, *Emergence,* 392–93.

48. Greenville *News,* June 20, 22, 29, July 16, 20, 1933.

49. Ibid., June 13, 1933.

50. Ibid., August 6, 1933, December 15, 1934.

51. Ibid., September 13, 19, 1939; December 2, 1937; November 24, 1940.

52. Ibid., September 29, 1935.

53. Ibid., March 3, 4, 1933.

54. Ibid., May 13, 27, July 1, 9, August 3, 15, 1933; May 12, 1934.

55. Tindall, *Emergence,* 473– 77.

56. Greenville *News,* November 24, 1933; April 24, 1934; December 9, 1933.

57. Ibid., May, July 22, August 27, September, 1933. Details on the program of the CCC is in John A. Salmond, *The Civilian Conservation Corps, 1933–1942: A New Deal Case Study* (Durham, N.C., 1967).

58. Greenville *News,* December 21, 1934; April 7, June 14, August 19, October 29, 1935; December 16, 1935.

59. Ibid., July 16, 1937.

60. Ibid., March 18, April 8, September 11, 1934; January 27, 1935.

61. Ibid., July 9, 1933; February 20, 1935; July 13, 27, 1939.

62. Ibid., November 20, December 29, 1933; September 14, November 3, 1935.

63. Ibid., September 28, October 10, 21, 1933; November 18, 1934; August 30, September 5, 12, 1935; February 29, 1936.

64. Ibid., March 1, 1933; April 3, June 23, 1934; February 5, 1935; March 19, 1936.

65. Ibid., November 8, 1936; September 28, 1937.

66. Ibid., October 24, 1936; April 11, July 28, 25, 1937.

67. Ibid., July 29, August 4, 6, 1933.

68. Ibid., August 12, 6, 1933.

69. Ibid., August 2, 1933.

70. Ibid., August 1, 1933.

71. Ibid., December 29, 30, 1935; February 11, 19, 1936.

72. Ibid., February 24, 1936.

73. Tindall, *Emergence*, 505; Greenville *News*, May 25, July 1, 1933.

74. Greenville *News*, June 21, July 6, 1933.

75. Ibid., July 15, 1933.

76. Ibid., August 5, 1933; Tindall, *Emergence*, 509.

77. Greenville *News*, January 22, March 22, 1934.

78. Ibid., April 16, 22, 23, 1934.

79. Tindall, *Emergence*, 510; Greenville *News*, August 23, 27, 1934.

80. Greenville *News*, August 31, 1934.

81. James A. Hodges, *New Deal Labor Policy and the Southern Cotton Textile Industry, 1933–1941* (Knoxville, Tenn., 1986), 100; Tindall, *Emergence*, 511.

82. Greenville *News*, September 3, 4, 1934; Hodges, *New Deal Labor Policy*, 90.

83. Greenville *News*, September 4, 1934.

84. Ibid., September 4, 1934.

85. Ibid., September 5, 1934.

86. Ibid., September 6, 1934.

87. Ibid., September 6, 7, 1934.

88. Ibid., September 7, 1934.

89. Ibid., September 7, 8, 1934.

90. Ibid., September 11, 12, 1934; Hodges, *New Deal Labor Policy*, 107–108, 112–18.

91. Hodges, *New Deal Labor Policy*, 130–31; Greenville *News*, October 1, 1934; Dunlap, "Victims of Neglect," 88.

92. Greenville *News*, September 12, 1934.

93. Ibid., July 23, 1933; August 13, 1939.

94. Joseph T. Drake, "The Negro in Greenville, South Carolina" (M.A. thesis, University of North Carolina, 1940), 38–40.

95. Drake, "Negro in Greenville," 40–42.

96. Ibid., 43–48.

97. Ibid., 48–49.

98. Greenville *News*, March 18, 19, 1933.

99. Two comprehensive studies of lynching in South Carolina in the twentieth century are Jack S. Mullins, "Lynching in South Carolina, 1900–1914" (M.A. thesis, University of South Carolina, 1964) and Susan P. Garris, "The Decline of Lynching in South Carolina, 1915–1947" (M.A. thesis, University of South Carolina, 1973). The Greenville County lynching victims were Sam Hudson, of Greer, June 26, 1905; Andrew Thompson, December 18, 1905; Jesse Fuller (white) and Joe Barker, both of Greenville, December 26, 1909. Mullins, 143–44.

100. Greenville *News,* November 18, 1933.

101. Ibid., November 29, 1933; November 1, 4, 1934.

102. Edwin D. Hoffman, "The Genesis of the Modern Movement for Equal Rights in South Carolina, 1930–1939," *Journal of Negro History* 44 (October 1959): 346–69 and Robert W. Bagnall, "Lights and Shadows in the South," *The Crisis* 39 (April 1932): 124–25, cited in Idus A. Newby, *Black Carolinians: A History of Blacks in South Carolina from 1895 to 1968* (Columbia, 1973), 229–32.

103. Greenville *News,* July 6, 7, 1939.

104. Ibid., July 7, 1939.

105. Ibid., September 14, 25, October 2, 16, November 22, 1939.

106. Ibid., April 27, July 24, 26, 1940.

107. Drake, "Negro in Greenville," 206–208.

108. Ibid., 216–18.

109. Greenville *News,* September 17, 1935; January 28, 1936.

110. Ibid., June 25, July 5, 1936.

111. Ibid., February 29, June 11, July 4, 1936.

112. Ibid., December 6, 1938; William E. Leuchtenburg, *Franklin D. Roosevelt and the New Deal, 1932–1940* (New York, 1963), 267–68. Walter J. Brown, then a columnist for the Greenville *News,* gives a colorful account of "the purge" in *James F. Byrnes of South Carolina: A Remembrance* (Spartanburg, 1992), 66–76.

113. Greenville *News,* May 7, 16, November 6, 1940; August 7, 1941. Actually, Peace succeeded Alva Lumpkin of Columbia who had died two weeks after assuming Byrnes's seat.

114. Ibid., January 2, 1933.

115. Ibid., January 18, 19, 1933.

116. Ibid., July 15, March 23, 1933.

117. "James McDowell Richardson" *Biographical Directory of the South Carolina Senate* 2: 1363–65; Greenville *News,* August 2, October 11, 1933.

118. Greenville *News,* March 23, 1933; March 9, December 19, 1935; April 21, October 6, 1937.

119. Ibid., May 30, 1936.

120. Ibid., April 14, 15, 18, 22, 1933.

121. David D. Wallace, *South Carolina: A Short History, 1520–1948* (Chapel Hill, N.C., 1951), 686; Greenville *News,* October 13, 15, 28, November 8, 9, 1933; May 10, 15, 16, July 8, November 24, 1935.

122. Alfred S. Reid, *Furman University: Toward a New Identity, 1925–1975* (Durham, N.C., 1976), 31–61.

123. Reid, *Furman University,* 77–79.

124. Ibid., 89–90. Excerpts from Reid's longer study are incorporated in his "The Greenville County Council for Community Development: Furman and Greenville in Partnership in the 1930's," *The Proceedings and Papers of the Greenville County Historical Society* 6 (1975–1979): 78–88; Greenville *News,* February 12, 1939.

125. Greenville *News,* February 12, 1939.

126. Reid, *Furman University,* 91–92, 99.

127. Ibid., 92–95.

128. Greenville *News,* April 30, May 2, 1933.

129. Ibid., May 2, 16, 17, 21, 1933; October 13, 1935; February 16, 1936. B. H. Peace died on January 24, 1934.

130. Ibid., March 17, 1939.

131. Ibid., January 10, 20, June 24, 1927; January 10, 1929.

132. Biographical file, S.C. Room, Greenville County Library, Greenville, S.C.

133. Greenville *News,* January 10, March 16, April 18, May 15, 1929; October 8, 1933; October 15, 1934; August 19, 1937.

134. Ibid., October 14, November 1, 15, 1931.

135. "Faith Memorial Chapel, Cedar Mountain, North Carolina, Fifty-Second Year—1990" in possession of the author.

136. Lennie Lusby, "Music" in Alfred S. Reid, *The Arts in Greenville, 1800–1960* (Greenville, S.C., 1960), 43–44.

137. Greenville *News,* October 29, 1927; March 23, June 19, 1928; November 3, 1935.

138. Lila E. Earle and Evelyn P. Daniel, "Art: Architecture and Painting" in Reid, *Arts in Greenville,* 68–70.

139. Ibid., 70–71.

140. Ibid., 72.

141. Dorothy Richey, "Theatre Arts" in Reid, *Arts in Greenville,* 78–80.

142. Ibid., 80–81.

143. Ellen Perry, *Free Reading for Everybody: The Story of the Greenville Library* (Greenville, S.C., 1973), 19–22.

144. Ibid., 22.

145. Greenville *News,* May 5, 1940; January 14, 1941.

146. Ibid., February 26, March 16, January 22, 1939.

147. Ibid., February 25, 1937.

148. Ibid., September 17, 23, 26, 30, October 9, 11, 1939.

149. Ibid., July 7, 11, August 11, 1939.

150. Ibid., July 11, August 8, 1939.

151. Tindall, *Emergence,* 687–90; Greenville *News,* August 28, 1939.

CHAPTER TWELVE

World War II:
A Cauldron of Change

As Asia and Europe moved toward World War II in the late 1930s, the Greenville *News* urged the United States "in this, the world's dark hour, . . . to seek to preserve democracy here and keep that beacon light burning brightly." When Hitler invaded Poland on September 1, 1939, however, the nation's neutrality was severely tested. The *News* made it clear that "there may as well be frank recognition of the fact that American sympathies are strong and American opinions definitely formulated." Still, "that does not provide us with any reason for joining in this war."[1]

An eye-witness to the horrors of German Nazism was nineteen-year-old Max Heller, who arrived in Greenville from his native Austria in July 1938. On March 11 German troops had marched into Vienna, and anti-Jewish policies were quickly put into place. Heller had met a young woman from Greenville the previous summer, and he immediately wrote her to ask if she could arrange a job for him in the United States. Shepard Saltzman, who owned the Piedmont Shirt Company, promised the young man employment, and Heller arrived in Greenville with $1.80 in his pocket. He began work as a stocker, but was gradually promoted. When Heller's father arrived in Greenville, he went to work for his son at the shirt factory. The younger Heller became general manager of the company in 1943. Meanwhile, Trude Schonthal, whom he eventually married, escaped from Vienna with her family to Belgium. Her father was imprisoned for a time in a Nazi concentration camp in France, but he was able to escape. In 1942 the Schonthals came to Greenville, where Trude and Max were married. Some ninety members of their families died during the war—most in concentration camps. After World War II Max Heller formed his own company, and served as mayor of Greenville and as chair of the State Development Board.[2]

When the fighting in Europe began, Greenville County was caught up in a cauldron of change greater than any it had experienced since the Civil War. The economy quickened, demographic patterns changed, and the old system of segregation faced greater challenges. Out of World War II, the modern South was born.[3]

The effect of the war on Greenville's economy was instantaneous. According to the *News* in September 1939, "Europe's war and the resultant rise in prices in this country has caused Greenville merchants to place the heaviest orders they have since the boom days before 1929." With a flood of increased orders, textile mills stepped up production, and by mid-September they began to run eighty hours a week. The prices of "better mill stock" increased on the average of six to seven dollars in a week, and the price of cotton rose five to six dollars a bale.[4]

War relief efforts soon began. Ed B. Smith served as county chair for Finnish relief, and $1,875 was collected by March 1940. In June Mrs. A. Foster McKissick, chair of the Greenville chapter of the Red Cross, announced a plan for the enlistment of volunteers to make "bandages and garments for the war-stricken peoples of Europe." The program was formulated by Mrs. Marion Brawley. The first shipment of 716 items was made by the middle of August. Meanwhile, the Red Cross raised over ten thousand dollars for relief work in Britain and France. As Hitler waged the Battle of Britain in the summer of 1940, Mrs. Ellison S. McKissick, who was a native of Canada, became local president of Bundles for Britain. The first $1,350 sent to Britain was the cost of a fully equipped ambulance and its maintenance for a year. The Greenville group said "they sincerely hoped that these contributions will continue to help in winning this war for democracy."[5]

A greater step toward involvement in World War II for Greenville County residents came when Congress passed the first peacetime draft in American history on September 16, 1940. A month later, 19,142 men between the ages of twenty-one and thirty-six went to the local schools to register. On October 29 the draft lottery in Washington determined the order in which 122 men in the city and 177 in the county would be called. Those with the lowest numbers were John Robinson and Norris Connelley Campbell of Greenville, James Duckett Hammond of Fountain Inn, and Morris Charlie King of Tigerville. Not waiting for the draft, several hundred volunteered for the Army, Navy, and Marine Corps.[6]

At Furman, President John L. Plyler sought unsuccessfully to have a unit of the Army Reserve Officers' Training Corps (ROTC) located on the campus, but there was a shortage of officers to staff already existing units. In September 1939, however, Furman students began to participate in programs of ground and flight instruction under the supervision of the state Aeronautics Commission.[7]

In April 1941 a local steering committee, chaired by L. J. Walker, made plans to organize a Home Defense unit. The unit had an authorized strength of ninety men, forty of whom could be completely supplied with equipment at once. On May 28 forty-two men were formally inducted into the unit, and Guy B. Foster was elected captain of the company. Physical examinations were scheduled for thirty-five additional men the following week.[8]

War finally came to the United States on December 7, 1941, when the Japanese bombed Pearl Harbor and unleashed attacks on the Philippines, Guam, and Midway. The Greenville *News* reported that "Greenvillians gasped at first and then girded for action yesterday with the realization that America—and Greenville—are in a war." Residents listened by radio to the reports as they came in, and many "telephone calls poured into the News." An initial count numbered "at least thirty young men from Greater Greenville . . . known to have been stationed with the army, navy or marine corps, most of them at or near Honolulu and others at Manila in the Philippines and elsewhere in the Pacific." A day later the estimated number had grown to over one hundred.[9]

Not until Tuesday, December 16, did word of Greenville's first casualty reach the city. In a ritual that would be enacted many times in the next four years, Vardry (Turk) McBee of 16 Lavinia Avenue received word that his son, Kirk, had been killed during the Japanese attack on the battleship *West Virginia,* stationed at Pearl Harbor. The telegram from Rear Admiral Chester W. Nimitz began: "The Navy Department deeply regrets to inform you that your son, Luther Kirk McBee, seaman first class, USN, was lost in action in the performance of his duty and in the service of his country."[10]

Born on April 28, 1921, McBee was the son of Turk and Marie Goldsmith McBee and a great-grandson of Vardry McBee. He had attended Greenville High School and the Baylor School for Boys in Chattanooga, Tennessee. He enlisted in the Navy on August 1, 1940, and had been stationed in the Pacific for a year. A memorial service was conducted by Robert T. Phillips at Christ Church on December 19. The church was filled by "personnel of the local Navy recruiting station, men in the armed services," as well as family and friends.[11]

The editorial columns of the Greenville *News* reflected the resolution of the community: "If war had to come to the United States, it is fortunate that it has come in just the way it has—through the deliberately planned treachery and despicable aggression of the foe." Such an act "unifies the American people . . . in the grim determination to wage war with every resource at the nation's command—war to the bitter end of complete destruction of this menace to our security, regardless of cost or sacrifice."

In Washington Greenville Congressman Joseph R. Bryson denounced the Axis powers in a letter to President Roosevelt: "These states are all members of an unholy alliance . . . seeking world domination by brutal force and there should be no further waiting in declaring our intention to crush that aggression in all its parts."[12]

With a draft call-up imminent, one hundred men volunteered in two days for service in the Navy. Forty were rejected for disabilities; twenty were sent to Raleigh, North Carolina, for final induction; and physical examinations were scheduled for the remainder. The recruiting offices for both the Navy and the Army, on the second floor of the City Hall, received orders to remain open for twenty-four hours, seven days a week. The Army recruiters announced unlimited openings for the Air Corps and amateur radio operators. Satoshi Yagado, known locally by his American name as Norman, was the only Greenville resident of Japanese-American descent. An employee at the Piedmont Hatchery, Yagado announced that he was ready to join the Army. Soon service flags bearing blue stars for those in uniform and gold stars for those who had died appeared in churches all over the county.[13]

Typical of the World War II generation that was just beginning to assume leadership in the city and county, but who quickly went off to war, was Patrick Bradley Morrah, Jr. Born in Lancaster on June 13, 1915, the son of Patrick Bradley and Hessie Thomson Morrah, young Bradley Morrah moved to Greenville with his family in 1922. He graduated from Greenville High School and received a bachelor of arts degree from the Citadel in 1936. He graduated from Duke Law School in 1939 and returned to Greenville to practice. In 1940 he was elected to the state House of Representatives. Morrah enlisted in the Army on October 22, 1941, and resigned his seat in the legislature after Pearl Harbor. He was commissioned a first lieutenant in the Fourteenth Anti-Aircraft Artillery and was assigned to the Pacific theater of war. An intelligence officer, Morrah was attached to the Allied Air Force Headquarters in Brisbane, Australia, from February 18, 1942, to September 25, 1945. He rose to the rank of major and was awarded a bronze star.[14]

The normal course of life in Greenville was interrupted or modified by the war. Weddings, for example, had to be scheduled to fit the demands of the military, and uniforms were much in evidence. Mary Simms Oliphant and Second Lieutenant Alester G. Furman III were married at Christ Church on Saturday evening, April 4, 1942. The groom, along with two of his groomsmen, Dan M. Beattie and Preston (Pete) Marchant, had recently completed Marine Officer Candidate School and was stationed at Quantico, Virginia. Wedding or no wedding, Lieutenant Furman was back on duty at Quantico the following Monday morning.[15]

At Furman University students received deferments to complete the current academic year. Others accelerated their programs to finish in three years rather than four. In the fall of 1942 the number of male students dropped nearly a hundred, and ten male faculty members went into service. To keep the college open, President John L. Plyler negotiated for an Army program on campus. In September 1942 trainees from the Nineteenth Army Air Force Glider Pilot Training Detachment arrived. They took courses at Furman and received flight training at the municipal airport. By the next fall the Army trainees had virtually taken over the men's campus. Most civilian classes were taught at the Woman's College. There were only 658 regular students, of whom only 192 were men.[16]

Meanwhile the Greenville community took immediate steps to place itself on a wartime basis. Textile mills, local utilities, and the municipal airport employed extra security guards "to prevent sabotage." All civilian flying was temporarily canceled, and civilians were banned from hangars and airplanes. Mayor C. Fred McCullough, chair of the Greenville County Civil Defense Council, and Broadus Bailey, the director, led the local effort. W. B. Ellis was placed in charge of the utilities division. Ellis and A. C. Mann began to organize an auxiliary fire department, an auxiliary police force, blackout and air raid procedures, and guard details for local plants and utilities. Others leaders of the civil defense council included Glenn L. McCullough, J. A. McPherson, and J. P. Williamson.[17]

The two local draft boards, numbers 36 and 37, began a reclassification of men eligible for the draft. Approximately one thousand individuals were classified as 1-A and subject to immediate call for Army service. More than one hundred volunteers applied to teach Red Cross classes, under the direction of Mrs. Harry St. John. The initial classes were held at Dunean School, the DeMolay chapter, Furman, the Woman's College, and the YWCA. Civil defense instructions for air raids were distributed to the public schools.[18]

The South was a magnet for training camps and airfields because of the region's mild climate and vast open spaces. Eventually some 36 percent of the total expenditures for military bases went to the Southern states. On December 11 the creation of the Greenville Army Air Base was made public. The initial announcement indicated that the cost of the base would be about $7.5 million. The estimated air strength of the base was 130 bombers and pursuit planes, and the initial personnel would include four hundred command pilots and forty-five hundred men. In addition, there would be a large staff of civilian personnel.[19]

Lobbying furiously for the base had been Mayor McCullough, Chamber of Commerce President G. Heyward Mahon, Jr., and former U.S. Senator Roger Peace. They worked with the Chamber committee on defense projects, which included Alester G. Furman (chair), L. M. Glenn (secretary), John A. McPherson, A. C. Mann, R. F. Watson, J. B. League, R. A. Jolley, J. P. Williamson, Dr. Frank Kitchen, Frank G. Hamblen, J. S. Culpepper, Walker F. West, H. C. Harvley, J. B. Hall, Ben Meyers, and Dr. R. M. Dacus.[20]

The estimated monthly payroll of the officers and enlisted personnel alone was $250,000. As *Time* put it in a report entitled "Defense Boom in Dixie," such payrolls "bounced from one merchant's cash register to another."[21]

The air base was located on a two-thousand-acre tract 8 miles south of the city bounded on the west by Augusta Road and on the east by Fork Shoals Road. The city and the county delegation cooperated in the purchase of the land. Construction began immediately and was put out to bids from private construction companies. The original time estimate on completion of the base was from four to six months.[22]

One of the major contractors for the construction of the Greenville Army Air Base was the Daniel Construction Company of Anderson. World War II brought the company and its driving force, Charles E. Daniel, to Greenville. After 1945 he would become a major factor in shaping not only postwar Greenville but also the modern South.

Charles Ezra Daniel was born in Elberton, Georgia, on November 11, 1895, the son of James Fleming and Leila Mildred Adams Daniel. James Daniel was a millwright, and he soon moved his family to Anderson where he was steadily employed repairing textile mill machinery. During the summers the younger Daniel worked for the Townsend Lumber Company. After two years at the Citadel and service in World War I as a first lieutenant, he returned to Anderson in 1919 and went to work for Townsend full time. Daniel was determined to become a builder, and he began by building mill houses for the company. His goal was to build the houses better, faster, and cheaper than the competition, and soon he had contracts for constructing one hundred at once.[23]

By this time Daniel was working ten to twelve hours a day, seven days a week. In 1924 he returned to Elberton and married Homozel (Mickey) Mickel. Soon Mickey Daniel was accompanying her husband to construction sites, and she later became a partner in his business ventures. Daniel purchased stock in Townsend, and in 1927 became a vice president of the company. Daniel proposed expanding the company into industrial construction, but his partners balked. When the New Deal began to fund large projects, Daniel established the Daniel Construction Company in 1934. In

January 1941 he purchased a lot on North Main Street in Greenville which became the site of his company headquarters.[24]

Other Greenville businesses profited from wartime expenditures as well. When Poe Mill was sold in 1937, Nelson Carter Poe, Jr., turned his efforts toward two other family firms—Poe Hardware and Supply Company and the Poe Piping and Heating Company. During the war Poe received contracts for the mechanical work at twenty-six camps and other government installations. These included the atomic bomb project at Oak Ridge, Tennessee, where he lived for twenty-three months while the work was in progress.[25]

Less striking than the development of the construction industry at the time, but signaling a further diversification of industry, as well as a major change in the lifestyle of Greenvillians, was the opening of the Southern Margarine Company on the New Buncombe Road (later Poinsett Highway) on February 24, 1940. Hailed as the manufacturer of a "new state product," the corporation began the manufacture of oleomargarine. Soon "oleo" was replacing butter on local dining tables. During the first year the plant was scheduled to produce 3 million pounds, but its eventual capacity was double that amount.[26]

The economic boom in Greenville brought on by the war allowed a gradual shutdown of New Deal relief programs. On March 31, 1940, the CCC Camp at Paris Mountain closed, and the WPA rolls were reduced by 31.8 percent in the calendar year 1940. At the same time, the state Employment Service reported that private employment in Greenville County had increased some 43 percent. In May 1941 A. M. Moseley, the local supervisor of the National Youth Administration, announced that 268 young men and women out of a total of 450 in the county would be cut from the program. The aid program that survived the longest was the food stamp program. In March 1942 some twelve thousand dollars in free food stamps were distributed to five thousand people. But that program ended on July 1.[27]

New Deal farm programs, however, remained vital to the war effort. In May 1940 the Greenville County Soil Conservation District was established. Under the direction of W. R. Gray, the county farm agent, and H. J. Dowdle, the district conservationist, a soil conservation survey was made. Then a program of systematic crop rotation, strip cropping, contour farming, woodland management, and the planting of erosion-resisting vegetation began. In August 1944 more than a million linear feet of terraces had been completed in the county in the previous twelve months. Applications for an additional 12 million feet were still on hand.[28]

Greenville County farmers were called on to raise more food as a part of the war effort. Farm production goals were established by the county Farm War Board. G. D. Butler of the Mountain View community was chair. In 1943, for example, production increased as much as 400 percent over the previous year. Butler, who was forty years old, operated a fifty-acre farm. His prewar goal had been home consumption and sale of the surplus produce. With the war on, however, he aimed "to raise as much as possible. . . . The soldiers and defense factory workers have to eat." Mrs. Butler, who maintained the house and garden and raised chickens, supported the farm effort: "We've got to fight to the end to protect our free way of life and to preserve decency in this world. . . . My family is willing to sacrifice everything for our democracy."[29]

Rationing became a way of life in Greenville, as in the rest of the nation. Frank G. Hamblen, vice president of the Greenville and Northern Railroad, was appointed chair of the city rationing board. Assisting Hamblen were C. O. Milford, president of the Franklin Life Insurance Company, and Marion M. Hewell, secretary-treasurer of Fidelity Federal Savings and Loan Association. Leon Henderson was administrator of the local Office of Price Administration (OPA), located in the basement of the City Hall. The sale of automobiles was frozen by the federal government on January 1, 1942. Cars sold but not delivered at that time could still be obtained, and the general rationing of vehicles did not begin until February 26. At the same time automobile tires and tubes were rationed. The allotment for Greenville for January 1942 was 399 tires and 332 tubes.[30]

Under the rationing guidelines, lawyers, for example, were entitled to purchase two new tires. Attorney L. Larue Hinson, like many other citizens, purchased a bicycle. Soon he was regularly pedaling the 4 miles each way from his home off Buncombe Road to his office in Greenville each day.[31]

Food rationing began as a voluntary effort before it became mandatory. The price of sugar was set by the OPA at twenty-eight cents per five-pound bag to prevent the inflation which had occurred during World War I. Beginning on Saturday, January 4, 1942, local grocers asked their customers not to purchase more than 5 pounds of sugar a week. In May the rationing of gasoline went into effect, as well as sugar. Soon the OPA issued ration books for scarce items. Ration stamps and blue and red ration tokens became familiar sights in Greenville stores.[32]

Community drives for relief, the purchase of war bonds, and the collection of scrap became a regular part of life in wartime Greenville. The first Red Cross drive followed the attack on Pearl Harbor in December 1941. J.

E. Sirrine was general chair, and was assisted by Walter Greer, Jr., who was head of the textile division; E. E. Scott and P. M. McMillan, chairs of the commercial division; Margaret Keith, chair of the residential division; and Ernest Patton, chair of special gifts. The goal of the initial drive was forty thousand dollars, and was easily raised. Seven drives for the sale of war bonds were conducted in Greenville between 1942 and 1945. In August 1942 film stars Jane Wyman and John Payne lent their support to the local bond effort. In March 1944 a captured Japanese submarine was put on display. Salvage drives, under the leadership of P. D. Meadors, collected scrap metal, including automobile license plates and street car tracks. A rubber drive gathered 500,000 pounds of that scarce commodity.[33]

The Enemy Aliens Board for the Western District of South Carolina included Hoke B. Black, a local attorney, as chair; Roger C. Peace; Robert Gage of Chester; and Edward P. (Ted) Riley, the assistant district attorney. The board's responsibility was "to determine the status of enemy aliens in the district." On March 8, 1942, a surprise raid conducted by federal, state, and local officers seized "a quantity of guns and other articles at ten places in Greenville county."[34]

Air raid blackout drills were conducted under the leadership of Richard W. Arrington, commander of the Citizens Defense Corps, which included some one thousand trained volunteers. The first blackout occurred on May 25, 1942, and was declared 98 percent successful. The old city bell, which once marked the hours, was hung at the City Fire Department as part of the air raid warning system.[35]

To provide adequate recreation facilities for soldiers stationed in Greenville, the city council established a committee on clubs and centers. The members included Mayor McCullough, Dr. T. W. Brockman, William T. Potter, Mrs. J. Warren White, the Reverend C. O. Williams, Dyar Massey, Mrs. Francis Tindall, and John M. Holmes. A center for white soldiers opened at Textile Hall. A place for black soldiers at the Phillis Wheatley Center was operated by a subcommittee headed by Dr. E. A. E. Huggins. The downtown YMCA offered a range of activities for white soldiers, as did a number of local churches. The programs included organized game nights and dances.[36]

Holidays provided an opportunity for special activities for the troops. In November 1943 the Greenville Defense Recreation Committee sponsored a Thanksgiving program at the Army Air Force Training Center. On Thanksgiving morning Mrs. W. B. Mulligan, Mrs. R. N. Daniel, Mrs. A. D. Frye, Mrs. James Frederick, Kitty Means, Margaret Means, and Elizabeth Garraux decorated the tables in the mess hall with linen table cloths, holly, and fruit. Between 350 and 400 people attended the dinner and the Thanksgiving service afterwards in the base chapel. A floor show and dance followed, for which Mrs. Luther Marchant, senior hostess of the committee, had recruited forty local young women.[37]

At Christmas, the YMCA operated a "dinner exchange," organized by Sudie Mulligan, whose husband, W. B. (Monk) Mulligan, succeeded John Holmes as secretary in November 1944. Local families were urged to call the YMCA on Christmas morning and invite soldiers for dinner. Open House was held that afternoon in the lobby and club rooms of the YMCA, which had been especially decorated for the occasion.[38]

The beginning of the end of the war in Europe came with the Allied invasion of Normandy on D-Day, June 6, 1944. In Greenville the long-awaited announcement came early in the morning by radio. According to the Greenville *News,* "practically every car [radio] in Greenville and vicinity" was on. Later in the day "there were radios in practically every business establishment and every office as workers unable to be near their home radios followed the invasion over the air." Flags were displayed on Main Street, and the city alarm bell rang every hour, as did the whistles of the nearby textile mills.[39]

In September 1944 Commander H. F. A. Lange of the local American Legion Post planned a Victory Day celebration in anticipation of the German surrender. But the anticipation of victory was tempered with sorrow when the news reached Greenville on April 12, 1945, that President Franklin Roosevelt had died unexpectedly in Warm Springs, Georgia. Roosevelt had not only served longer than any other American president, but he had maintained the enthusiastic support of most Greenvillians through the twin traumas of depression and war. Furthermore, the presidential train had regularly passed through Greenville on its way from Washington to Warm Springs.[40]

On April 13 the train with the president's body on board stopped in Greenville from 6:30 to 7:07 P.M., while the two engines drawing the eleven-car train were switched. Some fifteen to twenty thousand people lined the tracks for a half mile on either side of the railroad depot. An honor guard of soldiers from Camp Croft, near Spartanburg, stood on both sides of the train. The Greenville State Guard was on duty to handle the crowds. Detachments of soldiers from Fort Jackson in Columbia stood at intervals along the railroad a mile north and south of the station. Mayor McCullough presented Steve Early, the president's secretary, with two wreaths—one from the city and another from Kate Finley. One was placed on the casket; the other in the funeral car.[41]

On April 15, the day of Roosevelt's funeral in Washington, seven hundred Greenvillians attended a memorial service at the First Baptist Church arranged by the American Legion Post. Major G. Heyward Mahon, Jr., spoke, and the service was conducted by H. O. Chambers, president of the Ministerial Union, and Leon M. Latimer, pastor of the church. The city bell tolled for five minutes at 4:00 P.M.—the hour of the service in Washington.[42]

Victory over Germany was not long in coming. The formal announcement of the surrender was made by President Harry Truman on May 8, and segregated mass meetings of celebration were planned for whites at Meadowbrook Park and for blacks at the Phillis Wheatley Center. Stores were closed for the remainder of the day after the announcement. The war against Japan continued until August, and the V-J Day celebration was much more emotional. "Greenville went slightly mad last night," reported the *News*, "when word came over the radio at 7:02 that the Japanese had thrown in the sponge." Stores, businesses, and banks closed on August 15, and churches scheduled services of thanksgiving at 8:00 P.M.[43]

At the end of the war, Greenville's highest-ranking officers in the armed forces were Major General Floyd L. Parks, commanding officer of the American Control Zone in Berlin, and Major General John Sloan. Within a few months, the war began winding down in Greenville County. The Army Air Base was placed on inactive status on November 30. The Chamber of Commerce quickly endorsed efforts to create a permanent airport at the site and to use the adjacent acreage for commercial and industrial development. The four draft boards in the county were consolidated into one. Service personnel began returning home at the rate of sometimes hundreds a day. The housing shortage became critical, and stores ran short of civilian clothes for returning soldiers. Local industries began the process of converting to peacetime status.[44]

To many returning veterans, their first Christmas home was bittersweet. December 24, 1945, brought Greenville a rare white Christmas, but the sense of living in a fairyland produced by the snow quickly dissipated. Two days later the *News* reported that "the majority of residents feel that if there are any more dreams of a White Christmas they will be something like a nightmare." There was no electrical power, no radios, and no telephones. Parties were canceled, and Christmas dinners were cooked on gas stoves by candlelight. "It was a bad day for the boys and girls who had received scooters, tricycles, wagons, fireworks, and other firearms."[45]

On the surface, Greenville seemed to have changed very little during the war years. To Schaefer Kendrick, home from the war, it was still "a textile *mill* town. The early morning whistles [of the mills] served notice to [their] constituents that it was time to get up and go to work. Between four and six in the morning the whistles made music that sounded like the works of some mad Russian composer." On Main Street the Woodside Building "stood vigil over Greenville like a lonely stalagmite, proud to be the tallest building in South Carolina, a fact we natives proclaimed on the slightest provocation or from no provocation at all." The city's greatest claim to fame, according to Kendrick, was still the Poinsett Hotel. He returned home with the memory of being in San Francisco "awaiting transportation to my new assignment on Okinawa. A native asked me where I was from. When I told him Greenville, S.C., he spontaneously exclaimed 'Poinsett Hotel and spoon bread.'"[46]

Samuel L. Zimmerman, a black Greenvillian, also found that little had changed. "Black veterans who chose to return to Greenville after risking their lives in defense of their country during World War II found postwar conditions virtually unchanged from what they left behind when going off to fight." For Zimmerman, however, the status quo was negative. "They faced unblinking segregation in almost every phase of public life. Often this segregation was backed by the full weight and power of the law—both state and local." Hundreds of black veterans and their families, "faced with the choice of remaining in Greenville to enlist in the struggle for change, or leaving to live under less onerous conditions," chose to leave. "Frequently they carried with them valuable skills acquired while in the military."[47]

But things were not quite what they seemed. On April 3, 1944, the United States Supreme Court, in the case of *Smith v. Allwright,* had struck down the white Democratic primary in Texas on the grounds that it violated the Fifteenth Amendment. Hoping to safeguard the South Carolina primary, Governor Olin D. Johnston had called a special session of the South Carolina legislature to transform the state Democratic Party into a "private club." South Carolina remained adamant in maintaining the old structures of segregation.[48]

But maintaining the status quo of antebellum ideals was more illusory than real. In the words of H. C. Nixon, an informed observer of the region, the South—and Greenville—emerged from World War II "with more social change and more unfinished business than any other part of the country." The economic growth and social dislocation of wartime demanded readjustment.[49]

Notes

1. Greenville *News,* August 30, September 5, 1939.
2. Ibid., Upstate Business section, December 13, 1992.
3. William J. Cooper and Thomas E. Terrill, *The American South: A History* (New York, 1992), 689; George B. Tindall, *The Emergence of the New South, 1913–1945* (Baton Rouge, La., 197), 731.
4. Greenville *News,* September 10, 11, 1939.
5. Ibid., March 22, June 9, 19, August 11, 20, 1940.
6. Ibid., September 17, October 16, 18, 30, 1940; November 28, 1943.
7. Alfred S. Reid, *Furman University: Toward A New Identity, 1925–1975* (Durham, N.C., 1976), 113–14.
8. Greenville *News,* April 18, May 29, 1941.
9. Ibid., December 8, 9, 1941.
10. Ibid., December 17, 1941.
11. Ibid., December 17, 20, 1941.
12. Ibid., December 9, 1941.
13. Ibid., December 9, 10, 13, 1941.
14. "Patrick Bradley Morrah, Jr.," in *Biographical Directory of the S.C. Senate, 1776–1985,* ed. N. Louise Bailey et al. (Columbia, S.C., 1986) 2: 1148–50.
15. Greenville *News,* April 3, 1942; Greenville *Piedmont,* April 15, 1942.
16. Reid, *Furman University,* 114–17.
17. Greenville *News,* December 10, 1941.
18. Ibid., December 11, 14, 23, 1941.
19. Ibid., December 11, 1941.
20. Ibid.
21. Ibid.; *Time* 37 (February 17, 1941), 75–80, cited in Tindall, *Emergence,* 694–95.
22. Greenville *News,* December 12, 1941.
23. C. R. Canup and W. D. Workman, Jr., *Charles E. Daniel: His Philosophy and Legacy* (Columbia, S.C., 1981), 8–10, 58–59.
24. Ibid., 9, 12, 28.
25. Greenville *News,* December 31, 1957.
26. Ibid., February 25, 1940.
27. Ibid., March 7, 1940; January 14, May 8, 1941; February 4, March 5, June 19, 1942.
28. Ibid., May 16, 1940; August 8, 1944.
29. Ibid., January 4, 1942.
30. Ibid., January 2, February 8, 1942.
31. Ibid., January 7, 1942.
32. Ibid., January 4, December 27, 1942.
33. Ibid., December 29, 1941; December 27, 1942; January 2, 1944; December 30, 1945.

34. Ibid., January 7, March 9, 1942.

35. Ibid., May 25, December 16, 1942.

36. Ibid., December 2, 1942; May 9, 1943.

37. Ibid., November 28, 1943.

38. Ibid., December 25, 1945.

39. Ibid., June 7, 1944.

40. Ibid., September 2, 1944; April 13, 1945.

41. Ibid., April 14, 1945.

42. Ibid., April 15, 16, 1945.

43. Ibid., May 8, August, 11, 15, 1945.

44. Ibid., October 23, December 30, 1945.

45. Greenville *News*, December 27, 1945.

46. Schaefer B. Kendrick, "What Kind of Place was Greenville in 1947," *Carologue* 8: 4 (Winter 1992), 7, 14.

47. Samuel L. Zimmerman, Sr., "Kruschev Can Eat Here. Why Can't I?" Ibid., 7, 15–16.

48. Tindall, *Emergence of the New South,* 726–27.

49. Ibid., 731.

The Emergence of Modern Greenville

The momentum of change in Greenville increased significantly after World War II and transformed the city and county into a modern industrial center. However, the movement into the postwar era did not come easily. In 1946 there was a shortage of clothes for men and women. Lines to buy shirts became standard in department stores, and socks, nylon stockings, and overcoats were in great demand. There was also a lack of building supplies. William R. Merritt, a Navy veteran, began constructing a house on Augusta Court, but for weeks there was no plaster available in local building supply houses. Returning veterans, attending college on the GI Bill, flooded local campuses. Between them, Furman and North Greenville Junior College secured over one hundred units of government surplus housing. The Parker District schools acquired buildings from the wartime training facility at the municipal airport. The effort to build a municipal auditorium had languished during the war, but a site was purchased on East North Street in July 1946. However, a series of delays postponed construction, and the Memorial Auditorium was not formally dedicated until May 1959.[1]

The year 1946 ended with the worst catastrophe in the history of the city of Greenville. On the night of November 19, shortly after the Christmas parade, there was a propane gas explosion at the Ideal Laundry on the corner of Buncombe and Echol Streets. Six people were killed, 120 injured, and ten homes were completely destroyed. Plate glass was shattered as far away as Main Street. The Echol Street Fire Station next door to the laundry had to be demolished.[2]

Agriculture

Agriculture soon declined in importance in Greenville County, as it did in much of the South. In December 1946 the Greenville *News* reported that farm tenants were almost a thing of the past. Families that were willing to live in rural areas only wanted housing and a few acres—preferring the commute to nearby industrial plants over farming. Twenty years later, in January 1967, the *News* indicated that agriculture was "in a back seat." Cotton production began to decline dramatically and peach and truck farming remained strong, but more and more acreage was put into grassland. Beef and pork production accounted for $1 million to $2 million annually in income, and milk and eggs $1.5 million each.[3]

Textiles

The textile industry continued to expand after World War II. In 1946 the total investment in textile mills in Greenville County was $39 million; in 1969 alone textile corporations invested $170 million. The Daniel Construction Company captured its first million-dollar contract in 1947. Mill owners upgraded their equipment, expanded their facilities, installed temperature controls, and built entirely new plants.[4]

Giant textile corporations emerged, such as J. P. Stevens and Company, which operated the four Victor-Monaghan mills, as well as the Dunean, Piedmont, and Slater Mills. Eventually, Stevens owned eighteen mills in the Greenville area and moved its manufacturing, personnel, and purchasing headquarters to the city. Chair Robert T. Stevens and Charles Daniel were firm friends, and "Charlie's Company," as Daniel Construction was widely known, did a brisk business with J. P. Stevens.[5]

Alester G. Furman, Jr., also closely associated with Robert Stevens, convinced him that the end of the mill village era had come. Younger workers were moving out of the villages into the suburbs. According to Furman, he once asked Stevens: "Bob, when are you going to sell your houses?" Horrified, Stevens answered: "Never, I'll never do that. We'd lose control of our workers." To which Furman replied: "We'll manage."[6]

On the whole, Greenville's mill workers had remained compliant since the General Textile Strike of 1934. There was only one local union, the Textile Workers Union of America Local 268 at Woodside Mill, headed by Jess Mitchell who had worked in textiles since he was fourteen. On August 15, 1950, after the installation of new equipment, union members at Woodside walked off the job charging a stretch-out by management. Within three days production was down by two-thirds. By the first week in September violence erupted. On September 15 the textile industry began to take action against the union in its own way. Southeastern companies, including Woodside Mills, announced an 8 percent raise to all workers not covered by union contracts. The strike ended on October 10. In March 1954 the state legislature joined other Southern states in passing a "right to work" law, which forbade the closed shop. Woodside Local 268 survived until 1955 when an organizing effort in the Carolinas, Operation Dixie, resulted in the wholesale firing of union members.[7]

The Southern Textile Exposition faced an uncertain future in 1946. Many exhibitors wanted to abandon the Greenville show, but the persistence of Bertha Green, who had been William G. Sirrine's assistant, brought the show an international reputation instead. Meanwhile, the Textile Hall corporation began planning for a new exposition center near the municipal airport and the new U.S. 29-Bypass. James H. Woodside became president and treasurer in 1950, and Yancey Gilkerson became executive vice president in 1961. The 1962 textile show was the last in the old hall, and immediately afterward the new building began to rise. The new Textile Hall opened on October 12, 1964, and in 1969 Greenville became the site of the American Textile Machinery Exhibitions. The number of international exhibitors and visitors caused Greenville business leaders to recognize that the old Textile Center of the South had become the Textile Center of the World.[8]

Industrial Growth

Charles Daniel became a major recruiter for industry for Greenville—and for the South. In 1945 the state legislature created the Research, Planning, and Development Board, and when J. Strom Thurmond was elected governor the next year, the board, the governor, and Daniel began to work together to increase the state's industrial base. That relationship continued through the administrations of James F. Byrnes and George Bell Timmerman. When Ernest F. Hollings became governor in 1959, he appointed Francis M. Hipp, president of Liberty Life Insurance Company, as chair of the reorganized Development Board, and the search for industry accelerated. A story in the October 1954 issue of *Fortune* described Daniel at work:

> By some mysterious method, Daniel learns that a northern manufacturer is planning to build a southern factory almost before the man realizes it himself. When this happens, Daniel appears in the executive's office, bearing an urgent invitation to visit Greenville and learn, "without obligation of any kind," the virtues of setting up shop in South Carolina.
>
> If the customer permits himself to be lured into Daniel's hometown, he is a gone goose.[9]

The efforts at recruitment began to pay off handsomely. Manufacturing in Greenville County expanded sevenfold from 1947 to 1976, and between 1960 and 1976 over $650 million in new industrial investment entered the county—much of it nontextile. At first, recruitment centered on textile-related businesses, such as chemicals and boxes. Then, diversification included electrical equipment, rubber, and aerospace. Between 1960 and 1975 the number of nontextile jobs doubled, from fifteen thousand to thirty thousand, and the share of textiles in the total value of products made in Greenville County declined from more than one-half to less than one-third.[10]

One business, developed after World War II, became nationally known. W. J. (Jack) Greer, a salesperson calling on local textile plants, saw the need for an all-purpose cleaner. In 1947 he established a laboratory in a former stable, and Texize Household Cleaner entered the market. Soon the company expanded to include bleaches, starches, floor cleaner, and liquid detergent. In 1955 Texize moved into a new plant in Mauldin, and eventually Texize became a division of MortonNorwich and then Dow Chemical Company.[11]

The Greenville News-Piedmont Company began to expand, as well, but control still remained in Greenville. In 1953 WFBC merged with WMRC to form the Southeastern Broadcasting Company. Roger C. Peace became chair of the board and Robert A. Jolley, president. On December 26 WFBC-TV went on the air as an NBC affiliate from a transmitter on Paris Mountain. Early in the 1960s, both companies—Southeastern and the News-Piedmont—began purchasing other stations and newspapers. On January 1, 1968, the two local companies merged to form Multimedia, Inc., with Peace as chair and J. Kelly Sisk as president. As the company expanded across the nation, entered the cable television business, and began producing television programming, Greenville became the headquarters of another major national corporation.[12]

Diversification came none too soon for the local labor market. The 1970s and 1980s brought further changes to the textile industry—environmental controls, worldwide inflation, and foreign imports. There were additional mergers involving local mills. For example, Dan River Mills of Virginia purchased Woodside Mills in 1956, but new investment went into the modern Beattie Plant at Fountain Inn. In March 1984 the eighty-two-year-old Woodside Mill shut down. J. P. Stevens and Company completely restructured itself by selling off a number of divisions involving many Greenville plants.[13]

One local company profited handsomely in the era of consolidation.

John D. Hollingsworth On Wheels, Inc., was established in Greenville in 1895, and in the 1960s Hollingworth's son began mergers with textile machinery companies in West Germany, Canada, Massachusetts, Britain, Brazil, and Mexico. In 1982 Hollingsworth took over both Platt-Saco-Lowell and Hergeth. An intensely private man whom few knew outside his own business, he became perhaps the largest manufacturer of textile machinery in the world.[14]

A Countywide Hospital System

City Hospital had expanded into Greenville General prior to World War II. But in 1945 a Citizens' Committee—Robert E. Henry, Richard W. Arrington, Ernest Patton, Roger C. Peace, and Fred W. Symmes—recommended the creation of a joint city-county hospital. Major construction began in 1949 at the old site, and Allen Bennett Hospital in Greer was opened in 1952. The next year Robert E. Toomey became administrator, and began to envision a countywide hospital system. In 1963 Hillcrest Hospital was built in Simpsonville.[15]

In June 1966 John I. Smith, chair of the hospital board, announced the purchase of a twelve-acre site on Grove Road, where a regional medical facility could be constructed. In 1971 Marshall I. Pickens Hospital, a psychiatric facility, opened, followed the next year by Greenville Memorial. North Greenville Hospital in Travelers Rest began to serve the upper part of the county. Shriners Hospital relocated to the Grove Road site, and the complex was known as the Greenville Memorial Medical Center.[16]

Donaldson: From Air Base to Industrial Park

The postwar development of the Greenville Air Base and its transformation into an industrial park was intertwined with the history of industry and the Cold War. After World War II the area expected the air base to close permanently, but the Defense Department retained it as headquarters of the Troop Carrier Command (later the Military Air Transport Command). But the federal government insisted on securing title to the property with no reversionary clause, and the county board of commissioners—Robert A. Jolley, Sr., B. A. Bennett, and Ansel Alewine—resigned in protest. The new board—James H. Woodside, J. C. Keys, Jr., and Alewine—secured such a clause in 1947. Some twenty-two hundred men were stationed at the base, and flew missions all over the world. In 1951 the base was renamed Donaldson in memory of Major John O. Donaldson, a native of Greenville who had served as a distinguished pilot in World War I.[17]

In November 1961 the federal government announced the closing of Donaldson, though it was postponed until 1963 because of the Berlin airlift. When the city and county regained control of the property, they immediately made plans to utilize the facilities for an industrial park. Such parks were springing up all over the South as a way of enticing industry into the region. A Donaldson Management Committee was appointed, with A. D. Asbury as chair. The first occupant of the park was Union Carbide, and by 1990 the Donaldson committee had transmitted to the city and county some $2 million. The employment at Donaldson grew to three thousand people, a thousand more than the air base had at its peak.[18]

Technical Education

The modernization of textiles and the diversification of industry challenged the labor market in the Piedmont, which was largely unprepared for these developments. In December 1960 Governor Ernest Hollings addressed the Greenville County Foundation on the critical need for training if additional industry were attracted to the state. Less than a year later, in May 1961, the legislature created a state system of technical education centers. Sapp Funderburk of Greenville represented the Fourth Congressional District on the board. A Greenville Area committee was established with Preston S. Marchant, president of the Chamber of Commerce, as chair. The Greenville County delegation in September 1961 approved the issuing of general obligation bonds of not more than $540,000, and the Greenville City Council conveyed to the center a site on U.S. 291.[19]

The Greenville Technical Education Center opened on September 5, 1962, with Harvey L. Haynes as director. The center's purpose, according to the first catalog, was "to provide technical training for qualified students, both young and adult, to meet the demand of a modern industrial society." Fifteen full-time and twenty-five part-time instructors taught some eighty day students and two hundred night students during the first session. Initially, the heaviest enrollments were in electronics, data processing, and metalworking.[20]

At the formal dedication on December 7 Governor Hollings invoked the spirit of the New South: "Today marks the beginning of a new educational age for the people of South Carolina. We are moving forward as never before in our history. . . . No longer quiet and self-satisfied, our cities and towns are alert to a new potential. They are determined to make South Carolina a productive community consonant with the technological needs of a new age."[21]

Clemson University began holding classes on the Greenville TEC campus, but in December 1967 the state Commission on Higher Education voted to transform the campus into South Carolina's first comprehensive community college. The Clemson program ended in June 1968 and Greenville Technical College opened in the fall. Thomas E. Barton became president of the college.[22]

Transportation Revolution

When Congress passed the Highway Act of 1956, its impact on Greenville County became as great as the coming of the railroad system in 1873. South of the city, Interstate 85 crossed the county from east to west not far from the site of the southern Indian path. Gradually U.S. 276, the old Laurens Road from Greenville to Mauldin which bypassed Simpsonville and Fountain Inn, was widened to connect with Interstate 26 near Clinton. These new highways became prime sites for textile mills and industrial plants. At the same time the older mill villages began to decline, and new housing developments were built on the eastside of the county and south along the Golden Strip.

A second development in transportation was the building of the Greenville-Spartanburg Airport. By 1957 it was apparent to Charles Daniel that the Piedmont needed a modern airport if it were to expand its industrial base. He enlisted the support of Roger Milliken of Spartanburg, and formed an ad hoc committee from the two counties, which included Alester G. Furman, Jr. Greenville Mayor J. Kenneth Cass gave his endorsement, and the group quietly financed a series of airport design and construction studies focusing on a site between Greer and Pelham equidistant from the cities of Greenville and Spartanburg. In November 1958 Daniel and Milliken unveiled their master plan.[23]

With the support of the two legislative delegations, the General Assembly created an airport district on March 25, 1959, and William T. Adams, Hugh Aiken, and John Rateree represented Greenville County on the board. The airport opened on October 15, 1962. In 1970, after his death, a fountain at the terminal was dedicated to the memory of Charles Daniel.[24]

Growth of the City and Downtown Redevelopment

Tremendous expansion of the Greenville city limits occurred in the years following World War II. In 1946 after a bitter fight, the annexation of the Augusta Road section added some ten thousand persons to the city. In the end, the Augusta Road residents approved annexation by a vote of

859 to 527. Two years later the Superhighway, Overbrook, Eastover, Laurens Road, and West Greenville areas were added. In 1950 Greenville was designated a metropolitan area by the Census Bureau. These additions brought major changes in city government and the shape of downtown.[25]

In 1950, under the leadership of Mayor J. Kenneth Cass and the city council, a referendum was held on the creation of a city manager form of government. The reorganization was approved, 1,575 to 442, and the following year Gerald W. Shaw became Greenville's first city manager. Former director of the Municipal Technical Advisory Service at the University of Tennessee, Shaw served the city of Greenville for twelve years until his death in 1966.[26]

Greenville, like cities across the nation, witnessed the development of suburban shopping malls. At first, they were small groups of connected shops with off-street parking, such as Lewis Plaza on Augusta Street which opened in 1948. Then, in November 1962 Wade Hampton Mall, touted as "a regional shopping center," with stores on two levels and a movie theater, opened. In November 1965 the Bell Tower Limited Partnership unveiled plans for an enclosed mall on 34 acres of the former Furman campus, and a month later the Caine Company announced the construction of McAlister Square at U.S. 291 and Laurens Road for $6.5 million. McAlister would be the largest mall in the state, anchored by Ivey and Meyers-Arnold department stores.[27]

The departure of those two major stores from Main Street accelerated the decline of downtown as a retail shopping center. As usual, Charles Daniel was already championing solutions to the problem. As early as 1957 he told the first meeting of the Downtown Greenville Association that the city was "unclean and neither attractive nor competitive with comparable progressive cities." Already the creation of new traffic patterns downtown was planned with the widening of Church Street and the building of Camperdown Way. That project, including the Church Street and the Reedy River bridges, was completed in October 1960. Charles Daniel's last public act was the ground breaking on June 29, 1964, for the twenty-five-story Daniel Building on North Main Street. When it opened in July 1967, it was the tallest building in South Carolina and a tribute to Daniel's personal contribution toward downtown renewal.[28]

Months before the Daniel Building was completed, the Greenville News-Piedmont Company announced its intention to build a new headquarters on South Main Street. The city itself initially planned to move City Hall to the site of the Greenville Woman's College but, after local protest, the council approved a modern glass and steel structure on Main Street. The campus site became a Civic Center (renamed Heritage Green), which provided space for a new county library, the Charles E. Daniel Theatre, and eventually the Museum of Art.[29]

Then, on February 28, 1976, the Chamber of Commerce formed the Committee for Total Development to spearhead renewal. The committee's leadership spanned two generations; Alester G. Furman, Jr., was chair, and Buck Mickel, Charles Daniel's nephew and president of Daniel Construction Company, was vice chair. In August 1967 the Greenville Area Transportation Study (GRATS) unveiled a $155 million program of highway construction, including freeways and a loop on the west side of downtown.[30]

Redevelopment found a champion in Max Heller, who was one of the founders of the Williamston Shirt Company and in 1948 established the Maxton Shirt Company. In 1969 Heller was elected to the Greenville City Council, and in 1971 he became mayor—a post he held until 1979. The fact that Heller was Jewish indicated the willingness of the local elite to become more inclusive. Under Heller's leadership, the Total Development plan became a priority. The old Woodside Building was replaced with a new glass and steel structure for the South Carolina National Bank. Change accelerated when Greenville received a federal Urban Development Action Grant of $7.4 million, one of the first in the nation.[31]

With these funds available and the active support of Buck Mickel and attorney C. Thomas Wyche, the son of C. Granville Wyche, the city began to acquire property on North Main Street near the Daniel Building. The first effort, in accordance with the Total Development plan, was the construction of hotel and convention facilities. Eventually, the Hyatt chain agreed to build a Regency Hotel, and the city assumed responsibility for the atrium, the parking garage, and the convention center—appropriately named for Max Heller. The success of the Hyatt Regency was the impetus for construction of the U.S. Shelter buildings directly across the street.[32]

Further development of Main Street followed. Revenue sharing funds of $1.5 million paid for widening sidewalks and landscaping. The Coffee Street Mall (later Piazza Bergamo) was constructed, and the old Meyers-Arnold building was transformed into a center for the sale of local arts and crafts.[33]

The School District of Greenville County

At the end of World War II, public education in Greenville was quite uneven. There were eighty-six school districts in the county, with the smallest having only a one-room school. The two largest—the Parker District and the Greenville City District—served two-thirds of the children of the county. In 1949 state Senator Ray R. Williams and the county legislative delegation appointed a committee of fifteen to study the problem of school equalization. Said Williams: "Something has got to be done and it seems to me this is late enough to start to do something about it." The committee proposed consolidation of the school districts, but it could not decide between two competing plans. One was the creation of a single district for the county; the other was the division of the county into three or four districts. In a referendum on July 11, 1950, the citizens rejected any change in the status quo.[34]

The following year, however, Governor Byrnes proposed a program of educational reform which he hoped might forestall the desegregation of the public schools then pending in the federal courts. Byrnes's program was based on the equalization of schools under the "separate but equal" doctrine upheld by the United States Supreme Court since 1896. By legislative act, the Greenville County Board of Education was empowered to create a consolidated school system. On August 23, 1951, the board, chaired by J. B. League, established the School District of Greenville County, and the legislative delegation approved the action. The county board appointed nine trustees, with A. D. Asbury as chair, and the delegation created a series of districts which would subsequently elect trustees.[35]

The implementation of consolidation lay in the hands of Dr. William F. Loggins, the new superintendent. In the nine years before his retirement in 1960, Loggins eliminated 102 small schools and proposed the construction of twenty-four new buildings. Slowly an educational program of greater equality began to emerge, as well as a cohesive district structure. But the scars of the swift consolidation of schools in disparate areas of the county remained, and though they were submerged in the 1960s and 1970s by the issue of racial desegregation, they reemerged in the 1980s compounded by the strength of the Religious Right.[36]

Higher Education: Bob Jones and Furman

Higher education in Greenville changed after World War II, as well. The Chamber of Commerce wooed Bob Jones College, a Christian fundamentalist institution, from Tennessee to a new campus on Wade Hampton Boulevard in 1947. The founder and inspiration for the college was Robert Reynolds Davis Jones, born in south Alabama in 1883. Bob Jones was a traveling evangelist in the mold of Sam Jones and Billy Sunday, but in 1926 he broke ground for a college in Panama City, Florida, which would become his institutional base. Bob Jones College survived the Great Depression and moved to Cleveland, Tennessee, in 1933.[37]

After World War II the college had no further space in which to expand, and plans were made to move. At that point the Greenville Chamber of Commerce became active in recruiting the institution. E. Roy Stone, chamber executive Kenneth B. Miles, Walter Goldsmith, and R. C. McCall of Easley led the effort. The chamber secured options on 180 acres of land on the Superhighway (now Wade Hampton Boulevard), and soon a new campus, costing over $3.5 million began to rise. By the time President Bob Jones dedicated the campus on Thanksgiving Day, 1947, it had been transformed into Bob Jones University. Soon it became the largest fundamentalist institution of higher education in the world.

A strong program of fine arts began on the Greenville campus. Besides music and drama, Bob Jones inaugurated Unusual Films, and in 1950 the university opened its Art Gallery of Religious Paintings. The collection of Baroque art grew rapidly and received international acclaim.

The forthright position of Bob Jones University in support of biblical literalism drew thousands of supporters to the campus, both as students and as participants in its annual Bible conferences. An ongoing controversy with Evangelist Billy Graham (a former student), the struggle to maintain racial segregation, and the school's ever-increasing involvement in politics kept the university in the local and national media.

At the same time Bob Jones University relocated in Greenville, Furman University entered a new era which transformed the state Baptist institution into a nationally known independent liberal arts college. The first step in that process was the consolidation of its two campuses and the construction of modern facilities. Enrollment grew rapidly after World War II and severely taxed existing buildings.[38] President John Plyler, board chair Alester G. Furman, Jr., and Dean Crain, pastor of Pendleton Street Baptist Church, envisioned a entirely new campus, and in 1950 the university purchased 973 acres near Travelers Rest. The architectural firm which had rebuilt Colonial Williamsburg—Perry, Shaw and Hepburn, Kehoe and Dean—was secured to design the campus, and the formal ground breaking occurred on October 6, 1953. Not until 1961, however, did both men and women students occupy the new campus.[39]

The second phase in the transformation of Furman was national recognition. Dean Francis W. Bonner began to build a strong faculty in the postwar decades, and Gordon W. Blackwell, president from 1965 to 1976, launched a major financial campaign aimed at "greatness by national standards." The first African-American students were admitted voluntarily, a new curriculum adopted, and in August 1973 Furman was granted a chapter of Phi Beta Kappa, the nation's most prestigious honor society.[40]

The third phase in creating a new identity at Furman was the university's break with the South Carolina Baptist Convention. President John E. Johns (1976–1994) watched warily as the national resurgence of fundamentalism invaded and then seized control of the Southern Baptist Convention, beginning in 1979. When the state convention began to name fundamentalists to the Furman board on a regular basis in 1988, the university reacted. On October 15, 1990, the trustees voted to amend the charter to allow the board, not the convention, to elect their successors, and Furman became independent of church control.[41]

The Willie Earle Lynching

Changes in race relations did not come easily or willingly to Greenville. Life in the segregated South resumed much the same pattern followed before 1941. But in 1944 the United States Supreme Court ruled in *Smith v. Allwright* that the white Democratic primary in Texas was unconstitutional. Even though the South Carolina legislature immediately acted to make the party a private organization, blacks formed the state Progressive Democratic Party to more political activity. On June 5, 1946, ten black citizens attempted to vote in the Democratic primary in Greenville, but they were turned away.[42]

Race relations took a violent turn in 1947 when a black man, Willie Earle, was lynched by a group of white taxicab drivers. On Saturday night, February 14, Earle, a twenty-four-year-old epileptic, hired Thomas W. Brown to drive him to his mother's home near Liberty, in Pickens County. About 10:00 P.M. Brown was discovered beside his wrecked cab, critically wounded. Pickens County officers shortly arrested Earle and transferred him to the county jail. On Sunday night, a group of Brown's friends gathered at the Bluebird Taxicab office, near the Greenville County Courthouse, and hatched a plan to lynch Willie Earle. Sometime after midnight some fifteen cars, mostly taxis, gathered for the twenty-mile ride to Pickens. At 5:00 A.M. they arrived at the Pickens County Jail, and a group of armed men called to Ed Gilstrap, the jailer, that they had come for "the Negro." Gilstrap unlocked Earle's cell, and the men drove away with the prisoner. About 6:25 A.M. Earle's body was discovered on Bramlett Road in Greenville County. Some six hours later Thomas Brown died at St. Francis Hospital. News of these events spread quickly through Greenville, to the state capital, and to Washington. Governor Thurmond, who had assumed office in

January, vowed to "exert every force at my command to apprehend all persons engaged in such a flagrant violation [of the law]." He notified the Federal Bureau of Investigation and gave his full support to state and local law enforcement officers. Eventually twenty-eight taxi drivers and three other individuals were arrested and indicted by the grand jury.[43]

The state attorney general, John M. Daniel, appointed Spartanburg attorney Sam Watt to assist Circuit Solicitor and later Congressman Robert T. Ashmore in prosecuting the case. The defendants were represented by four well-known Greenville attorneys—future U.S. Senator Thomas A. Wofford, Benjamin A. Bolt, John Bolt Culbertson, and future state Senator P. Bradley Morrah, Jr., The trial began on May 12 in a hot, crowded courtroom filled with some three hundred participants, families, spectators, and a large corps of journalists from around the world. Perhaps the most noted journalist was the British writer, Rebecca West, who represented *The New Yorker.* Locally, white opinion favored the defendants. Many people were angry that the case was being tried at all. Fruit jars appeared in stores and restaurants for contributions for the defendants' expenses. Talk on the street had it that they would never be convicted.

The jury consisted of twelve white males—nine mill workers, one farmer, and two salespeople. The first week of the trial consisted of reading the defendants' statements. Judge J. Robert Martin, later a federal district judge, acquitted three men for insufficient evidence and reduced the charges against seven others. On May 21 the jury began its deliberations, and five hours later reached its verdict. At 9:30 P.M. the court resumed to hear the verdict of not guilty on ninety-six separate counts.

Though the defendants were acquitted, the incident was a setback for the old order. Rebecca West sensed it when she wrote "Opera in Greenville" for the *New Yorker:* "The lynching trial in South Carolina and its sequels were a symptom of an abating disease. . . . There was a strange and dramatic tempo to be felt at the Greenville trial; wickedness itself had been aware of the slowing of its pulse. The will of the South had made its decision." A cartoon in the *Christian Science Monitor* carried the same message showing an acorn beneath the yard of a Southern mansion. The wording around the acorn read: "Greenville's Effort to Outlaw Mob Violence." The cartoon was entitled: "An Acorn Has Been Planted." Members of the black community determined that things would have to change. "This lynching disturbed us," recalled black leader Abraham J. Whittenberg; "nothing was ever done about it. So we felt we would have to come out for ourselves and stand up for our rights." The trial had a somewhat different impact on white Greenville. Schaefer B. Kendrick, then a young attorney, later recalled that "the real concern, down deep, of the white group, of which I was a part, was the effect the Earle lynching and resulting trial would have on Greenville's image as a progressive, cultural, growing city of the New South." The murder of Willie Earle was the last lynching in South Carolina and one of the last in the South.[44]

Changes in Race Relations

Change began accelerating in the late 1940s. In July 1947 Federal Judge J. Waites Waring of Charleston declared the South Carolina white primary unconstitutional, and the following year a large number of black citizens registered to vote in the Democratic primary. Whittenberg recalled that the blacks were not welcomed: "We were told by a lot of people we were not wanted. I went to a Democratic Party meeting in 1948 and I was asked to leave. But I wouldn't leave."[45]

In the spring of 1948 a group of black women requested the YWCA Board of Directors to open a branch for blacks. The board asked the Community Council of Greenville County to determine the need for such a branch. When the study began in July 1949, it had widened to a "Survey of Negro Conditions in the Greenville Area." Mrs. C. C. Withington and J. E. Beck, principal of Sterling High School, became co-chairs of a steering committee which supervised the work of eleven study committees co-chaired by interracial teams. The members included community leaders such as Wayne Freeman (editor of the Greenville *Piedmont*), Mrs. John M. Holmes, Dr. E. A. E. Huggins, L. P. Hollis, Noah Robinson, and Dorothy S. Welborn. In May 1950 the Community Council produced a comprehensive assessment at first entitled *Everybody's Business* and later *Greenville's Big Idea*. The assessment noted with optimism that there were already a number of efforts underway to improve the conditions of blacks, and it lauded "the greater feeling of understanding and cooperation between both races who participated in this study."[46]

But when the Supreme Court declared that segregation in the public schools was unconstitutional in *Brown v. Board of Education* in May 1954, white hostility toward blacks stiffened even more. South Carolina leaders declared their support of massive resistance, and Greenville made no effort to comply with the decision. Wayne Freeman, who had become editor of the Greenville *News,* vigorously defended the old order. He denounced the *Brown* decision as "an insult to the intelligence of White people." He called for closing the schools rather than desegregating them.[47] Bob Jones, Sr., proclaimed that intermingling the races was contrary to God's plan and that efforts to create "one world and one race outside the body of Christ has been of the devil." There was a resurgence of the Ku Klux Klan in the Greenville area with some meetings attracting several thousand people. A white Citizens Council was organized and included some prominent citizens, such as Dr. Thomas Parker, a member of the steering committee which had prepared *Greenville's Big Idea*.[48]

The most vocal supporter of compliance with the *Brown* decision was retired Parker District Superintendent L. Peter Hollis. Before and after *Brown*, Hollis called for cooperation between the races and criticized politicians for a failure of leadership. He urged blacks to vote and supported their representation on city council, the school board, and in the legislature. He was joined by the YMCA, the League of Women Voters, the American Association of University Women, and the Council of Church Women. The YMCA provided one of the few places where meals were available for interracial meetings. In 1956 a Greenville Council on Human Relations provided white liberals an organization in which they could communicate with blacks.[49]

Tension between the races grew even more with the inauguration of civil rights demonstrations. The first demonstration in South Carolina was held in Greenville in response to two events at the municipal airport. Early in 1959 Richard Henry, an African-American airman, was ordered out of the white waiting room. In October 1959, while Henry's case was pending, African-American baseball star Jackie Robinson spoke in Greenville at a meeting of the state conference of the National Association for the Advancement of Colored People (NAACP), and he was subsequently was asked to leave the white waiting room. On Emancipation Day, January 1, 1960, the NAACP sponsored a march from Springfield Baptist Church in downtown Greenville to the airport. Some 250 African Americans, led by the Reverend Matthew D. McCullom of Orangeburg, representing the NAACP, and the Reverend J. S. Hall, chair of the Greenville chapter of the Congress of Racial Equality (CORE), presented a resolution to airport authorities which denounced "the stigma, the inconvenience and the stupidity of racial segregation."[50]

Later that year groups of young African Americans began to test local segregation laws. On March 16, 1960, Robert G. Anderson, Jr., and Benjamin Downes were asked to leave the county library when they attempted to use the reading room. In July eight African-American students were arrested during a sit-in, and the library was closed. That same month there were demonstrations at the lunch counters at S. H. Kress, F. W. Woolworth, and W. T. Grant Stores on Main Street, and in August police began a series of arrests. A short time later a demonstration occurred at the white municipal skating rink in Cleveland Park.[51]

The responses to these actions was varied. In the library case, local African-American attorney Willie T. Smith, Jr., was joined by NAACP Legal and Defense Fund attorneys Jack Greenberg, Matthew Perry, and Thurgood Marshall. Before the case could be heard in federal district court, the chair of the library board, Romayne A. Barnes, announced that the library would reopen on September 19, 1960, "for the benefit of any person having a legitimate need." In the skating rink case, Federal Judge Ashton Williams ruled in October 1962 that by that time the principle that segregation in city parks was unconstitutional was clear.[52]

Meanwhile, a group of African-American citizens appeared before the Greenville City Council on January 10, 1961, and requested council "to act on segregation matters affecting our city." In response, a group of the white elite decided that it was time for some positive action—including Charles E. Daniel, Alester G. Furman, Jr., L. P. Hollis, and Thomas A. Roberts, the rector of Christ Church. This group was soon known informally as the Advisory Committee.[53]

A major signal that the attitude of the white power structure had begun to change came on July 1, 1961, when Charles Daniel, who had served briefly as a U.S. senator after the death of Burnet R. Maybank, made a landmark speech at the annual Watermelon Festival in Hampton. The Greenville business leader proposed an alternative to massive resistance. "The desegregation issue," he said, "cannot continue to be hidden behind the door. This situation cannot be settled at the lunch counter and bus station levels. We must handle this ourselves, more realistically than heretofore; or it will be forced upon us in the harshest way. Either we act on our own terms, or we forfeit the right to act."[54]

Events on the national level moved quickly. The University of Mississippi was ordered to accept an African-American student in the fall of 1962, and Greenvillians, like the rest of America, sat stunned before their television sets as they watched the outbreak of open warfare on the campus. "What has happened in Mississippi," said the Greenville *Piedmont*, "can happen [here]. . . . Thinking South Carolinians hope the lesson is being impressed upon the leaders of this state and upon all the people of this state."[55]

On a Sunday afternoon in the fall of 1962, a meeting convened at the home of Arthur Magill, president of Her Majesty apparel company which included Roberts; L. D. Johnson, pastor of the First Baptist Church; John Haley, pastor of Westminster Presbyterian Church; and David Cooley, executive secretary of the Chamber of Commerce. Those present agreed that the Chamber create a biracial committee of an equal number of African Americans and whites, subsequently co-chaired by Preston Marchant and Willie Smith. At first the biracial committee was composed of African American members A. J. Whittenberg, Mark Tolbert, J. Edgar (Tiny) Smith, E. L. McPherson, Harrison Reardon, Smith, Sampson, and Zimmerman; and white members Yancey Gilkerson, T. J. Mims, Schaefer Kendrick, Leonard Todd, Alfred Burgess, Hollis, and Johnson.[56]

The work of the biracial committee was intensive—operating under an agreement of secrecy with regular meetings scheduled. Emergencies often required additional sessions of both the full committee and its subcommittees. Alfred Burgess later estimated that about one-fourth of his time was occupied with biracial committee meetings in the beginning. Meanwhile a County Citizens Committee, broadly representative of the community and chaired by Furman Professor Ernest E. Harrill, began meeting as well. The success of the biracial committee was noteworthy. When the United States Supreme Court ruled that Greenville's trespass ordinances were unconstitutional, the committee recommended to the city council the repeal of its segregation laws. The council formally acted on May 27, 1963. After detailed planning, eleven eating establishments agreed to serve African Americans. On June 3, 1963, still recognized as a state holiday honoring Confederate President Jefferson Davis, L. P. Hollis and Alex Chambers, pastor of the Israel Metropolitan CME Church, met for breakfast at Woolworth. Quickly, other restaurants and lunch counters followed suit.[57]

Meanwhile, Bob Jones University continued its opposition to the civil rights movement. In March 1963 retired Major General Edwin A. Walker spoke on the campus. The year before he had been one of the major white leaders in opposing the integration of the University of Mississippi. In May 1964 Governor George Wallace of Alabama received an honorary degree from Bob Jones, and while in Greenville he called for support in his campaign to maintain racial segregation in the South.[58]

Public School Desegregation

In the summer of 1963 A. J. Whittenberg, president of the Greenville branch of the NAACP and a member of the biracial committee, along with the parents of five other African-American students requested their children be transferred to all-white schools. When their requests were denied, they filed suit in the federal district court. They were assisted by the NAACP

Legal and Defense Fund and represented by Willie Smith and Matthew J. Perry. The school district was represented by its attorney, E. P. (Ted) Riley, former chair of the state Democratic Party. In March 1964 Federal Judge J. Robert Martin, who had presided over the Willie Earle trial, refused to dismiss the case and gave the school board thirty days to reconsider. On April 14 the school board transferred the children to white schools under a limited freedom-of-choice plan. In July Superintendent of Schools Marion T. Anderson announced that fifty-five African-American students would be transferred to sixteen white schools.[59]

Community response to school desegregation was predictable. Wayne Freeman, writing in the Greenville *News* was blunt: "We are opposed to integration of the schools, now or in the foreseeable future. . . . For now we can only make the best of this inevitable situation . . . but disruption of the schools or the public peace and good order will not be tolerated." The Greenville Education Committee was formed by the parents of the African-American students involved in the court suit to build support for desegregation. To aid the students, the committee held a six-week program of tutorials to provide academic and psychological support. An interracial staff, headed by retired Furman Professor Sara Lowery, worked with the orientation program.[60]

The schools opened peacefully on September 1, 1964, though law enforcement officials stood by for several days. The African-American students were constantly harassed and consequently kept to themselves. Elaine Whittenberg's life was threatened repeatedly, and an FBI agent was assigned to protect her. But desegregation was still token and would remain so until further federal court action. The local civil rights movement received a boost on April 30, 1967, when Martin Luther King, Jr., spoke to a rally of thirty-five hundred people in Memorial Auditorium.[61]

Federal court action came in two waves. In May 1968 the state supreme court declared freedom-of-choice plans unacceptable, and in October 1969 the court ordered every school district to terminate dual systems at once. The Fourth Circuit Court ordered the School District of Greenville County to submit a plan for desegregation by January 23, 1970. Most white Greenvillians seemed to accept the inevitability of the situation.[62]

There were exceptions, however. White private Christian schools began to appear. Southside Christian School led the way in 1966, followed by Hampton Park (1968), Shannon Forest (1969), Washington Avenue (1970), and Boulevard Baptist (1970). Some Greenville citizens formed protest organizations including Citizens for Freedom of Choice, which held a meeting attended by some three thousand at Parker High School on January 22, 1970, and later opened an office downtown. Citizens to Prevent Busing was led by Carroll A. Campbell, Jr., a future congressional member and governor. On January 25 Campbell led a motorcade from Greenville to Columbia to lobby for freedom-of-choice legislation. Some three thousand people participated in that protest. African Americans who were concerned about loss of identity and the integration of the school administration formed Concerned Black Parents, chaired by H. L. Sullivan.[63]

The turbulence in the county was reflected in bomb threats to schools, hate mail and telephone calls to supporters of the school plan, and the burning of Davenport Junior High School in Greer. School board chair Harley Bonds asked for help from citizens. Ernest Harrill became chair of a biracial committee of thirty to assist the school district in the transition. Trustee William N. Page was the liaison with the school board, and Clelia Hendricks, coordinator of public information, provided staff support. Soon subcommittees were raising funds, sponsoring contests, providing orientation sessions for students and teachers, and enlisting volunteers.[64]

The plan, which affected the fifty-eight thousand students and five hundred teachers in the district, closed most all-African-American schools and then reassigned 60 percent of the African-American students and 10 percent of the white students. Seventy-five percent of the busing involved African-American students. Superintendent M. T. Anderson later admitted that the African-American community bore the brunt of desegregation.[65]

The schools of Greenville County reopened on February 17, 1970, after a long weekend of work in which furniture, textbooks, libraries, and classroom materials were moved. Some school buses were late, but there was no violence. The only pickets that day were at Armstrong Elementary School. Ernest Harrill made a statement that was broadcast by the national media: "I believe that Greenville can never be the same. We did what we had to, but the people have done it with grace and style; and out of it must come something better for all the community."[66]

Yet desegregation had been forced, and resentments still smoldered. In April African-American educators presented a list of grievances to the school board, and the following November there was violence at Berea, Greenville, Wade Hampton, and J. L. Mann High Schools. The board appointed ombudsmen to mediate between students and administrators. Harrill later commented: "Sad to say, we've been moved only by the law and not by our own spirit."[67]

Jesse Jackson

During this time, Greenville native Jesse Jackson became a leader in the civil rights movement nationally. Born in 1941, Jackson had grown up in the postwar era on Haynie Street under the watchful eye of his mother, Helen, and his grandmother, Aunt Tibby, while his stepfather, Charles Jackson, was in service. Jesse's father, Noah Robinson, lived next door, but he contributed little to his son's upbringing. When Charles Jackson returned from World War II, the family moved from Haynie Street to University Ridge, and eventually to Anderson Street. The combined salaries from Charles Jackson's work at the post office and Helen Jackson's work as a beautician placed the family in a relatively comfortable financial position in the African-American community. Always central to the life of the Jackson family was the Longbranch Baptist Church. Jesse once remarked: "That revolutionary Gospel I learned at Longbranch Baptist—I've found no higher truths."[68]

At Sterling High School Jackson was a good student and a superb quarterback. He spent his freshman year in college at the University of Illinois and transferred to North Carolina Agricultural and Technical College in Greensboro, where he became involved in the civil rights movement. Later as a student at the Chicago Theological Seminary, he became further involved, and he eventually went to work for the Southern Christian Leadership Conference and Operation Breadbasket.[69]

Jesse Jackson was honored publicly in Greenville on October 6, 1973, at a banquet at the Poinsett Hotel, where he had once worked. The banquet was billed as the largest interracial gathering in the state's history, and more than a thousand people came to hear Mayor Max Heller say that "Jesse Jackson is good for America." A decade later, in 1984, and again in 1988, Jackson was a serious candidate for the Democratic presidential nomination.[70]

The Growth of the Republican Party

The political complexion of Greenville, along with much of the South, began to change with the advent of the civil rights movement. When the National Democratic Party adopted a civil rights plank in the party platform in 1948, Governor Strom Thurmond joined the States Rights Democrats in forming a third party and became their presidential candidate. On November 2 Greenville County joined the state in casting South Carolina's electoral votes for Thurmond. Though African Americans voted in 1948 in greater numbers than ever before in the twentieth century, Greenville County cast 3,376 votes for Thurmond and 2,486 votes for Harry Truman. Republican Thomas Dewey received 844 votes, and Henry Wallace, another dissident Democrat, 30 votes.[71]

As yet, there were no wholesale permanent defections from the Democratic Party. The midterm elections in 1950 brought forth only Democratic candidates in Greenville, though the county convention tabled a resolution condemning the Truman administration. In the 1952 election many Democratic precinct meetings endorsed U.S. Senator Richard B. Russell of Georgia for president. When Russell's nomination failed, many local Democrats, including Mrs. Belton R. O'Neall, vice chair of the county executive committee, indicated she would vote for Republican Dwight Eisenhower on the Democrats for Eisenhower ticket supported by Governor Byrnes. The local Eisenhower campaign was well-organized, and eventually the Eisenhower independents carried the county with 17,092 votes. Adlai Stevenson, the Democratic candidate, received 11,963 votes. There were only 651 Republican ballots cast. South Carolina, however, remained in the Democratic column.[72]

In the 1956 presidential election, Eisenhower came within one thousand votes of carrying Greenville County on the Republican ticket—11,817 for Stevenson to 10,818 for Eisenhower. In the city the Republicans were triumphant—6,314 to 3,693. The state and local Democratic slate ran unopposed. Wayne Freeman, writing in the Greenville *News,* made the outcome clear: "Personalities and the race issue had a lot to do with the way South Carolinians voted." But Republicans were still fearful of deeply rooted Democratic loyalties, so Freeman added what became a part of the strategy to smooth the way to voting Republican for white Southerners: "It [the election] still represented a strong spirit of independence and should prove once and for all that this state is not 'in the bag' for any particular party." That theme was enlarged in the 1960 presidential election, when Senator Barry Goldwater, a leader of the conservative wing of the Republican Party spoke on behalf of Richard M. Nixon in Greenville in September. He offered the GOP "not as a permanent home, but one to live in until the South can recapture the Democratic Party." John F. Kennedy carried South Carolina narrowly, but in Greenville Nixon triumphed 22,179 to 13,720. The next year Charles Daniel welcomed Nixon warmly to his new estate, White Oaks, near the Furman campus.[73]

In the midst of the civil rights struggle, the presidential election of 1964 offered South Carolinians a clear choice between Goldwater and incumbent Democratic President Lyndon B. Johnson. County Republicans, cheered by the election of R. Cooper White, Jr., to the Greenville City Council the previous year, nominated a full slate of candidates for the state House of Representatives. Jeff Richardson, chair of the county Republican Party, denounced Democrats as "anti-Southern" and "anti-American." Goldwater spoke to a cheering crowd of twenty thousand people at the Greenville-Spartanburg Airport in September, and U.S. Senator Strom Thurmond, who switched to the Republican Party in September, wound up a series of speeches in the county with a fiery address at Parker High School. In the November election Goldwater swept Greenville County, as well as South Carolina. However, the county legislative delegation remained solidly Democratic.[74]

Sizeable Republican inroads in local offices occurred two years later, when the county convention again nominated a full slate for the House of Representatives, as well as candidates for selected county offices. In the election of 1966 only four Democrats maintained their House seats, and seven Republicans were elected, including Carolyn E. Frederick, the first woman elected to the legislature from Greenville County. But the gains were not permanent. In 1968, as Richard Nixon swept the county and the state, only local Republicans John Earle, Carolyn Frederick, and Mac V. Patterson held their House seats; Democrats won the rest. In 1970 the Republicans regrouped and won a majority on county council, but they remained in the minority in the House.[75]

The growing Republican success at the polls received a serious setback in 1976. The candidacy of Ronald Reagan for the Republican presidential nomination captured the allegiance of the Religious Right, a collection of fundamentalist and evangelical groups that advocated a conservative political agenda, and in Greenville visiting fundamentalist preacher Al Janney, speaking in a number of large independent Baptist churches (such as Southside and Hampton Park), urged his listeners to jump into the political fray. His listeners responded by packing the Republican precinct meetings and seizing control of the county convention with the use of floor leaders, walkie-talkies, and rigid discipline. The entire county Republican leadership, most of whom had come into the party during the Goldwater campaign of 1964, was voted out of office. They withdrew and formed a rival organization, the Piedmont Republican Club and blamed their ouster on the influence of Bob Jones University. Bob Jones III, who had become president of the university, was bitter: "The citizenry is awakened from its lethargy, but it was in every respect a movement of the people." The losers, he said, "inflamed bigotry against this institution." Nevertheless, until 1980 Greenville County had essentially two Republican parties, and the result was disastrous in local races.[76]

In 1980, with the prospect of Ronald Reagan's victory at hand, the two groups made peace, but it was not a comfortable truce. The fundamentalists and the business elite were from two different social and economic groups, but politically they learned to work together and divide the spoils of office. The fundamentalists became a mainstay of the Republican Party in Greenville County, just as African-American voters had become in the Democratic Party.[77]

Clement Haynsworth and the Supreme Court Nomination

Greenville came into the national spotlight when President Nixon nominated native son Clement Furman Haynsworth, Jr., to a seat on the United States Supreme Court in 1969. Born in 1912, he was the son and grandson of members of the Haynsworth law firm and the great-grandson of Furman President James Clement Furman. He graduated *summa cum laude* from Furman in 1933 and from Harvard Law School in 1936. Haynsworth returned to Greenville to practice law until he entered the Navy during World War II. In 1957 he was nominated to the Fourth Circuit Court of Appeals by President Eisenhower and eventually became chief judge.[78]

Elected president in 1968 by appealing to Southern white voters, Nixon promised to appoint conservative Southern judges to the Supreme Court. In 1969 he selected Haynsworth, and the first wave of reaction to the nomination was positive. The American Bar Association rated Haynsworth highly qualified, but a storm began to develop over a series of Haynsworth's decisions that were deemed hostile to organized labor, possible conflicts of interest, and questions about the nominee's views on civil rights. As the Senate Judiciary Committee hearings dragged on, opposition to Haynsworth grew among labor and civil rights advocates. Eventually, the committee recommended confirmation, 10–6, but the Senate voted to reject his nomination, 55–45. A bitter experience for Haynsworth and for Greenville, the judge continued to sit on the Fourth Circuit Court until a few months before his death in 1989.[79]

Changes in State and Local Government

Structural changes after 1960 brought greater diversity to state and local government. As a result of the "one person-one vote" ruling of the United States Supreme Court in 1964, members of the state legislature no longer represented counties, but represented election districts roughly equal in population. In 1975 the General Assembly created 124 single member state House districts, and in 1983 forty-six single member Senate districts. In 1974 African-American attorney Theo W. Mitchell was elected to the House and was succeeded in 1984 by Sara V. Shelton. In 1984 Mitchell won a seat in the state Senate.

Control of county affairs by the legislative delegation proved difficult, if not impossible, with reapportionment. In November 1968 Greenville County elected its first county council to handle local matters. At first, the county was divided into nine districts, and each member lived in a separate district, but was elected from the county as a whole. In 1975 the Local Government Act created single member districts, and local areas gained a voice in county affairs, while the business community in the city of Greenville lost its overriding influence. In the 1980s the two political parties were split fairly evenly on county council, and the members learned to conduct business more by compromise than by confrontation.[80]

The "one-person, one vote" ruling also resulted in minimizing the influence of small, rural counties in the state legislature and increasing the power of the more populous, urban areas such as Greenville. In the state House of Representatives, Rex Carter of Greenville succeeded Sol Blatt of rural Barnwell County as speaker in 1973. In 1979 Democrat Richard W. Riley became the first governor from Greenville since Martin Ansel left office in 1911, and Riley was succeeded by another Greenvillian, Republican Carroll A. Campbell, Jr., in 1987. Nick A. Theodore of Greenville became lieutenant governor that same year.

Richard W. Riley

South Carolina's chief executive from 1979 to 1987, Richard Riley was the first native born Greenvillian to serve as governor. Born in 1933, he was the son of E. P. (Ted) Riley, who served as assistant U.S. attorney and later as chair of the state Democratic Party. Riley was a graduate of Furman, the University of South Carolina Law School, and a Navy veteran. He served first in the state House of Representatives (1963–1966) and then in the state Senate (1967–1976), where he championed county home rule and constitutional reform.[81]

In 1974 Riley was unsuccessful in securing the gubernatorial nomination and retired from the state Senate. But in 1978 he was elected governor and served for eight years. The centerpiece of his administration was the passage of the Educational Improvement Act in 1984, which placed South Carolina in the forefront of national educational reform. In 1993 President William Clinton appointed Riley U.S. secretary of education.[82]

Cultural Life

Cultural activities revived after World War II, though religion remained dominant in the lives of most Greenvillians. The Greenville *News* reported in 1947 in the midst of the postwar building boom that there was $1 million in church construction planned over the next five years. The religious revival of the 1940s and 1950s resulted in the building of new churches and the expansion of old ones. Sunday closing laws continued to occupy the attention of the community, and in a referendum on March 1957 the city approved Sunday movies, while the county voted no. There were efforts to secure a Billy Graham Crusade as early as 1950, but not until March 4, 1966, did a Greenville crusade begin in Textile Hall. On the second day twenty-five thousand people attended, while many were turned away. So on March 9 two services began each day. By the end of the crusade on March 13 some 278,700 had attended—the last great interdenominational revival effort sponsored by the mainline churches in the tradition of the Second Great Awakening. Indeed, the fracturing of the evangelical Protestant establishment was indicated by the strong opposition to Graham's visit by Bob Jones University.[83]

In 1990 religion remained a major social force in Greenville County. Church members accounted for 64.9 percent of the population—more than the state as a whole, which had 61.9 percent, and the nation, which had 55.1 percent. Southern Baptist and African-American Baptist churches accounted for 40.7 percent of the membership. United Methodists were second with 7.2 percent of the population, and United Presbyterians were third with 3.4 percent. Since World War II the presence of Bob Jones University provided an institutional center around which the growing fundamentalist churches could coalesce.[84]

The Little Theatre was reorganized in December 1945 with Robert H. McLane, a talented drama teacher at Greenville High School, as director. At first the Little Theatre operated in a modest structure on Lowndes Hill Road, but eventually it moved into the handsome Charles E. Daniel Theatre. Bob Jones University joined Furman in offering a full range of artistic activities beginning in 1947. The Greenville Symphony was reorganized and gave its first concert in December 1948. By 1956 it had fifty-five members and employed Peter Rickett as its first resident conductor. The Art Association purchased the Gassaway Mansion as a permanent home, and in 1974 the art museum moved into a new structure adjoining the Little Theatre. The theater, the museum, and the new Greenville County Library shared Heritage Green, the site of the male and female academies and the Woman's College. The art museum enjoyed national prestige for several years in the 1980s when local industrialist Arthur Magill displayed his collection of Andrew Wyeth paintings.

The Peace Center for the Performing Arts

Greenville's role as a regional cultural center was greatly enhanced with the opening of the Peace Center for the Performing Arts with three performances on November 30 and December 1 and 2, 1990. The center had its roots in discussions among the supporters of the symphony, the Metropolitan Arts Council, the Community Foundation, and the city council. After the recapitalization of Multimedia, attorney David Freeman approached Elizabeth Peace Stall about funding for such a center by the Peace family. The Center for the Performing Arts Foundation was chartered in 1986 with Elizabeth Stall, president; Frances Graham McIlwinen, vice president; Etca Ramsaur White, secretary; Eric Amstutz, treasurer; and David Freeman, advisor. The foundation began with a $10 million gift by the family of Bony Hampton Peace. Constructed through a partnership with state, county, and city governments on the banks of the Reedy River, where Richard Pearis had originally settled, the center incorporated the remaining buildings of the old carriage factory and the Huguenot Mill. But the Peace Center was not only a facility for the performing arts; it served as the anchor for the future economic redevelopment of South Main Street. Thus, the center became a striking embodiment of Greenville's past, present, and hope for the future.[85]

Notes

1. Greenville *Piedmont*, December 26, 1946, January 3, 1960.

2. William D. Browning, *Firefighting in Greenville, 1840–1990* (Greenville, 1991), 99–104.

3. Greenville *News*, December 28, 1946; December 31, 1950; January 1, 1967.

4. C. R. Canup and W. D. Workman, Jr., *Charles E. Daniel: His Philosophy and Legacy* (Columbia, 1981), 35–36; M. A. Cross, "Today's Textile Scene in Greenville County" *Proceedings and Papers of the Greenville County Historical Society* (hereafter cited as *PPGCHS*) 4 (1968–1971): 17; Yancey S. Gilkerson, "1940–1950: War Effort Brings Maximum Production, Post-War Boom," *America's Textiles International* 16 (June 1987): 104.

5. Gilkerson, "1940–1950," 103; Canup and Workman, *Daniel*, 36–37.

6. Cliff Sloan and Bob Hall, "It's Good to be Home in Greenville," *Southern Exposure* 7 (Spring 1979): 1, 88–89.

7. James A. Dunlap III, "Victims of Neglect: The Career and Creations of John T. Woodside, 1865–1986" (M.A. thesis, University of South Carolina, 1981), 88–97; George C. Rogers, Jr., and C. James Taylor, *A South Carolina Chronology, 1497–1992,* 2nd ed. (Columbia, 1994), 137.

8. Gilkerson, "Textile Hall's First Sixty Years" *PPGCHS* 5 (1971–1975): 79–83.

9. Reprinted in Canup and Workman, *Daniel,* 57.

10. Ibid., 44; Sloan and Hall, "It's Good to be Home," 88.

11. Nancy Vance Ashmore, *Greenville: Woven from the Past* (Northridge, Calf., 1986), 240.

12. Greenville *News,* December 27, 31, March 19, 1986.

13. Gilkerson, "1970–1980: Fuel Shortages, OSHA Plagues Textiles in 70s—And Then Imports," *ATI,* 156–158, 182; Dunlap, "Victims of Neglect," 98–99.

14. Gilkerson, "The 1980s: Consolidations, Bankruptcies, Mergers, Buyouts, Imports, Imports, and—(Surprise!) Rejuvenation," *ATI,* 177.

15. Dave Partridge, "A Brief Highlight History of the Greenville Hospital System," *PPGCHS)* 8 (1984–1990): 182–83.

16. Ibid., 185–86.

17. Greenville *Piedmont,* December 26, 1946; *News,* December 28, 1947; Leonard Todd, "Donaldson Center Industrial Air Park," *PPGCHS* 8 (1984–1990): 133–35.

18. Todd, "Donaldson," 136–37, 140.

19. Greenville *News,* January 3, 1960; December 31, 1961.

20. Ibid., September 5, 6, 1962.

21. Ibid., December 8, 1962.

22. Ibid., December 31, 1967.

23. Canup and Workman, *Daniel,* 171–73.

24. Ibid., 173.

25. Greenville *News,* December 28, 1947; January 1, 1949; November 1, 1948; December 31, 1950. Expansion received a setback in 1950 when six areas—including Sans Souci, Park Place, American Spinning, and Poe Mill—defeated annexation.

26. Ibid., December 31, 1950; December, 30, 1951; January 1, 1967.

27. Ibid., January 2, 1949; December 30, 1962; December 30, 1965; January 2, 1966.

28. Ibid., December 29, 1957; Canup and Workman, *Daniel,* 195–96; *News,* January 1, 1961; January 1, 1967.

29. Greenville *News,* December 29, 1963; January 1, 1967.

30. Ibid., December 31, 1967; May 30, 1974.

31. Ibid., December 13, 1992; May 30, 1973; *Greenville Business* 2 (April 1994): 4, 31.

32. *Greenville Business,* 31, 34.

33. Ibid.

34. Marion T. Anderson, "Some Highlights in the History of Education in Greenville County," *PPGCHS* 5 (1971–75): 26–27; Greenville *News,* January 1, 1950.

35. Anderson, "History of Education," 27–28.

36. Ibid., 28–29.

37. R. K. Johnson, *Builder of Bridges: The Biography of Dr. Bob Jones, Sr.* (Murfreesboro, Tenn., 1969), especially Part III, Educational Endeavors, 171–270.

38. Alfred S. Reid, *Furman University: Toward a New Identity, 1925–1975* (Durham, N.C., 1976), 124–26.

39. Ibid., chapter 7.

40. Ibid., chapters 9 and 10.

41. On May 15, 1992, the state Baptist Convention cut all legal and financial ties with the university. A. V. Huff, Jr., "The Road to Independence," *The Johns Era, 1976–1994* (Greenville, 1994), 7–12 (copy in the University Archives, James B. Duke Library, Furman University, Greenville, S.C.).

42. Samuel L. Zimmerman, Sr., "'Khrushchev Can Eat Here. Why Can't I?'" *Carologue* 8: 4 (Winter 1992), 7, 15–16; Greenville *News,* June 6, 1946.

43. This account is based on Nancy Vance Ashmore Cooper, "The Narrative: Willie Earle Lynching and Trial, February–May, 1947," delivered at the Willie Earle Symposium, Furman University, November 27, 1990 (in possession of the author). A thoughtful contemporary assessment is Rebecca West, "Opera in Greenville," in *A Train of Powder* (New York, 1955), 75–114.

44. West, *Train of Powder,* 114; Cartoon reprinted in Ashmore, *Woven from the Past,* 157; Greenville *News,* March 19, 1986; Schaefer B. Kendrick, "What Kind of Place Was Greenville in 1947?" *Carologue, Bulletin of the S.C. Historical Society* 8 (Winter 1992): 4, 14.

45. Greenville *News,* March 19, 1986.

46. *Everybody's Business: A Self-Survey of Conditions Affecting the Negro Population of the Greenville Area* (Greenville, 1950).

47. Greenville *News,* May 18, 1954, June 2, 1955. A superb treatment of local school desegregation is Tomiko Brown Hall, "'Moved by Law and Not by Spirit': Public School Desegregation in Greenville, S.C., 1951–1971" (independent study, Furman University, in possession of the author).

48. Greenville *News,* March 5, 1956; September 18, 1960, cited in William Bagwell, *School Desegregation in the Carolinas: Two Case Studies* (Columbia, 1972), 143.

49. Bagwell, *School Desegregation,* 151–52.

50. Samuel L. Zimmerman, *Negroes in Greenville, 1970: An Exploratory Approach* (Greenville, 1970), 31–32; Greenville *News,* January 2, 1960.

51. Greenville *News,* January 1, 1961; Zimmerman, *Negroes in Greenville,* 25–26. Zimmerman details the treatment of civil rights cases by two local attorneys who were involved—Donald J. Sampson and Willie T. Smith, Jr.,

52. Zimmerman, *Negroes in Greenville*, 25–26.

53. Alfred F. Burgess, "Working Together for Integration," *Carologue*, 7.

54. Canup and Workman, *Daniel*, 182–83.

55. Bagwell, *School Desegregation*, 163–64.

56. Burgess, "Working Together," 7, 17.

57. Ibid., 17–18.

58. Greenville *News*, December 29, 1963; January 3, 1965.

59. Bagwell, *School Desegregation*, 171–77. A comprehensive treatment of school desegregation in 1970 is Betty Stall, "With Grace and Style: The Desegregation of the Greenville County Schools in 1970," *PPGCHS* 9 (1990–1991): 80–92.

60. Bagwell, *School Desegregation*, 178–79.

61. Interviews with A. J. Whittenberg, Willie T. Smith, and E. P. Riley, cited in Hall, "Desegregation," 22–23; Greenville *News*, December 31, 1967.

62. Hall, "Desegregation," 23–25.

63. Ibid., 26–29; Stall, "Grace and Style," 85.

64. Stall, "Grace and Style," 85–87.

65. Hall, "Desegregation," 32–33.

66. Stall, "Grace and Style," 89–91.

67. Ibid.; Hall, "School Desegregation," 35.

68. An anecdotal treatment of Jackson's years in Greenville is Barbara A. Reynolds, *Jesse Jackson: The Man, the Movement, the Myth* (Chicago, Ill., 1975), 26–36. A more recent treatment is Marshall Frady, "Profiles" *The New Yorker*, February 3, 10, 17, 1992. The quotation about Longbranch Church is from Ibid., February 10, 1992, 53.

69. Reynolds, *Jackson*, 36–40, 48–54.

70. Ibid., 41–44.

71. Greenville *News*, November 3, 1948.

72. Ibid., December 28, 1952.

73. Ibid., November 7, 8, 1956; January 1, December 31, 1961.

74. Ibid., December 29, 1963; January 3, 1965.

75. Ibid., January 1, 1967.

76. Alan Ehrenhalt, *The United States of Ambition: Politicians, Power, and the Pursuit of Office* (New York, N.Y., 1991), 97–98.

77. Ibid., 98–99.

78. John P. Frank, *Clement Haynsworth, the Senate, and the Supreme Court* (Charlottesville, Va., 1991), 17–18.

79. Ibid., passim.

80. Ehrenhalt, *United States*, 88–92; Greenville *News*, November 5, 1968.

81. Benjamin P. Bagwell, *Riley: A Story of Hope* (Pickens, S.C., 1986), 97–107; *Biographical Directory of the S.C. Senate, 1776–1985*, ed. N. Louise Bailey et al. (Columbia, S.C., 1986) 2: 1376–78.

82. Bagwell, *Riley*, 97–107.

83. Greenville *News,* December 28, 1947; December 31, 1950; December 31, 1950; December 29, 1957; January 1, 1967.

84. *Churches and Church Membership in the United States 1990,* ed. Martin B. Bradley et al. (Atlanta, Ga., 1992), 1, 31, 346.

85. Elizabeth Peace Stall, "Building the Peace Center: Using Historic Spaces in New Ways," delivered at the meeting of the Greenville County Historical Society, April 17, 1994 (in possession of the author).

Population
of Greenville County

1790	White	5,888
	Black	615
	Total	6,503
1800	White	10,029
	Black	1,475
	Total	11,504
1810	White	10,739
	Black	2,394
	Total	13,133
1820	White	11,017
	Black	3,513
	Total	14,530
1830	White	11,380
	Black	5,096
	Total	16,476
1840	White	12,491
	Black	5,348
	Total	17,839
1850	White	13,370
	Black	6,786
	Total	20,156
1860	White	14,631
	Black	7,261
	Total	21,892
1870	White	15,121
	Black	7,141
	Total	22,262
1880	White	22,983
	Black	14,511
	Total	37,796

1890	White	27,516
	Black	16,789
	Total	44,310
1900	White	33,999
	Black	19,488
	Total	53,490
1910	White	47,515
	Black	20,861
	Total	68,377
1920	White	65,034
	Black	23,461
	Total	88,498
1930	White	89,139
	Black	27,855
	Total	117,009
1940	White	105,679
	Black	30,432
	Total	136,580
1950	White	136,631
	Nonwhite	31,521
	Total	168,152
1960	White	172,823
	Black	36,786
	Total	209,776
1970	White	200,273
	Black	39,829
	Total	240,546
1980	White	235,210
	Black	50,842
	Total	287,913
1990	White	259,160
	Black	57,646
	Total	320,167

City of Greenville
Population

1850	1,305
1860	1,518
1870	2,757
1880	6,160
1890	8,607
1900	11,860
1910	15,741
1920	23,127
1930	29,154
1940	34,734
1950	58,161
1960	66,188
1970	61,208
1980	58,242
1990	58,282

Sheriffs

Ninety-Six District

1773–1775	Robert Stark
1785–1787	Edmund Martin

Washington District

1795–1797	Robert Maxwell

Greenville District

1787	Reuben Stringer
1771–1794	Hugh McVay
1795–1796	Larkin Tarrant
1796–1797	William Easley
1797–1800	George W. Earle
1800–1802	William Easley
1802–1806	William Anderson
1806–1810	Henry T. Walker
1810–1811	Thomas Payne
1811–1812	John Wood
1813–1820	Thomas Payne
1820–1824	Asa W. Crowder
1824–1828	Nimrod Underwood
1828–1832	James McDaniel
1832–1836	William Blassingame
1836–1838	James McDaniel
1838–1840	David Henning
1840–1844	William M. Goodlett
1844–1848	David Hoke
1848–1852	Messena Taylor
1852–1856	William A. McDaniel

1856–1860	David Hoke
1860–1864	John T. McDaniel
1864–1868	William T. Shumate
1868–1870	Austin B. Vickers
1870–1876	John L. Southern
1876–1900	Perry D. Gilreath
1900–1909	Jefferson D. Gilreath
1909–1912	J. Perry Poole
1913–1919	Hendrix Rector
1919–1920	Samuel D. Willis
1920–1924	Carlos A. Rector
1925–1927	Samuel D. Willis
1927–1928	Carlos A. Rector
1929–1932	Cliff R. Bramlett
1933–1936	Brazillai B. Smith
1937–1940	John A. Martin
1940	G. R. Richardson
1940–1952	R. Homer Bearden
1953–1956	R. V. Chandler, Jr.
1957–1972	J. R. Martin
1973–1976	Cash F. Williams
1977–	Johnny Mack Brown

Intendants and Mayors
of Greenville

1849–1851	Thomas M. Cox
1855–1857	H. Lee Thruston
1864	Thomas M. Cox
1866–1867	Dr. R. D. Long
1869–1870	Dr. W. R. Jones
1870–1871	Thomas C. Gower
1871–1872	James P. Moore
1872–1873	Henry P. Hammett
1873–1874	Samuel Stradley
1875–1877	William C. Cleveland
1877–1879	Dr. W. L. Mauldin
1879–1885	Samuel A. Townes
1885–1887	Dr. E. F. S. Rowley
1887–1889	Samuel A. Townes
1889–1891	Dr. E. F. S. Rowley
1891–1893	W. W. Gilreath
1893–1901	James T. Williams
1901–1903	C. C. Jones
1903–1909	G. Heyward Mahon
1909–1911	J. B. Marshall
1911–1913	Henry Briggs
1913–1915	J. B. Marshall
1915–1917	Charles S. Webb
1917–1923	H. C. Harvley
1923–1927	R. F. Watson
1927–1929	Alvin H. Dean
1929–1933	A. C. Mann
1933–1937	John McHardy Mauldin
1937–1947	C. Fred McCullough
1947–1961	J. Kenneth Cass

1961–1969	David G. Traxler, Sr.
1969–1971	R. Cooper White, Jr.
1971–1979	Max Heller
1979 (Jan. 31–July 9)	James H. Simkins
1979–1982	Jesse L. Helms (died in office)
1982–1983	Harry P. Luthi
1983–	W. D. Workman III

Index